L. S. Vygotsky and English in Education and the Language Arts

L. S. Vygotsky and English in Education and the Language Arts focuses on the hugely significant contributions of L. S. Vygotsky to research, theory, and practice in English and the Language Arts, exploring the relevance of Vygotsky's works for today's teachers and researchers.

Drawing on his 30 years of study, Smagorinsky interprets Vygotsky in relation to literacy education, teacher education, special education, and how life outside school has an impact on how people function within them. This insightful and accessible text firstly explores Vygotsky's early life to situate him historically and culturally and goes on to trace his understanding of human psychology as it relates to the social contexts of schools and pupils' lives at home. Vygotsky's pedagogical ideas are then discussed in depth, with specific attention on the role of emotions, the zone of proximal development, expanding textuality beyond writing, and his belief in the primacy of socialization. This book illuminates new areas of understanding, and challenges common perceptions available through limited and selective readings, establishing Vygotsky as a complex developmental psychologist rather than a classroom practitioner.

With points for discussion and reflection provided throughout, this text will be invaluable for student teachers, teachers, and academics in the field of English and the Language Arts.

Peter Smagorinsky is Distinguished Research Professor, emeritus, in the Department of Language and Literacy Education at the University of Georgia, USA, and Distinguished Visiting Scholar at the Universidad de Guadalajara, Mexico.

Key Thinkers in English in Education and the Language Arts
Series Editor: Andy Goodwyn

This truly global and all-encompassing series provides definitive knowledge about key thinkers in English language and literature teaching and research from around the world. Each volume is a key text to understanding the wider context to each thinker to the field, illustrating their continued relevance to contemporary approaches in English teaching and especially as it's applied to the classroom. Exploring key ideas and condensing complex theories in an easily digestible format, this series will be engaging, accessible and appealing to readers with a range of levels of interest in the field of English in Education and the Language Arts (EELA).

Titles in this series include:

L. S. Vygotsky and English in Education and the Language Arts
Peter Smagorinsky

For more information about this series, please visit: https://www.routledge.com/Key-Thinkers-in-English-in-Education-and-the-Language-Arts/book-series/KTEELA

L. S. Vygotsky and English in Education and the Language Arts

Peter Smagorinsky

LONDON AND NEW YORK

First published 2024
by Routledge
4 Park Square, Milton Park, Abingdon, Oxon OX14 4RN

and by Routledge
605 Third Avenue, New York, NY 10158

Routledge is an imprint of the Taylor & Francis Group, an informa business

© 2024 Peter Smagorinsky

The right of Peter Smagorinsky to be identified as author of this work has been asserted in accordance with sections 77 and 78 of the Copyright, Designs and Patents Act 1988.

All rights reserved. No part of this book may be reprinted or reproduced or utilised in any form or by any electronic, mechanical, or other means, now known or hereafter invented, including photocopying and recording, or in any information storage or retrieval system, without permission in writing from the publishers.

Trademark notice: Product or corporate names may be trademarks or registered trademarks, and are used only for identification and explanation without intent to infringe.

British Library Cataloguing-in-Publication Data
A catalogue record for this book is available from the British Library

Library of Congress Cataloging-in-Publication Data
Names: Smagorinsky, Peter, author.
Title: L. S. Vygotsky and English in education and the language arts / Peter Smagorinsky.
Description: Abingdon, Oxon ; New York, NY : Routledge, 2024. | Series: Key thinkers in English in education and the language arts | Includes bibliographical references and index.
Identifiers: LCCN 2023022218 (print) | LCCN 2023022219 (ebook) | ISBN 9781032449890 (hardback) | ISBN 9781032449876 (paperback) | ISBN 9781003374848 (ebook)
Subjects: LCSH: Vygotskiĭ, L. S. (Lev Semenovich) 1896-1934. | English language--Study and teaching--Research. | Language arts--Research. | Educational psychology--Research--History. | Psychologists--Soviet Union--Biography.
Classification: LCC LB775.V942 S63 2024 (print) | LCC LB775.V942 (ebook) | DDC 150.92--dc23/eng/20230715
LC record available at https://lccn.loc.gov/2023022218
LC ebook record available at https://lccn.loc.gov/2023022219

ISBN: 978-1-032-44989-0 (hbk)
ISBN: 978-1-032-44987-6 (pbk)
ISBN: 978-1-003-37484-8 (ebk)

DOI: 10.4324/9781003374848

Typeset in ITC Galliard Pro
by KnowledgeWorks Global Ltd.

Dedicated to Michael W. Smith

"People with great passions, people who accomplish great deeds, people who possess strong feelings, even people with great minds and a strong personality, rarely come out of good little boys and girls." (Vygotsky, 1997a, p. 232)

Contents

Series Editor Foreword by Andy Goodwyn   *ix*
Author's Preface   *xi*
Notes on Translation   *xviii*
Acknowledgments   *xxv*

PART I
Historical Matters in Understanding Vygotsky   1

1. Biographical Elements of a Short Life   3
2. Culture, History, and Society   23
3. Marxism and Vygotsky in the Soviet Context   35
4. Historicizing Vygotsky's Hierarchical Views   52

PART II
Factors in Human Development   69

5. Principal Themes of Vygotsky's Cultural-Historical Psychology   71
6. Phylogeny, Ontogeny, and Concept Development   92
7. Emotions and Reason in Human Development and Education   107
8. Play and Labor in Human Development and Education   122
9. The Next Zone of Development (Not the ZPD): A Genetic Understanding   142

PART III
Pedagogy   155

10. Vygotsky's Contributions to Pedagogy   157
11. Orientation, Interests, Attention, Memory, and Relevance   179

12	Teaching Literature	198
13	Teaching Writing	219
14	Vygotsky, "Defectology," and Inclusive Education	238

PART IV
Pedology 257

15	Vygotsky the Pedologist	259
16	The Pedology Decree: Vygotsky as Anti-Marxist Bourgeoisie	273
17	The Pedology Decree: Critiques of Method and Focus	291

PART V
Conclusion 309

| 18 | Conclusion | 311 |

References 315
Index 345

Series Editor Foreword

Andy Goodwyn

It is with great pleasure that I introduce the first volume in this series, 'Key Thinkers in English in Education and the Language Arts', an international series that aspires to provide truly comprehensive insights into the significance of a major author's body of work and their lasting importance to this field of Education. The series will initially focus on some key figures who were of great importance to Education generally and who have had strong influences on English in Education, and also on other leading authorities who are directly in the field itself.

At the beginning with Vygotsky, we start with someone from outside the field itself, but an unquestioned intellectual giant and hugely influential figure. It has taken many years, and many translations, for his work to become fully available to readers around the world and his reputation has steadily developed as a result and continues to do so. Like all, genuinely original thinkers, his work continues to offer new ideas and understandings, not least because translation is, in itself, a creative act, often amending and correcting interpretations and accepted views. The other factor is that over his short life, he produced a very substantial body of complex work in sophisticated prose and with dense packing of ideas that were always dynamic as his thinking changed and developed. Although he was strongly influenced by his times and the ideology of Marxism was ever present, yet his thinking had many other influences from European philosophy and a range of psychological contemporaries; and we should not forget he started out with a doctorate in the Arts, specifically theatrical performance. However much he used the lens of science to look at human development, there is something very much of the artist in his approach to words and concepts.

As Peter Smagorinsky makes very clear, he was of his time and he felt the intense pressure of the dogmas that emerged after the Russian Revolution. He came from a profoundly Jewish background and it seems his life was both physically precarious—he expected to die young and he did—and intellectually perilous—he attracted increasingly hostile criticism when many of his later ideas did not fit with Stalinist expectations. Ironically, had he lived longer and been healthier he might have disappeared into a dismal and tragic, Siberian oblivion.

Perhaps Vygotsky sounds, so far, like a tragic hero? There is an element of truth in that characterization, but we have his many and substantial works, he left us a great and generative legacy. A key principle of the series is to examine that work in the spirit of its both enduring, but also changing, significance. This volume is a perfect example of a vigorous and comprehensive review of the work and a challenging and fresh interpretation. The series does not offer just a tidy summary of received wisdom. This volume gives an immensely valuable account of Vygotsky's life and ideas, drawing on the vast amount of secondary literature now devoted to his oeuvre. In that sense, this account is an excellent summary of the interpretations of other scholars, those who influenced Vygotsky, his contemporaries, and the many academics and educators who have created their own perspectives on his significance. And this is no hagiography, for example, Smagorinsky is clear that some of Vygotsky's views were white and Eurocentric. Some contemporary assumptions inevitably affected his thinking and he must have been consciously aware that certain readers brought their own, more dangerous views to evaluating his work.

Many of his ideas have been hugely influential – except that quite often, as with all seminal thinkers, they have been distorted or misinterpreted. One great benefit of these volumes is that they challenge the lazy and easy simplifications that lead to a thousand cliches that, as is always related to Vygotsky, 'learning is social'. Peter Smagorinsky, is the ideal author for this volume as a lifelong scholar of Vygotsky's work but also as a fiercely independent thinker in his own right. His volume begins with a personal note since he discovered an actual family connection to the man himself. Like a fine piece of silk thread, this is a very long and thin connection, described with feeling and humor in equal measure. The book is a remarkable overview of Vygotsky, drawing on Smagorinsky's own long wrestle with understanding this most complex and, at times, contradictory of thinkers. As well as being informative, insightful, and scholarly, it is lively, accessible, and witty throughout. Vygotsky is illuminated and enlivened, his life and times, his cultural environment, and his intellectual energy, are constantly realized on the page. We are left in no doubt that he was a key thinker and deservedly a huge and enduring influence on the field of English and the Language Arts and we are also challenged to consider his ideas afresh as we make our own interpretations of his most important concepts.

Andy Goodwyn,
March 2023

Author's Preface

I learned while writing this book that I am a distant relative by marriage of L.S. Vygotsky's,[1] following from our shared home city of Gomel, Belarus. The city is alternatively spelled Gomel', and the nation has been known as White Russia, Belorus, and Byelorussia. Vygotsky was born there in 1896 and lived his first two decades in the region set aside for Jewish people, the Pale of Settlement. He moved to Moscow in the newly-formed Soviet Union in the 1920s. My grandparents, who were born in 1880 and 1885, lived in Gomel until they escaped the genocidal pogroms of the region and came to New York City. Tracing genealogy for such refugees is difficult, since they left their homelands with little baggage, and the only available information about their families has come from their memories, which I was able to draw on before they died. I was pleased, then, when the family tree website Geni turned up the following connection: *Lev Semenovich Vygotsky is your second cousin twice removed's wife's first cousin twice removed's wife's great uncle's wife's great nephew's wife's great aunt's husband.* These vast degrees of separation almost sound like a genealogical parody, and give me absolutely no authority in writing about Vygotsky. But I'm not turning it down.

My grandparents, Nathan and Dinah (DEE-nah) Smagorinsky, arrived in the United States in two shifts, with my grandfather arriving in New York City in 1913 to set up a business painting signs for local shops, and my grandmother arriving in 1916 accompanied by two sons born in Gomel. Their individual long and dangerous trips to the Scandinavian coast in the approach to and heat of World War I, with Revolution fomenting in Moscow and St. Petersburg, continue to amaze me, given that they carried what they owned and had no means of transportation; my grandmother's trip with two children is especially remarkable. Once in New York City, they had two more sons, including my father. My paternal family origins in Gomel have gotten me some friendly looks in Vygotskian circles, but the inheritance gives me no particular insight into his remarkable career.

This volume will focus on my understanding of the contributions Vygotsky has made to academic fields that are concerned with literacy, especially (but not confined to) the one known as Language Arts in the early years, and English[2] in secondary and tertiary education, focused on reading, composition, and language study. Although Vygotsky was primarily known as a developmental psychologist working from a cultural-historical perspective, his career began in his teens as a theater aficionado and critic. His doctoral dissertation, *The Psychology of Art*, which he began as a teenager and completed in his mid-20s, centered on Shakespeare's *Hamlet* and other fictional and theatrical texts and fables. He then built on these literary roots to conduct psychological studies of human development mediated by psychological tools—primarily and often exclusively spoken and written speech—a task with major implications for educators.

Vygotsky's work got wide circulation among English-speaking educators when Jerome Bruner coined the term "instructional scaffolding" to describe one very loose association he made from the first, and least accurate, translation of *Thinking and Speech* (Wood, Bruner, & Ross, 1976). With this association of Vygotsky with a short-term instructional technique, Bruner made a questionable version of Vygotsky available to teachers looking for immediate payoff for teaching efforts. This application runs contrary to Vygotsky's career project of developing a comprehensive developmental psychology, one far more concerned with maturation over time than it was with short-term teaching and learning (Smagorinsky, 2018a, 2018b; see Chapter 9).

In this book I reject this reductive understanding of Vygotsky. I see it as derived from out-of-context selectivity from one book, *Mind in Society*, which provided the entrée for many people to Vygotsky's work, and the endpoint as well. The book's editors' presentation of key essays has enabled people to take each out of the context of his work as a developmental psychologist. Isolating paragraphs from these essays, themselves taken in isolation, inevitably distorts their meaning and allows them to serve as the justification for various school lesson structures. Vygotsky (1997b) himself described this tendency among people of his own era, saying, "the juxtaposition of ideas plucked from absolutely different contexts distorts their meaning" (p. 314). Based on how I see him referenced, I believe that Vygotsky is often quoted selectively, but rarely read in full, or even in part, by people adapting his ideas to classroom instruction.

It's one thing to pluck an idea from one context and place it wholesale in another. At least the pluckers read the book, or perhaps the chapter, if not its broader context. Some people who undoubtedly never have read Vygotsky at all have explained him in cringeworthy terms. Here, for instance, is one representative online source's explanation of Vygotsky's contributions to educational research and practice:

> Vygotsky proposed that in order for a student to learn a concept or skill, the concept or skill had to be within what he called the student's "zone of proximal development." The zone of proximal development is a theory used to determine what a student is capable of learning. If a concept or skill is something that a student could do with the help of a "more knowledgeable other," then that concept or skill is something they could perform on their own after learning it with support. Vygotsky called the support that students receive in order to learn "scaffolding." (https://blog.udemy.com/vygotsky-scaffolding/)

This quote provides a bastardization of one section of one chapter from *Mind in Society*. It is wrong on virtually every point, especially the ridiculous idea that Vygotsky himself invented the practice of "scaffolding" in relation to the ZPD (which itself, as I'll argue in Chapter 9, is a poor and misleading translation). Vygotsky only used the term "scaffolding" in passing to describe how toddlers rely on furniture to keep themselves upright when first learning to walk. Yet this online resource, and many like it, provide the sort of shortcut to reading Vygotsky that many people have substituted for engaging with his corpus, reducing his extraordinarily complex understanding of human development to a teaching method between a teacher and a student designed to promote independent learning tomorrow.

This tendency to rely on snippets of his translated texts to produce a teaching technique has led to great misunderstandings about what he was after and what he left for others to ponder. Vygotsky himself (1997b) disdained[3] such misusage. He was critical of efforts to muscle a thinker into new times and spaces, saying that Karl Marx, the Soviet Union's foundational thinker,

> is willy-nilly being modernized, is drawn into the present debate, and most importantly, is grossly distorted by arbitrarily combining [his ideas] into a system [that relies on various] citations [of scholarship] found in different places. We might put it as follows: they are looking firstly, *in the wrong place*; secondly, *for the wrong thing*; thirdly, *in the wrong manner*.
>
> (p. 313; emphasis in original)

Nothing, he argued, "can be transposed from one theory to another" (1997b, p. 278) without distortions and misrepresentations. Such people are, he argued, "essentially eclectics and popularizers of other persons' ideas. Not only have they never engaged in the research and philosophy of their science, they have not even critically assessed each new school" (p. 292). The popularizer's goal is less to engage with complexity, and more to produce appealing, if erroneous, reductions to simplistic formulas: "The eclectics assimilated all they could from ideas that were hostile to them. The popularizers can be enemies to no one, they will popularize the psychology that wins" (p. 292).

Marxism itself is not immune from such distortions, and Vygotsky himself was ultimately accused of *pedagogical distortions* and also of being an eclectic, code for looking outside Marxism for ideas. Vygotsky's transgressions followed from what his critics asserted was insufficient attention to social class issues and excessive attention to non-Soviet thinkers considered anti-Marxist, anti-Leninist, and anti-Stalinist (e.g., as argued by Rudneva, 1937; see Part IV). Vygotsky presented himself as a committed Marxist, however, one who was concerned that theorists inserted Marxism into fields where it fit poorly:

> There is no unitary basic methodology of the epoch. What we have is a system of fighting, deeply hostile, mutually exclusive, methodological principles and each theory—whether by Pavlov or Einstein—has its own methodological merit. To distill a general methodology of the epoch and to dissolve Marxism in it means to transform not only the appearance, but also the essence of Marxism.... With an uncritical approach, everybody sees what he wants to see and not what is: the Marxist finds monism, materialism, and dialectics in psychoanalysis, which is not there.
>
> (1997b, p. 262, p. 265)

Among the challenges for a twenty-first-century English-language theorist is, as Vygotsky put it, that applying a Marxist outlook in a capitalist society produces unresolvable contradictions and errors. He argued that "It would be a historical miracle, of course, if a full-grown system of Marxist psychology were to originate and develop in the West, from completely different roots and in a totally different cultural situation. That would imply that philosophy does not at all determine the development of science" (1997b, p. 261). I place myself among those who should be alert to distortions following from my own socialization in the European-derived, individualistic, capitalist United States long after Vygotsky's death in the Marxist, collectivist, communist Soviet Union, albeit one whose officials found Vygotsky himself to be anti-Marxist.

I have been concerned since beginning to incorporate Vygotsky into my own studies that I am not getting it right. Virtually all of my Vygotskian writing has been an exploratory effort to think through what I think I know and orchestrate it into a cohesive whole in relation to the issues to which I apply his ideas. My thinking has shifted as his work has been translated anew, a project that is incomplete and so not fully available to inform this volume. I've also added complexity and nuance through my engagement with the contributions of people interpreting his writing, often based on their fluency in Russian. These sources have taught me to be skeptical of much of what is written in Vygotsky's name to inform teaching. There is sufficient disagreement surrounding him that one can never become too confident in one's own understanding, and his own career produced shifts in thinking on key issues, a common phenomenon in the maturation of a scholarly life.

The possibility that I might make mistakes is a logical consequence of the process I go through of *thinking through writing*, of using writing as a tool for thinking, a process Vygotsky (1987) outlined in compelling detail. Not only do I generate my understandings *as I compose and revise* written texts, I continually modify them as I engage with new readings and discussions, and with my own writing. In writing this book, for instance, I've reconsidered interpretations of some essential constructs that I've developed over the last 30 years. In fact, I've revised these ideas since beginning work on this volume, finding my own early drafts to include assertions that I have modified as I've engaged with his career and read newer ancillary translations and interpretations. This ongoing refinement raises the likelihood that what I think I know as a result of writing this book may be subject to revision the next time I try to apply the concepts to new problems.

I've thought of writing a book of this sort for several years now, and am happy to have this opportunity. I've re-engaged with most of Vygotsky's texts that are available in English and have read and re-read ancillary scholarship produced by people who have read his texts extensively in Russian. These sources will be generously referenced throughout this volume. Most of what I have tried to understand through this lens has concerned what happens in English and Language Arts classrooms, and other disciplines across the curriculum, in schools. Other investigations and thought pieces I've undertaken have explored his role in special education and human development across contexts, given how home life and school life are often at odds for cultural reasons.

In this volume, I synthesize that work and attempt to extend it and make it comprehensible and accessible to those interested in what Vygotsky has to offer. This synthesis will produce for me a provisional understanding that I hope helps me advance my thinking in the next go-round, and that I hope benefits readers in their own effort to grapple with the phenomenon of human development in cultural and historical contexts.

Complications in Reading Vygotsky in English

As I'll relate when discussing his personal history, Vygotsky spent much of his life fearing death from tuberculosis. He was often bedridden, reduced to dictating his ideas to family members. He was similar, in tragic ways, to the British Romantic poet John Keats from a century before. Keats died of tuberculosis at age 25, preceded in death by his younger brother Thomas from the same illness, causing Keats to live his short life in fear of death, which became a topic for his poetry, e.g., "On Death." Vygotsky similarly had a younger brother Dodik who died before turning 14, and a second brother who died of typhoid shortly thereafter, making Vygotsky constantly aware of and fearful of his own death, and shadowing his life with the specter of tragedy.[4]

The sickly young Vygotsky would, at times, dictate his thinking to a family scribe. Anyone who has attempted to write down another person's words knows that it's rare to reproduce them verbatim. In addition to what people wrote down at home, some of what was published under Vygotsky's name consists of lecture notes taken by attendees at his talks, again inviting distortion or abridgement of what he actually said. What is credited to Vygotsky, then, at times is another person's recording and no doubt reconstruction of his words, for better or worse.

Whether he wrote, dictated, or lectured the texts attributed to him, they underwent further change in the hands of others. In the Soviet Union, his works were edited by ideologues who would rewrite him to align his views with those of the Stalinist leadership. These corrupted texts then passed through the hands of English editors, who rewrote, reduced, and moderated his language for broad readerships. In retrospect, some—including the editors themselves (see Cole, 2009)—have critiqued the translation of an essential reading, *Mind in Society* (1978), for the efforts to make his forbidding prose more readable to an audience being introduced to his works for the first time. (See Notes on Translation in this volume for more extensive attention to the reliability of what is available in English.) I have defended this volume as the right book at the right time, appearing inadequate only after Vygotsky's reputation grew, more of his texts were translated and retranslated, and critical eyes re-examined this early effort to bring his work to a broader readership.

Once the texts are in an English speaker's hands, readers must wade through the prose of one who, to Van der Veer (1997a), rarely paused to consider the demands he was putting on them. In his "Translator's Foreword and Acknowledgements" to *The Collected Works, Volume 3*, Van der Veer says, "I have not attempted to improve Vygotsky's style of writing although it was at times difficult to refrain from doing so. It is clear that Vygotsky … never rewrote a text for the sake of improving its style and readability. Hence the redundancy, the difficulty to follow the thread of his argument, the awkward sentences, etc." (p. v). His texts are often reiterative, perhaps annoyingly at times. However, his tendency to spiral back to points multiple times can help readers struggling to follow him to reinforce what they think they know.

Vygotsky's reliance on the Hegelian and Marxist dialectic process of detailing a *thesis*, responding with an *antithesis*, and emerging with a *synthesis* can also be frustrating. Typically, in outlining a thesis he intends to disembowel, he will present it according to his source's logic. The reader might follow along and find it makes good sense. And then Vygotsky will turn on it—the antithesis—explaining its flaws and shortcomings as a way to engage with oppositional views in order to reach a new understanding, the synthesis. Ultimately, the knowledge is worth having, if a lot of work to achieve. The process of getting through each step of the dialectic procedure, however, may leave one intellectually exhausted.

The urge to reference a vague claim (e.g., "learning is social") to Vygotsky has, I believe, converted him to an academic meme. A meme refers to a replicable element of culture, one passed along and repurposed while retaining stable elements (Dawkins, 1976). In this sense, memes provide a simplified medium for the adaptation and spread of ideas. The ideas may or may not be valid. What matters is that they quickly signal an affiliation or perspective to which others' confirmation biases may be easily attached to promote a perspective through an appealing image, and to do so with the façade of authority.

Vygotsky has become a scholarly meme to buff up ideas. "Learning is social" is often accompanied by "Vygotsky (1978)" even though "learning is social" is so vague and banal as to be virtually meaningless. Nonetheless the claim acquires superficial status by the association with a famed, somewhat trendy, name that provides this piety with prestige. Not only is the claim so bland that it says nothing. It does so with authority. Vygotsky the meme carries intellectual weight, no matter how trivial the claim he is referenced to support might be.

Compounding this problem is the way in which schema-consistent information is favored in scientific communication, and communication in general. Researchers who are summarizing the details of scientific articles often read their sources selectively (Cazden, 1996) and distort the work they cite to make them more consistent with their prior beliefs. Vygotsky's zone of proximal development, coupled with Bruner's adaptation of scaffolding, often serves as a way to justify pedagogical moves that teachers were already making, yet that benefit from the veneer provided by an authoritative citation.

Along with others, I have argued that Vygotsky has been used in such a fashion by people who have read only a few chapters of *Mind in Society* (Smagorinsky, 2018a, 2018b), or no Vygotsky at all, relying on sources far removed from his own writing for their claims. Appearing thusly as a scholarly meme, he has been appropriated to justify whatever an author needs justified, attending to what suits their needs and ignoring the rest, such as his emphasis on long-term human development and not short-term learning. This meme often enables authors to claim a badge of membership in a community, such that people who reference Vygotsky become part of an exclusive club, or so they hope. Yet misrepresentations of Vygotsky in an effort to belong to his group suggests that the badge is made of tissue, and not of gold.

Proceeding with Caution

These many caveats, including my own reliance on Vygotsky's ideas in translation, call for some caution in applying his theory, a century later and lands apart, to the teaching of Language Arts and English. After spending graduate school immersed in a very different paradigm—cognitive psychology—I've spent over three decades trying to reorient my perspective to one grounded in culture and human development. I hope that, with the help of sources and interpreters I admire and have confidence in, this volume provides some idea of what Vygotsky has to offer readers who are interested in applying his theory to literacy education. These ideas go well beyond simplistic notions of the ZPD, scaffolding, play, and other bits extracted from the broad context of a deep developmental theory in which these means of mediation serve a longer process of human socialization and adaptation.

If I could summarize my project, I might rely on Vygotsky (1997b), who said of new volumes on old scientific problems: "they do not reveal the truth, but teach us the search for truth, although they have not yet found it. I also resolutely said that the importance of this book does not depend upon the factual confirmation of its reliability: in principle it asks the right question." Hegel, he continued, "went limping towards the truth" (p. 266) in search of answers. I hope that readers consider my inquiry into Vygotsky to be founded in good questions, investigated with care and good intentions. Even after many decades of trying to work with Vygotskian ideas, I remain limping forward on the quest, carrying a heavy load up a steep hill. Thanks for joining me.

Notes

1 The adaptation of Slavonic names in the Cyrillic script to the English alphabet has produced different spellings for names like Vygotsky (e.g., Vygotskii, Vygodsky, Vigotsky, Vygodskii). My choice of spellings from among these names is somewhat arbitrary, settling on the most common choice found in the scholarship. Although his name is often pronounced *Vie-Got-Skee* in the US, Russian speakers pronounce it *Vi-Gut-Skee* or *Vi-Got-Skee*, with a short rather than long i-sound for the first syllable. (See, e.g., Nikolai Veresov's YouTube videos on Vygotsky, e.g., https://www.youtube.com/watch?v=4OFIwzJ3TmY.) My own surname, Smagorinsky, is what an agent

on Ellis Island wrote down from whatever my grandfather said when being processed as an immigrant from Gomel, and has a different spelling from the names given by other agents at other ports to his relatives. See Snyder (2022a) for an account of the difficulties of pronouncing Russian and Ukrainian words in English.
2 Virtually every national school system has a discipline built around its linguistic heritage and national literature, often going by the name of the language.
3 Throughout this volume, I quote Vygotsky and his contemporaries in the past tense, and later scholarship in the present tense.
4 As described by his daughter Gita Vygodskaya (1998): "Toward the end of 1917 Lev ended his education at both universities, and in December returned to Gomel. At that time the city was occupied by German forces (World War I was still in progress—Transl.). It was impossible to find a permanent job under such conditions. The family was also going through a difficult time. Lev had two sick relatives on his hands: his mother recovering from a bout with tuberculosis, and his younger brother who also contracted the disease, and whose condition was deemed critical. The young boy needed constant care; Lev was his nanny and cared for him until the boy died before his 14th birthday. His mother, stricken by grief, fell ill again, and Lev once again had to care for her. Before the end of the year, another tragedy struck the family: Lev's second brother died of typhoid fever. And so ended his first year back to Gomel." (n.p.)

Notes on Translation

Before proceeding, I'll make what must sound like a shocking confession for someone attempting to write this volume: I've never read Vygotsky.

Vygotsky wrote in Russian primarily. He was also a fluent reader and competent speaker of German and Yiddish (likely spoken at home); could read Latin, Greek and Hebrew; had familiarity with English and likely French; and experimented with Esperanto to the horror of Soviet authorities (Van der Veer, 2022, June 24, personal communication). I only speak one language fluently, English. I'm the epitome of the old joke: "Those who speak three languages are called trilingual. Those speaking two are known as bilingual. People who speak one language are called Americans."

People like me are left to rely on the work of translators to engage with the ideas and his Soviet colleagues and tormenters. I have read Russian-language scholarship in translation, and a goodly amount of the English-language scholarship that has been produced to interpret and explain Vygotsky. But no, I have never read Vygotsky. If you meet anyone who claims to have read him, I suggest asking, *А на каком языке вы его читали?*[1]

Accuracy and Reliability

My knowledge of the theory I claim to employ is always at the mercy of the quality of the translations I rely on, a point I have made before (e.g., Smagorinsky, 2011a). Written translations of Vygotsky have been, by most accounts, questionable and unreliable (Mecacci & Yasnitsky, 2011; Van der Veer & Yasnitsky, 2016). Veresov (2017) finds that Vygotsky's mostly widely referenced and most beloved works have been dubiously translated, and with Kellogg (e.g., Veresov & Kellogg, 2019) is working on new versions of his texts, two of which have been published in time to help me with this volume.

Perhaps the easiest way to understand this conundrum is to look at the three different translations of his opus magnum, published as *Myshlenie i rech': Psikhologicheskie issledovaniya* (1934a) They are different lengths and have Vygotsky saying different things. The first, published in 1962, translated the title as *Thought and Language*, a mistranslation that carried over to the second (1986) version even as the translator, Kozulin, acknowledged its shortcomings. In a brief section titled "Note on the Title," Kozulin acknowledges that "Although *Myshlenie i rech* should be rendered in English as *Thought and Speech*, it has been decided to retain the rendering *Thought and Language*, which has become the standard English translation since the first MIT Press [1962] edition" (p. lvii). Yet this translation also has been found inadequate. These problems were addressed in the 1987 version, titled *Thinking and Speech*, which reflects the dynamic nature of the two elements, rather than positioning them as abstractions, as did the first two for "thought" and "language." These titular differences only hint at the discrepancies found across the three versions.

Van der Veer and Yasnitsky (2011) have argued that the problems in these translations originated in the compilation and editing of the Russian versions, and then were compounded in the hands of English translators:

> A full list of the literally hundreds of sometimes incomprehensible differences between the [Russian] editions of [*Thinking and Speech* in] 1934, 1956, and 1982 has not yet been published, but it would clearly and redundantly show that the later versions are corrupted and unfit to serve as the source for translation into English. Yet, this is precisely what happened with the American translation for the Plenum edition [i.e., *Thinking and Speech*]. As a result, this translation not only contains gross mistakes introduced by the translator [into English] but also numerous changes introduced [prior to translation] in the series of Soviet editions. The net result is a useless text. The proper thing to do would have been, of course, to take the 1934 [Russian-language] edition as the basis of translation and to note any discrepancies with the earlier articles that are at the root of the book.
>
> (p. 479)

And, I suppose the proper thing would be for me to learn Russian so I could read Vygotsky in his own words. But Duolingo Spanish is already beating me up badly enough.

Glick (1997) identifies another problem with translations: "Some of the works published in [Vygotsky's] name are pastiched selections woven into a seamless text but representing fragments from different years, snatched from more complete works which had not been published" (p. v). What is published under Vygotsky's name, then, is often not exactly what he wrote or intended for others to read; and combining fragments from different periods of his career might result in conceptually conflictual statements, given that his ideas developed over time.

I rely on Russian editors and English translators and editors to provide me with my Vygotsky, and their reliability matters in what I am given to read. It's worrisome, then, to read that

> As a series of recent studies and publications have shown, the texts of L. S. Vygotsky at our disposal, published after his death, are replete with editorial errors, censorship edits, distortions and outright falsifications. All these distortions and falsifications were found not only in Vygotsky's translated texts, but also, first of all, in his Russian-language publications, including the scandalous and odious six-volume collection of works of this author, published by the publishing house "Pedagogy" in 1982-1984 under the editorship of M. G. Yaroshevsky.
>
> In the light of numerous, systemic distortions of Vygotsky's texts in his Soviet editions, the only possible way out of the catastrophic situation with the scientific heritage of this author seems to be the only possible way out. Namely: to republish all his texts in a restored form, not distorted by the censorship of critics and faithful students and followers. The world's most famous Russian psychological journal [*PsyAnima*, the Society for Psychology & Allied Sciences] and publishing house "Our Everything" solemnly announce the official start of a new publishing project: PSYANIMA COMPLETE WORKS OF VYGOTSKY. https://psyanimajournal.livejournal.com/9491.html

Unfortunately, this project will not be available to inform my efforts here, so I am left with material considered useless, scandalous, odious, and distorted by people who know better than I do. Others have concurred with this dim view of the Vygotsky available in English. To Zavershneva and Van der Veer (2018a), "The Russian edition of Vygotsky's work in six volumes was an abysmal failure in many respects ... which is tragic because many Russian re-publications and foreign translations are based on that edition and thus repeat its many errors and falsifications" (p. xii). It's sobering to realize that the English translations based on the Russian versions, published by Plenum as a six-volume set of *Collected Works*, are among the best versions of Vygotsky available in English; and that they are based on an "abysmal failure," a disaster whose initial shortcomings at the hands of Soviet ideologues and revisionists are compounded when rendered into English.

Translators themselves have acknowledged that they have taken interpretive license that they considered appropriate at the time. Veresov (2017) has broadly been concerned that "Sometimes you wonder how hard translators try to turn Vygotsky into an activity theorist, even where it is absolutely inappropriate!" (p. 26). Cole, John-Steiner, Scribner, and Souberman rank among the first and most esteemed English-language contributors to Vygotskian scholarship. They edited and wrote the preface to *Mind in Society*, a collection of essential readings provided to Cole by A. R. Luria for rendering into English and global distribution. This book has now been referenced over 126,000 times, roughly half of the citations attributed to Vygotsky, a figure that does not include citations to individual chapters, particularly those concerned with the zone of proximal development and play. Cole et al. reveal that

> In putting separate essays together we have taken significant liberties. The reader will encounter here not a literal translation of Vygotsky but rather our edited translation of Vygotsky, from which we have omitted material that seemed redundant and to which we have added material that seemed to make his points clearer. As other editors have noted, Vygotsky's style is extremely difficult. He wrote copiously and many of his manuscripts have never been properly edited. In addition, during frequent periods of illness he would dictate his papers—a practice which resulted in repetitions and dense or elliptical prose. Gaps in the original manuscripts make them even less accessible now than they might have been at the time they were written. Because proper references were rarely given, we have supplied our best guess as to the exact sources to which Vygotsky referred. The process of tracking down and reading these sources has itself proved a very rewarding enterprise; many of his contemporaries were fascinatingly modern in important respects. We realize that in tampering with the original we may have distorted history; however, we hope that by stating out procedures and by adhering as closely as possible to the principles and content of the work, we have not distorted Vygotsky's meaning.
>
> (1978, p. x)

Glick (1997) is less sanguine about the consequences of those decisions, arguing that the "significant liberties" taken by the editors of *Mind in Society* may have imposed latter-day values on Vygotsky's writing of these papers several decades before and in a different context:

> *The processes of editing, clarifying, reducing seeming redundancies, eliminating polemical arguments of no contemporary interest and constructing volumes out of other*

volumes cannot but help to mold the author into a contemporary voice. The judgments of what is dated, what is redundant, what is unclear, and in what terms, are contemporary judgments, and, as is inevitable, contemporary construction addresses contemporary needs and understandings of what the core problems are.

(p. xii; emphasis in original)

I have little ability to make these discriminations myself, given my inability to read Russian, and am open to the criticism that I have marshalled considerable arrogance in attempting to write this book. I'm continually reminded how precarious a position I am in. My reading across the Vygotskian scholarship suggests that the challenges of translating Russian terms and concepts are colossal and raise cautions about taking any translation as authoritative without corroboration across sources.

Russian Naming Traditions

Russian naming traditions can be confusing to the English-only readers. Back when I read Dostoyevsky's novels, I had to maintain charts in order to keep track of characters who typically went by 3-4 different names, all without announcement. At the time there was no internet to help, such as https://wiki.ubc.ca/Names_in_Dostoevsky%27s_Novels. There were also no personal computers, so I created these charts by hand. I had to keep assiduous track of names and relationships in order to be certain who was being identified in the various passages in the novels.

Fortunately, this problem is less of an issue in Russian and Soviet psychology, where last names are typically used for sources. One remaining challenge concerns the lack of correspondence between the Russian Cyrillic Greek-origin alphabet and English Latin-origin alphabet. The Russian language has no basis in Latin, one of many reasons that Russians consider "The West" and Europe to be separate, hostile realms (Zamoyski, 2009). Russian names often appear in many English forms from different translators, e.g., Pavel Blonsky, Błoński, or Blonskii.[2]

Further, Russian names typically rely on initials rather than full first and middle names (e.g., L. S. Vygotsky). Twenty-first century conventions are moving away from the historic gender binary of male and female, yet I have endeavored to use pronouns appropriately when referring to individuals. I was unclear on whether to use masculine or feminine pronouns for some Russian and Soviet sources until I read Van der Veer's (2002) introduction to an issue of the *Journal of Russian and Eastern European Psychology*, in which he refers to one of Vygotsky's most severe critics, E. I. Rudneva, as "she." I wrote him and he provided the following rule: "Female surnames are made by putting an 'a' or 'aya' behind the male variant. Thus, Putin's wife or daughter is Putina and Vygotsky's wife or daughter Vygotskaya. Hence, females can be recognized by their surname ending on 'a.' Of course, there are exceptions (some Jewish names, e.g., Feldman or some Ukrainian ones, e.g., Stetsenko)." My takeaway: Don't assume that, just because many Russian and Soviet psychologists were men, all of them were.

There is thus a mostly-reliable way to infer an individual's sexuality by their name, if according to binary understandings prevalent at the time of their careers. Given that the Soviet Union only decriminalized same-sex relationships in 1991, those living outside the binary were unlikely to claim a nonconforming identity during Vygotsky's lifetime, or throughout the next half-century. In the post-Soviet era, Russia is ranked as "the least protective country in Europe for LGBT citizens" (The Council for Global Equality, n.d., n.p.), with repression expanding in the Putin era (Vernon, 2023). This authoritarianism has implications for Soviet scientists and how they are identified by pronouns, leaving only a binary available for referencing them.

Terms with No Clear English Translation or Meaning, or Whose Meaning Got Lost in Translation

Russian words don't always translate easily into English-language concepts, and require considerable plumbing to grasp in other cultural contexts. Cole (2009), for instance, devotes an entire article to the complications of translating a single term, *obuchenie*, whose disputed meaning in English broadly refers to the relation between learning and human development. This term is just one of many whose meaning may shift in translation, resulting in disagreements by different interpreters (see Fleer, González Rey, & Veresov, 2017). *Perezhivanie*, for instance, required an explanation from translators Kellogg and Veresov (2019) to clarify its meaning in different usages:

> In contrast to these terms which are left undefined in this first volume, *perezhivanie* plays a central role in Lecture Four on the environment, and it presents an immediate problem for the translator. It is both an everyday concept and a scientific [academic] one—that is, it has an everyday meaning familiar to every Russian, which is equivalent to undergoing an experience of some kind, but it is, in Vygotsky's pedological work, invested with much more precise and abstract content: a perezhivanie is a unit of analysis for the whole of human consciousness. For Vygotsky, it has the same relationship to the developing mind as an individual cell has to the growing body. At the same time, *perezhivat'* is a verb, meaning to have that experience. In these lectures, we have adopted the rather quirky solution of translating *perezhivat'* as "to experience" or "to undergo an experience" when Vygotsky uses it as a verb, particularly when he uses it in the everyday sense. When Vygotsky uses *perezhivanie* as a scientific concept, that is, as a unit of analysis, we have chosen not to translate it at all, but merely to transliterate it as *perezhivanie*.
>
> (p. viii)

I've wrestled with using *perezhivanie* in my own writing (e.g., 2011b), defining it as meta-experience, that is, how one experiences an experience such that it provides the framework for new experiences. But other people have used it in other ways, to the point where I've simply begun using meta-experience to describe how people's experiences of their experiences create emotional and cognitive frames for interpreting subsequent experiences.

I'll give one example of the problems of relying on translations to understand a concept developed in another language. One of Vygotsky's early influences, and at the time Russia's most prominent psychologist, Ivan Petrovich Pavlov, is immortalized in textbooks for identifying the *uslovnyi* or "conditioned response." As everyone knows, Pavlov's dogs learned to associate a sound or light, or even a painful electric current, with the arrival of food, causing them to salivate at the stimulus even when no reward followed. But "conditioned response" is actually a mistranslation that trivializes the phenomenon to suggest a mindless, knee-jerk reaction to a stimulus. Even the highly authoritative Cole et al. (1978) employ the original mistranslation in *Mind and Society*: "Whether reading, writing, or arithmetic is being considered, development is viewed as the mastery of *conditioned reflexes*" (p. 80; emphasis added).

The better translation is *conditional response*, which has begun to appear in translations of Vygotsky, if not necessarily in psychology textbooks. Vygotsky explained this phenomenon as an illustration of how both biology and environment are involved in the activity of both Pavlov's dogs and human beings:

> The most complex and subtle forms of human behavior ultimately rest upon very simple inborn behavioral mechanisms as their last source. However, no hereditary quality, no inborn property remains unchanged and the expression *conditional reflex* itself points to the change that the hereditary forms of behavior undergo under the influence of the *conditions* under which they manifest themselves.
> (in Van der Veer, 2020,[3] p. 7; emphasis in original)

It matters a great deal whether Pavlov was talking about mindless reactions to stimuli or responses cued by conditions that prompt, without determining, specific responses. The translation of *conditional* response shifts attention from reflexive action of the knee-jerk sort to externally prompted action, and thus to an environmental source. This conception changes the meaning from thoughtless responses largely of a biological origin to responses to factors in the setting, including the history of that setting. The response, while rapid, includes attention, the mediation available through a tool and thus a cultural dimension, and a degree of regulation; each of these factors is central to a cultural-historical approach. Understanding this distinction suggests the importance of how history (including training in psychological experiments) shapes the present and how people and dogs do more than simply react to stimuli without thinking. Pavlov's whole psychology can be, and typically is, reduced to a misunderstood point. As I'll argue in Chapter 9, Vygotsky's zone of proximal development has similarly been mistranslated and trivialized to depict short-term learning and essentialize him as a pedagogue with a single contribution, the scaffolding erroneously attributed to him via Bruner (Smagorinsky, 2018a, 2018b).

Trusting Sources

Why bother trying to understand Vygotsky, then, if what is available in English involves unreliable translations of questionable and ideologically edited versions of original texts? The answer is that there is a lot of help, along with a lot of dubious interpretations. Finding reliable, knowledgeable sources is key to getting closer to the "real" Vygotsky. I have relied on speakers of English (and other languages) who have read Vygotsky in Russian— Mike Cole, David Kellogg, Jane Knox, Alex Kozulin, Carol B. Stevens, Jaan Valsiner, René van der Veer, Jim Wertsch, Nicolai Veresov, and others—who have written many decades' worth of ancillary texts and translations to help me achieve the goal set by Van der Veer and Valsiner (1991) of *Understanding Vygotsky*. My indebtedness to them, and to many others working in this tradition, should be evident in my referencing throughout this book. These sources don't always agree, even as they often corroborate one another's versions of Vygotsky, giving me confidence in some Vygotskian claims and leading me to be cautious about the rest. I also include references to my own studies and thought pieces, the writing and discussion of which have helped me work my way toward whatever understandings I've arrived at to this point. Since these ideas continue to develop as I work them through, I'm sure they'll have evolved by the time anyone has read this book. If it's ever translated into another language, all I can say is, *caveat emptor*.

Notes

1 And what language did you read him in? Translation provided by https://www.deepl.com/translator
2 Pavel Blonsky (1884–1941) was a Ukrainian psychologist and philosopher who relocated to the Soviet Union after the Bolshevik Revolution. He was a major figure in pedology who was banned following the Pedology Decree of 1936 (see Part IV).
3 References to Van der Veer (2020), are made in accordance with the publisher's guidelines. As the reference to this citation indicates, Van der Veer translated and edited Vygotsky's *Pedology of the School Age*. Any references in this volume to (in Van der Veer, 2020) indicate a point or quote from Vygotsky himself in this text.

Acknowledgments

Vygotskian scholar James V. Wertsch has written about the *voices of the mind* that populate any individual's thinking. My effort since the early 1990s to understand Vygotsky has involved many hosts of voices, far too many to list here, as my lengthy reference list suggests. I would like to specifically thank the following friends for their critiques of individual chapters: Betsy Burris, Stacia Long, George Newell, David Reinking, Michael Smith, and David Yaden. I have also benefitted greatly from correspondence with René van der Veer and Michael Cole as I have tried to clarify my understanding of Vygotsky's career and theory during my writing of this book. Whether these voices have produced a cacophony or a symphony is up to readers to determine.

I also wish to thank Andy Goodwyn for recruiting me to write this volume and supporting its production; and my Routledge editors for their careful reading of the manuscript I initially submitted. I hope that it provides readers with a reasonably good understanding of, and does justice to the ideas of, L. S. Vygotsky, including both his remarkable and enduring contributions, and some areas in which his understandings require updates since his early death in a time and place far removed from the English-speaking world of the present.

Part I

Historical Matters in Understanding Vygotsky

Vygotsky's life and career took place in a tumultuous era, characterized by violence, oppression, revolution, hope, and paranoia. I review Vygotsky's biography in light of his historical context, then detail how this context shaped his views of people of different cultures and socialization. I also review Vygotsky's troubled relationship with Marxism, the driving motivation of the Soviet Union. Vygotsky claimed to be a devoted Marxist, but was ultimately suppressed because his Marxism did not meet Stalin's dogma. Understanding Vygotsky and his times benefits from contextualization culturally and historically, and suggests how he came to hold the views he did of society, psychology, and related areas.

1 Biographical Elements of a Short Life

I next present a brief overview of Vygotsky's short life, one that has resulted in his being dubbed "The Mozart of Psychology" by Toulmin (1978) upon his reading of *Mind in Society*. I am not a biographer or historian by trade and do not pretend that any of what I will present follows from my own historical investigations. Rather, I rely on various sources who have done this work well. I am especially indebted to Van der Veer and Valsiner (1991) for their detailed and, when appropriate, critical overview of his life. I also draw on various biographies included as introductory sections in books either by Vygotsky or about him, and on biographical articles and chapters from other sources.

I provide a selective account, focusing on biographical details designed to contextualize Vygotsky's humanity and the means through which his own development as a person helped to shape his worldview and beliefs about psychology. His early socialization was later modified through his critical reading of prior and contemporary thinkers, his engagement with findings from the clinical studies he conducted to test his theories and his experiences at the hands of Soviet repressionists. In providing this account, I hope to show that Vygotsky's theory of socially and culturally mediated human development, known in these pages as *cultural-historical theory* (see Chapter 5), applies as well to his own life trajectory, as it does to anyone's.

Notes on Geography

Those writing about the complex geographical area that includes Eastern Europe and the Soviet Union have relied on terms that require clarification, or at least attention. The first is "Europe," a continent whose borders are cultural as much as they are physical. The Soviets were adamant that they were not European, but rather a nation neither of the "West" nor the "East." Europe makes for a questionable generalization in that it includes a number of nations with distinct cultures. When the Soviet Union was launched between 1917 and 1923, European nations were involved in a Great War with one another. There was tremendous cultural variation among European nations as well. What bound them in the Soviet mind was their capitalist, and thus bourgeois, social organization. They were bundled with the United States as Western in the Soviet discourse that positioned capitalist and communist societies antagonistically, a hostility that these nations reciprocated.

Furthermore, the Soviets were in the odd position of rejecting European thought while grounding their worldview in the work of Marx, Engels, Hegel, and others from a Prussian-German society whose bourgeois orientation they found abhorrent. The Germans, under Nazi rule, made a tenuous pact with Stalin in the late 1930s to conquer Poland, but Hitler's expected betrayal of their agreement was central to the expansion of this conflict into World War II (Snyder, 2015). The Soviets of Vygotsky's era were enamored of Marxist critiques of capitalism. They found other Germans, along with most European and US psychologists and philosophers, to represent the worst in social inequity. Where "West" began and ended was a question open to interpretation, suggesting that the distinction is vague and that it rests on an intellectual framework about economic systems more than a separation of physical landmasses. To the Bolsheviks, the revolution they undertook in Russia was grounded in the belief that a global move to communism was impending, one that erased national borders and produced societies based on the will of the proletariat. As articulated by Leon Trotsky, "At the end of [The Great War] I see Europe recreated, not by the diplomats, but by the proletariat. The Federated Republic of Europe—the United States of Europe—that is what must be. National autonomy no longer suffices. Economic evolution demands the abolition of national frontiers" (quoted in Reed,[1] 1919a/2011, p. 134).

Reed (1919b/2011) accepted this axiom that "Today the workers of all countries are resolving to make an end of Capitalism. Bolshevism asserts that it is the Socialists, the trained revolutionary thinkers, who must point out the way, and lead the workers along it" (p. 68), a statement that includes the paradox that the workers will revolutionize the world's economies, yet will need to be led by "trained revolutionary thinkers" from what emerged as a new ruling class of Bolsheviks. Reed (1919c/2011) quotes Lenin as saying of this conundrum, "If Socialism can only be realized when the intellectual development of all the people permits it, then we shall not see Socialism for at least 500 years. The Socialist political party—this is the vanguard of the working class; it must not all itself to be halted by the lack of education of the mass average, but it must lead the masses, relying upon the Labor Organizations for revolutionary initiative" (p. 61).

The more conventional notion of an East and West is designed to bifurcate the world at the point where Europe bordered nations grounded in other sorts of cultures. Yet these borders have continually shifted over the course of history, complicating national histories and allowing Putin, for example, to claim that Ukraine never existed and has always been part of Russia, a belief with no historical substantiation (Snyder, 2018).

I have worked to address these complications in this volume, no doubt in unsatisfactory ways. I have tried to avoid the term "Eurocentric" because it overgeneralizes cultures and intellectual thought that defy generalization; I do use it when quoting sources. I find references to "European" to be inescapable, while recognizing the perils of including Greeks and Norwegians in the same broad category, and while aware that some nations have shifted over time in many ways, such as Poland's position vis-à-vis the Soviet Union and Germany. Instead of referring to "the West," I use terms like capitalist or bourgeois economies, and describe Vygotsky's version of Marxism as post-capitalist (see Chapter 3). Ultimately, these differences refer to those that were foundational to the stated goals of the Soviets—the formation of a communist society of greater moral certitude than could emerge under capitalism—rather than to any physical geographies in the nations from which ideas were developed.[2]

Mythbusting

Van der Veer and Valsiner (1991) review Vygotsky's ascent from Gomel, Belarus, to the center of psychological studies in Moscow after the formation of the Soviet Union. Their narrative contradicts what they refer to as simplistic accounts provided by many recorders of Vygotsky's life, including Vygotsky's own colleagues. His career did not, they assert, follow the sort of "Cinderella-type" (p. 12) narrative commonly related. This narrative is one of many oversimplifications of his life and work, as I'll argue in this volume. Van der Veer and Valsiner relate the "standard version" of the mythical account of his ascendance:

> in 1924 an unknown school teacher named Lev Vygotsky from a provincial town called Gomel'[3] delivered a talk at the Second Psychoneurological Congress in Leningrad that left the audience speechless. Vygotsky supposedly boldly and persuasively argued that psychologists should study consciousness, an argument in flat contradiction to the prevailing ideas of the time [which were enamored of Pavlov's reflexology]. [Leading Soviet psychologists] Kornilov[4] or Luria ... heard the talk and the decision to admit Vygotsky to the staff of the Institute of Experimental Psychology was immediately taken. Vygotsky moved to Moscow and very soon a troika of psychologists, Vygotsky, Luria, and Leont'ev[5], evolved. Working at the Institute of Experimental Psychology this troika developed the cultural historical theory, which quickly became the dominant theory in psychology, making Vygotsky one of the most well-known psychologists of his time.... Unfortunately, this story is untrue.
>
> (p. 39)

Rather, they say, Vygotsky was already an accomplished theater critic whose teaching had included various experiments, making his transition to Moscow smoother than his origin myth suggests. He did not suddenly appear in Moscow as a humble schoolteacher and lone genius but rather applied his intellect to a variety of challenges when young that provided the basis for his subsequent reputation as a cutting-edge if dangerous-to-the-state and thus marginalized, psychologist. He was a career-long collaborator and avid consumer of scholarship from across Europe and from the United States, a disposition that ultimately led to accusations of being a member of the debauched bourgeoisie[6] social class.

Yet his broad quest for understanding made him an international figure, more than simply a Marxist of the approved sort that populated Soviet psychological circles; and indeed, he met with their disapproval and condemnation (see Part IV). These more compliant Soviet psychologists were ever-attentive to state ideology and were painfully aware that dissent, or association with dissent, or accusations of dissent, under Stalin, typically resulted in execution, banishment to deadly labor camps, or exile (Solzhenitsyn, 1973).

Some were surely on board with Stalin's program to begin with; others surely modified their views to align with Party doctrine to preserve life and limb. "The history of Russia imposing a 'comply or die' policy against artists is nothing new. It has a history which spans for hundreds of years," said the Finnish-Ukrainian conductor Dalia Stasevska following the execution of Ukrainian conductor Yuriy Kerpatenko in October 2022 after refusing to participate in a concert in occupied Kherson. Ukrainian war crimes investigator Victoria Amelina compared Kerpatenko's assassination with that of Ukrainian playwright Mykola Kulish, who "was shot on 3 November 1937, near Sandarmokh, with 289 other Ukrainian writers, artists and intellectuals" she said, part of a long pattern of "brutal murders of a bright, talented, brave people whose only fault was being Ukrainian" (Higgins & Mazhulin, 2022, n.p.). These brave and talented people, whether their crime was being Ukrainian or something else, included psychologists and other members of the dreaded intelligentsia.

Vygotsky also departed from his mythic aura due to his conflicts with the other members of the famed "troika" or trio of collaborators, Luria and Leont'ev (Martins, 2013).

Leont'ev (1932/2005a) alludes to the status of their relationship in a letter to Vygotsky—he was 29 years old at the time, and Vygotsky was 35 and facing the prospect of death from tuberculosis—in which he laments the state of Soviet psychology and the divisions within their group:

> It seems more and more apparent that it will be necessary for me to leave ps[ychology]. I cannot work *alone* with A. R. [Luria]. I cannot cope on my own (I don't have the preparation, schooling, etc.), at least if I do not find an *exceptional* solution.... I *definitely* cannot continue with things as they have been in recent times (internally, in terms of ideas).... I'm glad that I wrote this letter. I have done everything here that I could. I am not asking you to answer me. I am free in a certain sense; I have done everything that I could, I have clarified everything *about myself* with you. I hope I will manage to do the same with A[lexander] R[omanovich] [Luria]. I do not need to tell you that I, least of all, could hold any grievances against you.
>
> (p. 76; emphasis in original)

Leont'ev did not abandon psychology. He went on to found activity theory, and after his death his sons disputed the severity of the falling out (Leontiev & Leontiev, 2003). Luria, three decades later, hosted Michael Cole, a young US psychologist who then served as Vygotsky's conduit to the world outside the Soviet lockdown on discrepant thinking. Leontiev and Leontiev interpret the conflict as less precipitous and more an internal disagreement, one soon left unresolved with Vygotsky's death and the Soviet Union's repression of alternatives to State ideology. As Van der Veer (2002) puts it:

> Vygotsky's position had become increasingly difficult by the time of his death. The posthumous criticisms and additional circumstances (e.g., the search of his widow's house by the secret police and the confiscation of his books, the disappearance of his publications from libraries) strongly suggest that he would not have been able to continue his work after 1936. Moreover, had he lived on, he might have been arrested and perished in the Gulag Archipelago. It is probable that his death from tuberculosis in a way saved him from a more horrible death. [Vygotsky faced] horrible options and was lucky to die of a natural disease in the company of his relatives. The disease killed him; otherwise he might have been murdered.
>
> (p. 8)

Ultimately, Vygotsky emerged as a polymath whose intellectual interests included medicine, law, history, philosophy, psychology, literary criticism, and special education. In each area, he pursued the goal of generating a comprehensive psychological framework that accounted fully for human development in all its manifestations and with all of its historical and immediate influences. He lived in continual fear of death from illness, and toward the end, from ideology. He reached these achievements before he died at the age of 37, albeit with much work to do to elaborate his theory.

Early Career in Context

Vygotsky's early life in Gomel found him to be a committed, serious, and industrious student and member of an oppressed Jewish community. His life coincided with extreme violence in Eastern Europe. The bloodshed had roots dating to the mid-19th century

(Figes, 1997) and continued with the 1904–1905 Russo-Japanese War, in which Japan defeated Russia in a dispute over control of Manchuria and Korea. This loss spawned the first Russian Revolution of 1905 against the Romanovs, a cause that failed. In a perilous and volatile world, and with the Tsarist government still precarious following the 1905 uprising, World War I broke out in 1914. This massive conflict set the stage for the second great Russian Revolution, which erupted in 1917. The Bolsheviks had been plotting to overthrow the Romanovs for several years, and the outbreak of war provided their opportunity. Their case for revolution was based on the premise that the entire war was a capitalist ploy to make money through the sacrifice of proletariat lives to serve the economic engine of battle (Gilbert, 1994).

Almost immediately after the Romanovs were overthrown, the Polish-Bolshevik War was fought in 1919–1920. The Bolshevik ascendance was hardly straightforward, however. Even among those seeking a socialist nation, there were violent disagreements among the Bolsheviks, Mensheviks, and Socialist Revolutionaries, with the latter two considered by the Bolsheviks to be corrupt hybrids of the old state and the new.

The overthrow of the Tsar produced a power vacuum that was contested in the Russian Civil War from 1917 to 1922, launched while World War I still ravaged the continent. The year 1924 produced the certification of the Soviet Constitution, Lenin's death, and the subsequent power struggle within the Politburo that produced a violent process of ascension for Stalin. Vygotsky's life and career unfolded during dangerous times, first through formal armed conflict throughout Europe and the East, and later through Stalin's purges and suppression.

Vygotsky's Path to Moscow

Vygotsky's journey from Belarus to Moscow, as Van der Veer and Valsiner (1991) note, was paved with obstacles. It was no Cinderella story. It involved his application of his intellect to both artistic and psychological studies, some good fortune in navigating a university entry system that created precious few spots for young Jewish men (and not women), and many influences. He was less a "lone genius" and more a person whose development carried many influences and collaborators (Van der Veer, 2007; Zinchenko, 2007).

Beginning in his teens, Vygotsky was heavily involved in Gomel theater scene, both in production and as a critic (Van der Veer, 2015). He wrote scores of theater reviews and undertook his inquiry into how art produces both emotional and intellectual responses in its readers, listeners, and viewers. His attention to art largely centered on drama and literature, a function of his primary orientation to words as psychological mediators.

While in Gomel he also began conducting psychological experiments, merging his interest in the role of (primarily literary) art in promoting sophisticated emotional and intellectual responses with his growing concern for a broader understanding of human development across the lifespan. This attention to long-term development began for Vygotsky with a focus on childhood and early socialization, his primary interest in his research. It also required generating a broader, more comprehensive theory capable of accounting for adult maturation and socialization in relation to cultural ways of being. To do so, he needed to challenge the reigning titan of Russian and Soviet psychology, Pavlov, who viewed human conduct as a collection of conditional reflexes,[7] enabling him to ignore the problem of subjective experience, i.e., consciousness. Vygotsky ultimately saw psychological tools operating between stimulus and response, bringing a Marxist dimension to Pavlov's reflexology. Leont'ev (1986) describes this formulation as shifting from the classic stimulus-response reflex pattern, "Not from stimulus to reaction, but from stimulus through a tool (represented by a triangle) to reaction" (cited in Holowinsky, 1988, p. 125). Understanding human consciousness in social, historical, and cultural contexts became Vygotsky's focus in generating cultural-historical theory, a name that suggests the ways in which the present is always a function of the past, creating the basis for newly emerging thinking, speech, and action (see Chapters 2 and 5).

Marxism

Vygotsky was influenced by Marxism, which was required of anyone hoping to survive in the Soviet Union. The record is full of dissidents and those found to have violated Party principles who were sent to labor camps or executed (see Daniels, Cole, & Wertsch, 2007; Solzhenitsyn, 1973). Ultimately, Party officials found Vygotsky to be insufficiently committed to the official doctrine and suppressed his work to the point that it was barely available in the Soviet Union. Smuggled and translated manuscripts in other languages provided his entrée to the global psychological community during the height of Soviet oppression.

Van der Veer and Valsiner (1991) conclude that he could not be considered as a pureblood Marxist—itself a chimera at best—even as Marxism contributed to his thinking, along with other theoretical and philosophical perspectives and sources of empirical data from the research of an international array of psychologists (see Chapter 3). Their interpretation is aligned with Wertsch's (1991) conclusion that

> several ideas in Vygotsky's writings are clearly grounded in Marxist texts. In the case of works such as Marxism and the Philosophy of Language (Voloshinov, 1973), there is also an obvious connection to such texts. In the final analysis, however, it seems to me that there is little that is necessarily Marxist in either Vygotsky's or Voloshinov's writings. In both cases the facts of each author's biography suggest that Marxist ideas played an important role in giving rise to their claims, but their crucial arguments are not uniquely and necessarily indebted to Marx.
>
> (p. 50)

This ambivalent embrace of Marxism helped provide the opening for Vygotsky to be specifically named as among the "wreckers" of Soviet society, those involved in subterfuge against the state (see the collection assembled by Van der Veer [2002] on the Pedology Decree, treated in detail in Part IV).

Vygotsky's Career in Stages

Vygotsky was both a person of his times, and a person under development. According to Kozulin,

> Vygotsky's earlier work, *Educational Psychology*, presents "Pavlov's theories in rather apologetic terms, claiming that reflexes ought to become the foundation of the new psychology" (p. 67). Moreover that text seems "peppered with quotations from the influential party leader and theoretician, Leon Trotsky" so that "at times the text is so far from Vygotsky that it looks like a page lifted from a popular communist propaganda brochure."
>
> (cited in Knox, 1993, p. 3)

This observation provides a reminder that quoting Vygotsky at one point in his career does not necessarily capture his thinking as it developed over time. As I'll relate in Part IV, among the criticisms he faced during the Pedology Decree was that he was Pavlovian, which did not characterize his work in the latter half of his decade in Moscow. Vygotsky, like many others, cannot be essentialized through single quotes. Reading widely across the span of his career will produce a much better appreciation for his willingness to challenge himself, along with the orthodoxies of his day, such that he progressed in his conception of human psychology well beyond the limits of his initial perspective and indebtedness to the leading thinkers of the late Tsarist and early Soviet Union periods.

Kellogg and Veresov (2019) review how

> [in] contemporary Vygotskian studies, there is a traditional and widely accepted scheme of [viewing Vygotsky's career]: Stage One (before 1927); Stage Two (1927–1930/31), with Stage Three … lasting from 1932 until 1934. This periodization of Vygotsky's life and work has created a common platform for generations of contemporary researchers for advancing and improving Vygotsky's theory. Interestingly, many are building their improvements on the second stage, the instrumental period in Vygotsky's evolution (e.g., Cole, Engeström, and Wertsch). In the last decade, a "revisionist" trend has emerged, claiming that in the last stage Vygotsky rejected this second period and returned to his early preoccupations with personality, fantasy, imagination and emotions (González Rey 2011, 2017). So recently published materials (Zavershneva 2010; Zavershneva and Van der Veer, 2018[a]) are cited as evidence that Vygotsky was moving in the direction of a new theory of consciousness that rejected the whole distinction between higher and lower mental functions and instead focused on the relations between functions and on understanding consciousness as a dynamic semantic system.
>
> (p. xvi)

Vygotsky was a work in progress, halted by tuberculosis as he approached his prime of life. He thus left an incomplete body of work that has been developed by others for nearly a century now, and no doubt will have impact for at least another.

Vygotsky's Jewish Heritage

Vygotsky was born to an affluent Jewish family—his father was a banker—in the Pale of Settlement in the city of Orsha in Belarus. His family moved to Gomel in his childhood. The Pale was situated on the western side of the Dnieper (also Dnipro or Dnyapro) River. Its shifting borders were indicated by "pales" or stakes (and thus fences), and comprised areas west of Russia in Belarus, Lithuania, Moldova, Ukraine, Poland, and Latvia. The phrase "beyond the pale" refers to being beyond the stakes defining an area, and thus in the wilderness; and being "impaled" characterizes being pierced with a stake, in the fashion of a vampire.

The Pale of Settlement was occupied by about 5 million Jewish people at about the time of Vygotsky's birth. It was where Jewish people in Tsarist Russia were required to live following its establishment by the Russian queen of German origin, Catherine the Great, both to segregate them from the purity of the Christian Romanovs, and to confine them for control and terrorism via pogroms. The problem of anti-Semitism in the region was not new, and has persisted through the fall of communism and rise of Putin (Zisels et al.,

2014). During the Khmelnitsky Uprising of 1648–1649, Russian Cossacks murdered much of the Jewish population in Gomel. The city was a little over half Jewish at the time of Vygotsky's birth (Vad Vashem, 2021), and during Vygotsky's upbringing in Gomel, the Jewish community was subjected to several deadly attacks.

Jewish Ostracism and Vygotsky's Inclusive Stance

Vygotsky's Jewish childhood during this threatening period helped to shape his view of societal and educational inclusion (Kotik-Friedgut & Friedgut, 2008; Smagorinsky, 2012a; Zavershneva & Van der Veer, 2018b). As I'll detail when discussing his role in Russian special education—known by the dreadful name of "defectology"— in Chapter 14, Vygotsky (1993) never took a pathological view of people whose lives were affected by what are known as "disabilities." Rather, he viewed them as normal people who needed other means of navigation (e.g., braille and walking canes for people lacking sight) so that they could participate in society as valued, productive members. This perspective enabled him to see the potential of all people to feel appreciated and included, and thus to undertake life with feelings of affirmation, belonging, and valued productivity. Such possibilities were denied to the Jewish people of the Pale of Settlement, except for the support they received from within their insular communities.

Vygotsky applied his inclusive vision to children who had been blinded, deafened, and cognitively diminished during the decade of war extending from the onset of World War I through the final conclusion of the Russian Civil War in 1920 and subsequent installation of Lenin as the head of government. Lenin was in bad health when he assumed Soviet leadership, and he came to power amid continuing political divisions and a devastating drought. These social challenges came atop the rubble of nearly a decade of continual war and the task of building a radical new communist society across a mammoth nation, the world's largest, occupying one-sixth of the globe's landmass. The Soviet Union had coasts on both the Pacific Ocean and Black Sea's portal to the Mediterranean world and Atlantic Ocean; a massive, frigid northern coast that connects the Atlantic and Pacific through the Arctic Ocean and its many seas; and a small coast west of St. Petersburg on the Gulf of Finland, which connects to the Baltic Sea and then the Atlantic. The north-south coordinates also span a great distance, ranging from the Arctic Circle to Afghanistan. Bringing this gargantuan land mass together as a single, unified society was an epic challenge, even as the Leninist goal was to eradicate national borders altogether and form a class-based continental entity.

Lenin's health declined, culminating with his death following a brain hemorrhage at the age of 53 in January 1924. Stalin's ascension to a reign of three decades had dramatic consequences for millions of people in Eastern Europe and the expanses of the Soviet Union (Snyder, 2010; Solzhenitsyn, 1973), including its psychologists and educators, who were considered to be among the "intelligentsia" who comprised a threat to Stalin's command.

Between his own experiences with ostracism in Gomel and his work in special education with children devastated by war, Vygotsky developed a compassionate view toward those often believed to have little societal worth. He understood life as a member of a despised cultural group that was excluded from opportunities in the broader society, one with which he strongly identified:

> Vygotsky combined an intense interest in and identification with the Jewish identity and history with a non-religious worldview. As so often happens in the case of Jews

and others who suffer discrimination, the outside hostility and harassments would almost have forced him to take an interest in his ethnic background had this interest not been there in the first place.

(Van der Veer, 2014, p. 16)

Evolutionary psychologists have taken an interest in how people view "the other," those from outside their kinship groups. Affluence, they have found, can isolate others from one's own vision and caring networks. Outcasts who have experienced rejection are more likely to develop empathy toward people from outside their social groups. Both extend empathy; one tends to offer compassion to people like themselves, while the other extends care in order to understand the feelings of outsiders, especially those experiencing trauma and discrimination (Castano & Giner-Sorolla, 2006; Dietze & Knowles, 2020; Kraus, Côté, & Keltner, 2010). It's therefore little surprise, then, that the ostracized Jewish Vygotsky was committed to the social well-being and psychological equilibrium of people considered inferior in the population.

Vygotsky's Secular Judaism

Zavershneva and Van der Veer (2018a), in their reading of Vygotsky's notebooks, conclude that Vygotsky, prior to his move to Moscow, was far more concerned with the state and fate of the Jewish people than he was to any Marxist ideology:

> the young Vygotsky rejected all contemporary ideas to save the Jewish people from discrimination and persecution by creating an autonomous state in Palestine or elsewhere. Instead, until well into 1917, Vygotsky [at about age 20] proposed the rather traditional option of strengthening the spiritual roots of the Jews by returning to the religious writings. Socialism was rejected, because it merely envisioned the compulsory redistribution of material goods and 'man lives not by bread alone'. It was only after the October Revolution that Vygotsky switched from arguments in favour of the religious faith in the Kingship of God to the communist belief in a Radiant Future.
>
> (p. 36)

The idea of establishing a Jewish homeland was in place well before World War II, with Palestine and Madagascar (under French control) considered possible destinations in Vygotsky's lifetime (Gilbert, 1994; Snyder, 2015). Hitler was the century's most virulent and violent opponent. But he was hardly alone in seeing Jewish people as not only subhuman, but bent on world domination, as described in the widely circulated forgery purportedly describing their evil intentions, *Protocols of the Learned Elders of Zion*. As many people sought a place to send them, Vygotsky hoped for an internal solution to the "Jewish problem" that nobody wanted them.

This dedication to the Jewish people was more secular than observant. Vygotsky was a member of the Jewish culture more than the synagogue, perhaps enabling his transition to the atheistic Soviet Union. As I'll review, Vygotsky became a Marxist, the problem being that there was no single way of being a Marxist; and in the Soviet Union, orthodoxies specified the sort of person one ought to be. Developmentally, Vygotsky grew up in a tight Jewish community that was banished from the mainstream of society and was periodically subjected to deadly pogroms, attacks that were condoned by the government. I postulate that this experience fundamentally shaped his view of the outsider whose life is degraded by the brutality of the mainstream, and whose sense of self relies on finding a valued role to play in productive, appreciated, and rewarded cultural work (see Chapter 14).

Vygotsky's Initial Soviet Idealism

Vygotsky was a product of the transition from the anti-Semitism of Tsarist Russia and its satellite nations to the formation of the new, unified, collectivist Soviet Union, albeit one layered atop a culture infused with anti-Semitism (Korey, 1972) that was not yet evident to the idealistic followers of the Revolution. Going from the oppression experienced by Belarusian Jewish communities to a society whose ideals called for full social equality surely disposed Vygotsky to embrace the new regime, and at the outset of the Soviet era, he surely did. He thus wrote, at times rhapsodically, about the possibilities afforded by communism and its celebration of the worker and the role of such institutions as the Young Pioneers and Young Communists in cultivating a new generation of good Soviet proletarian citizens destined to evolve as the New Soviet Man[8] (Vygotsky, 1993).

Soboleva (2017) recounts the development of this dramatic term, reviewing how it "ranged between two poles: the idea of the renewal of humanity according to socialist ideals, and the practical embodying of this idea in the Soviet Union. The first pole is marked with the utopian term 'New Soviet Man,' and the second pole with the sarcastic term 'homo sovieticus'" (p. 65). Furthermore, "The most perplexing problem raised by this phenomenon emerges from the inconsistent relationship between theory and praxis, and concerns the confusion of the concept 'Soviet man' with the empiric phenomenon" (p. 67). In this volume, I am wholly concerned with how Stalin provided the material reality for realizing this development, and not the ideals that surrounded its original conception, articulated both by Bolsheviks and foreign sympathizers like Reed (1919a/2020). Vygotsky himself, however, was swept up in the fervor for an egalitarian society promised by Soviet communists, one that would eradicate the discrimination he and his fellow Belarusian Jews had endured for centuries.

For example, Vygotsky spoke glowingly of the Young Pioneers and Young Communists, youth groups who were socialized into communistic ways to promote the future of Soviet society. Yet these groups, under Stalin, were given a role in starving the peasants to feed the proletariat, one drastic means of weeding out the undesirables to clear the path for the New Soviet Man to evolve. As described by Snyder (2010),

> Members of the Young Communists served in the brigades that requisitioned food. Still, younger children, in the Pioneers, were supposed to be 'the eyes and ears of the party inside the family.' The healthier ones were assigned to watch over the fields to prevent theft. Half a million preadolescent and young teenage boys and girls stood in the watch towers observing adults in the Soviet Ukraine in summer 1933. All children were expected to report on their parents.
>
> (p. 50)

Vygotsky's Panglossian optimism was soon dashed on the rocks of Stalin's totalitarianism and the latent anti-Semitism of Soviet society (Korey, 1972). But in his earlier writing, Vygotsky was an avid supporter of the new communist rule and its promise of an equitable society. The values and practices of Stalin's Soviet Union are often indistinguishable from those of neo-Stalinist Vladimir Putin, in whose Russian state children have been recruited to report adults who are not fully aligned with state decisions, such as invading neighboring nations (Whalen, 2022).

European Influence

Vygotsky's life as a Jewish man from an affluent family, in spite of how violently their human value was rejected by the Romanovs, shaped what might be considered his elitist, Western views of culture (see Chapter 4). It also likely contributed to his rejection by the Soviets as a Jew, an outsider, and a threat steeped in bourgeois Western influences (Van der Veer, 2002). The proto-Russian area of Rus was a medieval European society composed of an amalgamation of ethnic groups. The ruler of Kyiv in the 900s, Valdimar, was

> not a Russian. There were no Russians at the time. He was the leader of a clan of Scandinavian warlords who had established a state in Kyiv, having wrenched the city from the control of Khazars. His clan was settling down, and the conversion to Christianity was part of the effort to build a state. It was called "Rus," apparently from a Finnish word for the slavetrading company that brought the Vikings to Kyiv in the first place. It was not called "Rus" because of anything to do with today's Russia—nor could it have been, since there was no Russia then, and no state would bear that name for another seven hundred years. Moscow, the city, did not exist at the time.
>
> (Snyder, 2022b, n.p.)

In spite of these roots, and the fact that the Romanov Catherine the Great was a German with hopes of making Russia into a European empire, "the West" and its decadent capitalism and bourgeois ways have served as a monstrous Russian, Soviet, and post-Soviet bogey-person for ages. The Russians and Soviets thus are indebted to traditions emerging from European nations, while the specter of Western excess and its accompanying military threat has helped their leaders maintain a victim's identity for many generations (Snyder, 2018), including those in the post-Soviet era under the management of Vladimir Putin.

European Culture

Davydov (1997a) describes how Vygotsky managed the tension between being a devoted Marxist in the Soviet Union who is also a product of European intellectual traditions, saying that his research program must be viewed

> against the background of that of his contemporaries, reflexologists and "Marxist psychologists" and others who were ready to rearrange things in their mission to invent a new utopian science and society. What later distinguished Vygotsky was his ability to accept the task as it was posed by the turbulent Soviet social reality of the 1920s, but to approach it with methods informed by the Western intellectual tradition.
>
> (p. xv)

Among those traditions is the German notion of *kultur*, an appreciation of the finest work a society has to offer (Adorno, 2009). It elevates the compositions of Beethoven and Bach over the performance of the local school orchestra. In his doctoral dissertation,

The Psychology of Art, Vygotsky made it clear that he might have agreed with the satirical US 1960s songwriter Tom Lehrer (1965). When introducing a parody of the folk song "Clementine," Lehrer quipped that "the reason most folk songs are so atrocious is that they were written by—*the people*," spoken with a condescending sneer. To Vygotsky, "folk art" undertaken by "the people" is of lesser value than the sort of highbrow works produced by Shakespeare, Tolstoy, and other canonical literary greats. He arrived at this judgment even as he acknowledged the ways in which the production of texts is a potentially key means of psychological mediation for children, no matter how crude or unsophisticated the appearance of the products (see Chapter 13).

Vygotsky was influenced by European culture in an era when most societies were parochial, and travel and communication across distances were difficult. Transportation was unreliable, and the violence surrounding Eastern Europe in the first several decades of the 20th century damaged roads, relationships, and airwaves. People knew their surroundings, but lacked broader means of communication from afar to inform their beliefs. Solnick (1991) reports that telephone access in the early Soviet Union was minimal; and Lovell (2015) finds that early Soviet radio usage was spotty and controlled by the state. In such insular societies, people often viewed themselves as more culturally advanced than other societies, without knowing much about how others lived.

European Rationalism

Vygotsky was socialized in such a world to accept his society's culture, along with those European influences deeply embedded in pre-Soviet life, as the pinnacle of human civilization's progress. Although the Soviets viewed themselves as separate from Europe and the West, Vygotsky was among the inheritors of European traditions and assumptions, many of which were embodied in monarchial Tsarist Russia, with capitalistic authoritarianism among the reasons the Romanovs were threatened by revolutions in 1905 and 1917. These perspectives included the rationalistic values grounded in the Age of Reason, the Scientific Revolution, and the European Enlightenment, which valued dispassionate analysis and non-mystical interpretations of the cosmos suitable to life in an advanced, industrialized society.

Vygotsky accepted the rationalistic, Marxist premise that humans use their intellect to create cultural tools to control nature and thus reduce chaos and increase chances for collective human survival. Just as critically, he argued that cultural *psychological* tools—principally speech—enable the self-regulation of primal emotions (see Chapter 7). His emphasis on speech-mediated regulation was among the reasons he was dismissed as anti-Marxist and insufficiently oriented to material reality (see Part IV).

This rationalistic assumption was integrated into the ideas of the leading philosophers of the era—Marx, Bacon,[9] Spinoza[10]—and pervasive in Vygotsky's surroundings. His appropriation of such a worldview both illustrates his own theory of culturally mediated human development, and helps to explain his assumption that his own society was at the cutting edge of human progress. This belief in human progress, embodied in Soviet communism, may have been undermined by Stalin's Great Purge, including the Pedology Decree that shut down Vygotsky's career as he approached death. The concurrent effort to obliterate dissent, punish the intelligentsia, and elevate the working class was designed to eradicate the "wrecking" (i.e., undermining, sabotage) of Soviet society (described in detail by Solzhenitsyn, 1973).

Bakhurst (2007), rather than viewing Vygotsky's indebtedness to the rationalist tradition as limiting, writes in defense of Vygotsky's commitment to philosophical rationalism. Bakhurst was interested in the factors that drove Vygotsky's genius, rather than the traits that might tarnish his reputation as an elitist. Rationalism, argues Bakhurst, imbued Vygotsky's perspective with "Eurocentrism and his linear vision of historical progress" (p. 74). Bakhurst argues against the notion that "the fecundity of Vygotsky's insights depends on liberating them from this rationalist perspective, which, it is claimed, has a deleterious, indeed reactionary, influence on his thought" (p. 51). Rather, this orientation provided Vygotsky, powered by his formidable intellect, with the tools he needed to synthesize a complex host of ideas into a psychology that resolved the crisis of fragmentation that he found in the field of his day.

Modern-day educators who are concerned with equity are left to sort through this conundrum and decide how to evaluate the contributions of a man who aligned his vision with the practitioners of *haute couture* and viewed everyday textual production as having meager potential for promoting the development of Western higher mental processes. He thus valorized those ways of thinking that distill the values of the culture (see Chapter 2), while also arguing on behalf of developmental tools whose products typically have no archival value to society.

Vygotsky and Competing Intellectual Traditions

Vygotsky's intellectual heritage is complicated by its indebtedness to both European traditions and the Soviet view that "Western decadence" is among the means historically employed by Russians and Soviets to position Europe and the United States as eternal threats to the Motherland. Wertsch (2000, 2007) argues that other mixed heritages were at work as well. The inconsistencies he finds in Vygotsky's account of mediation follow from Vygotsky's simultaneous grounding in what appear to be contradictory ontologies in European thought (see Chapter 13). One view is centered on the role of "explicit" mediation (through observable means), grounded in the "designative" tradition consistent with Enlightenment or rationalist (Bakhurst, 2007) traditions. One is concerned with "implicit" mediation (through intangible means), associated by Wertsch with "expressivist" or Romantic traditions. These two traditions correspond roughly with "product" and "process" understandings of how people communicate, with one focused on the final appearance and the other centered on the generation of communicative texts. These seemingly contradictory epistemologies had influenced European thought for centuries at the time of Vygotsky's career.

Wertsch (2000) argued initially that Vygotsky seemed unaware of this contradiction and never resolved it. In 2007, he looks for more synthesis, arguing that "the two forms of mediation can be seen as part of a larger theoretical framework" (p. 191). This resolution addresses Taylor's (1985a, 1985b) concern that integrating these two traditions makes for bad philosophy: "there are very few of us who do not feel the force of both [designative and expressivist traditions].... [H]owever effective this compromise may be politically, it is a rotten one intellectually; it combines ... scientism (objectivism) with ... subjectivist forms of expression" (pp. 246–247). As I'll argue in Chapter 13, this "rotten" compromise is in fact dynamic and productive. It allows for a sophisticated interpretation of different acts of mentation that allow for both traditions to promote different but related cognitive and social acts.

Vygotsky in the Soviet Context

Following Vygotsky's move to the new Soviet center of Moscow, he became immersed in a society that had a specific revolutionary mindset and that was designed to produce one type of citizen. It was built around the ideal of equality and the noble character of the everyday laborer. I next review aspects of that society that provided the contexts for Vygotsky's career.

A Dictatorship of the Proletariat

According to Draper (1987),

> The phrase 'dictatorship of the proletariat' first appeared in a series of articles by Marx, later titled *The Class Struggles in France 1848–1850*, published in what was then Marx's own London magazine. The first article, written in January 1850, came off the press in early March. The expression or its equivalent appeared not once but three times—in each of the three installments (or chapters) that comprised the original series.
>
> This work was Marx's attempt to sum up the political meaning of the European revolution of 1848–1849. Marx had taken an active part in this revolution in the German arena, as editor of the leading organ on the revolutionary left, at the same time closely following the turbulent developments in France and Vienna in particular. The revolution was now over, and Marx was thinking over its lessons.
>
> (n.p.)

Draper (1987) proceeds to sort through shifting meanings for the term "dictatorship," which Marx and Engels used in more than one way. He reports Engels as saying, "Of late, the Social-Democratic philistine has once more been filled with wholesome terror at the phrase: dictatorship of the proletariat. Well and good, gentlemen, do you want to know what this dictatorship looks like? Look at the Paris Commune [the revolutionary government that seized power in France in 1871]. That was the dictatorship of the proletariat." Draper clarifies the tendency to attribute the wrong meaning to Marx's phrase:

> the reader must put aside the modern aura that makes 'dictatorship' a dirty word for us; for this aura did not yet exist. How do you counteract the primitive notion of dictatorship that was so common precisely among the people who wanted to be good revolutionaries? You tell them: *Dictatorship? That means rule. Yes, we want the rule of the proletariat; but that does not mean the rule of a man or a clique or a band or a party; it means the rule of a class. Class rule means class dictatorship.*
>
> (n.p.; emphasis in original)

Furthermore, as argued by Reed (1919b/2011), "as soon as the capitalist class has disappeared, the Dictatorship [of the Proletariat] automatically ceases" (p. 73). The French overthrow of the monarchy might serve as a model for Bolsheviks to get rid of the Romanovs and institute a more democratic society in which the workers owned the means of production and took control of society. Yet in the USSR, the meaning provided by Marx and Engels turned away from their egalitarian conception. "Thus," argues Draper (1987), "the antidemocratic interpretation of 'dictatorship of the proletariat,' repudiated by Engels when it was reported to him, was going to blossom in the Second International[11] and particularly in the Russian movement" (n.p.).

Yet the proletariat were not a singular group. Broadly speaking, there were urban industrialists and rural peasant farmers, considered to be of different and unequal sophistication. Reed (1919d/2011) wrote that

> Russia is not an industrial country; it is a land of peasants. The vast majority of the soldiers therefore, must be peasants. But it is the industrial workers who made, and who now lead and direct the Revolution. The peasant, infinitely backward in comparison with the city worker, followed the latter until he received the land. The peasant, as a general rule, wants to own his land, to have free markets for his products—this is his petty bourgeois psychology. He usually does not understand Communism, or the ultimate aims of the Revolution. The villages are far removed from the burning life of the great towns, and the peasant, being as a rule unable to read or write, and living far away from the front, usually knows very little of the causes of the war.
>
> If it were not for the incessant attacks on Soviet Russia and the terrible condition of the economic life, necessitating the straining of all resources of the conscious industrial workers, it would be possible to agitate and explain these things to the peasant; as it is, an enormous amount of education is carried on; but not enough. And in the meanwhile the peasant must be made to fight, so that the Revolution, and his own future happiness, may not be lost.... The draft [conscription] has proceeded, each time, without a hitch and the peasant in the Red Army will return to his village a revolutionist and a propagandist.
>
> (p. 89)

Reed (1919a/2011) relates Lenin's recognition that a proletarian revolution will require more sophisticated leaders: "While the peasants had been politically backward, still they had their own peculiar ideas, and they constituted more than eighty percent of the people of Russia.... Lenin's 'Instructions to Peasants' ... explained the Bolshevik revolution and the new Government in simple terms" (pp. 278–279). Ironically, the formulation of Marxist thought came from the educated class, the intelligentsia reviled by Stalin; and had its grounding in European thinkers and exemplars. The centralized planners in Moscow conceptualized a social order in which their own status would be diminished, an outcome only partially achieved in that the Revolution was undertaken from the top, and the state was run by its intellectual architects, not factory workers or rural farmers, those noble Soviets symbolized on the Soviet flag by the hammer and sickle. Hierarchies were thus built into the new society, with elite leaders using their privileged positions to purge enemies from interfering with their plans. Yet elitism was in turn considered bourgeois when practiced by others.

Vygotsky was contradictory in his view of such a dictatorship of the working class. His personal history might predict an inconsistent orientation to social class issues. Born into relative affluence and privilege, yet also born into subhuman assumptions as a Jew; raised to appreciate culture's most lasting art and theater, yet viewing children's crude art as developmentally important; educated in the most rigorous schools and universities, yet steeped in Marxism's claims to egalitarianism: He was a contradiction waiting to happen.

His elitist views created a chasm between him and Soviet doctrine, which elevated the status of the proletariat and privileged them over the intellectuals (at least, those intellectuals not involved in Soviet philosophy and rule), Stalin's despised intelligentsia. The Soviets' goal of creating a workers' paradise required a redistribution of power, one that relied on the elimination of the bourgeoisie through execution and banishment in order to even the scales. The Soviets' dedication to a class-less society also required psychologists to frame their work in terms of social class inequities, something Vygotsky addressed in his early pedological writing (Van der Veer, 2020) if not eventually to Stalin's satisfaction, even as his developmental theory has recently been employed to interpret social class differences (e.g., Moll, 2000).

The anti-intellectualism of the Soviet Union can be traced to Lenin himself upon the overthrow of the Romanovs. Solzhenitsyn (1973), a labor camp survivor, reports that Lenin's hatred of the intelligentsia was revealed in his 1919 statement that "In actual fact [the intelligentsia] are not [the nation's brains], but shit" (p. 328), a slovenly, pious, short-sighted, bourgeois, imperialist group who had, in Solzhenitsyn's ironic terms, "*betrayed the cause of the workers*.... This mockery of the intelligentsia, this contempt for the intelligentsia, was subsequently adopted with enthusiasm by the publicists and the newspapers of the twenties and was absorbed into the current of day-to-day life" (p. 328; emphasis in original).

In a letter to Comrade Kursky, Solzhenitsyn reports, Lenin felt that oppressing the intellectuals by any means was a necessary tactic. Lenin wrote,

> The court must not exclude terror. It would be self-deception or deceit to promise this, and in order to provide it with a foundation and to legalize it in a principled way, clearly and without hypocrisy and without embellishment, it is necessary to formulate it as broadly as possible, for only revolutionary righteousness and a revolutionary conscience will provide the conditions for applying it more or less broadly in practice. With Communist greetings, Lenin.
>
> (p. 353)

This sentiment was shared by such people as Nikolai Vasilyevich Krylenko, Prosecutor and ultimately People's Commissar for Justice of the USSR. He was a rabid prosecutor, who played a role in both Lenin's original "Red Terror" and Stalin's subsequent "Great Purge." Tuller (1996) reports Krylenko declaring that "We must execute not only the guilty. Execution of the innocent will impress the masses even more" (p. 6). Krylenko was a formidable enforcer of Soviet authority, and was among the architects of a legal approach in which a verdict and sentence for an accused crime were decided in advance. This policy, Krylenko explained, "shows the superiority of our system over the false theory of the separation of powers," that is, the theory of the independence of the judiciary. Rather, the system allowed Chair of the All-Russian Central Executive Committee, Yakov Sverdlov, to state that "It is very good that the legislative and executive power are not divided by a thick wall as they are in the West. All problems *can be decided quickly*" (Solzhenitsyn, 1973, p. 307; emphasis in original).

Krylenko himself had stated that "No matter how much is said here about the eternal law of truth, justice, etc., we know ... how dearly these have cost us.... No matter what the individual qualities [of the defendant], only one method of evaluating him is to be applied: evaluation from the point of view of *class expediency*" (Solzhenitsyn, 1973, p. 308; emphasis in original). A person could be prosecuted for offenses "in their *pasts*, in their biographies!" (Solzhenitsyn, p. 312; emphasis in original). Not only were violations to be prosecuted and punished in this fashion. People could be executed *for what they might do later*. As Krylenko said, "We protect ourselves not only against the past but also against the future" (Solzhenitsyn, p. 309).

Krylenko's life met its finale in 1938, and illustrated his own policies well. It began with a denunciation based on an accusation that he was a "wrecker" of Soviet life. He was immediately imprisoned, tortured, and put on trial, which lasted 20 minutes. Found guilty, he was promptly shot in the back of the head.

The intelligentsia were among those considered a threat to the Stalinist Soviet order. Solzhenitsyn (1973) quotes Victor A. Larichev, a Soviet engineer who was a member of the outlawed Industrial Party. He and many other engineers and scientists were subjected to a show trial in 1930 in which they were accused and convicted of plotting to overthrow the Soviet government (Gvozdetsky & Budreyko, 2021), leading to their imprisonment (most commuted from sentences to execution) (see Krylenko, 1930, for an account provided by the prosecutor). At the trial Larichev accused the intelligentsia in 1930 of being "mush.... [I]t has no backbone, and this constitutes unconditional spinelessness.... How immeasurably superior is the sensitivity of the proletariat," leading to "intelligentsia" being used "as a term of abuse" (Solzhenitsyn, p. 399). Rather, the everyday worker was elevated to a position of dominance and status. Solzhenitsyn poses the problem ironically:

> How could *engineers* accept the *dictatorship of the workers*, the dictatorship of their subordinates in industry, so little skilled or trained and comprehending neither the physical nor the economic laws of production, but now occupying the top positions, from which they supervised the *engineers*? Why shouldn't the engineers have considered it more natural for the structure of society to be headed by those who could intelligently direct its activity?
>
> (p. 390; emphasis in original)

Vygotsky's career in the Soviet Union spanned this period in which the proletariat were viewed as more knowledgeable than the bourgeoisie, which included the intelligentsia and other educated classes, although not the leadership class. Like the engineers and many others, Vygotsky fell into disfavor and faced the wrath of the authorities.

Between his independence, his elitism, his intellectualism, and other factors that violated the Soviet ethos, Vygotsky's work was suppressed during his life, and his legacy was buried after his death. Eliminating class distinctions produced new class distinctions. No matter how bent a society is on striving toward equality—a basic goal of communism—such social hierarchies always seem to emerge. Stalin's lockdown on academics like Vygotsky is emblematic of that pattern.

In capitalist Europe, the educated classes had been traditionally considered to be more advanced than the common laborers celebrated by Marxists. This belief in the value of education and expertise conflicted with the Party's belief that the proletariat has as much wisdom as the intellectual elites (to Lenin, society's "shit"), held back only by the artificial barriers of class distinctions. As is often the case in developing social concepts, this belief co-existed with the contradictory view available from the notion of *kultur*, the appreciation of great works, at least in Europe. Because they lack the shackles of class-based socialization, believed the Soviet leaders, communist laborers had developed greater insight than is possible through formal knowledge learned through academia. At least that was the official reason. There is good reason to believe that the leaders found the proletariat more loyal and easier to control than people from educated backgrounds (Fitzpatrick, 1979). This dynamic led to a situation in which

> institutional reforms often brought about the tragic dismissal of personnel who were often replaced by young Communists eager for self-advancement.... [T]hese

replacements were frequently people of inferior scholarship whose enthusiasm for social reconstruction led to their appointments [according to] a belief in the sound judgement of the vast flag-waving masses of daily workers as opposed to, for instance, the small minority of unconvinced "culturally refined intellectuals." ... The Party's task was to create trustworthy academics out of people of proletarian background and dubious education.

(Van der Veer & Valsiner, 1991, pp. 43, 93, 118)

In attempting to create a utopian society that liberated the worker from oppression, the Soviet leaders created a different social hierarchy that privileged and rewarded laborers (the proletariat) and considered academics (the bourgeoisie) to represent a suspiciously elite social caste.

Vygotsky and Soviet Communism

The contributors to Daniels et al. (2007) contextualize and historicize Vygotsky's career and work throughout their essays. They argue for a reciprocal conception of context, one that takes into account the etymology of "context" as derived from *contexere*, meaning "weaving together" (Cole, 1996). Vygotsky, then, while a product of his times, also helped to produce his times, even as Stalin's iron fist served to minimize the role of noncompliers in the direction society took. This sense of situated agency is critical to understanding a Vygotskian perspective, which relies on the premise that thinking is social in origin rather than being reliant solely on biological maturation (see Chapter 5), yet is not fatalistic about the implications of this condition for how individuals may potentially act on their environments.

There are additional divisions that complicate the notion of a unified Western culture. The foundational form of decadence in non-Soviet societies, to the Soviet mind, was its capitalist orientation, which produced greed, inequity, and social class distinctions that were difficult to dislodge or transcend. If the Soviets had a European influence, it came from Prussia, the boyhood home of Karl Marx (1867/1887; Marx & Engels, 1948), who also lived in a variety of European cities in the second half of the 19th century, including licentious London and Paris. Soviet society required a distinction between capitalistic and communistic social and economic organizations. Communism was, according to Marxist doctrine, a superior and inevitable economic and social system, destined to prevail over time as capitalism collapses due to its own internal contradictions and faults (Pannekoek, 1934). Marxism and communism were thus dogmatically assumed to provide the ultimate stage of human progress, a substantial stratum above capitalism.

As proposed by another European thinker, British naturalist and biologist Charles Darwin (1859), linear evolutionary progress was evident, in this conception, in the development of the species from primates through various human types and societies. The evolution of societies culminated with the establishment of classless, collectivist societies; that is, humanity reached its most advanced form in the formation of the Soviet Union. Embedded in this perspective was the premise that the white people[12] who occupied these supremely advanced societies were evolution's greatest achievement.

Soviet ideology focused almost exclusively on nurture in the nature vs. nurture dispute, one that remains in the air in such areas as reading research (Yaden, Reinking, & Smagorinsky 2021). As related by Van der Veer and Valsiner (1991), Vygotsky believed that "in a classless society—where people have the same chances and opportunities—inter-individual differences are likely to reflect genetic differences, whereas in a [capitalist] society such as the U.S. this was extremely unlikely" (p. 192). He "sincerely believed the utopian statements of leading Soviet ideologists and politicians about the future communist state.... [C]ommunist man would live without conflict.... [He agreed with Trotsky] on the possibilities of transforming the human being.... The unlimited plasticity of human material could be exploited by organizing the social environment in the right way" (p. 55).

That right way was through communism, a belief initially shared by Vygotsky at the outset of the Soviet Union's establishment. The New Soviet Man would emerge from such a society ever greater than before: "Man will set himself the goal of mastering his own feelings, of raising the instincts to the height of awareness, to make them transparent, of laying wires from the will to the hidden and the subterranean and thereby raise himself to a new level—to create a 'higher,' societal biological type, if you wish—a superman" ([Vygotsky, 1997a, pp. 351]; quoted in Van der Veer & Valsiner, 1991, p. 56).[13]

The "lower" or biological aspects of human personality play a limited, often nonexistent role in development in the Soviet conception. What is critical is how one's biological inheritance is mediated culturally, and ideally toward Soviet communism (which evolved differently than did communism in Maoist China and Castro's Cuba, providing each a distinct economic and political system; see Castañeda, 1997; Horowitz & Suchliki, 2009). In adhering to this latter belief, Vygotsky was aligned with Soviet ideology, in which eliminating social class barriers liberated the working class to rise in status and power, albeit at the expense of the previously dominant bourgeoisie. He simultaneously, in violation of doctrine, attended to nature, the biological inheritance that provided individuals with the material through which culture would do its developmental work.

Discussion

This chapter has provided a brief account of some of the key factors that helped to shape Vygotsky's thinking, speech, and actions in his tragically short life. His life illustrates cultural-historical theory, which views human development as a long-term, tool-and-sign-mediated process in which one both works within cultural contours and continually works in opposition to the environment and the problems it presents (Tulviste, 1991) to produce new conceptions. Given that environments are not unitary, but rather are complex and contentious, Vygotsky emerged from his various means of socialization as a complicated, at times contradictory human being, just like the rest of us (Smagorinsky, 2020a).

The chapters that follow turn to specific areas of inquiry that Vygotsky undertook. My approach will spiral back to key points and events outlined in this chapter, producing the sort of redundancy often practiced by Vygotsky. Whether this practice is useful to the reader, or annoying, is no doubt a subjective matter.

Notes

1 John "Jack" Reed was born into wealth, then became a Marxist who co-founded the short-lived Communist Labor Party of America in 1919 and served as editor for the *New York Communist* and *The Voice of Labor* newspapers. He was portrayed by Warren Beatty (1981) in the film *Reds*, for which Beatty was presented the Academy Award for Best Director. "Ten Days that Shook the World" is an on-the-ground, first-person, doctrinaire, unabashedly pro-Bolshevik account of the October Revolution of 1917. Reed was adamant that World War I was solely about financial profiteering that advantaged industrialists and was conducted at the expense of working class people conscripted into the military. He shared the Soviets' belief that a global uprising of

working-class people was necessary to end all wars and bring equality to the world. To escape indictment for sedition in the United States, Reed emigrated to Moscow, where he became disillusioned with the commitment of the Revolution before he died of spotted typhus in 1920 at age 33, with complications from a kidney disease. He was celebrated by the Soviets, among three Americans buried at the Kremlin Wall Necropolis. In 1987, he was commemorated with a Soviet stamp reading, "Worker of the American labor movement, internationalist writer, John Reed."

2   I'm indebted to conversations with Carol D. Lee for providing nuance to my use of Westernism and Eurocentrism in a separate project, which in turn required greater attention to overgeneralization in this volume.
3   Van der Veer and Valsiner (1991) spell the city *Gomel'* but I will use the simplified and more common *Gomel*, which Van der Veer uses in his 2014 volume *Lev Vygotsky*.
4   Konstantin Nikolaevich Kornilov (1879–1957) was a Soviet psychologist whose Marxist orientation led him to be called the first Soviet psychologist. He abandoned his effort to include reflexology when it produced ideological critiques.
5   Translated interchangeably as Leont'ev or Leontiev. I will arbitrarily use Leont'ev throughout for consistency's sake, except when quoting or referencing a source.
6   I will follow the usage of bourgeoisie and bourgeois, in which bourgeoisie is a noun that refers to middle and upper class people, and bourgeois is an adjective that references middle-upper class values and practices.
7   See the Preface to this volume where I review the mistranslation of *conditional reflexes* as *conditioned reflexes*.
8   Throughout this volume I rely on sources that use masculine pronouns to refer to humanity. I leave these references unedited, given that they represent diction that was considered proper at the time of authorship and translation.
9   Francis Bacon (1561–1626) was a British philosopher and statesman. He was known as the Father of Empiricism, arguing that inductive reasoning should inform all thought and that skepticism should be present in all investigations to avoid improper or superficial conclusions.
10 Baruch Spinoza (1632–1677) was a Dutch philosopher of Portuguese Sephardic Jewish heritage whose ideas were central to Rationalism and the Enlightenment. A Biblical critic considered radical, he was posthumously included in the Catholic Church's *Index of Forbidden Books*. He was a strong influence on Vygotsky (Roth & Jornet, 2017).
11 The Second International (1889–1916) was an organization of socialist and labor parties from twenty nations. It continued the work of the First International, or International Workingmen's Association, which organized various Marxist groups into a political body. The Second International abandoned the First's anarcho-syndicalism, i.e., its anarchist embrace of unionism to eradicate the inequitable working conditions of capitalism.
12 Jewish people were not considered white, but of a subordinate race.
13 Van der Veer and Valsiner's reference precedes the 1997a translation available in English, and so has different pagination. Here I use the pagination from the 1997a translation.

2 Culture, History, and Society

Vygotsky has been associated with theoretical perspectives going by a variety of names, all leading to a similar end. Moll (1990) describes Vygotsky's work as *sociohistorical* psychology, Berkenkotter and Huckin (1995) characterize his theory as *sociocognitive*, Wertsch (1994) uses the term *sociocultural*, Atherton (2011) views Vygotsky as being a *social constructivist*, Rodina (2006) describes him as a *social constructionist*, Mikhailov (2006) characterizes the theory as *cultural-historical*, Portes and Salas (2011) drop the hyphen for *cultural historical*, Leont'ev (1981, 2005a, 2005b) labeled his adjustment to collectivist understandings *activity theory*, and Cole (1996) has chosen the term *cultural-historical activity theory* (CHAT) for his own adaptation of Vygotsky to his explorations in *cultural psychology*.

Each of these terms is justifiable. I will use *cultural-historical theory* because of its historical dimension, one that I find lacking in invocations of Vygotsky's name I see in pedagogical writing. For several years I used *activity theory* or *CHAT* to characterize my work (e.g., Grossman, Smagorinsky, & Valencia, 1999), but found activity theory subject to doctrinaire interpretations I did not share. I have become content with considering myself a Vygotskian researcher in the cultural-historical tradition. I next introduce the key terms that help inform cultural-historical theory and provide it with its impetus.

Culture

The term "culture" is often invoked in references to Vygotsky. It's important, then, to come to an agreement on what it means. Kroeber and Kluckhohn (1952/1963) identified 250 definitions of the term *culture* prior to Vygotsky's introduction to the English-speaking world; their original 1952 edition was published shortly before Stalin's death and so during the Soviet suppression of pedologists like Vygotsky. This variation creates an imperative to define culture as specifically as possible in the context of Vygotsky's work. I'll begin with a source I trust, Cole (2002), who describes culture as humans' principal medium of human development. Cole accepts the definition that culture refers to the inherited aspects of a society's achievement that in turn frame the context of life in the present, and thus into the future. Kroeber and Kluckhohn's "omnibus definition" provides further explication, with culture including:

> patterns, explicit and implicit, of and for behavior acquired and transmitted by symbols, constituting the distinctive achievements of human groups, including their embodiment in artifacts; the essential core of culture consists of traditional (i.e.,

DOI: 10.4324/9781003374848-3

historically derived and selected) ideas and especially their attached values; cultural systems may on the one hand be considered as products of action, on the other as conditioning elements of further action.

(p. 181)

Cole (1996) departs from others in the Vygotskian tradition in his bundling of tools and signs (see Chapter 5) as *artefacts* "to make them synonymous with what Kroeber and Kluckhohn refer to as culture's essential core.... [A]n artefact is an aspect of the material world that has been modified over the history of its incorporation into goal-directed human action" (p. 306). Artefacts, he asserts, are both *ideal* (conceptual) and *material*, and these qualities become attributed to signs through their use over time. Artefacts, Cole (2002) argues, may be as explicit and mundane as a recipe, or as implicit (and also mundane, by which I mean everyday) as a pattern of discourse. Culture thus, to Cole, emerges as:

a structured, artefact-saturated medium that is simultaneously ideal and material, inside the head and in the humanly transformed environment, that serves to coordinate newborns with their caretakers within the overall circumstances of the social group. It transforms our notion of the transactional processes involved in development by adding a 'third force' to the ordinary dichotomous view of development as a transactional process.

(p. 307)

Cole thus describes culture as a set of assumptions that become second nature, leading societal members to implicitly perpetuate a culture's practices, artefact structure, worldview, hierarchies, and other values under the impression that they are natural aspects of human life, rather than products of socialization. His shift to the artefact is one of the few ways in which I disagree with Cole, one of my most important sources in understanding cultural-historical psychology. I see Vygotsky's distinction between sign and tool to have great value, even considering that words as signs can have a tool function when they enable action, and also as psychological tools for planning action and other capabilities.

Among the concerns of Marxist-era Soviets was emphasizing how people are different from animals, and how people are apart from and seek to control nature (see Chapter 5). Culture is a consequence of psychology that enables people to emancipate themselves from nature and acquire ways to manage it and shield themselves from its vicissitudes.

Social Hierarchies

I would argue that with nature under control, or held at bay, people turn to *control over other people*, both individually and tribally, to assert their dominance. The committed Marxist would say that such an outcome is a consequence of capitalism and its social class distinctions and inequities, and thus competition and degradation. Yet power issues have driven Russian and Soviet ambitions, and human relationships within their society, through both their communistic and more recent kleptocratic periods. It seems more a human problem than one resulting from ideological economic systems, both of which position societies hierarchically and produce systems of subordination. In Stalin's Soviet Union, the unwanted were disposed of through execution, exile, or the Gulag (and thus, typically, death), suggesting an unequal society. Urban industrialist proletariat workers were believed to be more politically sophisticated than rural agrarian proletariat, all of whom were superior in character to the bourgeois. One set of hierarchies replaced another in the Bolshevik quest for equality.

The need to dominate other people produces societal discord and, ultimately, results in social hierarchies within communities and schools when a dominant culture establishes itself as the optimal version of the human species and treats all others as deficient, problematic, and in need of remediation toward dominant norms. This problem is evident in societies with colonial heritages, when inequity was instituted by the invaders when they first planted a European flag on foreign soil (Izzard, 1999). Capitalism produces a system that in turn creates competition designed to result in winners and losers, even as rhetoric and philosophy suggest that everyone has equal access to an affluent and prosperous life. This persistent condition creates different challenges for schools in English-speaking nations, then, who don't exterminate or banish the parts of the population deemed inferior or threatening. Or they subordinate and remove them anyhow, as many US charter schools do when they methodically de-enroll students whose performances don't match the school's rhetoric (Taylor, 2015).

Prolepsis and Telos in Development

Cole's (1996) uses the term *prolepsis* to characterize tacit means of structuring experience. Prolepsis helps account for subtle forms of mediation that work in concert with explicit rules, laws, and conventions that guide development. Wertsch and Sohmer (1995) provide a complementary notion in describing the role of *telos* in the organization of societies. A teleological end is one that is conceived of as the ideal way to complete a process. To the Soviets, the New Soviet Man, the good Soviet citizen of proletarian roots, embodied that ideal. Peters (1956), writing shortly after Stalin's death, reports that this value held steady throughout Stalin's period of rule:

> As early as 1923, the Soviet Education Law laid down the basic pattern and enunciated the objectives of the Soviet school. It stated: "All the work in the school and the whole organization of school life should promote proletarian class consciousness in the minds of pupils and create knowledge of the solidarity of Labor in its struggle with Capital as well as preparation for useful productive and political activity."
>
> In 1946, Pravda reported on an All-Union congress of educators which took place in Moscow. Their resolution, duly forwarded to Stalin, read: "We professors and instructors, obligate ourselves so to conduct our work that every day spent by a student in a higher educational institution will nurture in him Bolshevik ideology, broaden his political and cultural horizon, and enrich him with knowledge of his specialty."
>
> More recently the minister of education of the Russian Republic outlined the achievements and the final objective of Soviet education: "By educating the young in the spirit of Communism, our Soviet school has become the instrument of a cultural revolution, a weapon for the rebirth of society. For the first time a great reformative function was imposed on the school. It was confronted with the task of the nurture of a new man, free from the slavish psychology of capitalist society."
>
> (p. 421)

Peters concludes that over the course of Stalin's rule, "the objectives have remained remarkably constant" for the conduct of education (p. 421). These objectives represent the teleological end anticipated for Soviet schoolchildren, in turn shaping the experience of education in their schools.

In US schools, the white upper-middle class standards that were infused in schools by Horace Mann from the outset as a means of assimilating diverse immigrants into a unified society remain in place (Smagorinsky, 2021a). These psychological hierarchies are reinforced through various structures that I have called the *deep structure of school*: the institutionalized curriculum and assessment, dress codes, codes of conduct, approved speech genres and social languages, conventions for interaction, composition of administration and faculty, physical arrangement of schools, hidden curriculum, and other structural factors that organize the educational process according to a specific value system (Smagorinsky, 2020a, 2020b). Such cultures take on a façade of a natural, normalized social system, but are in fact ideologically constructed and maintained.

The role of these standards and structures is to establish the teleological destination for all students: "The child's social environment includes a variety of 'ideal forms' of the end-product of development (adult forms), and the developing child starts from the lack of possessing these forms. These 'ideal forms' guide the child's experiences with the social world, that is, his 'cooperation' with others, and direct the child's construction of meaningfulness in his relationship with the world" (Van der Veer & Valsiner, 1991, p. 317). The Soviet effort to force an entire population of a land mass encompassing 8.65 million square miles populated by roughly 150 million people[1] in Vygotsky's adulthood into a single mold proved a challenge, one requiring the extermination of millions of dissidents, suspected dissidents, accused dissidents, and collateral damage (Solzhenitsyn, 1973), and the re-education of those compliant people from newly incorporated lands. One could similarly argue that the effort by US schools to produce a single type of person based on the white middle class ideal has worked to the detriment of those from nondominant cultures, if not to their mass execution.

Culture and Education

Vygotsky himself associated culture with education (Van der Veer & Valsiner, 1991), with the well-educated person being a person of culture, of a specific type. This belief is engrained in other cultures as well. In the United States, Horace Mann's mass education program was designed to reshape the conduct, speech, appearance, faith, and other aspects of culture of the multiethnic European immigration wave of the mid-1800s. His goal was to assimilate a new generation of uniformly educated American citizens through schooling (Smagorinsky, 2021a). Educational uniformity to promote citizenship is an ancient practice. King Alfred The Great, king of the West Saxons and of the Anglo-Saxons, translated Latin texts into English in the late 800s and made required reading of "those books most necessary for all men to know" in order to develop wisdom and virtue. Similarly, the late-19th-century Mexican dictator Porfirio Díaz endorsed what might today be called Mexican cultural literacy à la E. D. Hirsch (1987) or a common core curriculum: "If all Mexicans learn the same thing," he is reputed to have said, "they will tend to act in the same way."

Uniformity, not diversity, has long provided the structure of mass education (Smagorinsky, 2022). Working against this deeply engrained conception of education as a medium for producing a particular sort of citizen (or for those who don't shape up, punishments) requires a strong rationale and a will to fight an entrenched institution that is supported by many stakeholders. Efforts at multicultural education and other challenges to the status quo have often been met with ferocious opposition (Pollack & Zirkel, 2013). This phenomenon requires a shift from Vygotsky's focus on the superiority of Soviet communism (see Chapter 4) and the role of schooling in promoting a devotion to it, to his account of cultural mediation. These oppositional perspectives—cultural-historical theory's attention to how cultures develop in relation to their environments, and Vygotsky's belief that some cultures are better than others—provide tensions for anyone hoping to find a way to resolve the availability of relativistic conceptions of the ideal society with the likelihood that that they prefer one over others.

Instruction is typically concerned with what teachers and students can demonstrate in short segments. Students are often positioned as generic, with the same problems being considered equally accessible to all students, regardless of their socialization and experiences in life and in school regimens. This assumption of a "problem isomorph" (Newman, Griffin, & Cole, 1989) and concurrent assumption of a *human isomorph* embody the idea that all people have identical access to solving a task, and that this task provides a sample for the rest of their capabilities.

Such conceptions pay little attention to the historical development of the students, the institution, the surrounding community, the teaching method, and other issues that help to produce a cultural phenomenon. It's important to remember, then, that cultural-historical theory would predict that well-entrenched institutions like schools are difficult to change, and difficult to work within if one is misaligned with what the school is designed to process and produce (Smagorinsky, 2010a). The Vygotskian instructional ideas I relate later in this book (see Part III) thus would always require contextualization, which is one reason I have argued against the notion of "best practices" (Smagorinsky, 2009b, 2018c) that might be effective in one setting, but not in another. It can't be "best" if there are places where it doesn't work well.

A focus on cultural mediation turns attention to the process by which consciousness is mediated by cultural signs and tools that communities of practice have developed over time (see Chapter 5). This historical view could in turn identify those aspects of an environment, including a school, that shape the thinking, speech (or other means of expression), and actions of the people who comprise its population. In a sense, this approach would allow for an understanding from within the institution of how it is structured to afford a particular kind of experience. This recognition could in turn suggest what sort of student is best served by that structure, and which ones do poorly because of a cultural mismatch with the institution (Moll, 2000; Portes & Smagorinsky, 2010; Smagorinsky, 2017).

Education in European and the colonized English world's schools typically relies on individual learning performances for assessment (Moll, 1990). Vygotsky's use of cultural-historical theory insists that people do not act alone, but instead enact cultural practices with historical roots, and do so in relation to the human artifacts of their environments. People need not be immediately present in order for an occasion to be social; the artifacts they leave behind help to structure the environments and infuse them with human values and implied practices. The environment itself is not the focus of attention: "paedology [pedology] studies the environmental structure as it relates to the psychological organization of the developing child, and is not interested in the environment as it exists in itself…. [This] relational emphasis … dominates any study of development" (Van der Veer & Valsiner, 1991, p. 315). What matters is how people subjectively construct, interpret, and assign meaning to the settings of their development (Smagorinsky, 2010b).

Culture and Collective Evolution

This attention to culture and history is central to a Vygotskian perspective. People have evolved in relation to social contexts, typically in collective ways, in contrast with the "survival of the fittest" beliefs that followed from Spencer's (1864) interpretation of Darwin (1859). Spencer's conception suggests that individual humans are engaged in a continual struggle against one another for dominance. But Darwin (1859) understood that people survive as groups, not as individuals. This fact explains how such a slow, weak, hairless creature—one lacking sharp teeth or claws, one largely helpless in infancy and early childhood—as a human being could outlast saber-tooth tigers and other fierce, hungry predators. A superior intellect and the tool of speech helped enable group survival, and simple intelligence is often offered as a reason for the enduring survival of homo sapiens. But in ancient times, talking didn't help an early human outrun a leopard or giant hyena. Rather, collective efforts in organizing and perpetuating cultures enabled groups of humans to survive their predators. These societies employed tools to construct protective environments and other assets and pass them down across generations, modified over time to meet new exigencies and employ more durable materials.

In this sense, people survive because they work as social units against the more powerful forces of nature, and accumulate cultural artefacts that help them perpetuate their domains. People are mutually indebted to one another for their personal survival and to ensure survival across generations. These groups in turn tend to work as social units against other social units, resulting in internecine and inter-group conflicts.

Through these networks of relationships, groups of people also become cultural beings and members of reciprocating, interrelated communities. South African literacy scholar Makalela (2019) has drawn on *ubuntu*, an African term that characterizes the essence of human communities. This concept is embodied in the expression "(I x We): I am because you are" (Makalela, 2019, p. 237). To which I'd add, We are because of what came before; and to which Makalela adds, "Ubuntu refers to an African humanism and cultural patterns that value overlaps, continuity, and cross-overs between communities. It finds expression in the slogans: 'I am because you are; you are because we are; visitor please come to my home so we are complete' to value complex and multi-directional interdependence between people" (pp. 239–240).

Vygotsky appears to have embraced such a view as well, saying, "I am conscious of myself only to the extent that I am another to myself" (1997b, p. 77). He described this relational view of human development as follows:

> through others we become ourselves, and this rule refers not only to the individual as a whole, but also to the history of each separate function. This also comprises the essence of the process of cultural development expressed in a purely logical form. The individual becomes for himself what he is in himself through what he manifests for others. This is also the process of forming the individual. In psychology, the problem of the relation of external and internal mental functions is posed here for the first time in all its significance. Here, as has been said, it becomes clear why everything internal in higher forms was of necessity external, that is, was for others what is now for oneself.
> (1997c, p. 105)

He situated this social orientation as a factor in human development, focusing on the principal medium of communication, *speech*, and its communal origins: "the meaning of the word exists objectively first for others and only later begins to exist for the child himself. All basic forms of social intercourse between the adult and the child later become mental functions" (1997c, p. 105). This phenomenon, as I will relate later (see Chapter 5), serves as the ultimate distinction that has favored human beings in evolution.

Culture and Power Differentials

Vygotsky (1997a) sounded remarkably like Makalela discussing *ubuntu* when he said, "we know ourselves insofar as we know other people, or, more precisely, that we are conscious of ourselves only to the extent we are other for ourselves, i.e., somehow alien to ourselves" (p. 172). My reference to *ubuntu* raises another conundrum in understanding Vygotsky, because undoubtedly he would have regarded the African people whose communities are organized around *ubuntu* as backward, as Luria did with the Muslim peasants in Uzbekistan. In his early writing Vygotsky said that "Investigation of so called primitive peoples is one of the richest sources for psychology. Certain peoples of the uncivilized world, being on the lowest rungs of cultural development, or usually called primitive or primal people in, of course, the relative sense of the word" (1997a, p. 82). Vygotsky simultaneously believed that cultures develop according to their own conditions and needs, thus making any social group's culture worthy of the people it serves; and that cultures like his own were more civilized and more highly culturally developed than those of "primitive or primal people."

It's hard to know what he would have believed had he lived a normal lifespan, dying in about 1970 instead of 1934, or until 1980, as did Jean Piaget, born the same year; and had he formulated his views in a different context. The resemblance to *ubuntu* follows from his imperative that people engage with their social environments to develop higher mental functions, those that are learned through cultural practice and validate an individual within a social group. The insularity of communities, however, tends to work against inter-group cooperation and respect. This problem greatly affects US schooling and its multicultural makeup, resulting in battles over the content of the curriculum, the most appropriate means of instruction, the makeup of the faculty in relation to the students, and many other points of contention. African people should not be viewed romantically; inter-tribal wars have long produced violent clashes, and colonial impositions have subordinated their communities to external values (Clegg, 2021). *Ubuntu* thus appears similar to Western notions of community in which people are bound together within groups, but not necessarily across them.

Cultures also inevitably produce power differentials. To Wertsch (1998), "Sociocultural settings inherently involve power and authority" (p. 64). He continues,

> The emergence of new cultural tools transforms power and authority. It is not as if cultural tools, in and of themselves, operate as independent, causal factors, but they can have a potent effect on the dynamics of human action, including the power and authority relationships involved in it…. [I]nstead of engaging in endless arguments over whether it is either the agent or society that really exists and is the foundation of power and authority, a focus on mediated action and the cultural tools employed in it makes it possible to "live in the middle" and to address the sociocultural situatedness of action, power, and authority.
>
> (p. 65)

Power is not always exerted with moral persuasion. In social conflicts, it's more often a bludgeon. Tools of conquest, such as the guns, germs, and steel described by Diamond

(1997), have provided the means by which one society comes to dominate another, rather than a superior morality or culture. These initial forms of brutality may then be converted into discriminatory laws that create advantages for those most similar to the power figures who construct them (Glaude, 2016; Lipsitz, 2009). Schools inevitably manifest these broader forms of discrimination in their structure, making them better suited to meet some students on their own terms than others.

Populations from outside the norms established by those with power often get pathologized as deficient in comparison to the developmental schedules determined from the research samples. It is well-established, for instance, that non-white people are typically judged to be in arrears of white people because they often don't develop according to the same mediational environment, leading to deficit conclusions (e.g., Herrnstein & Murray, 1994). By being different, and being measured by methods established by white researchers with white population samples in white settings, they are deemed deficient. As a result, racist policies designed so that "no child is left behind" are designed to reroute the development of those on the demographic margins of school structure so that they are aligned with what a researcher's (typically white, reasonably affluent) sample says they ought to be like (Freeman, 2005).

Research on developmental differences between males and females is also typically reliant on sampling errors. Kohlberg's (1958) research on hierarchies of moral reasoning, for instance, was conducted with participants who were all males at Harvard University,[2] introducing both gendered and social class biases. Yet his formulation held sway until Gilligan (1982), once his research assistant, replicated his work with women (also at Harvard), challenging and complicating Kohlberg's masculine moral reasoning stages, if not the affluence of his sample. Gilligan later included working-class women and women of color in her research to avoid the elitism of her initial study and extend her critique of Kohlberg and male psychology in general (Taylor, Gilligan, & Sullivan, 1997). Gilligan (2020) described her entry into the field as daunting:

> I was teaching at Harvard with Erik Erikson, a psychoanalyst working in the Freudian tradition, and Lawrence Kohlberg, a cognitive-developmental psychologist working in the tradition of Piaget. To all these men—Freud and Erikson, Piaget and Kohlberg—women appeared deficient in development. Women's investment in relationships was considered to be at the expense of a clear sense of self and women's emotional responsiveness was said to compromise their capacity to think rationally and judge objectively. Thus the paradox noted in *In a Different Voice* [Gilligan, 1982]: the very qualities that distinguished women's moral goodness, their relational sensitivity and empathic concern, marked them as deficient in development.
>
> (n.p.)

As a result, those influenced by these dominant men accepted their conclusion that women are underdeveloped, less capable versions of men, a belief that affected their prospects for success in the working world, the political environment, and in schools.

Cultural Phylogeny

Vygotsky's attention to cultural phylogeny helps identify inequities between people of different socialization and the causes for inter-group conflict. Cole (1996) finds this problem to be behind the earliest efforts at undertaking cross-cultural studies by Herodotus in the ancient Mediterranean world, and he made it a concern of his Laboratory of Comparative

Human Cognition at the University of California-San Diego. Understanding cultural phylogeny is important in apprehending all forms of conflict and discrimination. Racism, for instance, is historical and institutional (Crenshaw, 1988; Lipsitz, 2011). Culotta (2012) identifies racism as one of many instantiations of tribalism, which positions people as either with or against us, as *us* or *them*. The term "barbarian" originally referred to outsiders, who were considered less civilized than those inside the gates.

Racism has been around since the first meeting of people of different skin colors and bodily features, since the first meeting with outsiders. Attention to both the historical development of the human species as oriented to tribalism and intercultural conflict, and of the individual lives that develop through the mediation of different communities, can help expose why there are social insiders and outsiders, social hierarchies, discriminatory practices, generationally transmitted hate, and other problems that produce bias in schools and classrooms. These include efforts in the 2020s to ban Critical Race Theory from US schools, where it wasn't being taught but which signified attention to racism, whose existence was denied (Schuessler, 2021).

But to take a Vygotskian perspective, it's important to address why students from different sorts of cultures arrive at school with different worldviews and genre understandings (Majors, 2015). Here I take a more relativistic stance than Vygotsky, who saw technologically advanced societies as culturally superior, and communist societies as both morally and institutionally stronger than capitalist societies (see Chapter 1). The relativistic perspective seeks to understand how some of those cultures are advantaged in schools, and how to create conditions that make education a more equitable experience.

In doing so, it is important to keep in mind that although Vygotsky is very useful for understanding how people develop within cultural contours, his elitism also produced his belief that human phylogeny produced Soviet civilization as its pinnacle, rather than seeing cultural phylogeny as producing many worthwhile ways that are appropriate for organizing life to meet specific community needs (see Chapter 4). The modern-day educator remains caught between these strands of thought, one that sees progress culminating with societies predicated on European Enlightenment rationalism (and to Vygotsky, communist structures), and one that sees cultures evolving to address the problems available in their environments (Tulviste, 1991) and so fitting to their surroundings. Each of these perspectives remains in the air, with ideological conservatives in the English-speaking world tending, like Vygotsky, to assume the superiority of industrialized and technological societies, albeit from a capitalist perspective (e.g., Pearce, 2017); and multiculturalists asserting the value and legitimacy of the many cultures that assemble in schools (Milner, 2010).

Education in a Complex and Contradictory World

These questions are longstanding, and Vygotsky himself provides a paradoxical account. He was enthusiastic about schooling's possibilities for evolving the New Soviet Man in a national monoculture, while also explaining why people from different cultures develop in relation to different environmental challenges. I would not expect readers to be any more flawlessly coherent than Vygotsky, or than I am, given the many traditions that surround humans in general and that inevitably produce ambivalence and internal contradiction in people (Smagorinsky, 2020a). They illustrate the complexity of undertaking a cultural-historical perspective while being a subjective human whose experiences produce growth and cognitive change over time in relation to shifting and contradictory environments. I next review issues affecting education in light of cultural-historical factors.

Teachers who value both long-term development and short-term learning face a dilemma in the way their work is structured to meet short-term goals and deadlines. There is much pressure to submit grades, and no opportunity to see the fruits of long-term development. Rather, teachers are urged to prevent "learning loss" that might occur if students "fall behind" in their progress through the curriculum. Addressing the ontogenetic needs of students is challenging when teachers are bombarded with deadlines to meet: grades to submit, "progress reports" to issue, Individualized Education Plans to complete, bells to signal that learning has begun and ended, parents to call, and countless other schedules to follow. One teacher I know was required to make 20 phone calls to parents each month. She only made 18 in one month, and had her deficiency included in her professional work file.

Schools are not designed for teachers to address long-term human development, aside from the scope and sequence and pacing charts that schedule teaching and learning opportunities. These curricular features may or may not actually serve students' best interests in their long-term development, or follow their various developmental processes. Such imposition of dominant-culture values on minoritized members of communities is involved in extracurricular activities as well, such as when an African American wrestler in the United States was threatened with disqualification from a match because the referee didn't approve of his long, braided hair (Stubbs, 2019). The referee attempted to derail the student's cultural trajectory and replace it with something better aligned with historical white hair-stylings and their presumed role in developing a finely cultured person.

Vygotsky and Piaget: Environment and Biology

Vygotsky formulated a sociocentric psychology in response to the cognitive emphasis of his day, most notably in his critique of Piaget's publications in that time. Piaget formulated a classic "nature"-based understanding of human development, one that proceeds along age-based stages and the growth they demonstrate. These stages presumably apply to everyone developing at a "normal" pace. Vygotskian psychologists find early Piaget—whose works were heavily critiqued in Vygotsky's writing—to be problematic for a variety of reasons. Basing an understanding of human development solely on advances in age, or studying thinking as a disembodied act, overlooks the ways in which culture shapes thinking in different ways, and creates norms based on how a sample of humanity responds to psychological tests. Given that researchers often study population samples that represent their own demographics (Zyphur & Pierides, 2020), they are susceptible to sampling errors, i.e., unwarranted generalizations to populations different from those in the research. Piaget studied his own children, producing one of history's most misleading sampling errors, yet producing a neat developmental schedule that remains instituted in schools and psychologies (e.g., Borst & Spann, 2023; Ojose, 2008).

Vygotsky and Piaget are often presented as taking oppositional views. Both were born in 1896, albeit in different national settings (for Piaget, the politically neutral Switzerland, savaged by Soviet critics as bourgeois). Piaget is typically characterized as having a biological approach to human development, with psychological states maturing according to age-based stages. Vygotsky is generally characterized as taking a social approach, with thinking shaped by social engagement that produces "higher mental functions" that represent the ideology and practices of a cultural group. I have represented them in this fashion myself in prior writing.

My reading of Vygotsky's oeuvre for this volume has complicated my understanding of both Vygotsky and Piaget. Ultimately, I think that Vygotsky took a balanced approach between nature and nurture, being highly attentive to bodily maturation and such hereditary and traumatic conditions as blindness. Vygotsky rejected strict age-stage theories while acknowledging general patterns in which the body changes simultaneously with, if not as a stimulus for, the development of higher mental functions. Such factors as sexual maturation, the emergence of teeth, and other biological aspects of maturation are often accompanied by changes in cognition, such as the capacity to develop a world view, which is not available in infancy, emerging instead in adolescence.

Piaget, who outlived Vygotsky by nearly 50 years, gravitated toward a social perspective. As described by Leont'ev (1997), "Piaget himself read *Thinking and Speech* only in the late 1950s and largely agreed with Vygotsky's critical remarks" (p. 25). Piaget (1973) confirmed this conclusion, saying, "The human being is immersed right from birth in a social environment which affects him just as much as his physical environment. Society, even more, in a sense, than the physical environment, changes the very structure of the individual ... Every relation between individuals (from two onwards) literally modifies them" (p. 156).

Their differences aside, Vygotsky (1998) found much to admire in Piaget's developmental account, saying,

> the remarkable studies of J. Piaget on speech and thinking in the child and his judgments and social deductions leave no doubt.... [E]xtremely clever and penetrating studies.... Piaget shows what an enormous role social factors, to use his expression, play in the development of the structure and function of the child's thinking.
>
> (pp. 61, 63)

Their differences were far more subtle than nature vs. nurture. Vygotsky argued, for instance, that "In contrast to Piaget, we believe that development proceeds not toward socialization, but toward converting social relations into mental functions" (1997c, p. 106). From this distinction, Vygotsky saw Piaget firmly grounded in age-based developmental stages—which Vygotsky also saw in noting the changes that accompany key biological developments such as the emergence of teeth and the onset of puberty—to the extent that socialization is a function of biological maturity. Vygotsky's departure came in seeing socialization as the molding medium through which means of mentation develop.

Discussion

> [T]o formulate the goals of education in a scientific fashion means to have in mind, in an entirely specific and exact form, the particular system of behavior we wish to realize in our student. We only have to glance over the various educational systems in their historical development in order to discover that the goals of education have, in fact, always been entirely specific and fundamental, and have always corresponded to the ideals of the epic and of those particular economic and social structures of society that defined the whole history of the epic. And if these ideals have been formulated in new ways each time, this has always been because of the scientific helplessness of the particular philosopher, or because of the class based pretense of the epoch.
>
> (Vygotsky, 1997a, p. 55)

This quote provides a good summary of some of Vygotsky's major points. Educational systems are embedded in a cultural history, one that is specific to the development of the schools within them. They are ideological (tied to the ideal of the epic) and responsive to such superstructures as economic capitalism or communism. They have in mind a finished product, a child, youth, or young adult whose thinking—whose higher mental functions—develop in accordance with the "behavior we wish to realize in our student." This alignment of young people with adult models and adult priorities produces a socialized citizen, one who will both internalize the values of the environment and in turn help to adapt them to emerging contingencies and pressures.

These efforts at adaptation can be contentious. In the 2020s, some groups are pushing to provide a liberatory education, others in the English-speaking world are seeking to maintain their status by preventing social class movement and prohibiting the advancement of oppressed people. Among the chants heard in the 2017 Charlottsville, Virginia "Unite the Right" rally of white supremacists was a refrain of an old Nazi slogan, "Jews will not replace us!" Nor will black and brown people or people with nonbinary sexual orientations. And women had better watch out, too.

And herein lies the conundrum faced by 21st-century educators: Should schools serve to maintain stability that maintains inequity, or to relieve people of oppression and unlock their potential? My own preference would be to maintain useful traditions and question those that are discriminatory, with the understanding that there would be disagreement over which are which. There would also be disagreement over what constitutes a beneficial change, given that some see requiring Christian iconography in schools to be a positive move, and others see it as imposing one belief system at the expense of others. In 2022, Texas passed a law forcing schools to display "In God We Trust." To State Sen. Bryan Hughes (Republican), "The national motto, In God We Trust, asserts our collective trust in a sovereign God." To others the law represents a "blatant intrusion of religion in what should be a secular public institution" (Riess, 2022). Cultural relativism surrounds schools no matter how relativism is interpreted. These factors, outlined well in Vygotsky's work even if practiced unevenly in his own vision, make schooling every bit as complex and contentious as this century's conflicts suggest it is.

Notes

1 The population fluctuated through growth and death during wars and purges: "The population of the USSR changed as follows over the years: 86.3 million on Jan. 1, 1870, 124.6 million on Jan. 28, 1897, 159.2 million at the end of 1913, 147 million on Dec. 17, 1926, 194.1 million on Jan. 1, 1940, 178.5 million on Jan. 1, 1950, 208.8 million on Jan. 15, 1959, 241.7 million on Jan. 15, 1970, 262.4 million on Jan. 17, 1979, and 266.6 million on Jan. 1, 1981. Despite the enormous loss of life as a result of the two world wars and the Civil War, the population grew quite rapidly. By 1940, the population of the USSR was 22 percent higher than that of Russia in 1913. More than 20 million people of the USSR died during the Great Patriotic War of 1941–45 [World War II]; indirect losses to the population through a lower birthrate and increased mortality were also considerable. It was not until 1955 that the prewar population figure was attained" (The Great Soviet Encyclopedia Wiki, n.d., n.p.).
2 Harvard did not admit women before 1977, when it merged with Radcliffe College.

3 Marxism and Vygotsky in the Soviet Context

According to Leont'ev (1997), "Vygotsky's creative work was first of all determined by the time in which he lived and worked, the era of the Great Socialist October Revolution.... . The new psychology should proceed from the philosophy of dialectical and historical materialism—it was to become a Marxist psychology" (p. 10). In this chapter, I contextualize Vygotsky's career by situating it within Soviet society during Stalin's reign, especially in the volatile 1930s.

Vygotsky came of age during the October Revolution of 1917 (also known as the Bolshevik Revolution). He was 21 at the time of the overthrow of the Romanovs and experienced the Polish-Bolshevik War and the subsequent Civil Wars through which the Bolsheviks filled the ensuing power vacuum. He believed himself to be a true Marxist psychologist. But he eventually ran afoul of the authorities, along with millions of others. Was he a Marxist, as he believed; or a bourgeois heretic, as charged during the Pedology Decree (see Part IV)? It depends on what one thinks Marxism to be.

Marxism has had more than one interpretation and application, helping to explain how Vygotsky could claim a Marxist orientation while being banned for his anti-Marxist, anti-Leninist, and anti-Stalinist attention to scholarship from Europe and the United States, among other violations. It is important to sort through the issues at stake, to understand both the foundation of Vygotsky's Marxist psychology, and the reasons he was ultimately on the brink of being purged as among the "wreckers" of Soviet society, a process typically involving some combination of accusation, arrest, torture, starvation, trial, and execution or exile (Solzhenitsyn, 1973).

My goal here is not to explain Marx, whose legacy is a subjective construction. I am persuaded by Zamoyski (2009), who, speaking of the politicization of historical writing about the relationship between Poland and the Soviet Union, asserts that "Not only did nationalism or dominant state orthodoxy select and distort facts; various interpretations of Marxist theory reinvented them to suit visions of the future" (p. xx). With this caveat in mind, my task is to investigate how Marx has been interpreted and applied, with special attention to Leninism and Stalinism and their doctrinaire imposition of their use of Marxism to advance and sustain their political ends. I next review the terms of this dispute and how Vygotsky and other pedologists got caught in the crossfire between competing notions of Marxism. In this crossfire, one side had much bigger guns and used them with a vengeance to silence all others. In what follows I review the complications arising from theorizing and putting into practice an understanding of materialism, disagreements over the role of tools and signs in human development, the problem of seeking a dialectic understanding in a society with a singular official doctrine, and the question of social class in psychology and education.

DOI: 10.4324/9781003374848-4

Dialectical Materialism

Materialism, which places human engagement with the physical world at the center of analysis, was described by Vygotsky (1999) as involving "a connection of physical processes and includes mental facts in them" (p. 230). Natural science begins with "the assumption of an objective reality which exists outside of us, in conformity with certain laws, and which can be known. And this is, as Lenin has frequently pointed out, the very *essence* of materialism" (1997a, pp. 298–299; emphasis in original). Marx believed that any attempt to reconcile materialism with idealism—those theories that considered the mind or spirit to be independent of the material world—as inherently wrongminded. Materialism was thus positioned in opposition to the idea of pure ideation. Without an exclusively materialist focus, no psychology could be considered Marxist to the Leninist interpreter. I next review aspects of dialectical materialism that both figured into Vygotsky's understanding and led to his rejection in the 1930s.

The Roots of Dialectical Materialism

Marx derived his understanding of dialectical materialism from his fellow Prussian, Georg Wilhelm Friedrich Hegel. Hegel, like many historical thinkers, provides a complicated heritage, especially if one values his ideas yet hates his national origins. First, he was from Europe, a geographic and ideological area reviled by the Soviets. Yet was also a foundational thinker in the Marxist theory that animated the Soviet worldview. Of greater concern to modern-day multiculturalists who draw on Vygotsky is Hegel's racism (Basevich, 2022), a charge disputed by some (e.g., McCarney, 2003) yet substantiated by others (e.g., Bernasconi, 2003a, 2003b). It would surprise few to find that a Prussian living from 1770 to 1831 looked down on non-white races. This period was characterized by a slave trade with deep roots in European history, and was not confined to the enslavement of Black Africans, over 10 million of whom were kidnapped and sold throughout North, South, and Central America and the Caribbean to people of colonial heritage; also enslaved were the original people of these continents. European colonization was typically carried out on lands occupied by non-white people, suggesting a belief in their inferiority and ripeness for subordination.

If we assume that Hegel harbored racist beliefs, the question then becomes, is he a worthy figure to draw from in understanding human development and Vygotskian thought? It's a dicey ethical question, similar to the dilemma facing classical music lovers who must decide whether it's acceptable to listen to music composed by the Nazi Richard Wagner, or the vexation confronting literary readers who like Ezra Pound's poetry but not his fascism, or more recent conundrums over whether J.K. Rowling's transphobia should affect readers' enjoyment of the Harry Potter series. For my purposes, it's inescapable that Vygotsky drew explicitly on Hegel via Marx, and that Vygotsky viewed people from non-industrialized societies, often composed of people of color, as less advanced than were those occupying communist Soviet Union. My task here is less to express moral outrage over people from other times and places, and more to get to the bottom of Vygotsky's cultural-historical theory. I thus proceed with some caution, yet with confidence that understanding Hegel helps to illuminate much about Vygotsky, their proneness to prejudice notwithstanding (see Chapter 4).

Dialectic Synthesis

Among the enduring legacies of Vygotsky's Marxist orientation was his reliance on the Hegelian/Marxist dialectic of thesis-antithesis-synthesis as a way to transcend one's current state of knowledge. Vygotsky accepted the premise grounded in Hegelian and Marxist thought that all of human development is built around this union of opposites as people engage with the world around them, which is always in flux and changing in relation to social and earthly environments. He embraced the Hegelian notion that "great genius develops with the help of another great genius not so much by assimilation as by clashing. One diamond polishes another" 1999, p. 121). This phrase could have appeared in the *Hebrew Bible*'s (*Old Testament*) Proverbs 27:17, which proclaims, "As iron sharpens iron, so one person sharpens another."

Vygotsky employed this method to critique his antecedents and contemporaries—his antitheses to their theses—to produce new insights. As Leont'ev (1997) put it, "Internal dialectics, in principle, always formed the characteristic feature of [Vygotsky's] thinking.... [Vygotsky sought] to discern two polar, struggling sides in a phenomenon when he analyzed it and to regard this struggle as the moving force of development" (p. 19). Marx's notion of the "struggle" between economic and social classes infiltrated the discourse of the day, referring to any dialectical engagement of opposites, and is often invoked in 21st-century discourse to characterize ongoing efforts to make societies egalitarian from a Marxist perspective (e.g., Gómez, 2018).[1]

If people had nothing to work against, if people were not embedded in contradictory environments requiring resolution, they could not develop into something new. This phenomenon is known to Vygotsky as *compensation*, which he described as occurring when

> some function of the child's organism develops in response to a difficulty or obstacle that it encounters... the child at every turn discovers an insufficient adaptation to the surrounding milieu. The child at every turn encounters obstacles and difficulties, and the fact that the child is not adapted forms the starting point for a whole series of compensatory processes that develop because of it.
> (in Van der Veer, 2020, pp. 7, 9)

An antithesis needs to be well-grounded in order to have growth potential in the form of a synthesis. Simply opposing something is insufficient. Rather, it needs to be informed and based in some empirical reality, in the tradition of the European Age of Reason and the Marxist insistence on a materialist orientation. From a Marxist perspective, it also needs to eschew capitalism, as described by Sewell (2005):

> Capitalism is now a thoroughly degenerate social system, which must be overthrown and replaced by its opposite, socialism, if human culture is to survive. Marxism is determinist, but not fatalist. The victory of socialism will mark a new and qualitatively different stage of human history. To be more accurate it will mark the end of the prehistory of the human race [the capitalist phase], and start a real history [of socialism or communism].
> (n.p.)

Vygotsky said something similar: "We are all dialecticians. We do not at all think that the developmental path of science follows a straight line, and if it has had zigzags, returns, and loops we understand their historical significance and consider them to be necessary links in our chain, inevitable stages of our path, just as capitalism is an inevitable stage on the road toward socialism" (1997b, p. 336). The inevitable demise of capitalism has yet to occur, and its fate is far beyond my non-prescient ability to forecast. The capitalist kleptocracy that Russia became in the wake of the Soviet Union does not substantiate the idea that the world remains in a prehistory that awaits a communist or socialist regime. Perhaps that day will come, but if empirical reality is the basic requirement, it hasn't yet, as the roar of neoliberalism—capitalism with a vengeance—in the US indicates.

What matters from Vygotsky's materialist standpoint is how a dialectic synthesis is central to human development, if not necessarily the clash of civilizations through which capitalism will collapse under its own weight and give way to socialism or communism. A clash of civilizations often does not produce "diamonds polishing diamonds," but instead results in a victory based on the number of corpses the triumphant side creates among its opposition. More in line with Vygotsky's use of the term, at the personal level, writing this book has been for me a process in search of a dialectic synthesis. I have been referencing Vygotsky in my research for over 30 years now, and am well short of being an expert, on this topic or any other. I hope I never reach the point where I believe I'm an expert, which to me is a sign of stagnation, of stasis, the end of growth. I agree with Vygotsky that without an obstacle to overcome, growth is not possible. I have too many obstacles to understanding to declare that my expedition is over.

I am approaching my composition of the chapters in an exploratory way, as a process of thesis-antithesis-synthesis. My own prior understandings and publications comprise my establishment of a thesis, or more accurately, a large set of related theses. My reading of new material, and revisiting of old, along with some helpful conversations and correspondence, have produced an antithesis consisting of better expressions of ideas I have been working toward, corrections of inaccuracies in my conceptions, and other forms of opposition. These sources have also confirmed some ideas on which I've had a tenuous grasp. The resulting synthesis is what has emerged through my composition of these chapters, in which I mix ideas that are well-rehearsed with efforts to reach better understandings through the process of composition in light of competing ideas. This synthesis is provisional, no doubt subject to further refinement as international colleagues continue to generate translations and interpretations that challenge my present state of mind.

This illustration demonstrates the notion of a dialectical synthesis. English teachers will be pleased to see that Vygotsky's fascination with *Hamlet* is based in part on the protagonist's ambivalence, the tensions he experiences between action and inaction and the need for resolution. Van der Veer and Valsiner (1991) titled their archival book *Understanding Vygotsky: A Quest for Synthesis*, as emblematic of Vygotsky's own method, and the authors' own quest to learn by exploring his career. The synthesis of concepts is a major goal and mediator of human development. Vygotsky's own analytic process was dialectic, a means by which he examined perspectives, critiqued them, and resolved and synthesized them into a higher understanding.

He in turn applied this process to his laboratory research, challenging theory with empirical data. He assumed that development becomes available through engagement with opposition and obstacles. At the same time, a wall of obstacles, such as those faced by society's dispossessed, undoubtedly stifles development, even with resilience opening up possibilities for goals to become available and be reached (Young, 2003). Vygotsky's account of human development thus went beyond what was available in the psychology of his day, through dialectic interrogation of his era's leading psychological thinkers, using a Marxist lens to seek his own synthesis, one that was insufficient and downright erroneous and bourgeois to Soviet authorities. His departures eventually led to his suppression, an antithesis that crushed any possibilities for synthesis.

Vygotsky extended his own dialectical process to all of human development. He hoped that his pedagogical approach would contribute to the rapid evolution of the New Soviet Man through education. Van der Veer and Valsiner (1991) describe Vygotsky's conception of human development as following from "a dialectical struggle between 'man and the world' where the hereditary constitution is not smaller than that of the environment.... . Vygotsky saw definite limits to the possibilities of transforming human beings by societal reforms and was by no means an extreme environmentalist" (p. 54). That is, his understanding of the role of contexts in shaping and steering human development was not deterministic, even as he believed in the possibilities of a new classless society in reforming human nature via forced evolution brought about by a shift to communism. To Vygotsky, the environment mattered a great deal, but could not in and of itself create a worker's paradise (see Lyons, 1967, a Russian Empire [now Belarus] native who grew up a socialist in New York City and ultimately soured on the Soviet Union). But the Soviets disagreed.

Vygotsky's reliance on Hegel's formulation was streamed throughout his writing. He found the progress of science to involve a union of opposites that took into account prior conceptions, evaluated them, challenged them, and pushed forward into new territory. He viewed the foundation provided by psychologists from the decadent West to provide a launch point from which a new psychology could be undertaken. In Vygotsky's Preface to German gestalt psychologist Kurt Koffka's *Foundations of Mental Development* (1934), he wrote that the book served as "a culmination point of European psychology which we must dispense with (that is, on which we must rely while at the same time rejecting it)" (1997b, p. 196). This statement positioned Vygotsky as a post-capitalist psychologist, in the sense that any "post" perspective is designed to shift to a new paradigm without wholly escaping vestiges of the old.[2]

Vygotsky's Balance of Materialism and Idealism

Vygotsky (1997a) found that any binary in which opposing poles never engage is by definition insufficient. He said, "a one-sided, physiological materialism is as far from dialectical materialism as the idealism of empirical psychology. It confines the study of human behavior to its biological side, ignoring the social factor" (1997a, p. 60). Soviet Marxists asserted that biological psychologies—in that time, Piaget and his age-based stage theory provided a good example—work in service of perpetuating social class differences, given the tendency to account for workers' low station in life by attributing it to their weak biological inheritance. They thus rejected biology as a factor in development. Yet Vygotsky found both biology and environment to have important roles in human life.

Vygotsky was clear not to conceive of psychology as all about behavior (e.g., Watson's[3] [1930] US-based behaviorism) or disembodied cognition (e.g., Husserl's[4] [1913] phenomenology), or only about the material environment, the required focus for Soviet Marxists. Dialectical psychology, he wrote, involves

> unique psycho-physiological unitary processes. These represent the higher forms of human behavior, which we suggest calling psychological processes, in contradistinction to mental processes and in analogy with what are called physiological processes.... . Dialectical psychology studies [thinking] as a unitary and integral process [involving mental and physiological sides].
>
> (1997b, pp. 113–114)

Here Vygotsky violated the Leninist-Stalinist dictum that only materialism matters in a society built around the notion of everyday labor. Rieber and Wollock (1997) argue that Marxism,

> from its own particular point of view of dialectical materialism and social struggle, is a radically humanist philosophy; radical in that it not only emphasizes the human, but by removing God from the traditional God/man nexus inevitably throws all emphasis on the human. Moreover, the emphasis placed on human society means that the latter virtually replaces God in explaining the end, nature, and motivating force of humanity. Finally, it is human society at any given historical moment, not God, that is seen as the final cause of nature itself, in the Hegelian sense that society is the highest development of the dialectic of nature and that man's knowledge of nature is a historically mediated social construct. In Marxism, therefore, the opposition between nature and society is transcended by the unity of the historical dialectic.
>
> (p. ix)

The Soviet Union was explicitly atheist, removing God from the equation while retaining some elements of mysticism in its claims to be elevating the human soul via the creation of contexts that nurture the spirit. Vygotsky (1987) wrote that "The very attempt to approach the soul scientifically... contains in itself the entire past and future path of psychology because science is the path to truth, albeit one that passes through periods of error" (p. 428). Rather than looking to the heavens for answers, Marxists sought them in human material productivity, with working class people in collective farms and factories the most valued members of society, at least theoretically. Meanwhile, the Party leaders, as satirized by George Orwell (1945) in *Animal Farm*, reserved for themselves luxuries and privileges denied to the masses, from factory workers to the reviled intelligentsia.

The rejection of God or other non-material spiritual North Star captured the Soviets' more general prohibition of psychologies other than those related to corporeal tools and their use for physical labor. Vygotsky (1993) rejected Christianity for many reasons. His own positionality as a Jewish man suggests the complications of living in socially complex societies that hope to integrate people of different cultural heritages into a national identity with a common frame of mind. It is especially fragile when a single worldview, including all of its details, is imposed from above on independent thinkers.

Vygotsky's Marxism as Post-Capitalism

In Vygotsky's mind, a Marxist psychology could not be bootstrapped into existence, instead requiring growth from the ruins of bourgeois psychologies previously established in Europe and the United States. Vygotsky wrote in his 20s that "Marxist psychology does not yet exist. It must be understood as a historical goal, not as something already given" (1997a, p. 340). Soviets saw communism as the eradication of capitalism altogether, with any remnant a betrayal of Marx, Engels, Lenin, and Stalin. Vygotsky described his engagement with US and European scholarship as follows:

> The development of scientific ideas and views proceeds dialectically. Opposite ideas concerning one and the same subject replace each other in the process of development of scientific knowledge and a new theory is often not a direct continuation of the preceding one but its negation, a dialectical negation, however. It includes all the

positive achievements of its predecessor which have stood the test of time, but it itself strives in its constructions and conclusions to transcend its predecessor's boundaries and to conquer new and deeper layers of phenomena.

(1997b, p. 175)

This passage reveals Vygotsky to have had respect for his antecedents and contemporaries, including those verboten in the USSR. He found some investigators from bourgeois nations to have had ideas worth considering, among those "positive achievements of its predecessor which have stood the test of time." Vygotsky found the differences to be significant and of long-term effect, if not incommensurate points in a binary conception. He expressed his disavowal of bourgeois psychology as follows:

Our science could not and cannot develop in the old [Tsarist] society. We cannot master the truth about personality and personality itself so long as mankind has not mastered the truth about society and society itself... . In the future society, psychology indeed will be the science of the new man. Without this the perspective of Marxism and the history of science would not be complete. But this science of the new man will still remain psychology. Now we hold its thread in our hands. There is no necessity for this psychology to correspond as little to the present one as—in the words of Spinoza [1677/1955, p. 61]—the constellation Dog corresponds to a dog, a barking animal.

(1997b, pp. 342–343)

Capitalist and communist psychology needn't be wholly different in every aspect to Vygotsky. He was confident that bourgeois psychologies were inherently flawed. He specifically named one nation as exemplifying the ills of working from the wrong premises: "the psychology of behavior [i.e., Watsonian behaviorism]... is false, for the new psychology wants to know the mind as well; it is a philistine, everyday term, which is why it attracted the Americans" (1997a, p. 339). His post-capitalist orientation thus did include remnants of the kinds of societies he found objectionable, as charged by the Soviets, while allowing space for what was, to use one of his frequent terms, *correct* in prior conceptions. Whether the Soviet authorities were correct to use such a stern litmus test is open to discussion.

Van der Veer and Valsiner (1991) take a sober look at the claims for Soviet communism as the ideal human society (here, using a different definition of "ideal," one referring to optimal rather than non-material): "It would take the Second World War and later general environmental pollution to make people seriously doubt these [idealistic] claims" about the likelihood that the Soviet Union would produce "the image of man as the self-conscious creator of his own destiny and the new society of prosperity and eternal bliss" (p. 221). The Gulag was not the chosen destiny of Soviet intellectuals, and communism didn't produce a classless society. Those in the Politburo did not spend their days mucking around in the mud on the collectivist farms celebrated in communist ideology, lore, and propaganda (Figes, 1997). Indeed, the leaders lived relatively luxurious lives (Davies, 2007). Missing from their conception was a dissident voice, an antithesis to the propagandic thesis provided by the Kremlin, one that might produce a more realistic synthesis of understandings of the effects of the Soviet means of social organization. Opposing views were missing because they had been banished to Siberia.

The woke 21st-century literacy educator might be uneasy with this emphasis on gravitating to the norms of the collective, given that in the United States and other colonized nations, this dominant culture has been built on the bones of people who preceded them on the world's continents, and those who were enslaved to labor on colonial invaders' lands. The idea of a dominant national culture was critical to the formation of the Soviet Union, and was also central to Horace Mann's vision in founding public education in the United States. It remains an adamant value of politically conservative people who are dedicated to maintaining a hierarchical social system. And it remains the bane of multiculturalists who find the imposition of a national collective on diverse people to be inequitable and violent toward those from outside the circles of power.

Class Analysis

Among the issues that led to Vygotsky's fall from Soviet grace were the accusations that he focused on the wrong dimensions of human psychology. A Marxist approach, to many in the Moscow scientific circles, should focus primarily, perhaps exclusively, on social class issues, and not ethnicity or other cultural factors; and not at all on biology. Vygotsky was again out of step with the Leninist/Stalinist interpretation of Marx and Engels.

Vygotsky's oeuvre shows that social class was among his interests, if not a primary one. He referred to "two phases of interests in a working-class adolescent," for instance, saying that "for the proletarian adolescent, youth begins later and ends earlier and ... the passage of this whole period of development is either compressed or extended depending on unfavorable or favorable economic and social-cultural conditions" (1998, p. 17). Here he described how the socio-economic environment shapes development among capitalist working-class adolescents, a point of comparison for him in his writing. The onset of adolescence, he said, is accompanied by immersion in ideologically organized, economically structured environments, such that

> societal ideology is represented most of all as connected with one position or another in societal production... . [W]e must also present class psychology not as suddenly arising, but as gradually developing. It is understood that we have its full development as early as during youth when a man already occupies or is preparing to occupy one position or another in societal production. The history of the school-age child and the youth is the history of very intensive development and formulation of class psychology and ideology... . Class psychology cannot, of course, be created by external imitation. The process of its formation is undoubtedly deeper. Class psychology in the child is created as a result of his working with those around him ... as a result of common life with them, common activity, common interests. Let us repeat, class cohesion is formed as a result not of external imitation, but by shared life, activity, and interests... . It is understood that sharing of life, work, and interests places before the adolescent a number of problems; in the process of solving them, class psychology develops and takes shape.
>
> (1998, p. 43)

Although Vygotsky was found to be bourgeois and inattentive to social class issues in his research by the Soviet authorities, there is much in his work that suggests that class analysis was part of his program, just not the principal focus. Vygotsky (1998) addressed the ways in which social class affects development, making a point that surely went against Soviet orthodoxy: that social class may be limiting in the development of people's intellects. Instead of positioning the proletariat as the most glorious Soviet citizens outside the leadership class, he saw a different outcome. First, social class is a critical factor in human development: "the process of intellectual maturation in different social strata presents a very different picture. External factors that form intellectual development assume a decisive significance in the transitional age [adolescence]: the intellect acquires methods of action that are the product of socialization of thinking and not of its biological evolution" (p. 76). Socialization thus matters, and takes the biological inheritance in class-mediated ways.

The limits of humble circumstances, he argued, confine the ways in which an intellect may grow:

> in a peasant environment, we frequently encounter adults who have not gone beyond the intellectual level of a schoolchild. Over their whole life, their thinking has not moved beyond the sphere of the visual, never made the transition from specifically logical thinking to its abstract forms. Since soon after finishing school, the adolescent enters the kind of environment in which higher forms of thinking have not been mastered, it is natural that he himself does not reach a higher degree of development, although he displays great ability. It cannot be more decisively confirmed that the formation of concepts is the product of the cultural development of the intellect and depends in the last analysis on the environment.
>
> (1998, p. 77)

With his premise established that the social environment shapes cognition, Vygotsky specifically addressed how such factors as schooling produce differential effects: "the child's development and his movement along the stages is determined by social-cultural conditions. A comparison between those studying in public schools and those studying in privileged schools discloses substantial differences" (1998, p. 81). Ultimately, a person is somewhat bound by socialization, such that there is

> a close connection between the environment and the adolescent's self-consciousness.... [T]he vital form of the adolescent's personality depicted by Spranger[5] refers only to an adolescent from a certain type of environment. Its transfer to other social strata is not borne out by facts. Transferring this structure to proletarian and peasant youth is completely inadmissible.
>
> (1998, p. 173)

The implications of these changes are evident, he asserted, in the personalities of children and youth socialized to different class-based cultural practices:

> With respect to self-consciousness, the working-class adolescent is not simply arrested at an earlier stage of development in comparison with the bourgeois adolescent, but is an adolescent with a different type of personality development with a different structure and dynamics of self-consciousness.... [T]he roots of these differences must be sought in the class to which the adolescent belongs and not in one degree or another of his material well-being. For this reason, putting adolescents who belong to different classes into one group ... seems to us to be wrong.
>
> (1998, p. 178)

These perceptions are not only the view of the psychologists who study how environments shape human development. They become internalized by the people being depicted, a theme that Vygotsky extended in his work in defectology (see Chapter 14) when he described how people with atypical makeups—principally the blind, deaf, and cognitively impaired—take on debilitating, dysphoric views of themselves in relation to how they are treated by an ableist society.

Vygotsky may have made Soviet authorities nervous with his characterization of proletarian children as having less-developed higher mental functions, given the goal of elevating their status to occupy positions of authority in society. Of course, communism would eliminate class boundaries; and of course capitalism would exacerbate them. Vygotsky was criticizing how social class orientation in inequitable societies produces further inequities by the sorts of environments constructed for students of different socioeconomic circumstances, resulting, he believed, in limited ways of comprehending the world. More modern researchers (e.g., Moll, 1990) have argued that working class children are continually solving sophisticated problems in home and community life using skills and strategies that are not evident in school tasks. Skeptical beliefs about the valorization of the working class would contradict both Soviet orthodoxy (the idea that people all have equal potential, which is limited by circumstances alone), and pro-working-class scholarship that finds that the work and thinking of the proletariat are far more sophisticated than they appear (Rose, 2004; Scribner, 1985).

Multiculturalists of the 21st century would undoubtedly be sympathetic to research that documents the intelligence of the blue-collar worker. What matters in this perspective is how intelligence (and presumably higher mental functions) develop in relation to environmental demands. Vygotsky's points about working class potential, even if confined to capitalist societies and not the communist regime, may have been disturbing to Soviet authorities who conflated his beliefs with the idea that biology produces such differences, not environments. This belief in the superior biological inheritance and determinism of the affluent classes was among the illusions they hoped to dismantle. This view also might concern 21st-century multiculturalists and equity-oriented educators who agree that the problem is how working class people are interpreted, not how much potential they have. This potential becomes limited through school tracking that presumes their lack of sophisticated thinking (Oakes, 2005). Yet to Vygotsky, their socialization has great effects:

> The parents' social position creates a whole set of conditions, which in their turn slow down or accelerate the child's growth and weight gain: different nutrition, different air volume depending on the living circumstances, different hygienic conditions—all this stands *between* the social factors and children's physical development. We thus see that the social factor that influences the organism *determines the action of a great number of biological factors* and by means of them, by creating a particular configuration, influences the child's process of growth and maturation.
> (in Van der Veer, 2020, p. 33; emphasis in original)

One might object that the biological can shape the social. For instance, a competitive athlete can create a new social status and economic status, as they did in Soviet sports to the point of promoting cheating through the use of performance-enhancing drugs, a practice that has continued well past the fall of the USSR (Whorton, 2015). Biology also has social consequences following from involuntary traits such a skin color and gender identification that produce the social discrimination faced by people whose bodies don't conform to norms or preferences grounded in race, gender, physical makeup, or mental makeup, an ongoing problem in many nations colonized by Europeans. Soviet ideology emphasized that such forms of bias would disappear in a classless society, a belief contradicted by their own enduring anti-Semitism (Brent & Naumov, 2004), racism (Law, 2012), and sexism (Mamonova, 1988).

Vygotsky's observations anticipate Tulviste's (1991) conclusion that people develop in relation to the conditions and problems presented by their environments, making social class an inevitable area of investigation. He applied the same principle to gendered socialization, saying that

> The purely psychological differences between boys and girls, such as different capacities for certain subjects, for example, the notorious incompetence of girls in mathematics or in activities that require assertiveness, likewise are not primarily conditioned facts, but rather are derived from the special historical role of women in which the division of social functions condemned women to the limited path of the four K's [translated as children, cooking, dressmaking, church].
>
> (1997a, p. 79)

Vygotsky asserted that "the formation of concepts discloses before the adolescent a world of social consciousness and leads inevitably to intensive development and formulation of class psychology and ideology" (1998, p. 44). Social class produces a worldview, and sense of self in the world. Furthermore,

> the adolescent is not only the son of his social class, but is already himself an active member of that class. Correspondingly, the years of adolescents are the years of forming the adolescent, primarily his social-political world view.... Problems that life itself poses for the adolescent and his decisive entry as an active participant into this life require for their solution the development of higher forms for thinking.
>
> (1998, p. 45)

These "higher forms for thinking," the higher mental processes, are those cultural ways of thinking that people develop through social participation (see Chapter 5). The higher mental processes that surround the educated, monied classes are, in many ways, different from those that develop among working class people. Vygotsky's various endorsements of Marx and communism and his many comments about the inequities of capitalism were consistent with Marxist critiques of capitalism in relation to social class and environmental factors, and took on an ideological dimension. As Vygotsky and other Soviet psychologists often pointed out, European and US psychologists embedded capitalist, bourgeois ideologies into their conceptions of development. Psychology, like other disciplines, can't escape being a product of the worldviews of its practitioners.

Vygotsky's attention to social class factors suggested to him that economically advantaged classes have far greater potential for developing sophisticated ways of thinking, in contrast with working class people who are the inheritors of a position in society that is oriented to material labor, the Marxist ideal. This perspective has been evident in the more recent work of British linguist Bernstein (1960, 1971), who spoke of the *linguistic determinism* of working-class discourse through the restricted codes they use (1960). As stated by Vygotsky (1997b):

> Heredity, says, Blonsky (1925), is no simple biological phenomenon. We must distinguish chromatin [genetic in the DNA sense] heredity from the social heredity of

the conditions of life and social position. It is on the basis of this social, class-based heredity that dynasties are built. In a highly productive, rich class society with high material security and high fecundity of these dynasties, their chances to produce a great quantity of talents are enhanced. On the other hand, continual heavy work, physical labor, and poverty give the hereditary genius of the working masses no chance whatsoever to manifest itself... . [T]he same social reasons that led one's parents to commit a crime usually remain operative in the second generation as well and determine the fate of the children as they first determined the fate of the parents. Do not poverty, unemployment, being unattended, etc. and other well-studied factors of criminality act upon the children with the same irresistibility as they did upon their parents?

In exactly the same way those social conditions (material security, the cultural conditions of domestic life, leisure, etc., etc.) which at the time guaranteed the grandparents and parents good marks in their school education will on average guaranteed the children of these parents the same good marks.

(pp. 171–172)

I should note as an aside that criminality is not the sole province of lower economic classes. Robber barons, kleptocrats, and scammers have stolen more money than millions of poor people pilfering a loaf of bread could imagine. And the top 10 post-Soviet Russian kleptocratic oligarchs, as of this writing, have a net worth of $186 billion (Bloomberg, 2022).

Readers, like Soviet critics of pedology, might see Vygotsky pathologizing working class people who are bound to replicate the conditions of their childhood in their adult lives, with the same limitations. Much research has documented the generational ways in which poverty and values are transmitted (Moore, 2011); and many examples are available of those who either rose from humble origins to accumulate wealth, and those who squandered their inheritance and led lives of misery.

Vygotsky's social class analysis has consequences for schooling. He described conditions that have changed little over time and across borders:

Education has, at all times and in all places, born a class-based character, whether or not its adherents or apostles were aware of it. In fact, in human society education is an entirely well-defined social function whose direction is defined always by the interests of the dominant class, and the freedom and independence of the lesser artificial educational environment from the greater social environment is essentially a matter of very relative and very conditional freedoms, and to an independence that exists within certain narrow limits and boundaries... . From the psychological point of view, therefore, it does not make sense to speak of different abstract and general goals of all education in general. Each form of education has its own goals, indeed, one might say that every epoch has its own form of education, and however these goals are expressed, they will always develop certain aspects and a form of behavior which this education would like to bring to life.

(1997b, p. 56)

His remarks here suggest that his critique was aimed at pre-Soviet or capitalist education in which social classes are dominant or subordinate. His perspective went off the rails in the USSR when he spoke to the local, situational character of an appropriate education. This view was evident in the pedologists' use of diagnostic tests to sort students into categories for specific types of schooling (see Part IV), disqualifying him from being Marxist in good standing in the Soviet Union.

Vygotsky's class analysis suggests that social class orientation is virtually fateful, providing little or no means of upward mobility in capitalist societies and imposing limitations on the degree to which higher mental functions are possible. In the United States, Horace Mann's vision of schooling as society's great equalizer has never been achieved. Soviet society sought to create a nation of economic equals in which such matters were not of concern. Critiques of capitalism helped pave the way for Marxism to govern Soviet life under a doctrine that celebrated the moral superiority of the working class people whom Vygotsky described as being limited by their circumstances. Yet other accounts indicate that the Soviet system only created different forms of inequity and oppression (Orwell, 1945; Solzhenitsyn, 1973).

Of social class, Vygotsky (1998) argued that

> the character and method by which the child recognizes his own existence and activity depend to a high degree on how his parents consider and value themselves. Value scales of adults become the value scales of the child himself... . [I]n the sense of being conscious of one's own personality from the social-class aspect, the working-class adolescent will, of course, reach a higher stage of self-consciousness than the bourgeois adolescent. In other respects, he is slower. But we cannot say anything in general on the lag and movement forward where the paths of development form completely immeasurable qualitatively different curves.
>
> (p. 179)

The generous interpretation with this statement is that Vygotsky was describing a capitalist society in which different social classes are availed different sorts of experiences and trajectories; that he was talking about pernicious capitalism and not equitable communism. To the Soviets, stating these outcomes associated him with the societies whose consequences he outlined and positioned him as bourgeois, as among those who benefit from social class castes.

Vygotsky found capitalism to be only the latest economic structure to separate social classes in a system of domination and subordination. He wrote that

> The concepts of the social category of class and class struggle ... are revealed in their purest form in the analysis of the capitalist system, but these same concepts are the key to all pre-capitalist societal formations, although in every case we meet with different classes there, a different form of struggle, a particular developmental stage of this category. But those details which distinguish the historical uniqueness of different epochs from capitalist forms not only are not lost, but, on the contrary, can only be studied when we approach them with the categories and concepts acquired in the analysis of the other, higher formation.
>
> (1997b, p. 235)

This higher formation was Marxism, which provided the terms for his critiques. Marxism also provided the basis for Soviet critiques of Vygotsky and pedology, often on his lack of fidelity to their doctrinaire reading of Marx on the question of social class. Given how there are many Marxisms that are incorporated into many worldviews and ideological and historical settings, it's easy to see how Vygotsky could be a Marxist in one conception (including his own), and anti-Marxist in another.

Vygotsky and Capitalism

Vygotsky (1998) positioned himself as a Marxist who was suspicious of bourgeois researchers and their assumptions, even as he routinely consulted the work of Dewey, Piaget, and other dissolute capitalists upon whose ruins a Marxist psychology might be formulated. Only a communist nation could produce a truly Marxist perspective, he argued: "We do not at all expect to find a finished system of Marxist psychology in Western science. It would be almost a miracle if it emerged there" (1997b, p. 83). Perhaps that is why some US Marxists charge so much in honoraria for speeches railing against the decadence and inequity of capitalism.[6]

Vygotsky more specifically critiqued capitalism's shortcomings in discussing the role of crises in development, for which he was excoriated by Soviet peers. Crises refer to "abrupt and major shifts and displacements, changes, and discontinuities in the child's personality [such that] the child changes completely in the basic traits of his personality. Development takes on a stormy, impetuous, and sometimes catastrophic character" (1998, p. 191). To Vygotsky, psychologists in capitalist societies misunderstand such periods: "They are more inclined to take them as 'diseases' of development because of its deviation from the normal path. Almost none of the bourgeois investigators could theoretically realize their actual significance" (1998, p. 191). Rather than being aberrant acts of naughty and dissolute children, such volatile behavior is a normal part of development.

Bourgeois researchers, he said critically, tend to study people like themselves—from their own often-privileged social class and often from their own race, gender, and other demographic categories—and generalize from what they observe. This sampling inevitable leads to deficit constructions of lower-class people, a complaint that some might apply to Vygotsky himself for his characterization of the peasant and proletariat. He more directly argued that

> bourgeois research is wholly incorrect, or incorrect to some extent at least... . [B]ourgeois investigators have a very limited range of observation, that is, they always observe the child in conditions of the bourgeois family with a certain type of rearing. Facts show that in other conditions of rearing, the crisis occurs differently.
> (1998, p. 295)

Vygotsky both took the Marxist position that the bourgeoisie are decadent in their self-interested perpetuation of social class distinctions, and also pointed out the limits of lower-class socialization. The Soviet doctrine, however, positioned the proletariat as morally elevated and the monied class as fundamentally corrupt; and the proletariat as more qualified than the bourgeois to operate a society. Suggesting that their social upbringing was limiting, rather than illuminating, and doing so as part of his belief in developmental crises, no doubt helped the Party marginalize Vygotsky and bury his contributions from further availability.

Another factor that may have contributed to Vygotsky's rejection in Moscow concerned his somewhat deterministic account of the consequences of social-class-based upbringing. He said in his early educational writing that

> In modern society, every person, therefore, whether he likes it or not, is inevitably a spokesman of a particular class... . "Thus," writes Blonskii, "there are no invariant and obligatory laws of human behavior in society whatsoever. In class society the concept, 'man,' is generally an empty and abstract concept. Man's social behavior is

determined by the behavior of his class, and each person is inevitably a person from a particular class." In this regard, we must be profoundly historical and must always present man's behavior in relation to the class situation at a given moment.

(Vygotsky, 1997a, p. 212)

Human development thus inevitably involves socialization such that the idea of a unitary human species is an illusion. Rather, consistent with cultural-historical theory (which was in its early stages when Vygotsky authored this text in his 20s), social class boundaries can be very difficult to transcend, both for the limitations placed on potential by those with greater capital, and for the ways in which a working class life limits conceptual growth (a contentious issue then and now). Vygotsky linked this phenomenon to the Marxist notion of labor, the tool-mediated activity through which people participate in cultures (see Chapter 5):

Human labor, i.e., the struggle for existence, assumes, by necessity, forms of the social struggle and, accordingly, place this whole mass of people under the same conditions, forcing them to develop identical forms of behavior. These identical forms of behavior are made up of all those widespread religious beliefs, ceremonies, and customs, within which a given society lives. Thus, whether we like it or not, education is, either consciously or unconsciously, always guided along class lines. This should be kept in mind whenever present day pedagogics confronts the old question as to what constitutes the ideal of education, whether an international type that would be suitable for all mankind, or a national type. It is essential to keep in mind the class nature of all ideals, and recall that the ideals of national, nationalism, patriotism, and so on are only masked forms of the class trend of education.

(1997a, p. 212)

Schools have been celebrated in both capitalist and communist nations as mechanisms for equality across social classes (Smagorinsky, 2022). To capitalists, communists are attempting to create a single class out of many, thus producing mass mediocrity and straightjacketing the society's most talented people to produce equality. The Kurt Vonnegut short story "Harrison Bergeron" illustrates this perspective with a gifted 14-year-old boy whose abilities must be contained in order for him to be the equal of others: "THE YEAR WAS 2081, and everybody was finally equal. They weren't only equal before God and the law. They were equal every which way. Nobody was smarter than anybody else. Nobody was better looking than anybody else. Nobody was stronger or quicker than anybody else." His satire proceeds to depict such a society as stagnant, mired in its own need for conformity to the lowest common denominator.

To communists, the capitalists are making upward economic mobility the emphasis, inevitably producing corruption and lower social classes whose members face obstacles to escaping their circumstances. The Soviet authorities concluded that Vygotsky's attention to social class limits made him bourgeois, no matter how critically he examined Europe, the United States, and capitalism.

Vygotsky and Other Intellectual Traditions

Psychology was among several intellectual structures within which Vygotsky developed as a person and psychologist. Whether consciously or not, he worked within competing intellectual traditions that shaped his thinking, under the management of his own intellect. His attention to both bourgeois and Soviet thinkers tainted his development into the sort of Marxist approved of by the authorities. But there were traditions beyond the tension between the Soviets and the European-US axis, between communism and capitalism, that provided Soviet Marxism with its primary center of gravity. As described by Wertsch (1998),

> Vygotsky had a difficult time resolving this issue and as a result ended up being ambivalent about the telos [ideal endpoint] of human development [Wertsch, 1995, 1996]. At certain points in his writing he was quite clear in positing a kind of enlightenment rationality as the ideal outcome of human mental development, but at other points he seems to have envisioned the "harmony of imagination" as the ideal endpoint. Such complexity and ambivalence characterize most accounts of development, but my point in noting this is to provide a reminder that, when we discuss development, we typically are positing some ideal endpoint or points.
>
> (p. 37)

This reminder applies well to Soviet society, which had a very clear ideal endpoint in mind for the Soviet citizen. In many areas of his writing, Vygotsky was well-aligned with that vision. His wide-reaching interests also immersed him in other traditions as well, producing at times hybrid conceptions that were dismissed as eclectic (a dirty word among Soviets because it lacks Marxist purity) and bourgeois.

In my own work drawing on Vygotsky, I've argued that it's impossible for human beings to be consistent, given the many directions in which they are pulled. Multiple, often competing ideal endpoints surround them as they navigate society (Smagorinsky, 2020a). It's to be expected, then, that he would both change over the course of time, and change in relation to different, often competing ideological systems and worldviews; and in the process, be beholden to ideas of conceptually different origins.

Discussion

This chapter has reviewed issues Vygotsky faced as a post-capitalist Soviet psychologist whose Marxism was informed by, and thus contaminated by, a small set of European (often Prussian-German) and US philosophers and psychologists. Life in the Soviet Union was governed by orthodoxies that permitted no departures, relying on the eradication of dissident views in varying forms. In this sense Soviet thought lacked the dialectical dimension so central to Marxism, instead using blunt force to obliterate any antithesis to the official interpretation of Marx available through the Soviet "revolution from above."

There are many Marxisms (Ratner & Silva, 2017). My task is not to pick a winner in who is more right about what, but to review how Marxist interpretations have arisen, become ossified to promote different ideologies, and weaponized against dissident thought. Part IV of this volume reviews how Soviet ideologues took exception to Vygotsky's version of Marxism, leading to his intellectual interment around the time of his physical death. Vygotsky was among millions of casualties left behind in the construction of the Soviet state in the image of Stalin. Among other atrocities at around the time of Vygotsky's death, over 100,000 Soviet citizens were shot during the Polish Operation of 1937–1938 as Polish spies, "the largest peacetime ethnic shooting campaign in history" and largely the consequence of a conspiracy theory of little substance (Snyder, 2015, p. 57). It is extraordinary that his oeuvre is available to later generations at all.

Notes

1 "Struggle" was also Hitler's autobiographical term, with *Mein Kempf* translated as *My Struggle*, although of a different sort.
2 Thanks to Joe Tobin for helping me understand that the "post" in post-colonial and other post perspectives does not mean "above and beyond and leaving in the dust" but rather an epistemology that follows in the wake of a problematic predecessor without eliminating it. For example, I have drawn on post-colonial scholarship and have incorporated it into my own outlook. Yet I own a property and home on lands occupied by the Creek Nation before the European invasion.
3 John Broadus Watson (1878–1958) was a US behaviorist psychologist who studied how to train animals and educate children. His infamous "Little Albert" study created fear in a disabled boy to demonstrate behaviorist principles.
4 Edmund Gustav Albrecht Husserl (1859–1938) was a Jewish Prussian-German atheist, philosopher, and mathematician known as the founder of phenomenology.
5 Eduard Spranger (1882–1963) was a holistic German philosopher and psychologist with an interest in personality development (e.g., Spranger, 1914).
6 One such US Marxist was invited by our graduate students to speak, and said that his fee for three days was $15,000. When the students said that their budget was very limited, he said he could fly in and out on the same day for $5,000. Their treasury would not accommodate that amount either, and he told them he was therefore not available.

4 Historicizing Vygotsky's Hierarchical Views

Human development must be understood, in cultural-historical psychology, as a function of various histories. Historical antecedents have created the worlds and societies into which people are born and within which they develop. As William Faulkner (1951) put it in a quote often recited in Vygotskian studies, "The past is never dead. It's not even past" (p. 73). The past is present in virtually all areas of human life as people are shaped by their traditions and the historical narratives that surround both the customs and themselves. Vygotsky (1997c) spoke to the role of history in the present, saying,

> many are still inclined to present the idea of historical psychology in a false light. They identify history with the past. For them, to study something historically means necessarily to study one fact or another from the past. This is a naïve conception—seeing an impossible boundary between historical study and the study of present forms. Moreover, *historical study simply means applying categories of development to the study of phenomena. To study something historically means to study it in motion. Precisely this is the basic requirement of the dialectical method.* To encompass in research the process of development of something in all its phases and changes—from the moment of its appearance to its death—means to reveal its nature, to know its essence, for only in movement does the body exhibit that it is. Thus, historical study of behavior is not supplementary or auxiliary to theoretical study, but is a basis of the latter.... . Blonskii expressed this in the general statement: behavior can be understood only as the history of behavior. This is a truly dialectical point of view in psychology.
>
> (pp. 42–43; emphasis added)

This history takes place at two levels (at least). Past history produces the cultures, traditions, teleological directions, proleptic means of mediation, and other factors that a human enters upon birth or relocation, and whose influence shapes the direction of societies. The history of any individual within this process is the second level; Vygotsky's comments above speak to this factor in human development. Both matter. In this chapter, I am concerned with both long history in creating social contexts in which the present unfolds, and Vygotsky's own history within these contours.

The interpretation of history is undertaken through a cultural lens, so understanding a nation's or individual's history is always a subjective project. Soviet history has been especially prone to revision so that, according to an aphorism related by Wertsch (1999), "Nothing is more unpredictable than Russia's past" (p. 268). As is now well known, the United States has also been subject to historical revisionism in order to paper over the many inequities and horrors visited on Native, Black, Asian-origin, and Brown people domestically

DOI: 10.4324/9781003374848-5

and the oppression of people abroad (Yacovone, 2022). The task of historicizing a society, or the people within it, is shaped by an ideological lens provided by "collective memory" bound by schema, habit, and narrative, one that may distort past events to suit present needs (Wertsch, 2021). Different ideological positions produce different histories of the same events, making judgments about any of them a relativistic endeavor. Furthermore, a nation's history may be warped by what Snyder (2021) calls "memory laws": "government actions designed to guide public interpretation of the past. Such measures work by asserting a mandatory view of historical events, by forbidding the discussion of historical facts or interpretations or by providing vague guidelines that lead to self-censorship." Although "Early memory laws were generally designed to protect the truth about victim groups.... [T]hese early laws could be defended as attempts to protect the weaker against the stronger, and an endangered history against propaganda" (n.p.). Yet in many forms, they serve propagandistic ends designed to maintain inequity and power differentials. Snyder finds these "memory laws" to be at work many societies, including the United States and its 2021 efforts to promote the "1776 Project," initiated by President Donald Trump to instill a "patriotic education." This effort was undertaken by a commission that included no historians of US history. This commission

> defined its task as the "restoration of American education." ... It is a perverse goal. Teachers succeed if students do not understand something.... The new memory laws invite teachers to self-censor, on the basis of what students might feel—or say they feel. The memory laws place censorial power in the hands of students and their parents. It is not exactly unusual for white people in America to express the view that they are being treated unfairly; now such an opinion could bring history classes to a halt.
> (Snyder, 2021, n.p.)

And indeed it has, with even school librarians now threatened with criminal charges if their libraries include books considered "obscene" over any depiction of sexuality, especially that which provides favorable depictions of non-binary youth (Tagami, 2023). Those making these decisions represent a minority in the population; according to Tagami, "All but one of the senators who co-sponsored SB 154 are male, and all are white."

In this chapter, I situate Vygotsky's career within the historical context of his lifetime. This environment provided a setting in which hierarchical views of societies were common. Vygotsky both explained societal variation as a function of cultural mediation, and positioned some cultures as more advanced than others. He thus provides a complex source to draw on for multiculturalists who see Vygotsky as a relativist without recognizing his hierarchical views. Yet the latter is part of his intellectual and social heritage, and benefits from analysis and explication.

Cultural Evolution

Vygotsky's attention to the historical evolution of cultures led to his belief that communist societies represent the peak of human phylogenetic evolution. Lenin explained how cultural perspectives become established, asserting that ideologies are repeated countless times over the course of a society's existence, becoming naturalized in a worldview:

> human experience, repeated billions of times, is fixed in the consciousness of man by figures of logic. These figures have the stability of a prejudice, an axiomatic character

specifically (and only) by virtue of those billions of repetitions.... . In the phylogenetic plan ... speech evidently played a decisive role in the process of fixing in the human consciousness logical figures repeated billions of times in human experience.

(quoted in Vygotsky, 1998, p. 119)

These billions of iterations are fundamentally cultural, serving to reinforce and reproduce both an outlook, and the structures and processes that sustain them over time. Vygotsky's entry into this phylogenetic, self-perpetuating, ethnocentric series of repeated logics undoubtedly helped to shape his view that "primitive" people's higher mental functions were not as "high" as those of the Soviets.

Societies promote the development of higher mental functions that fit their ideologies and make their perpetuation more likely. These higher mental functions pre-exist any individual's arrival on earth, providing the antecedent values into which individuals grow over time. Human development, to Vygotsky, takes place within cultures that have, over many iterations, developed higher mental functions suitable to their societal needs (see Chapter 5). He stated that

Human behavior is the product of development of a broader system than just the system of a person's individual functions, specifically, systems of social connections and relations, of collective forms of behavior and social cooperation... . [E]very higher mental function was formerly a unique form of psychological cooperation and only later was converted into an individual method of behavior, transferring into the psychological systems of the child the structure that, even in the transfer, retains all the basic traits of symbolic structure, changing only its situation basically.

(1999, p. 41)

This symbolic structure is composed of signs specific to a culture's historical needs and related developmental pathways. Both individual development and the development of societies are products of social histories that shape what is possible to think in given contexts. The history of higher mental functions, Vygotsky asserted, involves "the history of converting means of social behavior into means of individual-psychological organization" (1999, p. 41). In this sense, socialization to historical ways of cultural thinking produces the higher mental functions that in turn enable fruitful participation in a society's organization and processes. In a monoculture, this phenomenon may enable many individuals to function according to the same assumptions, codes, manners, goals, and other aspects of a collective society. In multicultural social groups, there is a tendency for one culture to dominate, and the rest to either assimilate or exist in subordinate ways. This condition produces the inequities that typically characterize societies where colonialism has produced social tiers, where immigrants are regarded as inferior and deficient, where enslavement has created an oppressed class whose status is difficult to change well beyond the era of subjugation, where gendered assumptions produce social tiers, and where other problems commonly found in 21st-century nations are continually present.

Yet, to Vygotsky, not all human societies have learned to think in concepts or develop higher mental functions. The human brain, he stated,

having a ready inventory, did not produce thinking in concepts itself at primitive stages of development of humanity and the child; of course, there was a time when thinking in concepts was a form unknown to humanity. Even now, there are tribes that do not have this form of thinking. We ask, should we assume that they, like the aphasics, are suffering from a disturbance of the basic brain function?... a concept is a historical, not a biological category in the sense of the function that produces it. We know that primitive man had no concepts.

(1998, p. 133)

Homo sapiens first appeared over 300,000 years ago, and were preceded by protohumans millions of years before that. They also developed at the same time as other humanlike species that became extinct, even as traces of their DNA remain in living humans (Sankararaman et al., 2014). It's not clear how anyone could know the conceptual understandings of "primitive" people who could surely distinguish their own tribe from another, could make tools and use them to solve problems in their environments, could make plans based on their abstraction of local knowledge to generalizations, and could meet other definitions of conceptual thinking described by Vygotsky.

The Problem of Religion

In accordance with Soviet doctrine, Vygotsky accepted the primacy of a nation that eschewed capitalism, and that organized society to elevate the status of the humble worker, the noble proletariat of Marxist ideology and lore. Soviet citizens from many of the previously independent areas of the new, expansive Soviet Union were understood as underevolved. They lacked prior Soviet education and guidance, were stunted in social and intellectual progress, and were in need of Soviet-style social organization in order to reach an enlightened state of being in the fabled communist Workers' Paradise.

The study conducted by Luria (1976) in remote areas of the Soviet Union therefore found the Muslim peasants to be "backward" in large part due to their adherence to the Islamic religion. These communities, Luria concluded, ought to be replaced by Soviet collective farms, bringing their "Third-World" economies under the umbrella of communism, one of the first two economic "worlds," the other being the odious capitalism. The lands of wealthy pre-Soviet Russians who were accused of capitalist tendencies were also seized by the state, which made them available to the proletariat in collectivist farms. What both the Muslims and the bourgeoisie needed was a Soviet culture that would remove the advantages (and moral disadvantages) following from wealth, and the eradication of religion that distracted its adherents from the material realities of life and substituted mythological abstractions of no pragmatic value.[1]

Other groups were considered inferior as well. Vygotsky (1993) took a dim view of Christians, whose religion, he felt, obscured clear thinking with fairy tales valorizing what they saw as their own superior culture. From such an elevated position, he believed, Christians took on a patronizing disposition to view the downtrodden with pity and charity, rather than creating for them opportunities for inclusion. In the Soviet Union, religion was considered, as phrased by Marx (1843),

> the sigh of the oppressed creature, the heart of a heartless world, and the soul of soulless conditions. It is the opium of the people. The abolition of religion as the illusory happiness of the people is the demand for their real happiness.

In the absence of religion, Soviet psychologists often drew on poetry and other forms of mysticism to imbue their psychological theories with soul and spirit (Smagorinsky, 2009a).

Vygotsky (1997a) stated the point clearly: "In the rigorous sense of the word, psychology denotes the science of the soul. This has been its definition from the very beginning" (p. 2). Given Vygotsky's interest in how art mediates emotional development, he was able to find an outlet for his literary interests that coincided with his emphasis on long-term human maturation. He thus had spirituality, if not a professed belief in and devotion to the Old and New Testament or Qur'anic deities.

Vygotsky's Jewish heritage created obstacles to higher education and placement in Soviet psychological circles, given the anti-Semitism practiced in Soviet society (Tartakower, 1971). To borrow a phrase often repeated by Vygotsky, taken from Psalm 118:22–23 of the Jewish sacred text, the *Hebrew Bible* or *Old Testament* (later claimed by the Jewish prophet Jesus, per Mark 12:1–11) "The stone the builders rejected has become the cornerstone" of a new edifice (Psalm 118:22). His own membership in a scorned community perhaps represented to him that rejected stone, one upon which a new psychology and society could be built.

In the Soviet context, "Jewishness was viewed as an embarrassing obscurantist diversion from the class struggle. This failure of vision was part of orthodox Marxism's wider failure to adequately grasp *any* oppression that was not directly reducible to class" (Johnson, 2019, n.p.; emphasis in original). The Soviets had to address "the Jewish question" as the Nazis rose in the 1930s with the goal of removing Jewish people from Germany, Europe, and ultimately the Soviet Union and the globe. However, the Soviets' focus was on social class, not race or ethnicity, which allowed anti-Semitism to fester, ignored as a factor in developing a society based on equity.

Religion, then, was a complex issue for Vygotsky, if not a problem at all to the Soviets except for the need to eliminate it. He did view non-Jewish religions as flawed, especially in combination with capitalism. What is available in his writing in English includes scant attention to the role of Jewish people in the USSR. Johnson (2019) reports that the fate of the Jewish people was a major concern of Leon Trotsky, a Soviet architect of Jewish heritage who was banished and ultimately murdered in Mexico in 1940. Vygotsky was surrounded by hierarchical understandings of religion that either dismissed religion altogether, or positioned one's own religion as the apex of spiritual life. His view of Christians and Muslims was consistent with the Soviet purge of religion, if not their persistent anti-Semitism.

Nonetheless, while the Nazi movement was growing stronger in Europe, a belief circulated that the Bolshevik Revolution had been insinuated by a powerful Jewish cabal in pursuit of world domination (Ruotsila, 2000). Judeo-Bolshevism, the belief that Jews had penetrated and controlled the Revolution and Soviet government, developed as a conspiracy theory that inflamed anti-Semitism around Europe (Hanebrink, 2018). This belief in Jewish ambitions to rule the earth via secret cabals infiltrating global leadership persists in the 21st century (Flores, 2022), with anti-Semitism a growing problem in the United States and other nations (Boorstein & Clement, 2023), in spite of the absence of any evidence that they have ever attempted world conquest or, especially, have ever succeeded.

Monoculturalism and Multiculturalism

Vygotsky has often been recruited to support multiculturalism in today's schools. Progressive educators have found his account of cultural mediation to legitimize pluralistic cultures, without attention to Vygotsky's own reluctance to accept multicultural equity. Meanwhile, US social conservatives assert, similar to Vygotsky, that "Western culture" is inherently superior to all others (Bonnett, 2004), albeit because of the greatness of the Judeo-Christian heritage and not a Marxist, materialist, rationalist perspective. In the United States—where the solution is capitalism, not communism—the conservative view has long been at the center of schooling, dating to the founding mass education in the United States. Those who hope to conserve Judeo-Christian dominance view progressive multiculturalism as a threat to social stability and cultural continuity (Grzymala-Busse, 2019), or at least the continuity of the culture engrained in the structure and process of public education. Vygotsky, in this sense, was more monocultural than the 21st-century progressives who claim his influence, including me. He lived in a more parochial world than the 2020s now afford, such that the prospects for being worldly were less available to him than to those in a modern connected world.

The tensions that follow from naming him as a source to justify pluralism are not simple to resolve, given his own elitist views on art and culture. Vygotsky, as related by Van der Veer and Valsiner (1991), "viewed non-Russian cultures in the USSR as being at a lower level in their historical development, and expressed the sentiment that the building of the 'new society' opened new developmental possibilities for them... He argued for the re-education of the children of 'national minorities' as it could be the mechanism of cultural change at large" (p. 324). The woke modern reader will no doubt find his view paternalistic and ethnocentric, and illustrative of George Bernard Shaw's quip that "my country is the best because I was born in it," or if not born in, reluctantly adopted by.

Yet this recognition of Vygotsky's own cultural blinders does not stop theorists from drawing on him to argue for the respect of all cultures. I can accept his account of mediated development as a justification for multicultural education, while also recognizing that he did not apply these principles to his own society, and couldn't have done so even if he'd wanted to, given that it would comprise a violation of Soviet doctrine and thus earn a trip to the Gulag, or a bullet to the head. The contradictions are inevitable, and must be kept in mind when considering Vygotsky as a source in educational conceptions.

Ethnocentrism

The shaping force of societies is evident in what is, inescapably, Vygotsky's ethnocentric perspective. If growing up in parochial communities produces a limited understanding of the outside world, then Vygotsky's formative years were decidedly insular. He lived in the Pale of Settlement among his own kind, according to their values and practices. In his era and in the 21st century, people from non-technological societies were typically viewed in industrialized nations as developmentally behind, more like children than adults socialized to living in a modern technological society (see Chapter 6).

Vygotsky's uncritical quotation of Georgi Valentinovich Plekhanov, the Russian-Soviet revolutionary and philosopher who was among the leading Marxists of his era, is indicative of how he and his society viewed "the other" as barbaric: "The Australian *savage*'s whole existence depends on his boomerang just like the whole existence of contemporary England depends on its machines" (1997b, p. 180; emphasis added). His account of people from non-technological societies characterized them as "half-primitive" people who benefit from exposure to technology. He wrote that as they engage with

> European civilization and receive objects of European general use, they begin to take interest in them and to value the possibilities they bring with them. These investigations show that primitive people initially have a negative opinion about the reading

of books. After they have received several very simple agricultural tools and have seen the connection between the reading of books and practice, they began to evaluate the white men's work differently.... . On the one hand, several new systems are not just linked with social signs but also with ideology and the meaning which some function acquires in the consciousness of people. On the other hand, new forms of behavior develop from the next content picked up by the person from the ideology of the surrounding environment.

(1997b, p. 98)

His assumption appears to be that the intercultural exchange is peaceful and that European and especially Soviet ways are simply better and thus to be aspired to. This approach, however, was not evident in European colonization, where the imposition of European ways was achieved through violence, disease, and cultural genocide. It was not evident in the ruthless imposition of communism on the Soviet Union's many peoples. The process rarely involves aspirational rising to the technology of the colonizers. Instead, "primitive" cultures tend to be obliterated and replaced. They rarely take on the ways of an oppressor volitionally in hopes of a better life, other than to adopt their tools of warfare in order to improve their chances for cultural survival.

"Primitive" People

Vygotsky's English-language translator Knox (1993) provides a sympathetic reading to Vygotsky's use of terms like "primitive" to characterize people from early societies or current cultures operating without technology or industry. Their practices were not "rational" in the Enlightenment sense, but had their own logic among the people who used them. Knox (1993) notes how the terms primitive and cultural

> must be defined not from today's perspective, but from the context of the first two decades of the Soviet Union, and particularly from around the time around the Russian Revolution.... . Early 20th century literature and art considered the "primitive" to be natural and superior, and "cultural" as something artificial, removed from the primary unnatural. Indeed, in his description of the development of primitive people Vygotsky refers to the "Baldwin effect"[2] whereby evolution is always accompanied by involution.

(in Vygotsky and Luria, 1993)

Against this popularized notion of primitivism, Vygotsky himself redefined these terms in the light of his own theory of development:

> as man progresses over history and a child through stages of development in his or her lifetime, the primitive or natural stage is not replaced by later cultural stages, rather the latter was superimposed like scaffolding on top of the former, changing, restructuring, and adapting these natural processes. Thus the psychology of a cultural man is not superior or inferior but different [from] that of a primitive man, just as the psychology of an adult is different from that of a child, particularly a child without schooling.

(Knox, 1993, pp. 9–10)

Although Knox absolves Vygotsky of the problem of pathologizing "primitive" people through such characterizations, she relates how Vygotsky at times found parallels between phylogeny, the development of the species, and ontogeny, the development of individuals within the species. Nonetheless, Wertsch (1997) writing in the same volume, concludes that "Vygotsky and Luria take a very strong anti-recapitulationist position" (pp. x–xi) (see Chapter 6).

To Knox (1993), Vygotsky was not creating a cultural hierarchy. Rather, he was creating an analogy between the "primitive" mind's development and that of a child. With a different upbringing, these "primitive" people could develop culturally according to Enlightenment notions of intellectualism. Whether becoming Soviet urban factory workers or laborers on collectivist farms established on depleted soil would represent an improvement is beyond the scope of my analysis.

Knox (1993) locates Vygotsky's view of "primitive" people in the broader society, both of "Europe" and "the West" and of the Soviet Union:

> Vygotsky's treatment of the higher stage of cultural development is, however, essentially Eurocentric: he follows the lead of other Western psychologists who saw Enlightenment and, rational, or scientific thought as the latest and most advanced (hierarchically speaking) step in psychological development. Still, he did not ignore the importance of the type of thinking characteristic of the "primitive" mentality that can still be found in cultural adults of differing degrees.
>
> (p. 12)

To Knox (1993), Vygotsky saw how Soviet adults could retain vestiges of childish thinking, just as post-capitalist Soviet society might retain vestiges of the bourgeois cultures that they sought to replace. Developmentally, a child cannot yet be an adult, and so can only think in relatively simple ways until both biology and socialization contribute to the formation of higher mental functions. The "primitive" people similarly cannot start out as rational, ideally communistic people, but must go through stages to develop those capacities. Significantly, it is not either-or when it comes to logical and prelogical systems of thought. Rather, heterogeneity is inevitable, producing hybrid ways of thinking following from immersion in multiple influences that accrue through experience. It's not clear if Vygotsky saw hybridity in the thinking of remote peasants living in cultural isolation. The presence of multiple cultures appears to be required for different thought systems to be available for appropriation, if not clean integration.

Vygotsky's drawing of a parallel between "primitive" people and young children produced an infantilized depiction of both ancient and current populations whose societies were predicated on other values and affordances. His portrayal of "primitive" or "tribal" people works against the ways in which he has subsequently been referenced to support multicultural respect and validation. He asserted that "higher mental functions arise from collective social forms of behavior" (1998, p. 168), which surely these "primitive" societies developed primarily to survive.

Vygotsky documented how people from different cultures develop differently, while also creating cultural hierarchies positioning Soviet communism and its ideal citizen as the ultimate human form. Such cultural mediation produces differences in how various social collectives engage with the world and learn to interpret it. This *sociocultural history*, in Wertsch's (1985) terms, might be termed *cultural phylogenesis*, the lifespan of the culture, which is at work in societies in ways that produce differences, conflicts, and perceived hierarchies that are determined by those with the greatest power, those who institutionalize their own ways of being as optimal.

Luria (in Vygotsky & Luria, 1993) did find that "primitive" people were advantaged in situations calling for survival in nature:

> If we compare these processes in a cultural man—say an average modern Parisian—with those in an Australian who is at a very primitive stage of development, we will see that the cultural man is inferior to the latter with respect to almost all the simplest psychological functions... . [I]n all these natural functions, the primitive man is incomparably superior to the cultural man, and nevertheless we still know that the mental life of the latter is much richer, that he is much more powerful, and that often he is much better oriented in his environment and controls the environmental phenomena.
>
> (p. 169)

Biologically, in the battle to live with and subordinate nature, the "primitive" person is best equipped. Luria's remarks appear to romanticize the "noble savage" (Rousseau, 1762), that uncorrupted being who is incomparably superior to the "cultural man" who thinks in abstract concepts and so is not always directly engaged with the natural, material world and its social structures and processes.

British novelist H. G. Wells's (1895) *The Time Machine*, published the year before Vygotsky's birth, featured a contrast between two separately evolved human species: the weak and childlike Eloi who developed from the upper class and whose unchallenging lives have degraded their intellects and human spirit; and the savage Morlocks of lower class descent who must innovate to survive and emerge as the stronger species. They are superior in the sense that Vygotsky and Luria (1993) conceived, better able to survive life's harshness through physical domination and the force of will. They are inferior in their limited capacity for developing intellectualized higher mental functions. I can find no evidence that Vygotsky read this novel, yet his and Luria's conclusions in this case are similar in lauding the survival capacities of people who rely on material engagement with the world, unmediated by technology, perhaps suggesting a zeitgeist in the wake of Darwin.

Assumptions about the best means and destinations of development are cultural constructs that typically position one's own kind at the highest level of progress and judge other ways as deficient. Even those taking a cultural perspective are prone to this tendency, including among the most thoughtful and intensely knowledgeable people of their era. The quality of a cultured worldview is evident in the concepts that people develop in the course of development. These take place at both the phylogenetic and ontogenetic levels: Societies develop governing conceptions of optimal living within their own contours, and individuals adopt those conceptions through their participation in social life.

Cultural Unity and Variation

Vygotsky (1998) was clear about the mediational role of contexts in human development: "The complex syntheses that arise in the process of the child's and the adolescent's cultural development are based on other factors—mainly on societal life, cultural development, and work activity of the child and adolescent" (p. 36). This sort of statement, taken out of context, might be used to justify Vygotsky as a cultural relativist, which he is often considered to be (Moll, 1995). More specifically, however, his comments became judgmental and hierarchical.

Vygotsky's accounts of people from non-industrialized societies can trouble the 21st-century mind. He referred to cultures in which the mysteries of the world are accessed through dreams or games with what appeared to him to be coincidental outcomes. He said of a "primitive" people,

> why should one study and think when one can see in a dream or throw dice [to answer a question?] Such is the fate of all forms of magical behavior: very soon they are turned into an impediment to further development of thinking, although they themselves at a given stage of historical development of thinking are the embryo of certain trends.... . [T]he magical character of the operation, rooted, as Lévy-Bruhl[3] demonstrated, in the depths of primitive thinking, compels us to reject instantly the idea that we have before us a purely rational, intellectualistic device of the primitive mind.
> (1997c, pp. 46–47)

He distinguished between the role that dreams play *for us* and *for them*:

Dreams play a completely different role in the life of primitive man then they do *for us*. The connection of dreams with other mental processes, and, derived from this their functional significance in the general structure of the personality, are completely different. Almost everywhere, dreams were at first a guide which was followed, an infallible companion, and frequently a master whose commands were not disputed.
(p. 183; emphasis added)

Vygotsky referred to how dreams often function in non-industrialized societies, populated by *them*, as visions foretelling the future. He viewed this function as the province of "primitive" people who lacked rationalist tools for interpreting the world. Yet a reading of "indigenous" scholarship—not available to Vygotsky—gives dreams a much more sensitive reading, and makes them relevant in the 21st-century world. Native American scholar Jacobs (1998), for instance, recounts his experiences living among the Rarámuri shamans of Mexico, and their attention to the futures available through dreams. Rather than being in a primitive state in which dreams are "at first" visionary guides abandoned once technology is accessible, they remain powerful sources of interpretation among the shamans. These societies still exist and have their own vitality and relevance to the people who inhabit them, and whose worlds are far less polluted and riddled with vice than the "rational" societies viewed as more advanced. They might indeed find it hard to adapt to the imposition of a rationalist regime; but that might be more a problem with the regime than with the people upon whom it is forced.

Indigenous scholarship asserts the validity, and at times superiority, of societies that have not developed according to what might be characterized as "white" notions of progress (e.g., Brayboy & Maughan, 2009; Cajete, 1994; Kanu, 2011; Kimmerer, 2015; Smith, 2005). This perspective was not available to Vygotsky, who wrote that

> The laws of dreaming are the same everywhere, but the role which the dream fulfills is completely different and we will see that such a difference not only exists between, let us say, the Kaffir *and us* [per Lévy-Bruhl, 1922]. The Roman believed in dreams as well, although he would not say in a difficult situation "I will dream about

it,"—because he stood on another level of human development and would solve the matter, in the words of [Roman historian and politician Publius Cornelius] Tacitus, "with arms and reason and not like a woman through a dream."

(1997a, p. 97; emphasis added)

"The Kaffir" refers to Black South Africans, originally of Bantu ethnicity but later, in the mid-1900s, a term applied to all Black residents as a pejorative. The idea of dreams serving an assessment and planning role comes from Lévy-Bruhl's report that, when presented with a complex challenge, "each of us would reply: 'I will think it over.' The Kaffir says: 'I will dream about it.' For him the dream fulfils the same function as thinking does for us" (Vygotsky, 1997a, p. 97). And apparently, women use dreams in this irrational manner as well.

The Kaffir are depicted by Vygotsky and Lévy-Bruhl as different from "us," in what today would be considered a form of "othering." The weak portrayal of women further suggests social hierarchies; as Swindle (2003) argues, Tacitus "always ties [woman characters] closely to a male counterpart, be it a son, a lover, or a husband"(p. 106), indicating a subordinate or ancillary role. This status assignment should not be surprising from Tacitus, who lived from the years 56–120. The next 1,800 years or so did not advance women's rights sufficiently to be adopted by Vygotsky or most men of his time; and the United Nations (2022) predicts that equality is nearly three centuries away from the present time.

It's also not clear how taking up arms constitutes an act of reason, although to someone who survived the first four decades of the 20th century, perhaps it did.

Dreams remain vital sources of understanding among modern-day people from outside technological and industrial societies (Jacobs, 1998; Kracke, 2006). The biology of dreams, as Vygotsky notes, remains constant, but their roles shift culturally, and different conceptions of dreams have served, among many means, to create cultural hierarchies constructed from the perspective of those making the judgments. To Vygotsky, "thinking" has an intellectual dimension that is not available to a dreamer, making the Kaffir's reliance on dreams to envision possibilities a lower order of cognition. Yet Vygotsky's contemporary, Swiss psychologist Carl Jung (1875–1961), found dreams to provide indirect access to one's emotional state of mind, albeit following from reflection under the guidance of an analyst.

Wertsch (1997), in his "Preface" to *Studies on the History of Behavior*, notes that developments since the volume's authorship have provided a better perspective on the issues than was available to Vygotsky:

In addition to advances, there are simply differences between 1930 and today that count as legitimate and interesting areas of inquiry. There has been something of a paradigm shift away from evolutionary approaches toward cultural analysis, and from linguistic analysis toward linguistic and cultural relativism. Figures such as Boas[4], Sapir[5], and Whorf[6] lead the way in rejecting the kind of evolutionary ranking of languages and cultures that plays such an essential role in [Vygotsky's] argument.

(p. xiii)

Vygotsky's attention to how societies shape development thus had an ethnocentric dimension that produced these evolutionary rankings of cultures in ways that contradict how he is often recruited to promote cultural relativism, something to which I've contributed (Smagorinsky, 2013b). Rather, his general account of mediation has helped generate an understanding that industrialized societies don't set the standard for other cultures to ascend to; that they are developing in relation to the challenges that their surroundings present to them. This understanding has led more recent ethnographers working in the Vygotskian tradition to eschew hierarchies and argue for legitimacy and appropriateness of the situated knowledge developed in communities, often from outside the traditions practiced by those who position them as "primitive" or underdeveloped (e.g., Moll, 2000; Rogoff, 2011).

Wertsch (1997) finds that Vygotsky's association of "primitive" minds with the minds of children to be too stark. He argues that

> the boundaries between genetic domains are, in fact, not so neat as Vygotsky and Luria assumed. Recent findings in physical anthropology and archaeology indicate that hominidization involved an extended period of overlap (something on the order of two million years) between phylogenesis and sociocultural history. This contrasts with the view generally accepted when Vygotsky and Luria were writing. In their view, phylogenesis is assumed to have culminated with a final qualitative transition giving rise to the organism of Homo sapiens, and this, in turn, allowed sociocultural history to begin. The massive overlap now generally accepted as existing between these two genetic domains means that cultural or proto-cultural development provided part of the context for, and hence influenced, organic evolution during hominidization. The fact that we now know a great deal more than what was known in 1930 about languages of the world, for example, indicates that some of the authors' generalizations about levels of linguistic complexity are no longer accepted. The same critique applies to many of their general statements about cultural complexity as well.
>
> (p. xi)

The knowledge generated by researchers after Vygotsky's death makes some of his propositions dated and questionable. The cautionary tale here is that simply quoting Vygotsky as the arbiter on all matters can reinvigorate ideas that have been questioned and revised over time. Just as he interrogated his contemporaries and antecedents with intellectual vigor, his own corpus is open to questions and revision by those who have access to a near-century's worth of scholarship and opened accesses for communication.

View of Animals

Vygotsky's diction, even in translation, reveals a difference between his time and the present. In his day, research on animals was conducted routinely, often in ways that would have People for the Ethical Treatment of Animals (PETA) and American Society for the Prevention of Cruelty to Animals (ASPCA) protesting in the streets. Here, for instance, is one of many matter-of-fact accounts he provided of an experiment on the nervous system:

> Sherrington[7] ... cut [dogs'] vagus nerve and the spinal cord and cut off all the main internal organs and large groups of skeletal muscles from the influence of the brain. In this way, in his experiments, the main bodily manifestations of emotions which arise through reflexes were excluded by surgical means. However, there was no doubt that under appropriate conditions, the experimental dogs exhibited emotional reactions without noticeable changes in the manifestation of characteristic symptoms that are usually taken as signs of anger, fear, satisfaction, or aversion.
>
> (1999, p. 87)

Vygotsky referred to Pavlov's studies of dogs in similarly detached terms, recounting one such study by saying,

> The classic example of such a "perversion of instinct" is demonstrated by Pavlov's experiment where a conditional reflex is developed in a dog by cauterizing its skin with an electric current. The animal's first response to pain is a violent defensive reaction; it strains against its harness, it bites the device with its teeth, and it fights with all its might. But as a result of a long series of experiments, where pain stimulation was accompanied by food, the dog's response to burns on the skin began to be that very same reaction with which it usually responded to food.
>
> (1997a, p. 43)

We can only hope that Vygotsky would, in current times, be concerned about the effects on animals following from experiments by people. It is instructive in any case, to keep in mind that Vygotsky's world and the 21st century's imperative for ethical research did not always dovetail. Different worldviews have emerged to provide the lenses through which events are interpreted. This phenomenon goes by the name of the Overton Window,[8] which refers to the range of beliefs, attitudes, and dispositions considered acceptable at any given time. This window shifts with new understandings and moods to accommodate broader changes in perspective. It's important to keep in mind the Overton Window through which any individual could envision possibilities during their era of existence.

Eras are but one factor in how animals are viewed. Regional and national values matter as well. I watched the delightful film *The Adventures of Milo and Otis* (Hata, 1986) with my children, and we were charmed by the dog's and kitten's adventures of survival. We then learned that the Japanese film responded to different rules about animals' treatment, with about 30 kittens killed during the shoot, including one scene in which a kitten falls from a high cliff, with a different kitten used for each of many takes to replace the one who had died in the previous one.

How, then, to judge Vygotsky's dispassionate descriptions of animals being tortured in lab research? The notion of *presentism* is always useful to keep in mind when reading a person from a different time and place. Presentism refers to using a modern frame of mind to judge people's actions from prior eras that had different conditions, sensibilities, and values. At times it makes good sense to re-evaluate a prior belief system and its artifacts, such as the 2020s movement to tear down US Confederate monuments, rename buildings, and remodel buildings to erase the glorification of those who acted traitorously in the past, yet who were glorified by Southerners whose historical revisions continue to animate school textbooks (Bohan, Bradshaw, & Morris, 2020). One might ask then, should Vygotsky be shunned because he reported cruelty to animals uncritically? I'll leave readers to think through that dilemma and arrive at their own determination.

What this problem indicates is that cultural experience produces an ideological stance toward the social and natural worlds. Vygotsky (1997c) concluded that "World view is that which characterizes a person's behavior as a whole, the cultural relation of the child to the external world" (p. 242), which might include gravitating to a culture's norms, even when they appear wrong-minded in retrospect. Wertsch (1999) sees worldviews as responsible for Burke's (1966) notion of *terministic screens*, which act as lenses that both focus attention and limit it, such that cultural experiences both create possibilities and impose blinders. Wertsch concludes that "By using the cultural tools provided to us by the sociocultural context in which we function we usually do not operate by choice. Instead, we inherently appropriate the terministic screens, affordances, constraints, and so forth associated with the cultural tools we employ" (p. 55).

George Washington, "The Father of His Country," was a slave owner, as was typical of people of his station in the 1700s United States, especially the South. In the 2020s, his view of Black Africans as his property, and his harsh treatment of them, has become a topic of concern to the point where some advocate the renaming of his namesake, George Washington University (Francois, 2022[9]). Is it presentist to "cancel" George Washington because he appropriated the terministic screens, affordances, constraints, and so forth associated with the cultural tools of his day? Is it racist not to cancel him? These are vexing questions that also arise in taking into account the various hierarchical views that appear in the pages of Vygotsky's writing, even if his shortcomings fell far below the level of enslaving other humans.

Male Bias

It's possible to detect a masculine bias in Vygotsky's worldview, which would be consistent with the values of his time, and ours. His work, for instance, viewed the emotions as the fount of all human thinking (see Ellis & Solms, 2018, for a contemporary confirmation of this view). He asserted, however, that the task of the intellect in an advanced society is to subordinate emotions, to regulate them. This view might position the emotional orientation of many people as inferior, a problem identified by feminist psychologists (e.g., Gilligan, 1982, 2020) as built into the fabric of psychology of the 20th century. Vygotsky (1999) wrote, for instance,

> Women have much readier emotions than the stronger gender owing to a strong excitability of the nervous system, particularly its vasomotor section. The same thing is noted in children compared to adults. The general rule is that, like individuals, whole nations are more subject to emotions the lower their level of education.
> (p. 152)

Emotional expression was, to Vygotsky, a sign of insufficient self-regulation aligned with the intellectual development specified in Enlightenment values; and women were more likely to exhibit it than men. This assumption permeated the research on moral reasoning by Kohlberg (1958), the male researcher whom Gilligan (1982, 2020) challenged with her feminist psychology. Vygotsky (1999) further associated high emotional states with low levels of civilization, showing his bias in favor of advanced technological and industrial societies based on scientific principles guided by reason, in spite of the emotional ways in which policy is developed in the 21st century (Haidt, 2012):

> The so-called wild people are more irascible and indomitable, more unbridled in their joy, more depressed by their grief than civilized peoples. The same kind of difference is noted between different generations of one and the same tribe. We are more peaceful and gentle as compared to our barbaric predecessors who got greater pleasure in yielding to reckless outbursts and bellicose fury, but who fell so easily into dejection at any failure that they killed themselves because of trifles.
> (p. 152)

The 21st-century reader might rightfully recoil at such characterizations, which easily lead to racist interpretations of non-industrialized people. Whether Vygotsky was sexist and racist or not is more a question on the degree to which his worldview was aligned with the perspectives of his time and place. During my work on this book, I became convinced that Vygotsky's career in a male-dominated field inevitably produced a belief in the primacy of men, a phenomenon that has been observed in many scientific fields. Yet "hidden figures" are now being excavated from obscurity to show the often-uncredited role that women have played in developing science.[10] When I posed this possibility to René van der Veer, a person whose knowledge in these matters has earned my highest respect, he replied,

> I don't think you can make the case that early Soviet psychology was a man's endeavour. Men formed the majority, of course, but especially Jewish women entered the field in substantial numbers. Moreover, Vygotsky cited them and worked with them. Think of Vera Schmidt, Tamara Dembo, Blyuma Zeigarnik, Maria Ovsyankina, Birenbaum, Bozhovich, Sabina Spielrein, etc. Neither do I think that in his research he focused on boys. See the chapter on difficult children in his Notebooks. That he always used "the child, he" was indeed a convention [of using masculine pronouns universally]. Vygotsky's sisters also had academic training and became good researchers in their own right. So, I would argue that he was perhaps less a male chauvinist than others in his time. In his own cultural environment, that of learned Jews, it was increasingly normal that women played an intellectual role.

I'm content, then, to consider Vygotsky "less a male chauvinist than others in his time." It would have been highly unlikely for him to be a 21st-century woke feminist in his own time and place. It appears he may have been ahead of his time in including girls in his research and women among his colleagues. I'm sure that he could be subjected to a harsh, presentist critique nonetheless. I'm equally sure that if anyone pays attention to anything I say a century from now, I'll be open to plenty of criticisms (see Klosterman, 2016, for an elaborated view of how today's certitude becomes the future's head-scratcher).

Discussion

In considering Vygotsky's elitism and how it might fare in more democratic circles, I'm reminded of a remark made by current US cultural critic Cornel West, who has recorded rap music and appeared on funk albums (e.g., Bootsy Collins's, 2020 *The Power of the One*), while also being a faculty member at some of the world's most high-status universities. During a discussion with Henry Louis Gates on the 2019 program *Reconstruction: America After the Civil War*, they reflected on the contributions of civil rights champion and NAACP founder W. E. B. Dubois, a man of great sophistication and accomplishment—he was the first African American to be awarded a doctorate—who looked down on jazz and other pop culture media of the sort beloved and practiced by West. West acknowledged that, although he had unlimited admiration for the role played by DuBois in advancing civil rights, as a person he felt little affiliation with him because his taste did not accommodate the contributions of everyday people and the creators of content consumed by the masses.

Rather, DuBois felt that an intellectual elite, the "talented tenth" capable of inspiring "racial uplift" through formal education, should be cultivated to lead the Black population to equality in society. Vygotsky appeared to share such elitist tastes in art and intellect, one that might be off-putting to those who share West's appreciation for popular culture and those who produce and consume it. West could respect and cherish DuBois's stance on civil rights while rejecting his highbrow taste in the arts and patronizing view of less-talented 90%, just as a modern-day reader might have concerns about Vygotsky's dim view of "primitive" people and their childlike ways, yet still admire his enduring contributions.

Should Vygotsky be cancelled because some of his views fall short of 21st century sensibilities? That's up for readers to decide. My own view is that he is a worthy topic, in spite of holding views that met the spirit of his times and not the present, at least not the progressive wing of the 21st-century population. Drawing on scholarship from yesteryear is a complex undertaking that benefits from careful thought and as respectful a stance as is possible, with presentism ever lurking, and self-righteousness over the sins of the past often providing the lens for viewing history.

Notes

1 I am an atheist. But I might be wrong.
2 The Baldwin Effect is credited to US evolutionary psychologist James Mark Baldwin (1861–1934). It posits that the ability to learn new behaviors, typically in response to external stress, affects a species' ability to survive, and ultimately, *its genetic makeup*. Its premise that behaviors can produce genetic changes has been both rejected and confirmed since its introduction in Baldwin (1896), although some find antecedent beliefs in the years following Darwin's *On the Origin of Species*.
3 Lucien Lévy-Bruhl (1857–1939) was a French philosopher, anthropologist, sociologist, and ethnologist who distinguished between "primitive" and "modern" people's thinking, with primitives conflating the supernatural and material worlds and modern people relying on reflection and logic.
4 Franz Uri Boas (1858–1942) was a Prussian-German–American known as the Father of American Anthropology. He helped develop the fields of historical particularism and cultural relativism.
5 Edward Sapir (1884–1939) was a Jewish, US-based anthropologist and linguist.
6 Benjamin Lee Whorf (1897–1941) was an US linguist who, with Sapir, is credited for the Sapir-Whorf hypothesis, which posits that a language's structure shapes how a speaker conceptualized the world (also known as the principle of linguistic relativity).
7 Sir Charles Scott Sherrington (1857–1952) was a British neurophysiologist who won the Nobel Prize in Physiology or Medicine in 1932.
8 Named after Joseph Overton, who first proposed the idea early in the 21st century to describe shifts in public policy that follow from changes in acceptability.
9 Published, ironically, in *The Washington Post*.
10 I'm pleased to include my mother, Margaret Smagorinsky, among these hidden figures. Married to a noted meteorologist, she herself was an accomplished statistician who, along with other scientists' wives, made uncredited, significant contributions to the development of the science. To test the Electronic Numerical Integrator and Computer (ENIAC)'s accuracy as theorized by the Barotropic Equation, a task requiring computations of considerable complexity, meteorologists needed to get consistent results in comparisons between forecasts and actual weather. Prior to doing the computations with the computer, the team had a set of three statisticians analyze them by hand. As described by Steve Easterbrook (2020), "The actual calculations for this were handled by a team of three women, led by Margaret Smagorinsky, who was, at the time, a meteorological statistician with the US Weather Bureau. The three women hand-calculated over a hundred 24-hour forecasts for this one-dimensional model, using data from the Weather Bureau to initialize the forecasts. So credit for performing the first successful numerical weather forecast doesn't belong to ENIAC at all: it belongs to three "human computers": Margaret Smagorinsky, Norma Gilbarg, and Ellen-Kristine Eliasson."

Part II
Factors in Human Development

This section reviews Vygotsky's role as a developmental psychologist. He was never a pedagogue of the sort he's often made out to be through references to scaffolding. Rather, he was concerned with overall human development as it is mediated socially. This section details the factors that figured into his developmental conception, some of which are based in schools, some of which originate elsewhere. All have a cultural-historical basis, suggesting the need to know the history of cultures and how they shape action in the present and provide trajectories for the future. This review further looks at Vygotsky's views on emotional life and how play (not fun) is an essential formative experience in preparing children and youth for the labor that will characterize their subsequent lives. Finally, this section reviews the mistranslation and misunderstandings of what is commonly known as the zone of proximal development, and repositions it as a long-term developmental zone and not one in people's heads or a teaching method designed to help students learn incremental skills.

5 Principal Themes of Vygotsky's Cultural-Historical Psychology

My understanding of cultural-historical theory did not involve a rapid grasp of the concepts and is still under development. I began my exploration a couple of years after getting my doctorate in 1989. I had been immersed in cognitive psychology throughout my graduate studies. My reading began with the Vygotsky translations available at the time, mainly *Mind in Society* and the newly translated versions of *Thought and Language/Thinking and Speech* in 1986 and 1987. Of the latter, I began with the 1986 Kozulin translation, which was a lot more affordable in paperback than was the hardback-only Plenum version. I was an assistant professor who'd taken a substantial pay cut to leave my high school job, where I'd built up over a decade of seniority, for a starting university position, and had two young kids at home.

I also began to read ancillary scholarship that began in earnest in the 1980s and has grown exponentially since. As a learner, I first wrestled intellectually with the concepts, many of which concerned the ways in which the human mind is not an insular organ inside the skull, but is extended throughout the body neurologically and into the environment by means of tools and signs. I began to develop a different understanding of the human mind, one in which it is distributed rather than encased in the head, as outlined by Salomon (1993) in a volume whose publication came during this process. Intellectually, this phenomenon began to make a good deal of sense to me.

But I don't think I really started to get it until I developed a *felt understanding* of sociocultural processes. I began to feel my mind's interconnectedness with people, cultures, tools, signs, and bodily functions. This latter issue, mind and body interrelatedness, became very evident in my coming to terms with my severe chronic anxiety and how it affected my thinking and physical presentation. In addition, I began to feel more connected to things outside myself. My own understanding was thinly intellectual until it became embodied, until I could feel myself extended into my surroundings and my historical antecedents. Cultural-historical theory was no longer an abstract system. It was how I lived.

This chapter details essential aspects of Vygotsky's cultural-historical psychology. Wertsch (1991) identifies three principal themes that underlie Vygotsky's conception of human development, grounded in a historical understanding of how cultures develop and function: "1) a reliance on genetic, or developmental, analysis; 2) the claim that higher mental functioning in the individual derives from social life; and 3) the claim that human action, on both the social and individual planes, is mediated by tools and signs" (p. 19). These themes are realized in his attention to concept development, among the overarching tasks of human social life (see Chapter 6). They are also "closely intertwined in Vygotsky's work, and much of their power derives from the ways in which they presuppose each

DOI: 10.4324/9781003374848-7

other" (Wertsch, p. 19). Although they are inevitably interrelated, they may be treated separately, although in an integrated fashion. I next address each of these themes as explored by Vygotsky and those whose scholarship has relied on his conception.

Human Development Is a Primary, Encompassing Concern

> [D]evelopment is a process of forming the person or the personality, which is accomplished by a path along which at each step there is the emergence of new qualities, new human-specific formations, each prepared by all of the previous development but not contained in a finished form in any earlier step.
>
> (Vygotsky, 2019, p. 19)

Vygotsky's "genetic" or developmental focus is essential to those claiming him as a source. The term "genetic" can initially be confusing to those who learned the term as indexing "genes," suggesting biology and DNA as his focus. Although Vygotsky was highly attentive to biology—indeed, his dialectical psychology involves the tension between nature and nurture (Vygotsky, 1997b), as I'll review in this chapter—he saw socialization as the most critical factor in the shaping of biological cognitive capabilities into "higher mental functions" that embody a cultural outlook: "All higher mental functions are the essence of internalized relations of a social order, a basis for the social structure of the individual" (Vygotsky, 1997c, p. 106).

Among my assertions in clarifying a Vygotskian perspective is that *if it's not about long-term human development, then it's not Vygotskian*. Short-term instruction and its consequences were incidental to his attention. As Vygotsky phrased it to open *Pedology of the School Age*,

> The principal fact that we face when we study the child is development. The child is a being that grows and develops. He is in a constant process of change. Therefore the process of development is the first thing to understand when you begin to study the child.... . [C]hild development often resembles not just the quantitative enlargement of what was given from the very beginning, but the qualitative transformation of one form into another. In this sense, child development often resembles the transformation of the caterpillar into the pupa and the pupa into the butterfly.
>
> (in Van der Veer, 2020, p. 1, 4)

Vygotsky undertook a comprehensive and important project of formulating a developmental psychology that situates the human mind amid a host of competing influences, each with historical antecedents that require attention to culture. Simply helping learners today so they perform independently on a task tomorrow ignores culture and history, which are at the heart of his understanding of human development. And reducing him to "learning is social" rather than "development is social" misconstrues what he means by "social," limiting it to the immediate present and ignoring the long-term processes he emphasized. The "social" in Vygotsky's sense constitutes history in the present (M. Cole, personal communication, 5-20-21). This deep sense of the social, rather than the immediate sense of talking to someone in the present, characterizes Vygotsky's perspective, and integrates well the Bakhtinian notion that discourse is a historical phenomenon, and not simply immediate talk (Wertsch, 1991).

The Historical and Cultural Nature of Being Social

Vygotsky understood social and cultural in specific ways. Human development refers to "the unfolding of something new" (1997b, p. 198). This unfolding has both biological dimensions—bodies grow over time and experience such changes as the onset of sexual drives—and, of great interest to Vygotsky, social foundations. Vygotsky related how

> The word "social," as applied to our subject, has a broad meaning. First of all, in the broadest sense, it means that everything cultural is social. Culture is both a product of social life and of the social activity of man and for this reason, the very formulation of the problem of cultural development already leads us directly to the social plane of development.
> (1997c, p. 106)

Vygotsky's sense of the social is deeper and more complex than most claims that reference him suggest. It is deeper in history, and deeper into the present environment, which is a product of historical social developments. A cultural person need not be in the company of others to be social. Because a cultural person is saturated with the means and ends of a historical process, "a Tibetan monk contemplating issues of jealousy in the isolation of his cave is involved in as much a socially constructed endeavour as a psychologist leading a discussion on the same topic at a conference" (Van der Veer & Valsiner, 1991, p. 395). I made a similar point about readers:

> readers reading alone in the solitary confines of their dens similarly engage in text construction.... . [T]hey produce mental representations that, while not tangible, linger yet. Though alone, they engage in culturally mediated processes, in dialogue with the great history of texts, contexts, intertexts, and intercontexts. Though alone, they act in relationship with other readers and readings, participating in communities of practice where social positioning and powerful readings have consequences for others.
> (Smagorinsky, 2001, p. 163)

A child sitting quietly at a desk doing a worksheet is a cultural person involved in a socially constructed endeavor. The classroom is structured according to a longstanding tradition that positions the teacher and texts in authoritative roles, and places students in subordinate roles working on problems in isolation from other students. The child might appear to be solitary and non-social, but is marinated in culture through artifacts, traditions, scripts, and practices. In the Bakhtinian sense, it is dialogic, even though the students appear isolated and solitary, because they are immersed in a historical type of setting with traditions, rituals, and other cultural factors that shape the present moment. The present is always in dialogue with the past, building on its precedents and perpetuating them into the future.

This historical dimension suggests the need to pay attention to both phylogeny—the development of a whole species, such as humans, or cultures within a species—and ontogeny, the development of a single organism within a species (see Chapter 6). Both of these phenomena point to Vygotsky's focus on long-term development as the means by which people become cultural members of societies. To Vygotsky (in Vygotsky & Luria, 1993),

> The behavior of modern, cultural man is not only the product of biological evolution or the result of childhood development, but also the product of historical

development. In the process of mankind's historical development, change and development occurred not only in the external relations between people and in man's relationship with nature; man himself, his very nature, changed and developed.

(p. 81)

Understanding what Vygotsky was talking about—socially mediated, long-term human development emerging from historical antecedents—is critical to applying him to current educational problems. To simply say "learning is social" with a Vygotsky citation misses the whole point of cultural-historical psychology and pedology.

Challenges in Being a Vygotskian Educator

Understanding how schools shape thinking, more than how the brain operates independent of culture, was central to Vygotsky's views of nature and nurture, biological and social. It would be worthwhile to inquire into a school's orientation to human development, which as I'll review in Part IV was a central concern of pedology. Is a school structure based on stages representing short age ranges, suggesting that everyone ought to be proceeding at the same pace, and that everyone has the same access to the ideology of the curriculum and thus an equal chance of succeeding academically? Is it cultural along the lines described by Vygotsky, suggesting that different sorts of students will make up classrooms in ways that do not all align with the school's established norms? And if this understanding should be in effect, do educators address diversity by forcing uniformity in accordance with mass education's historical emphasis on assimilation? Or should they try to create a school that is diverse in students' cultural knowledge and socialization, and as a result diverse in teaching and learning genres, and thus no doubt more difficult for an administrator to manage or a testing agency to assess? These questions speak to the need for a cultural-historical developmental emphasis that seeks to understand the settings in which people grow into their cultures' ideologies and processes: the "higher mental functions" that are appropriated from society and enable fruitful participation in its activities.

Vygotsky's developmental focus thus went beyond how the human body reaches capabilities through the biological process of aging. Social history and cultural surroundings mediate how people develop worldviews, ideologies, habits and practices, assumptions, problem-finding and problem-solving methods, and other frames of mind adapted from the people around them. I next explore more specifically what Wertsch (1985) calls *the social formation of mind* in Vygotsky's cultural-historical theory.

Higher Mental Functioning Derives from Social Life

The piety "learning is social" has justified just about any classroom practice that involves multiple speakers. Such a conception greatly shortchanges the ways in which historically grounded societies shape how people learn to think culturally. In this section I review a set of points that contribute to Vygotsky's understanding of how people develop higher mental functions in social settings: those ways of thinking that embody a cultural worldview and related set of practices.

Imitation in Socialization

Vygotsky's notion of cultural assimilation requires a degree of imitation of what is modeled by more experienced members of society. Imitation is often viewed as robotic, characterized as "mindless" and zombie-like in much educational writing. Vygotsky argued, however, that imitation is an active form of learning in which constructivism is at work. Operating in this tradition, Scribner (1985) studied assembly line workers, themselves often characterized as mindless automatons, and found that their daily work appeared repetitious, but in fact required continual decision-making and adjustment. Together, Vygotsky and Scribner make a strong case that people are rarely reduced to mindless action, even when assigned busywork or heavily scripted or routine tasks requiring little apparent constructive thinking. Their work suggests that if students are assigned busywork, their minds are actively involved in thinking about something, perhaps their resistance to boring instruction, perhaps their imagination of a better alternative, perhaps their insight into a problem such that a single correct answer is insufficient.

Vygotsky (1998) took the view that these social relationships involve the imitation of the practices that surround a person during development. His view of imitation was more complex than the typical association of it with simple-minded mimicry and mechanistic reproduction of behaviors. Rather, imitation enables one to take on the persona that social relations are promoting:

> aided by imitation, the child can always do more in the intellectual sphere than he is capable of doing independently. At the same time, we see that his capability for intellectual imitation is not limitless, but changes absolutely regularly, corresponding to the course of his mental development so that at each age level, there is for the child a specific *zone of intellectual imitation* connected with the actual level of development.
> (pp. 201–202; emphasis added)

I have yet to see claims in pedagogical writing referencing Vygotsky that instruction has been motivated by the *zone of intellectual imitation*, even as many celebrate the *zone of proximal development* for what they see as a way of teaching short-term learning. His account of the zone of intellectual imitation actually sounds quite similar to the oft-quoted way in which he described the zone of proximal development in *Mind and Society*:

> Everything that the child cannot do independently, but which he can be taught or which he can do with direction or cooperation or with the help of leading questions, we will include in the sphere of imitation.... . What the child can do himself, with no help on the side, reveals his already mature capabilities and functions.... . [[T]here is] a strict genetic [developmental] pattern between what a child is able to imitate and his mental development.
> (1998, p. 202)

This fluid, constructivist notion of imitation helps explain cultural transmission, as people replicate and grow into the practices through which they have been socialized. If imitation were strict and unyielding, cultures would never change. Yet they continually evolve and develop, as asserted in Marxist dialectical formulations, indicating how imitation provides a general way to act while allowing for innovations and reconstructions of the environments that provide the contours for individual and social group development.

Nature and Nurture in Human Development

The roles of nature (biological) and nurture (socially environmental) have often been pitted against one another, as if only one can be a factor in human development. This bifurcation appeared in Soviet doctrine, in which only nurture mattered; and in more recent psychologies such as that informing the Science of Reading, in which only nature matters. To Vygotsky, they were complementary aspects of maturation, although not necessarily at peace with one another. Vygotsky (in Van der Veer, 2020) challenged the notion that either nature *or* nurture is the proper force of human development:

> There are two opposite viewpoints about quite a number of aspects of child development in science. One is called nativism, that is, the theory of hereditary or congenital origin, the other empiricism, that is, the theory of experiential origin. The first theory considers some aspect in child development as determined by heredity and reduces the process of development itself to the unfolding of some inborn qualities. The other theory, on the contrary, attempts to explain the development of the child's properties or phenomena not by the unfolding of innate qualities but from elements of the child's experience.
>
> The principle of convergence attempts to rise above the extremes of both viewpoints and to combine both claims into one. According to this principle, every process of child development, says Stern[1], is not simply the appearance of inborn properties and neither the simple perception of external influences but the result of the convergence of internal qualities and external conditions of development. Convergence stands for the crossing, intersection, or concurrence of characteristics laid down in the organism with the external conditions in which these characteristics manifest themselves.
>
> Child development can only be explained and understood from the conjunction of these two causal series. "Not about one function or property," says Stern (1927, p. 27), "we should ask whether it comes from inside or outside, but we must ask: *what* in it comes from inside and *what* from outside, because both always participate, albeit in different proportions, in its realization."
>
> (p. 6; emphasis in original)

Among Vygotsky's stated aims was to resolve the "crisis in psychology" of the day. There were too many psychologies operating from different assumptions, methods, conceptions, etc. for psychology to be useful; and the fragmentation of psychologies across paradigms continues today. Vygotsky challenged the psychological tradition of studying behavior independent of mind, of studying mind independent of society, of isolating the mind from the rest of the body, of detaching emotions from cognition, and of relying on other divisions that worked against the goal of achieving a dialectical unity of opposites. Vygotsky felt that "psychology seemed a hodge-podge of unrelated or contradictory research findings without any unifying idea whatsoever" (Van der Veer & Valsiner, 1991, p. 143). He sought in contrast to develop a meta-theory, or integrative theory, that potentially takes advantage of, and synthesizes, both nature and nurture (Overton, 2015; Yaden, Reinking, & Smagorinsky, 2021).

Vygotsky emphasized that both biological and cultural factors are at work in human development. Significantly, the two are not only both present, they are interrelated, as Vygotsky outlined:

> the biological and the social sometimes appear to be not two distinct entities but one and the same thing considered from different sides: the former turns out to be the otherness of the latter. In this sense we must not think that, say, the child's reactions,

or the facts of his development, are *divided* into biological and social ones. They do not exist next to each other or on top of each other but within each other.

(in Van der Veer, 2020, p. 31; emphasis in original)

From the standpoint of dialectical materialism, a struggle is always present, one seeking resolution in the development of personality. Vygotsky (1997b) stated their relationship when he posited that "Nature has provided man with an aesthetic need, it enables him to have aesthetic ideas, tastes, and feelings. But precisely which tastes, ideas, and feelings a given person in the society of a given historical period will have cannot be deduced from man's nature; only a materialistic conception of history can give the answer" (pp. 243–244).

People's frames of mind emerge from the history of the culture within which they grow, giving the natural disposition to take on a perspective a shape and substance. Yaroshevsky and Gurgenidze (1997) ground this understanding in Soviet thought: "The principle of practice entered Vygotsky's thinking from Lenin's theory of reflection, from Lenin's 'Philosophical Notebooks,' where it was emphasized that human practice builds the 'formulas' which are 'repeated billions of times and become stamped in human consciousness as the figures of logic' (Complete Works, Vol. 29, p. 198)" (pp. 357–358). The society one enters has developed ways of being that are presumed natural because of their countless repetitions over time. People have a natural inclination to eat; but both physical and social contexts shape what people eat, how they prepare it, and how they enjoy it. At the same time, I can't imagine a historical epoch in which I'd have found lima beans to taste good.

Nature

Vygotsky found biological maturation to be a factor in human development. A child of five is not given Vygotsky to read or calculus problems to solve, because bodily maturation has not yet provided the cognitive skills needed to grasp them. Vygotsky's explanations revealed a knowledge of anatomy: "From the biological aspect it is characterized by an intensified activity of the hypophysis and the thyroid gland, which influence the growth of the sex glands and in this way prepare for sexual maturation" (1998, p. 25); and "the childhood of permanent teeth can be considered to be the time when the child becomes civilized, the time when he assimilates modern science, beginning with writing and modern technology. Civilization is a somewhat recent acquisition of humanity in order that it might convey itself by inheritance" (1998, p. 35).

Biological phenomena *in utero* even figured into his conception such that "it is necessary to consider the laws and data of genetics, that is, the science of heredity … [Psychology needs to address] the influence of heredity and uterine development of the child on the process of his social development" (1998, p. 195). His insights might have helped inform pregnant women about the dangers of smoking, drinking, and doing drugs, with the first two common behaviors in women through at least the 1950s, and the phenomenon of fetal alcohol syndrome a continuing problem (Berridge & Loughlin, 2005). Nonetheless, biological development is insufficient in explaining human psychology, especially the age-based stages described by Piaget and believed by many to comprise human development. Vygotsky (1998) maintained that

> the child's chronological age cannot serve as a reliable criterion for establishing the actual level of development… . This is the outcome, the result, the final attainment

of development for the period passed. These symptoms indicate rather how development occurred in the past, how it was concluded in the present, and what direction it will take in the future [suggesting a trajectory].

(pp. 199–200)

To Vygotsky, age matters as a very broad category, but without the specific chronological triggers identified by Piaget. Biological factors such as the onset of puberty—itself variable in age—produce fairly predictable stages, such as the turmoil of adolescence. What gives these periods shape is social engagement. On the broad level, the Soviets believed that a communist society would provide each citizen with equitable circumstances and so shape worldviews into a collectivist mentality. They contrasted this ideal with the decadence of capitalism, which they asserted can only produce selfishness, competition, and cruelty. They envisioned a monoculture that would produce a society of equals. That is, they sought to construct a culture that shaped human development, and ultimately evolution, toward a specific sort of nation and citizen. I next review how culture shapes development in Vygotsky's psychology.

Biology and Social Norms

Biological stage development has been critiqued in the field of "special education," the field of educating children and youth whose development is considered "behind" that of their peers. Although it is difficult to generalize across the whole field of special educators, there is a tendency to follow the biologically oriented "medical model" of diagnosis in which differences from age-based norms are viewed as deficiencies. The Lovaas Applied Behavioral Analysis (Lovaas, 1987) method for autistic children, for instance, claims that it will, through behaviorist punishments and rewards, make autistic children "indistinguishable from their normal friends" (p. 8). His article, in just 7 pages, employs the terms "normal" and "abnormal" 45 times in promoting ABA, which has been critiqued as torturous and traumatic from within the autism community, where more compassionate norms prevail (Autistic Self-Advocates Against ABA, 2020).

This goal of forcing assimilative behaviors away from "abnormal" conduct enforces biological norms with the understanding that anyone who develops according to a different schedule is developmentally behind those "normal friends." The medical model of special education has been roundly criticized from within the Disability Studies in Education movement (e.g., Baglieri, 2017) as focused on difference constructed as deficiency, obsessed with norms instead of diversity, inattentive to how social environments shape human development, and in need of reform and humanity. My colleagues and I have found this tendency to be an overgeneralization, one that does not apply to the many devoted and caring special education teachers we know (Smagorinsky, Tobin, & Lee, 2019). As I'll review in Chapter 14 on "defectology"—an atrocious name for a socially oriented approach to educating learners who lack typical functioning—Vygotsky (1993) provided one of the most coherent approaches to a sensitive, humanistic, developmentally concerned special education available.

What matters here is that biology has social consequences. "Ableist" assumptions follow from the ways in which able-bodied people find deficiencies in those who exhibit differences. Skin color produces prejudicial judgments across races, and within them as well, as evidenced by the "lightness standard" applied to people of color, often *by* people of color, with lighter skin affording greater social acceptance and status. People with mental health differences are often constructed as threatening and too weird for inclusion. Blonde hair is often idealized as the epitome of pulchritude; and in the colonized world, the texture of sub-Saharan African hair is frequently subjected to often-painful, likely health-threatening straightening processes to meet the standards of white beauty (National Institutes of Health, 2022). Biological factors thus are implicated in a person's development in ways shaped by culture.

Nurture

Cultural development, Vygotsky (1998) argues, plays a "central and leading function" in a person's maturity:

> The fate of this function confirms as clearly as is possible the law of transition from social to individual forms of behavior, which might also be called the *law of sociogenesis of higher forms of behavior*: speech, being initially the means of communication, the means of association, the means of organization of group behavior, later becomes the basic means of thinking and of all higher mental functions, the basis means of personality formation. The unity of speech as a means of social behavior and as a means of individual thinking cannot be accidental. As we have said above, it indicates the basic fundamental law of the construction of higher mental functions.
>
> (p. 169; emphasis added)

The primacy of speech will be addressed in greater detail in the third part of this review, which treats Vygotsky's emphasis on the role of tools and signs—both being capabilities of words—in human development. For now, it is important to understand the consistent argument that Vygotsky made across the span of his career about "higher" functions, by which he means the ways of thinking that best serve cultural ends:

> the structures of higher mental functions represent a cast of collective social relations between people. These structures are nothing other than a transfer into the personality of an inward relation of a social order that constitutes the basis of the social structure of the human personality. The personality is by nature social.... . [N]ew behavior of many becomes behavior for himself; man himself is conscious of himself as a certain entity.
>
> (1998, pp. 169–170; p. 172)

Vygotsky's (1997c) account of how people learn from their environments is neatly expressed when he says that "The child begins to apply to himself those forms of behavior that adults usually apply to him, and this is the key to the fact of mastery of one's own behavior" (p. 88). Development, he wrote in one of his first major educational texts,

> is not a simple maturation, but cultural metamorphosis, cultural rearmament. And if we wish to analyze the memory of an adult person, we would have to examine it not from the form nature gave it, but in the form that culture created.... . [W]hen we study the memory of cultural man, strictly speaking, we do not study an isolated "mnemonic function"—we study all the strategies and techniques aimed at fixing experience in memory and developed in the course of cultural maturation.
>
> (1997a, p. 186)

80   *Factors in Human Development*

Vygotsky concluded that the first two years of life are subject largely to biological development. At that point children's speech begins to exert control over their actions; and this speech is learned from the people who surround them, rather than being an independent function. Culture then becomes increasingly paramount:

> at a certain moment, which comes at an early age (around two years), the lines of development of speech and thinking, which until that time went apart, cross, coincide in their development, and give rise to a completely new form of behavior that is most characteristic of man. In this phase thinking becomes verbal and speech becomes intellectual.
>
> (in Van der Veer, 2020, p. 113)

Cole (1996) offers a correction of this view, locating this convergence at the first human contact, when the process of socialization begins implicitly. Cole's evidence is compelling, if based on a small sample of infants in hospital nurseries, where adults would bounce babies in blue diapers and attribute manly virtues to them, and handle babies in pink diapers gently and describe them in terms of beauty and sweet temperaments (see Rubin, Provezano, & Luria, 1974).

Cole (1996) thus sees *tacit socialization* as beginning with the first human contact. Vygotsky, while acknowledging this phenomenon, was more interested in how speech develops and becomes a means of regulation according to social influence. Undoubtedly the two work in conjunction. A male infant who is tacitly directed to adopt manly interests would, at around age 2, begin to use speech to ask for manly toys and do manly things. This same child might ultimately grow up to realize a different identity, creating a vexing conflict between biology and socialization that would be subject to social judgments such as the ban on LGBTQ+ books in 2020s libraries and cancellation of extracurricular school activities that would validate their lives.

These examples illustrate some of the many biological and cultural intersections that contribute to how a person develops frames of mind, and how they are often in conflict requiring dialectical synthesis. They also illustrate how the world occupied by Vygotsky did not anticipate how values would shift to include such things as sexuality beyond the binary he and his contemporaries assumed; that is, how the Overton Window would shift beyond the bounds of what was available to think in his day. This shift is only beginning and faces violent resistance in most parts of the world.

Higher Mental Functions

Vygotsky (1997c) described his research program as involving "*the concept of higher mental functions, the concept of cultural development of behavior, and the concept of mastery of behavior by internal processes*" (p. 7; emphasis in original). Higher mental functions do not develop on their own. They are appropriated through engagement with others in the social world, and in turn serve to regulate thinking.

To Vygotsky, human development is dynamic and takes place within conflicting environments. Child development is dramatic given the continual struggle through contradictions faced in engagement with other people and their social structures. This assumption fits the "unity of opposites" in dialectical materialism, with the drama both between and among people, and within their psyches as they wrestle with conflicting conceptions. My example of the male-genitalia infant growing into a different sexual identity illustrates how a dramatic conflict can be both external (in relation to societal values and assumptions) and internal as the individual wrestles with contradictory messages from the social world. These tensions contribute to the development of higher mental functions, the cultural ways adapted from one's social surroundings, including those forged in opposition.

Higher mental functions, Vygotsky (1998) argued, "are the basic nucleus of the personality being formed." Their development follows, he continued, "the law of *the transition from direct, innate, natural forms and methods of behavior to mediated, artificial mental functions that develop in the process of cultural development*.... [H]igher mental functions arise from collective social forms of behavior" (pp. 167–168; emphasis in original). Wertsch (1991) has stated the matter as follows: The human "'mind goes beyond the skin': the agent of mediated action is seen as the individual or individuals *acting in conjunction with mediational means*" (p. 33, emphasis in original). Those mediational means might be external to the body, such as when I rely on the texts I consult, engage in conversations with others, and use my computer to type these words to produce a text that is simultaneously outside my body, an extension of my mind and its historical development, and a means to stimulate further thinking in myself and possibly others.

Human Action Is Mediated by Tools and Signs

Leont'ev argued that Vygotsky's cultural-historical approach led to an emphasis on labor, and thus tools, both staples of a Marxist philosophy (see Chapter 8). Vygotsky's project comprised

> an attempt to apply Marx's historical method in psychology. Thus, for Vygotsky the determinants of human mental development are ... human *tool-mediated labor activity*.... The study of the formation of the higher mental functions in ontogenesis and phylogenesis as structures which develop on the basis of elementary mental functions and are mediated by psychological tools became the major theme of the research of Vygotsky and his collaborators.
> (Leont'ev, 1997, p. 21; emphasis in original)

Of particular concern to Soviets was the practical labor of the proletariat. Vygotsky (1998) noted that "Hegel repeatedly tried to consider human practical activity, and specifically the use of tools, as putting logical inferences into action" (p. 119). Leont'ev (1997) traced this perspective across Vygotsky's career:

> Vygotsky's idea was clear—the elaboration of the theoretical methodological foundations of a Marxist psychology must begin with a psychological analysis of the practical, labor activity of humans on the basis of Marxist positions.... Vygotsky did not turn to the examination of mental phenomena in themselves, but to the analysis of labor activity. As is well known, the classics of Marxism saw this activity as first and foremost characterized by its tool nature, the mediation of the labor process by tools.... [H]is own hypothesis ... rested upon Marx's theory of labor activity.... [T]he problem of activity ... was central to Vygotsky.
> (pp. 16–18)

As I'll detail in Chapter 5, Vygotsky wholly accepted Engels's (1925/1978, p. 449) proposition that "labor begins with the manufacture of tools" (quoted in Vygotsky, 1997b,

p. 180). "During the transitional age [adolescence]," Vygotsky argued, "an extremely important leap is made in the development of practical, goal-directed human activity; here for the first time possibilities open up for actually mastering professional work, the concrete realization of practical thinking" (1998, p. 110).

I next review key issues in Vygotsky's emphasis on the role of signs and tools in human labor in human development. I begin with what might seem a strange topic in this context: the early psychological problem of figuring out how people and primates are different from one another, thus providing insights into human psychology. This topic provided the central focus for Vygotsky and Luria's (1993) book-length *Studies on the History of Behavior: Ape, Primitive, and Child* and recurred elsewhere in his writing. Studying primates and what they cannot do helped to foreground what humans can do in contrast. Making this distinction was central to developing a psychology of human development.

People, Primates, Tools, and Signs

The problem of distinguishing people from primates, not just to Russians and Soviets but to global psychologists, was particularly keen in the years following Charles Darwin's (1859) outline of evolution. This theory helped psychologists to situate cultural psychology's emphasis on individual human development within the histories of cultures and species. Psychologists of, and prior to, Vygotsky's era were concerned with the question: If people and primates have evolved from a common ancestor into different species, what distinguishes the two?

Biologically, people and primates are very similar. People and chimpanzees share a genetic inheritance that is almost identical (Diamond, 1991). Their genes differ by just 1.6%, while chimpanzees and gorillas differ by 2.3%, leading Diamond to call humans the "third chimpanzee," following (1) the common chimpanzee and (2) its close relative, the bonobo. To anthropologist Jane Goodall, "Chimpanzees, more than any other living creature, have helped us to understand that there is no sharp line between humans and the rest of the animal kingdom. It's a very blurry line, and it's getting more blurry all the time" (quoted in LaBerge, 2018). What, then, makes them so different? Inquiring psychologists needed to know.

Some explanations are biological. People walk upright, while primates rely on all four limbs to get around, a capacity that also enables climbing trees and other structures. Humans have 46 chromosomes, but chimpanzees have 48. Monkeys (but not apes) have tails that allow them to balance and that provide a fifth limb for climbing and grasping. Primates have thick fur coats; humans are relatively sparsely covered except on their heads and genitalia. As great as these differences are, they are dwarfed in importance by a critical biological difference: the capacity of the human larynx, and absence of "vocal lips" endemic to other primates, to produce sounds that may be used to form words (Nishimura et al., 2022). This ability has enabled people to evolve culturally, relying on words to guide their societies' and individuals' intellectualization of their worlds (Lieberman, 2007). What gives words meaning is culture, those social structures and processes that provide the contexts for human development.

Both people and primates use tools to act on their environments. In Vygotsky's day, researchers were aware of tool use in non-humans, if not in the sophisticated way it has become understood in the century since (Chittka, 2022; De Waal, 2017; Sanz, Call, & Boesch, 2013). What humans, but not animals, can do is *invent and manufacture new tools*. Animals adapt available materials (sticks, etc.) to carry out various actions (e.g., knocking fruit from a tree) without creating improved forms through their production from raw materials. Primates use tools, but lack human speech and its capacity for creating a sign in the form of words, which became of paramount importance with the development of labor and its associated tools. The availability of tools and signs to people using them volitionally and planfully suggested to Vygotsky (1997b) that "it is free intention—an absolutely essential element of genuine tool use—which distinguishes man from animal" (p. 208). A macaque might use a stone to break open a crab to eat, but can't create a new form of tool through the imaginative mental projection of a future possibility, and can't use words to articulate the process to share with other macaques to plan a greater tool development program. Vygotsky (1997a) argued that

> the whole difference between man and the animals may be summed up by saying that man is an animal that makes tools. From the moment labor, in the human sense of the term, i.e., the deliberate and intentional intervention in the workings of nature and on the part of man, for the purpose of regulating and controlling vital processes between nature and himself, became possible—from this very moment mankind ascended a novel biological stage, and something novel that was foreign to his animal ancestors and to his fellow creatures became part of his experience.
>
> (p. 32)

Humans further have the ability to speak, a capacity that enables them to use words as semiotic signs. Parrots can imitate the sound of words, but cannot use them intentionally and to regulate their behavior, communicate with other parrots for collaborative action, or think about things. Verbal representations enable the intentional capacity to plan for the future, a uniquely human capacity, Vygotsky (1997a) argued:

> The aggregate of our thoughts seems to organize our behavior ahead of time, and if I think first and only then do something, this means nothing less than a duplication and complication of behavior in which the internal reactions of thought initially prepare and adapt the organism, and then the external reactions carry out what had been established and prepared in thought ahead of time. Thought always plays the part of an advanced guide of our behavior.
>
> (p. 166)

Vygotsky (1997a) attributed this notion to Marx, whom he quotes as saying, "Were a person to construct a [beehive] cell out of wax, [in contrast with bees] he would first construct it in his mind. At the end of a process of labor, a result is obtained that, even before the start of this the process, existed ideally, i.e., in the imagination of the worker." Vygotsky continued,

> The structure of the spider's web, or the cells of a beehive, still pertain wholly to forms of instinctive behavior, i.e., the passive adaptation of the organism to the environment, which in no way differs from exactly the same mechanism of digestion in the human stomach or intestine. Man's behavior, in fact, encompasses an essentially new component, *the preliminary presence in the mind of the results of work*, a guiding stimulus of all reactions. Our concern here, quite obviously, has to do with nothing less than the kind of duplication of our experience. Thus, duality is at the very foundation of this volitional act, and this duality becomes especially prominent and vivid whenever several motives, several opposing strivings, clash in our consciousness.
>
> (p. 167; emphasis added)

This quote, from Vygotsky's early pedagogical writing, retains a Pavlovian influence in its reference to stimulus-response reactions, albeit one that includes a volitional dimension required for anticipating and planning for future circumstances and consequent actions. Vygotsky's identification of signs as a principal means of distinguishing people from apes was well crystalized in his belief that "As Marx said, [people] first build their creation in their imagination. The result of the labor process existed in an ideal form before the beginning of this work. This perfectly indisputable explanation by Marx refers to none other than the *doubling of experience* that is unavoidable in human labor" (1997b, p. 68; emphasis in original). People's first level of experience is the imaginative projection of a plan of action; the second is the subsequent act itself, which may include variations from the plan. Further duplication might occur if the person both acts and reconceives future action at more or less the same time. The doubling of experience is a uniquely human capability, enabled by speech although in many cases enabled as well by the ability to project images, as in a blueprint for constructing a home.

Tool-mediated labor (beyond using found materials to dislodge food from trees) is central to understanding human beings and human societies. Vygotsky's interest in human speech enabled him to take a fundamental Marxist principle, the identification of tools of labor as critical mediational means, and apply it to human speech as a *psychological tool*. Relatedly, he identified verbal signs—the completed utterance that embodies meaning and enables communication between and among people—as not only critical to human development, but as among the most significant capabilities distinguishing people from primates. He argued that

> The most essential feature distinguishing the psychological tool from the technical one is that it is meant to act upon mind and behavior, whereas the technical tool ... is meant to cause changes in the [external] object itself. The psychological tool changes nothing in the object. It is a means of influencing one's own mind or the behavior or another's. It is not a means of influencing the object. Therefore, in the instrumental act [of verbal thinking] we see activity toward oneself, and not toward the object.... . [B]y acting on external nature and changing it, he at the same time also changes his own nature and acts upon it. He subordinates the workings of his own natural forces. The subordination to oneself of this "force of nature," i.e., of one's own behavior, is a necessary condition of labor. In the instrumental act man masters himself from the outside—via psychological tools.
>
> (Vygotsky, 1930, n.p.)

Tools and signs thus are of different sorts, and have several characteristics. Tools and signs by themselves have no agency. Rather, they are infused with cultural meaning in labor activity undertaken volitionally and intentionally, with a future orientation grounded in cultural history.

Signs serve as external means by which to communicate and manage life, and ultimately as the internal means of regulation (Leont'ev, 1997). Signs are inscribed with meaning that enables abstractions through which people see beyond the immediate situation and project possibilities imaginatively. A dolphin might use a sponge to protect its sensitive snout when skimming food from an abrasive sea floor, but could not speak or write about it to help subsequent dolphins adapt to their environments, or invent and manufacture a better sponge for the same purpose. Vygotsky, in Vygotsky and Luria (1993), concluded that "Describing the splendid examples of the use of tools by human-like apes, [Köhler[2]] showed, in subsequent studies, how futile were all attempts to develop in animals even the most elementary sign and symbol operations" (p. 13). Vygotsky (1999) concluded that

> As soon as speech and the use of symbolic signs are included in the manipulation, it is transformed completely, superseding the former natural laws and engendering for the first time properly human forms of using tools. From the moment the child begins, with the help of speech to master situations, having preliminarily mastered his own behavior, a radically new organization of behavior arises, as well as new relations to the environment. Here we are present at the birth of specifically human forms of behavior that, having broken away from animal forms of behavior, subsequently create intellect and then become the basis for work—specifically the human form of using tools.
> (pp. 14–15)

Signs enable the abstractions that humans can generate and comprehend, but primates cannot. Signs are a form of abstraction in that they stand for something else; the word "goat" is not a sentient creature, but a collection of squiggles or a sound that people learn to represent the familiar barnyard animal. Luria, in Vygotsky and Luria (1993), wrote that

> in the mind of the cultural person, abstraction is a necessary, integral part of any type of thought process, a technique fostered in the process of the development of personality, and a necessary condition and tool for one's thinking.... The process of abstraction develops only with the growth and cultural development of a child; his development is closely tied to the initiation of the use of external tools and to the working out of complex techniques of behavior. Abstraction itself can in this case be examined as one of the cultural techniques implanted in children during the process of his development.
> (pp. 193–194)

This abstraction comes in the form of a semiotic sign. It might be musical, or a religious icon, or to the ancients, constellations representing earthly or mythic figures. To Vygotsky, human speech had the most complex and important role in sign usage, not only enabling symbolic use but allowing complex thought and articulation beyond what most signs afford. I next address issues involved in the use of speech as a mediational means.

Speech

Vygotsky himself was almost exclusively oriented to three principal means of semiotic mediation: "words, words, words" (Van der Veer, 1997b, p. 7). Speech is learned from surrounding speech communities, and over time becomes available for private, self-regulatory thinking in the form Vygotsky called *inner speech*. Inner speech does not resemble the spoken speech learned from social contexts; rather, it is more chaotic, less expressed in complete sentences. Vygotsky described inner speech as something that would make no sense to another person if it were somehow transcribed. It achieves a more coherent public form through articulation into spoken or written speech.

Words are among the semiotic signs that embody meanings to people, grounded in the cultures in which they have matured. Vygotsky was oriented to the ways in which a person's meaningful associations with a word indicate the unity of a concept (see Chapter 6). He especially was interested in the movement of concepts, their increasing development over time as people become enculturated to ways of investing meaning in cultural artifacts. Among these artifacts are words, themselves invested with meaning by the people who use them. Vygotsky placed a premium on investigating "the way words acquire significative meaning, the way they transform into symbols" (Van der Veer & Valsiner, 1991, p. 259). This continual attention to movement, activity, and development is central to a Vygotskian perspective, and derived from Marxist thought.

Speech operates at two levels: as a sign when it stands as a spoken or written text, or as a tool when it serves as a medium of generating new ideas, an emergent process in which thinking takes shape through the process of articulation (Vygotsky, 1987). A completed word can also serve as a tool, such as when I read the writing of Vygotsky and his interpreters and use their understandings to advance or challenge my own, thus acting in the world with text-derived ideas. This double, often related capacity has produced the notion of the *artefact* for Cole (1996), a term he applies to any residue of culture that both represents prior human social organization and enables members of cultures to participate in its activities. Yet I see each having a distinctive role, suggesting the value of their separation.

Vygotsky was consistent throughout his career in positioning speech as the key to human development. Luria wrote the following in Vygotsky and Luria (1993): "The convergence of thinking and speech constitutes the most important moment in the development of an individual, and precisely this connection places human thought at an unprecedented height" (p. 201). As children learn to speak according to their social surroundings, they learn to think in the terms represented by those words: "Speech takes a commanding height; it becomes the most used cultural tool; it enriches and stimulates thinking, and, through it, the child mind is restructured, reconstructed" (Luria, in Vygotsky & Luria, 1993, p. 205). This capacity produces the result that "The highest cultural forms of intellectual activity are achieved by human preliminary verbal planning" (p. 206). I next review specific areas that Vygotsky emphasized in his investigations into the role of speech in human development.

The Tool of Tools (and Sign of Signs)

Vygotsky is associated with *semiotics*, a term first appearing in the 17th-century in the writing of the English philosopher John Locke. It emerged more as a field of inquiry in the late 19th and early 20th centuries under competing versions developed by the Swiss linguist Ferdinand de Saussure (1916) and the US philosopher Charles Sanders Peirce (1931–1935; 1958). Semiotics is concerned with the function of signs: human constructions that represent something. Words were the most important signs to Vygotsky, who positioned them as the keys to concept development. Yet Yaroshevsky and Gurgenidze (1997) note that

> Vygotsky includes in the category of cultural signs not only language forms, but also different bearers of a significative function—schemes, maps, algebraic formulas, works of art, etc. These signs are special psychological tools by means of which the individual organizes his behavior and learns to direct them voluntarily. Just like tools of labor, they act as an intermediate link between the activity of the persona and the external object and mediate the relationships between them. But whereas the tools of labor are directed toward the object and change it according to a consciously set goal, the signs change nothing in the object, but serve as a means by which the subject can influence himself, his own mind.
>
> (p. 350)

More recently, signs have been interpreted broadly in such fields as multiliteracies and multimodality, which view any sign—a word, a graphic design, a musical composition, a numerical formulation, and so on—as having similar semiotic potential for expressing and communicating an idea. Vygotsky featured words that, as non-material except when printed, are an "ideal" form (and some find their uttered form as having evanescent materiality; see Bleich, 2013). Since then, others working in Vygotsky's tradition have elevated the importance of other sign systems. John-Steiner (1987) has described psychological tools in other modes as well; Wertsch (1991) has used the metaphor of the *cultural tool kit of mediational means*; I've drawn on their work to outline the possibilities of other sign systems in specific cultural activities, such as interpreting literature through art (Smagorinsky, 1995a, 2001, and others); and others have tied semiotics to both economies and technology (New London Group, 1996).

Wertsch (1999) concludes that "In outlining his account of mediation, Vygotsky focused primarily on language, but he recognized other semiotic phenomena as well. Among the signs and systems he mentioned are language; various systems for counting; mnemonic techniques; algebraic symbol systems; works of art; writing; schemes, diagrams, maps, and mechanical drawings; all sorts of conventional signs" (p. 30). His attention to them, however, is principally confined to passing references. Even his doctoral dissertation on *The Psychology of Art* (1971) focused on verbal art, particularly drama (with its accompanying physical expressions and representations), fables, and stories. Vygotsky's emphasis on speech might now be seen as limiting, perhaps as a form of colonization, to those who have been socialized to structure their worlds via other sign systems (see Belgarde, LoRé, & Meyer, 2010).

Words as Paramount, in Contrast with Multimodal Understandings

Words, to Vygotsky, serve as the "tool of tools," a phrase that he attributed to Dewey (quoted in 1997c, p. 61). Vygotsky (1998) asserted the dominance of speech in the process of conceptual maturation. In adolescence, youth use words to embody concepts, with reliance on other semiotic systems receding in importance:

> the process of intellectualization, like the transition to thinking in concepts, narrows more and more the circle of visual thinking in concepts and thinking in graphic representations. This leads to a demise of the method of thinking which the child uses, with which the child must part, and to the construction of a completely new kind or type of intellect in its place.... [Ach][3] asks whether the transition from graphic thinking to thinking in concepts is the basis of the fact that eidetic[4] tendency ... is found significantly less frequently at this stage than in the child.
>
> (p. 39)

Vygotsky (1998) long preceded the 21st-century concern with multimodal sign systems, emphasizing speech as the key to maturation into a culture's ways. The child is more likely than an adult to think in images (eidetic thinking) that linger as memories upon which to build understandings. These operations will "usually disappear with the end of childhood, but do not disappear without a trace, but are converted, on the one hand, into a visual basis of ideas and other the other, enter into perception as component elements" (p. 154). Images of this sort thus serve a developmental role, but do not enable conceptual thinking. "With the transition to thinking in concepts," he maintains, "eidetic images disappear, and we must assume a priori that they disappear before the period of sexual maturation since the latter marks the transition from the visual concrete method of thinking to abstract thinking in concepts" (p. 155). Vygotsky made a link between how individuals mature in their lifespan, and how the human species has evolved over time (see Chapter 6):

> Jaensch maintains that not only in the ontogenesis, but also in the phylogenesis of memory were eidetic images dominant at the primitive stage of human culture. Gradually, together with cultural development of thinking, these phenomena disappeared, yielding their place to abstract thinking, and were preserved only in primitive forms of thinking of the child. In later development ... the significance of the word became more and more universal and abstract. Probably, hand in hand with the interest in concrete images, eidetic tendency moved to the background, and the change in the character of language resulted in eidetic instincts being pushed back farther and farther. The pushing back of this aptitude in cultured man must be the result of the appearance of cultured language with its common meanings of words which, in opposition to the individual verbal knowledge of primitive languages, limit more and more the attention directed to sensorially perceived fact.
>
> (p. 155)

Phylogeny and ontogeny work in similar ways in Vygotsky's presentation. In his conception, early people thought in images but not in concepts, much like the Soviet children he studied, and the German children studied by Jaensch (1930). Images continue to have a role in promoting imagination and fantasy, he argued, "thus changing their basic psychological function" (1998, p. 156). Yet he disregarded "the possibility of the appearance of anything like a true concept in processes of visual thinking" (p. 160) even as "visual thinking ... has great significance in the development of the intellect" through its role in imaginative thought. This capacity is transformed under the influence of verbally articulated concepts that give images meanings. These concepts are represented in words, leading Vygotsky to conclude paradoxically that "to think without words, humanly, means basically to be supported by the word" (p. 161). This phenomenon is evident in the tendency of teachers to require of student art that it be accompanied by a verbal explanation that clarifies the intent of the text and, not insignificantly, gives the teacher something that can be graded according to conventional criteria.

Vygotsky described this shift from eidetic imaging to verbal representation as a matter of both biological maturation and cultural experience. One possibility that I see in promoting the cultural side of this understanding is that Vygotsky was simply describing social effects and attributing them to biological maturation. To refer to terms from earlier in this volume, school has a proleptic effect realized in a hidden curriculum that promotes verbal thinking at the expense of other means, and does so toward the teleological ends of a culture. This point was later made by Gardner (1983) in his exposition on "multiple intelligences" that provide a set of ways of thinking and acting in the world beyond the verbal and logical/mathematical ways that saturate school learning and are implicitly positioned as the most important ways of thinking.

It's possible that the narrowing of the semiotic field to verbal thinking and expression is a function of what is valued in school, and that Vygotsky could be describing educational effects that follow from school's focus on speech. It's not possible to say confidently what accounts for the conclusions he drew. What is possible, however, is that the schools of both Tsarist Russia and the Soviet Union emphasized what Vygotsky believed to be paramount—verbal conceptualizing—and that he in turn described those effects as biological, emerging in conjunction with sexual drives. This value, as Gardner (1983) has argued, remained in effect in US schools, with little reason to believe that much has changed, in spite of the hortatory efforts of multimodalists to expand the semiotic repertoire available in school. Gardner's *Frames of Mind*'s subsequent editions in 2004 and 2011 suggest that his critique remains viable.

Hearing, Speech, and Signs

People who can't hear typically rely on sign language, leading some in deaf education to see Vygotsky (1993) the defectologist as a multimodalist (e.g., Skyer, 2022; see Chapter 14), in keeping with recent semiotic trends. Yet hand signals are a form of speech consistent with Vygotsky's emphasis on words, rather than serving the 21st century trend toward multimodalism:

> We have become accustomed to the fact that man reads with his eyes and speaks with his mouth. Only a great cultural experiment which showed that it is possible to read with the fingers [braille] and speak with the hand [signing] discloses the whole conventionality and mobility of cultural forms of behavior. Psychologically these forms of rearing can do what is more important: specifically, they can accustom the deaf-mute and the blind child to speaking and reading.
>
> It is important that the blind child reads just as we do, but this cultural function is facilitated by a completely different psychophysiological apparatus than we use. In the same way, for the deaf-mute child, most important from the point of view of cultural development is the fact that universal human speech is facilitated for him through a completely different psychophysiological apparatus.
>
> (Vygotsky, 1997c, p. 228)

These "roundabout" means (Vygotsky, 1993), in spite of being undertaken by hands and not tongues, represented a form of speech to Vygotsky. Vygotsky was both highly sympathetic to blind and deaf people, and at times less understanding. Deafness, said Vygotsky (1997c), "is one of the most serious obstacles [in development]. Circuitous paths of speech development result in new, incomparable, and exceptional forms of behavior" (p. 25). Van der Veer and Valsiner (1991) note that to Vygotsky, "thoughts not embodied in words would merely be Stygian shadows" (p. 360). His view of those lacking normative evolutionary features might sound alarming to modern-day sensitive ears. He accepted Potebnya's[5] conclusion that "deaf-mutes without speaking teachers (or trained teachers) would remain almost animals forever" (1998, p. 74). Vygotsky's verbal orientation led him to conclude that

> the further development of speech becomes possible only thanks to the development of thinking. We have already seen that the child's active widening of his vocabulary proceeds on the basis of thinking, that meaningful use of the word in general, as a means to communicate or a means of thinking, is in essence an intellectual operation. Although thinking and speech develop from different roots, this is why their higher development becomes impossible if they are separated from each other.
>
> This is brilliantly proved, on the one hand, by deaf-mute persons, whose thinking hardly rises above the level of the primitive or natural stage despite the fact that their

intellect has all the natural material to develop. The absence of speech makes the cultural development of the intellect impossible. The opposite situation we see in idiots whose underdeveloped intellect leads to an underdevelopment of speech. The idiot does not experience the greatest discovery about which Stern speaks, and therefore his speech remains on the primitive level characteristic of animals or the child in the first one and a half years of his life.

(in Van der Veer, 2020, p. 116)

"Idiot" was an acceptable diagnostic term of Vygotsky's day, along with "moron," "imbecile," "retarded," and other terms now verboten in respectful discourse. He was simply using conventional language for the era, and not violating 21st century norms in presentist fashion. Nonetheless, his view of the limited intellectual potential of people lacking speech is best left to his time and place, and not as a viable notion in times of greater awareness of the deaf or mute experience.

Discussion

This chapter has concerned essential aspects of Vygotsky's cultural-historical psychology. His genetic (developmental) emphasis is concerned with the ways in which the tool of speech and sign of the completed word (or words), learned through cultural engagement and shaped through ideology, produce the higher mental functions that are realized in concepts. Understanding Vygotsky, to use Van Der Veer and Valsiner's (1991) titular term, requires understanding what his overarching task was. This chapter is designed to be clear about his career project and what it entailed, and to be clear about what it was not, and did not entail.

I've included attention to problematic aspects of how Vygotsky delineated his perspective on human development. Understanding Vygotsky requires attention to all of his beliefs, not just those that are convenient to arguments about the present times that one hopes to make with his citational sanction. If anything, his own points of confusion or contradiction provide useful stimuli to those either formulating new theories or extending old ones. If the goal is the construction of a comprehensive psychology of socially mediated human development, one that avoids the fractures that follow from focusing on different areas (behavior only, cognition independent of context, etc.), then the task is extraordinarily complex and difficult to manage with all its moving parts accounted for. It's also difficult to conceive of a theory in one time and historical place, and have it survive intact a century or more later in another.

At the same time, these principal themes laid out by Vygotsky remain durable and informative to later psychologies in later eras. One might quibble, in the context of the multimodality ethos of the 21st century, with his emphasis on words, but would probably do this quibbling with words. One might reject his view that cognitive development among deaf people requires extreme measures to overcome the lack of spoken words to represent the world and its meaning. But then, wrestling with these questions is a valuable way to clarify what a 21st century educator needs to take into account when seeking to think comprehensively about human development.

The following chapters explore a set of specific issues that were central to Vygotsky as he worked toward an understanding of his own, a project cut short by his early death. It is now our task to take his foundational ideas and apply them thoughtfully to present and emerging concerns about how people grow into a culture's values and in turn help to create it anew for the next generations.

Notes

1 William Lewis Stern (1871–1938) was a German psychologist (born the year that Prussia was incorporated into Germany under Prussian Minister-President Otto von Bismarck) who was considered the founder of personalistic psychology and European psycho technique, and who was a pioneer in the fields of child, differential, educational, and forensic psychology.
2 Wolfgang Köhler (1887–1967) was a German psychologist and phenomenologist who helped develop the field of Gestalt psychology. He emigrated to the United States in 1935 after protesting the requirement that professors begin class with Nazi salutes, and rebelling against the dismissal of professors by Nazi leaders. He was a leading researcher of the mental lives of apes (Köhler, 1917).
3 N. Ach was a German psychologist of Vygotsky's time who was the founder of the school of Determinations Psychology.
4 Vygotsky's understanding of eidetic thinking drew on the work of the German psychologist Erich Rudolf Jaensch (1930), which ultimately drew the wrath of critics of pedology who considered European psychologists to represent a bourgeois outlook and helped build a case against both Vygotsky and pedology in the mid-1930s (see Part IV). Jaensch, not surprisingly for a German of the 1930s, was also a "committed Nazi" (Segal, 1986, p. 122).
5 Alexander Potebnya (1835–1891) was a Russian Cossack linguist with a strong interest in literature. Vygotsky, who was influenced by Potebnya, adopted his phrase, "The thought is not expressed but completed in the word" (Van der Veer & Zavershneva, 2018). One of Potenbnya's major works was titled *Language and Thought* (1862).

6 Phylogeny, Ontogeny, and Concept Development

Scientists have long noticed the somewhat odd relationship that exists between the ontogenesis and phylogenesis of organisms, i.e., between the development of the species and the development of the individual. In the human embryo, for example, gills, tail, scalp may be observed at a certain stage, a stage that is, moreover, analogous to those long gone stages of evolution when man's ancestors dwelled in the water and possessed tails. There is a multitude of facts that point to a correspondence between the history of the development of the organism from an embryonic cell and the development of the species as a whole. These circumstances lead Haeckel[1] to formulate the *biogenetic law* in roughly the following form: the history of the individual constitutes an abbreviated and compressed history of the species. Thus, the evolution of the organism repeats the evolution of the species [i.e., ontogeny recapitulates phylogeny], and in the course of their own development, the embryo and young of any species pass through all those stages through which the development of the species passed. Thus the embryo accomplishes a kind of truncated and accelerated path passage through the entire path of evolution… . The child's tendency to endow all objects with life, his love for everything imaginary, his attachment to fables, the primitive form of his drawings and language, all find their analogy in the animism of savages in primitive religious beliefs and in myths… . [T]his principle should not be taken in such definitive form, however, since we do not know enough about mankind's historical development to make judgments about analogies.
(Vygotsky, 1997a, pp. 65–67; emphasis in original)

Vygotsky's focus on human development was concerned with both the socially mediated individual (ontogeny) and the historical development of the societies they inhabit (phylogeny) that imbues an individual's life with a culture that provides the contexts for maturation (Gould, 1977). These changes take place within the four genetic [developmental] domains in Vygotsky's work (Wertsch, 1985). In addition to phylogenesis and ontogenesis, Wertsch identifies sociocultural history, which helps to shape both; and microgenesis that produces incremental changes.

As the quote that opens this chapter indicates, Vygotsky believed in his early educational writing that parallels exist, yet the jury was out on the question of whether ontogeny and phylogeny produce analogous lines of development. Over time, he both described common sequences of development and identified critical differences between the two. Among those comparable stages, Vygotsky (1997c) described the dominance of images (eidetic memory) among what he termed "primitive" (early, or non-technological) societies and young children, and the eventual dominance of speech in both.

At other times, however, he clearly distinguished between the two, dismissing the idea that ontogeny recapitulates phylogeny except in some very broad ways. Vygotsky (1997c) clarified that "we do not mean to say that ontogenesis in any form or degree repeats or produces phylogenesis or is its parallel. We have in mind something completely different which only by lazy thinking could be taken to be a return to the reasoning of [Haeckel's] biogenetic law" (p. 19), i.e., the belief that ontogeny recapitulates phylogeny. Rather, he concluded, *phylogeny provides the context for ontogeny*, which in turn develops in relation to both biological and social factors.

Vygotsky, Darwin, and Phylogeny

Knox (1993), the editor and translator of several of Vygotsky's manuscripts, situates Vygotsky's career in the stream of thought grounded in the evolutionary theory of Charles Darwin (1809–1882), a contemporary of and major influence on Karl Marx (1818–1883). Darwin found that life on earth develops in relation to contexts, with members of species making adaptations or taking advantage of attributes that help them survive environmental changes, without which they would perish. Typically for plants and animals, these adaptations are biological, depending on mutations or relying on specific affordances to survive changing environments. For people, these adaptations have had biological dimensions that produced the evolution of early primates into different species. The subsequent human species, a relatively recent life form, has relied on the biological advantage of its tongue, its large brain, and its development of languages. These affordances have enabled people to make deliberate, *collective* adaptations by making tools and constructing verbal signs to enable communication, planning, regulation, and agency for group survival that are not available to other species (see Chapter 5).

Humans employ signs and tools pervasively throughout their cultural activity, using them to understand the past and create their future, at times via deliberate efforts to force culture toward ideological ends. Van der Veer and Valsiner (1991) summarize the point by saying, "Human history is, then, on the one hand the history of man's growing dominion over nature through the invention of tools and the perfection of technology, and, on the other hand, it is the history of man's gradual control of the self through the invention of 'the cultural technique of signs'" (p. 220), especially speech.

A key contribution of Tulviste (1991) is his understanding that human thinking develops in relation to problems and challenges provided by natural and social environments. Without waterways, people would not develop boats to traverse them. Without the water surrounding them, or other societies to contend with, the island societies of Britain and Venice would not have become naval powers. How people learn to think is a consequence of what they need to do to survive within the conditions afforded to them by nature and cultures. Biology and social mediation, nature and nurture, are involved in how people engage with their settings of development. Showing Pavlov's influence, Vygotsky (1997b) linked the two explicitly, saying,

> The mechanism of the conditional reflex is a bridge thrown from the biological laws of the formation of hereditary adaptations established by Darwin to the sociological laws established by Marx. This very mechanism may explain and show how man's hereditary behavior, which forms the general biological acquisition of the whole animal species, turns into man's social behavior, which emerges on the basis of the hereditary behavior under the decisive influence of the social environment.
>
> (p. 59)

Factors in Human Development

These conditional reflexes are not simple knee-jerk reactions or mindless responses, but reactions that follow from the conditions surrounding human action, mediated by psychological tools.

Distinctly Human Development

Biologically, Vygotsky (1997b) found, humans have not changed radically over time, aside from such factors as growth potential that follows from better diets. Original humans were just as capable of thinking as any modern person:

> We have no reason to assume that the brain of primitive man differed from our brain, was an inferior brain, or had a biological structure different from ours... . [B]iologically speaking the most primitive man we know deserves the full title of man. The biological evolution of man was finished before the beginning of his historical development.
>
> (1997b, p. 97)

The development of cultures thus builds on the foundation provided by biology; and the development of individuals takes place in the context of cultures. The development of the individual and that of the species proceed in different ways, even as some parallels exist. Vygotsky (1997b) quoted Thorndike[2] (1906) to explain "the different order of the *same biological principles* in onto-and phylogenesis. Thus, consciousness appears very early in ontogenesis and very late in phylogenesis. The sexual drive, on the other hand, appears very early in phylogenesis and very late in ontogenesis" (1997b, p. 279; emphasis in original). These differences indicate how broad parallels may obscure critical differences in the "lazy thinking" of those who do not investigate the matter thoroughly.

In Knox's introduction to Vygotsky and Luria's (1993) *Studies on the History of Behavior: Ape, Primitive, and Child*, in which they distinguish people from primates, and primitive people from what technologically oriented societies consider to be culturally advanced people, she notes that

> Among the ideological frameworks that shaped 20th century thought, perhaps none had such an influential impact as that provided by Darwin's theory of evolution of the species... . [F]rom Darwin comes the idea of development from lower to higher stages, whereby "primitive people," for example, are at a lower or, in other words, earlier stage in the historical evolution of man... . [H]owever, Vygotsky and Luria were interested in development not only over a lifetime (ontogenesis) but over the course of all human development (phylogenesis). In the strict sense of the word, they offer not just a cross cultural approach where various ethnic groups of preliterate people are compared, but a cross historical approach that examines the different stages of development through which the human species passes from its original beginnings in the anthropoid apes. For Vygotsky's theory of human development, the terms cultural and historical are important, however, more emphasis is placed on historical differences.
>
> (pp. 1–2)

Knox (1993) shifts the terms from whether or not ontogeny recapitulates phylogeny, to how each plays a role in human development. Both can occur without taking identical pathways. Given that the development of a society provides the context for the development of individuals within it, it's important to understand both. This understanding, however, needn't assume that their courses of development work in parallel.

Yet both ontogeny and phylogeny produce human concepts. On the broad level, over time a society constructs concepts to guide their collective action toward a social end, to give definition to their culture. Among the Soviet goals, for instance, was to take Marxist theory and build a society around its rejection of capitalism in order to evolve a society based on equity-based, leader-driven collectivism, at least in spirit. Within that society, individuals' personal thinking was mediated by social norms that impressed its value on their development of guiding concepts for life. I next review one of Vygotsky's major focuses in his account of human development, the ways in which people learn conceptual understandings derived from their social surroundings.

Concept Development

A concept is a generalization that enables one to interpret a category of experience through a cultural lens. A concept is not simply a classification, however. Rather, it enables a worldview, one that requires a consistency and relationship among its parts. Vygotsky (1987) illustrated concepts with the example of how a child learns to identify a fish, and then calls other fish-like things, such as a whale, a fish until learning that they are in fact biologically different. This distinction has real-world implications in many areas, if not necessarily with eliminating whales from the concept of fish. One who goes out to milk a cow, and instead attempts to milk a bull, is in for quite a surprise.

Biology provides such clear distinctions. But in a term like "hero" that is open to interpretation, it's important to be consistent so that heroes share the same properties, and villains are not included in the category (see Smagorinsky, 2013a, for an elaboration on ambiguous social concepts). These assignments of meaning are ideological in character. For instance, US President Abraham Lincoln may be a hero to some, and a villain to others, or both a hero and villain for different actions (presiding over the freeing of slaves while participating in the genocide of Native American people; see Green, 2021), depending on their value systems. National figures from British Prime Minister Winston Churchill to Australian Prime Minister Scott Morrison have similarly been interpreted widely, with severe critics calling for their cancellation (a fate also met by Lincoln in 2021, when schools in San Francisco removed Lincoln's name from the curriculum). I next review how Vygotsky understood concept development, a factor in both phylogeny and ontogeny.

Spontaneous (Everyday) and Scientific (Academic) Concepts

Vygotsky identified two general sorts of concepts. Spontaneous or everyday concepts are those developed through engagement with one's environment, without the benefit of formal knowledge. For example, I might understand weather patterns from growing up in a particular geographic region. If I lived in Oklahoma, I would learn to anticipate the tornado season in the spring and summer, and that knowledge would serve me well in protecting the lives of me, my loved ones, and my property (part of my own bourgeois, colonial heritage). But if I moved from Oklahoma to Alaska, where there are few tornados but many earthquakes and volcanos, I might undertake inappropriate preparations.

Spontaneous concepts, therefore, are limited to the contexts in which they are developed. In contrast, people may learn more broadly governing principles through formal education that produce what Vygotsky called scientific or academic concepts. A scientific concept will help me understand the conditions under which tornados develop as general weather systems, and provide me with knowledge as a tool for anticipating tornadoes in various regions. Typically, this sort of concept is learned through formal instruction in school, or other such setting.

Vygotsky (1987) stressed the need for integration of these two conceptual planes in order to ensure powerful learning and developmental experiences. Formal instruction in principles will not result in the development of a durable concept, and might (as often happens in school) simply produce a psittaceous repetition of words (e.g., "Britain's government is a parliamentary democracy and constitutional monarchy"). In order for a concept to have value, the learner needs an experiential basis from everyday life to invest a formal concept with meaning. The development of a concept relies on *interplay between the learner's conceptual fields*, with a relation developing between scientific and spontaneous concepts to enable "Scientific concepts [to] restructure and raise spontaneous concepts to a higher level" (Vygotsky, 1987, p. 220). The formal principles of the scientific concept create *cultural schemata* (Cole, 1996) that enable a greater understanding of worldly experience and ability to act in relation to the world in confident, systematic, reliable ways.

To Vygotsky, "Practice (praxis) is the strictest test for any theory" (Van der Veer & Valsiner, 1991, p. 150). It provides the basis for a dialectic to produce the tension that leads to a synthesis that enables concepts to be transformed in the process of attempting to refine them. Schooling serves as a major site for the learning of formal concepts that embody a culture, although often without students' everyday knowledge recruited to bring them to life. Vygotsky thus foregrounded both abstract theoretical knowledge as the means of elevating experience to higher levels, and experience as the ultimate arbiter of theory.

The Twisting Path of Concept Development

Concept development does not follow a simple, straightforward pathway, but instead involves fits and starts, what Vygotsky (1987) called a *twisting path* (see also Smagorinsky, Cook, & Johnson, 2003). My own decades-long effort to take a Vygotskian perspective has followed such a route. Vygotsky characterized these intermediate stages of concept development the *complex* and the *pseudoconcept*, those that appear to provide a unitary generalization but include inconsistencies. There is no clear demarcation between where a complex ends and a pseudoconcept begins, and there might be regressions along the way.

I view these stages as having utility in outlining how the refinement of a concept occurs over time and includes errors of inclusion or exclusion during the process that are, ideally, gradually reduced or eliminated over time. I might hear the word "police officer" as a young child and apply it to anyone I see wearing a uniform. As time goes by, I might learn to distinguish between a police officer and a member of the military, a guard at the mall, a British Foot Guard, and others in uniform. Ultimately, I might assign social meaning to police officers based on my experiences with them, interpreting them as the guardians of public safety, an insular racist organization, or other meaningful designation, depending on their actions. The pathway to this understanding could be quite uneven, depending on the actions of police officers, the discourse surrounding their conduct, the images available in the media, and other factors.

The theory-practice binary, then, provides a misguided way of thinking about human activity (Smagorinsky et al., 2003). Rather, argued Vygotsky (1997b), practice "pervades the deepest foundations of the scientific operation and reforms it from beginning to end. Practice sets the tasks and serves as the supreme judge of theory, as its truth criterion. It dictates how to construct the concepts and how to formulate the laws" (pp. 305–306). One who only thinks abstractly, without grounding in practical activity, is not likely to generate ideas that can be put into earthly action. Bookish knowledge, then, while important, is inadequate; and notions generated through practical work without abstraction have only local applications. Schooling, along with other formal sites of learning, enables the adaptation of practice-based knowledge to new situations through generalized knowledge that transcends the immediate context of learning.

Lower and Higher Mental Functions

Vygotsky's attention to multiple levels of development led him to view biological development as a "lower mental function." Biological development provides the functions through which concepts become available. A biological inheritance, while useful in catching food and climbing trees, is less useful in organizing a society and planning its future. The adaptations leading to survival enable species and individuals to perpetuate their kind across generations. For animals, these adaptations are not consciously undertaken. A finch does not decide to change its beak to break open seeds after an environmental change (e.g., a drought) alters available food sources. Rather, those with favorable biological features survive and reproduce, thus altering the species' developmental trajectory. Those unable to adapt die out, or fly off in search of a more suitable environment, which might in turn require adaptations across generations in order for survival.

Uniquely, in contrast, humans have the capacity to expand their minds via concepts, which enable adaptations via higher mental functions that don't require a fortuitous biological makeup. To Vygotsky (1997b),

> the biological purpose of mind becomes understandable. By introducing tremendous complexity into man's behavior, by giving it endlessly varied forms and by providing it with enormous flexibility, mind turns out to be the most valuable biological adaptation. Mind is unequalled in the whole organic world and it is to mind that man owes his dominion over nature, i.e., the higher forms of his adaptation.
>
> (p. 57)

"Mind" is a complex phenomenon. It includes biological elements emerging from a physiological inheritance that matures over time to enable such possibilities as conceptual thinking. These "lower functions" are mediated by society, producing higher mental functions that are central to becoming a cultural person.

Words in Developing Higher Mental Functions

As I've reviewed in prior chapters, Vygotsky identified a singular sign (which may act as a tool), *words*, as the most significant advantage of being human, and the means to developing higher mental functions. Word meaning, to Vygotsky (1987), was the unit of analysis for understanding human concept development. It embodies all of the themes identified by Wertsch (1991) concerning Vygotsky's emphasis on a developmental approach, the role of social mediation in shaping human development, and the role of tools and signs in becoming a cultural person (see Chapter 5). Van der Veer and Valsiner (1991) describe how the meaning ascribed to words is a function of cultural indoctrination:

> after a course in communist thinking an everyday (lower) concept such as "farmer" would still refer to the same set of objects but would have changed its meaning (intension). The [Sovietized] child would now understand that a private farmer is not a man growing corn, etc., but a proletarian misled by the false kulak[3] ideology. The feedback effect ... of higher mental operations does not undo the results of earlier operations but retains them in a peculiar way.
>
> (p. 277)

Van der Veer and Valsiner (1991) describe what I have proposed as a post-capitalist frame of mind: One that moves beyond an ideology without being able to discard it altogether. Vygotsky (1997a) referred to the social origins of word meanings as "collective social experience" in which "Each person makes use not only of those conditional reactions that have formed in his or her individual experience, as happens also with animals, but also by means of conditional relations that have formed in the social experience of other peoples" (p. 32). This early view of Vygotsky's was indebted to Pavlov, while also suggesting how reactions are socially mediated, perhaps indicating a post-Pavlovian frame of mind. In making this break, Vygotsky paved the way for cultural-historical understandings of human psychology by grounding any human response in the history of a society's ways of responding.

Vygotsky laid out how signs are not universal, but products of how cultures position natural and human elements around ideologies. Veresov (2017) makes the key point that "the sign itself does not mediate; it is the [individual, culturally situated person] who mediates, when creating new signs or using existing ones" (p. 25). That is, a sign is only a sign to people who interpret its meaning according to cultural understandings. Like any other text, it has no autonomous meaning (Nystrand, 1986). And like any other text, its meaning is not fixed, but is interpreted by people from ideological positions, and changes in relation to increasingly sophisticated understandings of social worlds.

Further, speech involves more than individual word meanings. Wertsch (1991) synthesizes Vygotsky and Bakhtin (1986) to detail the role of social languages (e.g., the language conventions used in cultural niches, such as lawyers, police, tennis players, etc.) and speech genres (the typified ways in which discourse is used situationally, such as lectures in school or documents prepared for legal disputes). Speech genres themselves serve as mediational means, such that the conventions that govern how people talk in "restorative justice" interventions to resolve behavioral transgressions rely on listening and respect, in contrast with punitive interventions that are inflexible and top-down (Winn, 2018). The genres thus govern, if not determine, appropriate ways of thinking, acting, and speaking in certain settings.

Wertsch (1991) clarifies, saying that "Although it may appear straightforward to characterize speech genres as being tied to types of situations and social languages as being tied to types of speakers, these two ways of categorizing utterances are in reality often connected in complex ways" (p. 77). The social language of lawyers might involve the speech genre of the opening statement. What matters is how participation in speech genres indicates an affiliation with their governing ideologies, and performance of membership in cultural groups. Ultimately, these uses of speech embody meanings that provide the lens through which a speaker or group of speakers interprets the world. They also signal one's membership and acceptance in the social groups with whom these conventions are shared.

Concepts as Cultural Schemata

Through the development of concepts, people develop schematic knowledge that guides their participation in societal activities. In information processing theory, where the term was coined, a schema refers to the ways in which the brain structures knowledge based on past experience or second-hand knowledge, such as that learned in school. Entering a typical classroom draws on schematic knowledge of how classrooms operate and how to act within them, with violators disciplined or expelled. Cole (1996) adapted the construct and modified it, referring to *cultural schemata* that are appropriated from social environments. These schemata correspond to growing concepts about how to act within societal parameters. When they enter fields operating under different regimes and orders, people may act inappropriately and get disciplined, as Black children often are in US schools (Hines & Wilmot, 2018).

Given that people seek social status and inclusion (see Chapter 14), their gravitation to social norms provides them with a sense of belonging, attachment, and homeostasis (cf. Damasio, 2021). Or the social norms may make them feel alienated and unwelcome, as many members of non-dominant cultures often do in school, even among Black students in primarily Black schools (Bell, 2020), or highly successful Black students in white spaces (Everett, 2018). Concepts in this sense are always cultural and historical and available first in society, and then gravitated toward or resisted by people through their experiences with others. Vygotsky (1998) maintained that

> the concept not only results in a system and serves as a basic means of recognizing external reality. It is also a basic means for understanding another, for adequate assimilation of the historically constituted social experience of humanity. Only in concepts does the adolescent systematize and comprehend the world of social consciousness for the first time. In this sense … to think in words is to join one's own thinking to thought in general. Complete socialization of thought is contained in the function of concept formation.
>
> (p. 48)

I read this reference to "humanity" as local, rather than universal. That is, people gravitate to local norms rather than ascending to a shared human outlook, and are more likely to extend empathy within kinship groups than with people from the outside (Von Vugt & Van Lange, 2006). If a universal frame of mind were available, cultures would not come into conflict, as they have done historically (see Cole's [1996] tracing of cultural psychology's genesis to Herodotus's effort to understand why Mediterranean societies clashed with and battled one another, written in 430 B.C.E.). In Vygotsky's Soviet Union, there was only one social conception to gravitate toward; developing toward other ends was a deadly path to take. More pluralistically inclined nations involve both assimilation and resistance, which can be interpreted as divisive, recalcitrant, or uncivilized to those who hold power and authority; see the white supremacist response to the Black Lives Matter movement (Taylor, 2018). Living within conflicting ideologies complicates concept development from a social perspective under the assumption that ideologies are in place in the setting and are appropriated by individuals. When multiple ideologies are in the air, developing sturdy, consistent concepts is unlikely (Smagorinsky, 2020a).

Concept Development in Adolescence

Adolescence, which Vygotsky called the *transitional age*, is a time of conceptual maturation. For the young child, social concepts are concrete and tied to the immediate environment. In contrast, Vygotsky (1998) said, "the adolescent's main successes in the development of thinking are in the form of cultural development of thinking" (p. 75). He expanded on this phenomenon, saying,

> Spranger is fully justified in calling the transition age [adolescence] the age of growing into culture. When they say that the adolescent discovers his internal world with its possibilities, establishes his relative independence from external activity, then, from the point of view of what we know about the cultural development of the child, this may be designated as mastery of the internal world. Not without reason, the external correlate of this event is the development of a life plan as a certain system of adaptation that is first realized by the adolescent. Thus, this age crowns and completes the whole process of cultural development of the child.
>
> (1997c, p. 251)

Adolescence, then, involves *more than* developing via general cognitive stages, such as those posed by Piaget (1973): (1) sensorimotor intelligence, (2) preoperational thinking, (3) concrete operational thinking, and (4) formal operational thinking. This is not to say that Piaget's stages are wrong. Rather, a biological stage theory is insufficient from a cultural-historical perspective that is interested in the ideology of cultural cognition, and is too explicitly tied to specific age ranges rather than the mediation of cultural experiences. Adolescence is a time when cultural self-regulation, mediated especially by both public and private speech, begins to shape the personality in ways that enable the developing youth to exercise control and self-discipline in relation to social expectations: "the social situation of development is nothing other than a system of relations between the child of a given age and social reality. And if the child changed in a radical way, it is inevitable that these relations must be reconstructed" (Vygotsky, 1998, p. 199). The means by which they are reconstructed are the tools and signs developed by societies to act on their environments (see Chapter 5).

Concepts provide the understandings through which people perceive and interpret the world. Vygotsky (1997b) argued that a concept serves as

> a system of judgments brought into a certain lawful connection: the whole essence is that when we operate with each separate concept, we are operating with the system as a whole.... [O]nly in adolescence does this function finally take shape.... Adolescence is the age when world view and personality take shape, when self-consciousness and coherent notions of the world develop. Thinking in concepts is at its basis. For us the whole experience of contemporary civilized mankind, the external world, the external reality and our internal reality are represented in a certain system of concepts. In concepts we find that unity of form and content which I

mentioned above. To think in concepts means to possess a certain ready-made system, a certain form of thinking which in no way predetermines the further content at which we arrive.

(1997b, pp. 100–101)

Part of the developmental process, then, involves growing into the higher mental functions, the cultural conceptions that bind together a society whose trajectory is suggested by its teleological ends. Adolescence is a particularly important stage in which conceptual growth takes place, a conclusion drawn by a variety of developmental researchers who see this period as one of both expanded worldviews (Adelson, 1972) and the capacity for stepping back to get "distance" on oneself and one's situation (Sigel & Cocking, 1977). Vygotsky (1998) argued that concept development

> results in basic changes in the content of the adolescent's thinking. First, thinking in concepts leads to discovery of the deep connections that lie at the base of reality, to recognizing patterns that control reality, to ordering the perceived world with the help of the network of logical relations cast upon it. Speech is a powerful means of analysis and classification of phenomena, a means of ordering and generalizing reality. The word, becoming the carrier of the concept, is … the real theory of the object to which it refers. The general in this case serves as the law of the particular. Recognizing concrete reality with the help of words, which are signs for concepts, man uncovers in the world he sees connections and patterns that are confined in it.
>
> (p. 48)

To Vygotsky (1998), the stage of adolescence is when a "revolution" in thinking and consciousness occurs. In this formative stage, not only the content of thinking changes, but more critically, the forms it takes and processes it goes through undergo development as well. Although growing into various aspects of a culture can be piecemeal, the aggregate changes involve maturation into the integrated sets of normative conceptual thinking that produce a reasonably unified cultural worldview. Here Vygotsky knit together both biological and social development, finding this intellectual capacity to emerge simultaneous with the onset of sexual maturation:

Before the onset of sexual maturity, the child has no potential for forming abstract concepts… . [D]ue to the effect of training when educational material is assimilated that consists for the most part of general positions that express some law or rule, through the influence of speech, attention is diverted more and more in the direction of abstract relations and thus leads to the formation of abstract concepts.

(p. 39)

Teachers of middle and high school, then, engage with students at a time when their ideological formation is underway, and social concepts become ripe areas for inquiry and development. As I write today, US schools are clamping down on what sorts of ideologies are available, shutting down discussions of race, sexuality, and related topics that are considered "divisive" because they depart from the dominant white heterosexual culture's worldview and threaten their status at the top of the social food chain (Stitzlein, 2022). In a pluralistic society, arriving at consistent understandings of the world can be fraught with conflict and peril. And pluralism can be viewed as a threat to social stability by those in dominant positions.

Worldviews begin to come into focus through the maturation realized in adolescence. Adolescence, to Vygotsky (1998), is a critical period of life from an ideological perspective, one centered on social concepts learned through engagement with others. He wrote that

> Convictions, interests, world view, ethical norms and rules of behavior, inclinations, ideals, certain patterns of thought—all of this is initially external, and becomes internal specifically because as the adolescent develops, in conjunction with his maturation and the change in his environment, he is confronted by the task of mastering new content, and strong stimuli are created that nudge him along the path of developing the formal mechanisms of his thinking as well.... Together with the transition to thinking in concepts, the adolescent is confronted by a world of objective, societal consciousness, a world of societal ideology.... [E]ven the child assimilates scientific facts, and the child is imbued with a certain ideology, and the child grows into separate spheres of cultural life. But an inadequate, incomplete mastery of all of this is characteristic for the child, and for this reason, the child, perceiving the established cultural material, does not yet actively participate in its creation.... [T]he adolescent ... begins actively and creatively to participate in various spheres of cultural life that open before him.
>
> (pp. 42–43)

This "incomplete mastery" indicates that concept development is not a straightforward or rapid process, but one that goes through stages in which concepts become increasingly refined. Further, the effects of socialization are tacit in childhood and come under greater awareness and self-control, first with the emergence of speech during the toddler period, and ultimately in adolescence. Refinement is available through engagement with other people, originating outside the individual. It provides the means through which people become cultural as they appropriate worldviews available through concepts. This thinking becomes more conscious and deliberate, enabling the youth to act volitionally and become part of the construction of culture, rather than as minted products of socialization. Vygotsky (1998) described this process as involving the "Progressing socialization of internal speech and progressing socialization of thinking[, which] are the basic factors in the development of logical thinking during the transitional age, the basic and central fact of all changes that occur in the adolescent's intellect" (p. 72).

Ideology and Concept Development

Words have multiple roles. Conceptually, they embody meanings. These meanings typically originate in society and are appropriated by individuals in a process of concept development. Van der Veer and Valsiner's (1991) example of how a "private farmer" (i.e., a capitalist, land-owning, bourgeoisie tiller of the earth) might be understood as an odious "kulak" according to Soviet doctrine illustrates how a culture's ideology impresses specific meanings on objects that are open to different interpretations. These meanings are not static, but change over time in relation to the maturation of thought, itself developing in relation to shifting social environments.

As changing conceptions across generations have shown, the stability of dogma is subject to change as attitudes shift in relation to growing knowledge and sensibilities. Slavery was common in ancient societies and throughout much of human history. It was outlawed in the United States through military superiority, not moral superiority. Even those taking the moral high ground were inconsistent; most abolitionists were not also integrationists, believing that slavery was uncivilized but not pining to have Black neighbors (Potter, 1977). Globally, the United Nations General Assembly adopted a Universal Declaration of Human Rights in 1948 stating that "No one shall be held in slavery or servitude; slavery and the slave trade shall be prohibited in all their forms." These shifting sensibilities and environments have provided the contexts within which people adopt their ideologies and relational thinking and action in the world. The Overton Window provides an understanding of how changes in society produce changes in perception, if not universally so, as indicated by the ferocious backlash in the 2020s against assertions of LGBTQ+ rights and dignity (Golec de Zavala, Lantos, & Keenan, 2021).

Van der Veer (1997b) observes that for Vygotsky, "word meanings or concepts embodied the contribution of culture or society and as such formed co-constituents of human development in that specific culture or society" (p. 6). This role helps account for the diversity of cultures, if not the sort of hierarchical positioning of societies that often follows from such distinctions (see Chapter 4). Van der Veer (1997b) maintains that "Vygotsky arrived at a sort of 'linguistic psychology'":

> Mental development was now largely seen as the result of the development of word meanings acquired in instruction. Likewise, the theme of the systematic structure of mind became actually a way to describe how word meanings gradually come to dominate all human mental processes. Finally, in the realm of epistemology, he still held that scientific terms or words as proto-theories co-determine our view of reality.
>
> (p. 7)

Words thus achieve more than indexing a sound to an object. Rather, words embody ideologies and cultural values. Van der Veer, in emphasizing the role of schooling in the attribution of meaning to words, refers to the ways in which different types of settings promote different kinds of thinking. The primary signs for developing concepts are words. The word, argued Vygotsky (1997b),

> fully reflects the processes and tendencies in the development of a science. A certain fundamental unity of knowledge in science comes to light which goes from the highest principles to the selection of a word. What guarantees this unity of the whole scientific system? The fundamental methodological skeleton... . The word is a philosophy of the fact; it can be its mythology and scientific theory... . [T]he very statement of the questions, the use of one or the other psychological term, always implies a certain way of understanding them which corresponds to some theory, and consequently the whole factual result of the investigation stands or falls with the correctness of falsity of the psychological system.
>
> (pp. 288–289)

As reviewed earlier, words have little import unless they are linked to practical activity, the labor that is central to Marxist thinking. Leont'ev (1997) captures this referential idea as follows:

> Instead of the biblical "In the beginning was the word," Goethe writes "In the beginning was the act." For Vygotsky, in the problem of the genesis of thinking the

logical emphasis is transferred to the words "In the beginning." Thus, *in the beginning* was the act (practical activity), which became mediated by the word.

(p. 25; emphasis in original)

Vygotsky (1997b) noted how not only children, but experienced adults immersed in a field of endeavor, build concepts through words. The field of psychology itself, including its competing conceptions, reveals its understandings through its terms:

> If one would like to get an objective and clear idea of the contemporary state of psychology and the dimensions of its crisis, it would suffice to study the psychological *language*, i.e., the nomenclature and terminology, the dictionary and syntax of the psychologist. Language, scientific language in particular, is a tool of thought, an instrument of analysis, and it suffices to examine which instruments a science utilizes to understand the character of its operations.
>
> (p. 281; emphasis in original)

Given how this process develops throughout the individual lifespan and across generations in societies, the analysis of concept development in professional fields, leisure activity, and other areas of endeavor is an appropriate extension of Vygotsky's principal emphasis on childhood and adolescence as developmental periods. I've adapted his principles to teachers' development over time (Smagorinsky, 2020a), my own experiences with learning about life and nature through gardening and landscape design (Smagorinsky, 2023a), and my attention to how societies have used mass schooling to promote national identities (Smagorinsky, 2021a, 2022). Understanding the process of concept development is useful to one's own concept development, especially if conscious awareness and self-regulation are to serve as factors in acting agentically within societal bounds.

Abstraction, an outcome of formal schooling, is often a target of criticism when ideas do not match the material world (Van Oers, 2001). Yet Vygotsky (1998) saw abstraction as the means by which future action may be planned and undertaken, assuming that it is grounded in material reality:

> those who consider abstract thinking as a removal from reality are wrong. On the contrary, abstract thinking primarily reflects the deepest and truest, the most complete and thorough disclosure of the reality opening up before the adolescent... the awareness of one's own internal activity.
>
> (p. 47)

Here he described a phenomenon similar to the notion of *metacognition*, i.e., thinking about thinking or learning how to learn, which is a central proposition of information processing theory and among its most valuable constructs. What is missing in that conception are the ways in which learning how to learn is a cultural phenomenon, not one solely executed by the brain, as Cole (1996) realized in his use of *cultural schemata* to indicate their social origins, rather than *schemata* located inside the head. Vygotsky continued,

> Just as the word is a means for understanding others, it is the means for understanding oneself ... for the apperception [prolonged and focused attention; see Chapter 11] of one's own perceptions. Because of this, only with the formation of concepts does an intensive development of self-perception, self-observation, intensive cognition of internal

activity, the world of one's own experiences, occur.... [O]nly together with the formation of concepts does the adolescent begin to truly understand himself and his internal world. Lacking this, thought cannot attain clarity and cannot become concept.

(1998, p. 48)

These concepts are not personal inventions, but are adapted from the surrounding culture. Vygotsky clarified that

The concept begins to be understood not as a thing, but as a process, not as an empty abstraction, but as a thorough and penetrating reflection of an object of reality in all its complexity and diversity, in connections and relations to all the rest of reality.... . The concept taken in action, in movement, in reality, does not lose unity, but reflects its true nature... . [W]e must seek the psychological equivalent of the concept not in general representations, not in absolute perceptions and orthoscopic diagrams, not even in concrete verbal images that replace the general representations—we must seek it in a system of judgments in which the concept is disclosed... . [A] concept turns out to be a long activity that includes in itself a series of acts of thinking.

(1998, pp. 55–56)

This process begins to take important shape in adolescence and continues across the lifespan in relation to social contexts. It is not strictly linear, responding instead to inevitably shifting cultural landscapes, reinforcing the Marxist notion that the world is continually in flux and requires adaptations to new developments. As I write, for instance, fewer people appear to believe that global warming is a hoax (Deeg et al., 2019), because the evidence is ubiquitous and incontrovertible: It keeps getting hotter and "thousand-year" events are becoming commonplace (Wallace-Wells, 2022). These changes reflect how both the biological and social worlds often overlap—meteorologist John Knox recently told me that his field is becoming a social science along with its historical role as a natural science— and contribute to how people conceptualize their worlds.

Soviet society was predicated on the evolution of the New Soviet Man, a specific sort of individual. Although many people in the 21st century also believe that only one human type—their own—ought to be cultivated, a multicultural society involves the confluence and collision of people socialized to divergent ways of being. This meeting of different minds makes the challenge in schools different from, and more complex than, those immersed in a society in which a single future is envisioned; unless that narrow sense of destiny is manifested in the school as well.

Discussion

Vygotsky (1998) allowed that "I do not want to make a mistake and, in pointing to the relation to the environment, to consciousness, to speech, I do not want to reduce everything to speech" (p. 259). As I have noted, he gave some attention to other sign systems. Yet his view that developing concepts relies on word meanings, and not other sign systems and their potentials, suggests a heavy orientation to speech as the means by which societies advance. This phenomenon affects the long-term development of cultures as they use speech to give meaning to life and generate possibilities for the future, and to individuals within cultures who engage with others in speech and other semiotic activity to grow into an ideology and related set of practices.

106 *Factors in Human Development*

The problems remain with how the collision of cultures in schools and elsewhere in society can be managed in such a way that a society maintains a sense of balance, cohesion, and purpose while allowing local cultures to prosper and develop possibilities that may enrich the greater society. The emergence of alternatives can threaten those with inherited power, as is evident in the ways in which schools of the 2020s are fraught with contention over how students dress, what they may read and discuss, who is entitled to self-definition, and many more issues. Vygotsky is an excellent source for understanding how these various cultures have come into being and, as Herodotus might investigate, what to do when they come into conflict.

Notes

1 Ernst Heinrich Philipp August Haeckel (1834–1919) was a Prussian-German polymath, with a reputation as a zoologist, naturalist, eugenicist, philosopher, physician, professor, marine biologist, and artist. In addition to the biogenetic law, he was known for his roles in scientific racism and social Darwinism.
2 Edward Thorndike (1874–1949) was a US psychologist working from the behaviorist tradition. He is credited for describing the Law of Effect, in which responses producing a satisfying effect in a particular situation become more likely to recur in future such situations.
3 From Wikipedia: "Kulak ... was the term which was used to describe peasants who owned over 8 acres (3.2 hectares) of land toward the end of the Russian Empire. In the early Soviet Union, particularly in Soviet Russia and Azerbaijan, *kulak* became a vague reference to property ownership among peasants who were considered hesitant allies of the Bolshevik Revolution ... *Kulak* originally referred to former peasants in the Russian Empire who became wealthier during the Stolypin reform of 1906 to 1914, which aimed to reduce radicalism among the peasantry and produce profit-minded, politically conservative farmers. During the Russian Revolution, *kulak* was used to chastise peasants who withheld grain from the Bolsheviks. According to Marxist–Leninist political theories of the early 20th century, the kulaks were considered class enemies of the poorer peasants. Vladimir Lenin described them as "bloodsuckers, vampires, plunderers of the people and profiteers, who fatten themselves during famines", declaring revolution against them to liberate poor peasants, farm laborers, and proletariat (the much smaller class of urban and industrial workers). Under [Stalin's] dekulakization, government officials seized farms and killed most resisters, deported others to labor camps, and drove many others to migrate to the cities following the loss of their property to the collectives."

7 Emotions and Reason in Human Development and Education

Arthur Conan Doyle's (1890) *Sherlock Holmes*, in "Sign of the Four," states unambiguously that good thinking relies on a purely analytic mind: "The emotional qualities are antagonistic to clear reasoning." This value on "cold cognition," absent the corrupting influence of the passions, was contested by the funk band Parliament (Worrell, Collins, & Clinton, 1975), who assert that what matters in life is how you feel, not what you know. These polar views of the role of emotions in human cognition provide a tension that is important in exploring Vygotsky's simultaneous belief that emotions are primary in thinking, yet become disciplined by the rational intellect: "Let us take the thinking of modern man. As for Spinoza, for one, thinking is the master of the passions, and for others (those described by Freud, people autistically oriented and closed within themselves), thinking is the servant of the passions" (Vygotsky, 1998, p. 183). A Florida sheriff recently found a very concrete illustration of this tension between reason and emotion, saying that road rage incidents are created by people who "let their emotions get the best of them, and they don't really think about the consequences of their actions or what could happen as the result of their stupidity." This chapter explores how reason and emotion are fundamentally related in the drama of life on the social stage, both in Vygotsky's conception and in more current views that question his ultimate confidence in the intellect in disciplining emotions.

In societies grounded in the assumptions that emerged during the Age of Reason and its subordination of passion, the emotions have often been thought to corrupt clear thinking. Enlightenment philosopher Immanuel Kant, according to Vygotsky (1999), believed that "affects actually are only diseases of the soul… an abnormality and a sickness" (p. 151). The architects of the James-Lange theory of emotions[1] shared this view that emotions corrupt cognition:

> James also is inclined to consider affects as pathological phenomena, harmful to the beings experiencing them. Lange gloomily tells of the fate of passions' dying breed. James is also forced to consider them as rudimentary vestiges that were initially useful, but deteriorated in the course of development and were converted into useless, meaningless adjuncts of our mental apparatus connected in no way with the rest of the activity.
> (Vygotsky, 1999, p. 155)

Emotions, as these perspectives show, have long been considered to be the enemy of clear thinking, at least by men who have opined on the subject. One might point to Sherlock Holmes as the epitome of a mind that operates without the distortion of emotion. It's easier to do when you are a fictional character, however, rather than a human being. Yet even the Star Trek character Mr. Spock, celebrated for his withering logic, is torn between his Vulcan (logical) and human (emotional) sides, a dialectic that has produced the tensions that have helped make him a character of enduring interest (Asher-Perrin, 2019).

Vygotsky, as his critique of Lange and James suggests, was firmly committed to understanding the role of emotions in both human thinking and human development. He managed to adopt this perspective in spite of the overwhelming influence of the European Enlightenment, whose valorization of reason required a view that emotions are the antagonist of logic. This belief has been reinforced by stereotypes, such as the view that rational men make better leaders than emotional women (Lopez-Zafra, Garcia-Retamero, & Berrios Martos, 2012) and that educated white people, led by reason, are more logical and therefore more reasonable than people from other cultures and ethnicities who engage in disagreements with passion (Kochman, 1981). Reason has also been pitted against religion and its reliance on faith (Flavell, 2022). These beliefs have become entrenched in many people's understandings of the subordination of emotion to reason.

Vygotsky saw important roles for both emotions and the intellect, although in a hierarchical relationship in which reason comes to regulate passion. Emotions, he argued, begin in biology: "the interactions of the cortical and subcortical centers are considered to be the basis of emotion" (1999, p. 113). He did not see emotions as inherently corruptive of thinking, however. At the same time, he viewed them as ideally subordinated to reason, a capability that comes with maturation of the sort that the Florida sheriff found lacking in road rage combatants. "What is higher in man," Vygotsky believed, is "his free and rational will and his control over his own passions" (1999, p. 173) such that "the victory of the will over passions appears to be not a victory of a higher nature of the soul over a lower, of exalted passions over base, but a victory of the will over passion, of freedom over necessity, of the spirit over nature" (1999, p. 176). "Nature" here refers to biology and the capacity of any creature to feel anger, satisfaction, and other emotions. What makes humans distinctive, among other traits, is their ability to learn how to control emotions through verbal regulation. Vygotsky never wrote about subduing emotions through physical acts such as deep breathing (Homma & Masaoka, 2008), unless he implied that such actions follow from verbal bodily regulation during the effort to promote relaxation.

Vygotsky characterized his approach as integrative, consistent with his quest for psychological unity. Human passions, he argued, "undoubtedly reveal the indisputable fact of unity of spirit and body in one phenomenon, in one being.... Our affects make it clear to us that we, together with our body, are one being. It is specifically passions that form the basic phenomenon of human nature" (1999, pp. 163–164). It should be no surprise that Vygotsky sought synthesis of all functions to account for human development, consistent with his view that psychology was in crisis in large part because of its fragmentation into subfields, and that the integrated field of pedology could produce a developmentally centered education.

This chapter explores Vygotsky's views on the relation between emotion and reason. As the previous quotes suggest, he found that both are involved in human thinking, with one developing control over the other. I locate his belief in Enlightenment thought rather than empirical findings from his research, and rely on more recent research by Haidt (2012) to question the degree to which he accurately depicted both emotion and reason (see Smagorinsky, 2021b).

The Drama and Passion of Human Life

Vygotsky was a theater critic in his teens, and a theater afficionado throughout his life (Van der Veer, 2015). His exploration of drama—the topic of both his theater criticism and among the featured genres of his doctoral dissertation on *The Psychology of Art*

(1971)—provided the basis for his view that life itself is dramatic, inevitably tragic, always emotional. Vygotsky believed that the principle focus of psychology should be on personality, "a character of the drama of life on the social stage" (Yaroshevsky, 1989, p. 219), with drama emerging in relation to other people in social settings. Dramatic tensions are also present within individuals as they engage with a conflictual world. The development of personality is thus a consequence of the internal and external dramatic struggles a person experiences in everyday life. These tensions are grounded in emotionally based contradictions that are central to the development of personality.

Yaroshevsky (1989) argues that Vygotsky viewed human drama and theatrical drama as closely related. Art provides a vehicle through which to understand and regulate human emotions (see Chapter 12). The development of personality is fundamentally dramatic, and experiences with art are inherently psychological. Both are involved in the development of consciousness, and both are intensely emotional: "The emotions are one of the features which constitute the character of an individual's general view of life. The structure of the individual's character is reflected in his emotional life and his character is defined by these emotional experiences" (Vygotsky, 1987, p. 333). Emotion is central to human development, even that of the amoral psychopaths described by Kennett (2002), if in selective and limited ways (Blair et al., 2006). Development without emotion is not possible, Vygotsky asserted: "Our affects make it clear to us that we, together with our body, are one being. It is specifically passions that form the basic phenomenon of human nature.... [A] theory of emotions that excludes the possibility of development inevitably leads us to admitting emotions to be eternal, inviolable, changeless essences" (1999, pp. 164, 203). These emotions provide the basis for the dramatic tensions that characterize human life and mediate developmental trajectories over time.

Emotions as the Source of Human Thinking

Vygotsky took as axiomatic that emotional life is primary for humans, and has a primitive basis in the emotional life of animals. Although he looked specifically at how emotional responses shape responses to art—particularly literature (Vygotsky, 1971)—he spoke generally about how emotions provide the basis for how people engage with life. In his early work in *Educational Psychology*, he stated that

> Regardless of whether a cause is real or unreal, the emotion associated with it is always real. If I cry over the fictitious hero of a novel, or if I am frightened of a strange monster that comes to me in my sleep, or, finally, if, in an affected state, I hallucinate a conversation with a brother who was long gone,[2] in all of these instances the causes of my emotions do not, of course, exist in reality, but my fear, my grief, my compassion remains an entirely real experience regardless. Thus, fantasy is doubly real, on the one hand, by virtue of the material it comprises, and on the other, by virtue of the emotions associated with it.
>
> (1997a, p. 150)

Vygotsky's emphasis on the emotions positioned them as primal, but not ultimately primary:

> Emotional reactions, thus, perform a highly important function in behavior. They are reactions that emerge in the critical moments of a disturbed balance, turbulent reactions, that in strong degrees can become an affect leading to a genuine behavioral

storm and affect the deepest layers of our internal and external activity. Precisely because the emotion emerges in a critical moment of behavior it dictatorially controls our behavior, determines the whole condition of the organism, fundamentally changes even our internal organic functions, such as respiration, blood circulation, and internal secretion. Research shows that emotional reactions are rooted in instinctive reactions. Emotions such as fear and anger are echoes of the turbulent reactions of fight and flight elaborated by animals in the long process of adaptation. That is why the meaning of emotions in behavior is that they refer to the degree of adaptation or non-adaptation, balance or imbalance between the organism and the environment.

(in Van der Veer, 2020, p. 136)

There are hints at Vygotsky's early indebtedness to Pavlov's reflexology in this conception, one that Vygotsky revised as he recognized the limits of seeing behavior as a strictly reflexive way of engaging with the world. He later argued that "emotion is not simply the sum of feeling the organic reaction, but primarily an urge to act in a certain direction" (1999, p. 93), with the inclusion of will shaping emotional responses. Throughout his own growth as a psychologist, he was steadfast in seeing emotions as the basis for thinking, if not the endpoint. As this quote reveals, he also saw emotions as central means of helping people working toward a state of equilibrium, a process that is more of a quest than an achievable state. If Vygotsky is right that tensions and contradictions drive development, a state of equilibrium would signify the end of development, even as people continually strive toward it. Emotions are, as I review next, held in check by the volitional work of the mind's intellectual control, a regulatory function that helps work toward the homeostasis that Damasio (2021) feels is important to living a contented life, even if total psychological balance is likely not actually possible.

Emotions and the Intellect

Emotions are the source of people's engagement with the world. But to Vygotsky, they are in need of intellectual regulation. His work in his early pedagogical volume, *Educational Psychology*, addressed the need to moderate and direct emotions through education:

the ideal of emotional education would appear to consist not in the development and reinforcement of the emotions, but, on the contrary, in their suppression and attenuation... . From simple observation, we know how the emotions complicate and vary behavior, and how far an emotionally gifted, refined, and educated person towers over an emotionally uneducated person.

(1997a, p. 100)

Because Vygotsky developed his ideas over the course of his career, it can be difficult to assume that what he said in this early work would be sustained over time. His debt to Pavlov is evident in his characterization of emotions as reactions: "emotion should be understood as a reaction that occurs at a critical and catastrophic moments of behavior, as points of disequilibrium, as the ultimate end outcome of behavior, having a direct impact on the forms assumed by subsequent behavior at every moment" (Vygotsky, 1997a, p. 101). Emotional reactions, he continued, are "a powerful guide of behavior. It is in an emotional reaction that the purposefulness of our organism manifests itself. Emotions would not be needed if they were not purposeful.... But their inner role as guides of all behavior, what had been their initial role to begin with, still remains" (p. 102).

Post-Pavlovian Vygotsky never rejected Pavlov's account of reaction altogether, only its exclusive role in prompting a response and the absence of tools and signs in mediational roles. His account of the emotional reaction positions it as the source of human engagement with the world, which is consistent with his later understandings. Emotions have a principal role in initiating an action, and remain in play in relation to the intellect's effort to control them. "It would be wrong," he wrote, "to imagine, as some believe, that emotion seems to be a purely passive experience of the organism, and does not itself lead to any sort of activity. Thus, the primordial regulation of the reactions arises from the emotions. The emotion associated with a reaction guides it and regulates it, depending on the overall state of the organism" (Vygotsky, 1997a, p. 103). There is a reciprocal relation between the emotions and the intellect, with each affecting the other in a developmental process.

Emotional Control as Indicator of Maturity

Vygotsky, as always, tried to understand emotions as part of long-term developmental processes. He associated greater emotional expression with primitiveness or immaturity and insufficient education of the feelings. Emotionally driven ideation, he argued, is both childlike and characteristic of under-development, as in the "primitive" people he described: "When a person does not realize what he is doing and acts under the influence of an affective reaction, you may again infer his internal state and the character of his perception from his motor behavior. You can observe the return to a structure characteristic of early stages of development" (1997b, p. 93). He associated unbridled emotionality with underdevelopment, either of an individual or a whole people, an echo of the parallels he saw between ontogeny and phylogeny (see Chapter 6):

> The young child's logic is also subordinated to his emotional life. "The main trait of the most primitive mind," says Blonskiy (1925/1930), "is its emotionality. The logic of this mind is the logic of what is pleasant and what is unpleasant. Everything that is pleasant is accepted, everything that is unpleasant is rejected" (p. 124). The child cannot escape the power of the immediate interest that possesses him in this moment like he cannot direct his behavior other than with a view to the closest and direct satisfaction of his need. The line of development of the child's behavior goes in the direction of a decrease of this undivided power of the emotion and already in the preschool age, we see that the child's emotionality is receding to the background. The new suppression of emotionality—this time relegated to a minor role—characterizes the beginning of the school age.
>
> (in Van der Veer, 2020, p. 137)

Education, Vygotsky believed, plays a key role in the emotions, in the development of intellectual capabilities to moderate emotional spikes. He disagreed with the widely held view of his time that emotional reactions diminish as a person ages. Rather, he argued, emotions

> undergo deep internal changes. They form connections with new and more complicated forms of behavior. This is what constitutes the real evolution of emotional life in the school age. The first symptom is that the emotional reactions lose their direct

dictatorial power over the child's behavior. Blonskiy (1925/1930, pp. 160–161) is completely right when he says that this must lead to an important conclusion for education. Only for early childhood we can justify teaching based on the child's immediate emotions, his subjective interest, by trying to trigger his immediate pleasure and laughter, in particular. Teaching the schoolchild "must not at all try to amuse the child." However, it would be dangerous to fall into the opposite mistake, as the older [Tsarist] school did, and to ignore the child's interests completely by making the school subjects difficult and unpleasant for the child. "Teaching must neither be unpleasant for the child," because this as well, by causing a strong emotion in the child, delays his development on a lower level where his behavior is ruled directly by emotions.

(in Van der Veer, 2020, pp. 137–138)

Emotions, he maintained, provide the basis for growth, but require self-regulation to do so productively. In school,

a pedagogue must not ignore the child's still fairly powerful emotionality but rely on it in order to overcome it. This is why we get the somewhat paradoxical conclusion that says that the more difficult work the pedagogue presents to the children, that is, the further he leads them along the line of development and the more he requires of their seriousness, the more he must rely on their emotionality.

Thus, this rule about the increasing seriousness of instruction also has its exception. The younger the child is, the more emotionality must form part of the lessons. With retarded[3] children, who have not yet finished their preschool development, the lessons must rely more on emotionality than with children who went ahead.

It is explained by the fact that when the child faces a more difficult task he, as it were, goes down in his development. "When the child performs difficult mental work, he again begins to show all the properties of a younger age" (Blonskiy, 1925/1930, p. 125) and, thus, we must use pedagogical methods proper for a younger age, that is, strengthen the emotional aspects of the pedagogical work.

(in Van der Veer, 2020, p. 139)

Vygotsky associated unbridled emotional response with immaturity, such that a frustrated and angry teen (or, in my experience, an adult) who cannot easily complete a task becomes childlike, with a cascade of feelings that may inhibit further progress. In this sense the learner "goes down" in development, reverting to child-like emotional reactions that would benefit from maturational regulation. His point was that children of nonnormative development may exhibit frustration more easily than their age-group peers, and so resemble children of younger age and degree of emotional regulation.

Emotions and Socialization

Emotional life, in cultural-historical theory, has a deeply social dimension. How people feel is in large part a consequence of the setting in which an emotion develops and is expressed:

Emotion grows as a function of the audience that experiences it. Shame experienced in front of a crowd of thousands is thousands of times more powerful than shame experienced in front of a single person. The same may be said of the emotion of satisfaction, which directs all our reactions to an ultimate goal, which grows and increases in magnitude the larger is the group in whose channel it travels.

(Vygotsky, 1997a, p. 192)

As might be expected, Vygotsky found emotions to not simply be reactions, but conditional responses that are socially mediated over time. To use modern examples, people of different cultures learn to display emotions in appropriate ways to meet social expectations within their frames of reference. As Lim (2016) describes it,

In Western or individualist culture, high arousal emotions are valued and promoted more than low arousal emotions. Moreover, Westerners experience high arousal emotions more than low arousal emotions. By contrast, in Eastern or collectivist culture, low arousal emotions are valued more than high arousal emotions. Moreover, people in the East actually experience and prefer to experience low arousal emotions more than high arousal emotions.

(p. 105)

These learned emotional expressions can be relearned when people immigrate and must adapt to new expectations (De Leersnyder, 2017). Vygotsky described the process by which such cultural differences are manifested in the expression of emotions as they are mediated culturally:

Together with the growth of the child's social experience, these emotions become more and more social. While we can characterize the range of emotions of the young child as egocentric, the range of emotions of the schoolchild have a social character, even when these emotions are egoistic. This means that the emotional reactions of the young child are primarily concentrated around aspects connected with personal behavior and determined by organic needs and drives. The emotions of the schoolchild are characterized by the growth of the objective and social aspect. They last longer and become more stable. The schoolchild develops what we call permanent interests, that is, interests directed at an activity of longer duration, sometimes maintained for a whole year or longer. This interest is not so much directed at the satisfaction of immediate organic needs but at the observation of the surrounding world and some activity in this surrounding world. Emotions connected with cognition, such as curiosity, inquisitiveness, the interest in everything that is new, and emotions connected with an activity, such as the emotions of coping, effort, success, triumph, come to the fore.

In exactly the same way, the child's personal emotions become more and more connected with his social life. The child finds personal satisfaction in the emotions of contest, competition, self-assertion, respect, friendship, leadership, and so on. In other words, the emotional life of the development of the will [i.e., volition and self-regulation] itself, that is, the mastery of one's behavior, becomes possible on the basis of the social development of the child's personality.

(in Van der Veer, 2020, pp. 139–140)

Emotion, cognition, imagination, and personality are intertwined with the cultural historical context: "the movement of our feelings is closely connected with the activity of imagination. A certain construction may turn out to lack reality from a rational perspective.

Nonetheless, this construction is real in the emotional sense.... Imagination is a necessary, integral aspect of realistic thinking" (Vygotsky, 1987, pp. 347, 349) (see Chapter 8). Vygotsky's relation among imagination, emotion, and cognition suggests that people's capacity to project a trajectory for themselves, to set a path toward a social future, is culturally mediated. It is important to understand, then, the kinds of mediation that provide both the emotional foundation and cultural sense of propriety for their trajectories, and the sorts of mediation that potentially limit their possible conceptions of trajectory.

Reason and Emotion

Vygotsky (1997b) drew on one of his major influences to conclude that "thinking is at first, in the words of Spinoza [1677/1955, p. 187] the servant of the passions, but that man who has reason is the master of his passions" (p. 97). Spinoza was, he argued,

> a determinist and, in contrast to the stoics, claimed that man has power over his affects, that the intellect may change the order and connections of the passions and bring them into accord with the order and connections that are given in the intellect.... That I think about objects that exist outside myself does not change anything in them, but that I think about my affects, that I place them in other relationships to my intellect and other processes, changes much in my mental life. To put it more simply, our affects act in a complex system with our concepts and he who does not know that the jealously of a man who is bound up by the Islamic concepts about women's fidelity and of a man who is bound up by a system of opposite conceptions about women's fidelity is different, does not understand that this feeling is historical, that it changes its essence in different ideological and psychological environments, although there undoubtedly remains a certain basic biological component on the basis of which this emotion develops. Thus, complex emotions emerge only historically. They are combinations of relationships that develop under the conditions of historical life. In the process of development the emotions become fused.
> (p. 103)

Emotions, he argued in Pavlovian fashion, constitute reactions. People who are in balance with their environments, who may be carrying out mundane routines, have little to emote about as long as there is no disruption. However, he argued, "As soon as this balance is disturbed an emotional reaction immediately emerges" (in Van der Veer, 2020, p. 136). He continued,

> Emotional reactions, thus, perform a highly important function in behavior. They are reactions that emerge in the critical moments of a disturbed balance, turbulent reactions, that in strong degrees can become an affect leading to a genuine behavioral storm and affect the deepest layers of our internal and external activity. Precisely because the emotion emerges in a critical moment of behavior it dictatorially controls our behavior, determines the whole condition of the organism, fundamentally changes even our internal organic functions, such as respiration, blood circulation, and internal secretion.
>
> Research shows that emotional reactions are rooted in instinctive reactions. Emotions such as fear and anger are echoes of the turbulent reactions of fight and flight elaborated by animals in the long process of adaptation. That is why the meaning of

emotions in behavior is that they refer to the degree of adaptation or non-adaptation, balance or imbalance between the organism and the environment.

(in Van der Veer, 2020, p. 136)

There is no shutting down the emotional flow. One's feelings are profoundly implicated in how people think. But, to Vygotsky, how people think has an effect on how people's emotions affect them. The emotions, he argued, are intellectualized in order to regulate and subordinate them, both in relation to art (see Chapter 12) and in the drama of everyday life. He accepted the belief that

> One should always attempt to control one's emotions and subject them to the control of the intellect... . One should never give way to the lower passions, but rather climb the rational ladder and be more refined and detached in one's judgments... one should never become the victim of one's moods.
>
> (Van der Veer & Valsiner, 1991, p. 15)

Emotions, he believed, need to be controlled and disciplined in order for an advanced rational society to be possible. Most people are not like dogs who ceaselessly bark at every passing car. They have the capacity to recognize emotions and use their intellects to moderate extremes and act as rationally as possible, according to cultural traditions, to control them. The triumph of the intellect might be best expressed in Vygotsky's (1997b) statement that "the actions of a mathematician ... represent the most perfect model of human thinking" (p. 225), one that rises above the passions to calculate the world precisely. Yet STEM fields have an emotional dimension, as when architecture is designed to produce an affective response (Shemesh et al., 2016) or when anxiety affects one's ability to carry out mathematical functions, leading to feelings of frustration (Luttenberger, Wimmer, & Paechter, 2018). It seems that Vygotsky's remark would apply more to the abstract mathematician doing problems than a mathematician solving a real-world problem like disproportionate educational opportunities for people of different racial groups.

Vygotsky's claim here is consistent with the idea that "rocket science" represents the highest form of human intellectual activity, rather than being highly empathic or being a superior sculptor. I should note that designing the rockets launched in time of warfare might not meet the definition for sublime human behavior, even as I marvel at the new James Webb space telescope and the images it provides of the cosmos. It's possible to value more than one thing at the same time. It's also possible that the same disposition or stance can be construed differently in different settings. The British "stiff upper lip," culturally designed to suppress emotional expression, might be viewed as inappropriate in a culture that values emotional displays. Tsai (n.d.) summarizes the cultural dimensions of emotional expression well:

> Lutz (1988) argued that many Western views of emotion assume that emotions are "singular events situated within individuals." However, people from Ifaluk (a small island near Micronesia) view emotions as "exchanges between individuals" (p. 212). Social constructivists contended that because cultural ideas and practices are all-encompassing, people are often unaware of how their feelings are shaped by their culture. Therefore emotions can feel automatic, natural, physiological, and instinctual, and yet still be primarily culturally shaped.
>
> (n.p.)

Vygotsky argued from available understandings that more recent work has begun to complicate. It's useful to keep in mind that his account of emotional life was a function of where and when he lived, and that in some areas, this limitation made a multicultural outlook less available to him than modern investigators have access to.

Education of the Feelings

The role of education in the subordination of emotions to the intellect, argued Vygotsky, is great. Academic concepts, he maintained (Vygotsky, 1987), enable one to develop abstract knowledge that enables the adaptation of what is learned in one context to another (see Chapter 6). School is among the critical settings in which children become socialized to cultural expectations that they learn to apply in moving from place to place, and that they learn have general principles that enable their adaptation. Through schooling, "the novel component which emotion contributes to behavior is wholly reducible to the organism's regulation of every one of its individual reactions" (1997a, p. 103). Education helps to foster developmental changes in individuals and social groups:

> If nothing changes, then nothing has been taught. What are the educational changes that must be introduced into the feelings? Above, we saw that every feeling is nothing other than the mechanism of a reaction, i.e., a particular reaction of the organism to some stimulation from the environment. Consequently, in its general outlines, the mechanism for the education, the feelings, is precisely the same as for all other reactions. By connecting together various stimuli, we can always form new relations between an emotional reaction and some element of the environment, thus altering all those stimuli. A reaction is associated with the first step in education.
>
> (1997a, p. 104)

Pavlov's influence is clear here, and in ways that I think Vygotsky would not have agreed with later in his own development. He stated in this early writing that emotions are reactions that trigger new reactions, and a person is the sum of these reactions. My interpretation is that the intellectualization of the emotions is less a reaction, and more an act of deliberation, of will, of self-induced intentional cognitive action undertaken with psychological tools to reduce the impact of an emotional reaction.

This disagreement does not dismiss the idea that emotions are types of reactions, and that much of life comes in reaction to the environment and the challenges it issues. Reactions are both biological, as in knee-jerks in response to a tapped nerve, and social, in that reactions are culturally shaped, including the distinct and influential culture of each individual's family. Educators can help create environments that foster emotional development in culturally appropriate ways. They also might do considerable damage by responding to a student's emotional outburst in hostile, insensitive ways. The abstractions available in school settings are ultimately what enables self-regulation: "Hence, the first rule for the education of the feelings: Try to so organize a child's life and the child's behavior in such a way that he encounters those stimuli between which such transfer of feelings is typically to be created as often as possible" (1997a, p. 105), often through verbal formulations of emotions.

The socialization of emotions fit with the Soviet doctrine that the cultivation of nationalism, or at least of the Soviet doctrine surrounding Marxism, is of utmost importance in schooling. Undoubtedly the New Soviet Man was lurking beneath Vygotsky's assertion that

> we can easily lift out of the narrow circle of personality all the self-centered feelings, i.e., teach the child to respond with anger, not to the wrongs done to him personally, but to the wrongs done his own country, his own social class, or his own craft. It is this possibility for the broadest possible transfer of feelings which also constitutes the surest guarantee of the education of the feelings, which may be expressed as the possibility for the creation of entirely new relationships between the individual and the environment. This is why there can be no unacceptable or undesirable emotions, from the teacher's standpoint. On the contrary, the teacher must always start from what are thought of as the lowest or self-centered feelings, understanding them to be the most primitive, the most basic, and the most powerful of all feelings, and just on the basis of those feelings, lay the foundation of the emotional structure of personality.
>
> (1997a, p. 105)

Two points are available here. First, Vygotsky's idealism was on display in his assertion that there are no unacceptable emotions. Teachers have often been faced by verbal assaults from students, no matter how sensitively they organize the environment. School violence remains a threat to the stability of an education, and is a reflection of broader societal workplace violence (Smith, Singer, Hoel, & Cooper, 2003). Whether the cause is individual students or the school culture—no doubt Vygotsky's explanation—incidences of violence continue. Regardless of cause, a hostile student's assault on another, either verbal or physical, would be difficult for a teacher to view as acceptable or desirable. Actor Will Smith's infamous slap of comedian Chris Rock during the 2022 Academy Awards event, following Rock's effort to elicit laughs by mocking Jada Pinckett Smith's alopecia, and Will Smith's subsequent decade-long banishment from future award ceremonies, illustrates how the acceptability of angry emotional responses is a cultural phenomenon.

Second, the education of feelings, in Vygotsky's conception, followed from the general task of socialization to Soviet culture. Schools were arranged to promote this socialization by the creation of developmental pathways that benefitted the culture, and toward which the child was most fruitfully led:

> the educational mechanism reduces to a special organization of the environment. Thus, the education of the feelings is always, basically, a re-education of the feelings, i.e., a variation in the direction of an emotional innate reaction [known in psychiatric circles as a "corrective experience"]... . [T]he emotions have to be considered as a system of anticipatory reactions that inform the organism as to the near future of his behavior and organize the different forms of this behavior. For the teacher, therefore, the emotions become an extraordinarily valuable tool for the education of various reactions. No form of behavior is so vigorous as when it is associated with an emotion. If you would like to induce in a student certain desirable forms of behavior, therefore, always be sure that these reactions leave an emotional trace in the student. No moral sermon educates like real pain, like a real feeling, and in this sense, the apparatus of the emotions seems like an expressly adapted and subtle tool by means of which behavior may be influenced effortlessly.
>
> (1997a, pp. 105–106)

Vygotsky's idealism appears to have led him to the conclusion that "effortless" influences are possible. No doubt such work would require considerable effort. Nonetheless, he argued that the emotions are thus central aspects of human development, and are amenable to re-education in school:

> Emotional reactions turn out to have a substantial influence on absolutely all forms of our behavior and on all the components of the educational process. Whether we wish to help students achieve a better memory or whether we wish thinking to proceed more successfully—in either event we must take care to stimulate the particular activity emotionally. Experience and research have shown that an emotionally tinged fact is remembered more strongly, more firmly, and longer than one that is neutral. Every time you tell a student something, take care to engage his feelings. This is needed not only as a tool for better recall and better assimilation, but also as an end in itself.
>
> (1997a, p. 106)

Vygotsky made a case that would please the modern educator: That how people feel about what they do is a critical factor in their engagement with learning. He argued that the educational traditions of his day, especially in Tsarist or many European schools, were lifeless and dry, focused on facts more than feelings:

> Everything that we lost as a consequence of this education, the spontaneous sensation of life and, incidentally, the lifeless, uninspired method of teaching all the different subjects played no small role in this disengagement from the world and in this destruction of feelings. Who among us has not thought of what an inexhaustible source of emotional stimulation is concealed in an ordinary course of geography, astronomy, or history, all we have to do is think of ways of teaching these subjects that go beyond all dry logical schemata and make of teaching not only an object and labor of thought, but also a labor of feeling.
>
> (1997a, p. 107)

An education must have an emotional foundation in order for students to want to learn. Banishing emotion from learning will banish learning itself, because there will be no basis for engagement:

> Emotion is no less important a tool than is thinking. The teacher must be concerned not only that students think about and learn geography, but also feel deeply about it. Such a thought usually does not come to mind for one reason or another. And teaching that is emotionally felt is a rare visitor to our schools, and is associated, for the most part, with an impotent love for one's own subject on the part of the teacher who doesn't know of any way of imparting this love to his students, and therefore, usually has the reputation of being eccentric.
>
> Meanwhile, it is precisely the emotional reactions that have to serve as the foundation of the educational process. Before communicating a particular piece of knowledge, the teacher should induce the appropriate emotion in the student, and take care to associate this emotion with the new knowledge. Only new knowledge that has passed through the student's senses may be inculcated. Everything else is lifeless

knowledge that diminishes every vital relationship to the world. Of all the subjects taught in school, only in the teaching of literature, and there only to an insignificant degree, was the presence of an emotional component recognized as an essential element of the educational process in the classroom.

(1997a, p. 107)

Emotions are foundational to engagement in school. Ultimately, Vygotsky argued, emotions can be counter-developmental when unrestrained by reason. I close with a consideration of Vygotsky's faith in reason as the final arbiter of how emotions contribute to human thinking and action in society.

A 21st Century View of Reason as a Chimera

Nearly a century after Vygotsky wrote about emotions, Haidt (2012) studied how people respond to the hypothetical dilemmas about moral action and found that people do not generate ideas through rational analysis. To Gilligan (1982), this tendency is especially likely among women; Haidt does not make a gendered distinction. His inquiry followed from his observation that people on the political left and political right tend to consider one another to be illogical and emotional, while they themselves are logical and morally accountable. To interpret this paradox, he argued that emotions, rather than reason, are responsible for the positions people take. Enlightenment assumptions enabled them to believe that their logic is what produced the beliefs, rather than serving in a subordinate role to account for the passions.

Vygotsky (1971) postulated that people first and foremost respond through gut reactions, passions, emotions. Contra Vygotsky, Haidt (2012) found that these emotions produce the thrust and substance of their thinking, which they then rationalize through whatever justifications they can come up with. They thus subject their gut reactions to confirmation bias, the tendency to marshal information in a way that confirms or supports how a person feels. Reason, Haidt says in agreement with Hume, is the slave of the passions, rather than the means by which emotions are regulated. Although "cold cognition"—a logical, emotionless sorting through of facts in order to arrive at a sound conclusion—underlies Enlightenment conceptions of reason, it is a chimera (Roth, 2007). Rather, people respond primarily through gut-level, often unconscious feelings that they then justify with whatever logics they can produce to give their emotions the appearance of rational support.

Haidt (2012) describes the belief in logic to be "the rationalist delusion" (p. 103), a misconception he might claim to plague Vygotsky (Smagorinsky, 2021b). Haidt argues that the rationalist delusion implies that "the rational caste (philosophers or scientists) should have more power, and it usually comes along with a utopian program for raising more rational children" (p. 103). And thus schools take on the task of chasing the rationalist mirage, and muffling the emotional lives of students and teachers.

Haidt (2012) provides a compelling challenge to Vygotsky's faith in reason, one worth considering. The first two decades of the 21st century have provided a good bit of support for his views, as political polarization ramps up passions that are in turn rationally justified, no matter which side one falls on. Van der Veer and Valsiner (1991) note the ways in which history has disconfirmed Vygotsky's belief in rationality on several fronts, such as resistance to the science behind climate change, and more recently, global pandemics, immigration, sexual politics, racism, and other contentious topics, all politicized and subject to different forms of reason to justify the driving emotions. They point out that

> The optimistic conclusion to be drawn from Vygotsky's account of human history is that one could see definite progress in two respects: modern man surpassed his precursors through (1) his superior domination of nature through technology, and (2) his improved control over the self through "psychotechnology." It would take the Second World War and the later general environmental pollution to make people seriously doubt these claims.
>
> (pp. 220–221)

Vygotsky's faith in Enlightenment rationalism was not a product of his own research. Rather, he appears to have adopted the values of his era and place, where rationalism was valued and emotions were viewed as corrupting influences. His identification of emotions as critical aspects of thinking departed from the rationalist mood of the Age of Reason, yet he ultimately turned to reason as the means by which emotions are disciplined. I believe that Haidt's (2012) reliance on his research to question the "rationalist delusion" (p. 103) behind conceptions like Vygotsky's provides him with a stronger basis from which to make his points. In either case, the tension provided by their opposing views can be very generative to those seeking to advance their understandings of the related roles of emotion and intellect in human development and action.

Discussion

I conclude with the belief that Vygotsky's account of emotions is both significant and incomplete. Vygotsky (1997a) described the "'lifelessness' of school" (p. 127) in his own time. Goodlad (1984) later described school life as emotionally *flat*, a conclusion that seems to have survived the decades. In test-driven schools of the 21st century, in which discussions of social issues are being forbidden by legal mandates of the 2020s, they have gotten no livelier.

Vygotsky's observation that interest is critical, and that interest has an emotional basis, suggests that the re-inscription of formalism into the school curriculum, and elimination of "controversial" topics from discussion, will be detrimental to schooling and learners (see Chapter 11). His concern might be acted on in many different ways by educators of different persuasions, with disagreement among them. In spite of the great likelihood that Vygotsky was right, and that education must begin with students' emotional investment in their work, policymakers appear bent on making school as dull and lifeless as possible, and as comforting as possible for those in the dominant culture, whose peace must not be disturbed by "divisive concepts" that threaten their status in the social order.

Vygotsky's view of emotions as developmentally critical, and subject to cultural mediation, is consistent with the project of cultural-historical psychology. One might take issue with the value of Soviet schooling and its effort to evolve the New Soviet Man through the cultivation of a Soviet mindset. My reading of Solzhenitsyn (1973), Snyder (2010, 2015, 2018), Figes (1997), and other critics of Soviet society leads me to question the value of using schools to produce a narrow, ideologically oriented, specific sort of citizen. At the same time, given that schools have historically served a national socialization agenda in a variety of nations (Smagorinsky, 2021a, 2022), it is not surprising that he would advocate such a view, especially at the optimistic launch of the Soviet Union. In pluralistic nations, that project continues, in spite of attempts by multiculturalists to expand the cultural repertoires available to engage with the curriculum, and alter it to reflect greater diversity. Applying a belief in an educational monoculture that prepares students for participation in the mirage of a singular national character and common theological basis has, in the view of many, done more harm than good (Mampaey & Zanoni, 2016).

The question remains whether or not emotions are controlled by reason, or whether reason is a post-hoc rationale for emotions. I have been persuaded by Haidt (2012) that people are not rational; that they are driven by emotions and use evidence selectively to produce logical afterthoughts to explain their gut feelings (Smagorinsky, 2018d). I'm sure that taking this position would make me an odd creature in an Enlightenment-inspired school. But it's an orthodoxy that I think merits attention and interrogation.

Or, perhaps the dichotomous nature of the question obscures the ways in which emotions and cognition co-develop. At times the emotions, especially at fraught moments, overcome reason; and at times reason can temper emotions. Undoubtedly they work in concert, and in different ways in different circumstances. In schools governed by the assumption of reason, however, the emotions remain, as Kant believed, diseases of the soul, an abnormality and a sickness. In this chapter, I have made the case that emotions are fundamental to being human, contribute to personal development, are the genesis of one's response to the world, and should play a central role in education. Reason matters too, and in conjunction with emotionality figures into how and what students learn in school. I'm reminded of an adage available in the question of whether or not schools should allow prayer: As long as there are math tests, there will be prayer in school. You can ban it, but you can't stop it. Emotions are similar: They are always there, openly expressed or not. Ignoring them shuts down a critical avenue to school participation, and dampens the potential available from engaging with school emotionally in order to advance academically, and emotionally as well.

Notes

1 The James–Lange theory was developed by John Dewey and named for William James and Carl Lange. It is based on the premise that physiological arousal produces emotions (e.g., smiling itself may produce good feelings), rather than emotions producing bodily effects.
2 Recall that Vygotsky lost one brother to tuberculosis and another to typhoid in their youth.
3 As I have noted throughout, Vygotsky employed terms acceptable in his day that sound harsh and inappropriate to the 21st century ear, and it would be presentist to judge him for being a person of his time.

8 Play and Labor in Human Development and Education

Many people in the English-speaking world might think that play and labor are mutually exclusive; that play is merry, and labor is work. From Vygotsky's perspective, however, both play key, related roles in human development. Play isn't always fun, and labor is more than work. Play enables an understanding of boundaries that are essential to undertaking labor. I next detail his perspective on these fundamental aspects of human development. I first address Vygotsky's account of play, including its key feature of imagination and its application in games. I then shift to the role of labor in human societies, a fundamental Marxist notion that both figured heavily into Soviet life and accounts for collective action in societies that involve industrialization.

Play

"Play" is among those issues that are included in *Mind in Society*, which has provided the lion's share of citations to Vygotsky's contributions to psychology and education. Like any idea extracted from a great investigative program without attention to the broader thrust of the work, it has been trivialized and used to support other agendas, such as making classrooms "fun" (e.g., Singer, 2013). But fun was never Vygotsky's game.

What comes across overwhelmingly when reading Vygotsky's available corpus in English is what a serious person he was. I don't get a sense that Vygotsky spent a lot of time playing beach volleyball or yukking it up with friends at the neighborhood tavern. Even his great interest in the theater was less as a means of entertainment, and more of a serious effort to understand human psychology and its relation to art, to improve theatrical performances through criticism, and to fortify his theory of human development by attending to the emotional dimensions of art under the management of the intellect (see Chapter 7). Vygotsky (1998) referenced Stern's concept of *ernstspiel*, that is serious play (p. 268), a phenomenon that he argued has a transitional role in leading to socialization to cultural norms. To Vygotsky, play is serious work, and may not be fun at all. It ultimately socializes the maturing child to the demands of collective human labor.

Defining Play

Vygotsky defined play in a number of places throughout his *Collected Works*[1] and other texts. He rejected simplistic notions that were in circulation in his day:

> The old definition of play as every activity of the child that does not pursue getting results regards all types of children's activity as being equivalent.... [P]lay is a unique

relation to reality that is characterized by creating imaginary situations or transferring the properties of some objects to them. It would be dangerous, it seems to me, not to see a substantial difference between this "play" and play in the true sense of the word during preschool age—with the creation of imaginary situations.

(1998, pp. 266–267)

Vygotsky's notion of play referred to experimental, imaginative activity designed to create possibilities that in turn help a child learn boundaries. He specifically rejected both play-as-nonproductive-activity, as in the previous quote; and play as a source of enjoyment or amusement (Hedegaard, 2007). Vygotsky (1966) was clear on this point, saying,

We know that the definition of play on the basis of the pleasure it gives the child is not correct for two reasons—first, because we deal with a number of activities which give the child much keener experiences of pleasure than play. For example, the pleasure principle applies equally well to the sucking process, in that the child derives functional pleasure from sucking a pacifier even when he is not being satiated. On the other hand, we know of games in which the activity process itself does not afford pleasure—games which predominate at the end of preschool and the beginning of school age and which only give pleasure if the child finds the result interesting; these are, for example, sporting games (not only athletic sports, but also games with an outcome, games with results). They are very often accompanied by a keen sense of displeasure when the outcome is unfavourable to the child. Thus, defining play on the basis of pleasure can certainly not be regarded as correct.

(p. 6)

Of course, play *may* be fun. Yet to Vygotsky (1978) play is a developmental medium. Through play, children become socialized to the cultural practices that are epitomized in games, which represent broader values built into societies. Playing the real-estate acquisition game Monopoly within such a rule-bound setting, children learn competitive values and the benefits of accumulating and trading property, all built into US capitalist culture. The PBS program American Experience aired, in 2023, *Ruthless: Monopoly's Secret History* (Ives, 2023), a documentary that explores the game's "folk" prototype, originally patented by its designer, Lizzie Magie, in 1904. Her game was anti-monopoly and promoted revenue sharing rather than the cutthroat annihilation of opponents' finances. Fittingly, the game was pirated and sold to Parker Brothers in its more pitiless and feral form. Later, the game Anti-Monopoly was developed, with players taking the role of trust-busting lawyers filing lawsuits against monopolies. The appeal of these alternative versions of Monopoly in the United States suggests that there have been multiple views of capitalism in play within the nation over the last century. The PBS program includes attention to how children's understanding of finance would take on different trajectories, depending on which game they learned to play.

Monopoly was adapted in the Soviet Union in 1988 under a name translated as Manager, in which it was given a "socialist twist" (Shevchenko, 2021, n. p.). Shevchenko's (2022) reports on Soviet board games found both board-based versions of competitive games (basketball, soccer), and games in which children play "war games aimed to inculcate a spirit of patriotism in the future defenders of the Soviet Motherland" (n.p.). As Vygotsky would predict, the games played by children socialize them to the values of the cultures they are being prepared to enter.

The US child playing Monopoly would not learn how to act collectively toward greater societal ends, a communistic value available in Manager. Beyond the collectivist, labor-oriented emphasis of Vygotsky's work during this regime, play enables the individual child to develop means of mental self-regulation so as to become part of the social whole, a factor available regardless of national ethos or economic system. Play enables growth within social contours: "In play a child is always above his average age, above his daily behavior; *in play it is as though he were a head taller than himself.* As in the focus of a magnifying glass, play contains all developmental tendencies in a condensed form; in play it is as though the child were trying to jump above the level of his normal behavior" (1978, p. 102; emphasis added).

Play enables people to experiment with possible trajectories and mediums and the borders they provide, all with a developmental purpose. Vygotsky (1978) argued that

> Though the play-development relationship can be compared to the instruction-development relationship, play provides a much wider background for changes in needs and consciousness. Action in the imaginative sphere, in an imaginary situation, the creation of voluntary intentions, and the formation of real-life plans and volitional motives—all appear in play and make it the highest level of preschool development.
>
> (pp. 102–103)

To Vygotsky (1978), "play involving an imaginary situation is, in fact, rule-based play.... [T]here is no such thing as play without rules and the child's particular attitude toward them" (p. 94). Moreover,

> whenever there is an imaginary situation in play, there are rules—not rules that are formulated in advance and change during the course of the game, but rules stemming from the imaginary situation. Therefore, to imagine that a child can behave in an imaginary situation without rules, i.e., as he behaves in a real situation, is simply impossible. If the child is playing the role of a mother, then she has rules of maternal behavior. The role the child plays, and her relationship to the object if the object has changed its meaning, will always stem from the rules, i.e., the imaginary situation will always contain rules. In play the child is free. But this is an illusory freedom.
>
> (p. 95)

There is more to play than imagining situations and acting appropriately within them. Holzman (2008), along with Vygotsky, argues that human life is fundamentally emotional, and that play is infused with emotions. Her theatrical orientation is evident in her view that life is also performative, an everyday dramaturgical presentation consistent with Vygotsky's association of theatrical interpretations and performances with the drama of life (cf. Goffman, 1959).

Vygotsky (1978) argued that play is not free of restriction, and indeed is designed so that children learn how to navigate rules and boundaries. Beyond game parameters, play takes place within the context of contradiction, an oppositional force, an obstruction, a dialectical problem. Games are *played against something* in order to promote socialization, and so comprise a developmental necessity. Play, he concluded, must involve "the imaginary, illusory realization of unrealizable desires... . Like all functions of consciousness, it originally arises from action. The old adage that children's play is imagination in action can be reversed: we can say that imagination in adolescents and schoolchildren is play without action" (p. 129). Once play is undertaken in the material world, one can use the imagination mentally—in individual thinking that has a future orientation—in relation to the rules of socialization learned through social play.

Play and a Future Orientation

Play is a complex activity that promotes what Vygotsky (1978) felt was critical to psychology: To see human development as the unity of biological and social elements and not to fragment it into separate realms, such as behavior, memory, emotion, and other component parts. He incorporated play into his comprehensive cultural-historical psychology in saying,

> the essential attribute of play is a rule that has become an affect. "An idea that has become an affect, a concept that has turned into a passion"—this ideal of Spinoza's finds its prototype in play, which is the realm of spontaneity and freedom. To carry out the rule is a source of pleasure. The rule wins because it is the strongest impulse (cf. Spinoza's adage that an affect can be overcome by a stronger affect). Hence it follows that such a rule is an internal rule, i.e., a rule of inner self-restraint and self-determination, as Piaget says, and not a rule the child obeys as a physical law. In short, play gives the child a new form of desires, i.e., teaches him to desire by relating his desires to a fictitious "I"—to his role in the game and its rules. Therefore, a child's greatest achievements are possible in play—achievements that tomorrow will become his average level of real action and his morality.
>
> (pp. 99–100)

The imaginative spontaneity of play, while having degrees of freedom, is ultimately subordinated to the developmental process of developing a social consciousness that enables cultural participation. Play is thus a developmental medium that helps with socialization through the imaginative engagement with tasks, settings, etc. and their rules and boundaries. Within this structure, a person can "become a head taller" by performing in relation to presumed cultural trajectory that the play is designed to advance. This play has a strong affective dimension, one that Vygotsky believed could come under the control of the intellect during the process of maturation (see Chapter 7).

Play has more than immediate effects. Vygotsky's psychology was forward looking; he rejected aspects of Freud, for instance, because of his fixation on the distant past. Vygotsky in contrast took a developmental approach that saw any moment in a person's life as embodying both a personal and cultural past, and that situated the individual within a future-oriented pathway. Children's play takes on meaning through "its connection with the future activity of this young [person], with the future forms of adaptation and the struggle for life, with the future that awaits the young or child with the advent of maturity." Like a youthful animal, a playful child "exercises and develops the functions and strengths that it will need in its future life" (in Van der Veer, 2020, p. 6).

Play and Collective Labor

Vygotsky saw play being primarily characteristic of younger children, before they move into the world of labor. Collective labor is the endpoint toward which playful interactions point a child:

> While the roots of play lie in an instinctive need, the content of child play is always taken from the surrounding environment and this inborn, instinctive playful education constitutes the main function of this age. It stops when this dominance of play activity ends with the division of play and work. With this division into serious activities and activities for oneself, begins the school age—which can be characterized as the age of cultural formation par excellence.
> (in Van der Veer, 2020, pp. 47–48)

Learning to play by the rules produces a willful, volitional gravitation to social norms; "it teaches the child to steer his behavior and master it" (in Van der Veer, 2020, p. 141). Play comes in response, not to spontaneous impulse, but "along the line, along which the whole playing collective determines the progression of his behavior" (p. 141) by providing purpose, discipline, process, goals, tools, and other means by which a child becomes a cultural person. The playful child is working toward socialization and the ability to regulate the self in response to norms: "He is learning to adjust his behavior to some children and to oppose others. In play the child goes through a first and serious school of collective behavior" (p. 141).

Disciplined play produces the cultural laborer who acts willfully to occupy a role in a social collective, monitoring and regulating one's actions so as to perform within rule-bound environments. In doing so the child

> is lifted to a higher level [as] the mechanisms of labor mature in play.... . Thus the will is the antithesis of the [playful] instinct, although it develops from it. Therefore, from the genetic [developmental] viewpoint, we must not contrast play and labor. We must consider them as two genetically [developmentally] connected stages in the development of child behavior.
> (in Van der Veer, 2020, p. 142)

This "higher level" is a cultural endpoint. The New Soviet Man would presumably develop differently than does the capitalist of what the Soviets considered the decadent bourgeois European-based societies against which communism was launched. Developmentally, then,

> The changes that take place in the play of the schoolchild can be traced back to three basic aspects. The first is that in this play the aspect of social emotions—contest, competition, self-assertion—more and more comes to the fore. The second is the growing collectivity and complex collective organization of these competitive team games. Finally, the third is the growing meaning of the playing rule as the basic mechanism for the training of the will.
> (in Van der Veer, 2020, p. 143)

School plays a role in the process as a formal means through which development occurs, providing channels of activity through which play becomes a serious means for developing into a cultural being. In the Soviet Union, those contours oriented its citizens to collective action. Vygotsky argued that "In the school age the child goes through an important critical stage in his cultural development. Labor becomes possible for him and with it the voluntary behavior that distinguishes the labor of man from the instinctive forms of labor of animals" (in Van der Veer, 2020, p. 143). Becoming a part of the collective was a Soviet priority, and children's collectives were the social medium through which they developed into good Soviet citizens, ideally the New Soviet Man. Soviet orthodoxy required psychology to orient itself to the collective, to the everyday laborer, to the Soviet mission, so Vygotsky aligned himself with the dogma that state leaders demanded. Within a children's collective, "Every playing child occupies his 'play position' and performs his role. Characteristic of schoolchildren are the games with rules that regulate the complicated interaction of the playing collective" (in Van der Veer, 2020, p. 146).

Symbolic Play, Words, and Self-Regulation

Vygotsky tied play to his semiotic emphasis on word meaning and its role in concept development, articulated most fully in *Thinking and Speech* (1987). Play, he argued, becomes subject to self-regulation through the use of verbal signs that help children orient themselves conceptually to cultural systems of thought through which governing rules emerge. Play

> is the main channel of cultural development of the child, and specifically of the development of his symbolic activity. Experiments show that in play and in speech, consciousness of conditionality, of the arbitrariness of uniting sign and meaning, is foreign to the child. In order to be a sign for a thing, a word must be supported by the properties of the thing signified. Not "everything can be anything" in the child's play. In play, real properties of the thing and its symbolic significance exhibit a complex structural interaction. In the same way, for the child, the word is coupled with the thing through its properties and is interwoven in their general structure. For this reason, in our experiments, the child does not agree that the floor might be called a tumbler ("you couldn't walk on it"), but he makes a chair a train, changing its properties in the game, that is, treating it as a train. The child refuses to change meanings of the words "table" and "lamp"[2] because "you could not write on a lamp and a table would burn." For him to change the name means to change the properties of the thing.
>
> (1999, p. 9)

To Vygotsky (1997c), "a child's symbolic play may ... be understood as a very complex system of speech aided by gestures that supplement and indicate the meaning of individual toys" such that they ultimately take on a symbolic meaning (p. 135). This symbolic quality, available through the self-regulation learned through play via verbal means, contributes to a child's personality development via social experience. This process critically involves

> the formation of internal speech that now becomes the child's main tool for thinking. If at the stage of play, the child thinks and acts in a mixed way and thinking of some activity embodied in signs, moves directly to dramatization, that is, to a factual carrying out of the activity, then the thinking and action of the school-age child are more or less separated from each other. In play, we see a unique form of using signs:

for the child, the process of play itself, that is, the use of signs itself, is still closely linked with entering into the meaning of these signs, into imaginary activity; in this case, the child uses the sign not as a means, but as a goal in itself.

(1997c, p. 250)

Play is thus fundamental to human development. Through play, a child learns how to articulate in words the symbolic environment that guides the socialization process. Play, Vygotsky (1999) contended,

> is the basic path of the child's cultural development and specifically the development of his sign activity. Experiments show that in play and speech, the child is far from recognizing the voluntary established connection between the sign and the meaning. In order to become a sign of a thing (word), the stimulus must be supported by the qualities of the object itself that is denoted. Not all things are equally important for the child in such play. The real qualities of the object and their sign meaning enter into complex structural interrelations in the play. Thus, for the child, the word is connected with the object through its qualities and included in a common structure with it. For this reason, in our experiments, the child does not agree to call the floor a mirror ... but converts a chair into a train, which acquires its qualities in his play, that is, he manipulates it as a train.

(p. 52)

In this sense, the imagination may enable a broom to become a mounted horse in that it can be adapted to horse-like actions; yet the broom would be difficult to imagine to be a floor to be walked on. Vygotsky allowed that "in play anything can be everything" (p. 135), although some correspondence to its referent is necessary for a tool of play to serve a specific social purpose. In play, argued Vygotsky (1997c), "some objects can very easily represent others, replace them and become their signs. We also know that in this case the similarity that exists between the toy and the object that is represents is not important. Most important is its functional use, the possibility of using it to produce the representing gesture" (p. 134).

Play is thus not a strictly physical activity engaged in by children to exercise their bodies and personalities. Play initiates, in contrast,

> the beginning of ideational behavior. The play activity of the child proceeds outside real perception—in an imaginary situation.... . [T]he very essence of child play is the creation of an imaginary situation, i.e., a certain semantic field which transforms the child's whole behavior and forces him to be governed in his actions and deeds solely by these imaginary situations and not by the visual situation. The content of these imaginary situations always indicates that they develop in the world of adults.

(1997b, p. 229)

Ultimately, he argued, "Play is self-education; what corresponds to it in the adolescent is a complex and long process of transforming tendencies into human needs and interests [via] a complex and real synthesis of the one and the other, a transformation of tendency into interest is the true key to the problem of the transitional [adolescent] age" (1998, p. 28). In adolescence, he asserted, biological maturity enables children to turn inward, to play mentally with ideas without a material playground to accommodate the imagination.

This age is thus critical for socialization, for turning the cultural intent of games into real, self-regulated understandings and actions that advance both the individual and the social group.

Imagination

Vygotsky's perspective emphasized the role of the imagination in envisioning possibilities within constraints. As is the case with emotions (see Chapter 7), the imagination—to Vygotsky, the capacity to envision what is not materially present—and creativity—an application of the imaginative function—are subject to the temperance of the intellect. This self-regulation develops over time in relation to social experience. The young child, contrary to popular understanding, is less creative than a mature adult, who has developed a wide range of experiences and thus has more possibilities to project an image to govern present or future action.

Furthermore, adult cultural conceptions follow from imaginative projections constructed during play. Vygotsky (1998) related how "one of the essential changes that fantasy undergoes during the transitional age [adolescence] is actually a liberation from purely concrete, graphic factors and, together with this, a penetration into it of elements of abstract thinking" (p. 157). Abstract thinking, which is promoted in school, which is a socializing institution, represents the cultural values and perspectives of a social group, and so varies by community of practice. What is imagined, then, is suggested by how the social environment shapes students' development. Vygotsky asserted that one could not develop a collectivist frame of mind in a capitalist society founded on individual competition and the hoarding of goods; nor could Monopoly be adapted to Soviet society without a socialist twist. What was imaginable to the sequestered Soviet mind thus was distinctively a product of the broader societal values and practices of the nation, even as the Bolsheviks sought to produce a revolutionary continent based on proletarian class affiliation rather than nationality.

As a child moves into adolescence, imaginative play is increasingly a mental phenomenon. It develops initially in material engagement and, through the use of meaning-laden signs—especially words—becomes possible strictly in thought. A child, he argued, can distinguish between the real world and the play world. The child knows intellectually that a broom is not a horse, even if it can be imagined to be one. This distinction ultimately enables material playthings to be discarded, with the mental tasks shifted to symbolic thinking during adolescence. The child "replaces play with imagination [i.e., the child plays mentally more than physically]. When the child stops playing [in the physical world], he really rejects nothing other than seeking support in real objects. In place of play, he now fantasizes" through the imagination (1998, pp. 157–158).

During this process the adolescent's imagination loses its dependence on the immediate concrete situation, either of a play situation or other activity in which the imagination is at work in the present environment. Vygotsky (1998) was adamant about

> the progressing abstractness of his fantasy... . [T]he child's fantasy is significantly poorer than the adolescent's fantasy, that only owing to the easy excitability of feelings, the intensity of experience, and uncritical quality of judgments does it occupy a greater place in the behavior of the child and for this reason seems to us to be richer and well developed. Thus, we see that the fantasy of the adolescent does not become poorer, but becomes richer than the child's fantasy.
>
> (p. 161)

In adolescence, "the abstract enters as a requisite constituent into the activity of imagination, but is not the center of this activity" (1998, p. 163). This capacity for (to Vygotsky, largely verbal) abstraction allows for communication, planning, and goal-setting. These abstract abilities allow humans to coordinate action to exert greater control over their environments:

> Not only artistic works are produced with the help of fantasy, but also all scientific inventions and all technical constructions. Fantasy is one of the manifestations of man's creative activity, and specifically in the transitional [adolescent] age, approaching thinking in concepts, it undergoes broad development in this objective aspect.... In fantasy he anticipates his future and, consequently, also creatively approaches its construction and implementation.
>
> (1998, p. 165)

Here Vygotsky revealed his reliance on both social and biological maturation to account for changes during the life cycle. In adolescence, he argued,

> on the basis of sexual maturation, a new and complex world arises with new tendencies, strivings, motives, and interests, new movers of behavior and its new directions; new motive forces push the thinking of the adolescent forward, and new tasks open before him. We saw further that these new tasks lead to the development of the central and leading function of all mental development—to the formation of concepts—and we saw how on the basis of the formation of concepts, some completely new mental functions develop, how on the new base, perception, memory, attention, and practical activity of the adolescent are restructured, and *what is the main thing, how they unite in a new structure, how gradually a foundation is laid for higher syntheses of personality and world view*. Now, with an analysis of imagination, we see again how these new forms of behavior, bound in their origin to sexual maturation and connected with it by drives, serve the emotional strivings of the adolescent, how in creative imagination, the emotional and intellectual aspects of the adolescent's behavior find a complex synthesis, how in it are synthesized abstract and concrete points, how sexual drive and thinking are complexly combined in a new unit—in the activity of this creative imagination.
>
> (1998, pp. 165–166; emphasis added)

Among the facets of imagination that some might find surprising is the degree to which imitation is involved (see Chapter 5). As emphasized throughout his writing, Vygotsky viewed human socialization as central to development. People become like the people who surround them, especially in their formative years. Children from infancy mimic the behavior of the adults around them, which is why a person growing up in the United States Bible Belt is much more likely to become a Christian than is a person in Saudi Arabia. People become socialized through their adoption of the behaviors and thought patterns that surround them, and this appropriation comes in large part through imitation.

He did not see imitation as unthinking mimetic activity, however. Rather, he saw imitation as a constructive, imaginative way of adopting social norms. He rejected the belief "that reduces the essence of imitation to the simple formation of habits and to recognize imitation as a substantial factor in the development of higher forms of human behavior" (1997c, p. 96). These higher forms of behavior are the cultural ways of engaging with the world learned through social experiences. The adoption of norms is both imitative and creative, each serving as an important dimension of human growth in social contexts.

Games

"Gamification" is a relatively recent addition to the educational vocabulary. Gaming involves learning through what Gayol, Rosas, and Smagorinsky (2020) have called *ludic* activities: Those that include learning through playful activities that feature game-like characteristics, such as rewards, levels of achievement, and other elements undertaken either cooperatively or competitively, or in cooperative teams competing against one another or against the game itself. Gamification involves "learning content and practicing literacy skills as if they were playing a game, making the educational experience both challenging and fun" (Kingsley & Grabner-Hagen, 2015), although to Vygotsky, "fun" is not the point of playing games and may not be involved at all. Such "serious games" (Van der Spek & van Oostendorp, 2011, p. 741) are being adapted from video games, board games, and other gaming platforms to enable greater engagement in school learning (Johnson & Kim, 2021).

Games also may socialize youth into worldviews that may work against other forms of socialization. Cooper and Zimmerman (2011) report that a host of studies conclude that violent video games are associated with a range of anti-social, often violent real-world actions. In simpler times, the "Cowboys and Indians" game I played in childhood with finger guns positioned Indians in subordinate roles, a hierarchical depiction that we internalized, reinforced by the many such images in the media of the day, exacerbated by the absence of any Native American people to disconfirm the stereotypes. I was amazed when I lived in Oklahoma in the 1990s, a US state with a high Native American population, and during playtime little kids played "Cowboys and Indians," with Native American kids playing Cowboys and shooting up the designated Indians. Vygotsky might have envisioned such a possible form of socialization as this latter example provides, even though he didn't write about it in the works I consulted; he tended to view socialization as positive, as the means by which a national identity around an ideological position could be cultivated. He could never have imagined the 21st century video game market and games like Grand Theft Auto, in which players engage in all manner of criminal activities. In 2013, an 8-year-old boy in Slaughter, Louisiana, killed his 88-year-old grandmother after playing the game (Russell, 2013), suggesting that Vygotsky's favorable view toward games requires exceptions in the online era.

In Vygotsky's (1997a) early work in educational psychology, he advocated for a strong role for games in school learning, tied to the Soviet industrial project of the 1920s and 1930s. An occupational education, he argued,

> teaches subordination and mastery simultaneously, illuminating all the moral drawbacks of both. In this sense, the educational effect of industrial labor fully recalls the educational effect of games, where the child senses himself forever linked to a whole network of complex rules, and where, in addition, he is taught not only to obey these rules, but also to subordinate the behavior of others to these rules and to act within the strict guidelines established by the conditions of the game period.
>
> (p. 192)

As a form of play, a game involves learning the boundaries set by rules and by social relationships that are managed in group settings, even as anarchy might be available to the

21st-century video gamer. "Children's games," Vygotsky maintained, "are very nearly the most valuable of all tools for the education of the instincts" (1997a, p. 88), because

> nearly all of our most fundamental and most characteristic reactions are created and developed in the course of the games we play as children. It is this which is the meaning of the element of *imitation* in children's games; the child deliberately copies and assimilates what he sees in adults, thereby learning about relationships, and develops his earliest instincts, instincts that he will have need for in his future activity.
>
> (1997a, p. 89; emphasis in original)

Vygotsky saw rule-bound games as providing the socialization for how to grow into a cultural adult. His notion of the cultural adult as a model might come into conflict with the development of Nazi board games, such as Juden Raus! [Jews Out!], in which

> Using crude antisemitic stereotypes and imagery, the game's themes reflect racial hatred, forced deportations, and confiscation of Jewish property. The board shows a walled town, through which players move to round up Jews and deposit them outside the city walls, where a slogan reads "Auf nach Palästina!" (English: "Off to Palestine!") The winner is the first to remove six people.
>
> (The Wiener Holocaust Library, n.d.)

The instincts Vygotsky described were learned, not inborn dispositions such as those which move birds to migrate and salmon to swim upstream to their natal spawning grounds. Children aren't born Nazis, but can be socialized by games and other means to become Nazis. The games might be competitive, or might involve individual play with props and tools. A girl playing with dolls, he noted,

> learns not how to relate to a real-life child, but rather what it feels like to be a mother. This is how to view those elements of imitation that are brought into games; that is, they promote the child's active mastery of various aspects of life and, along the same lines, give a sense of discipline to his inner experience. Other so-called building games, i.e., those involving working with materials, teach us how to make our movements precise and sure-footed, develop thousands of the most valuable habits, and diversify and multiply our reactions. These sorts of games teach us how to set ourselves a particular goal and how to organize our movement so as to guide ourselves to the realization of this goal. Thus, these games provide the first lessons in systematic and rational activity, in the coordination of movement, and in the ability to guide one's own organs and control them. In other words, they are the guides and teachers of our external experience, just as the former games serve as guides of our inner experience… . Such a game is a vital social and collective experience of the child, and in this sense it constitutes an entirely irreplaceable tool for the inculcation of social skills and habits.
>
> (1997a, p. 90)

The progressive 21st-century reader might find Vygotsky's gendered assumptions about girls and dolls to be archaic; and that is because they are. More modern conceptions of gendered identity not only have changed expectations within the traditional male-female binary, they have expanded understandings of sexuality that enable different roles for any individual, unless politicians develop laws that enforce heteronormativity. In Vygotsky's day, and continuing into the present, however, there remain gendered assumptions, including "gender reveal" events in which a child's sex is established in gestation, setting a gendered identity trajectory prior to birth, likely reinforced in multiple ways throughout their upbringing. Vygotsky's life and career ended well before more current sensibilities emerged; and those sensibilities are not shared by all, either in the English-speaking world where LGBTQ+ rights are continually under attack by social conservatives, and in Putin-era Russia where old homophobic tropes are being used to justify his invasion of Ukraine and other geopolitical actions (Edenborg, 2022).

Games serve more than the development of individual motor skills and emotional regulation. They enable one to function socially. Education, Vygotsky (1997a) wrote, ought to contribute to

> the development and polishing of particularly subtle forms of social interaction. In fact, social relations in the present epic have become vast not only in terms of scale, they are also vast in terms of degree of differentiation and complexity. Formally, social relations were confined to a small group of stereotypical relationships, and the course of man's social behavior encompassed more or less completely the ordinary rules of everyday courtesy. Together with the growing complexity of life, the individual now finds himself involved in increasingly more complicated and more highly diverse social relations, he is a member of the most diverse social groups, and therefore the full multiplicity of modern man's social relations cannot be confined to any sort of preset collection of skills and habits. Rather, the goal of education is to develop, not a definite quantity of skills, but particular creative capacities for rapid and skillful social orientation.
>
> (p. 91)

As is the case of every generation, the children of Vygotsky's time were faced with a society of growing complexity to which adaptations were necessary. Society's complexity and diversity may have multiplied exponentially a century later, along with the availability of the digital gaming industry. Games thus have had a role in socialization regardless of epoch. Games promote social engagement, and social engagement enables more complex gaming and thus greater socialization. To Vygotsky, games were key means of enabling more mature thinking in relation to a multiplicity of experiences with others in imaginative action. Games teach people how to be members of communities of practice and citizens of the social groups with which they participate, for good or ill. Within the confines of rules and practices governing games, those playing them are met with virtually infinite possibilities and outcomes—although being a socialist Monopoly player might prove challenging—that require their social coordination with others, and rely on flexibility and creative thinking. Few areas of education, he believed, enable such developmental possibilities.

Vygotsky (1997a) emphasized the regulatory function of playing within rule-bound settings. This dimension enables both social participation according to expectations, and self-regulation during the game and in its aftermath. Verbal control in inner speech becomes available for reflection and the planning of future action. He argued that "By subordinating all the behavior to special conventional rules, games are the first medium to teach the child rational and conscious behavior." He continued,

> Games are the child's first school of thought. Every form of thinking arises as a response to a particular difficulty, as a consequence of a new or difficult encounter with

the elements of one surroundings. Wherever there is no such difficulty, wherever our surroundings are fully known to us and our behavior proceeds effortlessly and unimpeded, as if it's simply a matter of adjusting to our surroundings, there is no thinking, there wherever one looks are gears and linkages turning. But as soon as the environment presents us with any kind of new and unanticipated position on the board that requires in our ways of behaving likewise new moves and new reactions and quick reorientation of our activity, there thinking arises, as a special anticipatory stage of behavior, as an internal ordering of more complex forms of experience whose psychological essence reduces ultimately to choosing, from out of the set of all possible reactions that present themselves to us, only those that are needed in light of the basic goal which behavior is now called upon to achieve.

(p. 92)

Games require schematic knowledge of the game's features, which tend to represent some real-world activity (e.g., the real estate knowledge built into Monopoly, and the socialist twist required for its conversion to Manager). These schemata are cultural (Cole, 1996), situated within value systems and histories. They enable the metacognitive application of this knowledge to new situations with the help of abstract thinking that enables adaptations to changes in the field of play or endeavor.

As noted, Vygotsky (1997a) saw games as being both individual (a child playing with a toy, such as a doll, which socializes the child to a worldview and related role) or competitive. The competition of games, to Vygotsky, has particular salience in promoting development. Although collaboration and cooperation have often been asserted as ideal means of being educated (Laal & Laal, 2012), Vygotsky argued that people develop *against obstacles*, such as the actions of opponents in competitive games. Contrast this emphasis on overcoming obstructions with the ways in which many adults act as helicopter (hovering), lawnmower (creating unobstructed pathways), and jackhammer (blasting away perceived barriers) parents to create easy pathways to success for their children (Treleaven, 2022). Using language that indicates his early indebtedness to Pavlov, Vygotsky argued that

Thinking arises out of a clash of reactions and out of a selection of some of these reactions under the influence of anticipatory reactions. But it is just this clash and just this process of selection which makes it possible—once, that is, certain rules are introduced into a game and the possibilities of behavior are, thereby, restricted, where, in addition, the child's behavior is given the task of attaining a definite goal, all the child's instinctive capacities being strained to the utmost and his interest being stretched to the highest degree—that it becomes possible to induce the child to discipline his behavior in such a way that it obeys certain rules, that it points in the direction of a single goal, that it solves certain problems deliberately.

(1997a, pp. 92–93)

Games in this sense are not leisure pursuits or distractions from the serious business of learning. Durkin and Barber (2002) review how many adults believe that video gaming is a diversion from schoolwork and responsibilities, a mindless distraction, and an impediment to the development of social skills. They take the opposing perspective that video games, as Vygotsky asserts, are instead developmental tools through which players learn social conventions. This perspective runs contrary to what many believe about how excessive videogaming affects children, youth, and adults in ways that stunt their social and emotional growth and produce violent behavior (Dunckley, 2015). Vygotsky's attention to games long preceded the more addictive forms of gaming via video platforms (Griffith, Kuss, & King, 2012), often with violence as a key feature, and this factor figures into how people interpret gaming in the 21st century.

Regardless of how one understands the value of electronic games, to Vygotsky a game using material means encourages

> a rational and appropriate, methodical, and socially coordinated system of behavior or consumption of energy, subordinated to different definite rules. Thus does it disclose its complete analogy with the consumption of the adult's energy and work, the features of which fully coincide with the features of a game. The only difference is that the results which, in the labor process, are expressed in a definite, objective outcome, which one also has in mind ahead of time, in the game are expressed in a certain conventional affective satisfaction, which is resolved subjectively within the individual player himself, in the form of pleasure which he gains from winning a game. Thus notwithstanding all the objective differences that exist between play and work, which would even lead us to consider them polar opposites, they possess absolutely the same psychological nature. This underscores the fact that games are the natural form of work in children, a form of activity which is inherent to the child, as preparation for his life in the future.
>
> (1997a, p. 93)

Gaming, then, is a form of socialization to the demands of labor, a paradox that represents the dialectical understanding of human development that runs throughout Vygotsky's writing.

Games and Moral Development

Games are an early form of the labor through which a person develops as a social being. This socialization includes learning the principles underlying moral action. Vygotsky (1997a) saw play and gaming as a means for the development of morality in relation to social norms, under the assumption that moral codes are local to societies and not universal, as has often been claimed in US character education programs (e.g., Lickona, 1991). Vygotsky believed that following a moral command is ineffective; that presenting people with rules to follow will never enable them to internalize those rules to guide their own conduct. "This is why," he claimed,

> the worst of all pedagogical techniques is to insistently and earnestly introduce into the mind of the student and awareness of those deeds he must not do. Telling him, 'Don't do that' is already an incitement to carrying out this deed, simply by virtue of the fact that it introduces into the student's mind the thought of this deed, and consequently, the inclination to carry it out.
>
> (1997a, p. 160).

Rather than following adult didactic imperatives and commands in school, he argued, "The idea that the child's own will is his best teacher is still very much alive in pedagogics" (p. 234).

People thus need to *feel* the moral understandings they reach in deep, psychological ways. They need to develop moral codes inductively (cf. Smagorinsky & Taxel, 2004, 2005) both to meet cultural standards, and to satisfy their own notion of virtue. Vygotsky (1997a) wrote, "The authoritarian principle and morality from which this authority must have emanated in one way or another must be demolished, and in its place something entirely new must be erected." Moral education requires "the social coordination of one's own behavior with the behavior of the group, and here obedience must be replaced throughout by free social coordination." A moral code comes about through a recognition that rules provide a fair playing field, and so requires self-discipline to maintain the integrity of the game, and eventually of labor. "Pedagogical singsong" is inadequate to enabling

> the free adoption of those patterns of behavior which will vouchsafe the consonance of all of behavior.... . Nowhere is the child's behavior so regulated by rules as in play, and nowhere does it assume such a free and morally instructive form as in play. Nowhere in play do we find any patterns whatsoever that an adult might have prescribed and which the child only enact. On the contrary, games are the natural seedlings of future moral behavior. The child obeys the rules of a game, not because he is threatened with punishment or, on the other hand, because he is scared of failing in something or losing something, but only because observing the rules—which is a promise that he renews from one minute to the next—vouchsafes him the inner satisfaction that comes from playing a game, because here he acts as part of the general enterprise that is formed out of a group at play. Breaking a rule does not represent any threat whatsoever, other than the fact that, at that moment, the game has not worked out, and the child has lost interest in it, and this is a powerful enough incentive for regulating the child's behavior.
>
> (p. 233)

Vygotsky believed that games ought to play a greater role in education for all of these reasons. In his conception, the moral dimensions of playing games would obviate the possibilities of cheating, an outcome that unfortunately is often violated; indeed, a "cheat" is often available to video gamers as a shortcut. It doesn't help that adults provide models of how to cheat, which is not just a problem in capitalist societies; Solzhenitsyn (1973) reports countless instances of Soviet prison employees stealing from incarcerated dissidents (or accused dissidents). Although games are often thought to be trivial and a distraction from real intellectual work (Okamura, 2013), Vygotsky found them to have tremendous potential for promoting learning in school. Whether they promote moral behavior no doubt depends on how they are managed, and whether or not the game itself and the society it epitomizes have a moral foundation.

Games and Emotions

In Chapter 11, I review Vygotsky's understanding of how interest should be central to schooling, and no doubt games are very interesting to young people (and old). Yet this focus on their capacity to engage a player may suggest to some that games are not part of a rigorous academic curriculum; that they serve to amuse more than to educate. Vygotsky (1997a) took issue with such thinking as part of his critique of the abstract nature of schooling, one that both distances learning from praxis, and reduces the emotional investment a child has in learning. Regulating emotions through the intellect's conscious attention, he argued, does not suppress feelings. It subordinates them such that

> feelings are bound up with the other forms of behavior and guided in the appropriate directions. One example of such rational employment of the feelings we might cite are the intellectual feelings, i.e., feelings such as curiosity, interest, wonder, and the like which arise in immediate association with intellectual activity and which guide this activity in most explicit fashion. [Games constitute] the best means of disciplining emotional behavior. The child's games are always emotional, there are always strong and vivid feelings in these games, though they teach the child not to follow emotions blindly, but to make them conform to the rules of the game and to the ultimate goal of the game period. Thus, games are the first forms of conscious behavior, arising on the basis of instinctive and emotional behavior. They are the best tool for the integrated education of all these diverse forms of behavior and for establishment of the proper coordination and interdependence between them.
>
> (p. 109)

Games enable children to experience winning and losing, and doing so within the bounds of cultural expectations. A "tennis brat" who has never learned how to cope with obstacles and loss can be a pitiful sight, screaming at officials and opponents without the temperance of emotions that Vygotsky found to be a critical component of maturation. Both winning and losing in respectable ways involve graciousness and respect in the broader culture. Learning how to respond to a game's outcome is a matter of enculturation, and thus comprises a key developmental form of action leading to inclusion in a society's ways.

Labor

A Marxist perspective is oriented to continual change in the world. Even inert material like stone is constantly eroding, if imperceptibly. Heraclitus told his student 2,500 years ago, "You cannot step into the same river twice," to which his student replied, "Not even once, since there is no *same* river." The flow of life does not allow for a static conception of how the world works.

For humans, labor serves as a key instrument of change undertaken volitionally by people. Vygotsky, like virtually all psychologists of his time, felt the need to distinguish humans from other animals (see Chapter 5). Labor, in a Marxist conception, is an exclusively human capability. An animal might build a dam, dig a hole, build a nest, raise a brood, and otherwise act on the world. They might do so through the use of material tools, such as when New Caledonian crows extract grubs from tree holes using twigs that they strip and sharpen (Seed & Byrne, 2010). Such actions, however, do not meet the Marxist definition of labor.

Vygotsky accepted the Marxist principle that "'work created man himself' (Marx & Engels, [1985], p. 486), that is, created the higher mental functions that mark man as man. Using a stick, primitive man masters from outside, with the help of a sign, processes of his own behavior and subordinates his actions to a goal, making external objects serve his activity" (1999, p. 64). The crow using a sharpened twig might be said to be doing the same thing, yet without such conscious attention and deliberate, future-oriented action. A crow has never imagined that nest-building might be expanded, that perhaps a crow condominium community might work more effectively than a single nest to produce a more secure avian society.

Labor involves more than the use of the tool itself. What enables labor to become possible is the use of *signs*, such as the speech that helps plan and coordinate activities, the graphic plans that might guide construction in the future, and other means of symbolic expression that allow for humans to orient themselves to a future not available through immediate perception. Vygotsky (1997a) described how vocational education can serve psychological growth into a culture's norms:

> the student's own movements are restored to him in the form of the finished product of the work. This permits him to monitor his own activity and to evaluate his own labor on the basis of the indubitable and objective results of work, and, what is most important, to create the opportunity for realizing a concluding moment of satisfaction, of exultation, of conquest in some sense, thanks to which our strivings and all forms of activity are aroused in essential ways.
>
> (p. 191)

Labor requires a product, which again might describe a crow's use of sticks to nab a tasty grub. A person, however, sees meaning in labor, and that meaning is typically expressed through verbal signs. Meaningful processes and products ought to drive occupational education, Vygotsky argued, rather than the incentive of grades, so that "The more the student's strivings and interests are bound up with this ultimate point of his labor efforts, the more powerful and the more effective will be the coordinating and connective effect of these efforts within the overall system of his reactions" (p. 191). Undoubtedly, the crow is satisfied by the scrumptious reward of the grub, but such contentedness is fleeting, and it will soon go back for more. The human product of labor, in contrast, has a meaning that can be projected into the future.

Labor, argued Vygotsky, enables humans to grow as communities. Animals, too, often live communal lives, from bees to bears. What they can't do is sustain and grow their communities into cultures that advance both within and across generations. Vygotsky claimed, in accordance with Soviet dogma regarding the veneration of the proletarian worker in factories and on collective farms,

> even the most primitive forms of labor require, of necessity, a certain degree of coordination of effort, a certain degree of skill in reconciling one's behavior with the behavior of other people, and in coordinating and monitoring one's reaction so that they can become a constituent component of the general fabric of collective behavior. This is why labor, especially in its higher end industrial forms, always signifies the greatest school of social experience. One psychologist has said that nowhere does man learn genuine courtesy and foresight as in the modern factory, since it teaches everyone to coordinate his own movements with the movements of others in as meticulous a fashion as possible.
>
> (1997a, p. 192)

Undoubtedly, this account of the value of factory work has a very Soviet ring to it. Yet the modern capitalist member of a technology company might make the same claims about learning how to coordinate activities with others (Tripathy, 2018). What is critical is the distinctively human notion of labor that Vygotsky's Marxist account provides. Animals may hunt in packs, and colonies of insects have a division of labor that works in factory-like fashion. Teamwork in the natural world is abundant. What this teamwork lacks is the human capacity for conscious awareness of how to work collectively toward ends that are not within their sensory range. Seeing beyond the palpable enables humans to anticipate and prepare for future events that are not yet discernable. The use of imaginative play enables, according to Vygotsky (1997a) "a form of behavior directed towards forms that have not yet occurred in our experience" (p. 153), and thus serves a developmental role in one's socialization to cultural labor and a future orientation.

His view of labor as a means of learning social relationships and collective action led Vygotsky to be a great advocate of "occupational education," a good fit with the Soviet industrial emphasis that gave the proletariat status and constructed the bourgeois as enemies of state to be annihilated. "In occupational education," he said, "there occurs a fusion and integration of the entire pedagogical process, an organic unification of all its components into a single whole, and this cyclic character of occupational education emphasizes even more clearly that all the successive stages of this process form and complete close a complete circle" (1997a, p. 194).

Trade school and occupational education, Vygotsky (1997a) believed, enable "an entirely new view of labor, understood as the very foundation of the educational process. In such a purely trade school, labor is introduced not as a subject of teaching, nor as a method or tool of teaching, but as the very substance of education. In the felicitous phrase of one educator, not only is labor introduced into the school, but the school is introduced into labor," a possibility that "underlies the Soviet system of education" (p. 182).

This focus was consistent with his materialist view that action in the world is a critical means of growth, a belief that influenced his view that schooling that emphasizes abstraction, with little practical application, is hollow. He held this view even as he maintained that the capacity for abstraction, and thus future planning, is a distinctly human capacity that should be cultivated in school. "The only criterion of knowledge," he argued, "is its vital value, its need in the real world, i.e., the principle of practicality" (1997a, p. 198):

> every pedagogical science that has treated knowledge in isolation from praxis has virtually always produced entirely unwarranted efforts and, from the psychological point of view, has acquired the character of fruitless Sisyphean labor, like pouring water into a bottomless pit. The common perplexity of gymnasts [teachers in the most advanced of the three types of German secondary schools] underscores, quite eloquently the meaninglessness of the labor that falls to the lot of students.
>
> (p. 195)

Simply doing problems assigned by a teacher, he argued, "is quite pointless, is not needed for anything, and is, for all intents and purposes, worthless" (1997a, p. 195), leading students to reject school learning, which devalues their labor. Praxis—the enactment, embodiment, or realization of abstract or theoretical thinking in practical action—is what matters most. The intellect serves as the guide of praxis, but without material action, it amounts to little: "Praxis constitutes the ultimate test that any scientific discipline may be subjected to" (p. 200). But in school, truth is presented "in the form of an abstract theoretical rule, attained not in the course of a search and of labor, but as if in purely mental work period. It was never related to the vital needs that gave rise to it, nor to the vital conclusions that flowed from it" (pp. 200–201).

Material productivity, action in the physical world, is the final and greatest outcome of thinking, and this productivity comes from labor. Here Vygotsky sounded like a rank-and-file Marxist and advocate for Soviet industrial society, with collective farms (which worked better in theory than in practice, in which many millions of Soviets perished; see Snyder, 2010) a critical arena for putting labor to good use. Social and political changes, he argued per Engels, follow from changes in economics of the period, the means of production and distribution, not changes in people's minds or in philosophy.

It may be paradoxical that Vygotsky critiqued philosophy through the writings of a philosopher, and that he elsewhere (Vygotsky, 1987) asserted the importance of learning abstract thinking in school, albeit always grounded in practical action. Vygotsky—still in his 20s when he wrote the account from which I have quoted—articulated views that were entirely consistent with the views of Marx and Engels, the architects of communist ideology. He appears to have maintained his value on labor, on human action in the world, across his own development as a psychologist, and during his own fall from Soviet grace as Stalin undertook his deadly purges of dissent from orthodoxy (see Part IV). Human labor, Vygotsky maintained during his career, enables the construction of the material and psychological worlds in ways that contribute to the development of societies through the intentional action designed to bring nature, society, and the self under greater intellectual and material control. Play in childhood provides the formative developmental process that leads to human labor.

Discussion

This chapter has concerned play and labor, two developmentally critical forms of action that appear quite different, but in fact are fundamentally related. Vygotsky's early, optimistic, idealistic view of the new Soviet society undoubtedly led him to underestimate the ways in which power corrupts ideologies and idyllic conceptions of the optimal society. In some of his earlier writing, he spoke rhapsodically about Soviet communism in ways that were easily contradicted by Stalin's genocidal personality, and his murder and imprisonment of anyone considered a dissident, or a friend of a dissident, or an acquaintance of a dissident, or an innocent citizen who was named by someone after a lengthy, brutal interrogation (Solzhenitsyn, 1973).

Nonetheless, Vygotsky's notions of play and labor as cultural activities have resonance beyond the confines of Soviet society. Socialization requires young people to take on the outlooks and practices of their elders, which involves imitating their speech and actions without being slavishly dependent on them, and ultimately relies on adapting those imitated thoughts and actions to new conditions via individual thinking independent of corporeal activity. Games embody these outlooks and practices, requiring gamers to learn how to play according to moral codes that result in fair play, again with the caveat that not all games serve moral development or the creation of a fair and just society. This ideal has often been violated by coaches and parents who model bad behavior, who then pass it down to children under their supervision (Shields, Bredemeier, Lavoi, & Power, 2005).

Ideally, the immediate sensory environment provides feedback that enforces boundaries—physical, interactional, and psychological—that are learned and eventually become available in the mind as guiding structural constraints and affordances. This internalized set of conventions is represented symbolically—to Vygotsky, primarily with meaning-laden, conceptual words—in mental activity that enables people to envision possibilities beyond the immediately perceptible, especially as future action is concerned. Play, games, imagination, emotion, and labor thus figure prominently, and in concert, in how people learn how to engage with and act on their cultural worlds.

Play is serious work that leads to serious labor that contributes to psychological development. Beyond Vygotsky's interest in vocational or occupational education designed to produce a productive workforce in industrial settings, the principles he outlined apply to other forms of play in other sorts of societies. Treating his notion of play as anything less contributes to the trivialization of his work in psychology. Simply taking a term he used, such as play, and crediting to him a misrepresentation of his aims only further perpetuates the problem he found with too much social science research, theory, and practice: The selective extraction of points and words and their application to contexts in ways that overlook or distort his meaning.

Notes

1 The six volumes comprise collected works, not complete, and so do not include much of Vygotsky's oeuvre.
2 Vygotsky's lamps were not illuminated by electricity, but by flames.

9 The Next Zone of Development (Not the ZPD)
A Genetic Understanding

As a doctoral student in the 1980s, I was primarily influenced by information processing theory. I had never heard of Vygotsky and was a bit annoyed that a new name had surfaced during my studies that people were fussing about. By the early 1990s, Vygotsky was on the tip of everyone's tongue, and I knew I needed to get out there and learn something about him. The mysteriously named "Zone of Proximal Development" had crept its way into countless publications and was invoked behind the podiums of every conference I attended and splashed across conference screens via the technology of the overhead projector. This "ZPD" appeared to be a panacea, along with its conjoined twin "scaffolding." The terms became synonymous with Vygotsky then and remain so now. Earlier this year, a neighbor who does autism research asked me what I was up to, and I responded that I was working on a book about Vygotsky. "Ah," he said, then carefully enunciated, "The Zone of Proximal Development." He wasn't sure what it was. But he knew that it meant "Vygotsky."

But back to my post-doctorate days. After seeing and hearing so many references to Vygotsky, I decided to read *Mind in Society*, the first and most widely referenced of Vygotsky's collections to be published in the United States, to see what everyone was talking about. I was especially interested in the now-ubiquitous Zone of Proximal Development, which had the profession abuzz. When I read the chapter featuring the ZPD in the collection, "Interaction between Learning and Development," I approached it almost in awe: I would finally find out the meaning behind this exotic term, in the words of this celebrated educator and psychologist. I hoped to learn about instructional scaffolding, the term developed by Jerome Bruner based on his reading of the earliest translation of what was rendered, in 1962, as *Thought and Language*. To Bruner, scaffolding embodied a pedagogical manifestation of the ZPD. And that's how the educators interested in psychology erroneously came to know Vygotsky: As a pedagogue of the sort he never was.

When I read this chapter, and its phrasing of the ZPD construct, I felt great affirmation of myself as a teacher, especially given how Bruner adapted Vygotsky to teaching through the scaffolding metaphor. I felt so good in large part *because I was already scaffolding instruction in my teaching*. I had learned to teach by providing initial support of learning a skill or building an understanding, having students work on related problems in small groups as a "weaning" stage, and then having them perform independently to indicate how well they'd adopted the knowledge in their own thinking and writing.

I was also pleased that the description of the ZPD in *Mind and Society* authenticated my belief that students have potential that can be fostered through carefully planned instruction, rather than having an intelligence quotient, or fixed ability that they carried across the lifespan. I'd seen many students perform above their presumed ability levels, and many

DOI: 10.4324/9781003374848-11

more perform beneath what their school status suggested was their intelligence. I was convinced that people's capabilities could be fostered through the right methods, that the right methods were available to me via scaffolding, and that by scaffolding I was a Vygotskian teacher. To have my instruction validated by Vygotsky, Bruner, the ZPD, and the use of scaffolding gave quite a retroactive boost to my teaching and provided me with a way to talk about instruction as a teacher educator in universities. I was fully on board with this program, as were the others studying along with me and my major professor, who claimed a Vygotskian influence through his emphasis on instructional scaffolding (Hillocks, 1995).

Several things happened to disturb my contentedness. First, in attending both research and practitioner conferences, I found that no matter what they were doing, everyone claimed to be a Vygotskian ZPD-inspired instructional scaffolder. Any way in which a teacher helped kids learn something was represented as Vygotskian. Scaffolding had come, in short order, to mean all things to all people. The affirmation I'd felt in my own teaching was shared by every teacher whose students were learning from the instruction—the point of instruction—all through scaffolding via Vygotsky. I was concerned that once a construct becomes diffused in this fashion, it loses real meaning.

Relatedly, I began a more extensive reading program of both Vygotsky and the people producing scholarship around him. I'd been tantalized enough by reading *Mind in Society* to read beyond its contents, which were comprised of chapters taken outside the context of their original production. As I ultimately learned, the chapters in *Mind in Society* were translated and edited to provide a smoother read for novices like me (see Notes on Translation). Cazden (1996) has argued that most references to Vygotsky are selective, and employed to fortify an author's pre-existing beliefs. I was guilty of that too, justifying my own practice rather than reconceptualizing prior understandings through a careful and extensive reading of his work.

The more I read, the less I believed that Vygotsky was talking about designing effective lessons that start with support and end in independent performance. His larger body of work was concerned with long-term human development, not lesson planning. It just didn't make sense that his greatest contribution as a developmental psychologist working in a cultural-historical tradition would be to provide a way to structure classroom lessons where the teachers designed sequences for learning strategies and skills for short-term learning.

Since then, a great many more of Vygotsky's works have been translated, and the scholarship base interpreting his ideas has tremendously expanded. I have met few people outside hardcore cultural-historical researchers who have read them or even know about them, however. My own thinking has grown in relation to my engagement with this scholarship, along with my contributions to it. I learn a lot by writing. Although I realize that it might be taken wrong, when I was asked for a feature at my university's website what my "favorite" books were, my response was, "the ones I've written" (https://news.uga.edu/smagorinsky-peter/). They are my favorites not because they are so good, but because I learn the most by putting my thoughts into written words, which fits well with my understanding of Vygotsky's approach to tool-and-sign-mediated human development.

In this chapter, I detail why I reject not only the idea that scaffolding is Vygotskian, I question the translation of his phrase *zona blizhayshevo razvitiya* as the Zone of Proximal Development. The translation itself is misleading and has led to the oversimplification of Vygotsky, reducing him to a lesson planner. It has wrongly and unfortunately changed Vygotsky from a pedologist (concerned with the whole "science of the child" in human development) to a pedagogue (concerned with everyday instruction) through selective, incomplete reading (see Part IV). I next review the issues that have moved me to this conclusion.

The Next Zone of Development

In a set of articles in which I challenge the idea that Vygotsky=ZPD=scaffolding (Smagorinsky, 2018a, 2018b), I borrow a translation from a BBC (1990) broadcast, *The Butterflies of Zagorsk* (a city near Moscow now called Sergiev Posad). The documentary features a school of "defectology" (see Chapter 14) serving blind and deaf children (the titular "butterflies"), in which they learn how to communicate by rapidly spelling words on one another's hands, a long and laborious process complicated by the fact that the children enter with no alphabetic knowledge. Producer Michael Dean's narration refers to the instruction as working within the *Zone of Next Development* (ZND), which I found to be a much clearer representation of what Vygotsky was after than does the established ZPD. That translation's use of "proximal" is confusing because it suggests adjacency rather than human growth into a new stage. The BBC translation makes it clear that long-term development is the focus of the construct, not classroom lesson planning.

More recently, Kellogg and Veresov (2019) have improved on this translation, calling it the *Next Zone of Development* (NZD). They critique the conventional translation by saying,

> the meaning of the Zone of Proximal Development cannot be derived, as has too often been done in educational research, from the constituent parts: "zone" does not refer to a level but rather to the relationship between two different pedologically defined levels; "proximity" must be measured in developmental years rather than in calendar or "passport" years; and "development" is never reducible to learning to do some task without some outside help ... . [S]omething we often see in educational research: the ZPD becomes little more than the belief that the child will learn to do alone whatever he or she is able to do with assistance (something that is both trivial and manifestly untrue of many important interactional skills such as conversation).
> (pp. vii–viii; p. 2)

"Passport" age refers to age as determined by a birth certificate; all Soviets were required, beginning at age 16, to carry an internal passport through which they could be identified by Soviet authorities. Kellogg and Veresov (2019) elaborate on the trivialization promoted through the translation as the Zone of Proximal Development, one that obscures Vygotsky's actual definition of a developmental zone in years and not moments or days:

> Vygotsky's zones of proximal development are not age periods themselves: they are the zones that link and separate the age periods—the zones of potential or possible development for a given child or a group of children and for a given social situation of development. This zone between age periods is likewise measured in years (and this is another detail which often escapes those who have tried to use the ZPD in educational work), but these years are likewise not "passport" years but developmental years.
> (p. 153)

Kellogg (from the United States, now in S. Korea) and Veresov (from Finland, now in Australia) are reputable translators with extensive reading in several languages—Veresov's publications have appeared in 10 languages to date—and are reliable in interpreting their sources. I could be guilty of confirming my own bias by endorsing their perspective, as I was in accepting the Vygotsky=ZPD=scaffolding conflation at the outset of my investigations into his body of work. But I'm confident that their deep reading of Vygotsky in

Russian and translations into English give them authority in these matters. And to them, Vygotsky was not talking about short-term learning.

I have come to see the notion of the NZD as an embodiment of Vygotsky's developmental theory. It is quite different from the daily lesson planning companion that the ZPD has become. It is forward-looking in the deep sense, anticipating development's movement into its next phase, mediated by the social environment as a whole. To a pedologist like Vygotsky (see Part IV), it involves the full "science of the child" that takes into account a wide range of factors in the process of maturation. A set of lesson plans is a relatively minor aspect of that mediation. I next turn to how Vygotsky's developmental approach has been corrupted and minimized by the misdirection provided by the version of the ZPD popularized by Bruner and taken up in educational writing.

Vygotsky, Bruner, and Scaffolding

Vygotsky himself only used a scaffolding metaphor once, employing it to describe how toddlers use furniture for support when first learning to walk:

> Let us recall how the child gradually learns to walk. As soon as his muscles are strong enough, he begins to move about on the ground in the same primitive manner as animals, using a naturally innate mode of locomotion... . The transition to walking is usually not clear-cut. At first the child makes use of external objects, by holding on to them: he makes his way along holding onto the edge of the bed, an adult's hand, a chair, pulling the chair along behind him and leaning on it. In a word, his ability to walk is not yet complete: it is in fact still surrounded, as it were, by the scaffolding of those external tools with which it was created. Within a month or two, however, the child grows out of that scaffolding, discarding it, as no more external help is needed; external tools have now been replaced by newly formed internal neurodynamic processes.
>
> (Vygotsky & Luria, 1993, p. 202; reported in Van der Veer & Valsiner, 1991, p. 226)

Van der Veer (personal communication, August 13, 2018) concludes that Vygotsky's illustration of using furniture while learning to walk demonstrates his general principles that "(1) all higher psychological functions first go through a stage when the child relies on external sign usage; (2) external support can be seen as scaffolds which are no longer needed when the building is ready." There are many differences between Bruner's scaffolding and Vygotsky's example, however. As the above quote indicates, Vygotsky's toddler holds onto available furniture unprompted and with little foresight. Adults did not put the furniture there to support a child's attempts to walk. There is no support available from "adult guidance or in collaboration with more capable peer" (Vygotsky, 1978, p. 86) providing the furniture as support; it appears spontaneously to the child in the course of trying to walk upright.

Vygotsky did not coin scaffolding as a pedagogical term. It's worthwhile to see how the term was introduced to the field by the educational psychologist Bruner. Wood, Bruner, and Ross (1976) describe teacher-directed tutoring sessions that would appear quite authoritarian to many people who have used the scaffolding metaphor to justify an endless array of teaching practices. They came up with the term "instructional scaffolding" in the context of tightly controlled studies of tutoring sessions held for 30 three- to five-year-old children. In this setting, the tutors followed a common protocol for assisting the children's completion of tasks involving manipulatives. Wood et al. describe the tutors as carrying out a

> process that enables a child or novice to solve a problem, carry out a task or achieve a goal which would be beyond his unassisted efforts. This scaffolding consists essentially of the adult "controlling" those elements of the task that are initially beyond the learner's capacity, thus permitting him to concentrate upon and complete only those elements that are within his range of competence. The task thus proceeds to a successful conclusion.... . [T]he learner cannot benefit from such assistance unless one paramount condition is fulfilled. In the terminology of linguistics, *comprehension of the solution must precede production*. That is to say, the learner must be able to *recognize* a solution to a particular class of problems before he is himself able to produce the steps leading to it without assistance.
>
> (p. 90; emphasis in original)

Wood et al. (1976) argue that "Well executed scaffolding begins by luring the child into actions that produce recognizable-for-him solutions," enabling the tutor to "interpret discrepancies to the child... . [T]he tutor stands in a confirmatory role until the tutee is checked out to fly on his own" (p. 96). They explain that scaffolding involves a series of "functions": *recruitment*, which includes "enlist[ing] the problem solver's interest in and adherence to the requirements of the task; *reduction in degrees of freedom*, or "simplifying the task by reducing the number of constituent acts required to reach solution"; *direction maintenance*, or "keeping [the children] in pursuit of a particular objective" and "maintain[ing] direction by making it worthwhile for the learner to risk a next step"; *marking critical features*, or noting discrepancies between the child's performance and more appropriate problem-solving processes; *frustration control*, or reducing stress while not "creating too much dependency on the tutor"; and *demonstration*, or modelling solutions such that the task is idealized for the learner to envision and imitate (p. 98). This process involves the child following adult direction toward the adult's way of doing things. The process is tightly controlled and top-down, with the direction and content of learning set by adults ahead of time.

Langer and Applebee (1983) were instrumental in adapting Wood et al.'s support of children in writing tutorials to more general classroom instruction. Their references indicate that they drew on the same translation of *Thinking and Speech* (the 1962 version, translated as *Thought and Language*) as did Bruner (1978), with the more reliable 1986 and 1987 translations as yet unavailable to them. Wood et al.'s presentation of the scaffolding metaphor was thus relatively new and compelling, offering teachers a way to structure their instruction to provide support that leads to independent learning. Langer and Applebee wrote that

> we can derive a set of criteria for judging the appropriateness of the instructional scaffolding which teachers provide for particular school tasks. These criteria emphasize five aspects of natural language learning: intentionality, appropriateness, structure, collaboration, and internalization:
>
> 1 Intentionality: The task has a clear overall purpose driving any separate activity that may contribute to the whole. Eventual evaluation of students' success can be cast in terms of what they intended to accomplish.

2 Appropriateness: Instructional tasks pose problems that can be solved with help but which students could not successfully complete on their own. The most appropriate tasks will be those that involve abilities that have not yet matured but are in the process of maturation, or in Vygotsky's (1962) terms, abilities that are not so much "ripe" as "ripening."
3 Structure: Modelling and questioning activities are structured around a model of appropriate approaches to the task and lead to a natural sequence of thought and language.
4 Collaboration: The teacher's response to student work recasts and expands upon the students' efforts without rejecting what they have accomplished on their own. The teacher's primary role is collaborative rather than evaluative.
5 Internalization: External scaffolding for the activity is gradually withdrawn as the patterns are internalized by the students.

(p. 170)

Their conception is extrapolated from the very rigid approach described by Bruner (1978) and Wood et al. (1976). As the account reported above suggests, Wood et al.'s conception involved little student agency, a feature included in later adaptations of the scaffolding metaphor to account for teachers' support of students' writing (Hillocks, 1995), literary interpretation (Lee, 1993), and much else.

I am critiquing two things here. First, the initial conception of scaffolding is far more top-down than are many of its adaptations. Second, the translation converts Vygotsky from a pedologist to a pedagogue (see Part IV).

The preschoolers studied by Wood et al. (1977) were heavily directed in their manipulation of blocks and other materials, with guidance toward a pre-conceived endpoint. Such heavy-handed management of student learning is rarely involved in most accounts of scaffolding I'm familiar with, and indeed came under scrutiny by Dyson (1990), who offered the more agentive "weaving" metaphor to give learners greater authority in deciding which way to go, and how to get there. Similarly, Searle (1984) posed the question, "Who's building whose building?" to interrogate the top-down scaffolding procedures described by Bruner and colleagues.

I am not criticizing teaching and teachers who support student's learning in ways that lead to their independent performances. I think that the more agentive understandings of scaffolding provide teachers with a way to help students learn skills and knowledge that enable them to act effectively on their own, and have relied on such instruction in all of my pedagogical writing (e.g., Smagorinsky, 2018e; Smagorinsky, Johannessen, Kahn, & McCann, 2010). I just don't find it to be Vygotskian.

Vygotsky's (1978) notion of the *zona blizhayshevo razvitiya*, like many key ideas, has become trivialized in much educational writing. I can think of three reasons for this problem. First, people who refer to the ZPD have often only read selectively from *Mind in Society* and so take the chapter's content out of context and thus out of any resemblance to the rest of Vygotsky's writing. In doing so, they ignore Vygotsky's developmental theory, making such day-to-day adaptations dubious. Second, because teachers tend to be concerned primarily with short-term learning rather than long-term human development, this notion of "scaffolding" learning is quite appealing because it concerns the immediate results of instruction, which teachers must be accountable for demonstrating. Teachers tend to believe that they are preparing students for their lives beyond school; as tragically deceased teacher-astronaut Christa McAuliffe famously said before perishing in the

1986 Space Shuttle Challenger disaster, "I touch the future. I teach." Yet the pragmatics of schooling typically require them to show their effectiveness through performances on what is specified in the curriculum, and to do so often via frequent grades that amplify the importance of short-term learning. Vygotsky has thus been retrofitted to serve the ends of production-oriented neoliberal education.

The third reason that the ZPD has gone off the rails is that it gets explained in educational psychology textbooks—the source of learning for many readers—in its most reductive form as an information-processing, in-the-head phenomenon that is useful in short-term instructional planning, rather than the sociocultural, historically grounded, socially mediated developmental process that Vygotsky intended.

As a result, at least in educational writing, the ZPD tends to be viewed in this very limited sense of learning with guidance today, doing something similar independently tomorrow. I have found this conception of the ZPD to be problematic for several decades now (e.g., Smagorinsky, 1995b), along with Mercer and Fisher (1992), Chaiklin (2003), and others. Wertsch (1984) was concerned that trivial, uninterrogated use of the ZPD as an explanatory construct would lead it to "be used loosely and indiscriminately, thereby becoming so amorphous that it loses all explanatory power" (p. 7). And that's what's happened.

I have worked through different understandings, using the cultural-historical lens that Wertsch (1984) and others have provided to understand Vygotsky. I have often referenced Moll (1990), who positioned the ZPD as commensurate with "social contexts ... for mastery of and conscious awareness in the use of ... cultural tools" (p. 12), and with school as a context that pathologizes racially and ethnically minoritized students for their socialization to other processes. Moll departs significantly from those who consider the ZPD as a "cognitive region," as claimed by Wilhelm, Baker, and Dube (2001, n.p.), which locates it in the learner's brain rather than as a relationship between the more broadly distributed mind and the historically constructed environment, unfolding over time.

Moll's (1990) account pushed me to think outside the popular learn-today, do-tomorrow version of the ZPD and forced me to understand how any attention to immediate activity must take into account how the present has been formed by the past. Doing so requires that "the ZPD is a characteristic not solely of the child or of the teaching but of the child engaged in collaborative activity within specific social environments. The focus is on the *social system* within which we hope children learn, with the understanding that this social system is mutually and actively created by teachers and students" (Moll, p. 11; emphasis in original). Moll and Whitmore (1993) further propose that understanding learning in classrooms requires attention to social contexts, "on the sociocultural system within which children learn, with the understanding that this system is mutually and actively created by teachers and students. What we propose is a 'collective' Zone of Proximal Development" (p. 20).

Vygotsky was by no means a cognitivist, as suggested by claims that the ZPD is a "cognitive zone." His career project, as Moll and colleagues argue, could be said to be a fight against strictly biological and cognitive understandings of human psychology. Instead, he was primarily concerned with how human environments are established and perpetuated through social practices designed to guide action toward cultural goals. In other words, the ZPD is more than simply what a teacher can do to help a student become more independent by first working collaboratively; or in Wood et al.'s (1977) version, working under the teacher's heavy direction. It is far broader, deeper, and more complex than that conception. It has a developmental, historical, cultural, social, and future-oriented character that cannot be reduced to isolated learning episodes in classrooms. Moll and colleagues moved my thinking in this direction in the 1990s when I began to explore this question; and my subsequent engagement with the ancillary scholarship has been pushed me to expand my understanding further.

The translation as the ZND per *The Butterflies of Zagorsk*, and the *NZD* per Kellogg and Veresov (2019), has complicated Moll's (1990) equation of the ZPD with historically developed social contexts. These more recent interpretations have foregrounded stages (zones) of development over the course of time. The social contexts emphasized by Moll figure strongly into how development is mediated by cultural tools and signs, giving his conception a role in how people become cultural over time. I find the understanding provided via the translation as the NZD to enable the richest version of Vygotsky's concept and the one that fits best in the context of his career body of work.

A Misreading of the Buds and Flowers Metaphor

Vygotsky's (1978) most widely referenced account of the ZPD comes from the collection *Mind in Society*, disentangled from contexts that give it a developmental emphasis. According to this translation, the ZPD consists of

> the distance between the actual developmental level as determined by independent problem solving and the level of potential development as determined through problem solving under adult guidance, or in collaboration with more capable peers. The Zone of Proximal Development defines those functions that have not yet matured but are in the process of maturation, functions that will mature tomorrow but are currently in an embryonic state. These functions could be termed the "buds" or "flowers" of development rather than the "fruits" of development... . [W]hat is in the Zone of Proximal Development today will be the actual developmental level tomorrow—that is what a child can do with assistance today she will be able to do by herself tomorrow.
>
> (pp. 86–87).

This translation may be read in different ways. As I've argued, interpreting any one aspect of Vygotsky's writing requires contextualization with his career project; and removing this context enables selective readings that fit the reader's needs without matching them with Vygotsky's emphasis. The adaptation to scaffolding requires a selective interpretation of his metaphors to suggest a short-term process that in turn translates into a teaching practice. Yet the metaphors can also be read as accounting for the sort of maturation suggested by the *NZD*. The functions, Vygotsky emphasized, are *embryonic*, a developmental notion requiring long-term growth toward the *maturation* that he describes as the goal of instruction. Time and socialization occur between an embryonic and a mature state. Further, he referred to the *buds* or *flowers* of *development* rather than the *fruits* of *development*, using developmental rather than instructional language to indicate the maturation from buds to fruits, a process taking a season of growth in plants.

I surmise that Vygotsky's (1978, 1987) account of the ZPD in these sources has been reduced to short-term learning due to readers' greater attention to *today* and *tomorrow* than to his growth-oriented developmental metaphors suggesting "in the future." Vygotsky's account of the ZPD has been misinterpreted because the literal English-language meaning of "tomorrow" has dominated how his statement has been applied in research, theory, and instruction; and because the translation itself is amenable to a short-term conception and adaptation to school structures that is unavailable in Kellogg and Veresov's (2019) version. That literal reading of "tomorrow" has become embedded in the metaphor of instructional scaffolding, leading many, likely most, of the tens of thousands of references to the ZPD to refer to the wrong thing.

A developmental understanding of "tomorrow" as an indication of "the future" and not "on the very next day or very soon, when I have to issue a grade" leads to a very different conception of what he was proposing. Isolating his brief attention to the instructional possibilities of assisting learners in their move toward independence from this far more compelling, rich, and social view of how people learn to think during developmental stages has led to misunderstandings about who he was as a psychologist and what the actual implications of his formulation might be.

Vygotsky (1987) himself made it clear how inappropriate it is to focus on the dyad of teacher-student, or other limited social group, independent of how they are situated historically, culturally, and socially: "our research demonstrates that these sensitive periods [in which instruction is most likely to have effect] are associated with the social processes involved in the development of the higher mental functions" (p. 213). These higher mental functions take many years to develop through extensive experience with a culture's values and practices; and with contested social concepts like "patriotism" and "loyalty," are difficult to gravitate toward due to the different ways in which they are interpreted according to cultural assumptions (Smagorinsky, 2013a).

This expansion of the ZPD to account for the historical dimensions of any instructional episode (cf. Newman, Griffin, & Cole, 1989) is necessary to take what I consider to be a fully Vygotskian perspective, one signaled by the translation NZD. Simply putting teacher and learner together will not produce learning, as is well-documented in Moll's (1990) own work studying immigrant students' struggles to fit with school structures based on individual competition when the students' home cultures emphasize collective action (cf. Portes & Smagorinsky, 2010). Without intersubjectivity—the degree to which people interpret social situations in the same way—teaching and learning can produce deficit conceptions of the student or teacher as easily as it can promote new understanding. This long-term process of achieving intersubjectivity was part of the developmental emphasis of the whole of Vygotsky's career project.

What gets overlooked with the scaffolding metaphor is the problem of intersubjectivity between members of different cultural groups, as is often the case in US schools in which about 85% of the teachers are white and under half of students are white (Strauss, 2014). As many have noted (e.g., Groenke, Haddix, Glenn, Kirkland, Price-Denis, & Coleman-King, 2015), children of color are often at odds with the ways in which schools are taught. Assuming that instructional scaffolding will work because it is written into a lesson plan overlooks the possibility that teacher and learner will approach each other in ways that produce conflict over product and process, with the student inevitably losing, especially when Wood et al.'s (1976) top-down approach is employed. Scaffolding, then, needs to be viewed as an intensely relational process, one requiring mutual understanding and negotiation of goals and practices. This approach appears far more flexible than what is available from Wood et al.'s original formulation, and is rarely incorporated into what I often read when coming across the scaffolding metaphor in educational writing, where everyone starts out on the same page.

The *ZND* or *NZD* requires one to think in terms of long-term developmental processes, such as those illustrated in *The Butterflies of Zagorsk*. There, the goal is not to teach children something to do independently within a few days. It is to engage in a long-term process of enculturation to communication practices that both enable immediate communication, and allow those processes in turn to mediate development toward socially valued, culturally mediated conceptual ends. These frames of mind constitute the "higher mental processes" that Vygotsky believed are at the core of concept development. They provide the means by which human development is promoted toward cultural ends. Advancing through developmental stages is not simply a matter of getting older, as in conceptions still widely embraced in psychology, normative schooling, and special education. Rather, it involves engaging in social practices that allow people, regardless of the extent of their human capabilities, to participate in cultural activities so that they live satisfying lives, affirmed by others as valued and important in building a society over time.

Let us now return to Vygotsky's oft-quoted description of the ZPD in *Mind in Society*, making one critical change:

> The Next Zone of Development defines those functions that have not yet matured but are in the process of maturation, functions that will mature tomorrow but are currently in an embryonic state. These functions could be termed the "buds" or "flowers" of development rather than the "fruits" of development.... . [W]hat is in the Next Zone of Development today will be the actual developmental level tomorrow—that is what a child can do with assistance today she will be able to do by herself tomorrow.
>
> (pp. 86–87).

Simply substituting NZD for ZPD provides a much different reading of the construct, one that more clearly positions it as a stage of life, and not an instructional sequence. The buds don't mature overnight, but transform into their next stage of development in the form of the flower or fruit. Had this translation been available from the start, I suspect that the field would never have taken such a questionable direction in its understanding of Vygotsky. As a consequence, I believe, he would be referenced far less often, but far more accurately. And nobody, I suspect, would be happier with this outcome than Vygotsky himself.

Discussion

The ZPD remains a contested construct, as evidenced by the 2023 discussion on the xlchc-redux-g listserv hosted by the University of California-San Diego. Not all of the well-informed people in this discussion agree with me on my interpretation or how to apply it. Making sense of this construct has continued to vex some of the most knowledgeable people in the English-speaking world, including those fluent in Russian. Further reading would always benefit the inquiring mind in figuring out why the ZPD matters, if translating it as the NZD produces a different reading, and what to do with whatever knowledge emerges from this exploration. "Exploration" is a term I would apply to my own efforts to grasp the significance to a term developed in the Russian language for application to Soviet schools and their socialization mission. It's a foray into better understanding that I'll likely never complete as, like Hegel, I limp toward the truth by posing and trying to answer what I hope are worthwhile questions.

In this analysis I have attempted to demonstrate that conflating the ZPD/NZD with instructional scaffolding has taken Vygotsky's grand developmental project of understanding human development as a historically grounded, culturally oriented, socially mediated, long-term process, and reduced it to a teaching method, one that at inception in Bruner's work was quite top-heavy and teacher-controlled. Understanding Vygotsky's use of metaphor, including his use of "tomorrow" to indicate the future, helps to disentangle the two.

Instructional scaffolding remains a solid instructional principle. Yet nobody needs to reference Vygotsky to endorse scaffolding. Bruner (1978) is accurate, and his reputation is cemented among his century's most important educational psychologists. He provides a respected reference to support this instructional method, negating the need to add Vygotsky's name in unwarranted ways. If educational scholarship does not emphasize long-term human development in relation to the mediation of social contexts, then it's just not Vygotsky. Scaffolding has survived on its own for over four decades now, with Vygotsky getting tag-along credit due to misreadings of his metaphor, first by Wood et al. (1976), albeit working from the least accurate translation of Vygotsky's 1934 opus magnum; and then from those who, I believe, reference Vygotsky selectively or without having read him at all. Reducing his extraordinary career to a minor pedagogical point that I don't think he actually ever made has obscured his major contributions in developmental psychology.

Grasping Vygotsky's points about the roles of culture and socialization in human development could go a long way toward reconsidering the whole structure of schools that reify one social group's practices and values as standard and constructs others as deficient. A critical reading of Vygotsky himself would find that he did assume cultural hierarchies that positioned some societies, in particular his own, as developmentally more advanced than others; and some societies, first those considered "primitive" and then those from capitalist economies, as less advanced (see Chapter 4). A modified Vygotskian perspective that attends to cultures without ranking them could do more than allow students to learn through support. More importantly, his understanding of mediating contexts could make schools conceived in European traditions far more responsive to diverse students than their current orientation has thus far allowed.

I close this chapter with a quote from Veresov and Kellogg (2019). They make clear that Vygotsky was not the Vygotsky he's almost universally depicted to be. They take apart common assumptions attributed to Vygotsky, in so doing presenting him as he appears when his work is taken as a whole body and not partitioned into pieces read outside the context of his principles:

> The "generality" assumption is that there is a Zone of Proximal Development for everything—almost any skill or form of knowledge comes with a zone. In contrast, Vygotsky posits quite specific "neoformations", some of which are central to development (e.g., everyday speech in early childhood, sexuality in adolescence) and some of which are only of peripheral interest to development (everyday speech in adolescence and sexuality in early childhood). The "assistance" assumption is that the ZPD is brought into being wholly by the assistance available in the environment. Vygotsky, however, makes it very clear that the social situation of development includes the child himself or herself at every moment, and there are even critical moments where the influence of the child on the social situation almost seems to outweigh the influence of the environment on the child. Finally, the "potential" assumption is an equal and opposite reaction to the assistance assumption—it is that the ZPD is solely and wholly a potential that lies within the child. As Vygotsky set forth even in the very first of these foundational lectures, each step of development stands neither within the child nor within the environment. A step is not a stance at all: it is a process of linking stances, at first with assistance and only later—developmental years

later—alone. But just as Binet's[1] purpose was not to diagnose development but only to facilitate teaching, the purpose of the ZPD is not to facilitate teaching, but rather to diagnose development. In short, the ZPD is not pedagogical but pedological.

(p. 154)

I have acknowledged in this chapter that my own developmental path has included some of the errors detailed by Veresov and Kellogg. I bought into scaffolding as a Vygotskian method that could facilitate student learning in the short-term; I saw individual potential as a key component of the ZPD; I overlooked factors of socialization that troubled the intersubjectivity needed for instruction to be sensitive to cultural variation; I was focused on immediate learning more than human development. In this sense, my higher mental functions were at a crude state of formation; I worked at the level of the complex or pseudoconcept, rather than having the stronger conception that I have developed over time. It has taken me over 30 years of reading, writing, talking, and listening to overcome these misconceptions and understand what Vygotsky was talking about.

Veresov and Kellogg's (2019) closing statement is conveniently located for this point in this book. Vygotsky was a pedologist much more than he was a pedagogue. The first is concerned with the whole, developmental process, with attention to the role of schooling in socialization; the second involves more specific teaching methods. In the chapters included in Part III, I review Vygotsky's attention to pedagogy, which is more general than specifically about classroom practice. Later, in Part IV, I explore how and why Vygotsky the pedologist became *persona non grata* in the Soviet Union, banned by the state and shunned by its mainstream psychologists, to be revived outside the USSR decades after his death, only to be buried in a blizzard of misunderstanding.

Note

1 Alfred Binet (1857–1911) (née Alfredo Binetti) was a French psychologist who developed the Binet–Simon IQ test at the request of the French Ministry of Education, which sought a diagnostic way of identifying students who needed remedial education.

Part III
Pedagogy

This section includes five chapters that are concerned with Vygotsky's contributions to pedagogy. These themes and issues are not specifically instructional. Rather, Vygotsky's writing on pedagogy was broad. That is, he spoke of the importance of teaching to students' interests, without providing details on how to do so. This section then features two areas of the English Language Arts curriculum, teaching literature and teaching writing, that he specifically addressed in his publications, although not in any way that could be construed as a teaching manual. The final chapter in this section treats his work in special education, unfortunately under the misleading name of "defectology," in which he argued for inclusion and respect as the foundation of the education of children and youth developing outside the schedules of the typical young person.

10 Vygotsky's Contributions to Pedagogy

To Vygotsky (1993), "Communist pedagogy is the pedagogy of the collective" (p. 208), a judgment he made while writing his collectivist understanding of human difference ("defectology"—see Chapter 14). When he wrote this line in the late 1920s, the Soviet Union was established and a communist frame of mind was both in the air and embedded in policy. Prior to that, Vygotsky was admired for his teaching. According to his daughter, Gita L. Vygotsky (1998, n.p.), while he was still in Gomel,

> The newspaper in conjunction with the local Department of Education was looking for a nominee as the best teacher of the province. All were encouraged to send to the editor profiles of those teachers who seemed to be the most worthy of that title. Lists of names were published once a week. Soon after Lev Vygotsky's name appeared as the best teacher of the Gomel province. In one of the documents issued by the local Pedagogical Council, the significance of L. S. Vygotsky's work was highlighted as: "… showed pedagogical tact, eagerness, and erudition in teaching."

In this chapter I explore what Vygotsky had to say about teaching practice, presumably embodying the values that undergirded his own notable teaching. Ironically, he is known through his lectures, yet he endorsed practices that are well-aligned with progressive teaching per Dewey and others from outside the Soviet worldview.

Part III is centered on what Vygotsky wrote about pedagogy, the everyday practice of teaching. Pedagogy refers to the means of instruction, while pedology (see Part IV) refers to the cultural development of students, including the role of schooling. Vygotsky's specific instructional ideas were quite rare. Instead, he more generally argued on behalf of what I see as a pedagogical approach grounded in progressive values, often indistinguishable from those of US educational philosopher John Dewey.

Vygotsky's presentation of how schooling should be conducted was very idealistic. He depicted teachers as infinitely, almost preternaturally, patient; and students as avid, earnest inquirers into life's meaning. Vygotsky offered this conception as a rebuttal to the Tsarist education, where schools and classrooms were authoritarian and learning was rote. His alternative found that a major problem with Tsarist, European, and US schooling was its foundation in capitalism's competitive, individualistic emphasis. He hoped to replace bourgeois values with a more egalitarian, student-centered pedagogy that would help socialize children and youth to Soviet collectivist doctrine.

His early volume, *Educational Psychology*, embodies much of what he believed about school instruction. "The present book," he said in the introduction, "has as its goals chiefly

DOI: 10.4324/9781003374848-13

those of a practical nature. It is offered as a contribution to the Soviet school of pedagogy and to assist the rank-and-file teacher" in orchestrating students' experiences into a meaningful education (1997a, p. xvii). This book includes both enduring themes of his scholarship and positions he held in his 20s that he abandoned before long, such as his adherence to Pavlovian reflexology.

Educational Psychology provides much of what Vygotsky left as a pedagogue and will be the primary source I draw on in Part III for his pedagogical views. This chapter reviews what he provided for the teachers of the Soviet Union within the bounds of the goals of Soviet society. I begin by defining two key terms, education, and pedagogy.

Definition of Education

As in all things, Vygotsky viewed education as a mediational means for human development. Schooling thus has an immediate effect, but this influence matters primarily in how it contributes to a person's path in life. Education has historical and cultural dimensions that affect how a school is organized, which in turn suggest how classrooms should operate.

Vygotsky (1997b) saw "the instrumental method" as critical. This conception requires that a person employ "a number of artificial devices for mastering his own mental processes [known as] psychological tools or instruments" that are "analogous to the role of a tool in labor" (see Chapter 5). This emphasis on learning how to use cultural tools is entirely consistent with his account of human development across the span of human activity. Psychological tools, each with a cultural history, are the means by which people learn to mediate and regulate their thinking. They are not part of a biological inheritance, but are human constructions that stand as "artificial formations. By their nature they are social and not organic or individual devices. They are directed toward the mastery of [mental] processes" (p. 85). The instrumental method

> studies the child not only as a developing, but also as an educable being. It sees in this the essential distinguishing feature of the history of the human young. Education may be defined as the artificial development of the child. Education is the artificial mastery of natural processes of development. Education not only influences certain processes of development, but restructures all functions of behavior in a most essential manner.... . [A]ll natural functions of the given child are restructured at the given level of education. The instrumental method seeks to present the history of how the child in the process of education accomplishes what mankind accomplished in the course of the long history of labor, i.e., how he "changes his own nature ... develops the forces slumbering in it and subordinates the play of forces to his own power" [quote from Marx, [1867/1887], p. 192].
>
> (Vygotsky, 1997b, p. 88)

Vygotsky here spoke as a pedologist, describing the broad ways in which schools can serve children's development toward a culture's ideological ends. Although the modern educator might chafe at the notion that school is "artificial," in Vygotsky's parlance this term refers to a constructed tool or setting, rather than a biological feature. A tool of labor or thought is created socially, and not inborn; speaking a language is learned, not inherited. This constructed, "artificial" nature of schooling led Vygotsky to use Blonskii's definition of education as "a deliberate, organized, and prolonged effort to influence the development of an individual" (1997a, p. 1).

He elsewhere defined education as "the process of gathering and elaborating conditional reactions, a process of adaptation of hereditary forms of behavior to environmental conditions, a process of establishing new links between organism and environment, i.e., a process conditioned at every point of its path... . All education was always a function of the social structure" (1997b, p. 159). What often is overlooked in references to Vygotsky is the *prolonged* focus of his attention as a pedologist, as people develop over time within the constraints and affordances of their cultures, including the ones available in school.

Vygotsky (1997a) saw education as a key setting for growth. Humans change continually throughout their lives, as does all matter in a Marxist conception. Biologically, cells divide and people change physically. For the most part, however, he was interested in growth into a culture's higher mental processes. Education thus involves the

> preparation of the young for the complex and multifaceted activity of life. The term, "education," is applicable only to growth. Thus, education may be defined as a systematic, purposeful, intentional, and conscious effort at intervening in and influencing all those processes that are part of the individual's natural [biological] growth. Consequently only that formation of new reactions will be educational in nature which actually intervenes in growth processes to one degree or another, and steers these processes... . Education creates a social selection of the outward personality. Out of the individual, as biological type, it forms, through selection, man as a social type.
> (p. 58)

Education in school thus plays an important part in shaping the sort of person who emerges from the process, the concern of the pedologist. Schools have a deliberate design to foster that development, and the role of a teacher is to construct environments within which students learn how to direct and regulate their own activity within cultural contours. Education, Vygotsky posited (1997a),

> has always had as its goal not adaptation to an already existing environment, which may, in fact, happen anyway in the national natural course of events, but *the creation of an adult [through the process of education and development] who will look beyond his own environment...* . It is true that we educate for a life, that life is the highest judge, that our ultimate purpose is not to inculcate any sort of specific special academic virtues, but *to teach vital habits and skills, and that acculturation to life is our ultimate purpose...* . [I]t must be kept in mind that the elements of the environment may sometimes include effects that are quite harmful and destructive to a young child. Bear in mind that we are dealing not with a well-established member of the environment, but with a growing, changing, fragile organism, and much that would be entirely acceptable for an adult can be destructive to a child.
> (pp. 50–51; emphasis added)

One might find it disquieting to see schools formed upon such an ideological basis, designed explicitly to produce new generations of devoted Soviet communists. Yet that was the ethos of Vygotsky's time and place and was central to Stalin's view of the purpose of schooling. Socialization has been at the heart of mass schooling as a historical phenomenon across cultural boundaries.

Vygotsky's Soviet context emphasized the collective, and the patronizing role of the state (or "nanny state" in the U.K. and elsewhere in the English-speaking world, per Macleod,

1965). School could thus take on this socializing role, acting *in loco parentis*. US schools of the last half-century have experienced many battles over the degree to which teachers should govern the development of children and youth, in tension with what parents want for them. The implementation of outcomes-based education was accused, among other things, of shaping students' attitudes in violation of family values (e.g., Phyllis Schlafly Report, 1993). The storming of school boards in the 2020s has dramatically demonstrated how ferociously many parents oppose using school to produce perspectives and dispositions with which they disagree (Youngkin, 2022), no matter how well they suit the needs of other parent's children. States like Youngkin's Virginia have created Stalinist "tip lines" through which students and parents can report teachers whose ideology departs from their own (The Washington Post Editorial Board, 2022). Perhaps communism and capitalism are not such mutually exclusive systems after all; or, perhaps it's the people who govern them that matter most.

Pedagogy

Vygotsky described pedagogics as involving "integrated functioning." He was disturbed by notions of human development that looked at parts and not wholes. He was opposed to anything that suggested disjointed or mechanistic conceptions of human growth, or individual lessons that did not serve growth through zones of development (see Chapter 9). This disconnected view of a human being served to Vygotsky as a

> scrappy and fragmentary theory of development [that] was in great harmony with an equally mosaic-like pedagogics. A pedagogics which tore the internal organism of the growing child to tatters, to subjects and capacities. The new psychology takes as its point of departure the idea of mind's indissoluble link with all other vital processes of the organism and seeks the sense, meaning and laws of development of this mind precisely in the integral inclusion of the mind in the series of the organism's vital functions.
> (1997b, p. 153)

The psychology that Vygotsky believed should inform educational practice was *applied*, rather than theoretical or based solely on laboratory experiments. A cultural-historical psychology could not conceive of a body without a mind (e.g., behaviorism), or a mind without a body (e.g., phenomenology). Vygotsky approved of William James'[1] conclusion that "it is a pretty profound delusion to think that actual curricula, academic programs, or teaching methods could be taken right out of psychology for use in the school without further ado" (Vygotsky, 1997a, p. 7). Rather, he hoped to develop what Münsterberg[2] called

> a real, substantial applied psychology. And then such an applied psychology would no longer be a mere heaping up of such bits of theoretical psychology as could possibly be utilized for practical purposes. Applied psychology would thus stand in just the same relation to ordinary psychology as that in which engineering stands to physics. It would deal exclusively with the question: how can psychology help us reach certain ends? ... It must rely on its own resources. Simply to take over the ready-made material of general psychology would be useless.
> (Münsterberg, 1909, p. 95; quoted in Vygotsky, 1997a, p. 8)

Vygotsky's educational psychology was thus both practical and comprehensive. It required an application of knowledge of psychology to the exigencies of teaching, and attended not only to individuals but the psychological structuring of the whole school. Psychological theory would be put to the applied test at all times, with practice shaping theory at least as much as theory shapes practice:

> the psychological theory of public education not only does not mean prostrating oneself before education, but, on the contrary, signifies the ultimate in our mastery of the flow of educational processes. Thus does educational psychology become an extraordinarily effective applied science.... Least of all should we think of the educational process as one-sided, and ascribe all activity without exception to the environment, making nothing of the activity of the student himself, of the activity of his teacher, and of everything that must come into contact with education. On the contrary, in education there is nothing passive or inactive.
>
> (1997a, p. 52)

Vygotsky's educational psychology was thus designed, in classic Marxist manner, to study the flow and change of human development under the conditions available in school, and through tool-mediated labor. These conditions—those available in the environment—play a key, but not exclusive, role in an educational experience. What matters is how people act in relation to environments, individually and collectively. I next review the factors that Vygotsky emphasized in his early efforts to detail a practical, applied educational psychology to help facilitate the growth of students in the environment of school.

Activity-Based Practical Learning in Social and Historical Contexts

Vygotsky argued that development is shaped through social engagement, suggesting that learning serves to lead development in particular ways. Dewey (1897) is famous for the idea of *learning by doing*. Vygotsky similarly believed that people grow through action toward a culture's teleological ends (Wertsch, 1998). Children, he found contra Bruner in his scaffolding conception, are often "performing a task before they grasp the underlying principle" (Van der Veer & Valsiner, 1991, p. 335). This emergent, exploratory action allows them to learn how to solve problems by solving them, rather than by learning rules and then trying to put them into practice.

Cole (2005) provides a photograph of an ancient Sumerian classroom in which immovable stone benches face where a teacher might have stood. Teacher-centered instruction, he infers, is many thousands of years old and provides the dominant tradition in 21st-century schools, one that Cohen (1989) argues remains difficult to dislodge from people's images of classroom roles and relationships. Often, such classrooms are referred to as *monologic* (e.g., Nystrand, 1997) because speaking rights are governed by the teacher, whose speech is dominant, and the texts chosen by teachers (or curriculum designers from higher in the system) take authoritative roles in what students learn from. Bakhtin's (1986) construct of *dialogism* is typically referenced in opposition to the image of teachers controlling classroom discourse. Yet Bakhtin was a philosopher and literary critic, not an educational theorist or, as I bizarrely found him described in one source, a "child psychologist." His own teaching was characterized by lectures, not interaction (Vasiliev, 2018), raising questions about the relation between what he wrote and how it is interpreted, and how he himself taught.

Bakhtin himself provided different, oppositional accounts of monologism. He defined it on some occasions as the presence of a single dominant, hegemonic voice; his own mode of lecturing might fit that definition. But he also maintained that the historical notion of *dialogism* precludes the possibility of a monologic occasion. Because discourse is historical, it is always in dialogue with *prior utterances* more than immediate company. I review this point in Chapter 5 with examples of solitary monks and isolated students who are immersed in historical traditions, belying their solitary appearance.

Bakhtin's utterance might be a verbal text of any length, origin, or sort; or in more recent conceptions, texts in any mode, even as Vygotsky was almost exclusively oriented to verbal thinking. The child doing a mathematics worksheet in solitude is thus in dialogue with an ancient tradition of instruction that isolates students for assessment, perhaps covering information of little interest or use to the student. Bakhtin and Vygotsky converge on this point, making contexts a focus of analysis in Vygotskian thought. This imperative led Vygotsky to look at institutions and their histories to understand how classrooms within them function (Wertsch, 1991).

Foregrounding the Educational Environment

Vygotsky's cultural-historical theory replaced fragmented psychologies, the crisis of psychology he sought to resolve. He offered a conception that links mind, body, and environment. An educator's primary task is to design the social organization of the environment to promote long-term development, within a school that has been deliberately constructed in service of students' growth. "All education," he contended, "was always a *function of the social structure*. All education was essentially always social in the sense that in the end the decisive factor in the formation of new reactions in the child were conditions whose roots lay in the environment or—more broadly—in the interrelations of the organism with the environment" (1997b, p. 159; emphasis added).

Although Vygotsky is often described in terms of a dyad within the zone of proximal development (e.g., Kleinspehn-Ammerlahn et al., 2011), he went well beyond the assistance of a teacher or other "more capable peer" (Vygotsky, 1978, p. 86). His attention extended to the whole of the environment and rarely included any specific teaching methods or instructional relationships:

> In the old [Tsarist or European] gymnasium, seminary, or institute for girls of nobility, it was in the end not the teacher, not the form monitors and form-master who educated, but *the social environment established in each of these institutions*. This is why *the traditional view of the teacher as the most important and almost sole mover over the educational process cannot be upheld*. The child is no longer an empty vessel into which the teacher pours the wine or water of his sermons. The teacher is no longer a pump who pumps his pupils with knowledge. The teacher is even completely bereft of any direct influence, any direct educational influence upon the pupil as long as he himself forms no part of their environment.
>
> (1997b, p. 159; emphasis added)

Vygotsky predated Freire's (1970) "banking model" of education with his metaphor of filling empty vessels with teacherly knowledge, which both Vygotsky and Freire viewed as a bankrupt means of teaching (while being different in significant ways, in large part following from their Soviet and Brazilian national contexts; see Souto-Manning & Smagorinsky, 2010). Yet he violated a major tenet of current thinking, that "The most important factor affecting the quality of education is the quality of the individual teacher in the classroom," an oft-repeated claim made here by the Council for Education Policy, Research, and Improvement (2003, p. 1). To Vygotsky, however,

> the enormously large, exaggerated importance which the teacher had in the school was determined by the fact that the main motor, the main part of the educational environment was the teacher. And because of this he forgot his direct duties. From the scientific viewpoint the teacher is merely the organizer of the social educational environment, the regulator and inspector of its interaction with each pupil.
> (1997b, p. 159)

Vygotsky referred primarily to Tsarist and European teachers who took authoritarian roles, centering themselves and their knowledge more than the growth of their pupils. He found that:

> The traditional European school system, which always reduces the process of education and instruction to a passive apprehension by the student of a teacher's lessons and outlines, was the ultimate of psychological nonsense. The educational process must be based on the student's individual activity, and the art of education should involve nothing more than guiding and monitoring this activity. In the educational process the teacher must be like the rails on which trains travel freely and independently, receiving from the rails only the direction in which they are to travel. The school which has run on scientific grounds is inevitably a school of action.... [T]o educate means, above all, to establish new reactions and develop new forms of behavior.
> (1997b, p. 48)

Vygotsky's criticism of the European system of his day would apply to any top-down, rote memorization approach to education, including that widely practiced in 21st-century English-speaking nations (Brown, 2003) and elsewhere in the world (Serin, 2018). Rather than amplifying the role of the individual teacher in the classroom, Vygotsky *diminished* it in relation to the environments that school provides for student growth: "It was always the environment that educated," he argued. The educational challenge, then, becomes "how to reduce the role of the teacher as closely as possible to zero ... and how to base everything on his other role—the role of organizer of the social environment" (1997b, p. 160). Within this environment, "pupils are educated by what they themselves do and not by what the teacher does. It is not what we give but what we receive that is important. It is only by being independent that pupils change [due to] the role of the teacher as an organizer of the social environment" to promote student-generated, often autodidactic learning (1997b, p. 161).

Those who reference Vygotsky with phrasings such as "learning is social (Vygotsky, 1978)" are likely to do so in service of participatory classrooms, often in ahistorical ways. But as these quotes indicate, he was interested in student activity within the social environment of the whole school itself, not talking in class. Teachers who only promote talk under the assumption that doing so is Vygotskian miss his point that the environment is broad and historically deep; and that "social" means much more than talking in the moment. Anything *pedagogical* needs to have a *pedological* dimension:

> It is in his organism as nowhere else that there occurs the decisive engagement between all those different factors that determine his behavior for many years to come.

164 *Pedagogy*

> In this sense, education, in every country and in every epic, has always been social in nature, indeed, by its very ideology it could hardly exist as antisocial in any way.... . *[I]t was never the teacher and the teacher and the tutor who did the teaching, but the particular social environment in the school which was created for each individual instance.*
>
> (1997a, p. 47; emphasis added)

Minimizing the role of the teacher elevates the role of the student, a perspective available in Deweyan progressivism (1897, 1902, 1916). Emphasizing student activity is central to constructivist understandings of education in the progressive tradition, which is either the bane (Salyer, 2022) or salvation (Waks, 2013) of education, depending on whose perspective is consulted.

Vygotsky positioned teachers as supervisors of activity-based settings in which students do the work, and the teacher manages the environment. Davydov (1997a) concludes that in Vygotsky's view, "the teacher may educate students in deliberate fashion only by constantly *collaborating* with them, with their environment, with their desires and with their willingness to *themselves work* with the teacher" (p. xxiii; emphasis in original). Vygotsky opposed authoritarian teaching that positions the teacher front and center

> in accordance with his own instructional and educational goals without giving any thought to the child's motivations, interest, and willingness to undertake his own personal activity.... . Vygotsky viewed educational processes as they occur in the child as an internal foundation of his *development* and of the evolution of new forms of behavior in the child (the development of which in the appropriate period also constituted the principal goal of education).
>
> (Davydov, 1997a, p. xxiii; emphasis in original)

The environment thus provides the context in which students develop through their socialization in school, and is subject to reconstruction through student activity. The environment does not fatefully shape the destiny of students, but provides the setting in which they construct their own understandings, which are aligned with their culture's values as guides, but are subject to revision. This emphasis on student activity resonates in many ways with progressive conceptions that position the teacher as a "guide on the side" rather than the Tsarist "sage on the stage." I review his emphasis on activity next, adding a factor that was critical to Vygotsky but not always available in progressive thought: The importance of overcoming obstacles in learning and development.

The Role of Student Activity in the Midst of Obstacles

> "Je pense, donc je suis." [Later Latin version: "Cogito, ergo sum."] ["I think, therefore I am."]
> – René Descartes, 1637, *Discourse on the Method*

> "We think because we engage in action"
> – Hugo Münsterberg, quoted in Vygotsky, 1997a, p. 4

Davydov (1997a) reviews how "in the classroom the main figure, according to Vygotsky, is the child *himself* or *herself* as the *subject* of his or her own activity ... . [He emphasized] the special importance of the student's *independence* in processes of teaching and education" (p. xxii; emphasis in original). As a result, according to Vygotsky,

> The student's personal experience becomes the fundamental basis of pedagogical work. Strictly speaking, and from the scientific point of view, there is no other way of teaching... . Ultimately, the child teaches himself ... . [I]n the educational process, the student's individual experience is everything. Education should be structured so that it is not that the student is educated, but that the student educates himself... . The educational process must be based on the student's personal activity.
>
> (quoted in Davydov, 1997a, p. xxiii)

Within this environment, there is constant activity by all. Teachers are continually monitoring the students' progress. Their role as "guide on the side" is more active and agentive than it might appear to those who see this role as sidelining the teacher, avoiding the traditional curriculum, removing God from school, inviting anarchy in the classroom, and upsetting the established value system of the institution, each a historical criticism of Dewey (e.g., Lynd, 1953). In this vein, Vygotsky (1997a) stated that:

> The teacher fashions, takes apart and puts together, shreds, and carves out elements of the environment, and combines them together in the most diverse ways in order to reach whatever goal he has to reach. Thus is the educational process an active one on three levels: the student is active, the teacher is active, and the environment created between them is an active one. The educational process, therefore, may least of all be considered a benignly indifferent and straightforward process. On the contrary the psychological nature of the educational process discloses itself as a complicated struggle in which thousands of highly developed and heterogeneous forces join battle, as a dynamic, deliberate, and dialectical process that recalls not the slow, evolutionary process of growth, but a wavering and revolutionary process of unceasing combat between man and the world.
>
> (p. 54)

The modern educator might wince at this pugilistic depiction of the human condition, especially in light of school gun violence in US schools in the 21st century. School violence is a threat in other nations as well (Cowie, Hutson, Jennifer, & Myers, 2008). Concerned educators might worry that schooling is contentious enough already, and violence is a continual threat. So why depict education in such cataclysmic terms?

I read these metaphors of combat as indicative of Vygotsky's dialectical view that life is filled with tensions and opposition, which serve as the stimulus for response and growth. His metaphors depicting learning in school as warfare might be hyperbolic, or might be a dramatic way of representing how learning requires obstacles. Or perhaps he was using metaphors that reflected the incessant warfare of the early 20th century. Figuratively, these terms emphasized that generative learning and human development are not well served by pathways that are smooth and unfettered. Rather, people grow through their synthesis of opposites, through their overcoming of obstacles, through their management of dramatic tensions in life. The teacher's role is to stimulate students' approach to life actively as part of a continual struggle to engage in creative labor. I next treat more specifically his view that obstacles are important parts of human development.

Obstacles

Vygotsky saw human development as a phenomenon characterized by drama, tension, conflict, and opposition whose resolution produces growth toward a society's ideological ends. Without these conflicts, a person would have nothing to grow against, and would remain in a child-like state psychologically. Obstacles provide the means through which growth becomes possible. He observed this phenomenon in primates as well as people: "The ape's intellectual reaction appears always in response to some obstacle, delay, difficulty, or barrier" (Vygotsky in Vygotsky & Luria, 1993, p. 63). Pavlov, he continued, "stressed the obstacle's stimulation of a goal oriented reflex, which from this viewpoint, is the main form of life energy for any of us.... . [A]s Dewey demonstrated in his brilliant analysis of thought, any thinking develops from a difficulty. In theoretical thought, the difficulty from which we start is usually called a problem" (p. 64). In humans,

> Thought arises wherever behavior encounters a barrier. It is this difficulty, which we may understand as the basic source of thinking, that provide[s][3] a rationale for all those psychological analyses which establish that our thought is subordinated to a deterministic propensity, i.e., to a foreordained problem which has to be solved right away. Hence, also, all those elements of striving, of searching, orientation, and of all the other undeveloped and incoherent residues of adaptive activity that arise in thinking.
>
> (1997a, p. 173.)

Vygotsky was concerned about educational efforts that tried to smooth the path for student learning, a problem he found with education of his day:

> The pedagogics of the recent past was permeated through and through with this propensity. To make all of education easy, it sought to banish every difficulty and to make of it something entirely simple, carefree, and normal. This was an entirely healthy reaction against those backbreaking and superhuman exertions that had been the lot of students in the preceding epic.
>
> But together with healthy social propensities, a sizable proportion of psychological error also crept in. The demand that all of education be graphic, which we may think of as the highest expression of this pedagogics of facilitation, at the same time discloses all its weak points better than anything else. To make everything graphic means, above all, banishing every difficulty of thought beyond the child's reach. It means that everything that child is presented with has to be presented to him, first, in his personal experience, and second, in such an accessible, graphic, and facilitated form that the child has nothing left to guess at, nothing left to conclude, and only has to look and touch... . But it is far more important that such a propensity towards ease is in fundamental contradiction with the educational principles of psychology. It is virtually the same thing as insisting we not make it difficult for children in kindergarten to chew their food, and instead give them everything in half digested and liquid form. For us, it is far more important to teach the child how to eat than to feed them... . Meanwhile, it is necessary to take care to create as many difficulties as possible in the child's education, as starting points for his thoughts.
>
> (1997a, pp. 173–174)

This perspective runs against the grain of much current educational thinking, including that which has produced the scaffolding metaphor. It also may contradict Vygotsky's own point that education should begin with the learner's personal interests and experiences. Although "graphic organizers" and "advanced organizers" have been touted as means of building schematic knowledge—and I am among those who have advocated for such teaching (e.g., Smagorinsky, 2018e; Smagorinsky, McCann, & Kern, 1987)—Vygotsky found them to resemble predigested food that goes down easily. It's not clear if he would consider efforts to structure new learning on old knowledge as unwise, or if he would agree that procedural knowledge might have value in helping students navigate difficult topics. What is clear is that he believed that life and learning are hard, and that "*mesh[ing] with the sharp teeth of life's intricate gears*" is required for human development (Vygotsky, 1993, p. 73; emphasis in original).

In this spirit, Vygotsky (1997a) took a strong stand on the need for educators to make learning an obstacle-driven process. A child, he wrote, must learn how to "investigate the most complex and most involved circumstances. If you would like a child to do something well, take care to place obstacles in his path" (p. 175). He qualified this belief by acknowledging that too many obstacles would overwhelm learners:

> It goes without saying that it is not a matter of constructing deliberately hopeless situations for the child, which would only lead to fruitless and unsystematic expenditure of the child's efforts. We are only concerned with organizing the child's life, and teaching, so that the child confronts the two necessary elements for the development of thinking, as the highest forms of behavior. These two elements are, first, the difficulty, or, put differently, the problem which is to be solved, and, second, those elements and tools by means of which the problem may be solved.
>
> (1997a, p. 175)

This point has implications for schools in pluralistic societies in which people from the dominant culture are better prepared for the socialization available in school than are those from cultures originating in other ideological and discursive communities. Students from outside the cultural mainstream have many adaptations to make simply to fit in with the school's organization and behavioral expectations, and so enter with plenty of obstacles to overcome, if fitting in is the goal. Even highly successful students from such backgrounds may feel alienated in mainstream schools (Everett, 2018). Adapting Vygotsky to 21st-century schools in multicultural societies with inequitable distributions of power thus requires adjustment.

With this qualification in mind, rather than spoon-feeding children to avoid difficulties or filling student vessels with pre-established knowledge, Vygotsky changed the onus for learning from teachers to students. He offered the example of the Dewey-and-Montessori-inspired Dalton program of education (Parkhurst, 1922), founded in the United States during Vygotsky's Soviet career,

> which shifts the responsibility for finding and formulating scientific laws from the teacher to the student, which replaces the classroom with laboratories, which reduces the role of that teacher to nothing, to the extent that he can be replaced by books, manuals, pictures, and other instructional material, and which reserves for the teacher only the function of conductor and guide of the students' own experience—this program is, from the psychological point of view, the one that most accords with the nature of the process of educating thinking… . This system of teaching places the student repeatedly in the position of an investigator who is out to establish a particular truth and whom the teacher only guides.
>
> (1997a, pp. 175–176)

This guidance requires that students "be allowed to experience as many objects and phenomena as possible that could serve as a means for the acquisition of an appropriate piece of information" (1997b, p. 177). These affordances enable children to become their own teachers, which I review next.

Children as Autodidacts

Vygotsky's attention to students as the drivers of their own learning is evident in his account of how what was later called *metacognitive instruction* in cognitive psychology enables students to learn how to solve problems presented by their environments, a key issue in the directions that human development takes within cultural channels. Metacognition refers to thinking about thinking, or learning how to learn. The task of the student is not to repeat what teachers say or sit dutifully and follow instructions. Rather, it is to learn how to become an active citizen, to grow into a culture's values and ideology and participate in its cultural streams. The teacher's role is to create conditions for the development of ways of thinking that benefit the society, and not to implant ideas in the child's mind. "There can be no doubt," Vygotsky argued while still beholden to Pavlovian understandings, "every time such new types of reactions are formed in the course of everyday life, there is basically a psychological effect produced on oneself what may be thought of as a self-teaching process" (1997a, p. 57). The object is to participate "a head taller" than the birth-based or "passport" age that is often the means of determining a child's grade level in school.

Vygotsky offered an illustration of students using a think-aloud method to solve problems, a method typically associated with information processing yet presented here in a cultural-historical account of learning roughly 40 years before cognitive psychology cohered into a discipline. For Vygotsky, however, it was more a teaching method than the research method developed for investigating cognition from an information processing perspective. In spite of the many distinctions between cultural-historical theory's sociocultural orientation and information processing's conception of *mind as machine* (Boden, 2006), a chasm to which I have contributed (e.g., Smagorinsky, 1998), they are confluent on several points. Vygotsky (1998) offered:

> the proven device of all schoolteachers who make pupils who solve a problem incorrectly solve it aloud. The pupil, in solving this same problem to himself, gives an absurd answer. When he is made to solve the problem aloud, the teacher teaches him to be conscious of his own operations, to follow their course, to correct it sequentially, and to control the course of his thoughts. We might say that in making the child solve the same problem aloud, the teacher transfers the child's thinking from the syncretic plane to the logical plane.
>
> (Vygotsky, 1998, p. 71)

This depiction assumes that there is a correct or preferable answer, as in mathematics. It also illustrates what might be interpreted as a heavy-handed approach by the teacher that contradicts the idea that children teach themselves within the teacher's masterful construction of the environment. The think-aloud method might have more ambiguous consequences for ill-structured problems, such as literary interpretation, which is often subject to a teacher's imposition of an interpretation, including those who profess to conduct open-ended discussions (for examples, see Bickmore, Smagorinsky, & O'Donnell-Allen,

2005; Marshall, Smagorinsky, & Smith, 1995). Nonetheless, argued Vygotsky, "Ultimately, the child teaches himself" (1997a, p. 47), in this case guided by pointed questions and critiques from the teacher. Finding the right balance between intervening and allowing students to discover their own meaning continues to vex educators, often leading to contradictory thinking that is subject to the gravity of multiple conceptions (Smagorinsky, 2013a, 2020a).

The Issue of Age

Vygotsky's developmental emphasis, while attentive to biology, was primarily concerned with socialization. He was critical of the conflation of chronological age based on one's year of birth, and intellectual age involving the development of higher mental functions, saying that "Neither intellectual nor cultural age are chronological concepts" (1997c, p. 231). What is more important is the child's or youth's degree of socialization to cultural norms as evident in their development of higher mental functions that represent growth into a culture's ways and means. Age-based schooling is thus inadvisable, in his view. Schooling should instead be based on social maturation mediated by activity in environments designed to promote their growth. Among the gnarly tensions involved in this emphasis is that between being socialized into a dominant ideology and actively critiquing or reconstructing that ideology.

Yet at a broad level, age does matter. Although he did not believe that the passport age should determine a child's grade level in school, he recognized that biological maturation is required for some processes to become possible:

> Teaching a given subject, given information, habits, and skills is easiest, efficient, and productive only at certain age periods. This circumstance has for a long time dropped out of sight. The lower boundary for optimum times for teaching was established earliest. We know that an infant of four months cannot be taught to speak, or a two-year-old be taught to read and write, because at those times, the child is not mature enough for such teaching.
>
> (1998, p. 203)

Even with this observation, Vygotsky found chronological "age" to be a brittle means of thinking about growth and maturity. Among his targets in this regard was Piaget, whose age-based stage theory remains the foundation of much educational psychology in teacher education (Brainerd, 2003; Kaplan, 2018). Aspects of maturation might roughly correspond to one's chronological age, but the two might be quite different. To Vygotsky, maturation might include the self-regulation that produces self-discipline, a common understanding of a "mature" person. This capability does not appear like clockwork at a specific age, but follows from how a person is socialized across time.

From a developmental standpoint, what matters is the degree to which people have appropriated the higher mental functions valued in their communities and cultures, and have developed the concepts that guide life within them. This perspective applies to societies Vygotsky approved of, and capitalist societies as well. And as Vygotsky developed these ideas, to the west the Nazis were on the rise with their own vision of the ideal society, one in which Jewish people like Vygotsky were viewed as subhuman and best suited for deposit in a mass grave.

Within a society, the development of cultural ways of thinking might vary from person to person, making age-based schooling of questionable value in his vision. He would surely

170 *Pedagogy*

find it problematic that a curriculum is based on scope-and-sequence charts, universal standards for being "on grade level," exams that determine one's passage from one grade to the next, and the notion of "learning loss" that arose during the Covid pandemic of the early 2020s. Throughout the English-speaking world, however, these measures of educational attainment and advancement are the norm, even as multi-age classrooms exist and have strong advocates (Saqlain, 2015).

Education in Ethics and Morality

Education, argued Vygotsky, includes the stimulation of moral, emotional, and esthetic development. He concluded that "moral behavior is a form of behavior which is amenable to education through the social environment in exactly the same way as is everything else" (1997a, p. 221). This view of moral and ethical development is consistent with many conceptions of education, regardless of a nation's political economy. It had been practiced by the American continents' original inhabitants long before Europeans conquered their lands (Jacobs & Jacobs-Spencer, 2001). This subjugation was undertaken under the banner of the Christian cross and its moral system, one that allowed for genocide in the name of the Prince of Peace. More recently, various "character education" movements have been funded in the United States (Smagorinsky & Taxel, 2004, 2005) on the heels of many such programs over educational history (Howard, Berkowitz, & Schaeffer, 2004).

Vygotsky's views both resemble, and depart from, conceptions of morality still debated in English-speaking nations. He argued that it was not the role of psychology to define moral action, but to understand its implications: "It is not the responsibility of educational psychology to arrive at exact definitions of the form and content of those moral standards. This is the[4] something for social ethics, while the business of psychology is simply to find out whether it is even conceivable to put into practice in the real world" (1997a, p. 222). His approach was to provide an educational setting in which autodidactic students, under a teacher's management of the environment, arrive at moral understandings through their thoughts and action in situations requiring moral judgment. The activities include games and their moral dimensions (see Chapter 8).

Vygotsky's (1997a) early writing in educational psychology was produced during the foundational years of the Soviet Union, and reflected its worldview. A moral education or moral outlook, he stated, *could not be possible in a capitalist society*. Any remnants of Tsarist bourgeois influence must be eradicated from education. Vygotsky believed that "All that is left of bourgeois morality, like the corrupt legacy of a previous life, all this must be swept clear out of our schools" (1997a, p. 222). Vygotsky's post-capitalism thus did not include traces of all elements of bourgeois education; some aspects had to go entirely. Although he was ultimately found to lack a class orientation by Soviet authorities (see Part IV), he was clear in his 20s that he embraced the view that a society composed of hierarchical social classes cannot foster moral development. Impediments to moral development are "not a matter of culture in general, but of capitalist culture, in particular" (1997a, p. 223), he wrote before Stalin undertook his Great Terror.

There have long been disagreements regarding whether Marx's critique of capitalism included a moral imperative (Elliott, 1986). On the one hand, according to his contemporary Vorländer[5] (1904), "The moment anyone started to talk to Marx about morality, he would roar with laughter" (p. 22). On the other hand, the general Marxist view that Western society is inherently decadent suggests a moral dimension. It is not my task to resolve that question. What seems clear is that Vygotsky's understanding of Marxism and the inequities of capitalism led him to conclude that capitalism is fundamentally immoral, and that the equity available through communism or socialism will produce a society in which a moral education will be consequential in the development of virtuous proletarian citizens.

The behavior of many capitalists would support the notion that it fosters immoral conduct through its competitive encouragement of greed and subordination. Many current academics have professed such a view, often charging exorbitant fees to lecture on the evils of capitalism. Unfortunately, first-hand prison memoirs such as Solzhenitsyn's (1973) describe abundant corruption, theft, and bribery among Soviet officials and throughout the political and prison systems, suggesting that capitalism is not the only economic system in which immorality thrives. My goal here is not to argue on behalf of one economic system or the other, but to observe that capitalism is not unique in promoting bad behavior.

Rather, my task here is to report on Vygotsky and moral education within the confines of early Soviet schooling. In 21st-century character education programs, there is a tendency to either take a didactic approach in which values are impressed on children and youth by presumably virtuous adults; or to take a constructivist approach in which children and youth inductively work out how to behave morally in situations involving conflict, temptation, competition, and other sorts of settings in which virtue must be balanced against self-interest (Smagorinsky & Taxel, 2004, 2005). Vygotsky was decidedly constructivist when it came to moral education. Preaching morality, he argued, was somewhere between ineffective and counterproductive:

> Thorndike was quite correct in emphasizing the harm of those moral injunctions that are common in textbooks on ethics used in the French secondary schools. The real effect of all those descriptions of unethical actions the teacher would wish his students to avoid only brings to the mind of the student a certain urge and yearning to perform them. This is why, Thorndike concludes, it is extraordinarily damaging to present, as the authors of these textbooks have done, detailed explanations and accounts as to why it is wrong to commit suicide.
> (1997a, p. 161)

Moral injunctions against suicide, he felt, might provide students with a suicide option that they had not considered before. But simply using the lectern to explain and encourage moral conduct will not work regardless of the moral dilemma involved:

> All attempts at moral education, at moral sermonizing, must, for these reasons have to be seen as quite futile. Morality has to constitute an inseparable part of education as a whole at its very roots, and he is acting morally who does not notice that he is acting morally. Just like health, which we notice only when it is disturbed, like the air which we breathe, so does the way we behave in terms of morality arouse in us a whole series of concerns only when there is something seriously wrong with it. Hebart's[6] rule, "not to teach too much," is nowhere as applicable to this extent as in moral education. It is for this reason that we feel it is pointless to teach morality. Moral precepts, in and of themselves, will, in the student's mind, seem like a collection of purely verbal responses that have absolutely nothing to do with behavior.
> (1997a, p. 226)

Moral education is tacit, he believed, arising from real moral dilemmas; at the same time, speech-based self-regulation is a tenet of cultural-historical theory. Vygotsky is not clear on how such naturalized moral conduct is achieved without the speech-mediated self-discipline he described in his account of play and labor (see Chapter 8). Regardless of how a moral code develops, teacherly pontifications on morality, he believed, were no more effective than any other efforts to explain truth and reality to students. What should happen in school, in contrast, is that students discover how to act through the sorts of play that enable the learning of boundaries and social rules. His views on moral education thus were consistent with his inductive approach to learning, where the teacher's role is not to do the thinking for students, but to create environments that require them to think through social problems that mirror those they will need to adjudicate in their lives moving forward.

The Relation Between Learning and Morality

Among the claims of many 21st-century US character education programs is that instruction in virtue (typically didactic and hortatory) will produce better academic performance among students (e.g., Perles, 2013). Taking an inductive, constructivist approach, Vygotsky also argued that virtuous children will be better students than are those with moral shortcomings:

> There can be no doubt that consciousness exerts a decisive influence on our moral behavior, though there is no direct dependence whatsoever which can be established between the two. It was for this reason that Meumann[7] was able to show that moral development and the general level of education go hand in hand, while Witheft[8] established the rule that success in school has fundamental importance for the student's entire moral existence. The question has to be asked in such a way as to disclose the relationship between success in school and behavior, though this does not mean also explaining that relationship… . Nevertheless, we are still justified in claiming that there exists a profound relationship between the two, and that mental development is a propitious condition for moral education.
>
> (1997a, p. 225)

There are many questions about whether virtue produces good grades and better behavior, or whether an academic orientation promotes students' character, or whether the two go hand in hand, or whether one can operationalize virtue and measure it to make claims about its improvement, or whether every culture conceives of character in the same ways, or whether students from low-income homes, families of color, immigrant communities, and other often-marginalized groups get interpreted as having lower morals to begin with. Simply on the question of whether character interventions improve grades and behavior, the Social and Character Development Research Consortium (2010) studied the problem, and came to a solid conclusion. They don't.

Didactic character education approaches in the US lend themselves well to measurements involving pre and post intervention surveys, discipline data, and other sources through which improvement may be statistically claimed. Inductive approaches in contrast are open-ended and assume that developing a moral code would have multiple outcomes. Vygotsky might have seen a Soviet school suggesting, but not exhorting children to adopt, a particular moral code. At the same time, he saw socialization to his society's higher mental functions as a key task of schooling. No doubt what is necessary is a synthesis of these opposites, as Hegel and Marx would argue is necessary for achieving new insights.

I don't see Vygotsky reaching this synthesis, and assume that people who die at age 37 leave a lot of work unfinished. For instance, he never said what he meant by morality, ethics, virtue, or character, subjects that have been written about for thousands of years (e.g., Aristotle, 353 B.C.E.). Vygotsky's intent, however, was not to provide for others a ready-made definition of morality. Rather, he urged educators to build moral imperatives into academic inquiries so that moral decision-making was inevitable, and would contribute to the sort of person students are becoming through these experiences.

Vygotsky was adamantly opposed to using punishment as a way to enforce good behavior. He believed that developing discipline through play and labor were important, but that behaving out of fear of being punished for violations is counterproductive. One should not, he said,

> turn morality into the internal policeman of the soul. To avoid something out of fear still does not mean you are performing a good deed… . From the psychological point of view, chastity purchased at the price of fear sullies the soul worse than outright debauchery, inasmuch as it does not destroy all base wishes and desires in the child's mind, but only creates in his mind a petty and mean struggle between those desires and the no less humiliating and no less servile feelings of fear. Only that chastity has any value which is procured by a positive attitude towards action and by an understanding of its true essence. Not to do something out of a fear of dire consequences is just as immoral as to do it. Every unfree attitude towards things, all fear and dependence, already denotes the absence of any moral sensibility. In its psychological sense, the moral is always free.
>
> (1997a, p. 227)

What mattered to Vygotsky was not behavior, but personal transformation undertaken out of a desire to live a moral life. Punishments such as banishment do not allow a child or youth to participate in culturally affirming collective action—what I have called being swept up in a *positive social updraft* (Smagorinsky, 2016a)—but rather "is directed towards rendering him harmless and safeguarding the environment from his influence. Here, in contrast, our concern must be directed towards preserving and transforming the child's character and, consequently our goal is the most thoroughgoing re-education of the child" (1997a, p. 231). Punishment and the segregation of a misbehaving child are "entirely inappropriate for the education of moral behavior" because they do not include "the essential freedom of choice, which alone is capable of leading to moral behavior." Attending to the act and not the student's moral thinking leads a child "very quickly to understand that punishment is not at all necessarily related to his misdeeds, but that there is an additional and intermediate component here expressed in the intervention of adults, and he learns to avoid this intervention, to conceal his deeds, to tell lies, and so on" (1997a, p. 235).

Reasonable, experienced educators might debate whether Vygotsky is overly idealistic about children's nobility, or practically useful in figuring out to do with a student who disrupts the learning of everyone else. Perhaps Vygotsky would respond that in a healthy environment, disruption would not be appealing to a child. These educators further might wholeheartedly agree with his views of punishment, as do Osher, Bear, Sprague, and Doyle (2010); or view punishment as the way to shape children's behavior for their own benefit and that of the social group (Molloy, 2021). They might also debate such questions as who is most likely to be considered character-deficient and a behavior problem, given how race, gender, and income disparities have historically played a strong role in perceptions of behavior violations (Welsh & Little, 2018), along with mental health conditions that produce actions considered antisocial (Heekes, Kruger, Lester, & Ward, 2020). I do not aspire to resolve those questions, which I have wrestled with as a parent and teacher. I can easily conclude, however, that Vygotsky believed that punishment in service of promoting moral action and acceptable conduct in general might produce superficial compliance, but cannot produce a moral being.

Does moral development produce better academics, as character interventions claim? Does the appearance of moral development to placate a teacher indicate a superficial performance of acceptable conduct that masks thinking that would be considered morally corrupt, as Vygotsky believed? Do punishments only produce cynicism and not the inculcation of a moral code?

My review leads me to conclude that Vygotsky believed that there was a relation between moral development and intellectual development, and that it can only be cultivated with student action in response to situations requiring ethical choices. Vygotsky assumed, I believe, that moral development and academic development are enmeshed to the point of being the same channel of development. Schooling provides the setting in which important human development takes place in multiple areas: Socialization to a culture's ideology and practices, morality that emerges from invested inquiries into the concepts that shape their surroundings, practical content-area knowledge grounded in broader principles, physical maturation, participating as a good citizen in collective action, and more. His inductive approach would have students inquiring into questions requiring moral judgment to resolve moral conflicts, intellectual acts that provide a trajectory to a virtuous social future; and ideally, they would not only think about these dilemmas, they would act on them.

Teaching About Love and Sexuality

Vygotsky had much to say about both biological sexuality and social mores governing sexual behavior. I next turn to his views on two subjects that are broached in schools with delicacy, or not addressed at all, or are raised in the face of parental objections, or now may be forbidden to raise at all: The educational importance of teaching students how to love and understand their sexual maturation.

Rare is the reference to Vygotsky's (1997a) attention to love and sexuality. But he devoted a section of *Educational Psychology* to the subject, one that illustrates his synthesis of biological and cultural development in understanding the transitional age of adolescence. Like many 21st-century educators and parents, those of Vygotsky's day were squeamish on the subject of sexuality and the emergence of sexual desires. In his day, the issues were less complicated than they are now, given that binary understandings of boys and girls were the only conceptions available to talk about. Not surprisingly, the existence of LGBTQ+ people went unacknowledged in his writing during the 1920s. Wilkinson (2020) reports on how this population was somewhere between illegal and invisible in the USSR during Vygotsky's lifetime, and remains villainized under Putin's regime (Levesque, 2022). Vygotsky's world was dominated by the view of boys and girls as distinct sexes, and as the only options provided by either biology or social norms.

Vygotsky (1997a) felt that comprehensive sex education ought to be a fundamental part of schooling, and that "The elimination of sex education from the overall system of educational influence, the total expunging of this realm of life from the life of the young, the brazen and intrusive prohibition imposed on these questions, was the worst of all possible outcomes" (p. 72). Sex education remains controversial in terms of whether to teach it at all, how to teach it, and what to cover if it is taught (Hall, Sales, Komro, & Santelli, 2016). Vygotsky did not view it as a political problem, as the Culture Wars of the 2020s have positioned sex education (Izaguirre & Gomez Licon, 2022). He saw sexuality as a natural part of human development, one involving not only bodies and desires, but developmental trajectories. Like moral education, it cannot be avoided during adolescence's tumultuous changes. It can only be effaced from the curriculum.

The sex instinct, he argued, "requires adaptations to the social structure of life that would not cut into its already established forms, and the problem is not in the least one of suppressing or blunting the sex instinct; on the contrary, the teacher must be concerned with ensuring the full preservation and healthy development of the instinct" (1997a, p. 73). His views would be very unpopular in many 21st-century communities in which sexuality is to be suppressed via dress codes designed to mute sexual desire, especially that of boys toward girls (e.g., Downey, 2022; Raby, 2010). What is clear, however, is that sexuality was a taboo subject in Vygotsky's day, and remains one in the 21st century. Meanwhile, in both centuries and all others, the emergence of sexual desires and identities in adolescence remains a universal aspect of development.

Vygotsky views, unlike those motivating school board protests in the 2020s, were not grounded in in Puritanical conceptions of the human body or in views of sex as dirty, as the sole province of married couples, as a mortal sin involving fornication and sodomy, and as a topic to be silenced in polite company (e.g., Saunders, 2003). Absent a religious or political framework for considering sexuality as a school subject, Vygotsky concerned himself with sexuality as a normal, natural, and essential aspect of adolescence. Youthful love, he argued, "until recently, had been thought of as being inappropriate and harmful, and therefore assume the grotesque forms of courtship or flirtation." Yet

> in the eyes of the new psychologist, [love provides] the only means of humanizing the sex instinct. It teaches us to restrict the instinct and to guide it in only one direction, it teaches us how to build entirely exclusive relationships with one other person on a sound basis for the very first time, to isolate these relations from all other human relationships, and to assign to them an exceptional and profound meaning. Love in the time of youth is the most natural and most unavoidable forms of sublimation of the sex instinct. And the ultimate purpose of sex education is solely to teach the person how to love.
>
> (1997a, p. 74)

The polyamorous among us might find Vygotsky prudish for promoting monogamy as a social value; it's beyond my pay grade to provide a definitive answer on that question. He also never dealt with a persistent problem of current times: Teachers having sexual relationships with students (Johnson, 2008). And teacher squeamishness and lack of knowledge may torpedo any efforts to conduct sex education in ways that students benefit from (Pound, Langford, & Campbell, 2016). His attention to love and sexuality presumed a certain propriety and comfort level that are not always present when school and sex intersect.

Schools of Vygotsky's era were often co-educational, and the merits of such schools were debated. Burgerstein (1910), for instance, spoke glowingly of "The classical country for co-education in high schools in Europe … the grand duchy of Finland in Russia, a country of very great culture" (p. 3). Vygotsky's attention was thus centered on schools in which questions of whether boys and girls should be educated together were debated among educators. To Burgerstein, the fact that boys perform better in coeducational settings than boys-only settings justified the mixing of the sexes in school. Similar to dress code debates in the 2020s, the concern then was how the presence of girls affected boys' behavior and grades, a topic fraught with sexist underpinnings.

This issue aside, Vygotsky's belief that schools should emphasize the development of loving relationships that take sexual desire into account would run aground of the 2020s movement to restrict sex education to parental governance, and to eliminate it from the school curriculum. This movement does not address the question of love at all; it is concerned largely with muting both desire and the recognition that LGBTQ+ people exist and merit respect. Vygotsky instead saw attraction and desire as among the many drivers of relationships that students learn in school:

> Since establishing relationships in the school that would be needed later on in life is the fundamental psychological premise of our education systems, we must start by infusing the school with the network of nonsexual relationships that the child would need later on in life. This already presupposes the broadest interaction between the sexes in the school as the foundation of the educational system.
>
> (1997a, p. 80)

Similar to moral education in Vygotsky's conception, sexual education attends to developmental issues more than clamping down on behavior that deviates from expected norms. As he did in other areas, Vygotsky provided broad developmental outlines without saying exactly how to address them instructionally. Rather, he took the general progressive view that children and youth ought to construct their own understandings in relation to the mediational parameters of their educational environments.

In the 2020s, conservative parents and politicians have adamantly opposed such thinking. Morality, sexuality, and ideology are the province of home, not that of teachers who might challenge family values. Florida Governor Ron DeSantis stated the case unambiguously in justifying his "Don't Say Gay" legislation:

> "You know I hear some people say, 'Wow, school's coming up. But, you know, Florida, they have parent's rights in education, they banned CRT (critical race theory), all this stuff. People, how are they gonna know what to teach or whatever?' "And I'm just thinking to myself, you know, you teach reading, math, science, the basic stuff. And you don't teach gender ideology, CRT, the sexuality in the elementary schools. That's not very difficult to know and that's not very difficult to understand," he said.

This view would provide an educational context in which such topics are taboo, amplifying Vygotsky's contention that the whole school environment—in the case of Florida, the whole state environment—shapes what is possible for any individual teacher to do. Vygotsky's vision is only available in a generally progressive setting, restricting their application in many 21st-century schools.

Cross-Disciplinary Learning

Vygotsky's holistic perspective led him to conceive of schooling as one in which there are no "silos" separating fields and epistemologies such that synthesizing ideas across the curriculum is challenging and rarely required by content area teachers. Rather, he believed that the kind of instruction he advocated—one oriented to whole human development involving the integration of knowledge and socialization toward a culture's higher mental functions—was possible and necessary. Properly taught, a student resolves contradictions, gravitates toward cultural norms, and matures through the integration of biological and social factors. These processes enable a growing child or youth to make sense of the world in a fairly coherent way:

> There is a process of instruction which has its own internal structure, its own sequence, and its own emerging logic. At the same time, in the head of each pupil, there is an internal network of processes which are called to life and motivated in school instruction. These have their own logic of development however. Among the basic tasks of the psychology of school instruction is to clarify this internal logic, the internal course of development that is called to life by a particular course of instruction. Three facts have been solidly established in our experiments: (1) there is significant commonality in the mental foundations underlying instruction in the various school subjects that is alone sufficient to insure the potential for the influence of one subject on the other (i.e., there is a formal aspect to each school subject); (2) instruction influences the development of the higher mental functions in a manner that exceeds the limits of the specific content and material of each subject. Once again, this provides support for the idea of a formal discipline which is different for each subject but common to all. In attaining conscious awareness of cases, the child masters a structure that is transferred to other domains that are not directly linked with cases or grammar; and (3) the mental functions are interdependent and interconnected. Because of the foundation which is common to all the higher mental functions, the development of voluntary attention and logical memory, of abstract thinking and scientific imagination, occurs as a complex unified process. The common foundation of all the higher mental functions is conscious awareness and mastery. The development of this foundation is the primary new formation of the school age.
>
> (1987, p. 208)

Learning in disciplinary fragments thus is insufficient. Rather, each discipline should be taught so that it is related to and incorporates other parts of the curriculum. This interdisciplinary approach is difficult to achieve in schools in which subject areas are divided, school bells condition students to know when to stop being a historian and start being a mathematician, and teachers often view themselves as specialists in their content areas. His ideas would appear to apply more to the Dalton or Montessori schools he admired than to a conventional 21st-century school divided into disciplines and departments, often separated physically within buildings and requiring several minutes to navigate, without intellectual bridges joining them. Yet Dalton and Montessori schools tend to enroll students from affluent families (Meckler, 2018). Ironically, then, Vygotsky advocated for schooling perhaps best suited to bourgeois manners and practices.

Consistent with his other writing on pedagogy, Vygotsky offered general values and the assumption of avid commitments to learning, without explaining how to put them into practice. Putting them into practice is the hard part. Vygotsky's ideals on what makes for a developmentally appropriate schooling experience comes up against other value systems that impose authoritarian systems designed to impress an ideology and information on students and not to engage them in inductive inquiries through which they develop their own ways of thinking. If practice is what matters, then his conception, while no doubt inspiring to many, lacked a concrete plan.

Discussion

As this review shows, there is considerable validity in the perspective that Vygotsky was a pedologist and not so much a pedagogue. Vygotsky was interested in teaching, but not at the level of specific practices, and surely not at the level of scaffolding student learning of procedures and content in the short term. Rather, Vygotsky argued on behalf of a generally progressive approach to schooling, one quite similar to that available through Dewey, Montessori, and other "decadent" bourgeois educators. He often drew on European and US educators to inform his view, opening the door for rabid Stalinists to throw him under the school bus and silence his writing and influence in Soviet schools. Part IV reviews this sad conclusion to Vygotsky's Soviet career. Before detailing the Pedology Decree, I review areas of the curriculum that Vygotsky addressed across the course of his career.

Notes

1 William James (1842–1910) was a US philosopher who was considered the "Father of American psychology." He was a major contributor to development of pragmatism, radical pragmatism, and functional psychology.
2 Hugo Münsterberg (1863–1916) was a Prussian-German psychologist who emigrated to the United States to work with William James at Harvard University. He helped develop the field of applied psychology, which he extended into a variety of work settings. His support of Germany during World War I was controversial and affected his legacy.
3 I make this addition to correct a typographical error in the translated text.
4 I include this word, printed in the text, even though it is surely a typographical error.
5 Karl Vorländer (1860–1928) was a German philosopher who specialized in the work of Emmanuel Kant.
6 Johann Friedrich Herbart (1776–1841) was a Prussian psychologist and educational philosopher.
7 Ernst Friedrich Wilhelm Meumann (1862–1915) was a German educator, pedagogue, and psychologist. He founded experimental pedagogy, i.e., the theory and practice of learning in relation to the social, political, and psychological development of learners.
8 Neither Vygotsky nor the internet provides clarification on Witheft's identity; Vygotsky provides a reference for Meumann, but not Witheft. The name Witheft is of Russified German origin, which does not clarify his national origins. Witheft may be (per Van der Veer, personal communication, 10-25-22) the German educator W. H. Witthöft, who wrote about elementary school in the 1910s and 1920s, or Ivan Ivanovich Vitgeft. Or someone else.

11 Orientation, Interests, Attention, Memory, and Relevance

According to Vygotsky (1997a), "Memory functions best and its most intensive whenever it is attracted and guided by a particular interest. We learn best that which we look upon with the greatest of interest" (p. 143). Most US progressive educators would endorse this statement, grounding instruction in what students may explore with passion and commitment. This chapter looks at interest in relation to other constructs—orientation, attention, memory, and relevance—that speak to the need for an education to inspire a personal commitment to knowledge, personal development, and development within social contours.

Teachers often bemoan students' attention spans and lack of interest in school learning. As electronic devices become increasingly available, so have distractions for students. Robb (2019) reports that over half of the US kids own a smartphone by the age of 11. McLean (2022) finds that there have been jumps in device dependence during the Covid pandemic, among many other problems following from the shutdown and its aftermath. Parents report that, among kids 11 and under, 63% used a smartphone in 2020, a figure that rose to 71% in 2021. By then, 55% of five-year-olds were using smartphones. These figures coincide with Klein's survey (2020), which found that 85% of teachers and principals felt that the attention spans of children and youth were in decline.

Nearly a century before cell phones overtook the lives of children and youth, Vygotsky was concerned about how schools kill students' interest in learning by ignoring their heartfelt interests and placing them in passive, subordinate roles. In the pre-Revolutionary Tsarist schools, he believed, there was too much empty abstraction, too much teacher domination of floor space, too little of students' exercising agency over their learning, and too much emphasis on learning fruitless facts soon forgotten. Although Vygotsky himself appears to have largely been a lecturer in his teaching of older students and colleagues in Moscow, he emphasized activity and students' construction of knowledge in learning tasks aligned with their interests. He did not have to work against the distractions created by cell phones and other devices that enable internet usage and its endless fascination. His formulation comes from a time and place where pencil and paper were the most sophisticated literacy tools available, and where the classroom window provided the greatest potential for distraction. His conception thus does not provide a neat map for holding children's attention during eras of greater possibility for disruption. At the same time, he considered matters that remain salient to the 21st-century teacher, if in largely idealistic terms.

In this chapter, I look at the issues of orientation, interests, attention, memory, and relevance. Each plays an important role in students' engagement with their studies. I begin, in Vygotskian fashion, with the broad social context that helps to shape one's orientation to school, and then move the lens closer to see how, within that general stance, students

DOI: 10.4324/9781003374848-14

engage with a curriculum through their attentive involvement with relevant interests. Avid engagement in turn promotes their memory of what they learn.

Like much of Vygotsky's writing at the outset of the Soviet Union, his ideas reveal his unequivocal optimism for what lay ahead in a new society conceived to remove social class barriers and promote a nation of equals. These ideals glow with the possibilities afforded an education steeped in Marxist ideology and driven by students' genuine interests and concerns. Compulsory mass education has never actually worked ideally, however. Its challenges are infinite and complex and often expensive to address, and school funding has been in decline for some time (Leachman, Masterson, & Figueroa, 2017). Vygotsky nonetheless provides some general principles that might help a teacher understand how students experience school.

Orientation

Anyone who has maintained a garden knows the importance of orientation. A plant's orientation to the sun—the way it faces the sun in relation to its needs—has a great deal to do with its survival. A plant that requires full sunshine, when planted in the shade, will wither and die, or stretch to reach the sun in such a way that it becomes too distorted and unsustainable to support its requirements.

People are oriented to their environments as well, facing in some directions more than others, and often doing so with volition (or coercion) and mobility. To Vygotsky (1997a), "we have every right to speak not of a single orientation of our organism, but of a series of simultaneous orientations, one of which is the dominant orientation, and the others subordinate to it" (p. 128). A person takes a position in relation to various social centers of gravity, with the past shaping the initial stance, the present cultivating it, and the future predicated on how a person stands relative to the ever-morphing environment. Unlike plants, which have a single sun to face while rooted in a permanent location, students are pulled in many directions by many influences. And unlike plants, students have the volition to change their orientation to the diverse influences that populate their worlds, albeit amid pressures great and small to conform to a limited set of possibilities.

Vygotsky believed that the most important factor in education is the whole school itself: Its ethos, its emphases, its traditions, its pathways, its structure, its hierarchies, and much more (see Chapter 10). Many have found the school institution to be an unwelcoming place, leading to metaphors, such as prison, salt mines, and other indicators that they find it oppressive and a poor source for their orientation. Without an orientation to school, students have a difficult time engaging in any of what it has to offer. I've found in my own classroom studies that even classes designed to promote interest and literacy may struggle to engage students whose overall orientation to school is weak (Smagorinsky & O'Donnell-Allen, 1998a, 2000). A school where students feel uninspired, detached, distracted, or out of place at the building entrance is unlikely to include individual classrooms in which students eagerly engage with the curriculum, without that class uniquely serving an important emotional or social need. Understanding the concept of orientation, then, appears to be a central task of promoting students' approach to their educations. "Without fear of overstatement," Vygotsky asserted,

> one may say that orientation is the first condition where it becomes possible to affect the child through education. Certain teachers even suggest reducing the entire process of education to the development of certain forms of orientation, and thus

claim that every form of education is an education of attention, above all, so that the various modes of education differ from each other only by the nature of those acts of orientation that are to be fostered.... [I]n education we are always dealing not with the movements and actions that possess a purpose and goal in and of themselves, but with the development of skills and habits for future functioning and future activity.

(1997a, p. 119)

Future orientation is central to Vygotsky's developmental focus, an idea that held steady across other developments in his thinking across the span of his career. Orientation may characterize how one is positioned in the present, but in typical Vygotsky fashion, he saw the person's trajectory as grounded in the culture provided by history, and projected into future actions. School plays a role in helping to map the pathways students will take in life; "education means neither simply following an organism's natural inclinations nor a fruitless struggle against those inclinations" (1997a, p. 121). Rather, school helps to channel interests into a life path, what is known in Spanish as "El Camino." In the Soviet Union, that path required an alignment with State ideology, with the understanding that schooling is inherently ideological in relation to the politico-economic system in which it is undertaken.

Students' inclinations influence their orientation to school, yet are insufficient in and of themselves. School provides a setting in which inclinations, or an orientation, intersect with the social norms, classroom practices, and other features that provide socialization. The cultural flow of school might require adaptations from the ways in which students are enculturated at home. In Vygotsky's day, the image of the New Soviet Man provided the template for all pathways to socialization. Even with assimilation the goal of mass schooling in the United States and other 21st-century pluralistic nations, more recent multicultural education efforts have asserted the greater importance of preserving students' incoming heritages. This tension between developing a national citizen and preserving the cultures of diverse students remains in play in much of today's world. I don't think that Vygotsky resolved it in Soviet schooling, in that he both argued in favor of schooling designed to promote a Soviet identity, and schooling that emerges exclusively from students' interests and concerns, presumably shaped by the direction provided by Soviet culture.

Vygotsky (1997a) asserted that the student's inclinations should always provide the starting point for school learning: "Education cannot be conducted in any way other than through the child's natural inclinations; in all its strivings, education proceeds by taking as its starting point precisely those inclinations" (p. 121). Those inclinations only provide the beginning of formal learning. School then "intervenes actively in these natural inclinations of the child, brings them together, grouping them in whatever way one might wish, protecting some of them, stimulating some of them at the expense of others, and, in this way, introduces the spontaneous process of the child's inclinations into the organizing and shaping channel of the social environment in the school" (p. 121). If school only provided a setting in which children follow their inclinations without intervention, it would enable little of the socialization that Vygotsky saw as central to human development. In this sense, he departed from Montessori (1912), his contemporary who lived from 1870 to 1952, Graves (1983), and others who believe that teachers should follow the child without directing their activity, an individualistic conception that would not fit a Marxist collectivist system.

Children have been known to struggle moving from Montessori to conventional schools for their upper grades education (Ward, 2013). Their orientation to Montessori's child-centric, noninvasive approach to their self-directed learning undoubtedly makes adapting to greater structure and less agency difficult. Even for students socialized to a curriculum designed by people from well outside their range of interests, moving from class to class in upper grades requires continual reorientation. They also must reorient themselves away from social relationships (and cell phones) in order to pay attention to teachers and texts and the curriculum they follow. With this demand in mind, argued Vygotsky (1997a), teachers need to

> maintain the proper orientation [and] determine at every turn whether the subject matter he has introduced is in accord with the fundamental laws of activity and attention. Above all, this subject matter must be arranged and presented in such a way as to be in accord with the narrow range of the orienting reactions and, in terms of the nature of its effects, not be in contradiction with the duration of these effects. According to the simplest and most commonplace rules of pedagogical civility, a lesson should not last too long, nor should the teacher talk a mile a minute. Essentially, these rules express, in most primitive form, the very same demand for a correspondence between the subject matter and the students' adaptive reactions.
>
> (pp. 124–125)

Like much in *Educational Psychology*, this passage reveals Vygotsky's indebtedness to Pavlov's reflexology. The reactions, however, include conscious attention through the lens provided by orientation.

Different sorts of school activities are likely to produce different orientations toward school. To Vygotsky (1997a), "The meaninglessness and pedagogically destructive orientation toward examinations that was common in our Tsarist schools may serve as the simplest example of the import of such a fundamental orientation towards goals in the educational process" (p. 126). When school requires students to remember and take tests on facts from outside their orientation and interest, school is of little value. A trenchant fact here or there might spark a student's interest. But "Like a polished gem in a wasteland, this knowledge was unable to satisfy the simplest and most vital queries of the average and unassuming student" (p. 127).

What is absent from this ineffective education is attention to students' goals for learning. Education, he argued, must be "saturated through and through with such an orientation towards goals" so that teachers have "exact knowledge of the path along which a new reaction is to function" (1997a, p. 127). To shift this observation from Pavlovian to constructivist terms, teachers need to understand students' orientation to learning and anticipate how different pedagogical moves produce different responses in students and their reasons for learning something new. In Soviet education, students' inclinations ultimately needed socialization to Soviet ideology, producing another tension between free will and being subject to an enculturation process designed to create national unity around Marxist principles.

A final area of interest to Vygotsky with respect to orientation was the importance of habits. "It is clear," he said, "how important it is in education to establish habits. The process by which a certain action is turned into a habit and acquires the characteristic properties of automatic movement is called exercise.... [T]he goal of the teacher is to accustom the student to those habits which will be of benefit to him later in life" (1997a, p. 273). Exercise, or repetition, creates "a predisposition for optimal performance of this or that action" and so promotes efficiency. Vygotsky quoted Gaupp[1] to encourage "the facilitation of the overall direction of activity, expressed figuratively, in the creation of well-worn paths" (quoted in Vygotsky, 1997a, p. 274). He further quoted William James to make the point that

> "*we must make automatic and habitual as early as possible, as many useful actions as we can*, and as carefully guard against the growing into ways that are likely to be disadvantageous. The more of the details of our daily life we can hand over to the effortless custody of automatism, the more our higher powers of mind will be set free for their own proper work."
>
> (James, 1899, p. 48; quoted in Vygotsky, 1997a, p. 274; emphasis in original)

Routines, reinforced through repetition, produce habits that benefit one across the lifespan and enable an efficient way of navigating society, assuming that the habits fit with society's preferred pathways. This assumption is based on homogeneous premises about the best way to engage with society; Soviet life was designed for conformity, not diversity. Schools in the English-speaking world have pluralistic enrollments that make these pathways much easier for some students to follow than others. Students from outside the cultural mainstream may act in ways that are considered inefficient and detrimental to what schools expect, leading to differential treatment, discipline, and beliefs about potential.

Habits work best for those socialized to the ways and means of conduct institutionalized in formal settings. For those who are aligned, habits and routines promote a positive experience. The question for educators concerns whose habits predominate, and how to manage schools in which multiple forms of socialization produce different ways of acting, in and out of school (Crosnoe, 2011).

Interests

Interests provide one of the most important means of orientation a teacher can foster to promote students' engagement with the curriculum: "Together with inclinations and needs, interest is a tendency that stimulates activity" (Vygotsky, 1998, p. 10). Interests serve as "needs that set these mechanisms in motion" (p. 13). Needs are genuine and important aspects of development: "Needs disclose completely clearly expressed ontogenesis," including both innate needs and those "required in his adaptation to the environment, primarily the social environment" (p. 9). Vygotsky (1997a) argued that "Familiarity with the students' available store of experience is a necessary condition of pedagogical work" (p. 151). He continued,

> It is always necessary to know the soil and the material which we intend to build on, else we run the risk of putting up a flimsy structure on shifting sands. Therefore, the task of determining how to convey new material that is not part of the student's past experience in the language of his own experience becomes a matter of the greatest concern for the teacher.
>
> (p. 151)

Vygotsky's writing about school instruction makes him sound very much like a progressive educator from European or European-derived nations who plans activities that build on students' interests and knowledge:

> the fundamental rule demands that the entire educational system, the structure of teaching, be constructed on the foundation of children's interests, taken into account in exact fashion. The psychological law simply says that before trying to get a child

involved in some activity, get him interested in it, take care to discover whether he is ready for it, so that all the force is necessary for the activity are tensed, and the child is ready to act on his own, with the teacher left to simply guide and direct his activity.

(1997a, p. 83)

Knowledge from beyond current levels cannot, he believed, arouse interest. Rather, "for a student to relate to some object or event in a personal way, it is necessary to make the study of this object the student's personal affair, and only then can we be certain of succeeding" (1997a, pp. 85–86). To use a term from cognitive psychology, students' *prior knowledge* should always serve as the basis for new learning; and *prior interest* is the driver of what makes new learning possible. This view that readiness is critical to learning is not shared by all. Bruner (1960) argued in contrast that "any subject can be taught in some intellectually honest form to any child at any stage of development" (p. 33), which presumably would mean that a teacher could teach first-graders the difference between Karl Marx and Adam Smith (1776/1977), the sort of developmentally inappropriate teaching that Vygotsky explicitly rejected.

In contrast, teaching is possible, Vygotsky (1997a) argued, to the degree that it is built on students' interests, which involve knowledge. He was concerned "with how far this interest may be directed along the path of the actual subject being studied, and not only involve recourse to the influence of rewards, punishments, the desire to please, and so on, all of which are alien to it" (p. 84). Vygotsky argued against rewards and punishments to motivate students to engage with school learning. They are, he argued,

> psychologically speaking, entirely inappropriate techniques in the school. Besides all the other harmful effects we speak of below, they are also harmful in being useless, i.e., they are powerless to induce the form of activity we need, since they introduce an incommensurably more powerful interest which, we have to admit, forces the child into making his behavior coincide outwardly with what we desire, though internally he remains entirely unchanged.

(1997a, p. 84)

Vygotsky explicitly rejected behaviorism on many occasions, here embedding his critique in his view that rewards and punishments might produce apparent compliance without aligning thinking with action. Without incentives and disincentives to motivate students psychologically, teachers need to rely on interests to drive their learning. Yet teachers should not simply follow children's interests. Rather,

> In organizing the environment and the child's life in this environment, the teacher intervenes actively into the processes by which the child's interests evolve and acts upon them in precisely the same way he influences all of the child's behavior. His role, however, must always be: Before giving an explanation, arouse interest; before asking the child to do something, get him ready for it; before resorting to a reaction, prepare an orientation; and before communicating some new information, induce the anticipation of this new information.

(p. 121)

Elsewhere (see Chapter 13) Vygotsky made a case for grammatical study, the bane of literacy teachers around the globe. Here, ideals meet the stern response of reality, with the consequence that the imperative to begin with interests may lead to conflicts between what students want to know and the reality that some school learning is quite distasteful to many a student, especially those whose diction follows a different standard from the one imposed by school (Baker-Bell, 2020; Baker-Bell et al., 2020).

Assuming that students' interests provide some foundation for learning, teaching on their basis requires reflective practice so as to continually monitor their learning. "The teacher," said Vygotsky (1997a) "must not only observe the student, but also must make conjectures at every turn as to what is happening in the student, whether seen or unseen" (p. 124). Such teacher attention suggests the need "to subdivide the subject matter so that the most critical and the most important points will be reached, just as the force of attention rises, and that the least important parts of the presentation, those which do not suggest something new, occur as the wave of attention is falling" (p. 125). These lessons require continuity and integration; they "must incorporate a degree of give and take and allow for smooth development, i.e., [the subject matter] must be presented in a connected form that would make it possible for all of its parts to be perceived as a unified whole" (p. 125).

It's important to introduce a key problem facing the 21st-century teacher working in underfunded schools: Class size may be prohibitive in getting so involved with each student's developmental trajectory. I have not been able to find information on Soviet class size; and Peters' (1956) review of Soviet education finds that schools took on the task of specialization during Stalin's term, one that no doubt skews any averages. Class size averages in the United States can also be deceiving, in that small special education classes and large physical education classes get treated in the same computation. There is no question, however, that class size in the United States has increased as school budgets have declined (Leachman et al., 2017); and historically, budgets have not caught up with the demands of increased and compulsory attendance rules that have required schooling through higher ages. In my own city, teachers have total student loads approaching 200 students, many living in poverty, often in classes of about 40. Giving them all personal attention and building on their many and varied interests—those that are personal, social, salubrious, and culturally appropriate—is simply not possible. There are needs to be met as well, and on a limited budget that makes personal attention difficult to provide.

Vygotsky argued that the onset of adolescence, triggered by physical changes associated with puberty, is a time when interests matter greatly in students' engagement with school: "The key to the whole problem of the psychological development of the adolescent is the *problem of interests* during the transitional age [adolescence]" (Vygotsky, 1998, p. 3; emphasis in original). In adolescence,

> the problem of interests becomes exceptionally complicated. It is quite clear that if we do not create in adolescents positive attitudes toward certain impressions that interest them, we will not be able to master by pedagogical action the main part of those biological things of value that are involved at the transitional age. We can quite confidently point out that the problem of education and training at the transitional age [adolescence] is a problem of proper building of interests of the age... . [C]reation of habits alone or mechanisms of behavior alone without cultivating interests will always remain a purely formal education that will never solve the problem of the required direction of behavior... . All motivation for activity and for acquiring habits and knowledge is based on interest... . The problem of interest in teaching is whether or not children learn with interest; they never learn without interest: the question is what kind of interest it will be, what will its source be... . [W]e must not

consider nature as a reliable guide to ideals of education. For this reason, we can and must change interests, change their direction, switching the interests from one area to another, and we must cultivate and create new interests.

(1998, pp. 24–25)

Age-based stages—here described as nature, elsewhere as biology or heredity—provide only crude understandings of psychological maturity. Simply being 12 years old cannot predict a student's ability to engage with the curriculum; that possibility is a function of cultural age. Rather, at any age, what matters primarily is the degree to which teachers are attentive to what students want to know, and organize the learning environment to facilitate students' pathways to inquiry and understanding.

The interests driving adolescent activity are part of personality development, which to Vygotsky (1998) required that psychologists "understand the personality of the adolescent not as a thing, but as a process" (p. 15). This process in adolescence includes "growth, crisis, and maturation [that] determine the three stages of sexual maturation" (p. 16). Adolescence is widely considered to be a tumultuous time, such that "The process of maturation is composed of crisis and of synthesis.... Sexual maturation means the appearance in the system of organic tendencies, of new needs and stimulations—this is what lies at the base of the whole change in the system of interests in the adolescent" (p. 16).

These new experiences can produce emotional turbulence, with an adolescent's "negative, protesting, rejecting character" following from "the unfolding and dying off of formerly established systems of interests" (1998, p. 16). "Together with subjective experiences (depressed state, repression, and melancholy)," Vygotsky continued, "this phase is characterized by hostility and a tendency toward arguments and infractions of discipline" (p. 18). He was clear that not all adolescents experience these years the same; "not all children displayed negative attitudes to the same degree, and they manifested different forms of these attitudes in the family and in school" (p. 21).

Few teachers of middle and high school need Vygotsky to explain the vicissitudes of adolescence. But Vygotsky, ever taking an environmental and developmental approach, saw such psychological and behavioral disruptions to occur in relation to settings, and to emerge differently in relation to different conditions of the social world, including school. And teachers beware: "negativism may not appear in every life situation. To a significant degree, a sharp exhibition of these symptoms may be due to inadequacies of the pedagogical approach" (p. 22). As was always the case with Vygotsky, the biological aspects of maturation, which are important, are always only part of the story. The ways in which environments are structured elicit different responses, some more chaotic than others, especially during adolescence and the agitations that accompany bodily and social changes.

Attention

An orientation to school becomes available through a strong degree of equivalence between students' interests and the goals set by others, a phenomenon we have called *goal congruence* in our work (Smagorinsky & O'Donnell-Allen, 2000). Attention is the psychological function that then sustains this interest and supports progress toward goals. Paying attention in school has long been a problem for students. In one study, Csikszentmihalyi, Rathunde, and Whalen (1993), using a method by which "talented teens" reported their affective states and attentional focuses at various points during the day, found that in one large honors-level history class in a high-achieving school, during a lecture on Genghis

Khan's invasion of China, only two students were thinking about China. Of these two, one wondered why Chinese men wore their hair in ponytails; the other was thinking about Chinese food. Imagine, then, the challenges of holding students' attention when conditions are less conducive to engaging students in their learning.

One facet of attention that Vygotsky (1997a) found important is *apperception*, which follows from "the prolonged functioning of attention proceeding constantly in the same direction [such that] all of our experience is formed and developed in this very same direction.... [A]pperception denotes nothing less than the participation of our previous experience in the formation of current experience ... by virtue of already accumulated experience and of previous acts of attention" (p. 133). Apperception thus comprises "the accumulated capital of attention. But, in turn, it accumulates and forms a new reserve of our behavior, which has long since been referred to as *character*. Thus, the stages in this three-level formation of experience exist in the following sequence: Attention, apperception, character" (p. 133; emphasis in original).

A moral code built on the value of persistent application of the intellect to a task is thus available through the sustained attention to a topic that aggregates knowledge and experience into a worldview. Vygotsky found this moral dimension central to education (see Chapter 10), one that requires

> an even greater role for attention in education, since now attention is considered not as a means of facilitating a particular educational or classroom activity, but proves to be extraordinarily important as an end in itself. It never functions without leaving a trace, rather every time it leaves behind it a result. The set of results is collected into apperception, which strives to guide our behavior. Character is formed by the collection of apperceptions working together, which the subtlest educational measures are powerless to overcome. Thus, by guiding attention we take in our hands the key to the formation and development of personality and character.
>
> (1997a, p. 133)

Vygotsky thus saw attention as not simply paying attention to the teacher or a text, the most immediate teacher concern when conducting a class. Attention embedded in orientation and aggregated in apperception contributes to one's ability to focus and to moral development, and stands as a virtue to cultivate.

The typical student, however, does not simply pay attention because of a teacher's exhortations to concentrate. There has to be a high level of interest so that students desire to attend and learn. Goals, then, are not to found in the curriculum guide, from outside the students' range of interests and attention. They follow from why a young person would want to know something. It's important to keep in mind the imperative for Soviet schools to serve a primary role in evolving the New Soviet Man, a requirement of schooling that constrained freedom of choice. A student's desire to learn about a forbidden topic, such as the appeal of the affluence of the decadent West, might result in a sentence to "labor camps [operated] by the police for children between the ages of 10 to 16. These camps, distributed all over the Union, have for their inmates children serving up to ten year sentences, largely for petty thievery, but also for assault, participation in anti-Soviet activity, or vagrancy" (Peters, 1956, pp. 424–425). Anti-Soviet activity was broadly and ruthlessly interpreted, and was not an option for children or adults.

Romanticizing Soviet society based on Vygotsky's advocacy for conducting education according to students' interests and inclinations could easily lead to oversight regarding

Memory

> [Students] have to be made aware of the point of which they are learning and of the constraints that will be imposed upon the material subsequently. The greatest sin of the Tsarist school was not that there was little that was memorized there, but that memorization was performed in unneeded and fruitless directions, i.e., the point of memorizing something was always to respond to the teacher in an examination, all memorization was adapted only to this goal, and, accordingly, memorization turned out to be unfit for other goals.
>
> (Vygotsky, 1997a, p. 144)

School learning is highly dependent on memorizing information and reporting it back on tests, at both the immediate classroom level (Purdie & Hattie, 2002) and in high-stakes settings (Berliner, 2011). Rote learning permeated the Tsarist schools that Vygotsky hoped to reform, and remains an issue of concern in international schools in the 21st century (Bhattacharya, 2022a). Undoubtedly, remembering information is essential to developing conceptual knowledge (Nolan, 1973), the essence of human development in Vygotsky's (1987) vision. The problem is not one of remembering as a general concern. Rather, Vygotsky considered the ways in which schools require the memorization and examination of useless information, a problem of his day and the 21st century.

Memory is a complex phenomenon. Among the most common conceptions of memory comes from cognitive psychology, which depicts memory as a set of storage containers in the head, one for the short term and one for the long term (Repovš & Baddeley, 2006). In this representation, a memory may be retrieved from these containers into conscious attention, unadulterated, through neurological nodes and networks. Yet people commonly speak of memories as being warped, hazy, and obscured or altered over time. These experiences cannot be explained by memory as a retrieval system of events stored intact in a containment system. In contrast, Vygotsky (1999) described memory as a process that is socially mediated and thus subject to reconstruction. He argued that "the decisive factor is made up not on the strength of memory or the level of its development, but actually in combining, in building a structure, in perceiving relations" (p. 56). This relational structure mediates how an event is remembered.

Vygotsky (1997c) recognized that memory is not strictly an internal, reliable mental activity in which memories are retrieved from storage units in the fashion of a personal computer, the metaphor for the mind employed in cognitive psychology. Rather, memory is mediated by external factors that are either deliberately constructed by an individual, or prompted by environmental influences. Undoubtedly his favorite example of mediated memory was the knotted handkerchief, which is an external sign reminding a person of something to do. Many Soviet citizens apparently knotted many a hanky to remind them of obligations and responsibilities; and the knotted hanky reminder has remained of interest in psychology (e.g., Shanon, 2009).[2]

Vygotsky (1997c) concluded that a knot in a hanky serves as a deliberately constructed, purposeful, external means of regulating memory; that is, as a sign, an external meaning-laden construction created for the purpose of prompting a specific memory. He elaborated, saying,

> We call artificial stimuli-devices introduced by man into a psychological situation where they fulfill the function of autostimulation "signs," giving this term a broader and at the same time a more precise sense than in common usage. According to our determination, every condition[al][3] stimulus created artificially by man that is a means of mastering behavior—that of another or one's own—is a sign.
>
> (p. 54)

The ability to construct a sign is among the most unique features of the human species (see Chapter 5), and can be external and material (the knotted hanky) or internal and ideal (unspoken verbal ideation). Human behavior, Vygotsky (1997c) argued, typically involves biological processes—in this case, the brain's activity, perhaps in conjunction with physical manipulation of an object—in combination with social mediation. Humans create "artificial signaling stimuli," principally speech, which in turn control the cerebral hemispheres such that "the basic and most general activity of man that differentiates man from animals in the first place, from the aspect of psychology, is *signification*, that is, creation and use of signs" (p. 55; emphasis in original). Even the knotted hanky presumably requires some verbal addendum in order to ensure proper recall, e.g., "I need to take out the trash." As Vygotsky (1999) put it, "In the transition of activity inward, the replacement of functions itself leads to verbalization of memory and, in conjunction with this, to remembering with the help of concepts" (p. 56).

Twenty-first century people might have calendars on their devices, or write shopping lists, or engage in other external reminders to be where they are supposed to be and do what they supposed to do. They might also see a landmark they did not construct that brings back a memory or remind them where to turn. This turn is not just a physical reflex, however. It involves verbal sign-and-tool mediation, e.g., "Here's where I take a left." Memory is thus mediated by external signs and tools that enable what recall lacks, in conjunction with intellectual operations mediated by speech. In this sense, argued Vygotsky (1997a), a person's attention becomes directed attention.

In school, in contrast, memorizing and recalling information is a purely mental activity. Students typically can't rely on reminders to produce the answers the exam calls for. Rather, they might construct mental images—*iconic memories* in cognitive psychology terms—that serve the purpose of external reminders. To recall that the capital of Illinois is Springfield, one might imagine an *ill* person recovering in *spring*time in a flowery *field*, which invents a memory enhancer by making external knowledge an internal imagaic mental function, accompanied by verbal reminders. To remember the ways in which animals are classified for my recent Master Gardener Extension Volunteer status, I took the Kingdom-Phylum-Class-Order-Family-Genus-Species taxonomy and created a phrase, King Phillip Can Order Fabulous Greek Salads, which has nothing to do with the taxonomy but helps me remember it. Since students rarely are taught how to remember things, even as they are required to memorize much, they more likely repeat the facts many times in their heads in hopes that they will be able to repeat them during the examination. They might further employ flash cards to train themselves for the moment of recall in assessment.

As might be expected, Vygotsky found such devotion of mental action to recalling facts for a test but never using them purposefully to be a waste of personal and educational time. This problem was confirmed later in the United States, where Tyler (1949) found that the information memorized for school is mostly forgotten within a year, and almost entirely within two. It has since been re-confirmed by millions of students. Yet memorization of information remains a staple of education, in spite of mountains of research that demonstrate its ineffectiveness (Saavedra & Opfer, 2012) and student preferences for more agentive learning (Živkoviü, 2016).

Signs do more than serve as memory tools. They enable the imagination to *project future outcomes* through abstraction, planning, and anticipation based on prior experiences, another unique feature of being human. For the most part, a hanky knot, a fully external sign, is limited to the immediate mundane task of changing the laundry or picking up a loaf of bread. What enables a future orientation, he argued, is the use of words, the "tool of tools." Words, I would argue, further serve as the "sign of signs" given their infinite flexibility and capacity for expressing ideas in coherent detail. They also often come in conjunction with other sorts of signs, such as a map to a destination or schematic for a construction project, or in the current century, an electronic device that may employ multiple sign systems. Such use of semiotic signs enables a person to help construct a future world beyond the immediate range of perception.

There are aspects of Vygotsky's presentation that might be considered culturally insulated, a problem when disentangling any perspective from its time and place. He argued, for instance, that monuments are designed to preserve memories, and serve as mediated memory devices that contribute to historical narratives. He favorably referenced a contemporary psychologist's view that "the very essence of civilization consists in the fact that we purposely erect monuments and statues in order not to forget" (1997c, p. 59).

The Soviet Union was very big on monuments to their leaders and to the noble proletarian worker. But the heroes of leadership were more often commemorated than were the working class heroes. As reported by Bregman (2022), the nation had 15,000 Lenin statues in 1991, nearly a half-century after his brief rule and death. Lenin himself devised the system of *monumentálnaya propaganda* (propaganda through monuments), replacing Tsarist figures with monuments to Soviet heroes. These monuments have been more recently revived by Vladimir Putin, who stated in 2000 that

> If we agree that the symbols of the preceding epochs must not be used at all, including the Soviet epoch, we will have to admit then that our mothers' and fathers' lives were useless and meaningless, that their lives were in vain. Neither in my head nor in my heart can I agree with this… . So, let's direct all of our fervent energy and talent not into destruction but into construction [of statues commemorating Russian historical figures, especially the architects of Soviet society whom Putin hoped to emulate].
>
> (quoted in St. John-Bond, 2018, n.p.).

Aseyev (2022), a Ukrainian journalist writing during Russia's military invasion of Crimea during the second decade of the century, and later imprisoned and tortured for his dissident views, finds these monuments to represent propagandistic myth more than to achieve what Vygotsky believed to be the preservation of history:

> The Lenin that proudly towers over the main square in Donetsk and is now beautifully illuminated on the order of the local "republican" leaders is not the Ulianov [Lenin's birth surname] who founded the first concentration camps in Russia,

presided over the Council of Soviet Commissars [which both planned the rebuild after the Soviet takeover, and developed the Gulag], or was the tyrant guilty of the deaths of hundreds of thousands.

No. For them, Lenin is Kashtan ice cream for 28 kopeks and a warm May rally with their dads in 1979.

(pp. 102–103)

This sort of propagandistic use of monuments has occurred in the United States and other nations as well as a way to create memories consistent with a particular ideology. Loewen's (1999) study of US monuments reveals the ways in which Confederate heritage groups erected monuments following the Civil War, and well through the 20th century. These statues honor Klansmen, traitors, military failures, slave-owners, and other figures whose reconstructed images reinforced a history congenial to their noble and heroic "Lost Cause of the Confederacy" narrative. This history has been remarkably durable. It is embedded in school history books and continues to shape education that, in the 2020s, clings to mythology so as not to upset white students' sensibilities in schools and universities by suggesting that racism and gender discrimination exist (Moffa, 2022). Vygotsky's 1920s notion of preserving memories through statues assumes a sincerity that is often lacking in the ideological revisionist construction of historical monuments.

Memory may also be mediated emotionally. Damasio (2021) argues that memories both rely on the recall of events and involve their creative reconstruction: "When we relate and combine images in our minds and transform them within our creative imaginations, we produce new images that signify ideas, concrete as well as abstract; we produce symbols; and we commit to memory a good part of all the imagetic produce" (p. 47). This imaginative reconstruction is often undertaken in service of seeking equilibrium through affect. People yearn for homeostasis, the development of a stable state of mind and body for optimal functioning. The regulation of memories can contribute to the quest for stability through *emotions* (physiological responses), *feelings* (those mental experiences that follow from either the presence or absence of homeostasis, such as anger or joy), and *affect* ("the universe of our ideas transmuted in feeling" [Damasio, 2021, p. 79]), and subject to subjective construction.

This conception fits with Vygotsky's contention that people seek to regulate their mental states to achieve internal peace amid competing demands, both internally and in relation to their social situations. Damasio's (2021) view of homeostasis as a goal might contradict Vygotsky's dialectical method, which assumes that without obstacles to overcome, development isn't possible. Given that homeostasis might be unattainable, it represents a goal that is worked toward by never achieved. This possibility would allow, then, for Vygotsky's conception of the dialectical life to be consistent with Damasio's view that people seek equilibrium. It might be a Sisyphean task that never comes to fruition, yet has value in the process.

Vygotsky's criticisms of his contemporaries did not lead him to reject their understandings entirely, just as my disagreements with some of cognitive psychology's perspective does not lead me to dismiss the field's enduring contributions. Freud, with whom Vygotsky found fault for looking back in life more than developing pathways forward, offered the concept of *nachträglichkeit*, i.e., afterwardsness or retroaction. Emotion and memory are linked in the mind such that "what is stored is not a simple representation of the original experience. Retrieval of emotional memories is not analogous to extracting items from a memory bank" (Modell, 2005, pp. 557, 565). Memory thus becomes reconstructed as a person has additional experiences that emotionally affect how a memory is recalled so that "the subjective impact of an event is not given once and for all but is malleable by subsequent experiences" (Bistoen, Vanheule, & Craps, 2014, p. 668).

Memories thus rarely emerge intact, no matter how many times a fact is mentally repeated or how neatly the nodes and networks connecting memory containers are drawn in a figure. Vygotsky (1997a) argued that the effort to use memories as evidence of reality is fruitless. Wixted, Mickes, and Fisher (2018) report that "memory is *malleable*. With surprising ease, participants in a memory experiment can be led to believe, for example, that they saw a stop sign when they actually saw a yield sign (Loftus, Miller, & Burns, 1978) or that they became lost in a shopping mall as a child when no such experience actually occurred (Loftus & Pickrell, 1995)" (p. 324). "There can be no exact recollection of former experience," argued Vygotsky, "nor can there be any absolutely exact recollections, recall always denotes a certain reworking of what has been perceived, and consequently, a certain distortion of reality" (1997a, p. 148). These issues have great salience in school, especially as they relate to orientation, interests, and attention.

Memories are not only reconstructed, they are emplotted (Ricoeur, 1983) in a broader life narrative (Wertsch, 2022). Ricoeur describes three ways in which narrative emplotment functions. First, it weaves together assorted events into a meaningful, plot-driven narrative. Second, it assembles story elements into a familiar, established narrative structure. Finally, it provides the episodic structure of a narrative, editing out what doesn't fit and configuring the salient events temporally. Memories, then, can be reconstructed to fit a narrative that serves one's developmental trajectory. Vygotsky (1999) made a similar point, saying that

> the role of memory in the operation of the child affects not simply the extension of the segment of the past that actually is merged into a single whole with the present, but results in a new method of combining the elements of past experience with the present. A new method develops on the basis of including into a single focus of attention the speech formulas of past situations and past actions. As we have seen, speech forms the operation along laws different from direct action precisely just as it merges, unites, synthesizes the past and the present in a different way, freeing the action of the child from the power of direct remembering.
>
> (p. 35)

Vygotsky reinforced the role of speech in mediated memory, one that takes a memory and makes it part of a broader narrative. It might be the valorization of US Confederate leaders as part of a "Southern heritage" narrative in which the failed Civil War became the "Lost Cause" of a worthy battle, lost but morally right and not in vain. It might be a selective memory of an individual that amplifies some actions and elides others to create a coherent view that fits one's needs for personal cohesion and equilibrium. These memories cannot be lifted from cranial containers intact and in isolation. Rather, they are mediated, emplotted, and reorganized to fit a broader narrative.

Memorization through mental repetition is a crude and fruitless effort to recall information, used in school to pass an examination based on questions posed by someone else. Mediated memory through external signs, in contrast, provides a learner with a cultural cognitive map for organizing useful information, both for the moment and for future action. It is embedded in various sorts of narratives and related means of organizing information, events, emotions, and other factors into a meaningful whole. Vygotsky referred to medieval scholars who

> created imaginary mnemonic cities with many streets, squares, and houses, mentally placed in these cities names, designations, objects, and persons that had to be memorized, and this system of mnemonic cities met the requirements of the scholastic scientist. The contemporary schoolchild remembers with the help of a map, schema, or outline, but the mnemonic principle, that is, memory with the help of a sign, remains the same.
>
> (in Van der Veer, 2020, pp. 100–101)

Presumably, the child using a schematic external sign as a tool for organizing memories into useful intellectual structures would be interested in city planning, or at least navigating the neighborhood, for such signs to have educational value. Presumably verbal sign mediation is part of the process. This planning would in turn contribute to a developmental trajectory that involves the integration of parts into coherent wholes, often immersed in a narrative structure that gives meaning to experience.

This review of mediated memory complicates how memory serves the education of children and youth. In school, students are often tasked with memorization of facts that rarely cohere into a functioning whole, yet learn few strategies for remembering what they are tested on. Memory usage in school tends to look backward toward facts from lectures and textbooks. It lacks the generative, forward-looking function that Vygotsky saw as critical to a developmental perspective. It might follow teachers' frequent claim that memorized information will serve students' futures—e.g., Santayana's (1905) admonition that "Those who cannot remember the past are condemned to repeat it"—but that is unlikely if the facts are soon forgotten. As a result, memorization is required for low-level cognition, but not in service of orchestrating and synthesizing information, impressions, and experiences into a coherent, conceptual understandings that students find important, useful, or worth knowing. What is memorized is largely forgotten. What students might recall instead is how tedious and impractical their school learning has been.

Relevance

Vygotsky emphasized the need for schoolwork to be relevant if students are to be willing participants in education:

> Speech, writing, reading, counting and measurement must be intimately connected with the study of real-life phenomena and must not be taught at school as the separate subjects "arithmetic" and "Russian[4]." ... And not just the language habits and mathematical habits, but also the work habits, the social habits and the art habits must be acquired in the process of the school work.... . The old strict system of the development of arithmetical representations was more based on the logic of the subject itself than on the psychology of the child. The new programs, on the other hand, are pedocentric, that is, they focus on the child himself and the peculiar properties of his behavior and thinking. This is why in the complex method the *connection* between particular forms of activities and the *gradualness* in the learning of skills must first of all be pedological, that is, must have their basis in the psychology of the child. The arithmetical problems must be psychologically connected with the general

activity of the child through the *need* for arithmetical operations that develops in the process of work.... . We must only take care that it is indeed a real-life problem, which emerges in the process of the child's activity and not a dry, artificial problem from a textbook about swimming pools, banking operations, and so on that are incomprehensible for the child and foreign to him. This is the crux of "real-life arithmetic" and the crux of the whole work with the complex and the child's cultural development connected with it.

(in Van der Veer, 2020, pp. 168–169; emphasis in original)

Pedagogically, Vygotsky felt congruence with Dewey in yet another way, a belief in the value of project-based learning (cf. Kilpatrick, 1918):

The method of projects is essentially a method of problems that are systematically presented to the pupil. The formal habits, that is, reading, writing, and counting are the continuation of the development of speech. They are the highest cultural forms of behavior. How does the child develop the need for these higher forms of behavior? In the process of external activity, he stumbles upon a number of real-life problems that can only be solved by the elaboration of new forms of behavior and push the child to develop them.... . "The dialectical method," says Blonskiy [1925], "demands that phenomena are studied in connection with the practice of man, in connection with his transformative activity.... . The view of the child as a theoretician and investigator does not at all correspond with the pedological facts: he is first of all a doer and depending on how he acts, he more or less thinks. That is why only teaching that proceeds from the practical activity of the child collective is pedologically correct" (p. 189). This is why the earlier teaching of reading, writing, and counting, which was severed from the child's activity, deeply contradicts the peculiarities of childhood. Teaching in complexes, on the contrary, proceeds from the child's practice, from his external activity, and from there goes to the higher cultural development of behavior.

(in Van der Veer, 2020, pp. 169–170)

Although it provides no guarantees, a curriculum that continually returns to prior material in more advanced ways helps to reinforce and build the concepts involved, promoting relevance. Vygotsky (1997a) reached three primary conclusions about how to teach in relation to students' interests:

First, all the topics in a course must be interconnected, which is also the best way of ensuring that a common interest will be aroused and that this interest will collect around a single axis. Only then may we speak of a more or less prolonged, lasting, and deep interest, an interest that will not shatter into dozens of unrelated parts, making it impossible to grasp in a unified and general thought all the different subjects of study. [Second,] everything has to involve recourse to repetition, to memorization and assimilation of knowledge. But we all have come to realize how uninteresting is such repetition for children, how they dislike these lessons, even if they do not find them difficult. The reason for this is that here the fundamental rule of interest is violated and, consequently repetition turns into mere dawdling, constituting the most irrational and unpsychological of all techniques.

(p. 86)

Vygotsky worked according to a tension that can be difficult to resolve: How to promote the memory of whatever the student wants and needs to know, without doing so in such a tedious way that they lose interest in learning. He resolved this potential conflict by saying,

> The rule is to avoid repetition absolutely and to make instruction focused, i.e., to arrange the material in such a way that it may be gone over fully and all at once in the briefest and most simplified way possible; then the teacher may return to a topic but not to just repeat what has been already gone over but to review the same topic one more time in a more thorough and more all inclusive form, complemented with a wealth of new facts, generalizations, and conclusions, so that topics students have already studied are repeated anew, though unfolded from a new perspective, and this new aspect is so connected with what they are already acquainted with that interest is readily aroused all by itself. In this sense, just as in science as in real life, it is only a new view about what is old that may arouse our interest.
>
> Finally the third and final rule governing the employment of the child's interest mandates the construction of the entire educational system in the school in direct proximity to everyday life, to teach children in such a way as to interest them, to begin with what is familiar to the child and what arouses his interest in a natural way.
>
> (pp. 86–87)

This conception embodies what Bruner (1960) calls a *spiral curriculum*, one that continually cycles back to prior instruction so that knowledge is enriched, but not simply repeated. It further builds academic knowledge on the foundation provided by students' interests and experiences. Memorization in this sense is inadequate, fixed on knowledge without developing it, leaving little opportunity for authentic, pragmatic learning. Remembering information germane to interests is built into the learning that students want to do, reinforced over time and driven by engagement with new and increasingly challenging materials and concepts.

Discussion

Vygotsky's account of orientation, interests, attention, memory, and relevance undoubtedly would comfort the 21st-century progressive educator. He advocated for authentic learning, child-centered classrooms, learning driven by integrated conceptual understandings, a rejection of examinations to assess learning, and other features also available in the work of Dewey (1916). Dewey was, by the 1920s, in his 60s and a global star in educational philosophy, if considered bourgeois in the Soviet Union by virtue of his US location and presumed decadent capitalist stance. Both Dewey and Vygotsky might disturb those who view schooling as a place of subordination and submission to discipline, typified by Edmondson's (2006) title, *John Dewey & Decline of American Education: How the Patron Saint of Schools Has Corrupted Teaching & Learning*. Dewey has been accused of questioning traditional morality, abandoning the learning of information, undermining Christian values, valuing the collective over the individual through his advocacy for group work, and in general destabilizing the established societal order so that children may reinvent the world on their own terms. Given that such critiques of Dewey continue to be mounted by the conservative press (e.g., Benson, 2018), it's safe to say that the same battles that have been waged over the course and content of education internationally have budged little in the last century.

As one steeped in progressive values, I am untroubled by Dewey's and Vygotsky's perspective on how best to conduct a school. I do find the pure version of their progressive outlook to be overly ideal, however. Cohen (1998) concludes that Dewey's countercultural educational philosophy was never accompanied by a strategy for how to institute his ideas in schools that were conducted according to formalism and conformity. Vygotsky's and Dewey's shared perspective remains, for the most part, a vision more than a concrete plan.

A second complication concerns the ways in which some students, especially those socialized from outside the upper-middle class norms that govern schools, don't view school as the place in which their present is nourished or their future is formed (Eckert, 1989). Vygotsky's emphasis on orientation helps explain the problem. In order for school to thrive in the manner he describes, students would need to be oriented to school as a place of learning and fulfillment. I don't know if Soviet students felt so disaffected by school that they refused to engage with its tasks, but I do know that it's a common occurrence in the 21st century, and it troubled me as a teacher in the 1970s and 1980s. No matter how well aligned my instruction was with the vision I have described in this chapter, some students just would not participate wholeheartedly; and some would participate only with demonstrable resentment.

Among the issues at work, I believe, was a student orientation that found the whole business of schooling to be an alienating experience. Meanwhile, something outside school provides a primary orientation for many students: Jobs, personal relationship drama, social media, sports, celebrity life, music, etc. Some demographic groups are more likely to find school to be unwelcoming than others. I have argued that the students most likely to buy into and play along with school instruction are the ones whom schools were originally designed to accommodate: Relatively affluent white people (Smagorinsky, 2017). Perhaps teachers are to blame, as they are held accountable for everything else that goes awry in school and society. But the problem with the profession isn't teachers having bad days. The problem is, as Vygotsky and Dewey would argue, that school isn't designed to build on students' interests and motivations for learning. And it increasingly isn't designed or operated to make teaching a fulfilling profession.

The ardent prose in which Vygotsky describes his ideal school remains an illusion in mass public education due to students' orientations to other sirens toward which their interests are inclined. That problem does not make either Dewey or Vygotsky irrelevant; it makes them, instead, idealists whose ideas have currency, if not unproblematic application. Students' orientations to school remain critical, and with their attention distracted by so many temptations, maintaining a focus on school might challenge the greatest of teachers. Memorization remains both central to schooling, and questionable in promoting learning. Conceptual knowledge remains the key to human development, and cannot be advanced through the piecemeal and temporary memorization of facts in order to pass tests. People still remember what they need to know to learn what matters to them and forget the rest, and school still valorizes the curriculum over what students believe they should know to explore their interests.

The problems and challenges outlined by Vygotsky thus remain germane a century removed from his career in the Soviet Union. His idealistic presentation assumes that all students share his exceptional disposition to experience life to its fullest, which no doubt followed from his inborn disposition, his fear of impending death, his intense personality, and other factors that may be foreign to the great mass of students in school. Few students share that passionate dedication to their development, or his belief in schooling as a critical means to maximizing their potential. Too many school systems operate from the top down, making 21st century schools similar to the rote-driven schools of the Tsarist era that Vygotsky positioned himself against, much as Dewey formulated his views as a response to rote learning. This confluence of inflexible schools, and students oriented away from formal education, makes teaching especially challenging. Technology has been offered as both the salvation of education, and its greatest enemy (Cohen & Lippert, 1999). The problem with advocating for technology is that it assumes an isomorphic student, that is, one like all the others. Some students might indeed use technology only for academic purposes; yet for most, the temptations of online distractions make teaching students who have access to cell phones and tablets a challenging prospect. If technology were the magic wand, then it wouldn't be so problematic.

Even, however, with all these problems, Vygotsky's emphasis on grounding school in students' orientations and interests is a goal worthy of pursuing. Understanding the relation among orientation, interests, attention, memory, and school learning may not change the deep structure of school. But it may enhance teachers' understanding of how current schooling organization falls short, and suggest alternatives to conventional wisdom and practice.

Notes

1 Robert Eugen Gaupp (1870–1953) was a German psychiatrist and neurologist, and author of *Psychology of Children* (1908, or 1909, or 1918, depending on the source).
2 At home, I put a spatula on the kitchen counter pointed toward the utility room to remind myself to move the laundry from the washer to the drier. Sadly, I don't own a hanky.
3 I make the editorial adjustment here from what was translated as *conditioned* to the more accurate *conditional*.
4 Probably a course in Russian culture, literacy, and literature, comparable to "English" in English-speaking nations.

12 Teaching Literature

Literature mattered a great deal to Vygotsky, especially the theater. Since childhood, wrote Leont'ev (1997), Vygotsky "passionately loved literature and very early he began to deal with it on a professional level. His first works as a literary critic [in his master's thesis] grew directly from his interests as a reader [which] is why Vygotsky called his works a 'reader's critique'" (p. 13). As I will review, he shifted in his doctoral research to a more formalist approach. Ultimately, he found both readerly subjectivity and a formalist orientation to be involved in reading literature or engaging with the theater. As a young man in Belarus, he was a great aficionado of the stage, writing reviews of both Russian-language and Yiddish performances (Yasnitsky, 2012). Van der Veer (2015) reports that even as a young man, Vygotsky became

> an important figure in the control and organization of cultural life in Gomel and its surroundings. As a member of the so-called Art Council ... he had free access to all theater performances in the region and was responsible for the publications about these performances in the Soviet press. He also travelled around inside and outside the Gomel region and visited performances in other cities to contract troupes to play in Gomel.
>
> (p. 103)

Through this process he began to develop a theory of literary and performative reading, and in turn of how psychology develops in relation to the environment. From 1917 to 1924, he taught literature and became interested in his students' process of interpretation and response (Van der Veer & Valsiner, 1991). His doctoral dissertation focused on *Hamlet*, along with a variety of short stories, fables, and other fictional texts. His engagement with literary works provided the first stage of his psychological investigations, fittingly enough with a dissertation published as *The Psychology of Art* (Vygotsky, 1971), which Vygotsky had not wanted published, although he referred to its contents in his later writing. Vygotsky's conception of art was logocentric and included both emotional and intellectual elements. He focused for the most part on literature and the theater. This emphasis provided the foundation for his "linguistic psychology" (Van der Veer, 1997b, p. 7) and his view of the foundational role of speech in human development.

In this chapter, I will review his perspective on the role of literature as an art form through which psychological development is available. Vygotsky may not provide the ideal source for the 21st-century English Language Arts teacher, given his elitism and preference for canonical over everyday texts. He nonetheless generated insights that may illuminate much about reading, especially as an emotional and embodied experience. He produced

DOI: 10.4324/9781003374848-15

these understandings in his teens through his mid-twenties, a remarkable achievement that may excuse his snobbish views about literature. My purpose in reviewing Vygotsky's views on art (literature), emotion, and consciousness is to take this overlooked aspect of his career project[1] and examine it as a way to provide depth to his contributions to the field's understanding of cultural mediation, personality, and concept development.

This chapter focuses on Vygotsky's exegesis of literary reading in *The Psychology of Art* and later essays on emotions, including attention to how his socialization limited his vision. I address what he considered to be the essence of true art, the role of text and genre in literary production, the manner in which reading is fully embodied rather than an action conducted by eyeballs and brains, the emotional catharsis that readers undertake to produce understandings via "intelligent emotions," the emotions involved in both formal staged drama and everyday human drama, and attention to how Vygotsky's confidence in rationality may be an illusion given the primacy of emotions in human thinking. I close with some suggestions on how to think about teaching literature in light of what Vygotsky has to offer about the psychology of literary art.

The Psychology of Art

The Psychology of Art reveals Vygotsky (1971) in the formative stages of developing a comprehensive psychology of human development in its cultural-historical context. Art, he wrote, "is determined and conditioned by the psyche of the social man" (p. 12) and "systemizes a very special sphere in the psyche of social man—his emotions" (p. 13). He rejected the notion that an artistic response consists solely of a transaction between text and reader, such as that encouraged by Probst (2004), who urges readers to shut out culture in order to generate an unmediated personal response. In contrast, Vygotsky argued, "Between man and the outside world there stands the social environment, which in its own way refracts and directs the stimuli acting upon the individual and guides all the reactions that emanate from the individual" (p. 252). Individuals are always working within cultural and historical channels of practice that shape their perception of reality, including what they read and how they read it. There is no way to exclude the social environment or cultural history from a reading experience.

The Psychology of Art stands as a fascinating and impressive account of the qualities that distinguish what is art from what is not, and the ways in which art may engender responses in those who engage with it. It is also a youthful project that no doubt Vygotsky himself would have reconsidered had he lived long enough to revisit it, leaving such revisions up to his successors. His health during this period limited his possibilities to literary criticism rather than the active lab work he undertook subsequently, given that he produced *The Psychology of Art* during one of his many lengthy bed confinements due to tuberculosis, a period ranging from 1915 to 1922 that encompassed ages 19–26.

The Psychology of Art serves as what Leont'ev (1971), in his preface, calls a "germinal" exploration that Vygotsky never completed: To arrive at "the understanding of the function of art in the life of society and in the life of man as a sociohistorical being" (p. x). Although Vygotsky often referred to literary greats from Russia, along with Shakespeare, in his psychological writing, his formal literary criticism ended with his dissertation. The unique issues that he raised, however, remain relevant to the teaching of literature and the role of art and emotion in psychological development. Yaroshevsky (1989) describes this inquiry as "an attempt to understand man in the conflicts of his being in this world full of tragedy" (p. 215). Given Vygotsky's life experiences with anti-Semitic pogroms, two

Russian Revolutions, World War I, illnesses that took his brothers' lives and threatened his own, the Polish-Bolshevik War, the post–Romanov Russian Civil War, the institution of the Soviet Union as a radical social experiment, Stalin's Great Terror, and other upheavals of his time, life no doubt did appear to a sickly Jewish man from the Pale of Settlement to be a series of tragedies.

Limits of Vygotsky's Conception of the Psychology of Art

Vygotsky, while a titanic figure in the history of psychology, could not always see outside his own cultural limits (see Chapter 4). Few of us can, without contrasting possibilities. He was a man of his time and place, and those parochial contextual factors shaped how he viewed the world and limited his access to other possibilities.

Vygotsky's cultural limitations led him to interpret symbols in very specific ways, and to reach judgments about art and canonicity that matched those of his upbringing. In saying that "art is an expanded '*social* feeling' or *technique of feelings*" (emphasis in original), he approvingly quoted Hippolyte Taine[2] (1873), who wrote that "For seventeenth-century man there was nothing uglier than a mountain. It aroused in him many unpleasant ideas, because he was as weary of barbarianism as we are weary of civilization. Mountains give us a chance to rest, away from our sidewalks, offices, and shops; we like landscape only for this reason" (quoted in Vygotsky, 1971, p. 244).

This depiction of mountains as ugly, as serving only as a respite from social overstimulation, however, is not universal. Mountains are often hallowed sites to people from societies with sacred traditions, as exemplified by US Native American author M. Scott Momaday's (1969) *The Way to Rainy Mountain* and his characterization of the mountain as a spiritual source: "To look upon that landscape in the early morning, with the sun at your back, is to lose the sense of proportion. Your imagination comes to life, and this, you think, is where Creation was begun." This sacred role of mountains in cultures from outside the European sphere of influence has long been documented (e.g., Juluka, 1984; Wissler & Duvall, 1908).

Vygotsky's indebtedness to these traditions was characteristic of Soviets even as they, in Vygotsky's words, often distinguished between "the West" and "the USSR," setting themselves apart from capitalist Europe politically if not entirely culturally. Cultures from beyond the Northern and Eastern Mediterranean worlds (including the Soviet lands extending to the Bering Strait off the coast of the Russian Far East) were not included in his conception of "seventeenth-century man" as an arbiter of taste and standards. This provincialism is more difficult to sustain and defend in a 21st-century connected world in which access to multiple perspectives is readily available to those whose governments have not restricted internet and media access.

Even in "free" nations, parochialism is available to those who self-select information sources that feature ideologies with which they are already aligned. The early 20th-century limited knowledge to personal interactions and written texts, exposing Vygotsky to European and US theory and practice along with Soviet culture. He was shaped by his Jewish heritage (see Chapter 1), was immersed in both the Enlightenment (rational) and Romantic (spontaneous) traditions (Wertsch, 2000), had a Marxist influence that Soviet officials deemed inadequate, and, like all humans, was contradictory in spite of his efforts to be consistent (Dutton & Heath, 2010; Smagorinsky, 2020a). His brilliance could not overcome what his own cultural-historical theory would predict: That his thinking was social in origin, and that he was a product of his culture. He saw his society as optimal during the hopeful and idealistic formation of the explicitly communist Soviet nation, one that promised to legislate equality and eventually serve as the North Star for other societies to follow as international borders were eradicated and a global working-class society emerged from the ruins of capitalism.

The Essence of Art

Vygotsky's (1971) elitism was on display in his effort to distinguish what constitutes a work of art as opposed to a production of lower creative and aesthetic standards. He dismissed most children's literature as "a vivid example of bad taste, of the coarse violation of all notion of esthetic style, and of the most dismal misunderstanding of the mind of the child," due to its didactic emphasis characterized by "a hortatory tone, tedious copybook maxims, and unctuous preachiness" (Vygotsky, 1997a, p. 242). Art, instead, requires a careful formulation of appropriate materials, embeddedness in a suitable artistic genre, and topic of fitting emotional timbre. The modern teacher of literature is faced with a more complex terrain than this binary view of texts being either tedious and unaesthetic, or artistic. More recent excavations of this genre in Russia and the Soviet Union confirm Vygotsky's characterization of didacticism, while also complicating his binary perspective (Special Collections at the University of Washington Libraries, n.d.).

Vygotsky's earliest writing was well-aligned with 21st-century reader response theory. As reported by Van der Veer (2015):

> His Master's thesis at Shanyavsky University was an analysis of Shakespeare's *Hamlet*. Written in 1916, it was an entirely subjective analysis written from the viewpoint that readers are authors who are free to create their own interpretation of plays, novels and poems. In the years that followed Vygotsky changed his views—after the October Revolution anything that reeked of subjective or spiritual matters became suspect—and again [in his doctoral study, *The Psychology of Art*] tried to explain the effect of art in terms of the artist's technique.
>
> (pp. 106–107)

Whether he made this shift because he matured in his twenties to reach a new understanding, or pragmatically adapted his views on subjectivity to satisfy Soviet dogma, or did both or something else, remains unclear. Gravitating to Soviet orthodoxy was a life-saving measure taken by many citizens of the era (Daniels, Cole, & Wertsch, 2007). What is clear is that his early belief in the reader's free-range, idiosyncratic, highly personal responses to literature was displaced by a more formalist conception of art and its role in human development, albeit one that relied on emotions and imagination for response, analysis, elevation, and interpretation.

The Vygotsky (1971) who appears in his doctoral dissertation is thus different from the one in his master's thesis. In many ways, he became the sort of formalist given critical authority by the founders of New Criticism, locating artistry in the structure of a work. To this textual emphasis he added an affective dimension missing from New Criticism, the idea that a reader's response to a text begins with emotion, not analysis. He said of his task,

> I do not interpret [aesthetic] symbols as manifestations of the spiritual organization of the author or his readers. I do not attempt to infer the psychology of an author or his readers from a work of art, since I know this cannot be done on the basis of an

interpretation of symbols. I shall attempt to study the pure and impersonal psychology of art without reference to either the author or the reader, looking only at the form and material of the work of art.

(p. 5)

Vygotsky's (1971) focus on form led him to reject the view that meaning arises from "the psyche of social man" who "completes with his imagination the picture or image created by the artist" (p. 39), the very sort of reader whom he valorized in his master's thesis and who is positioned in reader response conceptions as a personal meaning-maker (Rosenblatt, 1938). Rather, he maintained, "the artist must never allow our fancy or imagination to perform an *arbitrary* addition or completion" (p. 46; emphasis added). These capricious elaborations, he said, are "the work of ignoramuses and laymen" (p. 46). In Vygotsky's conception, the psychology of art, unlike the changing psyches of people, "remains immutable and eternal. What changes and evolves from generation to generation is the way it is used and applied." Rorschach's inkblots, he continued, "show quite unmistakably that we give meaning, structure, and expression to the most absurd, random, and senseless accumulation of forms. In other words, a work of art by itself cannot be responsible for the thoughts and ideas it inspires" (p. 40).

Vygotsky disdained the manner in which many literary works have "fallen prey to commonplace and vulgar interpretation, the prejudices of which have to be dealt with every time one studies a familiar text" (p. 150). This conception no doubt goes against many more recent populist texts, such as those by Bleich (1975) and Probst (2004) that focus as much on, or perhaps more on, readers' subjectivity as they do on the contents of a literary text. Vygotsky was interested in subjective responses that emerge from engagement with textual codes, yet not unbridled responses. Indeed, these primary emotional responses become subject to the discipline of the intellect. His focus was on investigating how "qualitatively new emotional complexes arise in the course of reading" (Van der Veer & Valsiner, 1991, p. 32).

Vygotsky (1997a) distinguished between types of human works that can be considered art and thus to be canonical, and those that should not. He disputed Tolstoy's[3] view that children (aside, presumably, from prodigies like Mozart) are capable of producing art, asserting that their lack of technical skill prevents their creations, no matter how meaningful the texts might be to their personality development, from reaching artistic status. Tolstoy (1862) believed that it would be "odd and insulting" for him to critique the productions of 11-year-old children because such interference would violate "the natural properties the child's soul is endowed with from the very start" (p. 258). Vygotsky felt no such obligation to treat children's meaning-making with kid gloves: "No matter how sublime and how exquisite are those works [the children featured by Tolstoy] produced, their creative impulses were always of a different order than Goethe's[4] or Tolstoy's in their very essence" (p. 259) and in their technical achievement.

Such art might have developmental value to a child, but as art did not meet his lofty standards. Vygotsky (1971) believed in the developmental role of experiencing "the poetry 'of every moment'" available through "the creative reworking of reality, a processing of things and the movement of things which will illuminate and elevate everyday experience to the level of the creative." He considered the cultivation of this process to be among "the most important of all the tasks of esthetic education" (p. 261). But to be art, a work had to meet a high standard in its construction.

What, then, enables a work to be considered art? Vygotsky (1971) rejected strictly formalist and strictly affective accounts, looking instead to those structural aspects of a creation that enable a sense of profundity and new planes of emotional experience in those who transact with its substance. Form and material are critical to meaning in that they work together to produce an emotional state or experience capable of evincing a consistent type of elevated emotional experience in its respondents. This perspective assumes a common orientation to artistic conventions and no doubt privileges mature European and Russian works in that they conform to the traditions with which Vygotsky was most familiar. The problem with this conception is that it excludes works by other sorts of authors from being considered artistic, eliminating any status that might be available to women authors in a male-dominant critical society (Rabinowitz, 1987) or African artists (Vogel, 1997), who are often depicted in the white world as "crafts" producers rather than artists (Nettleton, 2010).

Vygotsky's (1971) dialectical attention to contradiction suggests the importance of considering the substance of the materials or language through which the art is constructed, which provide a paradox given the meaning they potentially suggest. Michelangelo's *Pietà*, for instance, evokes powerful emotions in large part because the poignant image of the crucified Jesus in his mother's lap is carved from a cold, hard block of marble. Tuscan artist Giorgio Vasari said of this sculpture that "It is certainly a miracle that a formless block of stone could ever have been reduced to a perfection that nature is scarcely able to create in the flesh," a possibility that Vygotsky contended cannot be produced from wax.[5] According to Leont'ev (1971), Vygotsky believed that

> Sensations, emotions, and passions are part of the content of a work of art, but they are *transformed* in it. Just as the artistic creation produces a transfiguration of the material of which the work of art is composed, it also causes a metamorphosis of feelings. The significance of this metamorphosis is, in Vygotsky's view, its transcendence of individual feelings and their generalization to the social plane.
>
> (p. vii; emphasis in original)

Just as an emotive sculpture like the *Pietà* may be carved from cold, dense stone, a literary work of art is constructed through the orchestration of otherwise humble words when they involve a paradoxical combination of form and material that contributes to the artfulness of a human creation. Art is not designed to replicate reality, but to present images that are structured to generate conflicting feelings in those who experience it. An article appeared in the news while I was drafting this chapter that speaks to this paradoxical quality of art whose weather patterns don't correspond to scientific reality:

> Some images didn't seem to make much sense, meteorologically. Van Gogh's 1888 "Starry Night Over the Rhone" combines the play of gaslight reflected in water and a sky full of blazing stars to suggest a transfigured sense of nocturnal solitude and ecstasy. But the details don't quite add up. The view of the city, in the background, is too clear and detailed for there to be enough moisture for the curious coronas that surround the stars. "It almost feels like he is trying to combine a different surface scene and a cloud scene" in a single image, Cappucci told me. But in other cases, contradiction or ambiguity led to deeper insights about an artist's intent.
>
> (Kennicott & Cappucci, 2021, n.p.)

These observations help to maintain two critical positions: That high art includes contradictions that generate a meaningful response; and that in the New Critical tradition, ambiguities are present that paradoxically don't undermine the unity of the text. As I'll review, to Vygotsky the point of reading literature was not to achieve unity. It is instead to mature through the experience of wrestling with contradictions, to engage in a dialectic process of response and interpretation.

Vygotsky's conception of art both shared formalist values and questioned them. His death in 1934 came right before the major works of New Criticism were produced by English-language literary critics. John Crowe Ransom (1937, 1941) was regarded as its principal architect. I majored in English Literature at Kenyon College from 1970 to 1974, and the Department of English was heavily influenced by Ransom, a pillar of the faculty and namesake of the college's main administrative building. Ransom's death when I was a student was a campus tragedy. I then got my teaching credentials at the University of Chicago in an M.A.T. program that required us to meet the requirements of English as well as Education, and with a faculty where the formalist Chicago School of criticism held sway, albeit a formalism that looked down on New Criticism's version.

When I began teaching high school English, I was issued a poetry collection, *Sound and Sense: An Introduction to Poetry* by Perrine and Arp (1956). The editors break down poetry according to its formal properties, and distinguish between canonical and noncanonical poems via the application of formalist criteria from New Criticism. I'll confess I didn't always understand the distinctions they made, and I'm sure my students didn't either, given that they preferred pop music song lyrics to canonical poetry for the most part.

Vygotsky's gravitation to masterworks suggests much about his own upbringing as a brilliant, educated, Jewish man from a nation influenced by European history. My own socialization through New Critical and Chicago School literary theory guided me toward an appreciation for the classics and for formalism's promotion of a "close reading" of literature (see Thompson, 1971, for a detailed treatise on Russian and New Critical approaches). My own literary interests in my heyday were, like Vygotsky's, canonical, including Dostoyevsky and Faulkner as my favorite novelists. I carried that bias into my early teaching, much as Vygotsky did to his, and at roughly the same age. What I lacked, among other things, was the ability to write a book elaborating a theory of the psychology of art, although I might have written one on the psychology of beer, about which I had developed considerable theory and practice. If only I'd gotten around to it.

Vygotsky found literary greatness to reside in a text's possibilities for bringing about an elevated emotional response in readers. This response requires readers to be socialized to the codification practices of artists who embed meaning potential into texts under the assumption that readers will be versed in how to read them. Vygotsky believed that only high quality art can produce this elevation of feelings, this metamorphosis. Toward this end, Vygotsky (1971) disparaged "trash literature" that appeals to "mass tastes" and satisfies "hidden and forbidden desires rather than aesthetic emotions and requirements" (p. 79).

He might not see much value for Young Adult Literature in a school curriculum, a violation of current taste that could make him *persona non grata* in some circles. Here, for instance, is a comment from an interview I conducted recently with a teacher as part of a longitudinal study of her development of a conception of good teaching. We were discussing her teaching of Angie Thomas' (2017) young adult novel *The Hate U Give*, written by an African American author based on her experiences growing up in poverty and also attending a white private school. The school the teacher taught in was an alternative high school enrolling primarily Latiné students, with additional white and Black populations, most sharing experiences with poverty that helped them resonate with protagonist Starr Carter. In discussing how well her students responded to the novel, the teacher said,

> By the time [my students] get to their senior year, they've been so beat down with, you know, the same *Romeo and Juliet* bull crap that they've always been accustomed to. But read something like [*The Hate U Give*], that curses and uses, you know, a real-life situation that we're seeing on the news constantly, they appreciate when you throw something at them that's relevant and current.

Shakespeare is archaic bull crap to the students; Thomas is fresh, vibrant, and relevant. It's not clear without research if the novel gives them the cathartic experience described by Vygotsky that is available through true art. It is clear, however, that they prefer it and see themselves reflected in it. It's hard to say how Vygotsky's would view the teacher's thinking or the students' ability to relate to the novel. It's hard to know what he would have thought if he'd lived beyond age 37 and into an age in which fiction written for teens is common, beloved, and possibly awaiting canonicity; and if so, canonicity on whose terms.

In a conversation with Michael W. Smith during the composition of this chapter, he made a good point about canonicity: Works often become canonical because of their limited potential for disruption of dominant culture values. Harper Lee's (1960) *To Kill a Mockingbird*, for instance, has become canonical at the school level because it presents racial issues from a sympathetic white perspective that both makes white people the agents of change, and leaves white readers' feelings of contentment intact. Vygotsky's emphasis on emotional responses to contradictions are contained within this conception, rather than having race being addressed more directly, as in *The Hate U Give*. My writing of this chapter comes during the conservative outcry against critical race theory (CRT), which conservative white critics view as divisive in its confrontation of the structures supporting white supremacy. If a CRT-friendly text emerges from this era as canonical, it would need to enter a very different surrounding discourse to become a classic as determined by school authorities. Canonicity thus has a profoundly local and ideological component, in spite of its stature as being timeless and universal, that might have been implied in Vygotsky's conception, but was not part of his expressed vision.

Vygotsky's early work had yet to achieve the cross-cultural dimensions that characterized his later research. More recent perspectives would make the reading of codes a function of socialization rather than having them serve as universal symbols, as might be implied by Vygotsky (Smagorinsky, 2001). His conception elevated the codifications that emerged from European, Russian-Soviet, and US literary criticism, which provides a critical advantage to works produced through those traditions. His more parochial world no doubt helped to reinforce that bias, one that limited an understanding of the conventions prized in Asian or African or Native American art, and in turn limited the degree to which such works could be appreciated. Vygotsky's (1971) premises about art, then, assume a common, canonical cultural framework for interpretation. Such frameworks are inherently ideological, enabling dominant groups to assert their authority over others by establishing the standards by which all works are evaluated.

Text and Genre

Vygotsky's (1971) account of the construction of the artistic text was well-aligned with what is now called *genre theory*. He was concerned with the features of a genre and how they cue particular and appropriate types of responses in readers, listeners, or viewers of the artistic text. Vygotsky's attention to genre anticipated the construct of *intertextuality*, the idea that each text takes on meaning in relation to other texts, and that texts are in dialogue with texts from the past and provide the groundwork for those that appear in the future (Bakhtin, 1973; Kristeva, 1969; Wertsch, 1991).

Vygotsky (1971) argued that "an author who puts down in writing the product of his creativity is by no means the sole creator of his work.... [Pushkin[6]] passes on the immense heritage of literary tradition," which depended on the cultural dimensions of the genres in which he wrote (p. 16). "Everything within us is social," he continued, "but this [premise] does not imply that all the properties of the psyche of an individual are inherent in all the other members of this group as well" (p. 17). Learning to read includes both biological factors (being blind requires alternative routes; see Chapter 14) and social mediation to understand textual codification.

Reading a text according to the textual codes of an inappropriate genre takes a reader away from its designed meaning. Such misreadings often follow from texts in which ironic codes are built in to indicate how the surface meaning is at odds with the presumed intentions of the author (Smith, 1989). In Jonathan Swift's *A Modest Proposal*, for instance, he proposes that Irish "*Persons of Quality* and *Fortune*" eat babies who are born into poverty, in that "a young healthy child well nursed is at a year old a most delicious, nourishing, and wholesome food, whether stewed, roasted, baked, or boiled; and I make no doubt that it will equally serve in a fricassee or a ragout." Reading other texts produced by Swift in which his views are compassionate would indicate that he is criticizing the inhumane treatment of society's dispossessed, and not providing dietary advice or presenting a plan for eradicating poverty.

Even in non-satirical texts, the focus of Vygotsky's analysis, misreading a genre's codes will produce an interpretation based on off-target indexing of textual cues. The reader would then miss the affective contradiction embedded in a text, the contradictions and paradoxes suggested by its structure and material. Such a reader would then likely not experience the contradictory feelings and emotions that a true work of art generates. Vygotsky (1971) concluded that the "affective contradiction and its solution, by means of short-circuiting contrasting sensations and emotions, represent the true nature of our psychological reaction to fables" (p. 143). Texts in which the author "develops its action on two contrasting, and frequently opposing, emotional levels" (p. 135) generate the "second meaning" that elevates a story to the level of art (p. 137) because "it forces us, by the strength and inspiration of its poetry, to react emotionally to its story" (p. 143).

Traditionally, Vygotsky argued (1971), formalist critics had sought to explain "the harmony of form and content" in artistic works, as subsequently New Critics would do to resolve ironic tensions, or Chicago critics would in finding unity in a work. In contrast, he argued that "form may be in conflict with the content, struggle with it, overcome it" to produce a "dialectic contradiction between content and form," introducing the thesis-antithesis-synthesis formulation into literary criticism. This inherent paradox, the "inner incongruity between the material and the form," is central to the effect of a work of art in that it produces conflicting emotions in the reader (p. 160). The presence of paradox is also central to New Criticism, although with the (to Vygotsky, mistaken) goal of unity, and lacking Vygotsky's emphasis on the emotions that contradictions produce in readers. Indeed, contrary to the technical, emotionless approach promoted by New Criticism and its effort to create a scientific literary criticism to legitimate literary studies (Gallagher, 1997), a work of art produces to Vygotsky "a state of emotional and philosophical complexity which does not succumb to rational analysis" (Van der Veer & Valsiner, 1991, p. 28), the task of the fully formalist approach.

This paradox is especially evident in a tragedy such as *Hamlet*, Vygotsky (1971) asserted, given that

> the task of art, like that of tragedy, is to force us to experience the incredible and absurd in order to perform some kind of extraordinary operation with our emotions.... . By forcing our feelings to alternate continuously to the opposite extremes of the emotional range, by deceiving them, splitting them and piling obstacles in their way, the tragedy can obtain powerful emotional effect [so that] *at any moment, [the protagonist] unifies both contradictory planes and is the supreme and ever-present embodiment of the contradiction inherent in the tragedy.*
> (p. 190, pp. 194–195; emphasis in original)

The presence of incongruent paradoxical combinations of form and material in the text thus has the effect of producing conflictual emotions, ironies that are central features of canonical works of art. What follows is an emotional experience that produces intellectual growth upon reflection. New Critics are similarly concerned with tension, irony, and paradox. In their reading, however, these contradictions are to be resolved for the unity and coherence of the work's meaning; that is, they are in the text for readers to find. Vygotsky finds these tensions intellectually irresolvable. They require a reader to respond to tensions emotionally, and then through reflection, to reach a higher plane of understanding in relation to the text, and ultimately to continue to grow on the trajectory provided by art as experience (Dewey, 1934).

The work of engaging with literature in such sophisticated ways requires the ability to make inferences. Vygotsky (1997c) found inferences to be necessary in virtually all areas of social life:

> The zoologist reconstructs a whole skeleton from an insignificant fragment of bone of some excavated animal and even a picture of its life. An ancient coin, which has no value as a coin, frequently reveals to the archeologist a complex historical problem. The historian, deciphering hieroglyphics scratched into a stone, penetrates into the depts of vanished ages. The doctor diagnoses illness from insignificant symptoms.
> (p. 41)

And so must the reader take fragments provided by literary artists, emplot them in familiar narratives, and make sense of them indirectly, that is, based on their assemblage more than on their literal meaning.

Vygotsky (1971) made a distinction between the events related in a narrative and the manner in which those events are depicted through a textual construction:

> the material is what is readily available to the poet for his story, namely the events and characters of everyday life, or the relationships between human beings—in brief, all that has existed prior to the story can exist outside of it or is independent of it. The form of this work of art is the arrangement of this material in accordance with the laws of artistic construction.
> (p. 145)

Vygotsky (1971) advocated for the undertaking of a "structural analysis" involved in the "composition" of events into a narrative sequence through which the text has the capacity

> to make life's events unreal, to transform water into wine, as always happens in any real work of art. The words of a story or verse carry its meaning (the water), whereas the composition creates another meaning for the words, transposes everything into a completely different level, and transforms the whole into wine. Thus, the banal tale of a frivolous provincial schoolgirl is transformed into the gentle breath of Bunin's[7] short story [taken up in the following section of this chapter].
>
> (pp. 154–155)

This composition of events into art creates the emotional effect that Vygotsky argued follows inevitably from a knowledgeable response to the artistic arrangement of form. Such a response requires the recognition of textual codes that move a text beyond the literal, that convert the water of material (words, stone, canvas; the mundane events of life) into the wine of a formally constructed work of art. The example of the distortion of meteorological science in paintings to construct emotional contradictions illustrates this phenomenon well.

Embodied Reading

Vygotsky (1971) saw reading as a fully embodied experience, rather than a solely intellectual process between a text and a reader's brain. This embodiment is socially situated, with contexts providing the contours within which embodiment occurs. His attention to emotional shifts points to a whole-bodied experience available from engagement with art. He rejected the Cartesian reduction of emotions "to a purely cognitive process" (p. 176). In contrast, argued Vygotsky, "Consciousness must not be separated from its physical conditions: they comprise one natural whole that must be studied as such" (p. 228). Consciousness is thus embedded in bodies and environments, illustrating the profound ways in which, as Wertsch (1991) phrases it, the mind extends beyond the skin. It also circulates throughout the body.

Vygotsky conducted a study of the ways in which a story's construction affects the breathing rates of readers. He devoted much attention to the short story translated in *The Psychology of Art* as I. Bunin's "Gentle Breath," but that Van der Veer and Valsiner (1991) translate as "Easy Breathing," in that "Vygotsky's emphasis was clearly on the process of breathing, not 'breath'" (p. 27). This sort of translation problem is similar to the faulty rendering of *Thought and Language* as an abstraction, rather than the more accurate *Thinking and Speech* as actions. Vygotsky was fundamentally interested in action (Wertsch, 1998), raising flags about translations that position him as an abstract theoretician.

Vygotsky assumed that breathing rates indicate emotional response to a stimulus. To test this hypothesis, he used a pneumographic recorder[8] to measure breathing rates of people reading "Easy Breathing." Van der Veer and Valsiner (1991) describe this relation between text structure and physical response as adapted from prior scholarship of the era:

> the *idea* of "easy breathing" became connected with Vygotsky's life-course in another significant way: it was the connection of that idea with Blonskiy's (1922) assertion that the literary text is emotionally received by the reader on the basis of the breathing rhythm while reading, that led Vygotsky into his first experimental study of the reception of literature.... . Vygotsky's particular interest in the breathing rhythms

while reading literature was linked to his idea that the author's construction of the text leads to the necessity of reading the text with a particular rhythm of breathing, which in its turn leads to the production of a corresponding feeling in the reader.

(p. 30; emphasis in original)

They proceed to quote Vygotsky's postulation of three points concerning "the psychic mechanism of poetry":

1) the speech rhythm of the text creates a corresponding rhythm and nature of breathing. Every poem or part of prose has its own system of breathing because of the immediate adaptation of breathing to speech. The writer creates not only the rhythm of words, but also rhythms of breathing.... . *[T]he person breathes in the way in which he reads.* 2) For each breathing system and rhythm there exists a specific organization of emotions, that creates the emotional background for the perception of poetry, specific for each work. *"The person feels like he breathes"* (Blonsky). 3) That emotional background of poetic experience is the same or at least similar to the one that the author has at the moment of creating, since in the writing of his speech his breathing rhythm becomes fixed. From here—the "infectious nature" of poetry. *The reader feels like the poet since he breathes in the same way.*

(1926, pp. 172–173; emphases in original; quoted in Van der Veer & Valsiner, 1991, p. 30)

The breathing patterns, however, are not necessarily harmonious with the author's construction of a codified text. Indeed, a reader's easy breathing in relation to the structure and content of Bunin's story, centered on murder and death, produces an affective contradiction such that "form is at war with the content, fights with it, *overcomes it*, and that in this *dialectical contradiction* between the content and the form the real psychological sense of our aesthetic reactions is hidden" (Vygotsky, 1925/1986, p. 204, emphases added; quoted in Van der Veer & Valsiner, 1991, p. 31).

To test this hypothesis Vygotsky recruited nine students in the Gomel Pedagogical School to read "Easy Breathing" silently and aloud, and also to listen to a reading by an experimenter. The pneumograph recorded their breathing patterns, showing high rates of correspondence between the breathing curves recorded by the machine and the structure of speech in the text as determined by its rhythms. Further, two texts ("Easy Breathing" and Gogol's[9] "A Terrible Revenge") produced different breathing patterns, suggesting that breathing rates do appear to follow from text structure and content, often in paradoxical ways that elevate the emotional quality of the response. Ultimately, according to Van der Veer (2015),

Vygotsky suggested that ... skilled authors can create special aesthetic effects by playing with the rhythm of the text and its content.... . It is not content as such that determines the recipient's aesthetic reaction, nor is it the style or form as such. Crucial is the artificially created conflict between form and content, perhaps induced by a paradoxical rhythm of writing.... . Crucial is that the readers or audience will feel contradictory emotions that are ultimately resolved in a new feeling.

(p. 107)

Vygotsky's study of breathing rates was both a novel study, and one that was grounded in a more sophisticated theoretical framework than the few subsequent studies investigating the relation to bodily conduct and reading. In the United States, Purves and Beach

(1972) found that "little has been done" to study reading experiences beyond post-hoc verbal reports, with only four studies of embodied reading available for their review. Peddie (1952) studied the reading responses of secondary school students with marked haptic tendencies—i.e., strong tactile or kinesthetic imaginations—and found "they were better able to perform than other students on a test in which they had to complete poems according to fitness of mood." Strother (1949) concluded that poems of fear provoked a higher muscle reaction than poems of happiness, hate, and tranquility. Nikiforova (1960) found that reading when accompanied by automatized speech produced a "decline in the quality of the students' judgments and drawings," suggesting that "constant articulation inhibits certain kinesthetic impulses" (Purves & Beach, p. 22). Kaiser (1967) studied the relation between metaphor and galvanic skin responses, finding that the metaphors in two stories did not produce different responses.

I also located the title of a study (Critchfield, 1938) that appears quite similar to Vygotsky's pneumographic study, but could not find a copy of the text, which is likely an unpublished doctoral dissertation (more a commentary on the limited publication opportunities of the era than a statement about its quality). I found two additional studies from outside the purview of Purves and Beach (1972). McGuigan (1969) reports a range of studies on bodily responses to various forms of interference, including those experienced during exposure to words of high and low imaging power, with responses "recorded from the tongue, lips, neck, non-preferred arm, horizontal EOG and EEG from the parietal and occipital areas" (p. 4). There is no report on how the "subjects"—the acceptable name for research participants in that era—responded to the research method itself, which I personally would have found quite distracting. The researchers concluded that "further work on the project, based on this pilot investigation, is feasible" (p. 4), if apparently never undertaken.

McGuigan (1969) reports another study in which the "verbal mediation group did in fact significantly increase the amplitude of tongue EMG from before the experiment until the phase in which the mediation test occurred. Furthermore, the increased amplitude of tongue EMG was significantly greater than for two other (control) groups," with no significant differences in the measure of responses taken from the right and left arm and right leg. Their interpretation is decidedly speculative: "It may well be that this heightened covert oral behavior was a direct measure of the verbal mediating response, as theoretically predicted" (p. 4). Finally, Angelotti, Behnke, and Carlile (1975) studied heart beats in relation to reading, finding that they are lower when a reader is heavily involved with a high-interest text (in their design, a science fiction story), and higher with a meh-interest text (in their design, a bland historical account). It is not clear how the investigators determined absolute levels of interest potential in the texts they selected for the study, although their distinction presumably indicates their own subjective preferences.

Although the notion of embodiment has become quite fashionable in literacy research, the actual physiological phenomena occurring during reading have little empirical documentation, as this small body of work from the 1930s to 1970s indicates. I find this paucity of studies surprising in the decades since, given the increasing sophistication of measurement technologies and the interest in embodiment. The questions raised by Vygotsky (1971) about embodiment never subsequently followed a theory that went much beyond "yes" or "no" to the question of bodily actions during reading.

Vygotsky's interest in contradiction produced a way of studying how breathing provides a contrapuntal pace that amplifies emotional responses. These initial emotional, embodied responses are then resolved intellectually. The feeling evinced in the respondent represents what Vygotsky (1971) called a *catharsis,* an Aristotelian term used "to denote the essence of aesthetic experience as cleansing the soul from affects and giving 'harmless' delight" (Yaroshevsky, 1989, p. 155). A catharsis serves as the social subconscious element of art's effect on the individual. Vygotsky's definition of catharsis is specific and departs from other meanings and conceptions. Freud, for instance, employed it to characterize the ways in which art serves as a vehicle for "living out forbidden desires" (Yaroshevsky, p. 155), a backward-looking approach to psychiatry focused on childhood and sexual impulses as formative and in need of reflection and interrogation. Vygotsky's forward-looking vision in contrast positioned art as a medium through which one may anticipate a social future channeled by cultural mediation. A cultural-historical theory locates this future-oriented vision in a historical context, so the past serves to help create the present and future. What mattered most to Vygotsky, however is what people develop toward within historically-established settings, and what mediates that maturation.

Vygotsky's (1971) catharsis involves *the generalization from personal emotions to higher human truths that becomes available through a transaction with a work of art*. Emotion and imagination, each indefinite and having potential to promote a raised awareness, are central to this process. An aesthetic response to art involves a delay in which the imagination elevates the response: "The emotions caused by art," he says, "are intelligent emotions" (p. 212). Consistent with Vygotsky's dialectic orientation, catharsis involves "an affective contradiction, causes conflicting feelings, and leads to the short-circuiting and destruction of these emotions" (p. 213). This process leads to "a complex transformation of feelings" (p. 214) that results in an "explosive response which culminates in the discharge of emotions" (p. 215). Art thus expands life's possibilities as a person overcomes, resolves, and regulates feelings through a process of generalization of those feelings to a higher plane of experience. This attention to regulation is consistent with the Marxist emphasis on the use of the intellect to monitor and control the natural environment, and ultimately to do so in social relationships formed within human communities.

Even with the formalist emphasis in his dissertation that largely displaced the subjectivity promoted in his master's thesis, Vygotsky (1971) attended to the emotional, subjective experience of the reader in this later (if still remarkably youthful and precocious) formulation:

> Emotions are not produced in us by a work of art, as are sounds by the keys of a piano. An artistic element does not introduce its emotional tone into us. It is we who introduce emotions into a work of art, emotions arising from the greatest depths of our being and generated not at the shallow level of the receptors but in the most complex activities of our organisms.
>
> (p. 207)

This subjectivity is not a free-for-all. It comes in relation to a deliberately codified artistic text such that the emotion suggested by a work of art is realized in a respondent in a process Vygotsky called *coaffect*. Art, then, potentially generates a heightened emotional response that produces an elevated plane of experience. This process is served by an imaginative extrapolation from initial feelings, particularly as they involve conflict and transformation. The art works in conjunction with a respondent's capacity to experience appropriate emotions, such that response varies, a problem that troubles any effort to claim that humanity experiences art in a single way. As the illustration of how mountains are subject to cultural interpretations shows, socialization produces readings of a particular type.

Further, some people are simply less empathic than others and have difficulty emoting in ways that correspond to Vygotsky's formulation. Sophisticated understandings of mental health were many decades from being developed (see Chapter 14). As he often did in this period, Vygotsky generalized from European and Russian high culture to all people, without a 21st-century understanding of mental health. As someone on the high-functioning range of the autism spectrum, I see merit in Kennett's (2002) conclusion that "the visual, literal and world-focused nature of the autistic person's thinking does not lend itself well to introspection or to the kind of abstraction required for seeing oneself as a being existing over time" (p. 357).

Like Vygotsky, Kennett (2002) sees reason ultimately prevailing in moral development, exceeding the passions; later in the chapter I will revisit their belief in reason as the ultimate arbiter of human conduct. Kennett's concern is not with reading processes but with the question of whether it's possible for autistic people to be empathic (her answer: Yes, possibly), and whether a psychopath's amorality can be equated with low autistic empathy levels (fortunately, no). The diminished capacity for empathy might create an exception for readers on the extremes of the autism spectrum, and perhaps conditions representing other departures from presumed norms, in achieving elevated states of knowledge through engagement with art.

The Emotion of Formal Drama

Vygotsky considered the problem of how actors produce convincing emotional performances that move audiences. Their acting comes even as they follow someone else's script repeatedly on the stage, might have a personality much different from the one whose role they play, and might despise the actor with whom they perform tender love scenes. Vygotsky was aware of Diderot's[10] (1830) "Paradox of the Actor," which is concerned with the ways in which actors play out emotions that they don't actually feel, and recite scripts so convincingly that viewers who are aware of the artifice of the theater nonetheless respond emotionally to the performance.

Technique alone is insufficient for the convincing replication of deep emotional states. A theater-goer needs to be attuned to the theatrical codes embedded in the performance. This awareness might follow from shared cultural and personal experiences that produce deep reflection on prior experiences and heightened awareness of how they affect one's developing personality. The kinds of emotions that are appropriate to express are learned, and are not simply reflexes as envisioned by Pavlov, whose influence at the time was great. They follow from a sense of propriety that is available through cultural practice, a cultural tool that intervenes between stimulus and response. Vygotsky described how socialization has a developmental effect on how emotions are felt and expressed:

> together with the growth of the child's social experience, these emotions become more and more social. While we can characterize the range of emotions of the young child as egocentric, the range of emotions of the schoolchild have a social character, even when these emotions are egoistic… . [T]he child's personal emotions become more and more connected with his social life. The child finds personal satisfaction in the emotions of contest, competition, self-assertion, respect, friendship, leadership, and so on.
>
> (in Van der Veer, 2020, pp. 140–141)

The social construction of consciousness extends to the theater itself. Vygotsky (1999) situated theatrical performances historically, arguing that actors' creative work changes "from epoch to epoch and from theater to theater (p. 239).... . [T]he psychology of the actor expresses the social ideology of his epoch and ... it also changes in the process of the historical development of man just as external forms of the theater and its style and content change" (p. 240). Different settings thus produce different psychologies for actors and directors, making the psychology of the actor "a historical and class category, not a biological category" (p. 240): "The actor creates on the stage infinite sensations, feeling, or emotions that become the emotions of the whole theatrical audience. Before they become the subject of the actor's embodiment, they were given a literary formulation, they were borne in the air, in social consciousness" (Vygotsky, 1999, p. 241).

An audience's response involves shared social understandings of what counts as tragic, triumphant, poignant, and so on, and how one appropriately expresses such emotions within particular, situated sets of conventions. Each iteration of a theatrical production, then, is situated in historical contexts that shape the interpretation of the script and directions, and affect both the performance and its reception. A theater-goer who laughs at the death of Polonius on stage might be considered a violator of decorum, unless the play is performed before an audience that finds murder to be a delightful event.

Discussion

This chapter has inquired into Vygotsky's earliest scholarship on the theater and the psychology of art, especially literature; and on his later writing on the role of emotions in human development. His attention to the emotional dimensions of the drama of life and its role in cultural life is relevant to his belief in the relation between life and art, between drama on the stage and drama in everyday life. His account is both fascinating and problematic; worth considering and worth reconsidering. I'll next lay out what I see as germane to the 21st-century English/Language Arts teacher in his formulation.

Although he was a teacher of literature, Vygotsky did not get into detail about classroom teaching; he was more pedologist than pedagogue. If he or others had provided more accounts of his teaching, we might or might not see the instruction that has been claimed in his name. He might be like Bakhtin, who is often invoked to promote participatory classrooms (Teo, 2016), yet who was a straight-up lecturer (Vasiliev, 2018). I don't think Vygotsky used small groups, as he is referenced to support (e.g., Erbil, 2020). I have only heard of his lectures. I don't know if, as a teacher of literature in Gomel, he lectured (which Csikszentmihalyi, Rathunde, & Whalen, 1993 found that most students don't listen to), or gamified his classroom (as is becoming popular in the 21st century; see Kim & Johnson, 2021), or had the students do projects (as described by Vygotsky's US contemporary Kilpatrick, 1918, and advocated for by Vygotsky), or did something else.

The *Psychology of Art* is a work of literary criticism, not a teaching manual. His contributions are more in offering what remains a unique perspective, one that integrates culturally-channeled textual formalism, human emotion as the primal driver of thinking, and the intellectual resolution of contradictory feelings. This process contributes to a reader's gravitation toward the teleological ends embedded in the ideology of artists, who manifest cultural history in their works. Equally at play is the ideology of the school, which constrains the types of interpretations available to students. There are implied pedagogical consequences for his conception, although not all readers might see the same possibilities.

It's inescapable that in Vygotsky's view, attention to textual form is paramount in having a fruitful experience with literature. This form is always intertextually related to genre traits that cue reading responses among those who have learned how to read them. Form, then, represents an ideology as well as a set of techniques. It's thus important to remember that studying metaphor, or irony, or other literary element as a technique is insufficient. Rather, Vygotsky would surely believe that readers need to know how, within a genre's conventions, a literary element is designed to function based on how its meaning is suggested by how it is socially and historically situated.

An old study of a student's apparent misreading speaks to this issue, challenging and complicating it in ways that trouble Vygotsky's conception. Hull and Rose (1990) studied a college student in a remedial writing course whose interpretation of an assigned poem departed significantly from canonical and conventional analyses. In particular, he read "wooden shacks" as dignified homes rather than as presumed indicators of a degraded life, because he and his family came from communities in which they were common. The authors infer that "Robert's background makes it unlikely that he is going to respond to 'a small cluster of wooden shacks' in quite the same way—with quite the same emotional reaction—as would a conventional (and most likely middle-class) reader for whom the shacks might function as a quickly discernible, emblematic literary device" (p. 293) indicating poverty. They go on to question whether they should (1) listen more alertly and sympathetically to students' unconventional readings based on their instantiations of different meaning to textual signs, or (2) help them become more attuned to the traditions that suggest specific meanings to those readers who, like the ones envisioned by Vygotsky, are socialized to understand meaning in specific ways determined by academic and cultural norms and traditions.

I see the tensions produced by this conundrum creating a fundamental dilemma for current-day teachers in multicultural classrooms: How should I treat responses that would differ dramatically from what my college professors and literature anthology editors would prefer and perhaps impose? How should I honor idiosyncratic literary responses and interpretations when the high-stakes assessments by which students and teachers are judged have a different correct answer in mind? How do I balance the logic provided by a student's socialization with the conventional interpretations generated from within the community of literary critics? How do I address the problem that many students (and adult readers) find canonical literature far less interesting than young adult literature or other contemporary texts?

Vygotsky, or at least the young literary critic who wrote *The Psychology of Art*, would adhere to canonical values, those that make textual construction of paramount importance. A modern-day literature teacher might have greater ambivalence about literary standards, seeing the cultural construction of signs by both authors and readers as situated within communities of practice. They might be oriented to the possibilities afforded by different schools of thought (Appleman, 2015) or from traditions from outside the European purview (Gates, 1988) that provide both forms of argumentation and a motivating ideology (Bazerman & Paradis, 1991). A reading might reveal as much about readers and their orientations as it does about texts and their creators, as Fish (1980) found when he told his college students that a list of linguists' names on a blackboard was a poem, and had them discuss it as one, which they did within the conventions of interpretive communities.

Vygotsky's world may have been too bounded to admit this proliferation of frames of mind to his conception. He appears to have believed that textual coding follows universal principles for producing emotional effects in readers, and that these tenets are grounded in the ideas of the men of the European Enlightenment. Undoubtedly his era's parochialism helped to suggest that his local values were universally shared. It's not clear how Vygotsky would react to this modern era and the expansion of possibilities for art and the responses it provokes. If he took an interest in readers' socialization, it was their socialization to those established literary codes, not to others. If they were developing a cultivated taste, it was to canonical works, not to the "trash" of popular narratives. His conception was similar to Rabinowitz's (1987; Rabinowitz & Smith 1997) concept of *authorial reading*, in which the first task of a reader is to engage with the form of the text. This form employs established codes and conventions that suggest a meaning within the bounds of an interpretive community. It is the task of Rabinowitz and Smith's ideal teacher to help students recognize these inscribed signs and how they suggest a set of possible meanings, and how those meanings fit with a literary tradition.

Rabinowitz and Smith (1997) depart from Vygotsky (1971) in providing the reader with more options, enabling them to contest a meaning once they understand an author's codification. They thus leave room for constructivist readings that reject an author's inscriptions, even when they are unintentional (e.g., when they embed a middle-class, masculine, ableist worldview). This shift departs from Vygotsky's belief that readers should learn how to participate in the cultural flow that governs life in their societies, and take on the trajectory it provides. To Rabinowitz and Smith, the student who learns that the author of *The Adventures of Huckleberry Finn* probably intended for his characters' racist speech to provide an ironic critique of racism might recognize and appreciate the author's technical orchestration of codes and traditions. This well-schooled reader might, after recognizing these structural elements and what they conventionally imply, then reject the text based on personal emotional experiences with racism that make the language painful to read. Whether teachers then proceed on the basis of the novel's canonical status or on the basis of how students respond to it emotionally is a choice between alignment with disciplinary traditions established by white authors and critics, or empathic responses to the personal feelings of hurt felt by students who are often, but are not exclusively, Black (Smagorinsky, 1992, 2016b). This latitude, however, is not evident in Vygotsky's account in *The Psychology of Art*.

The well-educated reader in both conceptions has a formalist obligation to read the text as written. The degree of formal knowledge required of the casual reader might remain in question. For English majors in college, knowledge of conventions and how they produce critically accepted meanings is likely essential. However, according to the U.S. Bureau of Labor Statistics (2021), about 16.5 million persons ages 16–24 (about 44% of the total cohort) were not enrolled in college in 2020. Chase (2009) reports that at the time of his essay, the percentage of college students becoming English majors was about 4% and dropping; Flaherty (2018) reports that from 2012 to 2018, they declined another 20%. Given current political movements to favor STEM fields and discourage "useless" majors, and the manner in which teaching has become so unattractive that many states now allow pathways for people without a college education to teach (Balingit, 2022), it's likely that this drop will only continue. In 2022, Saint Mary's University in Winona, Minnesota unplugged 11 major programs, including English, due to declining enrollments, part of a national trend in the United States (Barshay, 2021). Teachers of literature might then take into account the fact that hardly anyone they teach will become an English major, much less an English teacher. To what degree, then, should teachers prepare students to read as literary critics, when they may find it contrary to their needs and interests?

Vygotsky's formalist elitism might move him to promote the teaching of canonical works according to established conventions. The 21st-century teacher of English/Language Arts might not embrace canonicity, even as many surely do given the alignment of AP English and the Common Core State Standards with New Criticism and college preparation in general (see Shanahan, 2013, for an endorsement of these structures). No matter how one resolves the question, it's worth understanding the dilemma and wrestling with it to arrive at an approach for teaching in specific settings, including those in which students do not intend to go to college or become English majors; that is, most students.

It's hard to know what Vygotsky would have ended up believing if he'd lived into the 1970s, if he'd lived outside the Soviet Union, or if he lived in current times with all its connectivity affordances. Based on his only work of literary criticism, I assume that Vygotsky would support a college preparation education in established masterworks; other reading was somewhere between a waste of time and a frivolous but passing enjoyment. He might take a dim view of Young Adult Literature and popular culture, both of which are enjoyed by youth and many of their teachers. He might see school failing the students by denying them true artistic experiences and replacing them with stories of temporary interest and entertainment, but not historical or developmental significance. He was a person of his time, place, and upbringing. He was raised to be cultured in the Germanic sense of *kultur*, and he achieved at the highest levels throughout his life while beset by attacks of tuberculosis and the discrimination provided by anti-Semitism. It's hard to say he was on the wrong track. But it's easier to say that in a different time and place, other possibilities are available in terms of developmental tracks and life opportunities, and engagement with texts that do not meet his standards for canonicity.

A second area that Vygotsky's work might provoke teachers to think about concerns the role of emotions in literary engagement (and, as I discuss in Chapter 13, writing) and in classroom life. A lot of attention to Social-Emotional Learning (SEL) in schools is evaluated according to its effects on academic achievement. A meta-analysis (Durlak, Weissberg, Dymnicki, Taylor, & Schellinger, 2011) concluded that "evidence-based" teaching in SEL raises academic achievement by an average of 11 points on standardized tests. I see no relation between social and emotional learning and taking multiple-choice tests, but that's how these things are measured in school. I find that to be both a trivialization of emotional life, and a terribly misguided way of evaluating it.

Vygotsky offered a far richer, more complex understanding of social and emotional learning. In both art and human relationships, there is dramatic tension that produces emotional responses that provide the foundation for thinking. These emotions may emerge in conflicting ways that require some sort of reflection and development into a greater sense of self and surroundings. Whether this process represents a developmental stage by means of applying the intellect to make sense of the experience per Vygotsky (1971), or a post-hoc justification for those emotions per Haidt (2012), both does and does not matter.

It matters because Haidt's (2012) belief that there is a *rationalist delusion* would require a very different approach to teaching genres like argumentation (see Chapter 13). Teachers would have to listen to students' emotions in order to evaluate the content of their arguments and recognize that ideological differences are fundamentally emotional (Smagorinsky, 2018d). Rethinking the teaching of argumentation would be a healthy development in any case, given how researchers working from a sociocultural perspective are documenting not just the genre and its traits, but the means of persuasion that work situationally among people of different cultures yet that are diminished and dismissed in school as illogical (e.g., Majors, 2015).

It doesn't matter whether Vygotsky or Haidt is right to the extent that they agree that human thinking and action begin in a person's emotional responses to their surroundings.

This agreement shifts attention from "cognition"—thoughts generated by the computer-modeled organ in the skull that has no emotional sourcing or interference—to emotions as a primary focus of attention in school. It's no doubt idealistic to think that schools will be transformed by greater attention to emotional life. It's also idealistic to think that schools can proceed with the assumption that clear thinking is only clouded by emotions and still provide a sound education for their students.

Vygotsky's conception suggests that students' emotions would benefit from exploration as an initial stage of literary response. For some, this emphasis might be an end in and of itself. For Vygotsky it would not enable students to reflect on the dissonances of their reading experience and reach a catharsis. Teachers, he argued,

> must not ignore the child's still fairly powerful emotionality but rely on it in order to overcome it. This is why we get the somewhat paradoxical conclusion that says that the more difficult work the pedagogue presents to the children, that is, the further he leads them along the line of development and the more he requires of their seriousness, the more he must rely on their emotionality. Thus, this rule about the increasing seriousness of instruction also has its exception. The younger the child is, the more emotionality must form part of the lessons.
> (in Van der Veer, 2020, p. 139)

It's not easy to ascertain what Vygotsky would recommend that students should do in relation to their reading to represent their learning. Some might conclude that he implies a preference for a literary analysis that explains how the text's coding suggested a particular meaning. Others might say that he would begin with some expression of feelings and subsequent reflection as one who has experienced the art, and only later return to the text to identify why it made them respond as they did. Others still might consider that perhaps Vygotsky believed that assessment of such a profound emotional and developmental experience is misguided and ought to be jettisoned.

Vygotsky's thoughts on how emotions mature during human development are worth repeating. Emotions, he asserted,

> undergo deep internal changes. They form connections with new and more complicated forms of behavior. This is what constitutes the real evolution of emotional life in the school age. The first symptom is that the emotional reactions lose their direct dictatorial power over the child's behavior.... [T]his must lead to an important conclusion for education. Only for early childhood we can justify teaching based on the child's immediate emotions, his subjective interest, by trying to trigger his immediate pleasure and laughter, in particular. Teaching the schoolchild "must not at all try to amuse the child." However, it would be dangerous to fall into the opposite mistake, as the older school did, and to ignore the child's interests completely by making the school subjects difficult and unpleasant for the child. "Teaching must neither be unpleasant for the child," because this as well, by causing a strong emotion in the child, delays his development on a lower level where his behavior is ruled directly by emotions.
> (in Van der Veer, 2020, pp. 137–138)

Many have misunderstood Vygotsky's attention to the role of play, interpreting it to mean that school should be fun (see Chapter 8). I read Vygotsky as saying that school should be challenging but not discouraging, aligning his views with those of Csikszentmihalyi (1990) and his concept of *flow*, an experience that is available when challenges and abilities are well matched, producing a level of participation so great that one loses all track of time. Vygotskian flow comes through reading in which one's congruence with textual codes is aligned with emotional responses that are amenable to a catharsis that produces intelligent emotions that serve a developmental role. Both Csikszentmihalyi and Vygotsky associate such experiences with human growth over time as these remarkable experiences contribute to concept development within cultural contours.

Vygotsky thus provides much to challenge conceptions of reading a century after he developed his theory, while not getting into detail about what teachers should do pedagogically. As is the case with much of his writing, the work of planning and carrying out instruction is left to practitioners who engage with his work.

Vygotsky isn't easy. But neither is teaching. Oversimplifying either does neither justice. Applying Vygotskian concepts to classroom practice requires deep engagement with his writing—as problematic as it might be in both the Russian versions edited by Party loyalists and subsequent translations into English (see Notes on Translation)—and that of his knowledgeable interpreters, such as those I reference extensively in this chapter and throughout this volume. Otherwise, claims to a Vygotskian influence to justify commonplace teaching methods serve as a façade that avoids the complexity and reduces him to an academic meme.

Notes

1 As of this writing, Vygotsky has been referenced well over a quarter-of-a-million times in published scholarship. *The Psychology of Art* has been referenced 1,606 times, a good total for any publication, but a fraction of his total references.
2 Hippolyte Adolphe Taine (1828–1893) was a French historian, critic, and philosopher who influenced French naturalism, sociological positivism, and historicist criticism. He was known for his foundational work in literary historicism and for working to construct a scientific account of literature.
3 Count Lev Nikolayevich Tolstoy (1828–1910) was a Russian novelist who was often nominated for the Nobel Prize in Literature and the Nobel Peace Prize, yet never won.
4 Johann Wolfgang von Goethe (1749–1832) was a Prussian literary artist, scientist, and director.
5 The *Pietà* is my example, not Vygotsky's; his allusion to wax follows from his own examples.
6 Alexander Sergeyevich Pushkin (1799–1837) was a Russian nobleman famed for his poetry, plays, and novels. He is considered the founder of modern Russian literature and among the greatest Russian poets. He died at age 37, killed in a duel with his wife's alleged lover.
7 Ivan Alekseyevich Bunin (1870–1953) was the first Russian or Soviet author to be awarded the Nobel Prize for Literature.
8 A pneumograph records the respiratory velocity and force of chest movements as someone breathes, measuring the movements of the thoracic wall and movement of the chest wall against the closed glottis.
9 Nikolai Vasilyevich Gogol (1809–1852) was a Ukrainian novelist, short story writer, and playwright who influenced many of the major fiction writers of his era. His early death followed from a deep depression that led him to refuse food for nine days and burn his final manuscript.
10 Denis Diderot (1713–1784) was a French philosopher, art critic, and writer who became prominent during the Age of Enlightenment and who cofounded and edited the *Encyclopédie*, a volume embodying Enlightenment thought.

13 Teaching Writing

Vygotsky's writing about writing includes both groundbreaking insights, and ideas that spoke better to his era of handwritten script than to the 21st century and its device-mediated affordances. A century ago, most writing was undertaken with pen or pencil and paper for readers without immediate access to the text. Laboriously-produced handwritten texts designed for remote readers were subject to far more reflection than are social media posts, texts, and other modern compositions produced quickly and for prompt reading and response, with many formal conventions waived given the swiftness of the exchanges and informality of the medium. Vygotsky had no way of anticipating the rapid-fire manner in which writers send and receive messages in online environments, or of how online connectivity enables the co-construction of documents in real time. He undoubtedly could not have anticipated bots that do the writing for you.

He nonetheless arrived at some insights that have held up well. After considering some culturally-framed dimensions of Vygotsky's perspective, I review the developmental processes that Vygotsky saw involved in symbolic expression, a process that he believed begins with images, not words. This general background on Vygotsky's account of the role of writing in the process of human development in turn suggests issues facing teachers of writing.

Cultural Factors in Vygotsky's Conception

Among Vygotsky's postulations was that as people mature, they develop means of verbal self-regulation. The development of speech capabilities begins with social immersion that provides the language system used for thinking, including whatever variants a person might learn. As fluency with the act of speaking in this language increases and matures, speech in both spoken and written forms enables one to develop personal control over primal functions such as emotions (see Chapters 5 and 7). Through this process people learn not only a language system but its accompanying worldview, thus serving as a major factor in enculturation. This proposition became available from the hypothesis proposed initially by Edward Sapir of German birth and US upbringing in 1929 and subsequently developed by Benjamin Whorf, a US linguist. The Sapir–Whorf hypothesis (a.k.a. hypothesis of linguistic relativity) asserts that the structure of a language influences its speakers' worldview and thought processes to the point where their perceptions are shaped by their language system and its ideology.

Extrapolating from Vygotsky's life in Belarus and Moscow in the first one-third of the 20th century to life in 21st-century English-speaking capitalist societies inevitably produces disjunctures. The Soviet approach to establishing a monoculture, with an

DOI: 10.4324/9781003374848-16

ideological education serving as a critical medium, is both current and obsolete. It remains current in the United States, where many people assert that the nation is a monoculture based on the societies of Judeo-Christian people of European descent. In this conception, *e pluribus unum* (out of many, one) refers to the nation's unification under the Christian god (Cherry, 2007) and need for others to assimilate to its beliefs and practices. This belief is supported by the deep structure of schools (Smagorinsky, 2020a, 2020b) that creates pathways best suited for administrators, teachers, and students who fit that profile.

The assertion of a monoculture works against those from outside the dominant framework, those who must adapt or suffer the consequences. In 21st-century English-speaking nations, this belief in a singular Judeo-Christian heritage is challenged by the presence of people from other religious heritages (including atheists), racial groups, national origins, and other areas of human diversity. A monocultural system in a multicultural nation cuts people off from the many other mediational contours available to follow. In spite of superficial claims to supporting students' individual and cultural differences, US schools rely on a deep structure that continually imposes one set of norms across a diverse population. Developing self-regulation—a major task of human development to Vygotsky—in relation to someone else's culture is considered colonial and oppressive among progressive educators (e.g., Love, 2019). It remains perfectly acceptable and a matter of national responsibility for members of a dominant culture when their goal is to maintain control of society through such vehicles as schools.

At stake is nothing less than the vitality of a civilization, and the role of literacy in promoting it. Vygotsky spoke to this imperative by quoting Blonskiy, who wrote that "The period of civilization begins with the acquisition of letter writing: before that invention mankind stands at the level of barbarism, after it on the level of civilized mankind. Literacy is also a decisive moment in the history of the child's cortical development" (1925, p. 134), a point that sees both biology and culture at work in human development with the acquisition of literacy as a central mechanism, and ontogeny and phylogeny working in parallel. Vygotsky continued:

> This higher cultural development of the child becomes only possible on the basis of school instruction. Left to himself, the child usually advances with the greatest difficulty in this area and usually gets stuck at the earliest stages of culture. However, this does not mean that the mastery of written speech is given to the child exclusively from outside, by the school. On the contrary, it can be easily shown that the child in his development naturally arrives at a certain moment when the mastery of written speech becomes essential and possible for him.
>
> (in Van der Veer, 2020, p. 153)

This mastery of written speech coincides with development within a cultural framework, articulated in speech and advanced through writing. Significantly, Vygotsky emphasized that this acquisition serves the "higher cultural development of the child," the child's entry into the values and practices of a society. What is advanced, however, may be a narrow conception of a national culture, as the Soviet example illustrates, and as the United States and other colonized nations continue to reinforce.

Learning to write undoubtedly serves the socialization purpose that Vygotsky envisioned. Writing provides the means through which a worldview, regulated by both cultural influences and inner speech that embodies those values, may be developed and articulated at the highest possible levels. To Street (2003), this exclusive emphasis on a dominant culture's literacy practices produces an *autonomous model of literacy*, one that assumes that

> Introducing literacy to poor, "illiterate" people, villages, urban youth etc. will have the effect of enhancing their cognitive skills, improving their economic prospects, making them better citizens, regardless of the social and economic conditions that accounted for their "illiteracy" in the first place. I refer to this as an "autonomous" model of literacy. The model, I suggest, disguises the cultural and ideological assumptions that underpin it so that it can then be presented as though they are neutral and universal and that literacy as such will have these benign effects.
>
> (p. 77)

Street's (2003) critique raises questions about Vygotsky's unproblematic view of socialization through speech practices, undermining the belief that such a conception leads all toward the best possible outcome. This exclusive access to the best of all possible worlds has been claimed by societies as different as the United States, the Soviet Union, Native American cultures (Four Arrows, 2006, 2020), and others, suggesting that the notion of an ideal society is fundamentally ethnocentric.

The 21st-century progressive educator would argue that in contrast, multiple pathways lead to a more diverse, and thus more vital, society that grows in relation to the dialectic provided by contrasting points of view. This dynamic is one that Vygotsky might endorse, given his dialectical understandings of human development, even as he enthusiastically embraced Soviet monocultural communism as ideal before he found himself on the outs. Monocultures tend to be valued by the politically conservative; multicultures are the province of the politically liberal or progressive. To Vygotsky, writing serves as a way of adopting a culture's valued ways of being in ways that resemble the autonomous model described by Street:

> Learning written speech, that is, writing and reading, lifts the child to a totally new level of cultural development. Only on the basis of the mastery of this speech, the development of the child's abstract verbal thinking and his scientific education in the real sense of this word become possible. The child who mastered the book and writing makes a decisive step from primitive concrete-visual thinking to higher forms of abstract verbal thinking.
>
> (in Van der Veer, 2000, p. 168)

Verbal literacy is crucial to the development of scientific or academic concepts (see Chapter 6), which in Vygotsky's mind appear to have coincided with the indoctrination to which Soviet schools were dedicated. The literate Soviet citizen, specifically those of proletariat background, could best serve the nation through thinking in culturally framed ways and generating insights that could help build an equitable society free of social class differences. Vygotsky's intentions in promoting Soviet doctrine were guided by this promise.

Defining "Writing"

To Vygotsky (1997c), "written language [is] the most complex device of cultural behavior" (p. 140). Baroni (2011) provides a useful definition of "writing," one that encompasses both alphabetic and non-alphabetic scripts: "By writing, we mean a series of graphic symbols arranged on a surface (be it physical, like a sheet of paper, or virtual, like a screen), in a certain order and in a certain sequence, so that this series is likely to be interpreted (read) by an interpreter (reader) who knows how to decipher the meaning of these signs" (p. 128). This definition of writing fits as a subset in Scribner and Cole's (1981) still-relevant understanding of *literacy* as

> a recurrent, goal-directed sequence of activities using a particular technology and particular systems of knowledge … [a set of] socially developed and patterned ways of using technology and knowledge to accomplish tasks…. [Literacy consists of] a set of socially organized practices which make use of a symbol system and a technology for producing and disseminating it. Literacy is not simply knowing how to read and write a particular script but applying this knowledge for specific purposes in specific contexts of use. The nature of these practices, including, of course, their technological aspects, will determine the kinds of skills ("consequences") associated with literacy.
>
> (p. 236)

My references to "writing" will be based on Vygotsky's orientation to the Russian 33-letter Cyrillic alphabet, derived from the Greek alphabet and supplemented by about a dozen additional letters invented to represent Slavic sounds not found in Greek. As the next section indicates, however, alphabetic writing emerges from developmentally-appropriate images. Ironically, one does not initially learn to write by writing (McCutchen, Teske, & Bankston, 2008), a common belief among process-oriented writing teachers and theorists. Children first learn to write by drawing.

The Origins of Learning to Write

In the 1970s and 1980s, Graves (1983) reached the insight that children's use of alphabetic writing does not signal the beginning of their writing development. The first stage, he argued, is drawing pictures to represent ideas and objects. Understanding how an image serves to express ideas, represent them symbolically, and enable communication with others positions children to learn the ultimate achievement of the human race: The composition of texts via the symbol system of writing.

Vygotsky similarly argued that children first go through proto-compositional stages that involve images more than words. He described drawing "as a preparatory stage in the development of [the child's] written speech" because it is the medium through which a child produces, "according to its psychological function, unique *graphic speech*, a graphic story about something" (in Van der Veer, 2020, p. 154; emphasis in original). A drawing enables a child, according to Vygotsky's contemporary Bühler[1] (1922), to "draw speech, not just things" (quoted in Van der Veer, p. 276).

Vygotsky quoted Blonskiy (1925/1930) approvingly in noting the parallels between ontogeny and phylogeny in writing development: "Just like in mankind, writing emerged only at a particular stage of manual labor and drawing, i.e., at a particular stage of the development of the musculature of the fingers and the wrist, emerges the child's first writing, which is physiologically analogous to the archaic writing of mankind" (quoted in Van der Veer, 2020, p 142). The consequences of not engaging in drawing in early education are dire:

> Blonskiy (1925a) explains the fading of children's drawing on the threshold of the school age by the fact that mankind stopped exactly at this point of its development.

"If we do not teach the child drawing," he says, he will for the rest of his life remain in this stage, i.e., the adult as well will draw as if he were 7.5 years old. Thus, the drawing of the milk teeth child is instinctive and the permanent teeth childhood is the stage of training how to draw. Why? This is my opinion: having reached the [level of] drawing of a child of 7.5 years old, mankind continued on the path of pictography and writing[,] and drawing as such came to a standstill for the majority of mankind. Ontogeny repeats this. The drawing of the 7.5-year-old child signalizes that we can already teach this child how to write.

(pp. 156–157)

These ideas seem archaic, again suggesting that just because Vygotsky and his sources said it, that doesn't make it true in the here and now. Humankind has not, it turns out, abandoned drawing, even if I still draw as if I were 7.5 years old. But one needn't throw away the apple because it has a few bruises. Even for those who are skeptical about humans abandoning drawing or old people drawing like children because they weren't taught how to produce images, the idea that drawing serves as a form of proto-writing has staying power.

Vygotsky argued that drawing serves as both a symbolic act and a physical means of development. Preparing the human hand for writing requires exercise and usage: "In this development of the fine movements of the wrist, drawing and clay modeling play a very big role. This is why these activities, which strengthen and develop the hand, are a perfect preparatory stage for the teaching of writing. We thus see that written speech develops from the child's drawing" (in Van der Veer, 2020, p. 157). Once children develop this physical facility and understand that they can draw things that embody an idea, they may begin the transition to alphabetic writing.

Writing's origin in drawing implies that "the child first draws his letters [rather] than he writes them. This causes the child's handwriting to be extremely large" (in Van der Veer, 2020, p. 157). Because of this developmental phenomenon, Vygotsky argued, children should not be required to write between narrow lines as a way to discipline a more compact handwriting. Forcing them to write small when they are still at the large and loopy stage produces a developmental setback. Fine musculature is required for fine writing, and the physical and experiential development of the child requires patience as a child's writing becomes more appropriately smaller over time, with one centimeter in height serving as Blonskiy's (1925) point at which to begin writing instruction.

Although many educators consider the teaching of handwriting to be irrelevant given the likelihood that children will learn keyboarding skills and no longer need to write with a pencil (e.g., Bromley, 2010), Marquart, Diaz Meyer, Schneider, and Hilgemann (2016) describe the current handwriting crisis in apocalyptic terms:

For a long time now there have been reports of serious problems in schools with regard to learning to write and writing by hand. Many children do not hold their pens correctly or sit properly and write with excessive pressure. Cramp and pain are the consequences when writing at length. The children write too slowly and illegibly; they lack concentration and they tire quickly. Many children require additional support in the areas of motor development, language, learning, and behaviour. Problems with handwriting are the most frequent reason for schoolchildren to consult an ergotherapist.

(p. 82)

Many still find handwriting to be "a critical skill in any child's school journey" (Asselborn, Chapatte, & Dillenbourg, 2020, p. 1). Handwriting, then, can be seen as either obsolete or critical, depending on one's point of view. Those who see 21st-century writing through the lens of connectivity, a proliferation of genres, instant communication, keyboard affordances, and other electronic and digital tools might roll their eyes at the persistence of attention to handwriting in school. In much of the world, the progression no longer goes from drawing to oversized letter writing to more compact written expression, with the matter ending there.

Working on electronic devices begins for many students before they start school. According to the National Center for Educational Statistics (2005), 67% of nursery aged children in 2003 used a computer, and 23% used the internet. The American Academy of Pediatrics (2011), after concluding that the electronics industry was targeting children ages 0–2 and their parents as key consumers, soon thereafter recommended that for developmental reasons—e.g., their lack of memory to guide their actions—children under 2 years old should not be using digital media. The Pew Research Center (2020) surveyed parents and found that over a third with children under 12 report that they began using a smartphone before turning 5.

Whether handwriting remains an important developmental step, or one perhaps skipped by forthcoming generations, is a question for the future. Whether it promotes development toward something other than what Vygotsky envisioned—the mature citizen whose self-regulation helps to produce a cultured, rational mind—also awaits confirmation. The research review conducted by Galvin and Greenhow (2020) affirms that social media writing is quite different from traditional school writing, even as teachers continue to look for ways to include social media in their instruction to make school more relevant to students' immediate social lives, without the cell phones becoming distractions. The long-term impact of digital writing, however, remains to be seen.

Perhaps the shift to keyboarding has caused a decline in less-practiced handwriting skill; perhaps keyboards might be a good alternative for kids who are sloppy writers; perhaps writing bots, which are brand-new as I type these words all by myself without a bot, will make everything the field knows about writing obsolete by the time this book is in print. The fact is, however, that the world has changed in ways that make Vygotsky's views on the origins of writing development interesting, yet possibly less relevant than they were in the days before the electronics revolution. Vygotsky's conception therefore might be of interest to those who work with writers who have no technology through which to mediate their writing.

Like my drawing, my handwriting is stuck at about the age of 7.5. Fortunately, I have a keyboard to rectify the problem. Although typewriters became available in the 1800s and reached a standard form in the early 1900s, Vygotsky did not mention them. He produced his own manuscripts by hand or by dictation to a stenographer. I suspect that in his time and place, the typewriter was a transcription device from handwritten to typed texts, rather than a medium for generating a new text, as keyboard devices have become. Typewriter keyboards appear not to have been considered to be a writing tool. If Vygotsky's generation was like mine—my schooling took place in the US states of Virginia and New Jersey in the 1950s and 1960s—males didn't learn how to type. Typing was something women learned so they could type men's manuscripts for them. And the pre-electronic typewriters of yore were so clumsy that the QWERTY keyboard, still in use today, was developed to slow down a swift, skilled typist so the keys wouldn't arrive in a pileup caused by rapid, near-concurrent striking (Wertsch, 1991). No matter what, Vygotsky's references to writing are limited to marking paper with a pen or pencil; images from his handwritten manuscripts are easily available via internet searches.

What remains relevant is Vygotsky's view that the development of writing ability is central to other forms of literacy: "Just like manual labor and drawing prepare the development of written speech, writing in its turn prepares the development of reading" (in Van der Veer, 2020, p. 157). Drawing leads to writing, which leads to reading: "learning to write is much easier for the child than learning to read. Hereafter, they began to practice the simultaneous teaching of reading and writing at school," making learning to read easier than under prior approaches of his time (p. 157). This attention to the role of literacy in the development of higher mental functions remains a constant in Vygotsky's vision and is essential to any understanding of his conception of a cultural psychology (Cole, 1996), even as literacy educators working in the wake of Street (1984, 2003) might not define literacy in quite the same way. What is critical to a Vygotskian perspective is that literacy and writing need to serve the process of human development, along with their historical communicative and record-keeping functions (Woods, 2010a, 2010b).

The Production of Alphabetic Texts

Vygotsky's conception of the text follows general semiotic principles, in which inscriptions serve to indicate meaning. He referred to written words as being among "second order symbolic processes (such as writing, reading, etc.) or with such basic forms of behaviour as speech" (Vygotsky in Vygotsky & Luria, 1993, p. 136). Vygotsky devoted considerable attention to understanding how writing is distinct from spoken speech, and how spoken speech is distinct from inner speech. Inner speech represents the ideological discourse surrounding a child, which is appropriated for private thinking, self-regulation, concept development, and other affordances. It involves an inchoate swirl of thoughts that, if somehow transcribed, would make little sense to someone who had not thought them. In that they are addressed to the self, they are telegraphic, elliptical, and abbreviated.

Verbal speech provides an articulated version of the content, perspective, and emotion of inner speech, and does so for an immediate audience. The audience produces responses to an utterance that may serve as prompts for elaboration, retraction, or other provision of additional detail. There were no podcasts, or even many radio broadcasts, in Vygotsky's day. In contrast,

> Written speech is deployed to its fullest extent, more complete than oral speech. Inner speech is almost entirely predicative because the situation, the thinker always knows the subject of thought. Written speech, on the contrary, must explain the situation fully in order to be intelligible. The change from maximally compact inner speech to maximally detailed written speech requires what might be called deliberate semantics—deliberate structuring of the web of meaning.
> (Vygotsky, 1986, p. 182)[2]

Writers in his day addressed readers who were not present, those who would come across the text at a later time. To do so, writes Van der Veer (2007),

> the child must think carefully about what message he or she wants to express and what exact information the recipient needs to understand the message. Of course, in learning to write the children must also learn that sounds can be conveyed by symbols, that words consist of syllables, and so on. In that process, they become more

conscious of the structure of their own language. Finally, writing is different from speaking in that it requires a different motive... . Writing ... requires a conscious decision, a special motivation not called forth by an immediately preceding reply.

(p. 91)

Bakhtin (1986) might disagree with this last claim, given that his dialogic theory posits that all utterance comes in response to prior utterances. All texts are produced with *addressivity*, that is, they are addressed to another. *Hidden addressivity* occurs when the recipient is not present or has not explicitly prompted a response. Writing, then, may indeed be called forth by a preceding reply whose presence is not immediate or tangible. Much of what I've written for this volume has been a conversational turn prompted by the writing of others, or by my own prior writing, itself a turn in a long, multi-participant discussion over the course of time.

In any case, writing is a deliberate act designed to produce a text, one to be read later (in Vygotsky's day, usually much later). Even the digital environment produces delays, however brief, between writing and its reading. The pace of digital writing in relation to readers might make it a less deliberate action than Vygotsky conceived. Writing requires volition and a motive to produce, and it benefits from reflection and likely revision to be considered finished and ready for readers. This reflection might not be evident in ill-considered social media posts fired off in a moment of rashness. Reflection requires, and also helps to develop, a writer's conscious control of speech and its conventions, and ultimately the self as a member of a rational society and participant in the Enlightenment essayist tradition (Farr, 1993).

Writers thus develop linguistic meta-awareness through learning to write, which in turn contributes to their verbal self-regulation. As a result, "the main products of school instruction are reflection (*osoznanie*) and mastery (*ovladenie*)" (Van der Veer, 2007, p. 91). Although he was careful not to position writing as the exercise of a mental muscle such that writing makes one a better gymnast or car mechanic, Vygotsky did assert that learning one topic informs one's learning about other topics. This possibility is most likely when the topics share traits that carry over, or that promote "near transfer" in the words of cognitive psychologists (e.g., Sala et al., 2019). As a result, "instruction can have structural effects on cognition that go beyond the topic and knowledge taught. Thus instruction creates things that were definitely not there in the first place" (Van der Veer, 2007, pp. 91–92) and serves a leading role in human development via reflection and self-regulation.

Speech provides the principal means of undertaking these processes, and written speech is the most clearly articulated action serving development. These processes are culturally-channeled, undertaken with tools and signs that are appropriated from engagement with people whose traditions give them meaning. Further, Vygotsky (1987) argued, writing "requires conscious awareness of the very process of speaking. The motives of written speech are more abstract, intellectualistic, and separated from need" (p. 204). This intentional action distinguishes writing from the immediacy and spontaneity of spoken speech.

Self-regulation, reflection, and motivation are more the outcomes of learning to write than the mental operations of a beginner. Vygotsky (1987) argued that when instruction in written speech begins, the basic mental functions that underlie it are not fully developed. Indeed, their development has only just begun. An appropriate level of maturation prepares children for learning tasks, such that

> Instruction in writing can begin if the child's memory has reached a level of development that makes it possible for him to remember the letters of the alphabet, if his

attention has developed to the extent that it can be maintained on matters of little interest to him for a given period of time, and if his thinking has matured to the point that makes it possible for him understand the relationships between sounds and the written signs that symbolize them.

(p. 195)

This symbolic character makes writing an abstract form of expression, one that requires greater attention than spoken speech. Writing, argued Vygotsky (1987), "requires more than learning the techniques of writing," a point that suggests that both the muscle development required for handwriting and formalism as a pedagogy are inadequate to promoting students' writing as a vehicle for contributing to their development of cultural concepts. Its shortcomings are what promote its complexities:

Written speech lacks intonation and expression. It lacks all the aspects of speech that are reflected in sound... . . [The child] must abstract from the sensual aspect of speech itself.... . The abstract nature of written speech—the fact that it is thought rather than pronounced—represents one of the greatest difficulties encountered by the child in his mastery of writing.

(p. 202)

Vygotsky could not have anticipated the electronic affordances that enable intonation and expression in writing: Emojis, changes in font size and boldness, etc. Electronic speech can now be accompanied by sound effects and other embellishments as well. The times have changed, and Vygotsky's beliefs from the 1920s and 1930s need to be adapted to maintain their relevance.

Vygotsky's (1987) attention to the role of motivation might require revision as well. He invoked the idea that "motivation generally precedes activity... . Every conversation and phrase is preceded by a speech motive" (p. 203). Yet others might assert that motivation can emerge *from* activity, an idea that fits well with the practice of freewriting, in which students are told to start writing so that they can figure out what they want to say (Elbow, 1973). As I'll review later in this chapter, Vygotsky advanced this process-oriented view of speech without referring to its potential for generating a motive, rather than following one. I would add to this point the fact that even planned writing does not necessarily follow from motivation. At times during the composition of this book, I have felt sluggish and reluctant to write. But the act of writing has given me traction amidst the wheel-spinning such that I get into my groove and start rolling. Perhaps it is different with the beginning writers described by Vygotsky, but it's worth noting that other perspectives are available to consider the issues he raised.

Written speech nonetheless includes demands and conditions that make it a unique form of expression. Oral speech, Vygotsky (1987) says,

is regulated by the dynamics of the situation. It flows entirely from the situation in accordance with this type of situational-motivational and situational-conditioning process. With written speech, on the other hand, we are forced to create the situation or—more accurately—to represent it in thought. The use of written speech presupposes a fundamentally different relationship to the situation, one that is freer, more independent, and more voluntary.

(p. 203)

Vygotsky (1987) emphasized that teachers should not wait until processes have matured before attempting to teach children to write. Writing is too important a cultural and intellectual tool to delay, and thus should be taught as a matter of potential rather than prior developmental achievement. Again, learning precedes, rather than follows, development. The curriculum and instruction should be forward-looking, consistent with Vygotsky's developmental orientation. This look ahead is built on the past and present, on the cultural framework within which students grow in capability within the lower and upper thresholds of their possibilities: "Productive instruction can occur only within the limits of these two thresholds. Only between these thresholds do we find the optimal period for instruction in a given subject. *The teacher must orient his work not on yesterday's development in the child but on tomorrow's*" (p. 211; emphasis in original). I've argued (2018a, 2018b) that "tomorrow" is not a reference to the day after today. Rather, it more metaphorically refers to the future, consistent with his emphasis on long-term development (see Chapter 14).

Vygotsky's observations might easily describe 21st-century writing in many schools, or at least those whose teachers value the developmental potential of learning to write: "writing must make sense to the child, must be elicited by a natural want, a need, included in a lifelike task essential to the child. Only then will we be convinced that it will develop in the child not as habits of the hand and the fingers, but as a truly new and complex aspect of speech" (Vygotsky, 1997c, p. 145). Writing must mean something to the writer, a truism oft-repeated but often not practiced in scripted school instruction of the sort in vogue among administrators who see human development unfolding identically across all people, except for the laggards, and is thus subject to standardization.

Grammar

The teaching of grammar in English-language schools has had a troubled history. Several research reviews covering over a century of studies, extending back to the early 1900s, have found that the teaching of grammar in isolation from speech and writing produces curious effects. It generally results in no improvement in writing, and may actually produce regressions because the time spent on grammar could more fruitfully be invested in useful writing instruction (Braddock, Lloyd-Jones, & Schoer, 1963; Graham & Perrin, 2007; Hillocks, 1986; Weaver, 1996). A chart prepared by Hillocks (1987, p. 75) to depict the results of his meta-analysis of writing studies covering 20 years tells the story in dramatic images, showing the arrow for "Grammar/Mechanics" pointing to the left—below zero effects—and every other factor in writing proficiency pointing to the right of zero, showing some positive outcomes for student writers.

Every research-tested method of teaching writing to that point provides some advantage except grammar, which leads to declines in writing as measured in these assessments. It doesn't even improve students' spoken and written grammar (Hillocks, 1986). Critically, this overwhelming body of research refers to teaching grammar in isolation from usage in speech or writing, as an instructional end in itself. What matters in learning about syntax is how to use it so people can follow a speaker's or writer's train of thought.

Vygotsky's endorsement of grammar instruction might seem odd to progressive educators who reject formalism. He believed that a mastery of grammar contributed to the broader self-regulation that inner speech enables people to impose on themselves. Van der Veer and Valsiner (1991) write that Vygotsky's emphasis on the role of reflection (*osoznanie*) and control (*ovladenie*) as central to school learning suggests that the teaching of grammar may have the same beneficial result. As Vygotsky (1987) argued about writing, the learning of grammar follows from immature, rather than mature, mental processes: "Instruction in arithmetic, grammar, and natural science do not begin when the appropriate functions are mature. On the contrary, the immaturity of the required mental functions at the beginning of the instructional process is a general and basic law in all domains of school instruction" (p. 205).

Vygotsky (1987) addressed a movement of his day, the "agrammatical" effort "which suggests that grammar should be removed from the list of school subjects because it is unnecessary, because it provides no new speech capacities. If we analyze instruction in grammar and written speech, however, we find that it has tremendous significance for the general development of the child's thought" even as "he has already acquired the entire grammar of his native language…. [However] while he declines and he conjugates, he does not know that he declines and conjugates" (p. 205) due to a lack of conscious awareness. Children's knowledge is from everyday interactions, and so they do not develop or need the ability for the kind of abstraction that is learned in school as scientific or academic concepts. Nor does it involve the application of formal rules that guide one's use of conventions. A person having only informal, everyday knowledge of how to speak appropriately will likely have difficulty adapting (code-switching or code-meshing) everyday linguistic knowledge to new situations where other rules might apply, lacking conscious awareness and volitional control of the knowledge.

Vygotsky (1987) claimed that children can already speak with proper grammar when they enter school, raising questions about whether grammar instruction is necessary. It's not clear how he arrived at this assertion that children can speak grammatically at age 6, given how few adults speak wholly grammatical English, at least by textbook standards, and how many speak versions of English that don't conform to textbook rules. If the proposition that all forms of a language are rule-bound (Smitherman, 1977) holds up, perhaps that problem goes away. The issue in multicultural English-speaking societies is that grammatical departures from textbook rules are often constructed as cognitive deficiencies, ignorance, or laziness in both the popular (Wiens, 2012) and scholarly press (Van der Lely, Rosen, & McClelland, 1998), leading teachers to teach a single "Standard" English and punish those who don't master its intricacies.

Vygotsky's found that studying grammar as grammar to be "indeed a useless undertaking," aligning him with the researchers whose reviews found isolated grammar instruction to be not only useless but counterproductive. What does benefit the student is

> conscious awareness of what he does. He learns to operate on the foundation of his capacities in a volitional manner. His capacity moves from an unconscious, automatic plane to a voluntary, intentional, and conscious plane. Instruction in written speech and grammar play a fundamental role in this process [in that] both grammar and writing provide the child with the potential of moving to a higher level in speech development [via the development of conscious awareness and self-regulation].
>
> (p. 206)

Vygotsky (2004) saw a relation between grammar and logic, given grammar's logic: "the child's grammar develops before his logic…. [T]his lack of correspondence does not exclude the unity of grammar and logic in the development of the child's speech. In fact, this lack of correspondence is fundamental to the internal unity of meaning and word that is expressed in complex logical relations" (p. 74). Whether learning grammar serves a developmental role in the ability to think logically may depend on what one means by "logic."

Argumentation instruction (Hillocks, 2011; Newell, Bloome, Kim, & Goff, 2019; Toulmin, 1958) in Toulmin's tradition assumes that logical thinking can be taught and will lead to the best actions, at least according to the logic employed. I've contributed to this belief as well (Smagorinsky, Johannessen, Kahn, & McCann, 2010). As Van der Veer and Valsiner (1991) note, however, the Enlightenment rational thinking valorized by Vygotsky has not always been realized in human action. During the Covid pandemic, wearing masks has been interpreted as a personal choice and not a public responsibility. During rapid climate change, corporate deregulation is expanding. Preposterous lies and fabrications provide the foundation for political party platforms, and people in general think and act emotionally rather than rationally (Haidt, 2012). Logic in argumentation appears to be a quaint idea, at least in the public realm.

Cultural variations in speech conventions have complicated the belief that grammatical logic promotes gravitation to cultural logic. A recent call for Black linguistic justice (Baker-Bell et al., 2020) asserts the legitimacy of Black speech and the colonialism of efforts to make white textbook English the only form toward which speakers should aspire. Vygotsky's views on grammar were both consistent with this call, and violated it as well. He might be accused of linguistic hegemony for viewing cultures as monolithic, and societal ends as universally shared even as they privilege one way of being above all others. On the other hand, his conception might suggest that different grammars are embedded in different logics and cultural ways of being, such that the issues raised by Baker-Bell et al. could point toward the value of cultivating Black identities and social futures through the acceptance and fostering of Black speech.

One interpretation is limiting and impositional, the other liberatory and culturally responsive. Schools tend to take the more narrow of these perspectives, a situation that teachers should be aware of and reflect on as they consider how speech channels development, and how grammar and other areas of usage and mechanics produce specific logics that may not be cultivated in all homes and communities.

Products and Processes in Writing

The field of writing instruction took on a new cast in the 1960s. The research review of Braddock et al. (1963)—the first compilation and synthesis of writing research, undertaken at a time during which there were few writing research journals—found that research to that point had focused on written products. Researchers had studied such matters as how essays improved in some measurable manner after some form of instruction, often in comparison with other teaching methods; or what sorts of primary traits were essential to different forms of writing. This analysis of products, Braddock et al. felt, was insufficient, leading them to recommend that writing teachers and researchers ask, "What is involved in the act of writing?" (p. 53). This question helped to launch the writing process movement, one that shifted attention from the effects of teaching on the finished papers written by students, to the thinking involved in producing them and the procedures employed to generate them. Virtually all attention to writing by researchers came in the context of school learning, with the workplace, the community, the professions, and other areas not studied until the late 1970s.

Process vs. product became the name of the game, with attention to finished essays considered passé by many and a focus on text generation believed to be the proper emphasis of teachers, theorists, and researchers. In this sense, students benefit from learning procedural knowledge for how to generate the content of a piece of writing. Braddock et al.'s (1963) report came out almost simultaneously with the first translation of Vygotsky into English, the highly subjective and questionable 1962 version of *Myshlenie i rech': Psikhologicheskie issledovaniya* mistranslated as *Thought and Language*. Undoubtedly, the overlap between readerships of these two volumes was slim. Writing teachers and researchers were far more attentive to a major review of their field by some of their most prominent figures than they were to a volume from a long-dead Soviet psychologist whose suppression obscured his reputation at home and abroad, who was many years from being widely read via the publication of *Mind in Society*.

Had they discovered Vygotsky, and had they skipped ahead a half-century to the point where Vygotskian concepts had been far more extensively mined by global psychologists, they would have found much to appreciate. In *Thinking and Speech*, Vygotsky (1987) accounted for both process and product, albeit without explicitly making connections between them (Wertsch, 2000). Each emphasis, Wertsch found, had deep roots in European philosophical traditions that were often positioned at odds with one another. I next review the issues at stake and how they inform process-product debates whose dichotomous approach obscures the manner in which the two are complementary and essential to one another.

Murray (1980) captures the essence of the writing process movement in saying, "We do not teach our students rules demonstrated by static [product] models; we teach our students to write by allowing them to experience the process of writing. That is a process of discovery, of using written language to find out what we have to say... . We can let them discover how writing finds its own meaning" (Murray, 1980, p. 20). Murray was a highly influential writing guru of his era, providing impetus to this view of writing as a process. Writers, he argued, find meaning through the process of writing. Their products are almost incidental, and are likely to be revised or disagreed with at a later time, even by their author. In focusing on the generation of the text more than the product of the text, writers experience developmental changes of a highly personal nature. There was little sociocultural influence in this movement, which took place amidst a personal-growth, individualistic era in which people were encouraged to "Do your own thing." Diversity referred to individual human diversity, not cultural diversity, at a time when most people publishing their views were white. Writing, to Murray and other process authorities of the day, serves as a tool that enables individuals to discover personal meaning through the act of composing a text.

Murray exemplified the rejection of text-centered writing instruction based on formalist principles, which was likely the prime method of teaching writing in his day, often through the imitation of model essays comprised of five paragraphs (Johnson, Smagorinsky, Thompson, & Fry, 2003). In the same meta-analysis that identified the negative consequences of teaching writing by teaching grammar, Hillocks (1986) found that the imitation of model essays does improve writing somewhat according to the measurement criteria used in experimental studies conducted on writing instruction, although to a lesser degree than other methods of teaching writing. On the other hand, the freewriting that went hand-in-glove with Murray's position was only slightly effective too, at least in the experimental research included in the meta-analysis. Although Hillocks found the greatest effects with a "structured process" (Applebee, 1986) method that placed the teacher in a more critical designing role than the student-driven freewriting method, and that required clear criteria to guide teaching and assessment, for the most part the terms of the debate were set: Process is good, product is bad. These points were driven home in finely tuned journal articles and books in which the product did matter.

The process vs. product dispute in composition studies invokes long-standing traditions in European-derived thought (Wertsch, 2000), one tradition focused on how texts appear once produced (realized in formalism and product-based teaching and assessment) and one concerned with how ideas emerge (process-based approaches in the spirit of Romanticists like Rousseau). Yet the two are not at all in conflict; there is no text without a generative process (Barnes, 1992), and there is no process without a product being created.

It's easier to identify and grade a problematic product than to see an ineffective process, and so formalism's widespread emphasis in school is understandable, if not commendable. Products that don't meet school expectations have often produced deficit interpretations of the writers themselves. This complaint has been lodged against Ivy League students who are expected to have arrived socialized to academic discourse (Bartlett, 2003), "basic writers" considered cognitively deficient (Martinez & Martinez, 1987), the writing of non-white students that conforms to different speech traditions (Thomas, 1983), and others who do not reproduce textbook rules in their writing. It has generated the notion of "status errors," those violations of rules that leave the impression that a speaker or writer is of questionable breeding, ability, and achievement (Anson, 2000). Formalism is designed to defend the status quo of writing as presented in textbooks, and schools have embraced the responsibility with help from policies and public pressure.

The process movement got impetus from Britton, Burgess, Martin, McLeod, and Rosen's (1975) highly influential advocacy of the British "growth model" that foregrounds the need for education to serve the psychological development of students by emphasizing expression and activity. Moffett (1968) similarly argued that "Rendering experience into words is the real business of school" (p. 114), and Emig (1977) characterized writing as a "unique mode of learning" (p. 122) that promotes new thinking through the act of composition. Applebee (1981) describes writing "as a tool for exploring a subject" in which meaning is generated "at the point of utterance" (p. 100), an expressivist perspective that he prefers to "traditional" instruction that is teacher- and product-centered, even as the expressive perspective is also part of a tradition (an idea available in Applebee, 1974). These endorsements helped to promote "writing to learn" pedagogies that view the process of writing as a way of both expressing and developing ideas, regardless of what the product looks like, leading Yagelski (2007) and others to reject the value of the product entirely.

Langer and Applebee (1987)—the latter of whom studied with Britton and adapted his developmental perspective—conclude from a wide-ranging study of writers producing different sorts of texts that

> activities involving writing (any of the many sorts of writing we studied) lead to better learning than activities involving reading and studying only. Writing assists learning. Beyond that, we learned that writing is not writing is not writing; different kinds of writing activities lead students to focus on different kinds of information, to think about that information in different ways, and in turn to take quantitatively and qualitatively different kinds of knowledge away from their writing experiences.
> (p. 135)

Although it's easy to envision writing that does not produce new learning, their study of writing in school, where their research questions found fertile ground, provides empirical support for the learning available through the process of writing.

These endorsement don't mean, however, that products don't matter. A number of researchers have looked at written products as rich sources of meaning. They identify dynamic qualities following from the formal aspects of writing, raising questions about the rejection of product in the emphasis on process. A semiotic understanding of texts views them as bearers of a sign function, one that gives them a meaning potential. This meaning is not autonomous; it does not have an inherent meaning that readers are obligated to find. Meaning rather emerges from the confluence of reader, text, context, intertext (relations across texts), and intercontexts (relations across contexts) (Nystrand, 1986; Smagorinsky, 2001; Witte, 1992). Meaning may fluctuate depending on the cultural histories of those converging on a text. For example, the figure known as the *swastika* served as a mystical symbol in indigenous North American tribes, India, Japan, Persia, and other countries and cultures before becoming the Nazi emblem for genocide and terror. This example illustrates how cultural signs lack a fixed, objective meaning, instead being interpreted according to the contexts in which they appear by people socialized to read them in particular ways.

Writing serves the same cultural role when it is produced as a sign. Alphabetic writing is a set of squiggles on a surface or electronic document. Recognizing these squiggles as letters, words, sentences, and longer texts is something that people learn, and interpreting them also follows from following cultural conventions and practices. Written signs are replete with meaning potential, both to the writers of the texts themselves and to other readers, as long as they understand the conventions through which texts are produced. Writers may revisit their own texts and reflect on their form and what their form implies, and revise them if necessary, as I have done with this very sentence during an extended process of composition. In this sense, the sign of the provisionally finished text may in turn serve as a tool for further contemplation and composition.

Understanding one's own text is much simpler than understanding one produced by another person. People often lack intersubjectivity that enables a common understanding of written speech; that is, they lack a shared socialization that enables them to read texts and situations in the same way. Nystrand (1986) views "writing and reading [as] collaborative, social acts," with the text requiring a balance "between the expressive needs of the writer and the comprehension needs of the reader" (p. 47). This "reciprocity principle" requires that "*In any collaborative activity the participants orient their actions on certain standards which are taken for granted as rules of conduct by the social group to which they belong*" (p. 48; emphasis in original). A "good" written product does not have inherent, autonomous qualities that meet an objective standard. Rather, argues Nystrand, good writing is "in tune" with readers in terms of their shared expectations for tone, dialect, vocabulary, syntax, values, theme, and other traits.

Process and product, then, are not in conflict. Rather, they serve different, complementary roles in the meaning construction available through spoken and written speech. Although Vygotsky (1987) did not explicitly link them in *Thinking and Speech*, it's worth noting that this final volume of his career was produced under chaotic, life-threatening conditions that did not allow time for contemplation, revision, or follow up. Wertsch (2000) refers to Taylor's (1985a, 1985b) belief that mixing philosophical traditions represents a rotten compromise intellectually. My own view is that mixing philosophical traditions is inevitable and a consequence of living in a society in which many belief systems are in operation simultaneously, often in conflict with one another. People are thus destined to be inconsistent, to draw on traditions that serve needs, as teachers do in the pragmatic world of the classroom (Smagorinsky, 2020a). It's also possible that these traditions are less at odds than they might appear, given how both rationalism and romanticism may be at work in the production and consumption of the same text.

Discussion

Drawing on Vygotsky to inform writing pedagogy can produce wildly different understandings. The formalist might attend selectively to his attention to the sign function of language and his elitism and emphasize a writer's adherence to textbook rules for structure and language use. A process-oriented pedagogue might selectively read his chapters on the tool function of language and, like Yagelski (2007), believe that only the act of writing matters; that the finished text is disposable. Grammarians might read Vygotsky's views on grammar and believe that they are justified in emphasizing standard form as a way to promote not only acceptable forms of expression, but their logic and self-control as well. The early-grades teacher might agree that there is a handwriting crisis that needs to be addressed developmentally—perhaps with complementary clay modeling to promote dexterity—so that children's letters gradually decrease in size until they fit between the lines on their paper. The tech-savvy teacher might ignore Vygotsky's views on handwriting and emphasize keyboarding instead. Those who are convinced that verbal expression is paramount might embrace Vygotsky's emphasis on words and build a curriculum out of reading and writing alphabetic texts. The semiotician might reject the primacy of words and accept Wertsch's (1991) extrapolation of semiotic principles to promote a *cultural tool kit* of mediational means that expands the symbol systems beyond words. The person who has read Vygotsky lightly or relied on secondary sources who have read him lightly might claim that Bruner's notion of instructional scaffolding follows from Vygotsky's construct of the zone of proximal development and believe that whatever they are doing is an instance of scaffolding and is therefore Vygotskian (e.g., Nurfaidah, 2018) (see Chapter 9). These possibilities, and no doubt more, follow from the selective manner in which theorists, including Vygotsky, are often read (Cazden, 1996).

Vygotsky taken in convenient parts, however, is not Vygotskian, any more than chopping off one of his fingers provides you with his hand. What strikes me as important is understanding that he had a developmental perspective that began with a prehistory—in society, the shift from drawing to alphabets; in the lifespan, the movement from drawing to writing—and mature over time in relation to how cultures structure their environments.

The specifics of the developmental pathway afforded by literacy might be open to dispute. The exclusive role that Vygotsky assigned to speech might be contested by those who see other symbol systems being constructed and consumed according to principles that parallel those involved in writing while including other medium-specific dynamics as well (Bezemer & Kress, 2008). His extensive attention to handwriting and drawing, and apparent belief that they both suggest the need for hand-strength activities such as clay modeling, might have limitations for those who see composition in the future (and much of the present) being carried out on computers, tablets, phones, and other devices. When the sediment of these discussions settles, though, what is left is a conception of human development in which people become like the people around them ideologically and practically through both the tool use of written speech as a generative process, and the sign function of texts as the embodiment of ideas both personal and cultural, which in turn may serve as tools for advancing thought.

Vygotsky was surrounded by people who, in Gomel, emphasized formal knowledge of classic texts, leading him to see canonical art as having great potential for promoting development via the same channels that shape the production of texts (see Chapter 12). In Moscow he was part of a societal revolution that produced the world's first Marxist nation, one built on communistic principles of social class elimination, atheism, and other values.

These ideals were no doubt seductive to one banished during the previous regime because of his religion and culture. He was a product of the very developmental processes he described, without necessarily seeing how they confined his own outlook, a sort of myopia that all people share. The question arises, then, whether one can be religious, capitalistic, and open to popular culture, and still be Vygotskian. I think it's possible if one sees these ways of being as a consequence of living in the 21st century in a nation in which values and technologies are at work in ways that were not available in the early Soviet Union.

If I could offer some takeaways from Vygotsky's various exegeses on writing, they might be as follows. First, product and process are not in conflict, but comprise two aspects of a whole form of action. It's hard to imagine Vygotsky agreeing with Yagelski (2007) and his view that discarding a written product forces greater attention on the process of producing it, and therefore makes for good pedagogy. If I wrote something and you told me to throw it away, I'd discard you instead. Vygotsky's belief in the value of the written product was underscored by the severe shortages of paper in the Soviet Union; paper was too precious to dispose of. The process is generative, but so is the text once a reader, including and perhaps especially the author, begins to employ it as a cultural tool after engaging with its signs. The written form does have serious consequences, as people know from sending leap-before-you-look social media posts. Teachers might therefore proceed with the understanding that there are roles in classroom instruction for unrestrained writing as a way to generate ideas, the development of those ideas into more coherent drafts, and continued efforts to refine a text in light of the demands it makes on readers and possibilities for helping writers achieve their ends.

Vygotsky's attention to both the sign and tool functions of spoken and written speech remains compelling. The process movement perhaps overemphasized writing-to-learn at the expense of the structure of the text. A graduate student once approached me about being on her dissertation committee, describing a study that focused on the writing process of a set of teachers. I asked at one point, Does it matter if the writing is any good? Her response was to reject the question altogether, saying that she was in no position to judge another person's writing quality, and that her role was only to encourage writing in order to generate new ideas. At that time I was co-editor, with Michael W. Smith, of *Research in the Teaching of English*, to which well over 100 articles were submitted annually, with room to publish only about 12–16. I told the student that I decided whether writing is good or not all the time, assisted by reviewers who recommended publication or not, based on their judgment of the finished text's quality. She seemed horrified that I would be so judgmental, left our meeting, and never contacted me again.

I think it matters how the product turns out, as did Vygotsky. You would surely not be reading this page if I didn't have a great concern for the appearance of the product, something I've labored over for a few years during the conception, drafting, reorganization, revision, and final completion of the manuscript, followed by careful editing by my Routledge editors and my response to their suggestions to make the final product as clear as possible. The sign function of a text depends for communication on how its author structures it. It requires the sort of deliberation that Vygotsky described, and does indeed contribute developmentally to the socialization process afforded through literacy he recounted. I became an academic writer by studying the publications of people ahead of me in the business, by writing academic papers, and by learning from reviewer feedback (mostly). In so doing I became enculturated to certain scholarly ways. Indeed, the first paper I wrote as a doctoral student was returned with the pithy criticism: "You don't write like a scholar." I took that as an imperative to understand how scholars write, and to learn how to work within the conventions of academic publications in the social sciences. Over time I've also learned how to violate those conventions, giving me much joy.

This process has included many of the stages I've described, and has involved the dialectic process of thesis-antithesis-synthesis as I've positioned my writing both within and against the ideas of others, including Vygotsky's. I think that if he were to survey the current compositional landscape, much about his thinking would require refinement. However, I think that he would retain this dialectical dimension so that students' arguments, regardless of which conventions they followed, would be undertaken through an exploration of opposing ideas, through listening and engaging with others to reach a synthesis (Smagorinsky, 2023b).

Vygotsky's attention to the designative tradition does have implications, not all of which he foresaw. If texts embody the values of a culture, then it matters whose culture is treated as dominant in school. The early days of schooling were assimilative (Smagorinsky, 2021a), providing a structure that has endured through the present. This systemic institution of Enlightenment rationalism as the backbone of education has been celebrated by traditionalists and conservatives, and challenged by progressives and multiculturalists. Instituting a strict program of study based on Vygotskian ideas might suggest that school is properly conducted to promote assimilation to a dominant culture's ways, a major task of Soviet and US mass education. As a progressive, I see his views on promoting particular traditions as having greater resonance in his day and place than in ours; at the same time, as I survey the political environment of the 2020s, I see determined efforts to impose one tradition on all, including threats of violence at school board meetings, threats of termination to noncompliant teachers and incarceration of noncompliant librarians, and other drastic measures. Dominant cultures position outsiders as barbaric and deficient, rather than interpreting their differences as assets that might enrich and advance society. And Soviet society was not inclusive, and the barbarians were relocated outside the gates or beneath the ground.

The decades since Vygotsky's death have produced genre shifts that complicate his view that maturing toward a society's most valued sorts of texts helps to socialize a person to that culture's means and ends. Schools typically privilege the historical genres of argument/persuasion, description, narration, and so on. Not only that, they tend to teach restrictive versions of these modes based on old European notions of textuality. Yet cultural studies have found that not all narratives, arguments, etc. follow the same conventions. In the 21st century, people have access to many more modes of expression than were available to the ancient Greeks who identified these classic modes, and to the Enlightenment leaders who instituted them as the means of promoting rational thinking. No social media for them; no "world literature" from outside the English-language purview. Meanwhile, outside school young people are immersed in a textual world that is undergoing constant re-imagination and reconfiguration. As schools attempt to promote and enforce a monoculture based on old and exclusive traditions, young people participate in new and hybrid genres that they find more intriguing and engaging.

Vygotsky's beliefs therefore require adjustment, especially if schools are committed to a real diversity effort that lacks the assimilationist motive that has structured school in English-speaking nations since the inception of mass education. Monocultures assert the need to gravitate to their norms. The 21st-century multicultural educator might share Vygotsky's embrace of his developmental emphasis, but not his valorization of a single social structure. Such educators are at odds with policies designed to promote uniformity and conformity; that is, most educational policies. However, those concerned with honoring the cultures of students from diverse backgrounds would see merit in understanding how students from outside the cultural mainstream have learned to navigate their worlds, and think about how to accommodate their perspectives and practices within the framework of teaching whole classes in relation to a curriculum.

It's hard to say what Vygotsky would have thought of tweets, emojis, cultural dialects, and other compositional elements of the multicultural 21st century, especially in a society built around free-market capitalism and its rapid changes, and the inequities it inevitably produces. The 21st century provides more conceptual worlds beyond strict capitalism and strict communism, the "first" and "second" worlds that marginalize "third world" societies that lack an established industrial economy. These textual forms also illustrate the growing acceptance of nonverbal texts in the name of multiliteracies, multimodality, and other semiotic concepts that position alphabetic writing as one of many modes of expression and representation, and not necessarily the best for all authors and readers on all occasions.

Vygotsky, then, does and does not speak to writing teachers of English-speaking nations nearly a century later. His understanding of writing development is part of a broader theory of human development in which people's trajectories follow those of their society, mediated by the tools and signs that provide meaning and continuity to social life. Seeing writing as part of this pathway, one that helps formalize conceptual understandings and promote disciplined thinking within cultural bounds, has value even outside its original Soviet context. It helps me to know that I have become who I am, in many ways, through my efforts to write my understandings within academic genres that provide the structures and constructs within which I work. If I were a poet (I'm not), my writing within those communities would similarly shape my development as a person and citizen. Whether tweets and text messages have the same potential is to this point unknown. Whether writing bots will make everything to this point obsolete awaits resolution. Whether teachers should think about these questions is, I believe, of paramount importance.

Notes

1 Karl Ludwig Bühler (1879–1963) was a German gestalt psychologist and linguist who was among the founders of the Würzburg School of Psychology.
2 The "web of meaning" (1986) is translated in the 1987 version as the "fabric of meaning" (p. 203). I use the 1986 version because I like "web of meaning" better, in spite of the preference of many for the 1987 translation of the volume, which I have adopted based on the points made by various translators.

14 Vygotsky, "Defectology," and Inclusive Education

In 1994, I had the opportunity to attend the International Conference on Lev Vygotsky and the Contemporary Human Sciences in Golitsyno, a small town outside Moscow. There I gave my first paper with a strong and pervasively Vygotskian focus, shortly thereafter published as Smagorinsky (1995b). The conference was an exciting event for me as an assistant professor trying to make my way in the academic world, including the newly expanding niche occupied by Vygotskian studies.

After the conference, I took advantage of my only visit to Russia and went on a bus tour of the Moscow area that the conference organizers provided for us. We stood on the shoulders of history throughout this excursion. We visited where the "Russian White House" had been under fire just a year before during an event known as the 1993 Russian constitutional crisis, the 1993 October Coup, Black October, the Shooting of the White House, and Ukaz 1400, a revolt that President Boris Yeltsin turned back with military force.

This stop was not our only meeting with history. Our outing included a visit to Red Square and the Kremlin, although unfortunately, our trip couldn't accommodate a tour of its mammoth interior. We visited a Russian Orthodox church that had remained in operation throughout the communist era, even as at the point of the Soviet takeover, "Nearly all churches were closed down, church property was confiscated and thousands of clergy members were shot" (Daily News Egypt, 2016, n. p.).

We also wandered through a museum commemorating the tsars. My companion for much of the visit was Irving Sigel, a prominent Jewish Piagetian psychologist whose friendship with Jim Wertsch helped to create some listening space between devotees of Vygotsky and Piaget, two theorists often thought to be in opposition. Irv had been born in 1922, just as the Bolsheviks were beginning to consolidate their takeover of the Russian, and then Soviet governments. Irv had barely missed the Romanovs but was around for Hitler. As I admired some Tsarist jewels in the museum, Irv drew on our shared Jewish heritage and cautioned, "Always remember: They murdered your people." It was an educational experience in many, many ways.

Among our stops that week was a visit to a School of Defectology. When they told us of this destination, I remember thinking, Defectology? You must be kidding. Others on the tour complained about being forced to spend a few hours at this location. Many, if not most of us, had never heard of defectology and didn't like the sound of it. Vygotsky's (1993) writings on the topic, published as Volume II of his *Collected Works*, had been issued a year before, and with little fanfare and no readership among the conference attendees on the tour. I was unaware of its existence and would have put it on the bottom of my reading pile just on the basis of its name. Meanwhile, I was still trying to read what was already available—at that point, the offerings largely included three translations of *Thinking*

DOI: 10.4324/9781003374848-17

and Speech, *Mind in Society*, and *The Psychology of Art*—and the ancillary works produced by people at the conference and beyond. I sure wasn't going to read about "defective" people so early in the game, and wondered why Vygotsky would even write such a thing.

Furthermore, the School of Defectology we visited, although relatively recently built, had already fallen into disrepair, like much of the construction in the areas we visited. We never viewed teachers and students at work, and so never got a sense of what went on in the school's classrooms, or why it was called defectology. We walked around a deteriorating building, had little understanding of what we observed, and left a bit annoyed that we'd been taken to such a location by the autocrats who had planned our excursion and who were not interested in our opinions about what would meet our interests in touring the Moscow area.

And that was the last I heard of or thought about defectology for about 15 years. I had purchased the whole set of 6 volumes of the *Collected Works*, and Volume II was one that was always last in line to be read, if ever, given my aversion to the debilitating name of defectology. Another opportunity came up, however, that finally pushed me to set aside my bias and read Volume II. After reading it and some attendant scholarship, and after incorporating it into my own perspective on how to be an inclusive educator and citizen, I have ended up believing it may well be Vygotsky's most important contribution to the psychological literature, even as it is surely among his least read publications.

In October of 2022, I ran a reference search on Vygotsky. His scholarship had been referenced to that point around 265,000 times.[1] Of these, under 600 have been for Volume II of the *Collected Works*. Many people would be very happy to know that something they wrote has been referenced 600 times, but the figure is microscopic in comparison with other works from his oeuvre. The vast majority are to *Mind in Society* or its chapters (which are responsible for over half of Vygotsky's citations), or one of the three versions of *Thinking and Speech*. I think it's safe to say that Vygotsky's work in defectology is little known, little read, and little understood.

My own ignorance regarding defectology was mitigated in 2008, when I was recruited to write a review for *Reading Research Quarterly* of a new edited collection, Daniels, Cole, and Wertsch's (2007) *Cambridge Companion to Vygotsky*. It's a strong volume, and I was delighted to have the opportunity to read it carefully and share my views with the field in a review that was eventually published as Smagorinsky (2009a). When I submitted my initial draft of the review to my editor, Rose Marie Weber, she suggested that I look more deeply into a chapter I'd glossed over, Kozulin and Gindis's (2007), "Sociocultural theory and education of children with special needs: From defectology to remedial pedagogy." That suggestion helped to launch a line of inquiry for me that has now occupied about 15 years, and counting. Shortly after reviewing Daniels et al., I began writing about my family's history of autism, which I exhibit at what's called a high-functioning level. Although Vygotsky was mainly concerned with blind and deaf children, his outline of a theory of defectology fit my interest in atypical mental makeups very well.

This chapter is designed to help readers who are unacquainted with this robust field to understand its history and emphasis, and extract principles that I believe apply to all of life, including classrooms. Vygotsky's defectological writing is especially insightful in thinking about settings in which people have makeups that don't produce the sorts of behavior instituted in the system of rules, as in the case of autism. His ideas can also be extrapolated to populations that are not "disabled" or "disordered," but whose members are interpreted as such by those in dominant positions, as is often the case with people of color, people from low SES families, immigrants, people of nonbinary sexual identity, and others who may follow a different set of rules of engagement.

In my view, the badly neglected work in defectology serves as, to use the phrase adapted from the *Hebrew Bible* by Vygotsky, the "The stone which the builders rejected [that] has become the cornerstone." This chapter outlines how Vygotsky explicated the field of defectology and how its principles can inform any discussion of managing human diversity in school and society.

German and Soviet Defectology Prior to Vygotsky

The name *defectology* preceded Vygotsky by a few generations. McCagg (1989) reports that the term arose among Germans, who established the first special research and training centers and introduced the term "defective" to characterize children with special needs. The term's deficit-infused connotations bely the fundamentally empathic and nurturing approach that was later developed by the Soviets under Vygotsky's guidance. The early special education educators of Germany, however, viewed difference as a defect requiring medical interventions to cure. McCagg (1989) finds that the medical model for diagnosing difference was in place well before the emergence of German defectology. He reports such efforts as Austrian emperor Joseph II's 1700s asylums for "weak-minded children, as well as separate school institutions for the blind and deaf" (p. 43). The limited state of medicine contributed to the ignorance surrounding attention to anomalous bodies and minds, helping to produce the belief that they were to be treated as diseases or shut away to protect society from having to be concerned about them.

The goals and values of Vygotskian defectology and modern-day Disability Studies are often remarkably similar. Disability Studies, like defectology, is a deceptive name. For the most part, Disability Studies challenge the idea that a human difference is a disability, instead looking for ways to validate human lives that don't conform to evolutionary norms (Danforth & Gabel, 2007). This field often has a Marxist basis that makes it compatible with Soviet defectology, one predicated on a design to make society an equitable place, in word if not necessarily in deed (Smagorinsky, Cole, & Braga, 2017). Those who have embraced some form of Disability Studies, Critical Disability Studies, Critical Special Education, or related fields would undoubtedly see commonality between their work and that of the Soviet defectologists, in spite of their having emerged from different roots.

Many terms that are harsh to the 21st-century ear were once common in psychiatric and diagnostic circles, including retarded, defective, imbecile, and idiot. Vygotsky himself penned the following:

> This delay manifests itself to a different degree. Three basic types of the mentally retarded child are distinguished: the idiot, the imbecile, and the moron. The idiot is a backward child of an extreme degree who does not exceed in his mental development the usual range of a 2-year-old child. The educability of the idiot is extremely close to zero. Their fitness for future life is also close to this norm. Their higher psychological functions do not develop at all. Although the delay in mental development is the most striking, what completely lacks in the idiot, however, is his will, the mastery of his behavior.... . The idiot is a child who does not acquire speech. The imbecile acquires oral speech and, obviously, external speech. The highest form of speech, namely written speech, remains inaccessible to him. Finally, the moron masters written speech and counting and internal speech as well.
>
> (in Van der Veer, 2020, pp. 174–175)

This account sounds cringe-worthy to the 21st-century ear, yet was simply how people were named in Vygotsky's day. It's important to keep the notion of *presentism* in mind: The inappropriate use of present-day ideas and perspectives to interpret the past. Vygotsky would undoubtedly use different terms were he to have lived a century later.

Defectology came into being in a different time and place from the current world. Diagnostics were relatively primitive, especially with young children who often died before their conditions could be understood or treated. As a result, very broad terms were developed to account for blindness, deafness, cognitive impairment, and other conditions that were considered markers of inferiority to those representing the ableist norm. Situating a character in a wheelchair, for instance, signaled evil to a Hollywood film audience for many years, as Mr. Potter in the film *It's a Wonderful Life* (Capra, 1946) illustrates. Although this trope has been replaced recently by more sympathetic portrayals of disablement, there remain more subtle markers of disturbance associated with cinematic and televised autistic characters:

> Around the turn of the millennium, there was an outpouring of autistic representation in literature, film, and television. These resulted in a multitude of new cultural texts that reinforced damaging metaphors about autism that had previously emerged in medical discourse. In film and television, autistic people are portrayed through a variety of metaphors: as impenetrable fortress, missing puzzle pieces, confusing aliens, and as malfunctioning robots or supercomputers... . The *unfeeling machine* metaphor is personified through sound tracks that deploy a number of mechanical sound effects, including vintage typewriter or calculator sounds, binary code sound effects, as well as sound mixing techniques that evoke the supposedly mechanical, and computational nature of autistic behaviour and thought processes.
> (Felepchuk, 2021, p. 1; emphasis in original)

Like other forms of discrimination, the cinematic methods for depicting autism are baked into the profession's and the public's perspective, with a media genre emerging to suggest that autistic people are robotic and unfeeling. These subtle means of representation can have a pernicious effect on people who naïvely absorb these images and associate them with autistic people.

In Vygotsky's day, the European Enlightenment promoted widespread education in rational and scientific principles. Mass education tends to promote uniformity, leaving to schools the task of producing a particular sort of citizen to stabilize a society around nationalistic values. The Enlightenment brought about both a reliance on scientific solutions and a need for more universal education in Western cultural values. The pervasive ableism of societies tends to see those with special needs as a burden to this effort, rather than as a population in need of inclusion. Furthermore, all non-normative conditions were considered during this era to be the same, allowing authorities to manage the problem of variation through a single solution: Exclusion. Both mass education and medicine were fairly new and crude endeavors, and the use of medicine to disqualify atypical people from schools suggests that neither had yet matured enough to serve anomalous people well.

In the mid-1800s, Germans used the label of *retardation* for anyone not progressing according to age-group norms, including immigrant children deemed "retarded" by natives. The Germans' use of medical "curative" services led to the conclusion that anyone not considered developmentally appropriate was considered "retarded," whether they were deaf, blind, or cognitively behind their peers. Pathologizing a population based on their SES, bodily normativity, or immigrant status is still practiced today. Intelligence and morality are still associated with wealth, and those who are immigrants, impoverished, and socially othered are assumed to be deficient and in need of educational and moral reformation (Smagorinsky & Taxel, 2005). This dim view of nonnormative people helped to provide the context in which defectology came into being around the turn of the 20th century.

Defectology referred to a range of conditions including deafness, blindness, and various forms of "retardation." By the 1930s, "there was no going back for Soviet defectology. Perhaps its label was by then too well established, too revolutionary-national, to be cast aside" (McCagg, 1989, p. 42). The devastation following from World War I, the overthrow of the Tsars, the Polish-Bolshevik War of 1919–1920, and the civil wars that were fought to fill the post-Tsarist power vacuum produced widespread injury and need for special education in the Soviet Union. Under the influence of Vygotsky, Soviet defectology took on a new cast, one that jettisoned pathology and emphasized inclusion.

Vygotsky and Inclusive Defectology

The Bolshevik Revolution produced a purge of established Romanov-era psychologists, who were accused of being bourgeois and anti-revolutionary in Moscow (McCagg, 1989). In 1924, Vygotsky gave his celebrated talk at a Moscow congress that launched his career, if not quite as the culmination of the Cinderella narrative debunked by Van der Veer and Valsiner (1991; see Chapter 1). McCagg relates that "Vygotsky was an ardent, believing Marxist, and was possessed by a nigh messianic energy. He had a dynamic effect on the younger members of the institute. He soon seemed to incarnate the revolution there [in the development of] a specifically Marxist, high philosophical science" (pp. 52–53). From there the young Vygotsky was granted the revolutionary authority to establish a Laboratory for Study of the Psychology of Abnormal Childhood, which he modeled on a school he had set up in Gomel.

His laboratory abandoned the practice of depicting atypical children as uniformly sick and in need of medical interventions and cures. Indeed, his attention was less on the children themselves, and *more on the people who surrounded them*:

> The child's difficult behavior almost always points to difficulties in the environment: To remove the child's difficulty, we must therefore first remove the difficulties in the environment. This is why the education of such children must not fight the child's reaction but the causes that led to this reaction. Here the main rule for the teacher must not be to try to suppress the child's symptoms but to try to eliminate the causes that led to such a reaction.
>
> (in Van der Veer, 2020, p. 179)

The children themselves were often orphans and victims of the continual warfare between the beginning of the World War I and the end of the Russian Civil War, which left hundreds of thousands of damaged and traumatized children and youth, who in turn became the responsibility of the public education system. Their loss of typical physical capabilities did not indicate to Vygotsky a degraded life. Rather, it suggested the need for able-bodied people to help construct new and different developmental pathways to allow for participation in society's practices and processes.

This period coincided with Hitler's embrace of eugenics, a movement valorizing the Aryan gene pool. Eugenics originated in the United States and was adapted by the Nazis to meet Hitler's obsession with creating a master race (Black, 2003). Hitler sought to exterminate the Jewish people as a race, and to rid the public of anybody who did not meet the Aryan ideal. Vygotsky in contrast believed instead that the Jewish people are honorable world citizens, and that the deaf, blind, and disabled are just fine. Rather, it is *the people who surround them* who create a *social problem* of discrimination, leading to rejection and the feelings of inferiority that accompany it.

Defectologists sought to construct more humane settings to help cultivate the potential of those who were felt to have limited prospects for living a satisfying life or contributing to a broader society's possibilities. Their lives, according to conventional wisdom, lost personal and societal value when they departed from the norm. Their existence was defined by their differences, which were interpreted as deficiencies, creating limitations imposed on them by the ableists around them. In contrast, Vygotsky (1993) asserted that "a child whose development is impeded by a defect is not simply a child less developed than his peers but is a child who has developed differently" (p. 154).

Vygotsky's (1993) rejection of the Germanic quantitative assessments of difference was grounded in their reductive, normative way of establishing a proper, universal developmental growth trajectory from which deficits can be measured. His criticism resonates with critiques from the various Disability Studies fields with respect to modern-day special education that is based on a medical model. Too many people in the field of special education, say those in Disability Studies, are indebted to the Piagetian developmental conception based on biological stages that in turn produces diagnoses of developmental lags that require remediation. I should emphasize that Disability Studies professors who blanketly condemn the special education teaching force are caricaturing a lot of noble, dedicated, nurturing special education teachers as cold, callous technicians who do children harm. This overgeneralization from such insensitive practitioners to the whole field is unwarranted, something I say from knowing admirable special education teachers who have made a big difference in kids' lives.

Vygotsky's approach took into account both nature and nurture. Nature provides the biological differences: Blindness, deafness, and so on, even as they might have followed from human conduct by way of cataclysmic wars in the first decades of the 20th century. Nurture serves to cultivate human potential through the creation of settings that affirm, rather than debilitate, a person's sense of worth. Vygotsky's social orientation went against *disposition theory*, which is concerned with biological or organic dispositions. He instead worked with Adler's[2] *positional theory*, which provides a more social understanding of human personality and development by attending to how people of different stations in life are hierarchically constructed (see Harré, Moghaddam, Cairnie, Rothbart, & Sabat, 2009, for a more current view of positioning theory).

The social environment, however, needs to present challenges and problems in order for a human being to develop psychologically. Actually reaching a state of homeostasis would produce stasis and the end of development. Van der Veer and Valsiner (1991) conclude that to Adler, Vygotsky, Darwin, and Marx, "an organism that is fully adjusted to its environment would have no need to develop.... It is precisely the state of not being adjusted that causes species or individuals to develop and leaves potential for development and education" (p. 68). Yet the presence of too many obstacles requiring too many adaptations can be developmentally prohibitive. Lee (2008) argues that when adults encounter human difference in school, their tendency is to respond "to the challenges of academic achievement [by articulating] singular and normative pathways through which youth are expected to navigate the waters of the academic disciplines—and, by extension, singular and normative pathways through which teachers as adults may learn the complex and situated demands of teaching" (p. 269). Difference in most school settings is not to be cultivated, regardless of how nobly their mission statements trumpet their commitment to diversity. It is to be normalized.

To create space for a nurturing approach to educating children considered disabled due to bodily differences, Vygotsky (1993) made a key distinction that represents to me one of his greatest insights, one consistent with Adler's views on inclusion and feelings of self-worth and validation. From a biological standpoint, a difference such as blindness serves as a person's *primary disability*. The individual's biological state served as the sole focus of attention for the diagnosticians of the Germanic defectological tradition, a conception of difference that remains in effect today. Diagnosing deficiencies remains a staple of much special education, even as the means of educating children receiving these diagnoses have become diffuse enough that they are difficult to generalize about (Brownell, Sindelar, Kiely, & Danielson, 2010).

The primary disability is mainly a problem *when people in the environment treat the person as inferior*, as is typically the case in diagnostic searches for deficiencies. However, as Vygotsky noted, blind people don't know they are blind until they are treated as inferior by people with sight and learn that their ableist companions view them as handicapped. These negative judgments tend to produce dysphoria, feelings of inferiority imposed from without—from the Greek roots δύσφορος (dysphoros), δυσ-, *difficult* and φέρειν, *to bear*—in the person exhibiting difference.

This dysphoric emotional response produces the far more damaging *secondary disability* of feelings of low self-esteem. "Full social esteem," to Vygotsky (1993), "is the ultimate aim of education inasmuch as all the processes of overcompensation are directed at achieving social status" (p. 57). His sense of social and self-esteem is deep and rich. It lacks the sense of *noblesse oblige* that may accompany patronizing treatment saturated in pity. It is not the feel-good approach that has been practiced in the United States with many children who are celebrated no matter what they do, at times resulting in hedonistic and self-absorbed, and ultimately damaging effects (Brummelman, Thomaes, Orobio de Castro, Overbeek, & Bushman, 2014). Rather, Vygotsky referred to living a validated life based on contributions resulting from welcome, inclusive *social participation*.

I find the notion of the secondary disability to be among Vygotsky's greatest contributions to developmental human psychology, one that is applicable to any situation in which a person or social group feels ostracized for not fitting the social parameters of schools and other institutions. It reconceives difference as a *social problem* that requires a *re-education of the general population* so that they interpret a person's non-conforming body differently. If a person can exist as a sort of text, it matters how that text is read by others. If they look at a blind person and see a pathetic individual with no potential for making societal contributions, then they are part of the social problem that produces dysphoria when they treat the blind person as socially worthless and perhaps burdensome. In contrast, they might look at the same person and see someone of vast possibilities, one who requires changes in both the physical and attitudinal setting to advance, not only their own development, but the greater good of the communities in which they live. In doing so they become practicing defectologists who seek to eliminate the possibility of a secondary disability by working to validate the lives of others and help them feel like competent, welcome contributors to legitimate, worthwhile social activity.

Vygotsky's (1993) approach to the anomalous human makeup was thus positive, optimistic, and future-oriented, driven by his belief that "no theory is possible if it proceeds from exclusively negative premises" (p. 31). It was also idealistic; as Van der Veer and Valsiner (1991) say, "There were clear utopian undertones in his defectological writing of the time" (p. 62), consistent with Vygotsky's other idealistic views of the possibilities afforded by the new Soviet state. I prefer to err on the side of idealistic belief in the potential of my fellow human beings, when patronizing rejection is the alternative.

This future-oriented perspective was designed to help all people lead fully productive lives that, as cultural-historical theory would insist, are oriented to participating in goal-directed activity that has social value to themselves and others. Adler's (1933) notion of *social interest*, i.e., an individual's personal interest in furthering the welfare of others, informed Vygotsky's (1993) views on this communitarian approach to individual difference, as illustrated by his claim that "Cultural development is the main area for compensation of deficiency when further organic development is impossible; in this respect, the path of cultural development is unlimited" (p. 169). Vygotsky's approach was thus oriented to *assets* rather than *deficits*, a view aligned with modern-day Disability Studies and their attention to both the discursive environment of social interaction and the material means through which its navigations become possible.

This ethos of inclusion suggests the need for adaptive mediums to be developed through community efforts, such as the ways in which environments are structured with wheelchair ramps and other assistive technologies. It is further incumbent on the person requiring assistance to learn how to use such equipment to navigate environments with facility. As Kim (2012) has argued with respect to technology initiatives in school, alternative pathways rely on both material (technological) and psychological (verbal and conceptual) tools. Vygotsky (1993) reached a similar conclusion, saying that "the most important and decisive condition of cultural development [is] precisely the ability to use psychological tools" (p. 47).

Vygotsky (1993) shifted the terms of the debate *from re-mediation of the deficit* to *education of the surrounding community*. This attention to *settings* is a critical dimension of cultural-historical theory that emphasizes the necessary integration of all aspects of human development with one's affective engagement with the world. What matters is that children are provided the means through which they have the potential to develop higher mental functions—those that are developed within cultural contours and that distill value systems, appropriate practices, and teleological goals—even in the absence of a typical capacity. Indeed, developing higher mental functions that enable cultural participation is among the main drivers of the human capacity to develop psychologically. Providing inclusive cultural settings promotes such participation, which enables individual development to become enmeshed in the overall direction of a society, even as not all societies promote healthy relationships across all stakeholders, or for that matter, healthy teleological directions for whole societies.

The inclusion of those typically excluded from cultural activities may help enrich a community through the capacities for insights not available to those whose makeup does not require adaptation. These insights can help the broader social group learn to see the world through other means and from other perspectives. Vygotskian defectology not only helps typically-ostracized people feel included. It benefits the group by including perspectives not available to those enculturated to established norms, and by broadening the cultural workforce to take advantage of the assets provided by those often considered to be a burden.

Secondary Disability Beyond Disability Studies

My writing on the topic has detailed Vygotsky's approach to defectology, with the shift of applying his principles to mental health atypicality (e.g., Smagorinsky, 2012, 2016a, 2018f, 2019). In Vygotsky's day, mental health was poorly understood (as it often is today). Research into atypical mental makeups has advanced far beyond what was known in Vygotsky's day, with considerable nuance now in the identification of how to characterize a state of mind, if not throughout society, at least among most medical professionals. Applying defectology to mental health may not have been feasible in his day. But it is in ours.

I make this claim recognizing that the "mind" includes the whole body, as anyone trying to think while ravenously hungry or in terrible pain can attest. As Wertsch (1991) maintained, the mind also extends beyond the skin and into the mediating environment and its historical antecedents. In general, I have used Vygotsky's defectological principles to argue against common sorts of labels, such as autism spectrum *disorder*, obsessive-compulsive *disorder*, and chronic anxiety *disorder*, each considered a *disability*, all running through my own system and that of family members. From a Vygotskian perspective, *what is disordered and disabled is the mediating environment* that views human difference as a deficiency and treats those who don't exhibit expected norms as outcasts and rejects. This disordered environment views the atypical person as worthy only of pity or scorn (to Vygotsky, these are specifically Christian attitudes) but not worth an effort to change the behavior and beliefs of those who surround them, or the material conditions that are designed for typical makeups. (See Smagorinsky & Lang, 2023, for an account of preservice English teachers grappling with these issues after reading Heuer's [2007] *BUG*, a book written from a deaf perspective.)

In this work I have argued that any notion of "disability" is situational. If the lights go out and the room is pitch black, who is disabled, the blind person or those with sight? I have argued that rather than being disabled by the combination of Asperger's, obsessive-compulsiveness, and severe anxiety, I have an "Asperger's Advantage" in educational research because I have an unusual ability to concentrate and pay attention to detail that "normal" people lack (see Smagorinsky, 2014a, 2014b). I am, according to some definitions, mentally ill and disabled by my makeup. No doubt it does not serve me well in some areas of life. But for a career in social science research (or engineering, or other field requiring arcane knowledge and deep focus), I benefit from my "mental illnesses."

As was the case in the primitive days of special education, atypical mental makeups have often been grouped in overly broad categories. I have attempted to get to the bottom of how to understand different conditions experienced by people in my circle of family, friends, and students, and it's not an easy sorting process. I began using the terms *neurotypical/neuro-atypical* and *extranormal* before learning of the term *neurodiversity*, which had its own appeal. The more I read about what is and what isn't neurodiversity, the less sure I became about what I meant, or more broadly, what others meant. To some, it's a blanket term for any variation from a typical mental health makeup. To the National Symposium on Neurodiversity at Syracuse University (2011), neurodiversity specifically refers to autism, Attention Disorder Hyperactivity Disorder, dyscalculia, dyslexia, dyspraxia, and Tourette's Syndrome, a large and varied group of conditions. To some, neurodiversity largely refers to autism (e.g., Silberman, 2015). In order to be a useful term, however, it has to be something that people can agree on. I was on an organizational committee on neurodiversity, and the leaders disbanded it when we had trouble settling on a definition, much less an elaborated position.

To me, the amorphous nature of the term neurodiversity has made it a word to be wary of. It has become too diffuse to make sense of; and some of the conditions listed under its purview, such as dyslexia, are similar to neurodiversity in that they have become blanket terms for a wide range of conditions that may be far too different to be considered a coherent, empirically justified category (Compton-Lilly, Mitra, Guay, & Spence, 2020; Worthy, Lammert, Long, Salmerón, & Godfrey, 2018). Indeed, among the problems that mental health diagnoses have historically faced is the conflation of conditions for diagnosis and treatment, such as when autism was considered to be a case of childhood schizophrenia.

Other Areas of Historical Exclusion

Schools tend to be rigidly built for perpetuation of the historical culture it represents, sustained by a deep structure that is resistant to change (Smagorinsky, 2020a). Mission statements might emphasize diversity and inclusion, but a curriculum that rarely changes tends to support the sustenance of the *status quo*. As a result, many people feel excluded because they speak the wrong version of English, are of a different racialized socialization than are the dominant adults in the setting, and otherwise don't fit the mold that the school design accommodates (Smagorinsky, 2017). Note that I've said that many *people* feel excluded, because both teachers and students may feel alienated from the institution. It's common to lament the consistently white makeup of school faculties in the United States, which typically are found to comprise 80–85% of the teaching force. Many plans, such as pipelines for teachers of color, have been generated to change those demographics, and the ratios haven't budged. I infer that the problem is that people of color have bad experiences in school, such that becoming a teacher and returning to a site of extreme unhappiness never crosses their minds when they reach adulthood (Smagorinsky, 2020a). These demographic challenges may be exacerbated by the devastating teacher shortage of the 2020s, in which the problem is being addressed by the hiring of people without college degrees or any teacher preparation at all, as teachers (Balingit, 2022; Maxouris & Zdanowicz, 2022).

Ahmad and Boser (2014) are among those who wonder why there is such a "leaky pipeline" leading people of color into the teaching profession. I have responded by wondering if any sort of pipeline can possibly work when the destination is a sewer (Smagorinsky, 2021c), which many schools have become in an era of anger, politicization, and budget crises. I next review some issues that make school a place where particular demographic groups feel alienated and rejected. As is the case with virtually all demographic classifications, these tend to intersect with one another (see Crenshaw, 2023). That is, a Black lesbian woman has many shared experiences with Black heterosexual women, but also faces a unique set of obstacles to happiness within a discriminatory environment.

The LGBTQ+ (expandable to LGGBDTTTIQQAAPP) population was considered mentally ill until 1973 by *The Diagnostic and Statistical Manual of Mental Disorders* published by the American Psychiatric Association. I grew up within this environment and admit that I adopted these views growing up, rejecting them only in my 20s (I graduated college in 1974) when my worldview and experiences shifted toward greater understanding; my thinking has undergone continual modification as I've engaged with nonbinary scholarship and the people who produce it.

This attitude was widely shared among the heterosexual public, leading to terroristic treatment of this population in ways that persist to the present, as evidenced by the 2020s bans on LGBTQ+ books from libraries. For instance, in 2021 US politicians became apoplectic over non-existent problems, such as the specter of school sports for girls and women being overrun by trans women born with stronger and faster bodies. The presence of women or LGBTQ+ people in the military has produced accusations of wimping down the armed forces to undertake a "social experiment," as US Senator Ted Cruz (R-TX) complained after watching US Army recruitment videos that promoted a diverse military[3]: "Perhaps a woke, emasculated military is not the best idea," he said, distressed that "Dem[ocratic] politicians" and the "woke media" were trying to convert these fighting forces into "pansies."[4] This list of ignorant, stereotypical opinions could go on for pages.

A critical issue facing the inclusive educator concerns the public resistance from the dominant culture to opening up possibilities for others to thrive and participate. Being an inclusive educator, as cultural-historical theory would predict, takes place in the midst of overlapping contexts that maintain a commitment to exclusion. Being inclusive is a challenge to undertake when parents, administrators, colleagues, and a segment of the student population are committed to preventing the lives of LGBTQ+ people from being honored and respected.

In no way am I saying that LGBTQ people are "disabled" or "mentally ill," other categories I've included in this discussion. What I am saying is that each of these populations has experienced discrimination in similar ways. They share a family resemblance that leaves them dysphoric and punished through treatment that amplifies the secondary disability of feeling rejected and unworthy based on the negative environment in which their personalities develop. These pressures created by community members may make it difficult for institutions to embrace diversity, even when they want to. The inclusive educator might find subversive ways to improve the emotional lives of students and teachers from marginalized groups. But doing so in an institution designed to discourage such efforts, while papering over problems with the discourse of mission statements, can be perilous and exhausting work.

I have described the many ways in which students and teachers serve as "misfits" of education (Smagorinsky, 2017) in the sense that they do not fit conventional structures. Perhaps the most obvious are people of color. In school systems dominated by white people of relative affluence, people of color are often subjected to demeaning rejections of their human value. This problem is an old one. US schools were founded in order to assimilate immigrants to a unitary national culture, one that Black people, many still slaves in 1850, were not considered to be a part of. I don't fault Horace Mann for undertaking this task in the mid-1800s when a rapidly expanding US[5] was incorporating both territories and immigrants from throughout Europe and needed a unifying device to proceed as a nation. The problem is the way in which the production of a monoculture through education has persisted through eras in which uniformity often works against a community's best interests, as stagnation occurs around the preservation of a single culture.

The sense of "nation" and "national interests" that has prevented schools from adapting easily to population diversity refers to the colonial empire built on the bones of native people.[6] Early US schools were not available to anyone but white males. The primary goal of the "Indian Schools" to which Native youth were sent was to replace their historic cultures with white ways; 14,000 Native children were still enrolled in federal boarding schools as late as 1941 (Perrillo, 2019). For this cultural, ethnic, and racial group, the schooling experience has been one of colonization and oppression (Deloria, 1974). The monosexual, monochromatic, monocultural values instilled in US schools from the outset did not end with racial integration, the introduction of child labor laws, the access of women to the workforce and thus to more prestigious assignments in school coursework, or other changes in the school population. Rather, schools have simply forced new demographic groups to assimilate to the same established ways. The end result has been a stable institution that has accommodated the influx of new social groups poorly and often indifferently (Portes & Smagorinsky, 2010).

It would take several books to record simply the injustices done to people of color over time to demonstrate the obstacles to inclusive education faced by the modern teacher. Moll (2000) among others has done ethnographies of Arizona immigrant communities, finding that their daily lives include sophisticated reasoning and problem-solving, undertaken in cooperative groups; yet in school where they are isolated for testing on knowledge irrelevant to their lives, they are diagnosed as mentally inferior (cf. Rettig & Montoya Talavera, 2023). Their struggles in school have in turn served to create the impression that the Latiné population (which itself is quite diverse and difficult to generalize about) is intellectually weak, regardless of the intelligent work they do to survive as a community.

Kirkland (2014), also relying on community ethnographies, finds that when Black students are studied in their own spaces doing their own literacy work, they perform through compelling and highly sophisticated means of expression and representation. Yet in school, these same students are subjected to standardized tests designed by and for white people whose experiences, vocabularies, etc. are institutionalized in the assessments, making white students appear more intelligent and higher achievers, when in fact they are working within a more familiar discursive, assessment, and material environment (Robinson & Norton, 2019).

The areas I've reviewed here briefly are not comprehensive. Schools are exclusive in many ways, no matter how many diversity statements they issue or how woke their mission statement sounds. The deep structure of school makes it hard to adapt to changes in population, or populations unanticipated by the centralized curriculum. Communities tend to have dominant populations whose influence is disproportionate to their numbers, and whose goal is to preserve rather than question the *status quo*. As I write this book in the early 2020s, the schools in the United States are being besieged by parents opposing the teaching of critical race theory (CRT), which in fact isn't taught, but makes for a good bogeyperson as a proxy for any attention to racial discrimination. They also protest concern for social-emotional learning (SEL), which serves as a cornerstone of Vygotskian defectology. Conservative parent groups are also madly opposed to Diversity, Equity, and Inclusion (DEI) initiatives, making inclusion an officially verboten concept.

These systemic barriers to building school cultures that validate all students' lives are distressing and prohibitive, given how easily school boards and administrations are known to cave in to persistent parents, who often position themselves as victims when decisions do not accommodate their demands for their own values to be perpetuated (Bellamy, 2021). Meanwhile, the parents of marginalized children tend to be denied voice in decisions about how the school should work (Baquedano-López, Alexander, & Hernandez, 2013). As Abrams and Gibbs (2002) note, "cultural capital strongly influences home-school relations and dynamics of parental involvement in public schools" (p. 386). And those who have the capital are often quite willing to exercise it to the advantage of their own children, but not to those who threaten their status at the top of the heap.

Discussion

Vygotsky's work in defectology remains fresh and relevant in the context of 21st-century schooling. Children of difference still face negative social consequences of their conditions that lead to what Vygotsky called secondary disabilities, which in the long term is likely to trouble them more than the source of difference itself. The solution is to change the setting: To change perceptions, to allow for unconventional ways of thinking and acting, and to otherwise construct a more supportive and empathic context for children's development. The modern movement toward inclusion and welcoming has made progress toward this end, and yet remains stymied by the robust resistance to equity, inclusion, and social justice in schools by stakeholders in the system. And terms like "inclusion" are now under reconsideration in that they suggest that there is a social center to which outsiders may be admitted or accepted, positioning them in subordinate ways in relation to the dominant group, making "inclusion" a "normalising, hegemonic discourse and as a universalising concept" (Dunne, 2009, p. 42).

Here I'll sketch out some implications for teachers of Vygotskian defectological principles. The primary point of his conception is that people feel fulfilled in large part because of the ways that other people make them feel; and that the emotional side of social life is critically important to living a productive, fulfilling life. The United States and other English-speaking nations often have taken an individualistic, rather than collective, view of humans. People survive because they are individually smart, tough, innovative, insightful, and so on. This conception has misconstrued the "survival of the fittest" mantra from evolutionary thought to mean that each of us is on our own, that the United States is a nation of stout individuals (or weaklings who may be left behind).

Yet this Spencerian adaptation of Darwin overlooks the ways in which Darwin documented collective survival, which helps account for how the physically slow and weak human species has endured in the midst of far more physically imposing animals and forces of nature. This social dimension of survival is well illustrated in John Donne's 1624 poetic observation that

> No man is an island,
> Entire of itself,
> Every man is a piece of the continent,
> A part of the main.
> If a clod be washed away by the sea,
> Europe is the less.
> As well as if a promontory were.
> As well as if a manor of thy friend's
> Or of thine own were:
> Any man's death diminishes me,
> Because I am involved in mankind,
> And therefore never send to know for whom the bell tolls;
> It tolls for thee.

Individuals within this continental mass, in Bakhtinian dialogic fashion, are the sum of their antecedents (and more) and are inherently tied to their contemporaries, as suggested by the African notion of *ubuntu* that postulates that people exist only in relation to one another (see Chapter 2). These *voices of the mind*, to use Wertsch's (1991) phrase, inevitably produce competing values and perspectives, which in turn make it very difficult to be a consistent human being (Dutton & Heath, 2010; Smagorinsky, 2020a). This idea was well-expressed by another literary great, Walt Whitman:

> Do I contradict myself?
> Very well then I contradict myself;
> (I am large, I contain multitudes.)

Being social is a historical phenomenon, a tenet of cultural-historical theory that requires attention to both immediate contexts and the chronology that has produced them.

What, then, does Vygotskian defectology offer for the modern educator? Most obviously, I think, it suggests the need to pay attention to the cultures that dominate life in school, and the ones marginalized by the dominant cultures. These cultures originate outside the school, and are manifested in how the school day is structured and populated with practices. Just as individuals internalize the social understandings that surround them, schools serve as microcosms of the communities that populate them. And not all communities are wholeheartedly invested in inclusion as a societal and educational value. Downey (2021) reports the following scenes from recent school board meetings in my US state of Georgia:

> The social justice movement in America has prompted schools to apply an "equity lens" to reveal the effects on students from such societal ills as racism, sexism and homophobia. The angry crowds descending on local school board meetings suggest the equity lens is revealing something else as well—aggrieved white people.
>
> Unhappy parents—overwhelmingly white—in politically conservative districts in Georgia are packing school board meetings to voice alarm over what they decry as a liberal plot to divide the races by representing white students as oppressors and Black students as oppressed.
>
> At a school board meeting a week ago in Forsyth County, a father proclaimed to applause, "If you have materials that you are providing that say if you are born a white male, you are born an oppressor, then you are abusing our children."
>
> Two days later at a raucous meeting in Cherokee County attended by hundreds, with hundreds outside after the meeting room filled, parents booed when superintendent Brian V. Hightower explained equity means "recognizing that all students are equal and deserve equal access and opportunities for educational success and to feel welcome and valued." The crowd hissed when he reaffirmed Cherokee's commitment to social and emotional learning, which was borne out of concerns over rising rates of depression, self-harm and suicide. The crowd also shouted down parents who defended equity and social and emotional learning.
>
> (n.p.)

Downey's reporting reveals the obstacles facing teachers when they try to include marginalized students (and faculty), in part by adapting their classrooms to suit the dispositions and socialization of the students they teach (see Bass, 2019). Parents whose children stand to lose when others are given an equal chance will protest and label them purveyors of "educational terrorism," as Downey quotes a parent who opposes the frightful specter of CRT. These sentiments are shared all the way to the top of the state government. Tagami (2021) reports that

> The Georgia Board of Education adopted a resolution Thursday asserting that the state and country are not racist and that there should be guardrails around classroom discussions about race and controversial events. The 11-2 vote, with two of the board's three Black members in opposition, comes amid the latest flare-up in a decades-long culture war where the battles have often been fought in the schools. Gov. Brian Kemp last month urged the board to take "immediate steps to ensure that critical race theory and its dangerous ideology do not take root in our state standards and curriculum."
>
> (n.p.)

It's easy to dismiss their hysteria as the last gasp of a dying generation of racists, and a loud and noisome huff and puff at that. Yet racists are here in the present and oppose the whole idea of diversity, equity and inclusion. This opposition is accounted for in cultural-historical theory as a contextual factor grounded in historical means of discrimination that is part of the mediational environment. What it cannot provide is a set of tools for "dismantling," to use a popular term in these discussions, such an edifice.

Simply bringing logic to the discussion, and hoping to persuade people rationally that exclusion is unfair, has never changed much in society. These issues are emotional, not logical (Haidt, 2012). Cultural-historical theory is equipped to take this problem into account, without especially offering a handy solution. It's one thing to say that inclusion benefits outsiders, another thing to overcome strenuous objections to inclusion by a community's loudest, most powerful groups, those who are dedicated to promoting exclusion. Cultural-historical theory, including the principles available through defectology, helps to draw attention to whose values are insinuated throughout a public arena, the school building, as it becomes invested with the subjectivities of its constituents. Inevitably, everyone in the setting occupies a position that carries with it a degree of authority, often through the social groups they represent. This positioning manifests inequities of the sort that the activist parents described by Downey (2021) are dedicated to preserving to maintain their own status and that of their children.

I think that the first step toward undertaking an inclusive education that honors diversity and promotes equity—the DE&I that those white parents find outrageous and threatening—is to recognize why it isn't happening on its own, and to identify who is invested in denying its possibilities. Which social groups benefit from exclusive dynamics in schools? Which are disadvantaged? What cultural-historical factors have occurred to produce these inequitable positionings? Through what means are they instituted into the operation of the school, and how are they perpetuated? How is the curriculum constructed to support the heritages of a dominant culture, and how are other heritages suppressed or ignored altogether? What genres govern behavior and speech in schools and their classrooms, and whose values do they embody? How is resistance to the dominant culture's authority controlled and disciplined within the school system? Understanding these systemic barriers to DE&I is important if a counterculture is to be established that provides avenues for opportunities to students who have historically been denied access.

These questions can be undertaken by individual teachers or inquiry groups tasked with addressing issues of school climate. Such initiatives are already underway in many schools and at the district and state levels as well. The question is how much actual change they can effect when parents are opposing the whole idea of equity and inclusion, and when these parents think that schools should focus solely on "academics." This presumably academic focus often is based on mythology produced by textbook companies whose products are shaped by public input, with large states like Texas often providing the perspective and insisting on a selective history in which discrimination never has happened (Fitt, 2020). This problem leads to learning such bizarre "facts" as that slaves were happy and benefitted from the structure their masters imposed, along with free room and board. This sort of myth becomes ossified in the minds of students when they learn it in school and it in turn serves as the basis of their beliefs about diversity, equity, and inclusion (Springston, 2018). Nonetheless, there appear to be quite a few online examples of how school climate committees are structured and tasked and how they function, at least on paper.

I begin with these whole-school issues because it's very hard to be the only social justice educator in a building ruled by the *status quo*. Vygotsky believed that the whole school was the most important factor in education, rather than the much-lauded individual teachers bravely forging a way through the chaos (see Chapter 10). Those brave, rugged individualists might find themselves marginalized, outcast, questioned, and in states with no job protections (like mine), fired. Simply closing the classroom door, as teachers like to say, doesn't shut out this broad culture. It will come in through the vents and through the nostrils of students who exhale the detritus of their socialization.

It helps to have a school ethos within which equity education is valued in order to implement a caring curriculum that is designed to accommodate multiple cultures, enabling access for historically marginalized students through avenues that do not diminish anyone else's prospects for success. In many places, this vision is idealistic. For instance,

> Two Black students—Ikeria Washington and Layla Temple—were named valedictorian and salutatorian at West Point High School in Mississippi in 2021. Shortly afterward, two white parents questioned whether school officials had correctly calculated the top academic honors. Ultimately, the school superintendent named two white students as "co-valedictorian" and "co-salutatorian" on the day of graduation.
> (Donner, 2021)

Undertaking social justice in such communities can be difficult, and in states like mine, likely hazardous to further employment.

Where possible, whole-school inquiries can be built into the curriculum as critical explorations into school climate. Many themes of school instruction are amenable to inquiries into inequity: Success, cultural conflict, discrimination, and many others (for a lengthy list, see http://www.petersmagorinsky.net/Units/Unit_Outlines.htm). Each is both "academic" in that it involves engagement with challenging texts and ideas; and each addresses social problems that produce inequity and denied access. The two efforts are not mutually exclusive, and together they make literary study both formal and personal. And, together they might provide students with a means by which to question the fairness of the school institution, the community, and the people who populate them (Skerrett & Smagorinsky, 2023).

Again, however, such initiatives involve risks. Johnson, Chisam, Smagorinsky, and Wargo (2018) report a study of students in Virginia who participated in a *Letters to the Next President 2.0* campaign (letters2prez.org), an online platform created by the National Writing Project that was designed to promote critical inquiries into injustice. A number of students in the classroom they studied focused their projects on chronic areas of inequity in the school. The administration's response was to try to stonewall their findings in order to protect the school's appearance of being a fine place, filled with very fine people. This muffling of dissent has appeared often in schools and universities in relation to student newspapers that are critical of the institution, or other efforts to produce better, more inclusive circumstances (Chicago Tribune Editorial Board, 2018). Linnane (2021) reports on schools in Wisconsin where school administrators shut down recognition of Black History Month (February) because they felt it was "divisive" and did not send a "positive" message by raising awareness of race issues. These contextual factors create conditions that require alternative routes for inclusive educators to create.

Within classrooms, teachers can also look for ways to create alternative routes to meeting the demands of the curriculum (Bass, 2019). First, they need to be attentive to who is enrolled, where they come from, how they might have been socialized, how they have learned to think and perform, and other areas in which cultural diversity produces variation in how students do school. A defectological lens suggests that standardization is ill-suited to the task of addressing human diversity. Yet standardization is among the reasons that schools are resistant to change that invites a broader range of participation. Unfortunately, many schools now enforce standardization with a vengeance through assessment driven by culturally biased standardized tests, a culturally narrow curriculum that feeds into the tests, instruction that fits within the parameters of both, dress codes aligned with the fashion preferences of the dominant culture, speech genres based on the speech traditions of a single class of people, and more. The curriculum may be written from a centralized location, perhaps in the district, perhaps from an outsourced provider like the College Board or a publisher, perhaps elsewhere. I have found that the further from the generation of the curriculum a teacher stands, the less flexible it is in their hands (Smagorinsky, 2020a). Having a say in what's taught and how it's taught would likely be prerequisite to creating diversity-supporting flexibility in teaching and learning, of creating opportunities to participate in legitimate and valued ways in the construction of classroom knowledge.

My attention to creating avenues for inclusion is limited here, designed to illustrate how Vygotsky's work in defectology has implications beyond what he provided for the deaf, blind, and cognitively impaired children orphaned and sidelined by a decade of continual war in Eastern Europe. He sought to address their assets, rather than their "disabilities." He shifted responsibility from the individual "disabled" person to the environment that judges difference as deficiency. He made the collective responsible for the quality of life experienced by those on the margins. He rejected the whole idea of a handicap, other than the handicaps assumed in the ableist environment surrounding those who exhibit differences from the evolutionary norm.

Similarly, pathways for inclusion should be available to students on the margins of typicality and acceptability, a possibility I would create as well for teachers from underrepresented groups whose school experiences make it a prohibitive profession to consider. These pathways provide the *positive social updraft* that I believe is a necessity of inclusive schooling (Smagorinsky, 2016a). I'll close with an anecdote from a teacher candidate I had in a university class a few years ago. Because I always shared with my students my "Confessions of a Mad Professor" autoethnography (2011c) focused on my family's experiences with mental health, they often shared their own diagnoses with the class, which they said changed the tenor of the class for them. One young man confided privately that he experienced very high anxiety, and wondered if teaching might be the wrong profession for someone like him: He might stand out as weird, or might have a panic attack at work, or might experience some other consequences that would have an effect on his teaching. My response was that someone like him is desperately needed in schools, because kids have to have someone simpatico with their feelings and experiences, and he might be the only person in the building they feel they can talk with frankly. I hope he's still out there helping anxious kids who struggle to find their way in school.

A similar argument has been made on behalf of students and teachers of color and others from outside the 80–85% of teachers who are white (and mostly women). Kids benefit from having adults in the school with whom they share culture, racialized experiences, and other areas of intersubjectivity that are scarce elsewhere in the district (Milner, 2006). Simply creating pipelines on paper will not diversify a faculty if the experiences of marginalized people are negative enough that the profession isn't attractive; and that doesn't count the many other reasons that teaching has become a job that a lot of people undertake idealistically, and leave because it is emotionally exhausting, disrespectful of teachers' intellects and judgment, and materially unrewarding. Inclusion (or other term) is a pervasive challenge, not something easily done with a few simple measures. Rather, a school needs to be a place that people want to be in, where their self-esteem is reinforced through positive experiences and feedback, where they feel they are growing into a better person, where they feel that whoever they are and whatever they look like, there's a niche where they can feel respected and appreciated. Defectology is a horrid term. But defectologys lessons are profound and central to taking a Vygotskian perspective on school.

Notes

1 I report rough figures because the numbers continually change, and because the same publication may appear multiple times from different translations into English, and versions in other languages, making the exact number difficult to pinpoint.
2 Alfred Adler (1870–1937) was an Austrian physician and psychiatrist who developed "individual psychology" and who identified the concepts of the inferiority feeling and inferiority complex as formative in personality development. He departed from Freud in emphasizing the importance of feelings of belonging, family constellation, and birth order, concluding that contributing to others (Social Interest or *Gemeinschaftsgefuhl*) provides a person with feelings of self-worth and belonging.
3 Cruz himself, like a lot of tough-talking politicians, never served in the armed forces.
4 I always roll my eyes when "pansy" is used to characterize people as weak and fearful. As a gardener, I know that pansies are incredibly tough flowers, planted where I live in the fall so they can show all winter in weather that beats the life out of most annual plants.
5 I refer to the expansion of the United States with full awareness that it came at the expense of the people inhabiting the continents prior to European invasions.
6 Although my examples are from the United States, they apply to other colonized nations, including those throughout the English-speaking world.

Part IV
Pedology

The final major section of this book details Vygotsky's role in the pedology movement, that is, the "science of the child" in all its manifestations. After establishing Vygotsky as a pedologist whose attention to human development is comprehensive, I move to the last, tragic stage of his life and career, when Stalin imposed the Pedology Decree in which Vygotsky's field was banned over a host of presumed or fabricated violations, and in response to some criticisms that have merit. The 1936 Decree coincided roughly with Vygotsky's death, which many observers believe was merciful given the number of Soviet presumed dissidents who were shot during Stalin's Great Purge, and other times too.

15 Vygotsky the Pedologist

Vygotsky was deeply involved in the Soviet pedology[1] movement, which originated in Germany in the late 1800s, placing it on shaky footing in the anti-bourgeoisie Soviet Union. It involved the scientific study of child development in social contexts, with the school as a major area of environmental emphasis. In the early decades of the 20th century, pedology influenced psychological research in Europe and the United States (Depaepe, 1998). It was adapted by Russian, then Soviet educational psychologists, to understand the effects of schooling on the developing child and youth. Vygotsky's death coincided with the machinations that produced the Pedology Decree of 1936 and Stalin's Great Terror or Great Purge, and he was banned posthumously along with the field of pedology. This chapter will situate pedology historically and review its tenets. I include criticisms of pedology in this chapter. I reserve most for Chapters 16 and 17, with particular attention to its banishment when Stalin cracked down on real and perceived dissent of any kind, especially that from the despised intelligentsia and other previously elevated social classes.

Pedology (from Greek: πέδον, pedon, "soil"; and λόγος, logos, "study") was concerned with the developmental trajectories of students. The Bolsheviks initially made it a formal part of their educational plan, housing it in the Institute of Pedology, part of the Institute for Study of Brain and Psychical Activity. Byford (2021) describes its role in the new Soviet system:

> it was envisaged as an inherent part of the new education system, insofar as it was expected to replace a pre-existing functional component (the traditional school assessments, exams and reports). At the same time, this niche greatly exceeded the education system as such. Indeed, what pedological work measured and monitored was children's comprehensive biopsychosocial development. This included regular medical checks, anthropometric assessments, psychometric evaluations, the testing of general literacy and numeracy, the monitoring of the 'health' of the wider social environment in which the child was being raised, including family, school and neighbourhood, plus following up on the child's moral and political formation.
>
> (p. 6)[2]

Byford (2021) adds that "pedological work was initially positioned largely outside the schools themselves, in hubs removed from the day-to-day pedagogical work of teachers" p. 4). Pedologists were thus less concerned with classroom practice, and more concerned with child development broadly speaking. Their purview included how schools

DOI: 10.4324/9781003374848-19

are organized to cultivate students' development toward cultural ends, a dimension that Vygotsky considered the most important aspect of schooling. Ewing (2001) describes how

> "Pedology," the scientific study of children, had become particularly influential in the 1920s among Soviet educators and psychologists. Pedologists believed that studying the influence of environmental conditions and inherited traits on the mental and physical development of children would provide the empirical knowledge necessary to reform educational policies and thus progress toward the goal of creating socialism in the Soviet Union.
>
> (p. 473)

In the following two chapters, I will detail how pedologists' attention to "inherited traits" enabled their critics to construct them as anti-proletarian, accusing pedologists of considering working class people to emerge from intellectually poor gene pools. For this chapter, I focus less on Soviet critiques surrounding the Pedology Decree, and more on what the field entailed.

Pedology's purview included children's upbringing at home, the psychology of the child, the broad experience of education in school, and other long-term developmental influences. Indeed, it sought to assemble all knowledge of children from various sources into a synthetic whole, which Depaepe (1998) found to be an elusive goal in its many international settings:

> The content of the [paedology] movement, however, was far from being a coherent whole. In the first place, there was a considerable amount of conceptual confusion. Terms such as "child study", "paedology", and "experimental pedagogy" were not only used interchangeably as synonyms, but the definitions were also contradictory. Second, the experimental study of children was not seen as exclusively, and certainly not primarily, a matter for teachers and educators. Medical doctors and also psychologists, hygienists, and even sociologists, anthropologists, criminologists, jurists and others felt called to make their own contributions to the paedological movement.
>
> (p. 688)

This interdisciplinary approach was laudable in many ways, enabling pedology to be informed by a host of developmental factors and social perspectives. It also produced a cacophonous conception that made it hard at times to understand exactly what it was. And as a field that took on different forms in different national settings, pedology became quite eclectic, drawing from many sources. Van der Veer (2002)[3] notes that "eclectic" was among the terms used to discredit a Soviet scientist, especially when they recruited the insights of bourgeois European or US psychologists. The Prussian theorist Karl Marx—the son of a successful lawyer who lived in the debauched European cities of Trier, Bonn, Paris, Brussels, and London, and who drew on European sources, such as Hegel—was spared this condemnation. But Vygotsky's favorable references to Dewey and others helped to create a case that he was dangerously bourgeois and should be expelled from Soviet thought.

Ewing (2001) provides one useful account of Soviet pedology:

> In Russia, especially following the revolution of 1917, pedologists defined an ambitious agenda for their science. The progressive educator P. P. Blonskii referred to pedology as a "scientific synthesis" of knowledge about children, the eminent

psychologist A. B. Zalkind[4] defined pedology as "the discipline which absorbs and synthesizes valuable scientific material on the interconnections between the development of the human personality and the surrounding environment," and the innovative theorist L. S. Vygotskii defined pedology as "a general science of child development." By positioning themselves at the intersection of disciplines with a shared interest in child development, Russian pedologists believed that their scientific methods and social concerns would produce both academic legitimacy and public utility.

(p. 476)

Ewing situates this movement amidst the broader Soviet goal to solve practical social problems, apply Marxist understandings of historical materialism, and create a new Soviet society founded on Marxist principles. Holowinsky (1988, 2008) describes how pedologists predicated their work on biological, psychological, and sociological factors, and conducted research in three broad areas. *Pure* investigations studied the anatomy of children, physiology, child pathology, characterology, pedometry, and psychosomatic study. *Applied* research investigated child care, pediatrics, and child evaluation. *Auxiliary* studies looked into anatomy, histology, cytology, biophysics, general biology, psychology, and sociology. There was no clear consensus on which psychological theories should inform this massive project, although the Soviet leadership was clear on which sources were unwelcome: Any perspective emerging from a capitalist nation, with exceptions for Marx and Engels and exiled leaders like Lenin, whose Bolshevik agitations were produced while he lived in Munich, London, Geneva, and other cities in Galicia. Broad thinkers like Vygotsky, who consulted non-Soviet sources, found themselves on the outs with the State.

Pedologists "studied pupils' reading habits, after school activities, and family characteristics, including size, income, and hygienic practices. The goal was to understand how children's 'conditions of life' affected mental development and personal conduct" (Ewing, 2001, p. 477), a suitable focus for a cultural-historical psychology. Ewing reports that pedologists were especially concerned with

one of the most pressing problems of Soviet education, the so-called "difficult" children ... who were repeating grades, misbehaving, or otherwise acting "abnormally." In the early 1930s, Soviet children were "tracked" into separate classes and so-called "special schools" based on their ability, achievement, and behavior. In the language used by the Central Committee in 1935, the removal of "defective children" who "systematically disrupt school discipline, disorganize class instruction, and exert negative influences by their anti-social behavior" was the best way to restore order and discipline in education... . [S]ome pedologists recommended that "difficult children be included with "defective" and "mentally retarded" children in special schools, with the stated goal of "neutralizing the harmful influence of these children".

(pp. 477–478)

Pedologists were concerned with how to educate students considered to be difficult to teach: Those with cognitive shortcomings, those whose socialization produced disruptions in schools and classrooms, and those lacking typical functions like hearing and seeing. Their resolution to sequester them in special schools for targeted instruction in turn made the teaching of the remaining students easier in mainstream schools and classrooms.

The context, then, was both ideological and contradictory. The Marxist doctrine posited that all people are biologically equal and should be educated in egalitarian settings.

Some students, however, are disruptive, "retarded," or physically disabled and should be removed to promote the learning of others. Such confounds no doubt followed from the many, many angles and priorities influencing how pedology was conceived and undertaken. On the other hand, purging the undesirables was a Stalinist tactic for the whole of society. The egalitarian promise of the 1917 Revolution was applied unevenly, with a certain sort of person favored in the creation of the new workers' utopia.

The Soviet Political Context of the Pedology Movement

The punitive, exclusionary stance taken by Soviet authorities was evident in how scientists were treated under Stalin. Van der Veer (2002) reports that

> Individual psychologists had to take the right stance on these issues or risk suffering the consequences. In the 1930s in particular, the ideological pressure turned into genuine state terror, and no scholar could be sure that he or she had expressed the one and only "correct" viewpoint on a particular topic. Unfortunately, the infallible official viewpoints on these topics shifted repeatedly. That is why many intellectuals were prepared for the worst and always had a packed suitcase ready in case the secret police should arrest them (they invariably came during the night).... [A]ny allegedly negative feature in one's biography might be used against one, though it not necessarily always was (which, of course, increased the general atmosphere of confusion and insecurity).
> (p. 3)

The political climate of the 1930s included "the Stalinist system of control" of academics (Graham, 1987, pp. 167–168). The Soviet Union promised a worker's paradise in which the proletariat were unshackled from the bonds of a class-based society and released to reach their great human potential through the equity afforded by communism. Soviet society could provide the model for the rest of Europe to abandon its class-based inequalities and move toward more collectivist and participatory approaches to social organization, including the abandonment of national borders and creation of a class-based Europe built on proletarian initiatives (yet led by the leaders). Not only that, "Marxist reforms would bring about the necessary social revolution which would eliminate the factors hampering the free expression of sexual drives" (Van der Veer & Valsiner, 1991, p. 106). It was not only a utopian work environment. It would produce better sex as well. Meanwhile, as the philosophers and ideologues produced manifestos in European coffee shops and the Kremlin, for the most part peasant life went on with little change (Figes, 1997).

Among the goals of Stalin's USSR was the evolution of the enlightened proletarian worker known as the "New Soviet Man." This new breed of human could be cultivated through education, social rules, and ultimately, the murder of many millions of people who were found out of step with the Soviet imperative (Snyder, 2010). Once such rabble (including dissident or even mildly independent psychologists, or anyone accused of bourgeois leanings) was cleared, the Party assumed, the New Soviet Man could emerge as the crown of creation. For the rest, it was the Gulag, exile, or a bullet to the head (Solzhenitsyn, 1973).

Zinchenko (2007) reports that "Vygotsky's commitment to Marxist beliefs did not save him from criticism. His works were banned, denounced, and declared to be vicious and even evil. He was lucky to have managed to die in his own bed in 1934" (p. 213). Gustav Shpet[5] was dismissed from his academic positions on multiple occasions and subjected to "brutal interrogation and execution in 1937" by Soviet authorities (Wertsch, 2007, p. 184) due to his "freedom and dignity and the independence of his thought from Marxist-Leninist ideology, which at the time was growing stronger and stronger" (Zinchenko, 2007, p. 212). Shpet's literary contemporary Mandel'shtam,[6] who wrote a poem critical of Stalin, "perished in the Gulag a year after Shpet's murder" (Zinchenko, p. 231).

These dates and suppressions suggest the conditions under which Vygotsky undertook his career. The intelligentsia came under immediate suspicion of being counter-revolutionaries, a grounding that in and of itself was a cause for Stalinist concern. Solzhenitsyn (1973) reports one characterization of this class of dangerous pseudoscientists. Beyond landowners and capitalists of inherent moral decrepitude, those prosecuted included

> one additional social stratum, the social characteristics of which have *long since been under consideration* by the representatives of revolutionary socialism. This stratum is the so-called 'intelligentsia.' In this trial, we shall be concerned with *the judgment of history on the activity of the Russian intelligentsia* and with the verdict of the Revolution on it.
> (p. 327; emphasis in original)

Vygotsky was a person convinced of communism's potential for producing an equitable world. He frequently quoted Marx and Lenin, and spoke idealistically of a great future available in the Soviet Union. Solzhenitsyn (1973) is instructive on the perils of his oversight:

> just as the intelligentsia had never been overlooked in previous waves [of arrests and executions], it was not neglected in this one. A student's denunciation ... that a certain lecturer in a higher educational institution kept citing Lenin and Marx frequently but Stalin not at all was all that was needed for the lecturer not to show up for lectures any more.
> (p. 73)

Given the regime's emphasis on harsh and deadly punishment, it is unlikely that the lecturer retired to one of Stalin's luxurious dachas, one of many instances in which the Soviet rulers reserved privileges for themselves that were denied to the citizenry. As the allegorical narrator of *Animal Farm* reports—and author Orwell (1938) was a committed socialist—the original seven revolutionary commandments were, in short order, compressed into the single decree that "All animals are equal, but some animals are more equal than others" (Orwell, 1945, p. 42).

Vygotsky, too, found himself on the outs, repressed in the Motherland for promoting bourgeois values, according to his denouncers. His volume *Educational Psychology* (1997b) was "published in Moscow in 1926 but not reprinted for quite some time for purely ideological reasons" (Davydov, 1997b, p. xxi), a common fate for pedological writing. Tracing how Vygotsky went from celebrated psychologist to state pariah can require considerable unpacking. Yet a swift death awaited those who crossed a line, real or imaginary, or in some cases, those who might cross a line later. A Soviet might be a relatively innocent agent of anti-Marxist and anti-Stalinist beliefs and still pay the price. Kellogg and Veresov (2019) report that Vygotsky's lectures on pedology proved deadly to the dean who helped distribute them: "Shortly thereafter [Vygotsky's] lectures were made available to the students as mimeos by the dean, S. Z. Kazenbogen, who was then arrested as a 'Trotskyite' and subsequently shot" (p. v).

It can be hard to sort out these sudden turns of fate, and how one could go from authority to corpse in the blink of an eye. In spite of the collectivist philosophy of the Soviets, there was constant bickering among scientists and between scientists (and others) and the authorities. In contrast to the Marxist imperative to view the world as continually in flux and as driven by the unity of opposites, victory through the death of an opponent was often how disagreements were resolved. Van der Veer and Valsiner (1991) report that "In the 1920s ideological in-fighting slowly became the characteristic of most of Russian psychology, and became the dominant means of Soviet psychological discourse in the 1930s" (p. 120). Over the course of Vygotsky's brief career, he both embraced the utopian vision of communism, and asserted his independence from Party ideology by drawing on international streams of thought instead of staying within Soviet Marxist and Stalinist bounds.

More egregiously to the authorities, he approached psychology without the required exclusive Marxist framework for conducting a socioeconomic class analysis, which he subordinated to a more general understanding of context. As I have reviewed, he was attentive to social class issues. However, he included them among many dimensions shaping societies, rather than placing them without exception at the exclusive forefront. He was further found wanting for his insufficient attention to the workers' means of production. His emphasis on the tool of speech as the means by which people regulate their own thinking was viewed as a violation of the more proper attention to the proletarian use of material tools for acting on and bringing under control the natural environment.

Van der Veer and Valsiner (1991) describe the role reversal of the working and educated classes that the Soviet authorities demanded as follows:

> in 1921-2 there was a wave of reactions against "bourgeois" intellectuals and scientists, many of whom were sent to exile in the West in 1922 ... . The exile of these specialists was publicly explained by the need for educating the "proletarian intelligentsia" who would be ideologically fully devoted to the new regime, while being comparable in expert knowledge to the specialists with "bourgeois backgrounds." The latter "could not be trusted ideologically" and were denounced as anti-Soviet "schemers," charges supported by claiming that they had concealed their "scheming" by means of their passion of knowledge not available to the proletariat.
> (p. 125)

In spite of the great promise of communism's imperative for equality, inequalities proliferated, not only in terms of whose ideas were acceptable, but also within the Soviet universities and laboratories, predicated on Germanic traditions that produced hierarchical organizations that did not invite dissent. This reliance on European structures was one of many ironies circulating in Soviet society. The Soviet Union based their social organization on "the mixture of blind faith in one's own cherished dogmas and moral insensitivity towards nonbelievers typical of so many religious people in so many, far too many, historical periods" (Van der Veer & Valsiner, 1991, p. 246). Purges in the late 1920s increased in volume and ferocity, and were undertaken throughout the 1930s to crush academic and intellectual freedom so as to "oust bourgeois academicians of certain institutions in order to replace them with supporters of the Communist Party" (Graham, 1987, p. 9)

Vygotsky's emerging cultural-historical theory of human development both created controversy and produced rejection and criticism. He was left ultimately with few colleagues, as others gravitated to the imperative that "the writings of Marx and Engels had to be accepted as articles of faith" (Van der Veer & Valsiner, 1991, p. 199). Those who defied Marxist dogma, such as land-owning peasants known as *kulaks*, were executed to the tune of 14 million deaths, with 3 million Ukrainians starving in 1932–1933 alone. "Cancel culture" was practiced under Stalin with a vengeance. Those who were affected included Central Asians who, under Stalin's agricultural drive, were forced to abandon their historical itinerant cattle-breeding life and take up farming grain in soil ill-suited for its production. They were then subjected to demands for increased production, which resulted in immense suffering, with rapes, beatings, executions, and other punishments administered to those who resisted in any form or failed to produce yields in soil that could not yield them. Peasants ultimately resorted to cannibalism, prostitution, and other degradations to survive the famine that, ironically, occurred in one of the continent's most productive agrarian regions (Conquest, 1986), the Ukrainian land that was coveted by Nazis as well as Soviets for its productive black earth (Snyder, 2015) that nonetheless could not keep up with demands. Stalin tolerated no dissent, even from soil.

Vygotsky's Pedological Writing

These historical conditions help provide a context for Vygotsky's own account of pedology. His volume *Pedology of the School Age* (in Van der Veer, 2020) laid out his views on child development in relation to the practice of schooling. He argued in a way reminiscent of Darwin that schooling is in large part a process of adaptation: "the biological function of childhood is the child's learning of forms of adaptation that meet the complexity of his surroundings. Childhood is a period of change and formation, that is, indeed the age of plasticity" (in Van der Veer, 2020, p. 16). This malleability is subject to the influence of the environment, the shaping force that could produce a society of devoted Soviet communists. In the next sections I review aspects of his pedological work that were central to his project, yet controversial in his time and ours.

Diagnostic Tests

Pedology "is the science about the child as a natural whole... in his interaction with the surrounding environment. The main task of pedology is the study of the phases and periods through which child development passes. Establishing these periods allows pedology to distinguish the passport age and the real age of the child. These two ages do not coincide" (in Van der Veer, 2020, pp. 24–25). He here distinguished between the passport, or chronological age, and the "real" or intellectual or cultural age characterized by maturity in relation to the development of higher mental functions. This distinction identifies "different phases of their development" that reveal how "their actual [developmental] age will be very different" (in Van der Veer, 2020, p. 25).

This actual developmental age, the intellectual or cultural age, could be revealed through diagnostic tests that produced the proper placement of a child in the school's assignment to a learning track: "the study of the general child is the measure we use to measure the individual child's development. The norm of child development is the basis for the child's diagnosis" (in Van der Veer, 2020, p. 28). These diagnoses rely on a "synthetic method whose essence lies in the combination and juxtaposition of the heterogeneous data obtained by means of various methods. Its essence is to synthesize all these data and to derive on the basis of this synthesis a holistic and orderly characterization of each particular age as a unique real unity" (in Van der Veer, 2020, p. 51).

Properly diagnosed, a child had the opportunity to have an appropriate education. Education, Vygotsky maintained,

> is the influence exerted by us [educators] on the developing child, and the nature of this influence changes depending on the period of child development. Education may be defined as the mastery of the process of child development. In education man guides child development along a certain path according to goals scheduled in advance, creates the conditions for this development, and tries to master this process. The nature of this mastery itself turns out to be connected with the properties of one or the other period of child development. Educating an infant differs from educating a school child or preschooler. The explanation of this fact we must seek in a general thesis that characterizes all human activity directed at the mastery of natural or historical processes.
>
> (in Van der Veer, 2020, p. 51)

Schooling is thus a form of socialization to cultural practices, with general biological limitations and affordances. Vygotsky viewed age ranges as rough parameters for zones of development such that early childhood is too early for some sorts of understandings, and adolescence is a period that is ripe for such possibilities as ideological development. He departed from stage theories of development that take that approach more strictly, e.g., Piaget's (1973) four stages of cognitive development: Sensorimotor stage: Birth to 2 years; Preoperational stage: Ages 2–7; Concrete operational stage: Ages 7–11; Formal operational stage: Ages 12 and up. Vygotsky and other Soviet psychologists were more concerned with socialization as certain capabilities emerge over the course of biological maturation. Biology's affordances are therefore important, but not deterministic. Even so, he identified developmental norms that produced classifications for those who matured on different schedules.

Matters of socialization led Vygotsky to view cultures as difficult to compare, making him somewhat of a relativist, even as he could be judgmental about non-Soviet societies and their backwardness (see Chapter 4). Vygotsky could be contradictory on this question. He asserted that

> one should not confront people from other cultures with tasks taken from one's own culture and then draw conclusions from their possibly poor performance. For this would be judging them by our Western standards and seeing their thinking as a rudimentary form of our own... . [P]eople from different cultures have different higher mental capacities but do not differ essentially in regard to their basic capacities.
>
> (in Van der Veer, 2020, p. 208)

By locating Soviets among "Western" societies, Vygotsky worked against the Party view that "the West" is fundamentally corrupt and decadent. Meanwhile, the Central Asian research led by Luria (1976), with Vygotsky's support, reached pathologizing conclusions about the developmental levels of remote peasants who were puzzled by the tasks and the preferred answers of the research team. The problem was identified by Newman, Griffin, and Cole (1989), who demonstrate how differently organized "construction zones" produce specific value systems, and who argue that if learners struggle with a task, the problem may be the task or situation, not the learner. They critique the assumption that a research task is isomorphic, or identical across test-takers, and recommend changing the task to see if the result is different. This problem of using a single task to evaluate diverse learners under the assumption that it provides a sample of all capabilities remains a problem in standardized measures.

Cole (2022), who developed a close personal and professional relationship with Luria covering many decades, undertaken during the Cold War and its many perils, takes the view that Luria was far more sensitive to bias than his Central Asian research reports suggest. When Cole studied the learning of children considered to have prohibitive learning difficulties, he wrote that

> we realized that once we took up the challenge of teaching "these unteachable" children, our social obligations to the subjects of our research were altered significantly. Suddenly, we became responsible for the children's welfare. Our roles as objective experimenters were fundamentally breached by our obligation to make a difference. Now we had to do more than make claims about zones of proximal development based on average differences between groups of children on some standardized measure. Luria would have understood the difference.
>
> Luria ends his autobiography [Cole, Levitin, & Luria, 2006)] with a description of two case studies. These (one with a mnemonist, one with a brain injured engineer) were unlike his studies of Uzbeki peasant reasoning or the role of speech in the development of self-control, or even most patients he saw as a clinical neuropsychologist. Each case extended over many years and in each case, he acted as both diagnostician and therapist. It is through the mixing of these two roles that the form of psychological research he referred to as romantic science emerged.
>
> (p. 56)

Luria, like Cole, developed a sense of reciprocal responsibility to the people whose lives he studied. A "romantic science" includes both diagnostic tools and a commitment to the well-being of the people studied. Vygotsky argued that mental tests were inherently unfair when applied to people not socialized to their conceptual design. Yet he could be very judgmental about those from outside his own cultural purview in relation to tasks constructed from his own cultural experiences. His work in pedology thus both has multicultural appeal in its contention that people should be judged in light of their cultural experiences and not that of the investigator; and is hierarchical in the judgments he expressed about people from less technologically advanced societies.

Differentiating education to address students' specific needs required a sort of diagnostic testing that was deemed bourgeois and likely to perpetuate social class differences. This criticism might resonate well with modern-day educators' views of such practices as tracking, given that working class families' children are likely to be assigned to lower school tracks (Ozer & Perc, 2020). In the Soviet Union, social class was a far greater emphasis than race, which along with social class is often foregrounded in critiques of modern school tracking in societies grounded in European values (Mickelson & Everett, 2008).

These tests were part of a large-scale diagnostic regimen. Vygotsky was involved in a field known as "psychotechnics" that Kellogg and Veresov (2019) characterize as

> in some ways, the Soviet equivalent of business consultancy and human resource management. Because the USSR aspired to plan its labour market and especially because Soviet educational resources were scarce, psychotechnics was supposed to assure the maximal selection and professional training of particular "psychological types" for particular jobs.
>
> (p. xv)

In both school and in the workforce, then, diagnostic tests were used to categorize people and place them in appropriate situations, whether or not the diagnoses matched the people's own preferences or what a different sort of diagnosis might yield. During the 1920s and early 1930s, when pedologists had their greatest influence and then their abrupt decline, they undertook an effort to measure students' mental ability and learning potential. Vygotsky (2019) described how societal norms produced the standards by which a diagnosis was conducted:

> pedology utilizes what are known as standards and standard values to determine differences between the passport age and the pedological age. This standard value is a constant, taken as a measure in order to judge, by the deviation from this value, the degree of divergence between the expected course of development and the actual course of development as it occurs… . How then are these pedological standards obtained? They are obtained by means of a statistical study of children *en masse*… . There exists an average statistical value, which the mass of material will show us, i.e. when the average child of this mass will manifest a symptom. And with this mass value, I may compare each individual child and say, if the average of the mass of children shows this symptom at two years, and if my child shows this symptom at one year and eight months, then obviously he is developing faster than the average of the mass of children is developing… . [D]evelopment, although it unfolds over time, is not merely organized as a temporal process, but instead organized in a complex way; its rhythm does not coincide with the rhythm of time.
>
> (pp. 7–8)

A privileged background may prepare children better for IQ or other tests than a disadvantaged background, suggesting a class difference. Vygotsky believed in school's leveling effect, with proletarian children rising to the mean; it's less clear whether or not he expected bourgeoisie children to regress to the mean. Yet such a thing rarely happens. Schooling often exacerbates rather than closes gaps between social classes (Ceci & Papierno, 2005). Whether such an outcome is more likely in a capitalist society than a Marxist society is not clear.

There is evidence that Vygotsky was less of a leader in this aspect of pedology than his critics found him to be. Barrs (2017) argues that

> Vygotsky was an unrepentant pedologist but he was critical of some aspects of pedology, and in particular of its focus on mental testing, which came to be a dominating factor in the spread of pedology and was also implicated in its eventual downfall. Leontiev and Luria acknowledged that Vygotsky criticised the testing movement associated with pedology. However, 'they maintained that he committed an "error" by not criticising pedology as a field of study and by publishing some of his work in pedological journals' (Leontiev and Luria, 'Psychological Views of Vygotsky', 1956, quoted in Holowinsky 1988, p. 32). Leontiev and Luria both had to distance themselves from their affiliation with pedology (Yasnitsky 2009, pp. 73–4) and, in the case of Leontiev (who wrote an article criticising Vygotsky's psychology for its 'theoretical mistakes, inconsistencies of thought and individual idealistic views') from Vygotsky himself (Leont'ev, 2005b, 20).
>
> (pp. 354–355)

This comparative approach might justify the Soviet criticism that pedologists sought to pathologize working class people for having developmental paths that appear to lag behind those of the affluent classes. Vygotsky also, however, included a single-case comparative method that studied a child's progress through developmental stages:

> I compare not just different forms of child development to each other—I may do this as well, but *I mostly compare the child with himself at different stages of development.* Hence, the subject of my comparison is the different stages of child development. In this sense of speaking, we say that pedology employs a comparative-genetic method in its study; it presents comparative cross-sections of development at different age stages and, comparing them with each other, uses the means of comparison to represent the path of development of the child.
>
> (2019, p. 40; emphasis added)

Vygotsky (2019) made it clear that his notion of "age" is distinct from the "passport age" that details a date of birth and locates age on the calendar: "Such separate cycles of development, taken as a whole, are known as ages. An age is nothing but a given cycle of development, which appears as if set off by itself, separated from other cycles, which has its own specific pace and its own specific content of development" (p. 9). Age in this sense refers to a developmental point or period, which is complicated to identify given that maturation is not a smooth or direct process, but occurs along what he calls a *twisting path* (Vygotsky, 1987, p. 156).

Vygotsky's focus on the cultural individual within the bounds of the social collective positioned him at odds with official doctrine. Bakhurst (2007) argues that

> Despite his emphasis on the sociocultural foundations of psychological development, Vygotsky's thought remains centered on the individual subject conceived as a discrete, autonomous self. A cultural-historical approach, however, ought rightly to stress the dialogical character of the self. We do not just become persons through our interaction with others; *we are ourselves only in relation to others.*
>
> (p. 63; emphasis added)

Bakhurst is a respected figure in Vygotskian circles, but I don't entirely agree with this characterization. Undoubtedly, Vygotsky saw the cultural individual as the focus of his psychology. But he also emphasized the individual's "dialogical character." Bakhurst's reference to how "we are ourselves only in relation to others" could have been directly lifted from Makalela's account of *ubuntu* (see Chapter 2). I have found Vygotsky to be very well aligned with this concept, and so disagree with Bakhurst's (2007) conclusion that his attention to how individuals develop in relation to phylogenetic and historical factors prevents Vygotsky from being also concerned with collective understandings of psychology. To the Soviets, however, his attention to individual maturation within cultural and historical bounds might have been too great a departure from orthodoxy to allow him to remain influential.

The diagnostic tests of pedology came up against the Soviet belief that working class people are often mismeasured by tests normed in relation to a population that included people historically advantaged. Ewing (2001) argues that

> pedologists were pursuing a politically risky strategy by asking about obstacles to the further development of Soviet youth. In particular, their research suggested that even in a "socialist" system, certain categories of children, especially those in rural

areas and among "non-Russian" minorities, remained "backward" in their academic achievement. Soviet pedologists thus found themselves in the dangerous position of calling attention to shortcomings that contradicted the self-proclaimed "achievement" of equality among classes and nations in the Soviet Union.

(p. 479)

There is somewhat of a chicken-and-egg quality to Ewing's analysis. He contends that the diagnostic procedures might themselves be reliable and valid, leading to the exposure of the school system's shortcoming in promoting full-scale societal equity. Others might argue that the tests include biases that are bound to locate such differences by disadvantaging students from working class and non-Russian ethnic backgrounds, and miseducating them through remedial school placements.

These questions have concerned both recent equity-oriented educators in the English-speaking world who have critiqued academic tracking, and those who examine the Soviet pedologists' testing of children. The diagnostic expedition to remote areas published under Luria's name, and to which Vygotsky contributed, is perhaps the best-known effort to visit rural areas populated by isolated non-Russian minorities (Luria, 1976). Luria's concluding paragraph in the monograph refers to the "backward and remote region" of the Soviet Union, a conclusion reached because of the Muslim peasants' problem-solving approaches in Western-style categorizing tasks. This diagnosis violated Vygotsky's own statements regarding the ill-advisement of judging one culture according to another's conceptual understandings, tools, and signs. It also typified the ways in which pedologists viewed those for whom communist resocialization would be a formidable task. Luria's study has made many subsequent analysts uneasy about the judgments of cultural deficiency among outsiders to a society (e.g., Smagorinsky, 1995b).

The task of identifying cultural outsiders as deficient sounds familiar to those concerned with how tracking, special education, and school discipline policies in English-speaking nations have historically worked against the interests of racially minoritized groups, students of nonbinary sexuality, immigrants, low-SES people socialized to local ways, and others who are often assigned to these schools and tracks (Oakes, 2005; Tunç & Ülker, 2020). Various forms of discrimination continue to influence which sorts of children are likely to be assigned to which sort of educational track or program. This facet of pedology eventually proved to be their undoing in a nation whose ideals emphasized full equality for all, especially the proletariat; at least in theory.

Pedology and Higher Mental Functions

Pedology, as practiced by Vygotsky and his colleagues, had the broad developmental goal of cultivating a Soviet citizen through the mediational channels available in school. School ought to promote the higher mental functions that represent cultural understandings and appropriate actions (see Chapter 5). The concepts through which higher mental functions are articulated, to Vygotsky, are available primarily in words:

> a major factor in human mental development is the introduction of word meanings or concepts in instruction. It is instruction in the school setting that propels child development along lines that are each time specific for a certain culture or society.... [I]t is exactly the introduction of a new factor (i.e., culture in the form of word meanings) that announces a qualitatively new stage in development.
>
> (Van der Veer, 1997b, p. 5)

Concepts are what enable learners to connect and interrelate their knowledge networks coherently, and so were of great interest to pedologists. To Vygotsky (1998),

> the unified activity in which a concept is disclosed ... is logical thinking.... [T]he most important revolution in forms of thinking in the adolescent is the revolution that occurs as a result of the formation of concepts and mastery of logical thinking represents the second basic consequence of the acquisition of this function.
>
> (p. 57)

Formal Soviet education was designed to promote these higher mental functions, which would be fostered through schooling and developed under the influence of social reforms identified by the state.

School thus promotes logical thinking in the tradition of the Age of Reason, and educators should make analytic thought a big part of their teaching as a way to regulate the primal emotional response. Vygotsky (1998) argued that "Logical thinking becomes possible only when the child masters his thinking operations, subjects them to himself, begins to control and direct them ... logical thinking is characterized most of all by mastery and control" (p. 64). Self-regulation is thus a matter of logic, one that helps to bridle one's visceral emotional responses. Higher mental functions therefore not only represent cultural knowledge available through word meaning, but include a disciplining of the emotions through the application of logic:

> the whole mechanism of controlling and mastering behavior, beginning with propriocentric [from Latin *proprius*, meaning one's sense of the relative position of neighboring parts of the body] irritations that arise with any kind of movement and ending with introspection, is based on self-perception, on reflection on one's own processes of behavior. This is why the development of introspection is such an important step in the development of logical thinking, and logical thinking is certainly conscious and at the same time it is thinking dependent on introspection. But introspection itself develops late and mainly under the influence of social factors, under the influence of the problems that life puts before the child, under the influence of inability to solve problems of increasing complexity.
>
> (Vygotsky, 1998, pp. 65–66)

This reflection on one's learning and development becomes available through speech-mediated self-regulation in response to life's challenges. Vygotsky presented the process as an intellectual one, in spite of his attention to the fundamental role of emotions in thinking (see Chapter 7). Ultimately, however, these emotions become subordinated by the intellect so that they are expressed appropriately within cultural bounds. The pedologist's concerns thus included the interrelated functions of the intellect and emotions in social contexts, and how they follow from how educators organize their educational environments to socialize them in accordance with the values governing the setting.

Discussion

Vygotsky's central role in the pedology movement both made him a key player, and later made him a pariah to Soviet authorities. He would undoubtedly face a lot of criticism for some of his ideas by 21st-century progressive educators. These critics might admire his generally Deweyan orientation and developmental emphasis, but find his contributions to the diagnostic movement to be highly problematic. What I see is a contradictory stance. Pedology sought to provide optimal settings for student growth, informed by many fields of inquiry. However, this goal included the elimination of students diagnosed with behavioral, cognitive, or physical differences that resulted in their segregation in separate schools, such as schools of defectology (see Chapter 14).

As I write these lines, my colleague Usree Bhattacharya, the mother of a young daughter with Rett Syndrome, argues passionately for inclusion (Bhattacharya, 2022b) to help her daughter's socialization, growth, and emotional security. Her argument resonates with that of other advocates for mainstreaming that I am moved to embrace, even as I recognize that creating the conditions for such inclusion would be expensive and make new demands on teachers who—in this era of ideological hostilities, low pay, under-resourced schools, poorly socialized children following the Covid shutdown, micromanagement from administrators, threatening behavior from parents, hostile rhetoric in the public sphere, burgeoning class size, and other factors—are already leaving the profession in alarming numbers (Maxouris & Zdanowicz, 2022).

In the next two chapters, I delve more deeply into these issues, relying on Vygotsky's contemporaries to make the case against him. At times, such as their attacks on his diagnostic program, these critics make arguments that are worthwhile. At others the Soviets either appear to fabricate problems, blame Vygotsky for his early writing as if he maintained his youthful beliefs, read his work selectively, and otherwise mount an ideological argument against him using whatever evidence served their needs. In doing so I don't seek exoneration for Vygotsky, or attempt to vilify his accusers for their role in the demise of Soviet pedology. Rather, my task is to examine Vygotsky's pedological work and understand its appeal and its problems, and consider the extent to which it applies to 21st-century schooling in the English-speaking world and beyond.

Notes

1 Also spelled paedology.
2 Page numbers for Byford (2021) refer to the online version and not the book chapter.
3 The publication date I use here is the one preferred by Van der Veer. The issue of *JREEP* in which this article appears, along with all others in the issue, lists a 2000 publication date, but a 2002 translation date, indicating a 2-year lag between official date and actual date of publication. I am using the actual publication date in this volume.
4 Aron Borissovich Zalkind (1888–1936) was a Soviet psychologist, pedologist, and psychoanalyst. In 1931, he was accused of Menshevik-idealistic eclecticism, Freudianism, and "perversions at work," leading him to repudiate his career's work and causing his removal from the directorship of the Institute of Psychology, Pedology and Psychotechnics and from the editorship of *Pedology*. He died in the street of a heart attack after suffering heavy criticism, although may have committed suicide.
5 Gustav Gustavovich Shpet (1879–1937) was born out of wedlock to an Austro-Hungarian officer and a Polish-German aristocratic mother. He became a Russian and Soviet philosopher, historian of philosophy, psychologist, art theoretician, and interpreter with fluency in 17 languages. He was arrested during the Great Purge in 1935 on charges of "wrecking" and sent to Siberia, then re-arrested in 1937 as an alleged monarchist and executed in 1937.
6 Osip Emilyevich Mandel'shtam (1891–1938) was a Russian and Soviet poet of the Acmeist school, which emphasized an economical style.

16 The Pedology Decree
Vygotsky as Anti-Marxist Bourgeoisie

> "The Central Committee of the All-Union Communist Party (Bolsheviks) discussed the theory and practice of contemporary so-called pedology. The Central Committee of the All-Union Communist Party (Bolsheviks) deems that the theory and the practice of this pedology is based on pseudoscientific, anti-Marxist postulates." (From the resolution of the Central Committee of the All-Union Communist Party (Bolsheviks) entitled "On the pedological distortions in the system of the People's Commissariat of Education").
>
> (in Kozyrev & Turko, 1936, p. 44)

With this resolution, the Bolshevik Party banned pedology, leading to the suppression of Vygotsky and others. Declaring pedology to be "false science," the Decree eliminated university departments and dismissed, arrested, exiled, or executed their scientists. I will review the purge of pedologists in this chapter, and the next, with different focuses. This chapter treats what I consider to be the manner in which Vygotsky was constructed as bourgeois, with a focus on the Soviet political climate and the accusations of Vygotsky as anti-Lenin, anti-Stalin, anti-Marx, and a dupe of Western thought. Chapter 17 then addresses critiques of pedology's assumptions, also from a Stalinist perspective. To begin, I review the Pedology Decree of 1936 and why it was imposed.

The Pedology Decree of 1936

> A critique of Vygotsky's works is a timely matter, and must not be put off, especially as some of his followers have still not been neutralized (Luria, Leont'ev, Shif,[1] etc.). The resolution of the Central Committee of the All Union Communist Party (Bolsheviks) of 4 July entitled ["On pedological distortions in the system of the People's Commissariat of Education"] calls for exposure and eradication of all such theories as an obligatory condition for successful functioning of the Soviet school.
>
> (Rudneva, 1937, p. 94)

This judgment followed in the wake of the Pedology Decree of 1936, in which the field of pedology was forbidden in the Soviet Union. Not only was pedology to be banned, its practitioners would be "neutralized" in order to provide Soviet children and youth with a proper education. The Decree was issued during the thick of Stalin's Great Purge from 1936 to 1938. This period was driven by paranoia in Stalin's inner circle following an assassination and a belief that Stalin himself was on the hit list. It occurred simultaneously with the rising threat of Hitler, with whom Stalin created a brief alliance in order to invade and divide the lands of Poland in 1939, a pact that Hitler soon betrayed with an invasion of the Soviet Union itself.

Byford (2021) describes the political environment of the era, and its consequences for pedology, when it began to decline in favor in the early 1930s:

> At this critical juncture, the entirety of the Soviet scientific field was subjected to systematic politico-ideological scrutiny and intimidation by the rapidly Stalinizing Party structures (Krementsov, 1997). Party-political disciplining was designed to bring to heel and enforce Party-loyalty on all those in academic leadership positions who had assumed prominent positions in the nexus that during the 1920s formed between the Soviet state and the scientific field. The purpose of the exercise was to comprehensively subordinate those key domains of scientific activity that had during the 1920s been turned into a *de facto* extension of the Soviet state to the political will and authority of the Party, in which Stalin in turn sought to achieve full control. This meant that the entirety of pedology's scientific leadership, irrespective of the school of thought or methodological framework to which the researcher belonged, was at this point accused of one type of 'deviation' from the Party line or another (Umrikhin, 1991).
>
> (p. 6)²

And from there, things got worse. Among the ways that scientists, including psychologists, were contained was by having them "neutralized," a terrifying prospect during Stalin's Great Terror. Ewing (2001) reports that

> The power of the Stalinist state depended on the extent to which Soviet citizens could be persuaded to assume responsibility for making their own behavior conform to the requirements of the regime. Teachers' responses to the antipedology campaign suggest that a willingness to take on this responsibility transformed many of them, however unintentionally, into effective agents of dictatorship.
>
> (p. 493)

Teachers' involvement in the campaign against pedology, he continues, "contributed to the increasingly authoritarian nature of Stalinist schools in the 1930s" (Ewing, 2001, p. 475). Whether the teachers were avid adherents to Stalin's regime, or lowly citizens cowed by the threat of death in a labor camp, is beyond the scope of this analysis. Fear, however, was Stalin's calling card, and the ousting of pedologists and teachers

> brought a climate of terror to the world of schools and educational institutions. The fates of individual pedologists who were active in schools has not yet been reconstructed. However, this operation coincided with a wave of purges that invaded the world of schools: about half a million teachers were examined by special control commissions (which fired those whose social origins and political faith did not correspond to what was required by the Communist Party) and about 22,000 teachers were laid off following the arrest of family members from the summer of 1936 to 1940 (Ewing 2002, pp. 233–42; Holmes, 2005, p. 64). Among these there were certainly also pedologists, although the exact number at the national level is unknown. The Party directive of March 3, 1937, "On the defects of Party work and on the liquidation measures of the Trotskyists and others", marked the beginning of the "great terror", which was followed by a campaign of arrests. In Char'kov, Ukraine, from August 12, 1937, until April 6, 1938, 1341 educators were arrested, of whom

918 were shot, 402 were sentenced to ten years in prison in the concentration camps, and 21 were sentenced to eight years (Hillig, 2000, pp. 10–13).
(Caroli & Mecacci, 2020, p. 29)

Vygotsky was among those singled out for his "pedagogical distortions." Perhaps fortunately for him, he was dead by the time the Great Terror might have found him as guilty of anti-Marxism and anti-Leninism, and thus anti-Stalinism, as Rudneva (1937) accused him of being:

> One of the "pillars" of pedology, whose books have done great harm to the Soviet school, was L.S. Vygotsky.
> An analysis of Vygotsky's works published over the past ten years, beginning with *[Vygotsky's Pedology of the School Age]* and *[Thinking and Speech]* (1934), reveal the anti-Marxist character of his views and his organic link to the anti-Lenin "theory of the demise of the school."
> Vygotsky offers reactionary writings of bourgeois scientists as "novelties." These reactionary sources also nurtured the stupid anti-Leninist "theory of the demise of the school."
> The anti-Leninist theory of the demise of the school runs through all of Vygotsky's utterances.
> (p. 75)

Rudneva's essay is among those republished in a special issue of the *Journal of Russian and East European Psychology* edited by Van der Veer (2002) on Soviet criticisms of Vygotsky, especially his work in pedology. Those essays provide much of what is available on how Vygotsky went from celebrated founder of cultural-historical theory to one bound for the Gulag or executioner's pistol, spared only by death. I next review the major accusations mounted against Vygotsky and pedology by psychologists who were perfectly aligned with party doctrine and eager to snuff out opposing thought.

The Accusation of Anti-Marxism

Ewing (2001) reports how the Central Committee systematically discredited pedology and its practitioners in the 1930s,

> charging that pedological theory itself was based on "falsely-scientific and anti-Marxist foundations." In particular, any suggestion that children's fate was "determined" by "fixed" social or biological factors was condemned as directly contradictory to "socialist development," which had "successfully re-educated people." Such claims about environmental and hereditary influences allegedly revealed an "uncritical" borrowing of "bourgeois" theories intended to maintain the dominant positions of "exploiting classes" and "superior races" by perpetuating the "physical and spiritual doom of the working classes and 'inferior races.'" In the concluding section, the Central Committee instructed the Commissariat of Education to achieve "the full restoration of pedagogy as a science and pedagogues as its bearers and guides" by restoring teachers' responsibility for instruction, returning "the bulk of the children to normal schools,[3]" and eliminating the field of pedology by retraining specialists, withdrawing books, and abolishing courses.
> (p. 480)

The Decree ended pedology "and encouraged Soviet educators and psychologists to develop 'Marxist' child study," a move that shows how "pedagogical theories have been influenced by sociopolitical realities, philosophical attitudes and ideological considerations" (Holowinsky, 1988, p. 127). This list of influences could also include self-advancement and survival, given how careers waxed and waned in relation to a psychologist's adherence to the imperatives emerging from the top of the social order, the "revolution from above" in the Stalinist USSR (Tucker, 1990).

Ewing (2001) describes how on July 4, 1936, the Central Committee accused pedologists of disrupting "Soviet education by classifying vast numbers of children as 'unfit' or 'retarded.' ... the Central Committee declared that the establishment of socialism meant that inherited traits no longer affected the mental development of Soviet children" (p. 473). Not only is nurture more important than nature; nature is not a factor at all. Vygotsky (2019) contended that "never is a trait of development purely conditioned by heredity, a purely hereditary trait; i.e. the environment is always also involved in development. Consequently, development always has both hereditary and environmental aspects in unity" (p. 62). Wrong, said the Soviets. We are all born equal; only inequitable environments produce inequity and thus social class divisions.

Talankin (1931) concluded that "The Vygotsky and Luria group is undoubtedly talented. But it represents the danger of positivism and of uncritical transfer of various Western European psychological theories that are especially fashionable now, especially those that are very influential in the West" (p. 10). Referencing European and US psychologists branded one as anti-Marxist, and Vygotsky did cite many of them favorably, albeit in the context of his broader belief that a Marxist perspective could never come into being in a capitalist society. His criticisms of these sources mattered little in the charge that their influence rendered Vygotsky a hopeless bourgeois pseudoscientist.

These charges led the authorities to ban the reading of Vygotsky and his colleagues following his death, with the translation of *Thought and Language* into English in 1962 predating its availability in the Soviet Union by a dozen years. *The Psychology of Art* was never published in the USSR for ideological reasons, and also reportedly by Vygotsky's own preference. Kozulin and Gindis (2007) report that "For political reasons, any open discussion of Vygotsky's ideas was practically impossible from 1936 to the late 1950s" (p. 334). Daniels (2007) relates that Vygotsky's book *Pedagogical Psychology* [a.k.a. *Educational Psychology*; Vygotsky, 1997a] "was considered to be so politically unacceptable to the rulers of the Soviet state that one had to have a special pass from the KGB that would admit one to the restricted reading room in the Lenin Library where the book could be read" (p. 307). Cole and Jornet (2021) describe how

> For many years following the death of Stalin, Pedology remained unmentionable in Soviet society. Luria was himself a pedologist (Luria, 1928), but he never spoke of pedology and the various articles that appeared in the latter half of the 20th century appeared under dispersed guises with no mention of their Pedological origins. For example, the last three chapters of *Mind in Society*, and several essays in the English language edition of Vygotsky's *Collected Works* were originally part of Vygotsky's pedology project.
>
> (p. 285)

Yet these pedological chapters needed to be snuck into *Mind in Society* without mention of the term pedology (M. Cole, personal communication, July 8, 2022). Scientists like Luria lived in fear. Cole, Levitin, and Luria (2006) report that Luria, in addition to carrying a briefcase containing his papers, "carried with him a small suitcase with a change of underwear and toiletries in it. If he was arrested while on his way to or from work, [his former student] Lubovsky was to inform his family so that they would not fear he had been hit by a car and waste their time running around to hospitals to find him" (p. 252).

Stalinism shaped the careers of those who hoped to live another day in the Soviet Union. Shortly before Vygotsky's death, Leont'ev moved toward *activity theory* and its more collective emphasis. Whether Leont'ev made this shift to avoid persecution or because he found the move compelling and intellectually necessary is unclear. If the proof of the pudding is in the eating,[4] then Leont'ev's survival until his death in 1979 at the age of 75 suggests that his epistemological shift away from Vygotsky may have followed from more than intellectual differences.

The Problem of Diagnostic Tests

Vygotsky and his fellow pedologists undertook a controversial diagnostic program, using psychological tests to categorize students and adults according to the criteria built into the tests. Soviet historian Medinsky (1954), a scathing critic of these tests, wrote that "Intelligence and achievement tests were made with such calculations that the children of the indigent parents should appear as weakly endowed and nonachieving. Those tests claiming objective proof were in reality the means to enable the children of the bourgeois to continue their education and to accept the children of toilers" (p. 179). The tests, he argued in conjunction with other Soviet critics of pedology, were designed to perpetuate social inequity based on class differences, and thus were anti-Marxist and antithetical to the Soviet project.

Byford (2021) relates how the diagnostic program became problematic, and came under criticism from Leningrad Party boss Andrei Zhdanov,[5] who was assigned to evaluate the city's high schools. Zhdanov was alarmed by what he found happening to children diagnosed as having special educational needs:

> Among the most problematic issues to emerge was the pedologists' role in referring so many children to special schools. Zhdanov condemned the readiness with which children were being taken out of regular classes, arguing that such a policy disincentivized teachers from trying to improve pupils' performance and behaviour using their own methods and techniques. Moreover, the speed at which schools for the underachieving and the misbehaving were mushrooming had produced some unintended effects. The overall percentage of those relegated (somewhere in the region of 2%) was not huge, especially if one's understanding of underachievement was relatively fluid. However, by grouping such children into larger cohorts, and especially when they formed entire schools, these populations suddenly appeared much bigger. Moreover, managing schools populated entirely with the underperforming and the disruptive was a challenge, not least since providing such schools with additional resources and expertise, as was recommended by leading pedologists who promoted this type of triage, was not, in fact, within the state's means. The whole matter was made worse by the way in which such children were labelled. Though individual cases varied, they were invariably categorized using terms that carried stigma, not just for the children, but also their families, and ultimately the state. Zhdanov complained about the impression that the mass nature of such referrals gave of Soviet

society as supposedly experiencing 'degradation' (degradatsiia) and he blamed this on tests, describing them as pseudoscientific instruments that produced spurious diagnoses of 'backwardness'.

(pp. 10–11)

Zhdanov, along with Komsomol leader A. V. Kosarev, Commissar of Education A. S. Bubnov, and Commissar of Healthcare G. N. Kaminskii, soon were given the task of issuing a decree condemning the practice of pedology. Ewing (2001) reviews how the Decree was designed to purge such practices as using diagnostic tests to assess students' academic fitness that produced their differentiated assignments to school tracks:

> the Central Committee charged that pedologists' "pseudo-scientific experiments" had called excessive attention to "the most negative influences and pathological perversions" in children, their families, and surrounding environment. Such testing meant that "an ever larger and larger number of children" were assigned to special schools after being categorized as "mentally backward," "defective," or "difficult." In fact, the Central Committee declared, many of these children were perfectly capable of attending *normal'naia shkola* (normal [i.e., mainstream] schools), but once these labels had been affixed, they were considered "hopeless" cases.

(p. 480)

The 21st-century reader might easily see these charges as quite reasonable and in accord with more recent critiques of tracked schools (e.g., Oakes, 2005). Yet other agendas were at work. Political leaders were concerned that pedologists were "displaying 'pedological distortions,' succumbing to 'class-hostile elements,' and engaging in 'wrecking' activity with 'anti-Leninist' objectives" (Ewing, 2001, p. 472).

The Decree's recommendations were made as part of a broader move toward more repressive Soviet policies and government intervention in both science and daily life. This shift was no doubt influenced by the response to the rise of Nazis in the 1930s and threat of World War so recently after the resolution to the first major global conflict. Yet Stalin's authoritarianism could not be solely a response to Hitler, given the regime's effort to find a scapegoat for shortcomings of the Soviet school system, Stalin's valorization of the proletariat, and a growing distrust of "elite" intellectuals (again, Marx and Engels were not included among them, nor was Lenin): The "intelligentsia" and "society's shit" whose social status was viewed as the cause of proletarian subordination in society.

Among the major Soviet critics of pedology was Eva Izrailevna Rudneva, who was born in 1898 and lived through 1988. In a short Russian-language biography generously provided to me by René van der Veer, she is described as a historian with a high profile in Soviet educational policy. A Doctor of Pedagogical Sciences and Professor in a Department of Pedagogy and Educational Psychology, she was named Laureate of the Lomonosov Prize in 1961 (a highly prestigious award presented to some of the world's most distinguished scientists) and of the N. K. Krupskaya Prize (1968). The state awarded her medals "For Valiant Labor in the Great Patriotic War of 1941–1945" and "In Memory of the 800th Anniversary of Moscow," indications that she was a Soviet citizen of the highest rank. She was an accomplished thinker, publishing over 100 scholarly papers during her career. She wasn't just an attack dog unleashed on Vygotsky by the state. She was a highly respected figure who had status and influence in Soviet educational planning. Her refutation of Vygotsky and the pedologists thus carried weight, both for the respectability of the source and for her devotion to the official version of Marx provided by Lenin and Stalin.

As for her motives in launching a hostile attack on Vygotsky as the face of pedology, that question only has speculative answers, and her generation is long dead and unavailable for consultation. She might have disliked Vygotsky and viewed him as a rival. She may have undertaken the critique voluntarily, or by request, assignment, reward, or threat. Vygotsky's death a few years before may have made him a convenient target for her posthumous polemic. She may have done what one needed to do to ingratiate oneself to the authorities and thus have a career. And she may well have believed that the anti-Marxist, bourgeois Vygotsky represented a clear and present danger to Soviet society, even in death. What is evident is that she went after Vygotsky with unusual hostility and vigor.

Rudneva positioned Vygotsky at the forefront of the pedology movement she found so reprehensible. She used him both individually and emblematically in her effort to bury the field of pedology. She attacked Vygotsky for a great variety of violations of Soviet doctrine, some very real and clear, and some bordering on the fabricated.

The diagnostic tests used for classifying children were among her chief targets. She provided the basic problem in pedology's formulation: It relied to an extent on ideas emanating from Europe. She wrote,

> Following his bourgeois teachers, Vygotsky also took from them their method of investigation. Hence, the work of Vygotsky and his pupils on children has essentially been a mockery of our Soviet children and amounted to stupid, absurd tests and questionnaires associated with Piaget, Claparede,[6] and others. Thus, Vygotsky the pedologist combined his damaging utterances to both psychological and pedagogical issues, attempting to resolve such problems in education and upbringing.
>
> (p. 76)

Rudneva associated pedology with capitalism and its inevitable social class inequities, based on Vygotsky's selective borrowing from European and US sources. Vygotsky's agenda could therefore only be considered bourgeois. Razmyslov (1934), another severe critic of pedology and its practitioners Vygotsky and Luria, was blistering in his denunciation of Luria's expedition, and how the peasants were asked to do unfamiliar tasks and then evaluated according to inappropriate criteria:

> There are dozens of such protocols in Luria's expedition—dozens of protocols in which the experimenters literally tormented the respondents with their situational thinking; and when they did not find it, despite all their clever tricks, they drew conclusions such as the ones presented above [in which the peasants were judged to be intellectually and culturally backwards].
>
> Of course, there was no scientific experiment or scientific work whatsoever in Luria's expedition. No matter how much Luria and his comrades in arms have sworn that they were studying the problem of thought and collective farm workers in the ethnic regions in its historical development, this does not at all help them to conceal or disguise their reactionary theory, so hostile to Marxism.
>
> (p. 53)

In the Soviet Union, all things followed from Stalin's sense of collectivism. He hoped to create communities for all Soviets in state farm communities, or preferably in urban centers in service of creating a universal industrial culture. This goal to collectivize social life meant that efforts to study local cultures and ethnicities were considered to be "bourgeois nationalism." The state was concerned that individual groups might engage in what today would be called "identity politics" that fractured their national affiliation and made them less likely to engage in a Marxist class struggle to elevate the proletariat.

Vygotsky was surely guilty of the charge of studying ethnic and cultural groups, and categorizing them according to what he understood as the development of higher mental functions that best served a good Soviet citizen. Indeed, his contributions to Luria's (1976) research on peasant life in the outer reaches of the Soviet Union were designed to understand their cultural ways of living, albeit with the long-term goal of Sovietizing them.

Razmyslov's (1934) criticism was part of a growing view that the work of pedologists violated Marxist principles of lauding peasant life and avoiding any bourgeois influences that suggested that some were more capable than others. The modern educator will recognize this discourse in critiques of tracking, and they have legitimacy. The assumption behind the Committee's perspective is that all students are potentially capable learners and workers, and that pathologizing them through diagnostic tests creates the very social class differences that the Soviet Union believed could be overcome through education and societal structure. As a result, pedologists became viewed as hostile to the working class. Holowinsky (1988) reports that

> in the 1930s, at the height of criticism of pedology, Vygotsky's work was pronounced as 'eclectic' and 'erroneous' (Kozulin, 1986) and parts of his book *Thought and Speech* were prohibited from publication (Kolbanovsky, 1968). Vygotsky's work *Historical Meaning of Psychological Crisis* written in 1926 had not been published by 1979 (Radzikhovsky, 1979). The years of Vygotsky's professional activity (1924–1934) were the most turbulent in Soviet psychology.
>
> (p. 123)

Diagnostic testing and sorting thus violated a fundamental understanding in the Soviet Union, one predicated on eliminating affluence as a social advantage. Yet pedologists used such tests in their assessments of Soviet people from outside Russian culture, a problem that contributed to the demise of their field in a nation committed, in principle, to equality. Vygotsky believed, as interpreted by Van der Veer and Valsiner (1991), that "the natives' languages were definitely inferior as regards the formation and use of abstract concepts" (p. 213). This judgment is reminiscent of many more recent characterizations of working class (e.g., Bernstein, 1971) and minoritized racial groups' (critiqued by Moll, 2000) diction and problem-solving means.

Kellogg and Veresov (2019) report that "After Darwin, there was a strong tendency to think of this process of development from the phylogenetic side, in biologizing terms. Germans like Haeckel and Americans like Hall saw humanity not as linked human types but as higher and lower races" (p. xi), a criticism that Rudneva (1937) leveled at Vygotsky. Vygotsky, argue Van der Veer and Valsiner, characterized the national minorities as "backwards" and judged a "forced cultural development" to be essential in order to reach "a unified socialist culture" (p. 214), redirecting and shaping evolution to produce the New Soviet Man. They view Vygotsky's beliefs in this area as representative of Gould's (1981) conclusion that "many of the great men of psychology's history were prone to ethnocentrist and even racist reasoning" (p. 212).

The diagnostic project, to Razmyslov (1934), undermined the Soviet plan to use education to form a national identity:

> Instead of exploring the processes of overcoming egocentric thought in children under the conditions of the dictatorship of the proletariat and the building of socialism, Vygotsky and Luria ... derive this egocentrism not from the child's class environment, but from his biological nature. Instead of showing the process of development and cultural growth of Uzbekistan workers, they seek facts in support of their "cultural-historical theory" and "find" identical forms of thought in an adult Uzbek and in a five-year-old child and, under the banner of science, drag in ideas that are harmful for the work of building a national culture in Uzbekistan.
>
> (p. 51)

The tests, then, were highly problematic in Vygotsky's time, as they remain in 21st-century English-speaking nations and others. Concern for social class attention, and ultimately the elimination of social classes altogether, permeated Marxist thought. Schools played an important role in promoting state goals through the cultivation of a generation of Marxist citizens who would change history as they and their descendants helped demolish the capitalist edifice. Finding a Soviet child to be deficient ran against the State's belief that equality could be achieved if capitalism's cruel inequities could be eliminated, and if all worked equally on behalf of Soviet interests and values. The testing of children only perpetuated these differences, according to Rudneva (1937):

> The method for studying a child's intellectual development from Binet to Piaget's procedures, so widespread among pedologists, was the tool with which bourgeois psychologists attempted to demonstrate the intellectual superiority of children from the ruling classes over working-class children. And it was carried over to our conditions in a completely uncritical way.
>
> (p. 88)

Rudneva's critique has some resonance, given how European societies were built on centuries of social class immobility, typically in the sort of monarchial societies that the Bolsheviks had overthrown. Vygotsky was soiled by association with European and US psychologists working under the name of pedology, however:

> These "auxiliary means"—instruments, tools, signs—are considered by these authors in isolation from production relations in different sociohistorical environments and from the concrete labor of an adult and the practical activity of a child developing in a specific social-class environment; hence they have the same formal character as Werner's[7] undivided wholes. This disregard of the content of the concrete activity of the evolving human being also lies at the root of Werner's attitude toward the biogenetic law transferred to the psychology of Stanley Hall.
>
> (Abel'skaia & Neopikhonova, 1932, p. 40)

Stanley Hall was a prominent US psychologist at the time. He earned the first US doctorate in psychology at Harvard under the mentorship of William James, became the first president of the American Psychological Association, founded of *American Journal of Psychology*, and was the first president of Clark University, serving for over three decades as president, among many other achievements. He was also a practitioner in eugenics and promoted views of racial hierarchies. Hall had little use for poor, sickly, or disabled people, or people from non-white races; and believed that limited breeding and forced sterilization were appropriate to contain their proliferation. Providing them with assistance, he believed, inhibited the development of more advanced human types he called "supermen."

It is easy to see how Abel'skaia and Neopikhonova (1932) would find association with Hall to violate the Soviet ethos in relation to the working class. Associating Vygotsky's diagnostic tests with Hall's horrific sterilization program appears to be more hyperbolic than solid analogy, however. Hall, while occasionally mentioned, is not among the US sources that appear prominently in Vygotsky's writing. The criticisms, however, were designed to destroy a reputation more than to produce an intellectually sound argument.

Other concerns, however, have merit. Tests designed by people from affluent classes, those who tended to rise in psychological circles, were likely to be designed using tasks more familiar to people like themselves than to people with other forms of socialization. The critique maps on well to 21st century concerns about standardized testing, tracking, and other sorting mechanisms, at least in terms of rejecting the practice. Yet the concerns are grounded in different economic systems. The Soviet communists opposed diagnostic tests and placements because they were non-egalitarian and assumed that biology played a role in human difference. In contrast, they believed that environments that treated everyone the same, that eschewed diagnosing and classifying people, could produce a uniform communist society in which social class differences were eradicated. US critics of tracking have asserted that classifying people does not follow from sound diagnostic criteria and methods; they are the consequence of prejudices against the kinds of people who get identified as needing remediation. Ultimately, this process is circular: Low SES students get assigned to low tracks, their assignment to low tracks proves their intellectual inferiority, and their inferiority is what accounts for their low SES. The US critique is concerned with the ways in which tracking limits economic mobility. The Soviets hoped to eliminate the whole question of economic mobility.

The assignment to low academic tracks based on dubious gauges maintains them in low social positions for the duration of their schooling (Hallinan, 1996). Their low status in school in turn mitigates against future upward economic mobility. Vygotsky's contention that a capitalist society cannot produce a Marxist frame of mind helps explain how the same problem can be viewed as having different roots and consequences, even as many from outside communist and socialist nations continue to claim a Marxist perspective.

Social Class and Pedology

Rudneva (1937) and others valorized the working class and advocated for their greater role in running a society. They simultaneously accused the intelligentsia of maintaining social class separation through various means of oppression. Ironically, they did so from a highly privileged position in Soviet society. Regardless of the many contradictions between Soviet ideals and practices, their accusations often settled in a condemnation of the scandalous status of being bourgeois, as outlined by Razmyslov (1934):

> Vygotsky echoes Durkheim[8] when he says, "Everywhere, the development of the child's personality displays itself as a function of the development of the child's collective behavior; everywhere the same law is observed, namely, the transference of social forms of behavior to the realm of individual adaptation."

Vygotsky operates with the foggy concept of the collective in almost all of his books on pedology, and thus does not go beyond the development of the sociological thought of the neopositivists.

Wherever, in our view, he should be speaking of a child's class environment, his production environment, of the influence of school, his [Young] Pioneer group, and the Komsomol movement[9] as the conveyors of the influence of the Party and the proletariat on children, or that the categories of thought reflect and sum up the practice of social production, that they are the stages in our coming to know the world, Vygotsky instead speaks simply about the influence of the collective, neglecting to tell us what collective he is speaking about, or what he means by collective.

(p. 49)

The "neopositivists" in Europe and the US sought to identify objective reality through measures that produce statistical validations of hypotheses. My understanding of Razmyslov's criticism is that the purpose of such tests was to create differentiating methods, rather than to ensure the construction of environments that produce equality. Razmyslov's collective, then, might be the uniformly communist society, while Vygotsky's was more local. Either way, the critics were convinced that Vygotsky's consultations with European and US schools of thought were enough to characterize pedologists as anti-Marxist:

Instead of showing the process of "overcoming the vestiges of capitalism in the economy and the consciousness of the workers of Uzbekistan, and showing how, on the basis of the Party's general line and Lenin's national policy and under conditions of a lively economic and cultural boom in Uzbekistan, people are developing a new attitude toward work, the new man is being created and a communist consciousness is taking shape—instead of this, Luria attempts on the basis of "scientific and experimental" material from his expedition to Uzbekistan, to show that the collective farm workers of Uzbekistan think not in concepts, but complexly,[10] that they are unable to abstract from a concrete situation and are incapable of generalizations.

The workers in Luria's expedition and Luria himself assessed examples of a highly developed political consciousness among collective farm workers in Uzbekistan as examples of situational thinking, as an inability to go beyond narrow practice and move on the theoretical generalizations.

(Razmyslov, 1934, p. 52)

This characterization is quite accurate. The researchers' amazement at how the farmers grouped items, and their conclusion that they lacked the right higher mental functions, has been disquieting among even devoted Vygotskians. Among my own early efforts to work through his ideas (Smagorinsky, 1995b), I detail concerns similar to Razmyslov's. This example does confirm, I hope, that my interpretation of Vygotsky's sense of the collective as local, and his critics' sense of the collective as national, has some merit. But there's more to the Soviet critique than Vygotsky's sense of local collectives. Van der Veer (2021) reports that Vygotsky's contemporary Bikchentay[11]

voiced more explicit criticism, although he did not mention Vygotsky by name. Bikchentay noted that 80 languages were spoken in the Soviet Union and that pedological knowledge was largely based on the study of Russian children. Meanwhile, he said, we did not know enough about the ways to develop children into the new builders of a communist society. We must not study "memory," said Bikchentay (1931, p. 32), but children's readiness to join in the building of socialism. "We are not so much interested in the level of the primitive on the biological or even the historical ladder (all bourgeois researchers write about this). We are interested in the level of the former hunter in socialist production… we do not need tests for Tatar or Chuvash children, we need yardsticks to establish the productive level of children" (ibid., p. 33).

(p. 14)

I don't know the extent of Vygotsky's research samples well enough to determine whether or not he relied on Russian children exclusively, but the problem of generalizing norms from samples similar to the researcher, and thus building a sampling error into a research design, has long been a problem in educational research. Studies of all-white children in US schools, when applied to Black children, inevitably find them to be in deficit (Tate, 1995). In the case of Bikchentay's contemporary criticism of Vygotsky, he appears to endorse the official position that all that matters is creating the environment for the development of a Marxist ethos; one's prior experiences, including ethnic socialization, are irrelevant in a communist society in which equality follows from the elimination of capital.

The Ranking of Cultures

Van der Veer (2021) expands on how Vygotsky's hierarchical thinking about cultures contributed to the demise of pedology:

Vygotsky and Luria spoke of "superior" and "inferior" cultures, which was an unfortunate term since it suggested that cultures can be compared on a global scale and that European culture is best. The distinction they made between "mentally backward" and "culturally backward" or "primitive" children or adults was somewhat subtle, but in the sociopolitical climate of the 1930s Vygotsky and Luria's theory of cultural development became the subject of heavy criticism. As we have seen, to point out any differences between ethnic groups living in the Soviet Union became highly suspect, in particular when the persons belonging to these groups were politically active communists, and in the end not even explanations that referred to different living circumstances were acceptable, because it was claimed that negative living circumstances no longer existed in the socialist state. In this sense the 1930s differed dramatically from the 1920s when the popular authors Ilf and Petrov[12] could still portray extreme poverty, poor housing conditions, and begging street children during the New Economic Policy[13] (Ilf and Petrov 1980 [1928]).

(p. 17)

These cultures might be national, or might reside in social class status. Rudneva (1937) found Vygotsky to be hopelessly bourgeois, especially in his testing practices, which she argued were based on the assumption that affluent people have insights that are unavailable to the proletariat:

The resolution of the Central Committee of the All Union Communist Party (Bolsheviks) … revealed, with utmost clarity, the class intent of the antiscientific theory that the fate of the child is irrevocably sealed beforehand by the influence of heredity and the environment.

The Central Committee of the All Union Communist Party (Bolsheviks) establishes that this theory could have come into being only as a result of a noncritical transfer of the views and principles of antiscientific bourgeois pedology to Soviet pedagogy, the purpose of such pedology being to demonstrate that the exploiting classes and the "superior races" are especially gifted and have special rights to existence and, on the other hand, that the working classes and the "inferior races" are physically and intellectually foredoomed, the intent being to preserve the domination of the exporting classes... .

Vygotsky formulated very clearly this fatalistic determination of children's destiny by hereditary factors not only in his early works but also in his very last.

(p. 89)

Rudneva's critique here seems strained, premised on the presumed inherent contamination of Vygotsky's thinking by his references to European and US thinkers. Vygotsky was surely interested in biology, but not as the sole determinant of a person's prospects in life. Vygotsky (2019) stated unequivocally that pedology

studies the role of heredity in development... . [T]he pedagogue examines in what way the propensities that are laid down and transmitted according to the laws of heredity influence development itself while the laws of transmission of hereditary traits are studied by genetics and by general biology... . The problem of heredity in pedology is posed differently from the way it is posed in general biology or in genetics.

(p. 48)

The pedologist, he continued, "deals with complex traits that vary in development and emerge in development, for it is only in relation to these traits that we can establish the role that heredity plays in development" (2019, p. 49). His work in defectology (see Chapter 14) emphasized the promise of deaf and blind children through an appropriate education that takes into account their biological makeup and shifts the onus for their status on the able-bodied people around them. Vygotsky shared the concern that the environment may place limits on people born into working class families. Contrary to how he is depicted by these Soviet critics, Vygotsky (2019) did not claim that biology produces a social class orientation. In fact, he argued quite the opposite:

Let me give a simple study which has led to a number of misunderstandings. In Germany, Peters[14] studied the marks of school-age children for four generations in folk schools and discovered that there was a very high correlation between the good marks of a great-grandfather, a grandfather, a father, and a son, and between the poor marks of a great-grandfather, a grandfather, a father and a son. He concluded from this that the ability to do well in school and get good grades is, according to the formula of Pearson,[15] hereditarily conditioned.

(pp. 50–51)

Why, he asks?

Because the correlation between good and bad marks that we find between close relatives turns out to be closer than that which we find between other school children in the study. But we need only approach this study from a pedological point of view to see that this conclusion is wrong. Why? What does it take to get good marks in school? A series of conditions are needed. Say, if you just take wealthy farmers—and Peters studied mostly German farmers, the rural population—don't wealthy farmers with good incomes, other conditions being equal, have a better chance to have their children do well in school than non-wealthy, poor peasants? Of course, they do. Doesn't the very fact that the great grandfather, grandfather, and father were literate create the conditions for the fact that the grandson is literate? Of course, it does. It seems that when it comes to the development of traits that are very complex and not laid down at the outset, to traits which involve both hereditary and environmental moments, the fact that there are similarities and that these coincide with the degree of relationship can tell us nothing about their hereditary or non-hereditary nature.

(p. 51)

Vygotsky's argument concerns generational wealth and poverty, not inherent traits or Lamarckian evolution[16]; that is, a belief that a trait developed by an individual can be passed down genetically. Early in my education, one of my textbooks included a drawing of a well-muscled blacksmith pounding on iron with a large hammer. His large biceps, the text stated, could not be passed down to his children, because they had been developed through blacksmithing, whose consequences for musculature aren't hereditary. Although there is some evidence that factors like stress can be passed down at the cellular level to newborns (Lee, 2010), there is little reason to accept the Lamarckian premise widely.

In contrast, "conditional" factors are likely to produce the problem of social reproduction, an ongoing Marxist concern. Rather, however, than assigning all human differences to environmental categories and assuming that people are fundamentally of equal potential in any endeavor, Vygotsky included attention to biological factors that might produce different capabilities. He hoped ultimately for inclusive environments in both school and society, regardless of biological makeup (Vygotsky, 1993). Unfortunately, IQ tests have been used to assert that some races are more intelligent than others (e.g., Herrnstein & Murray, 1994), tracking assignments show a bias toward assuming that nonwhite students lack sufficient ability (Oakes, 2005), and tests in general are designed to separate the wheat from the chaff and provide a better world for the wheat. What I see as likely is that Vygotsky's use of tests might potentially veer into these problems, and that this possibility opened him up to criticisms that he believed in tests as a way for the elitists in the intelligentsia to decide who has value, and who does not. His broader career finds some support for this accusation, and contradictory evidence elsewhere. He was a complex person subject to a variety of environmental influences, some of which were in opposition to others. My conclusion from his inconsistencies is that he was, in many ways, a normal human being.

Vygotsky the Bourgeois

We have examined the "cultural-historical theory of psychology" and dwelled on the errors and distortions of Marxism committed by [Vygotsky and Luria]. But what are our conclusions? Undoubtedly that Vygotsky and Luria are objectively conduits for bourgeois influence on the proletariat. Not knowing Marxism, and not possessing the method of dialectical materialism, they are now constantly prey to these and other "fashionable" bourgeois psychological currents and distort and pervert the propositions of Marxism.

(Razmyslov, 1934, p. 57)

Soviet Marxism valorized the common laborer, and viewed affluence as a sign of corruption and decadence. Rudneva (1937) is explicit in naming the sort of intellectual company that Vygotsky kept, and why his consulting of non-Marxist (always presumed to be anti-Marxist) perspectives made him *personal non grata* in Soviet education. Although Vygotsky was highly critical of the names on Rudneva's following list of undesirables, his incorporation of elements of their ideas was unacceptable in Soviet doctrine:

> Vygotsky blindly followed every word of bourgeois psychology of the time. While attempting to "criticize" Piaget, Koffka, and others, he essentially followed the same path. He did not cast aside bourgeois psychological currents, but uncritically borrowed them. Eclecticism is very distinctly reflected in Vygotsky's concepts: it is difficult to find any current in bourgeois psychology that has appeared in the last two decades that has not found a place in his writings. Freud, Dewey, Levy-Bruhl, Adler, Werner, Piaget, Claparede, Koffka, Kohler, and Lewin—they have all, to some extent, found a place in his eclectic system.
>
> (p. 76)

Eclecticism that went beyond Marxism was bourgeois and anti-Marxist by definition. In finding Vygotsky guilty of seeing some merit in the ideas of some psychologists from capitalist nations, Rudneva is right, as any reading of Vygotsky easily reveals. What is missing from this critique is the extensive refutation provided by Vygotsky of aspects of their ideas that departed from his understanding of cultural-historical psychology's developmental thrust. During the Great Terror, however, even suspicion of having a bourgeois inclination might lead to expulsion or death; and as Van der Veer (2002) observes, Vygotsky's father's career in banking may have soiled him as bourgeois, and Jewish at that, in the eyes of Soviet officials.

Vygotsky's critics at times took ahistorical liberties in order to undermine his reputation. Rudneva critiqued Vygotsky as a Pavlovian reflexologist, for instance, a position true of his early writing, but modified through the inclusion of psychological tools in a reaction in the second of the three phases of Vygotsky's career. Rudneva (1937) argued that

> Vygotsky sees every mental function from the standpoint of reflexology. Attention is a system of reactions. Memory is, from Vygotsky's crudely mechanistic perspective, merely the connection between internal stimuli and a group of reactions. The entire learning process is based on reflexology, i.e., it is reduced to mere training.
>
> (p. 77)

I've made the case in earlier chapters that in his 20s, when he wrote *Educational Psychology*, Vygotsky was an outsider to Moscow's intellectual center. He was young, Jewish, and Belarusian. Pavlov was a Nobel Laureate, a national hero, and a giant in Russian and Soviet psychology. Being Pavlovian was expected, and taking on Pavlov would have been quite risky. Vygotsky ultimately found reactions to be inadequate and mechanistic, and added a critical dimension to the stimulus-response sequence: The intervention of a tool. Yet his early writing came to stand for his position in Rudneva's polemic. Ironically, among Vygotsky's criticisms of the behaviorists was their mechanistic approach, one he ultimately found problematic in Pavlov. Saying so upon his arrival in Moscow in his early 20s might have produced a different sort of career for Vygotsky.

Yet Razmyslov (1934) took Vygotsky's early reliance on Pavlov to indicate an anti-Marxist stance, quoting "his famous formula: 'Consciousness is only a reflex of reflexes'" and finding Vygotsky egotistical in hoping to surpass Pavlov as a reflexologist:

> But this is not enough for him. Bekhterev[17] and Pavlov seem to him to be insufficiently consistent reflexologists, and he wants to be a "greater reflexologist than Pavlov himself," "more papist than the Pope." He writes: "In claiming that consciousness, too, should be understood as a reaction of the body to its own reactions, one must be a greater reflexologist than Pavlov. So be it. If you want to be consistent, you must sometimes object to any half-heartedness and be more papist than the Pope, more royalist than the king. Kings are not always good royalists."
>
> (p. 50; Vygotsky quote footnoted to [*Problems of Contemporary Psychology*]. Giz., 1926, p. 42)

The criticism of Vygotsky as bourgeois, then, stands on both firm and shaky ground. He did indeed draw on psychologists from capitalist nations, which made him anathema in Soviet circles. He critiqued them as well, largely on psychological grounds rather than exclusively on their fidelity to Marx or Lenin. He was critical of capitalist notions of the human condition, saying,

> Pedology as it developed in the West and America is with all its roots connected with bourgeois education. Education, as is known, is one of the basic means of the class struggle in a class society. Connected with an idealistic philosophy, finding itself under the pressure of demands advanced by the theory and practice of bourgeois education, pedology absorbed many nonscientific elements.
>
> (in Van der Veer, 2020, p. 53)

European and US pedologists were bourgeois and bent education toward inequity; Soviet pedologists in contrast were concerned with the class struggle. Yet Vygotsky was ultimately deemed bourgeois himself. Whether he was or not may be a matter of interpretation, especially given his fervent belief in Soviet communism in many of his texts. From a Stalinist standpoint, consulting "Western" sources surely did condemn him as a capitalist flunky, as Kozyrev and Turko (1936) argued:

> An analysis of Professor Vygotsky's starting premises in the study of thinking and speech reveals that they consist not of scientific positions on that subject and that, although he does attempt to criticize bourgeois scientists, those attempts and that criticism are such as to make him an adherent to the idealistic statements of Kohler, Yerkes,[18] Learned,[19] Bühler, and others. Vygotsky explains the problem of development in subjective, idealist, and formal logical terms, completely disregarding Marxism-Leninism and not wishing, or being able, to approach and test critically the bourgeois legacy.
>
> (p. 62)

The debate over whether Vygotsky was or was not a Marxist raged in his day, and has been debated ever since. My sense is that Marx, like Vygotsky, can be interpreted selectively to fit agendas. Both might be interpreted differently in the US and Soviet contexts. My interest is more in these interpretations than in establishing a firm, faithful reading of

Marx by which others can be measured. In Stalinist Soviet circles, Vygotsky's attention to a subset of US and European scholars meant that he could not be a Marxist psychologist. Some of the criticisms leveled at him hold up over time; some appear to be polemics based on selective and ideological readings. Given how rare it is for any perspective to survive its own times intact, it is no surprise that Vygotsky's body of work includes some problematic assertions. I would include his early, Panglossian view of the possibilities for equity in communism's idealistic vision among his errors. I assume that the "20 million [Soviets who] died in labor camps, forced collectivization, famine and executions" under Stalin (Keller, 1989, n. p.) would agree.

Discussion

This chapter reviews the ways in which Soviet psychologists loyal to Stalin characterized and caricatured Vygotsky in the years surrounding his death. In their eyes, he did no good, and did considerable harm. The eclecticism of which he was accused allowed for no departures from state ideology, whose architects included no psychologists. To return to my early account of Bakhtin's explanations of dialogism and monologism: In the Soviet Union, there was in a sense a monologic muffling of all dissent, or suspected dissent, and thus no dialectic upon which to forge a new synthesis. The "Party line" was the only voice possible. In one sense, then, Bakhtin's own society was characterized by the monologism that he found troublesome.

But this single-voice society was also dialogic in the historical sense. The Party line was in dialogue with Marx's critique of the capitalism that provided Marx himself with a comfortable life in those decadent European cities. It was in dialogue, or at least in discursive conflict, with Tsarist imperialism. In a limited sense it was in dialogue with US and European scholarship, but not in Hegel's dialectical sense; rather, bourgeois thinking served as a body of work to be dismissed, not (as did Vygotsky) as a thesis against which to oppose an antithesis and from which a synthesis might emerge. As a result, the criticisms of Vygotsky both included legitimate concerns and complaints manufactured from selective attention to the many things he said and wrote. In the next chapter, I continue with this exploration of how Vygotsky was constructed during the Pedology Decree, producing an image that led to his suppression well after tuberculosis cut short his rich and detailed speaking turn.

Notes

1 Zb. I. Shif was among Vygotsky's students in Moscow. She was among those named during the Pedology Decree as an especially dangerous influence on Soviet society. Under Vygotsky's guidance, she wrote *The Development of Scientific Concepts in the Schoolchild* (1935).
2 I use page numbers for Byford that refer to the online version and not the book chapter.
3 "Normal schools" here appears to refer to "mainstream schools," in contrast with the use in European-based societies of "Normal schools." This latter usage describes teacher education universities in which teacher candidates learn how to shape students' behavior toward the white middle-class norm (Correa Arias, 2020).
4 This phrase is typically rendered incorrectly as "the proof is in the pudding," which makes no sense unless the proof is a spoon or the ingredients.
5 Andrei Aleksandrovich Zhdanov (1896–1948) was a Soviet politician, propagandist, and cultural ideologist who was considered to be Stalin's heir-apparent but died before Stalin. The Zhdanov Doctrine proposed that the world was divided into imperialistic (US) and democratic (USSR) types of societies, with Soviets being superior and the Doctrine asserting that "The only conflict that is possible in Soviet culture is the conflict between good and best."

6 Édouard Claparède (1873–1940) was a Swiss neurologist, child psychologist, and educator. He co-founded the journal *Archives de psychologie* and was its long-time editor.
7 Heinz Werner (1890–1964) was a German developmental psychologist. During the rise of the Nazis, he emigrated to the United States, where he worked at several universities, ultimately retiring from Clark University.
8 David Émile Durkheim (1858–1917) was a French scholar often credited with establishing the disciplines of sociology and the social sciences. He was interested in social structures more than individuals, and coined the term *collective consciousness*.
9 The Komsomol movement was a political youth organization established in 1918 within the All-Union Leninist Young Communist League. The Young Communists were the third age-based youth group, following the Little Octobrists who served children through age 9, and the Young Pioneers who served youth through age 14. The Komsomol movement was for youth and young adults through age 28. All were designed to socialize Soviet children and youth into a Marxist worldview.
10 I assume that "complexly" refers to thinking in complexes, a developmental stage on the way to thinking in concepts that also includes pseudoconcepts, those understandings that include elements that do not fit the concept. See Chapter 6.
11 Iroglo N. Bikchentai (also Bikchentai) was a Soviet pedologist whose career is detailed by Byford (2016).
12 Ilya Ilf (1897–1937) and Yevgeny Petrov (1902–1942) were a Soviet writing team from Odessa, active in the 1920s–1930s. They were commonly known as Ilf and Petrov.
13 The Soviet New Economic Policy was proposed by Lenin in 1921. It included both socialist and capitalist components as a way to help recover from wartime economic stress. It was abandoned by Stalin in 1928.
14 "Wilhelm Peters (1880–1963) completed his doctorate on colour perception under Wilhelm Wundt in 1904. He then joined the Würzburg school, where in 1915 he published the work on the correlation of school grades to which Vygotsky refers. ... Peters was from a Jewish family that had converted to Christianity; this meant that he lost his job during the Nazi years. He went to London and then Istanbul, and returned to Würzburg after the war, where he worked for learning-disadvantaged school children." (Kellogg & Veresov, 2019, p. 51)
15 Karl Pearson (1857–1936) was an English mathematician and biostatistician known for his adherence to social Darwinism, eugenics, and scientific racism.
16 Named after French naturalist Jean-Baptiste Pierre Antoine de Monet, chevalier de Lamarck (1744–1829), among the first proponents of such inheritances. See Lamarck (1914).
17 Vladimir Mikhailovich Bekhterev (1857–1927) was a Russian and Soviet neurologist, considered to be the founder of objective psychology. A reflexologist who was a rival of Pavlov's, he was the co-discoverer of the Bekhterev–Mendel reflex, indicating pyramidal tract lesions.
18 Robert Mearns Yerkes (1876–1956) was a US psychologist, ethologist, eugenicist, and primatologist involved in intelligence testing. He was prominent in studies of primate intelligence, and later became an advocate for eugenics and racialist theories.
19 Blanche W. Learned was a musician who collaborated with Yerkes to study the vocalizations of chimpanzees to provide an account of vocal expressions under different conditions. See Yerkes and Learned (1925).

17 The Pedology Decree
Critiques of Method and Focus

Vygotsky's controversial status as a Marxist provided the central material for much of the criticisms he faced as a pedologist. Soviet critics found him wanting in other areas as well, however. In this chapter, I review additional ways in which his Soviet critics found Vygotsky's pedological writing to work against the state's interests. Many of these criticisms are grounded in the principal issue reviewed in Chapter 16: That in relying on occasion on thinkers from the decadent bourgeois psychologists of Europe and the United States, he himself was corrupted and in need of erasure, of being neutralized. As I have done throughout, I do not defend Vygotsky against all accusations and complaints, some of which remain salient. At the same time, I try to expose those that involve distortions and selective reading and appear designed to ruin Vygotsky's reputation and obliterate the field of pedology, a goal reached through the Pedology Decree.

I review the criticisms in the areas of his inattention to details of research methods in his reports, his views on ontogeny and phylogeny, his account of the role of the environment in human development, and his inclusion of biology as a factor, the accusation that he viewed the onset of adulthood as the end of development, his account of spontaneous and scientific concepts and the charge that he embraced a view of thinking as verbal and detached from the material world, his reliance on the Nazi psychologist Jaensch for his formulation of eidetic memory (memory comprised of lingering images), and his vision of schooling as one day becoming obsolete and everyday life becoming the means of education.

Methodological Reporting

In a snarky subhead, Rudneva (1937) referred to "Vygotsky's Method of 'Investigation'" and said, "the experimental work in Vygotsky's investigations occupy a very limited place. He speaks much about the results of 'experimental investigations' and extremely little about the method that he used" (p. 88).

This critique has merit. As others have observed, Vygotsky only generally described his research methods in his publications. His clinical reports lack the specificity of current APA standards for explaining his investigative methods. Cole (1993) writes that "Vygotsky was not primarily an experimentalist. Luria said that his mentor's idea of an experiment is what we might call a pilot study, observations *pour voir* [to see]. Vygotsky was, rather what Russians call a methodologist, a scientist who worried about what kinds of methods could be brought to bear upon the theory in a relevant way" (p. 6). His reports would require greater detail to pass muster in a 21st-century refereed scholarly journal and were imprecise enough on specifics to find himself under the microscope operated by his contemporaries in the USSR.

Vygotsky did speak generally about the *double stimulation method*, in which he moved beyond the stimulus-response method common in laboratories dominated by Pavlovian influence. This method provides the research participant with a task that requires knowledge beyond what they enter the experiment with, comprising the first stimulation. The second stimulation comes in the form of tools and signs that enable the participant to solve the problem through reconstruction of the task, making the participant a designer of the task rather than a simple research subject. The participants' active role in changing the character of the task then becomes a phenomenon to study, with tool mediation, and not simply task performance or reaction, the unit of analysis. The method thus includes attention to volition in changing the task, and conflicts between motives. Yet Sannino (2015) notes that these procedures were not clearly spelled out in Vygotsky's reports:

> Often texts by Vygotsky and his colleagues refer to second stimuli but do not mention double stimulation or equivalent terms. No comprehensive account was left by these authors which would cover the different types of experiments conducted and the broad theoretical implications of their results. The fragmentation in these texts is due most likely to the academic, historical and political circumstances in which the works of these authors were conducted.
>
> (p. 1)

The Luria expedition also included attention to card-sorting tasks in which a participant was given cards representing a set of items, and told to group them, eliminating those that didn't fit. A hammer, a saw, an ax, and a log, to the researchers, are best grouped as a set of tools, with the log eliminated. But the farmers used a different logic, including the log in the set because a saw is useless without a log to cut (see Luria, p. 56). This method has produced harsh criticisms from those who see the method as culturally insensitive (Nell, 1999), a conclusion I drew in an early effort to understand Vygotsky (Smagorinsky, 1995b). Cole (personal communication, August 23, 2022), who knew Luria well, assures us that "Luria has an interesting discussion of his method and its rationale that showed he was very aware of the bias issue, but believed he had overcome it." Whether he did or not has been debated; my own view is that his judgment that the peasants were "backwards" due to their Muslim religion suggests a bias, even as I trust Cole's knowledge of Luria's approach and state of mind.

Vygotsky claimed a Marxist orientation in his approach to research, which provided him a rationale for the intensive study of small samples from which to draw great generalizations. He used the analogy of the drop of water that represents the contents of the ocean in one account (Vygotsky, 1987) to justify the intensive study of limited samples. He also drew on the adaptation of the dialectic approach, saying,

> When our Marxists explain the Hegelian principle in Marxist methodology, they rightly claim that each thing can be examined as a microcosm, as a universal measure in which the whole big world is reflected. On this basis they say that to study one single thing, one subject, one phenomenon until the end, exhaustively means to know the world in all its connections. In this sense it can be said that each person is to some degree a measure of the society, or rather class, to which he belongs, for the whole totality of social relationships is reflected in him… . [K]nowledge gained on

the path from the special to the general is the key to all social psychology. We must reconquer the right for psychology to examine what is special, the individual as a social microcosm, as a type, as an expression or measure of the society.

(1997b, p. 317)

It's useful to keep in mind that the world was a different place in Vygotsky's time than it is in the present. There were far fewer print journals available, and in the Soviet Union, paper shortages affected their production, as did the rise of the Nazi threat and the obsession it created for the Soviets, especially in the two societies' mutual interest in controlling Ukraine and its great agricultural bounty, a goal that has persisted through the Putin Era (Snyder, 2015). Nystrand (2022) reports how Bakhtin's major work on Goethe was destroyed in a 1940 bombing of his publishing house, with the few surviving pages ending up as rolling papers to serve Bakhtin's smoking habit. With few publishing outlets, with scant paper supplies, and with reporting conventions not yet developed, research was reported in a far more haphazard way than the 21st-century researcher has available, with online versions of the latest *Publication Manual of the American Psychological Association* easily available for proper form and content. The criticism that his research reports focus more on findings than on method thus has merit, but could likely be applied to much research of the era.

Ontogeny and Phylogeny

Rudneva (1937; cf. Razmyslov, 1934) accused Vygotsky of endorsing the notion that ontogeny recapitulates phylogeny (see Chapter 6). She said,

The whole of the so-called theory of cultural-historical development created by Vygotsky starts out from the premise that a child repeats the path of the whole of mankind in his development. The development of mental functions historically consisted in a transition from natural forms of behavior to cultural forms; an individual masters functions, and their use becomes voluntary and conscious—and all this takes place under the influence of tools and signs. In the stage of cultural development, the word plays the role of tool. For pedologists, including Vygotsky, slander of the children of workers goes hand in hand with slander of imperialists of the colonial peoples to justify the seizure of new territories in the name of "progress" and "culture."

(p. 92)

This critique attempts to place several factors in relation, and in questionable ways. First, Vygotsky was clear that, while some general similarities exist, ontogeny does not recapitulate phylogeny (see Chapter 6). Kellogg and Veresov (2019) state in their editorial notes that "What sets the ontogenesis of cultural behaviour apart from its phylogenesis (i.e. the origins of cultural behaviour in prehuman evolution) and even its sociogenesis (i.e. the origins of cultural behaviour in human history), is the presence and participation of a final form from the very onset of development" (p. 67). That is, a child can see and take after senior members of a society, but the teleological ends of a whole society are not visible, unless one sees them in an aspirational society that may or may be replicable elsewhere (typically, not; see, for instance, the different forms that communism has taken in the Soviet Union, China, and Cuba, described by Castañeda, 1997). Or perhaps only an ideal conception of an imagined society is possible, one not yet instituted among humans. Two notable experimental societies of this sort were (1) the participatory democracy produced by the US Revolution against Great Britain; and (2) the launch of a communist, Marxist nation in the Soviet Union at the expense of the monarchial Romanovs. Neither had a precedent, and both were justified by ideals that have been compromised by the behavior of their citizens and leaders many times over.

In contrast, for the individual child, argued Vygotsky (2019), "what should exist at the culmination of development, as the result of development, is already present in the environment from the very beginning" (p. 78) in the form of older members of the culture, and the culture they inherited and modified. Importantly, those elders are not static beings, nor is the society in which they live. What appears to be stable today may disappear tomorrow, creating developmental disruptions as person and environment interact and act on one another in ever-changing ways.

It is difficult to sustain the belief that Vygotsky found that individuals replicate the developmental patterns of their species. Kellogg and Veresov (2019) conclude that Vygotsky clearly distinguished between the two:

> Ontogenesis does not recapitulate phylogenesis and that is for two reasons. First of all, as Vygotsky says, ontogenesis includes the "final form" in its social situation of development. Secondly, even in sociogenesis, Darwinian laws are radically altered: the "Jennings" principle[1], that organisms are only capable of what their organs enable, is overruled by the use of tools, and we find that precisely those societies which are best able to look after the very old, the very young, and the very sick develop the best means of self-preservation.
>
> (p. 151)

These volitional acts of using tools to reconstruct their environments make humans uniquely capable of formulating plans to alter their circumstances, thus changing their trajectories. In spite of some general similarities between ontogeny and phylogeny, Vygotsky explicitly argued on many occasions that the two developmental paths are substantially different, raising questions about Rudneva's motives in making the criticism.

The Person and the Environment

> Everything Vygotsky said on questions of the environment and heredity are in glaring contradiction to the theory of Marx, Engels, Lenin, and Stalin. The conception of heredity Vygotsky borrowed from bourgeois scientists has produced an idea of development and education as a passive process. This conception of development inevitably leads to a denial of the role of formal education and upbringing. Marx and Engels saw human development as a single dialectic process in which there is a constant struggle between heredity and the creative side, adaptation, which breaks down what has been inherited.
>
> (Rudneva, 1937, p. 93)

Rudneva's critique began with an association of Vygotsky with bourgeois psychologists in contrast with the thinkers valorized by the state, whose ideas served as doctrine from a higher source. In spite of Vygotsky's many assertions that both heredity and environments are factors in development, and that pedology is concerned with the mediating role of schools on children's maturation, Rudneva depicted him as a bourgeois thinker who dismissed school as a socializing instrument. To Rudneva, "In this pseudotheory of Vygotsky's, the school and the teacher are completely unable to change a child's development. This becomes especially clear when Vygotsky discusses the influence of the school on intellectual development and on pupils' achievement" (p. 84).

Yet in modern interpretations, Vygotsky is often considered to be an extreme environmentalist in his attention to the sociocultural context of human development. Culture is central to his conception of how people develop in relation to their environments. However, he explicitly rejected the idea that environment is all that matters. He stated that

> Another developmental theory, counterposed to this and equally, it seems to me, incorrect, is that development is seen as a process which is not due to its own internal laws but as a process that is entirely determined externally by the environment. Such points of view have been developed in bourgeois science for a long time and have cropped up in Soviet pedology. They have held that the child is a passive product obtained by the action of the environment in a particular way; that development consists, in this way, of that which the child absorbs, incorporates into himself and acquires such features from other people which surround him in the environment.
> (Vygotsky, 2019, p. 17)

The accusation of being bourgeois was part of the arsenal of any Soviet citizen wishing to debase the reputation of another. Here, Vygotsky was accused of being bourgeois, and he in turn accused some Soviet pedologists of being bourgeois. Vygotsky's crime was to find that the environment works in conjunction with biological features during development, and to see school as having less-than-deterministic power to shape children into Soviets. But mentioning biology was taken to be a sign that he believed that inborn traits produce different social classes, a view embraced by racists historically who use IQ tests to make absolute claims about racialized intelligence (critiqued by Winston, 2020). Further, with schooling among the socializing mediums through which the Soviets hoped to rapidly evolve the New Soviet Man, questioning its strong role in development inevitably invited critiques from doctrinaire Soviet Marxists.

Kellogg and Veresov (2019) provide a footnote in which they assert that

> Soviet educators believed that children are born equal, and they become unequal only through an unjust and radically unfair social environment. Children can become equal again by providing them with a radically egalitarian, equal opportunity environment in which to develop. This view was given the status of an objective, physiologically based behavioural science by the work of the Soviet behaviourists Pavlov and Bekhterev, but also in the work of Marxist psychologists Kornilov and Zalkind under whom Vygotsky worked. But it is, as Vygotsky says mischievously, a bourgeois view. By this, Vygotsky means above all that it is American: Watson and Thorndike are using it to argue that American education, by providing an equal opportunity environment in which (white) children can develop, can easily avoid the injustice of feudal aristocracy, monarchy and the general inequality of European societies.
> (pp. 17–18)

Yet Rudneva (1937) found Vygotsky to be a fatalist in relation to the environment, and to believe that working class people were incapable of acting on it and changing it for the better. Note the contradiction between this critique and the assumptions behind

Vygotsky's double stimulation method, which is designed to reveal how volitional tool use alters both tasks and environments. Rudneva wrote that

> Vygotsky does not understand the Marxist-Leninist theory of the environment; he disregards the role of man in transforming the environment. The Menshevik "theory" of spontaneity, the right-wing opportunist "theory" of movement by itself, are evident in the role assigned to the omnipotent environment. In pedagogy, denial of the role of the individual person and a spontaneous understanding of the environment led to underestimation of the educational process and the role of the teacher, which is the basis of the anti-Leninist "theory" of the demise of the school. The founders of Marxism always struggled most vigorously against spontaneity, in whatever form and in whatever area it appeared. Marx and Engels's materialist conception of history underscores the creative role of the individual. Marx and Engels, Lenin and Stalin, repeatedly pointed out that the economic aspect is not the only factor in the course of history: other factors, above all man, act along with it.
>
> (p. 93)

The Mensheviks were one of three factions involved in the October Revolution of 1917, the others being Bolsheviks and Social Revolutionaries. Menshevism was banned in 1921, another violation of the dialectical value on thesis-antithesis-synthesis, with the antithesis outlawed and the thesis left standing. Menshevism was criticized by Lenin (1906) himself, who was "opposed on principle to all their tactics in general" and confident that their timidity—they sought a middle ground between capitalism and communism—could not contribute to "the victorious outcome of the bourgeois revolution in Russia ... in the form of a revolutionary-democratic dictatorship of the proletariat and peasantry" (n.p.). In Marxist terms, "dictatorship of the proletariat" refers less to the sort of dictator Stalin became, and more to a "conquest of political power by the proletariat" (Marx & Engels, 1848; quoted in Draper, 1987). The Mensheviks, as rivals to Lenin's Bolshevik party, had to be crushed in order to allow this political ascendance of the workers.

Rudneva argued that Vygotsky was ahistorical and that he felt schooling was ineffectual, a critique that is difficult to reconcile with Vygotsky's pedagogical writing, which he typically situated within the ideological project of evolving the New Soviet Man (see Chapter 15). Holowinsky (1988) describes a psychologist who gained influence under Stalin by maintaining "an extreme environmental and behavioral position. He disregarded information on past behavior and believed it possible to train a 'new person' by employing appropriate educational strategy. Such thinking was very appealing to Stalin, who had promised to build a 'new society'" (p. 127). This perspective denies the role of biology, assuming that education may itself form the character and ideology from the raw material that children and youth provided in schools. It further distinguishes between the "past behavior" of a society—the history that matters—and views the past behavior of the individual as irrelevant and subject to reformation in Soviet schools.

This effort relies on revolutionary actions by people, similar to the impetus behind the more recent critical pedagogy theories that view education as a process of learning investigative means for interrogating and changing society (Kompridis, 2006). Ultimately, critiquing Stalin would prove to be a deadly form of action. What needed critique to the authorities was capitalism and social class distinctions, absolute categories that required no intersectionality with gender, race, or other demographic factor (Crenshaw, 2023). Rudneva (1937) herself was well aligned with Stalinist views:

> Comrade Stalin underscored the Marxist conception of the active role of the individual. "It is people, albeit only insofar as they correctly understand the conditions that they have found in finished form, and only insofar as they understand how these conditions change, who make history" (From a conversation between Comrade Stalin and E. Ludwig, p. 4). Adoption of Stalin's constitution, the greatest document of our epoch, which sums up the results of the struggle and victory of socialism and, at the same time, reveals the perspectives of new victories and conquests, shows especially distinctly how the "law" that says that children are fatalistically ordained by heredity and social factors is alien and hostile to Marxist science and to our building of socialism.
>
> (pp. 93–94)

Here Rudneva summed up the problems with pedology: It includes attention to biology, fatefully seals people within social class boundaries, and overlooks human agency in changing society for greater equity. The extent to which Vygotsky in fact advocated for such outcomes, and to which the Soviets avoided them, is open for discussion.

Rudneva (1937) questioned Vygotsky's account of the environment on many points, including his view of human subjectivity and how people interpret their surroundings. I find Lave's (1988) account of environments useful. Lave makes a distinction between the *arena* and the *setting* that appears to be consistent with Vygotsky's formulation. The arena is the fixed environment, such as a building. This building might be a school one month, and a hospital in the next if the area is bombed. But it remains a building, unless the bombs say otherwise. The setting is the way in which people construct and interpret the arena, such as when a school is viewed as a workplace, a prison, a salt mine, a place to socialize, and countless other places to its various inhabitants (Smagorinsky, 2010b). Vygotsky (2019) described these two conceptions in similar terms:

> The environment should not be considered in this instance as a setting for development which, due to the fact that it includes certain qualities or certain properties, can thus objectively determine the development of the child. Instead, the environment should always be approached from the point of view of what relationship exists between the child and the environment at a given stage of development.
>
> (p. 68)

This relational view proceeds from the phenomenon that "the child is changing in the process of development" (p. 69), making neither the child nor the relationship with the environment (interpreted as a setting) stable. Rudneva (1937) found this formulation to be problematic in that it allows for subjectivity (interpreting the setting) in an environment with objective reality (the arena):

> Vygotsky "psychologizes" the environment. He speaks of changes in the environment in the process of subjective experience. In *[Foundations of Pedology]* (1934)[2] and elsewhere he mentions a case in which three children in the same environment

are in exactly the same conditions (difficult family circumstances, an ill mother) but react to them each in his own way. Here we have a subjective psychological change in the environment, but objectively it remains unchanged.

(p. 90)

Indeed it does, unless the children rearrange the furniture so classrooms become playgrounds, or in the United States, unless a shooter enters and it becomes a killing zone so shocking and traumatizing that the community decides to raze the building (Yan, 2022). To Vygotsky (2019), "the influence of the environment on the child's development must be measured according to, amongst other points, the influence of the degree of understanding of, awareness of, sensibility to what is happening in the environment" (p. 73). The evidence in support of human subjectivity in interpreting settings is overwhelming. Vygotsky here is guilty as charged. But I think he's right.

Vygotsky and his Soviet critics were at odds over the role of biology in the formation of a classless society. They both saw school as an ideological training ground, perhaps to different degrees. School environments have a motive—the broad destination toward which action is directed in a setting (Wertsch, 1985)—and the intent to produce a certain sort of citizen. Whether they are deterministic or not is questionable. They are undoubtedly influential, as reflected in modern-day critiques of tracking and the identification of school-to-prison pipelines. They are politically liable to top-down manipulation to produce a certain sort of citizen, as Florida Governor Ron DeSantis hoped to achieve in 2023 by eliminating references to racism and nonbinary sexuality from schools and universities in order to create a conservative citizenry, in part by intimidating teachers and professors into compliance (Craig & Rozsa, 2023). To Stalin and DeSantis, schools can channel students' development toward preferred ideals and doctrines through the organization of the environment, a belief shared by Vygotsky.

Vygotsky also, however, saw a role for schools in biological development. Not all biological features are amenable to the sort of development that interested Vygotsky. Fingernails, for instance, are part of the human biological inheritance, and they grow continually, but are not understood as developing into something new. They might ultimately take a social status, as evidenced by the horrified looks I get when people see my heavily chewed nails, or the symbolic stature of long nails in ancient China (Tingting, 2021). But for the most part, they remain made of the same material, grow in the same manner, and retain their form (assuming the absence of ornamentation) over the course of a lifetime and over the phylogenetic lifespan of the species.

Vygotsky was not so interested in fingernails, however, at least in his writing. He was mighty interested in how people develop over time, however, saying,

development does not simply realize, modify, or combine hereditary propensities; rather, development brings to those propensities something new. It mediates, as has been said, the realization of these hereditary propensities and in the process of development, something new arises, through which this or that hereditary influence is refracted.... heredity does not change during the development throughout the ages, but... the specific weight of hereditary influence may change during development if, as we said at the outset, development is really the rise of something new that is not contained in its finished form in inheritable propensities.

(Vygotsky, 2019, pp. 58, 60)

Had he been interested in fingernails, Vygotsky might apply these principles to the ways in which they take on status and meaning in social settings. They might signal to a physician the presence of various pathologies and thus the need for both interventions and new behaviors (Singal & Arora, 2015), or indicate socioeconomic status through the dietary practices suggested by their composition (Nardoto et al., 2020). Biology is thus socialized when people become involved.

Some hereditary features may be amenable to modification in school through the relation between a biological inheritance and the social environment, a relation that itself is continually undergoing change. In keeping with Vygotsky's materialist orientation and dialectic approach, he saw biology and culture acting on one another in a dialectical fashion, as opposites that are both linked and mutually influential.

Not so to Soviet critics, however. Ewing (2001) recounts how pedology became reinterpreted from the Bolshevik Revolution to the Pedology Decree:

> pedologists were undermined by cultural shifts which emphasized practical achievements and political loyalty at the expense of "academic" expertise and "scholarly" findings. Proclaiming the creation of a new type of hero, Soviet leaders rejected any suggestion that heredity or environment presented limits that could not be overcome with the proper combination of enthusiasm and dedication. The antipedology decree thus appears as a product of converging factors, including a rising tide of political repression, growing concerns about foreign influences, incipient conflicts between educational and political leaders, and changes in Soviet culture.
>
> (p. 482)

These changes shifted all attention to the environment. Had he not been a bourgeois US educator, Horace Mann might have been recruited with his claim in the mid-1800s that education serves as the "great equalizer of the conditions of men," capable of evening out all advantage and providing the means for disadvantaged people to achieve a state of equality, regardless of their biological inheritance or social origins. Rudneva (1937) in contrast found Vygotsky to be bourgeois in his attention to biology, accusing him of using the convergence of biological and environmental factors to promote the exploitation of workers:

> Stern's theory of convergence had the greatest influence on Vygotsky concerning questions of heredity and the environment. This theory, which mechanistically combines hereditary factors with the environment, was regarded by the pillars of pedology as very progressive.
>
> The theory of convergence, hereditary and environment predetermination, postulating two predetermining factors at the same time, is used by bourgeois scientists to demonstrate the superiority of the ruling classes and the backwardness of the exploited classes.
>
> (p. 90)

This charge has some support in Vygotsky's hierarchical thinking in relation to cultural norms (see Chapter 4). Researchers from technological and industrial societies have historically found that their culture is superior to those of societies less dependent on industry and technology (Escobar, 1995). Yet this criticism comes from within Soviet culture and is aimed at internal social class differences, not whole-society hierarchies, which the Soviets endorsed in their view of capitalist nations as incapable of providing the equality guaranteed by a communist economy.

The main evidence against Vygotsky on this point comes from his role in pedology's diagnostic program, and the criticism has merit. This view was reinforced by Vygotsky's occasional reliance on ideas emerging from the decadent "West," making him guilty by association with the bourgeois capitalists of Europe and the United States. Yet his involvement in testing and sorting in pedology, manifest in Luria's expedition to remote Soviet villages, likely had the effects identified by Rudneva of contributing to social class distinctions and the diminishment of people from the peasant and proletarian classes.

The End of Development

One of Rudneva's (1937) most curious criticisms concerns Vygotsky's understanding of development. In the following, she made the unwarranted claim that Vygotsky believed that development ends with adulthood, which I can find no basis for in Vygotsky's writing or lifespan. She wrote that

> The absurdity of Vygotsky's arguments reach the point where he says that development stops with the onset of maturity: the mind of the adult remains unchanged; it acquires no new qualities.
>
> Just as an optimal temperature of 37 degrees exists for the human body and any deviations upward or downward threaten to impair vital functions and ultimately cause death, so, with regard to formal learning, it has its own "optimal temperature" for teaching each subject. If we begin too early or too late, formal learning will be impeded to an equal degree. ([*The mental development of children in the formal learning process*].
>
> (p. 35) (Rudneva, p. 85)

Here, Rudneva was on point with Vygotsky's quote, in which he posited that there is a ripe time for learning matters of different complexities at different points of maturation. A child of three would not be given Dostoyevsky's *The Brothers Karamazov* to read, requiring the biological development to manage the task cognitively and the socialization to know how to read and understand the work as fiction. But Rudneva's interpretation is quite a stretch:

> One need not prove that this conclusion has been refuted by all the achievements of the cultural revolution in our country. Vast masses of workers, numbering many millions, in our country have risen up, and been aroused to participate creatively in the building of socialist society, and are mastering the most difficult areas of science. Vygotsky attempted to slander workers by establishing an "optimal" age for learning and trying to reduce the tremendous conquests of the Great October Socialist Revolution in the area of culture to nothing.
>
> (p. 85)

Rudneva's charge is more than just a philosophical disagreement. Accusations of being anti-Marxist, anti-Leninist, anti-Stalinist, and anti-Soviet could result in a death sentence (Kushen, 1993). Fortunately for Vygotsky, he was already dead at the time of Rudneva's accusation. Rudneva took Vygotsky's attention to the relations between level of maturation and demands of task and shifted them into a critique of his role as a psychologist in service of the revolution, which could produce nothing other than the rise of the proletariat. Rudneva's contention was that Vygotsky's focus on schooling meant that he believed in the rather absurd notion that development ceases at the point of adulthood, thus preventing the working class from reaching a higher state of consciousness in adulthood. Yet as I'll review, Vygotsky ultimately saw the workplace as a critical educational setting, bringing on the criticism that he did not believe in the possibilities of schooling in shaping a communist citizen. Once one became an enemy of the state, a psychologist of the era was doomed to lose the argument, and perhaps more.

The best evidence of Vygotsky's belief in the maturational possibilities of adulthood is his own career. Vygotsky recognized changes in his own conceptual direction in his shift from Pavlovian reflexologist to what might be considered a post-Pavlovian move beyond the idea that people are the sum of their reflexes, with tools intervening to give responses a cultural dimension. His career, as reviewed previously, can be divided into three periods, each representing new understandings. Had he lived longer, there surely would have been more developments in his thinking. The idea that he saw development as ending with the onset of adulthood is preposterous, and contradictory with the criticism that he saw factories as educational settings and thus didn't believe in the value of schooling. Yet such critiques had great sticking power, and potentially had deadly consequences in Stalin's Soviet Union.

Concept Development

Rudneva (1937) argued that "Vygotsky's division of concepts into scientific and everyday is artificial and contrived. It is difficult to surmise in Vygotsky's conception why 'cinema' is an everyday concept, but 'exploitation' is only scientific" (p. 80). This critique points to the perils of any bifurcated generalization. It's not clear where Vygotsky drew the line other than the site of learning: Spontaneous concepts are learned out of school in local, everyday life; scientific concepts are learned in school and have an abstract quality. Surely someone getting a degree in Film Studies is getting a formal, academic understanding of "cinema" through film theory; and the first school devoted to this discipline was the Moscow Film School, established in 1919 and undoubtedly known to Vygotsky, given his devotion to the theater and his knowledge of Stanislavsky's theory of the emotional portrayals of actors (see "On the Problem of the Psychology of the Actor's Creative Work" in Vygotsky, 1999).

This critique of Vygotsky's distinction between spontaneous and scientific concepts thus has merit, even as it's not clear that Vygotsky intended for the distinctions to be so hard and fast. Rather, he may have offered them heuristically, with the binary providing two poles on a continuum that might accommodate "cinema" as being available from more than one origin. It's also possible that Vygotsky might have sought the unity of opposites in his view that strong concepts involve both everyday and formal knowledge such that the theoretical has an empirical basis, and concrete actions in the world rest on a field of abstraction that lends meaning beyond the immediate. What is clear is that Rudneva provided the least sympathetic reading possible, locking Vygotsky into a binary that may never have been his intention to construct, if it is placed in the context of his abundant writing on concept development. Taking Vygotsky's quotes out of context, however, was a useful strategy if the goal was to discredit him. Taking Vygotsky's quotes out of context is also a tactic of the modern, selective quoters who are "eclectics and popularizers of other persons' ideas. Not only have they never engaged in the research and philosophy of their science, they have not even critically assessed each new school" (Vygotsky, 1997b, p. 292).

Rudneva (1937) further found fault with the centerpiece of Vygotsky's developmental theory, the relation between thinking and speech. She argued that this body of work

> consists of anti-Leninist, idealist positions. He regards the whole of man's mental activity not in the light of Lenin's theory of reflection, as a unified but complex dialectic process of active reflection of objective reality in the human consciousness, but as an idealist, immanent (internal, self-sufficient) process taking place independent of social-class relations and independent of people's productive activity.
>
> For Vygotsky speech is an instrument, a tool organizing the whole of mental activity. "An active consciousness whose object is the activity of consciousness itself is what becoming aware means" *([Thinking and Speech]. P. 193)*. According to Marx, the object of consciousness is conscious being; but for Vygotsky consciousness itself is an object: according to Vygotsky, higher scientific concepts are based not on the perception of tangible reality, but rather have speech as their source. The transition from one form of thought to another in the child is, according to Vygotsky, a self-developing process; and higher concepts such as scientific concepts "cannot be introduced into the child's consciousness from without" *([Thinking and Speech]*, p. 176). But, as we know, the development of thought in a child, his acquisition of the more complex forms of thought, takes place under the direct influence of education and upbringing as the child assimilates the cultural legacy of mankind. According to Vygotsky, however, attention and memory are the very special powers that we have within us. He disregards the material foundation of mental phenomena, though it is quite obvious that without a material substrate, we can neither understand nor explain psychological processes. Lenin attached tremendous importance to study of the material substrate of mental phenomena. He wrote: "Scientific psychology has discarded philosophical theories about the soul and jumped directly into study of the material substrate of mental phenomena-nervous processes-and produced, for example, an analysis and explanation of a variety of mental processes." Lenin considered study of the material substrate so important that he compared, to a certain extent, the revolution brought about in psychology by this study to the revolution Marx accomplished in the study of society.
>
> (pp. 76–77)

As somewhat of an aside, I would say that Soviet psychology ultimately had a strong ethereal, spiritual dimension. It is fairly common to come across references to literature and "the soul" in the work of later psychologists. I've argued (Smagorinsky, 2009b) that in an explicitly atheistic nation, one oriented to the material world, many people needed some avenue to spiritual life, and these vehicles provided it. Lenin's rejection of the soul thus was abandoned in post-Stalinist Soviet life, at least among some of its psychologists (e.g., Zinchenko, 2007).

Rudneva's (1937) critique provides one clue regarding how the merit of an idea could be measured: It must be aligned with what Marx and Lenin said. Their orthodoxies provided the foundation for what constituted proper thought about human psychology. Razmyslov (1934) plainly stated the ways in which adherence to the deities of Soviet psychology—political leaders with no training in psychology—should be total, and in which violations constituted an anti-Soviet disposition:

> Following the precise and clear instructions from Engels in his dispute with Duhring[3] (Anti-Duhring[4]), and following Lenin's statements on proletarian morals, in particular following his speech to the Third Congress of the Komsomol, it would seem that anyone who wants to be a Marxist should not err in his treatment of this question. But we who already know Vygotsky's views on the question of the school and other questions should, of course, be on our guard since he is a person who interprets the postulates of the founders of Marxism in his own way. And ... it turns out this is no idle matter. The whole of Vygotsky's interpretation of the conception of morality and moral education is alien to Marxism.
>
> (p. 56)

I've said earlier in this volume that my goal is not to get Marx precisely right, but to see how Marx had been interpreted and appropriated by various Soviets during Vygotsky's lifetime. As this quote indicates, there were doctrinaire readings that made Vygotsky's interpretation "in his own way" unacceptable in light of Lenin's pronouncements on the matter. The required alignment with doctrine at times produced some twisting of an opponent's thoughts. Rudneva (1937) properly distinguished between materiality and the ideal nature of inner speech as a means of developing higher mental functions, but ignored Vygotsky's value on practical activity in claiming that his inner-speech-mediated cognition lacked a pragmatic dimension grounded in worldly action. In fact, he was adamant that the two were mutually integrated and important in developing robust concepts (Vygotsky, 1987). Rudneva continued,

> Vygotsky's harmful system of development and learning is linked to the anti-Leninist "theory of the demise of the school," and should be exposed and discarded, not corrected. From a pedagogical perspective, Vygotsky's statement on formal learning and development serves the anti-Leninist "theory" of the demise of the school. Their methodological foundation is the Machist [characterized by machismo] understanding of intelligence, of the self-development of intelligence, its independence of the external world, and the metaphysical separation of thought from its content.
>
> (Rudneva, 1937, pp. 87–88)

Rudneva's critique positioned Vygotsky as one who would endorse thoughts thinking themselves, an idea that Vygotsky (1987) specifically rejected in his argument that practical, everyday concepts grounded in material engagement with the world are necessary for an ideal, academic concept to have any durability. Yet Rudneva (1937) dismissed Vygotsky's melding of spontaneous and scientific concepts, especially his value on speech as the principal means by which people make sense of, organize, and regulate their worlds:

> Vygotsky's division of concepts into everyday and scientific is totally wrong. According to Vygotsky's "theory," everyday concepts occur as a result of communication with the environment, whereas scientific concepts arise from everyday concepts in the process of formal learning. A scientific concept, according to Vygotsky, can arise only from an everyday concept, and, moreover—and this clearly contradicts the basic positions of Marxism—not through reflection of the objective world in our consciousness;

rather, it is generated by speech. Similarly, Vygotsky's conception of the nature of a concept is clearly at variance with Lenin's theory of a concept. Marx states quite definitely: "Dialectics of concepts is in itself only a conscious reflection of the dialectic movement of the external world" (Marx, "Ludwig Feuerbach and the end of German classical philosophy." *Collected works.* Vol. 1, p. 350). According to Lenin, a concept is a reflection of nature in man's consciousness... . Vygotsky's interpretation of the scientific and the everyday concept indicates that he understands the abstract and the concrete in the spirit of bourgeois psychology, which is based on formal logic. Vygotsky clearly is ignorant of the Marxist-Leninist theory of the abstract and the concrete. The dialectics of the transition from sensation to thought, from the singular to the universal, entails that the universal does not discard the singular, but preserves it.

(Rudneva, 1937, pp. 78–79)

The Soviet litmus test was whether a person matched the proclamations of Marx, Engels, Lenin, or Stalin. If not, the person under scrutiny was bourgeois. Further, Rudneva and other Soviet critics assumed that there is only one interpretation of Marx, and that conception may only come from Lenin or Stalin. Yet there are many ways to interpret and represent Marx (Worsley, 1982), some greatly at odds with one another, each grounded in a worldview that infuses Marx with the observer's biases.

Further, in Rudneva's (1937) conception, using speech to embody a worldly understanding is not sufficiently materialist. To Rudneva, speech may take on a form that is not identical to material reality. Logic is not real; it is a mental fabrication imposed subjectively on reality. And yet, one might say that Rudneva was doing precisely what she critiqued: Fabricating a reality through words that represented an abstract version of Vygotsky that was based on his perceived lack of faithfulness to Marxist-Leninist-Stalinist doctrine, and designed to produce an image available for rejection and neutralization.

Vygotsky and Jaensch

Vygotsky's position as a free-range thinker led to some seemingly inexplicable intellectual associations. He drew on Erich Rudolf Jaensch to understand "eidetic" memory, that which is based on images rather than words. Rudneva (1937) issued a scathing attack on both:

This arch-reactionary "theory" [of eidetic memory] was borrowed by Vygotsky from the German psychologist E. Jaensch, who at present functions as a direct agent of fascism. Among other things, Vygotsky, who knew foreign languages well and who had been abroad, could not have been unfamiliar with the zoological hate entertained by the fascist demagogue Jaensch for the Soviet Union and for Marxism. Nonetheless, he shamelessly dragged this nonsense onto the pages of our press.

(p. 83)

Rudneva's incessant polemics might lead one to doubt this characterization of Jaensch. Yet Jaensch was indeed a full-fledged Nazi with a special hatred of Jewish people like Vygotsky, and was among Germany's leading psychologists in the 1930s (Vine, 2009). Given the rising tensions between Hitler's regime and the Soviets in this decade (Snyder, 2010, 2015), it's not surprising that German psychologists of any kind would be viewed as the enemies of the USSR and Marxism. The lack of reflection on Stalin's own fascist rule is not surprising either, given the role of victimhood in Russian and Soviet history that has enabled the invasion of Ukraine in the 2020s, justified in part by claims of fighting back against a world of hostility and threat (Snyder, 2018).

Jaensch is surely worth criticizing for being an anti-Semitic Nazi from a society bent on exterminating Jewish people and others who did not conform to Hitler's Aryan ideal. Whether that disqualifies him as a source on the role of images in memory is a separate question. Simply being European doomed Jaensch to being anti-Marxist and thus *persona non grata*. Being a leading Nazi psychologist with a virulent hatred of Jewish people might be a disqualifier to a Soviet psychologist of the era, but Vygotsky found some merit in his account of imagaic memories, and referred to him in his work on memory (see Chapter 11). Vygotsky might to be admired for drawing on a psychologist who would have him exterminated as part of Hitler's eugenics program, and who, as a Nazi, viewed the Soviets as existential threats to the survival of nation and race. Or, Vygotsky might be questioned for aligning himself with a monstrous person elevated to the highest ranks of Nazi psychology.

Rudneva (1937) was more concerned with Jaensch's anti-Soviet position than his anti-Semitic position, as might be expected in a society in which Jewish people were initially accepted, but eventually on the outs (Azadovskii & Egorov, 2002). Whether Jaensch's influence on Vygotsky should lead to a ban on Vygotsky's psychological theory was easily resolved by Soviet doctrine. Whether that rejection remains salient in a different time and place is up to individual readers to determine.

The Demise of the School

What, ultimately, is the role of the school? To Soviet Marxists, the school was the breeding ground from which the noble Soviet communist proletariat citizen would emerge, The New Soviet Man, steeped in proper ideology and dedicated to Stalin's doctrinaire version of Marxism. Vygotsky saw education more broadly, with considerable learning taking place outside school, and with the workplace a critical site for socialization. His writing in this area contradicted Rudneva's accusation that he believed that maturation ends with the beginning of adulthood. Yet it also served as a way to claim that Vygotsky's embrace of workplace learning meant that he believed that schools were insufficient for indoctrinatory education, as if both could not work in concert toward the same end. Rudneva (1937) quoted Vygotsky as follows:

Vygotsky concludes:

> A preschooler already possesses all the basic grammatic and syntactic forms. In school, during formal instruction in his native language, the child does not acquire essentially new skills of grammatic and syntactic forms and structures. From this standpoint, learning grammar is truly a useless business. *([Thinking and Speech]).*
>
> (p. 213)

> These ultra-left-wing conclusions, which have done so much damage to the school, derive from Vygotsky's anti-Marxist "theory" of language. An analysis of Vygotsky's statements on higher mental functions and on other issues directly related to the process of learning shows quite clearly that vestiges of the anti-Leninist theory of the demise of the school, mentioned in the resolution of the Central Committee of the All-Union Communist Party (Bolsheviks) of 3 September 1935, are nurtured by Vygotsky's conception.
>
> (pp. 81–82)

One might contest Vygotsky's views on less ideological grounds. In pluralistic societies, children don't arrive at school speaking the same version of the same language. Historically, the standardization of spelling and other conventions became possible with the invention of the printing press, before which written documents produced a Babel of versions of the language that created challenges for people reading across texts, or in texts from outside their discursive communities (Howard-Hill, 2006). Mass schooling with ideological underpinnings—that is, all mass schooling—undoubtedly fostered standardization. Yet many types of English are spoken in each nation in which it serves as a national language. Indeed, linguistic variety in standardized schooling is among the challenges facing teachers in all such nations, including whether to adhere to textbook rules or whether to grant students the right to their own language (Kinloch, 2005). Grammar and language instruction are among the three strands of the English curriculum, along with literature (see Chapter 12) and writing (see Chapter 13), and are taught according to one syntactic system actually spoken by few people (Trudgill & Hannah, 2017). Where Vygotsky's view gains support is in the historical failure of grammar instruction to produce speech and writing that follow the rules specified in textbooks in the English language (Graham & Perrin, 2007; Hillocks, 1986; Weaver, 1996).

Rudneva (1937) took Vygotsky's view of workplace cognitive development as an indication that he believed that schooling is unnecessary, in spite of Vygotsky's also-maligned view that "scientific" or academic learning is a vital part of concept development. Rudneva explained how a Marxist-Leninist position emphasizes the role of school learning in human development, which from another point of view might be considered to be the essence of pedology. She said,

> Intellectual development is highly dependent on the organization and the method of teaching. The unity of the learning and upbringing process and a child's intellectual development follow from the Marxist-Leninist theory of cognition. Learning and development constitute a unity. Learning gives rise to and steers a number of processes of intellectual development. Acquisition of knowledge leads to the development and improvement of mental functions. For us, intellectual development is not so much a precondition for learning as it is its result. But pedological pseudotheoreticians have approached this question with their counterrevolutionary "law" that states that a child's fate is sealed.
>
> But on this question as well as on a number of others, Vygotsky remains the faithful pupil of bourgeois theoreticians, consistently reflecting the influence of Thorndike, Buhler, Piaget, Koffka, and others. Bourgeois psychologists, in accordance with their methodology, regard the development of intelligence as something separate from reality, abstracting it from the concrete conditions of the cognitive learning process, which results either in the separation of intellectual development from formal learning (Piaget), or in the dissolving of formal learning in development (Koffka) and an underestimation of school knowledge.
>
> Vygotsky says that formal learning and development are in unity, formal learning playing the leading role. Formal learning promotes development, but only if it is based not on matured functions, but on maturing functions, on functions that have not yet completed their development—not on development today, but on development tomorrow. The leading role of formal learning is apparent, imaginary; in reality, for Vygotsky, formal learning plays an external role relative to development and makes no alterations in a child's development. This is an absolutely invalid,

scurrilous affirmation. Every teacher knows very well how a child's development improves when he enters school, and that it is completely impossible to separate a child's development from formal learning.

(pp. 83–84)

It's difficult to reconcile this perspective with how Vygotsky characterized schooling, other than to acknowledge his understanding that learning leads development. He spoke of the relation between learning and development on a number of occasions. The critique of Piaget was accurate at the time in that he emphasized biological stages and not socialization; his views over time shifted to recognize the social dimensions of maturation. The idea that Vygotsky believed that learning and development are separate and mutually uninfluential is difficult to find support for (Cole, 2009). He wrote emphatically that two types of psychology were misguided: Those conceiving of a mind without a body (strictly cognitive approaches), and those conceiving of a body without a mind (behaviorism). Nonetheless, Vygotsky was depicted here as a naïve, faithful dupe of capitalist psychologists who did such things.

These various critiques ultimately positioned Vygotsky and the pedologists as anti-schooling. Razmyslov (1934) referenced Vygotsky as envisioning a future in which society is so marinated in learning and developmental possibilities that school won't be necessary; life itself will be the teacher. Razmyslov began by quoting Vygotsky:

[Vygotsky] writes as follows:

In the city of the future probably there will not be one building called a *school*, because school, in the strict sense of the word, means "leisure." But the school, which produced special people in a special building for "leisure" occupations, will become wholly a part of labor and life and will take place in the factories, on the squares, in the museums and the hospitals, and in the cemeteries.

And, once everything is in the public squares, in the museums, in the hospitals, and in the cemeteries, then, of course, there will be no need for instruction. Vygotsky even wrote about this: "As strange as it may sound, teaching as a profession is, from a psychological perspective, a false fact. It will undoubtedly disappear in the near future."

(p. 55; emphasis in original)

Rudneva (1937) made much of this futuristic vision of Vygotsky's as well:

In Vygotsky's opinion, there will be not one building in the city of the future adorned by the sign "school," since school will become wholly a part of work and life, and will exist in factories, on public squares, in museums, in hospitals, and in the cemetery. As we see, we find in Vygotsky complete concurrence with the "leftist" statements by V. N. Shul'gin[5], who campaigned for the stupid anti-Leninist "theory of the demise of the school." Even in his last works, *[Thinking and Speech]* and *[The mental development of the child in the process of formal education]*, Vygotsky denies the influence of formal education on development, and underplays the role of knowledge.

(Rudneva, 1937, p. 76)

And yet Vygotsky's pedological "science of the child" was centered on the developmental role of formal schooling on the conceptual worlds built by Soviet citizens. His attention to schooling makes it hard to accept the idea that he sought its demise. Speaking ideally, he may have been acting as a visionary, looking ahead to how the ideal Soviet society would unfold under the guidance of Marxist leaders, or at least of Shul'gin. During his corporeal existence on earth, however, Vygotsky was deeply concerned with schooling, the author of a textbook on *Educational Psychology*, and a leading pedologist focused on schools and the children who learn within their confines.

Discussion

This review details the attacks made on Vygotsky as a leading agent of pedology, and thus as a target of the Pedology Decree. He was simultaneously criticized for (1) believing in the demise of the school as it yields to everyday learning, (2) being a pedologist concerned with the role of schooling in development, (3) dismissing the learning of adults in proletarian roles, (4) believing in the value of words and speech as the "tool of tools" in human development independent of material reality, (5) being anti-Marxist, anti-Leninist, anti-Stalinist, and anti-Soviet by reading and incorporating the ideas of European and US psychologists and educational theorists, including those of whom he was often critical, (6) finding that biology figures into human development and that environmental factors are not solely responsible for shaping it, (7) believing that ontology recapitulates phylogeny, and (8) reporting his research findings with insufficient attention to method.

As I've reviewed, some of these criticisms are worth noting, while others appear to be polemics at times designed to distort his work and bury his reputation. My goal throughout this volume has not been to defend Vygotsky. Rather, it is to further my effort in, to paraphrase Van der Veer and Valsiner (1991), understanding Vygotsky through a quest for synthesis. As Vygotsky would surely advocate, this task involves a dialectic process in which ideas are engaged to produce a new conception. Engaging Vygotsky with his contemporary critics, current views, and my own interpretations has had value to me as one attempting to see his role in understanding a world separated by an ocean and a century. My hope is that readers benefit in similar ways from my exegesis, and from their own in response.

Notes

1. Herbert Spencer Jennings (1868–1947) was a US biologist, philosopher, and educator. For a biographical memoir, see Sonnenborn (1975). For Jennings's own views, see Jennings (1906).
2. Referenced in this volume as Vygotsky, L. S. (2019). *L. S. Vygotsky's pedagogical works: Volume 1: Foundations of pedology*. (D. Kellogg & N. Veresov, Trans.). Springer.
3. Eugen Karl Dühring (1833–1921) was a Prussian and German philosopher, positivist, economist, and socialist who was a strong critic of Marxism and a virulent anti-Semitist.
4. *Anti-Dühring* is a book by Friedrich Engels, first serialized and then published in 1878, that lays out Engels' Marxist perspective (written while Marx was occupied writing *Das Kapital*).
5. V.N. Shul'gin directed the Institute of School Methods in Moscow, where he was an advocate for the elimination of schools and the shift of the Soviet socialization process to the workplace.

Part V
Conclusion

This brief conclusion attends to the main points available from this investigation without an effort to belabor them, providing the readers an overview of the book.

18 Conclusion

My goal in this volume has been to interrogate the career of L. S. Vygotsky and come to some understandings of what he wrote during his lifetime, and what that work provides and implies for educators today. I hope in this final chapter to emphasize points I find worth thinking about, without belaboring points that I've already made abundantly throughout the preceding chapters.

One of my main contentions throughout has been that Vygotsky was a human being of his place and time. Like all people, he could be contradictory, especially in his career development as he grew in his understandings of human psychology and shifted positions. He also was, as cultural-historical theory would predict, shaped by his own contradictory circumstances. As an oppressed Jewish man during the reign of the Romanovs, he saw the Soviet Union in idyllic terms at the outset of communist rule, a view betrayed by the rise of Stalin and his paranoid drive to eliminate all resistance to his rule, his propaganda, and his interpretation of Marx. Vygotsky had conflicts with some of his dearest collaborators that appear not to have been resolved as he neared death. He participated in the pedology movement in ways that may have reinforced social class differences through the testing regimens used to sort students into appropriate learning tracks, anticipating the tracking dilemmas facing educators a century later. Perhaps most significantly, he died too young to develop cultural-historical theory toward its more mature current state.

This task has been left to his successors, including the many sources I've referenced to help advance my own understandings of what Vygotsky has to offer to 21st-century educators. If we are all standing on the shoulders of giants[1] in order to understand the world, then Vygotsky's broad shoulders have supported considerable weight over time, strengthened by the intellectual power of those whose tonnage he has borne.

Unfortunately, he has also been referenced by people whose selective, minimalist readings and non-readings have distorted his career more than applied its lessons. I hope that I've helped to puncture some of the misconceptions that have developed in relation to who Vygotsky was and what he provided. In particular, he was never the sort of day-to-day pedagogue designing lesson plans and scaffolding student learning of incremental skills. Rather, he was a developmental psychologist wholly concerned with overall human maturity following from both biological affordances and cultural mediation. One of my contentions has been that referencing Vygotsky to support classroom practices, including instructional scaffolding, is misguided and typically based on limited, selective reading of his large corpus of work or of second-hand sources who may have little understanding of what they claim to know. This problem results in what might be a peculiar conclusion to my analysis: *Vygotsky should be referenced by educators far less often than he is*, because most of what he's referenced for in education converts him from an early Soviet pedologist to a modern-day Western pedagogue.

Another area in which Vygotsky merits reconsideration is the perception that he was a cultural relativist. I find him to be less relativistic than he is commonly understood to be, including in my own prior writing. He is very useful for accounting for how people develop in relation to their surroundings; but Vygotsky was clear that some surroundings produce a better human being than others. In particular, communist economies produce better, more moral people than capitalist economies; and technological and industrial societies produce more advanced higher mental functions than do societies with tools and affordances of less technological and industrial complexity.

Each of these contentions is contentious. It's hard to say that the communist societies produced thus far have been kinder, gentler, and more moral places than those they displaced. Being the opposite of one thing (capitalism) does not make an alternative ideal; it instead provides avaricious people with different means of aggregating power, influence, and often wealth. Marx was an enduring, astute critic of capitalism, which doesn't make communism ideal, as its rhetoric asserts it must be. And Marxism has become somewhat of an inkblot, serving whatever purposes its viewer wants it to be, and punishing those whose interpretation violated the tenets set by dogmatic political leaders. Vygotsky was Marxist in one sense, and anti-Marxist in another, depending on the prism through which both Marxism and Vygotsky are viewed.

There's also a good case to be made that advanced technological and industrial nations have not produced advanced ways of thinking, but rather have accelerated the degradation of the planet through waste and the debasement of natural resources. As many indigenous people have argued, native ways oriented to living more harmoniously with nature are far healthier for individuals, communities, and the biota (e.g., Martinez, 2017). It really depends, then, on the teleological direction a nation or community has in mind for its development, the narratives generated to sustain that orientation (Wertsch, 2021), and the material and discursive surroundings within which development takes place.

A relativist would say that each approach has its own benefits and drawbacks. And yet the relativist would have a hard time justifying some cultural ways of being, such as the Nazi movement, which remains a factor and a leading force globally in perpetuating racism and brutality. Cultural-historical theory can explain how someone becomes a Nazi. Other perspectives are required in order to form a judgment about the phenomenon.

As I have argued, Vygotsky was a pedologist concerned with the whole science of the child in all developmental areas, and not a pedagogue with specific, practical ideas on how to run classrooms. Vygotsky may be salient to educators, however, even without attention to lesson plans and teaching methods. His focus on the interplay among play, labor, emotional life, interests, motivation, attention, and relevance suggests the importance of student-oriented classrooms where students, within the guardrails of societal expectations, define and pursue their own learning goals. Those taking a critical pedagogy perspective would argue that these guardrails limit possibilities and ought to be a subject of analysis and reconfiguration to produce a more equitable society. Yet the critical pedagogue owes us more than critique. If viable alternatives in the material world are to emerge, they can't work solely with ideals earnestly sketched on paper.

The imperative to undertake the pedologist's task and integrate all facets of human development into school organization and conduct is both inspiring and challenging. It is inspiring in gearing classrooms to the most heartfelt academic interests of children and youth. It is challenging given the frustrations that such open-ended, student-directed learning have often produced when students lack the sort of focus and intellectual drive that Vygotsky himself had (Smagorinsky, Wilson, & Moore, 2011). Vygotsky's embrace of methods that have largely been successful with students from affluent families in Montessori-style settings appears to be wrapped in the same optimism with which he endorsed Soviet communism for its great potential in creating equity. What remains for educators committed to such ideals is how to undertake such teaching in institutions that don't support them and with students who might not see school as a place where their human development is cultivated toward lifelong trajectories. One might argue that reforming schools would accommodate a greater range of students, resolving the problem. But given schools' stubborn resistance to change and the hostilities surrounding efforts to be more inclusive and respectful to those from outside the mainstream, that ideal is better suited to glowing academic publications than hard-fought public policy.

Vygotsky's attention to the issues specifically of importance to English Language Arts teachers is similarly uneven. His lengthy attention to handwriting, his view that student art has a developmental role but no lasting value, his dismissal of the popular culture of his day, his verbocentric orientation, his views on diagnostic testing for academic placement, and other values are worth considering and debating, and might have limited appeal to the 21st-century educator. On the other hand, in his early 20s, he generated an original, compelling theory of literary criticism involving a catharsis of conflicting elements into intelligent emotions. His outline of this process remains impressive and worth considering in the teaching of literature. Further, he provided, if not explicitly in detailing its implications, a view of textuality that involves both process and product. His process views helped to provide the foundation for Writing to Learn pedagogies in which writers find their topic and meaning by writing and speaking in an exploratory way (Barnes, 1992). Yet this process always comes in service of a textual product that serves as both sign to be interpreted, and a tool through which to construct new meanings. Without deliberately doing so, he resolved a problem that has troubled composition studies since the 1960s.

Vygotsky also took defectology and developed it into a field that transcended the notion of the defect and defective person. His notion of the "secondary disability" to characterize the negative consequences of being surrounded by the assumption of inferiority is tremendously insightful. He offered the idea that blindness, deafness, and cognitive impairment are not problems of individuals, but are social problems requiring able-bodied people to make adjustments and construct affirming environments. His understanding of emotional development lay at the heart of his deep commitment to how people feel about how they are treated. Feeling inferior both degrades their own lives, and limits their participation in useful cultural activity that benefits the collective. It also debases the lives of those who could do something but don't. Vygotsky's collectivist orientation requires shared obligation and responsibility for the greater good, a value that can be at odds with zero-sum beliefs often found in competitive capitalist societies that place individuals at odds with one another in the quest for material and cultural capital.

Vygotsky's compassion for the feelings of those considered inferior through bodily differences speaks to any ostracized social group. Those who face negative assumptions through minoritization based on race, culture, socio-economic status, gender, religion, and other demographic factors may experience the same dysphoria that Vygotsky described in children and youth damaged by war. These feelings follow more from how others treat them than from their points of difference from the preferred norm. Extrapolating Vygotsky's view that these are social problems and responsibilities of the mainstream population to address through the construction of empathic environments would contribute to a more secure, happy, and productive society. Such an effort would require empathic framing (Smagorinsky & Johnson, 2021), that is, making connections emotionally in order to reconsider people intellectually in terms of their human potential. Often this process involves reframing, given that people tend to be socialized to view "the other" as both inferior and threatening to one's personal order.

I set out neither to bury Vygotsky, nor to praise him. My hope in writing this book has been to take a deep dive into the large corpus of writing he left behind in his remarkable career, coupled with extensive reading of the deep divers who have preceded and accompanied me, and learn what I can from the exploration. Much of what he produced is praiseworthy and very relevant nearly a century later. Some of what he wrote has less archival value and remains an artifact of his time and place, a tumultuous time around the globe and in Soviet psychology. Some of what he wrote has been selectively extracted from the context of his career project and distorted to serve other ends. His work was distorted by critics in the 1930s (some of whom made legitimate points), and has been distorted by earnest educators who get their Vygotsky second-hand or through decontextualized excerpts.

From all this chaos and confusion, Vygotsky emerges as a fiercely intellectual man of great ideals and commitment, one that enabled him to work through a deadly disease throughout his teens and adulthood and propel his thinking as far as his deteriorating body would take him. Like every great thinker, he was limited by what his circumstances provided him with, compounded by the increasing authoritarianism of Stalin's Soviet Union. Like every person great or small, he was surrounded by contradiction and thus was contradictory himself. Unlike most people, he generated ideas that remain relevant a century later, and no doubt will be consulted for centuries hence. I hope that my effort in this volume helps to provide some clarity so that people claiming his influence moving forward will do so based on the whole of cultural-historical theory and not its most appealing applications to modern pedagogy.

Note

1 This phrase originated in the 12th century, credited to Bernard of Chartres, and became more broadly famous when Sir Isaac Newton said in 1675, "If I have seen further [than others], it is by standing on the shoulders of giants." I make no claims to seeing further, but do believe that I see better because of the work that has preceded me.

References

Aristotle. (353 B.C.E., date approximated). *Ethica Nicomachea* [*Nicomachean ethics*].
Abel'skaia, R., & Neopikhonova, Ia. S. (1932). Problema razvitiia v nemetskoi psikhologii i ee vliianie na sovetskuiu pedologiiu i psikhologiiu. *Pedologiia, 4*, 27–36. Republished in *Journal of Russian & East European Psychology* as "The problem of development in German psychology and its influence on Soviet pedology and psychology," 2002, 3838.
Abrams, L. S., & Gibbs, J. T. (2002). Disrupting the logic of home-school relations parent involvement strategies and practices of inclusion and exclusion. *Urban Education, 37*(3), 384–407.
Adelson, J. (1972). The political imagination of the young adolescent. In J. Kagan & R. Coles (Eds.), *12 to 16: Early adolescence* (pp. 106–143). Norton.
Adler, A. (1933/1964). *Social interest: A challenge to mankind.* (J. Linton & R. Vaughn, Eds. & Trans.). Capricorn Books.
Adorno, T. W. (2009). *Kultur* and culture. (M. Kalbus, trans.). *Social Text 99, 27*(2), 145–158. https://doi.org/10.1215/01642472-2008-028
Ahmad, F. Z., & Boser, U. (2014, May). *America's leaky pipeline for teachers of color: Getting more teachers of color into the classroom.* Center for American Progress. https://cdn.americanprogress.org/wp-content/uploads/2014/05/TeachersOfColor-report.pdf
American Academy of Pediatrics (2011). Media use by children younger than 2 years. *Pediatrics, 128*(5), 1040–1045.
Angelotti, M., Behnke, R. R., & Carlile, L. W. (1975). Heart rate: A measure of reading involvement. *Research in the Teaching of English, 9*(2), 192–199.
Anson, C. M. (2000). Response and the social construction of error. *Assessing Writing, 7*, 5–21.
Applebee, A. N. (1974). *Tradition and reform in the teaching of English: A history.* National Council of Teachers of English. https://files.eric.ed.gov/fulltext/ED097703.pdf
Applebee, A. N. (1981). *Writing in the secondary school: English and the content areas.* National Council of Teachers of English.
Applebee, A. N. (1986). Problems in process approaches: Toward a reconceptualization of process instruction. In A. R. Petrosky & D. Bartholomae (Eds.), *The teaching of writing. 85th yearbook of the National Society for the Study of Education* (pp. 95–113). University of Chicago Press.
Appleman, D. (2015). *Critical encounters in high school English: Teaching literary theory to adolescents* (3rd ed.). National Council of Teachers of English and Teachers College Press.
Aseyev, S. (2022). *In isolation: Dispatches from occupied Donbas* (L. Wolanskyj, Trans.). Harvard Library of Ukrainian Literature.
Asher-Perrin, E. (2019, September 17). *Spock and the myth of "emotion versus logic."* https://www.tor.com/2019/09/17/spock-and-the-myth-of-emotion-versus-logic/
Asselborn, T., Chapatte, M., & Dillenbourg, P. (2020). Extending the spectrum of dysgraphia: A data driven strategy to estimate handwriting quality. *Scientific Reports: NatureResearch.* https://www.nature.com/articles/s41598-020-60011-8.pdf
Atherton, J. S. (2011). *Learning and teaching: Constructivism in learning.* http://www.learningandteaching.info/learning/constructivism.htm

Autistic Self-Advocates Against ABA. (2020, April 13). *Problematic and traumatic: Why nobody needs ABA*. https://autisticselfadvocatesagainstaba.wordpress.com/2020/04/13/problematic-and-traumatic-why-nobody-needs-aba/

Azadovskii, K., & Egorov, B. (2002). From anti-Westernism to anti-Semitism: Stalin and the impact of the "anti-cosmopolitan" campaigns on Soviet culture. *Journal of Cold War Studies, 4*(1), 66–80.

Baglieri, S. (2017). *Disability studies and the inclusive classroom: Critical practices for embracing diversity in education* (2nd ed.). Routledge.

Baker-Bell, A. (2020). *Linguistic justice: Black language, literacy, identity, and pedagogy*. Routledge.

Baker-Bell, A., Williams-Farrier, B. J., Jackson, D., Johnson, L., Kynard, C., & McMurtry, T. (2020, July). *This ain't another statement! This is a DEMAND for Black linguistic justice!* Conference on College Composition and Communication Special Committee on Composing a CCCC Statement on Anti-Black Racism and Black Linguistic Justice, Or, Why We Cain't Breathe! https://cccc.ncte.org/cccc/demand-for-black-linguistic-justice

Bakhtin, M. M. (1973). *Problems of Dostoevsky's poetics* (R. W. Potsel, Trans.). Ardis.

Bakhtin, M. M. (1986). *Speech genres and other late essays* (C. Emerson & M. Holquist, Eds.; V. W. McGee, Trans.). University of Texas Press.

Bakhurst, D. (2007). Vygotsky's demons. In H. Daniels, M. Cole, & J. V. Wertsch (Eds.), *The Cambridge companion to Vygotsky* (pp. 50–76). Cambridge University Press.

Baldwin, J. M. (1896). A new factor in evolution. *The American Naturalist, 30*(354), 441–451. https://doi.org/10.1086/276408

Balingit, M. (2022, September 13). Wanted: Teachers. No training necessary. *The Washington Post*. https://www.washingtonpost.com/education/2022/09/13/teacher-requirements-shortage-jobs/

Baquedano-López, P., Alexander, R. A., & Hernandez, S. J. (2013). Equity issues in parental and community involvement in schools: What teacher educators need to know. *Review of Research in Education, 37*, 149–182. https://doi.org/10.3102/0091732X12459718

Barnes, D. (1992). *From communication to curriculum*. Heinemann.

Baroni, A. (2011). Alphabetic vs. non-alphabetic writing: Linguistic fit and natural tendencies. *Rivista di Linguistica, 23*(2), 127–159.

Barrs, M. (2017). Rediscovering Vygotsky's concept of the ZPD: Stanley Mitchell's new translation of 'the problem of teaching [obuchenie] and mental development at school age. *Changing English, 24*(4), 345–358.

Barshay, J. (2021, November 22). PROOF POINTS: The number of college graduates in the humanities drops for the eighth consecutive year. *The Hechinger Report*. https://hechingerreport.org/proof-points-the-number-of-college-graduates-in-the-humanities-drops-for-the-eighth-consecutive-year/

Bartlett, T. (2003). Why Johnny can't write, even though he went to Princeton: Many top colleges fear that their students lack basic composition skills. *The Chronicle of Higher Education*. http://chronicle.com/free/v49/i17/17a03901.htm

Basevich, E. (2022). What is an anti-racist philosophy of race and history? A new look at Kant, Hegel, and Du Bois. *Critical Philosophy of Race, 10*(1), 71–89.

Bass, C. (2019). Establishing a presumption of competence in the ELA classroom: One teacher's story of creating space for autistic culture. *Ought: The Journal of Autistic Culture, 1*(1), Article 14. https://scholarworks.gvsu.edu/ought/vol1/iss1/14

Bazerman, C., & Paradis, J. (Eds.) (1991). *Textual dynamics of the professions: Historical and contemporary studies of writing in professional communities*. University of Wisconsin Press.

BBC. (1990). *The butterflies of Zagorsk*. (M. Dean, Producer). Author. Retrieved July 17, 2017, from http://lchc.ucsd.edu/Movies/Butterflies_of_Zagorsk.mp4

Beatty, W. (Dir.). (1981). *Reds*. Paramount Pictures.

Belgarde, M. J., LoRé, R. K., & Meyer, R. (2010). American Indian adolescent literacy. In L. Christenbury, R. Bomer, & P. Smagorinsky (Eds.), *Handbook on adolescent literacy research* (pp. 415–429). Guilford.

Bell, C. (2020). "Maybe if they let us tell the story I wouldn't have gotten suspended": Understanding Black students' and parents' perceptions of school discipline. *Children and Youth Services Review, 110*, 1–11. https://doi.org/10.1016/J.CHILDYOUTH.2020.104757

Bellamy, P. (2021, May 19). Letter: Concerned Washougal parents kicked out of school board meeting. *ClarkCountyToday.com*. https://www.clarkcountytoday.com/opinion/letter-concerned-washougal-parents-kicked-out-of-school-board-meeting/

Benson, E. (2018, January 18). How John Dewey destroyed the souls of our children. *The Imaginative Conservative*. https://theimaginativeconservative.org/2018/01/john-dewey-edwin-benson.html

Berkenkotter, C., & Huckin, T. (1995). *Genre knowledge in disciplinary communication: Cognition/culture/power*. Erlbaum.

Berliner, D. (2011). Rational responses to high stakes testing: The case of curriculum narrowing and the harm that follows. *Cambridge Journal of Education, 41*(3), 287–302.

Bernasconi, R. (2003a). Will the real Kant please stand up: The challenge of enlightenment racism to the study of the history of philosophy. *Radical Philosophy, 117*, 13–22.

Bernasconi, R. (2003b). Hegel's racism: A reply to McCarney. *Radical Philosophy, 119*, 35–37.

Bernstein, B. (1960). Language and social class. *The British Journal of Sociology, 11*(3), 271–276.

Bernstein, B. (1971). *Class, codes and control: Theoretical studies towards a sociology of language*. Routledge & Kegan Paul.

Berridge, V., & Loughlin, K. (2005). Smoking and the new health education in Britain 1950s–1970s. *American Journal of Public Health, 95*(6), 956–964. https://ajph.aphapublications.org/doi/pdf/10.2105/AJPH.2004.037887

Bezemer, J., & Kress, G. (2008). Writing in multimodal texts: A social semiotic account of designs for learning. *Written Communication, 25*(2), 166–195.

Bhattacharya, U. (2022a). "I am a parrot": Literacy ideologies and rote learning. *Journal of Literacy Research, 54*(2), 113–136.

Bhattacharya, U. (2022b). UGA professor: We must stop segregating children with disabilities. *Atlanta Journal-Constitution*. https://www.ajc.com/education/get-schooled-blog/uga-professor-we-must-stop-segregating-children-with-disabilities/5IREQPUMKVHB3FILF7QKKIECGQ/

Bickmore, S. T., Smagorinsky, P., & O'Donnell-Allen, C. (2005). Tensions between traditions: The role of contexts in learning to teach. *English Education, 38*, 23–52.

Bikchentay, I. N. (1931). Ocherednye zadachi natspedologii [The next tasks of the pedology of nationalities]. *Pedologiya [Pedology], 4*(7–8), 31–36. [In Russian]

Bistoen, G., Vanheule, S., & Craps, S. (2014). *Nachträglichkeit*: A Freudian perspective on delayed traumatic reactions. *Theory & Psychology, 24*(5), 668–687.

Black, E. (2003, September). The horrifying American roots of Nazi eugenics. *The History News Network*. https://blog.fdik.org/2021-01/eugenik.pdf

Blair, K. S., Richell, R. A., Mitchell, D. G. V., Leonard, A., Morton, J., & Blair, R. J. R. (2006). They know the words, but not the music: Affective and semantic priming in individuals with psychopathy. *Biological Psychology, 73*(2), 114–123.

Bleich, D. (1975). *Readings and feelings: An introduction to subjective criticism*. National Council of Teachers of English.

Bleich, D. (2013). *The materiality of language: Gender, politics, and the university*. Indiana University Press.

Blonskiy, P. P. (1922). *Pedagogika*. Rabotnik Prosveshchenija.

Blonskiy, P. P. (1925/1930). *Osnovy pedagogiki*. Rabotnik Prosveshchenija.

Bloomberg. (2022, September 13). *Bloomberg billionaires index*. Author. https://www.bloomberg.com/billionaires/

Boden, M. A. (2006). *Mind as machine: A history of cognitive science*, 2 vols. Oxford University Press.

Bohan, C. H., Bradshaw, L. Y., & Morris, W. H. (2020). The mint julep consensus: An analysis of late 19th century Southern and Northern textbooks and their impact on the history curriculum. *The Journal of Social Studies Research, 44*(1), 139–149.

Bonnett, A. (2004). *The idea of the West: Culture, politics, and history*. Palgrave Macmillan.

Boorstein, M., & Clement, S. (2023, January 12). Survey finds 'classical fascist' antisemitic views widespread in U.S. *The Washington Post*. https://www.washingtonpost.com/dc-md-va/2023/01/12/antisemitism-anti-defamation-league-survey/

Borst, H., & Spann, R. T. (2023). Piaget's stages of cognitive development. *Forbes*. https://www.forbes.com/health/mind/piagets-stages-of-cognitive-development/

Braddock, R., Lloyd-Jones, R., & Schoer, L. (1963). *Research in written composition*. National Council of Teachers of English.

Brainerd, C. J. (2003). Jean Piaget, learning research, and American education. In B. J. Zimmerman & D. H. Schunk (Eds.), *Educational psychology: A century of contributions* (pp. 251–287). Erlbaum.

Brayboy, B. M. J., & Maughan, E. (2009). Indigenous knowledges and the story of the bean. *Harvard Educational Review*, *79*(1), 1–21.

Bregman, A. (2022, December 20). Soviet art returns amidst Russia-Ukraine War. *Forbes*. https://www.forbes.com/sites/alexandrabregman/2022/12/20/soviet-art-returns-amidst-russia-ukraine-war/?sh=f427e091d164.

Brent, J., & Naumov, P. V. (2004). *Stalin's last crime: The doctors' plot*. John Murray.

Britton, J. Burgess, T., Martin, N., McLeod, A., & Rosen, H. (1975). *The development of writing abilities* (pp. 11–18). Macmillan.

Bromley, K. (2010). Picture a world without pens, pencils, and paper: The unanticipated future of reading and writing. *Journal of College Reading and Learning*, *41*(1), 97–108.

Brown, K. L. (2003). From teacher-centered to learner-centered curriculum: Improving learning in diverse classrooms. *Education*, *124*(1), 49–54.

Brownell, M. T., Sindelar, P. T., Kiely, M. T., & Danielson, L. C. (2010). Special education teacher quality and preparation: Exposing foundations, constructing a new model. *Exceptional Children*, *76*(3), 357–377.

Brummelman, E., Thomaes, S., Orobio de Castro, B., Overbeek, G., & Bushman, B. J. (2014). "That's not just beautiful—That's incredibly beautiful!": The adverse impact of inflated praise on children with low self-esteem. *Psychological Science*, *25*(3), 728–735.

Bruner, J. (1978). The role of dialogue in language acquisition. In A. Sinclair, R. J. Jarvelle, & W. J. M. Levelt (Eds.), *The child's concept of language* (pp. 241–256). Springer-Verlag.

Bruner, J. S. (1960). *The process of education*. Harvard University Press.

Bühler, K. (1922). *Die geistige Entwicklung des Kindes* (3rd ed.). Verlag von Gustav Fischer.

Burgerstein, L. (1910). Co-education and hygiene with special reference to European experience and views. *The Pedagogical Seminary*, *17*(1), 1–15.

Burke, K. (1966). *Language as symbolic action: Essays on life, literature, and method*. University of California Press.

Byford, A. (2016). Imperial normativities and the sciences of the child: The politics of development in the USSR, 1920s–1930s. *Ab imperio*, *2*, 71–124.

Byford, A. (2021). Pedology as occupation in the early Soviet Union. In A. Yasnitski (Ed.), *A history of Marxist psychology: The Golden Age of Soviet science* (pp. 109–127). Routledge. https://dro.dur.ac.uk/31088/1/31088.pdf?DDD36+mzjs38

Cajete, G. (1994). *Look to the mountain: An ecology of indigenous education*. Kivaki Press.

Capra, F. (1946). *It's a wonderful life*. RKO Radio Pictures.

Caroli, D., & Mecacci, L. (2020). Forbidden science: The dismantling of pedology and the listing of the works of pedologists in the Soviet Union in 1936–1938. *European Yearbook of the History of Psychology*, *6*, 11–61.

Castañeda, J. G. (1997). *Compañero: The life and death of Che Guevara* (M. Castañeda, Trans.). Vintage.

Castano, E., & Giner-Sorolla, R. (2006). Not quite human: Infrahumanization in response to collective responsibility for intergroup killing. *Journal of Personality and Social Psychology*, *90*(5), 804–818.

Cazden, C. B. (1996). Selective traditions: Readings of Vygotsky in writing pedagogy. In D. Hicks (Ed.), *Child discourse and social learning: An interdisciplinary perspective* (pp. 165–185). Cambridge University Press.

Ceci, S. J., & Papierno, P. B. (2005). The rhetoric and reality of gap closing: When the "have-nots" gain but the "haves" gain even more. *American Psychologist, 60*(2), 149–160.

Chaiklin, S. (2003). The zone of proximal development in Vygotsky's analysis of learning and instruction. In A. Kozulin, B. Gindis, V. Ageyev, & S. Miller (Eds.), *Vygotsky's educational theory and practice in cultural context* (pp. 39–63). Cambridge University Press.

Chase, W. M. (2009, September 1). The decline of the English Department. *The American Scholar.* https://theamericanscholar.org/the-decline-of-the-english-department/#:~:text=English%3A%20from%207.6%20percent%20of%20the%20majors%20to,percent%20History%3A%20from%2018.5%20percent%20to%2010.7%20percent

Cherry, R. R. (2007, September 15). The Judeo-Christian values of America. *American Thinker.* https://www.americanthinker.com/articles/2007/09/the_judeochristian_values_of_a.html

Chicago Tribune Editorial Board. (2018, December 24). Student journalists get shut down. *Chicago Tribune.* https://www.chicagotribune.com/opinion/editorials/ct-edit-student-newspaper-arkansas-football-20181203-story.html

Chittka, L. (2022). *The mind of a bee.* Princeton University Press.

Clegg, J. (2021). *Scatterling of Africa.* Pan Macmillan.

Cohen, D. K. (1989). Teaching practice: Plus que ça change. In P. W. Jackson (Ed.), *Contributing to educational change: Perspectives on research and practice* (pp. 27–84). McCutchan.

Cohen, D. K. (1998). Dewey's problem. *The Elementary School Journal, 98*(5), 427–446.

Cohen, D. J., & Lippert, S. K. (1999). The lure of technology: Panacea or pariah? *Journal of Management Education, 23*(6), 743–746.

Cole, M. (1993, March-April). *Vygotsky and writing: Reflections from a distant discipline.* Paper presented at the Annual Meeting of the Conference on College Composition and Communication, San Diego, CA. https://files.eric.ed.gov/fulltext/ED360627.pdf

Cole, M. (1996). *Cultural psychology: A once and future discipline.* Harvard University Press.

Cole, M. (2002). Culture and development. In H. Keller, Y. H. Poortinga, & A. Schölmerich (Eds.), *Between culture and biology: Perspectives on ontogenetic development* (pp. 303–319). Cambridge University Press.

Cole, M. (2005). Cross-cultural and historical perspectives on the developmental consequences of education. *Human Development, 48,* 195–216.

Cole, M. (2009). The perils of translation: A first step in reconsidering Vygotsky's theory of development in relation to formal education. *Mind, Culture and Activity, 16,* 291–295.

Cole, M. (2022). Remembering Alexander Luria. *Cultural-Historical Psychology, 18*(3), 54–57.

Cole, M., John-Steiner, V., Scribner, S., & Souberman, E. (1978). Editors' preface. In M. Cole, V. John-Steiner, S. Scribner, & E. Souberman (Eds.), *Mind in society: The development of higher psychological processes.* Harvard University Press.

Cole, M., & Jornet, A. (2021). Background to the special issue on pedology. *Mind, Culture, and Activity, 28*(4), 285.

Cole, M., Levitin, K., & Luria, A. (2006). *The autobiography of Alexander Luria: A dialogue with the making of mind.* Erlbaum.

Collins, B. (2020). *The power of the one.* Sweetwater Sounds.

Compton-Lilly, C., Mitra, A., Guay, M., & Spence, L. K. (2020). A confluence of complexity: Intersections among reading theory, neuroscience, and observations of young readers. *Reading Research Quarterly, 55,* 185–195.

Conquest, R. (1986). *The harvest of sorrow: Soviet collectivization and the terror-famine.* Oxford University Press.

Cooper, R., & Zimmerman, M. (2011, August 24). Do video games influence violent behavior? *Michigan Youth Violence Prevention Center.* https://yvpc.sph.umich.edu/video-games-influence-violent-behavior/#:~:text=Researchers%20have%20reported%20experimental%20evidence,of%20child%2Dinitiated%20virtual%20violence.

Correa Arias, C. (2020). Action research, literacy, and teacher education in rural normal schools in Mexico. In Y. Gayol, P. Rosas, & P. Smagorinsky (Eds.), *Developing culturally and historical sensitive teacher education: Global lessons from a literacy education program* (pp. 245–266). Bloomsbury.

Council for Education Policy, Research, and Improvement. (2003). *Florida teachers and the teaching profession.* Author. http://www.cepri.state.fl.us/Documents/Meetings/TeachMP.pdf#:~:text=The%20most%20important%20factor%20affecting%20the%20quality%20of,are%20the%20most%20influential%20determinants%20of%20student%20achievement.

Cowie, H., Hutson, N., Jennifer, D., & Myers, C. A. (2008). Taking stock of violence in U.K. schools: Risk, regulation, and responsibility. *Education and Urban Society, 40*(4), 494–505.

Craig, T., & Rozsa, L. (2023, February 7). In his fight against 'woke' schools, DeSantis tears at the seams of a diverse Florida. *The Washington Post.* https://www.washingtonpost.com/nation/2022/02/07/desantis-anti-woke-act/

Crenshaw, K. W. (1988). Race, reform and retrenchment: Transformation and legitimation in anti-discrimination law. *Harvard Law Review, 101*(7), 1331–1387. https://doi.org/10.2307/1341398

Crenshaw, K. W. (2023). *On intersectionality: Essential writings.* The New Press.

Critchfield, R. (1938). *A study of pneumographic recordings of respiratory movements during overt reading and a correlation of the results with an objective reading scale.* Claremont Colleges.

Crosnoe, R. (2011). *Fitting in, standing out: Navigating the social challenges of high school to get an education.* Cambridge University Press.

Csikszentmihalyi, M. (1990). *Flow: The psychology of optimal experience.* Harper & Row.

Csikszentmihalyi, M., Rathunde, K. R., & Whalen, S. (1993). *Talented teenagers: The roots of success and failure.* Cambridge University Press.

Culotta, E. (2012). Roots of racism. *Science, 336*(6083), 825–827. https://doi.org/10.1126/science.336.6083.825

Daily News Egypt. (2016, September 22). Why Moscow's most iconic church used to be a swimming pool. https://dailynewsegypt.com/2016/09/22/why-moscows-most-iconic-church-used-to-be-a-swimming-pool/

Damasio, A. (2021). *Feeling & knowing: Making minds conscious.* Pantheon Books.

Danforth, S., & Gabel, S. L. (2007). *Vital questions facing disability studies in education.* Peter Lang.

Daniels, H. (2007). Pedagogy. In H. Daniels, M. Cole, & J. V. Wertsch (Eds.), *The Cambridge companion to Vygotsky* (pp. 307–331). Cambridge University Press.

Daniels, H., Cole, M., & Wertsch, J. V. (Eds.) (2007). *The Cambridge companion to Vygotsky.* Cambridge University Press.

Darwin, C. (1859). *On the origin of species by means of natural selection, or the preservation of favoured races in the struggle for life.* John Murray.

Davies, S. (2007). "Us against them": Social identity in Soviet Russia, 1934–41. In P. Waldron (Ed.), *The Soviet Union* (pp. 229–248). Routledge.

Davydov, V. V. (1997a). Editor's note. In L. S. Vygotsky, *Educational psychology* (L. S. Vygotsky & V. V. Davydov, Eds.; R. Silverman, Trans.) (pp. xiii–xv). St. Lucie Press.

Davydov, V. V. (1997b). Introduction. In L. S. Vygotsky, *Educational psychology* (L. S. Vygotsky & V. V. Davydov, Eds.; R. Silverman, Trans.) (pp. xxi–xxxix). St. Lucie Press.

Dawkins, R. (1976). *The selfish gene.* Oxford University Press.

De Leersnyder, J. (2017). Emotional acculturation: A first review. *Current Opinion in Psychology, 17*, 67–73.

De Saussure, F. (1916). *Cours de linguistique générale* (C. Bally & A. Sechehaye, with A. Riedlinger (Eds.). Payot.

De Waal, F. (2017). *Are we smart enough to know how smart animals are?* W.W. Norton & Company.

Deeg, K. S., Leiserowitz, A., Maibach, E., Kotcher, J., & Marlon, J. (2019, January 9). Who is changing their mind about global warming and why? *Yale Program on Climate Change Communication.* https://climatecommunication.yale.edu/publications/who-is-changing-their-mind-about-global-warming-and-why/

Deloria, V. (1974). *Behind the trail of broken treaties: An Indian declaration of independence.* University of Texas Press.

Depaepe, M. (1998). The heyday of paedology in Belgium (1899–1914): A positivistic dream that did not come true. *International Journal of Educational Research, 27*(8), 687–697.

Dewey, J. (1897, January). My pedagogic creed. *School Journal, 54*, 77–80.

Dewey, J. (1902). *The child and the curriculum*. University of Chicago Press.

Dewey, J. (1916). *Democracy and education: An introduction to the philosophy of education*. Macmillan.

Dewey, J. (1934). *Art as experience*. Capricorn Books.

Diamond, J. (1991). *The third chimpanzee: The evolution and future of the human animal*. Hutchinson Radius.

Diamond, J. (1997). *Guns, germs, and steel: The fates of human societies*. W.W. Norton & Company.

Diderot, D. (1830). *Paradox of the actor [Paradoxe sur le comédien]*. Société Française d'Imprimerie et de Librairie.

Dietze, P., & Knowles, E. D. (2020). Social class predicts emotion perception and perspective-taking performance in adults. *Personality and Social Psychology Bulletin*. https://journals.sagepub.com/doi/full/10.1177/0146167220914116

Donner, J. K. (2021, July 1). A Black valedictorian was forced to share the title after white parents complained. *Mic.com*. https://www.mic.com/life/a-black-valedictorian-was-forced-to-share-the-title-after-white-parents-complained-82377709

Downey, M. (2021, May 23). OPINION: Turning equity lens on schools exposes white unhappiness. *Atlanta Journal-Constitution*. https://www.ajc.com/education/get-schooled-blog/opinion-turning-equity-lens-on-schools-exposes-white-unhappiness/5YUPAKNZPRHONJP6JGEF4553AQ/

Downey, M. (2022, August 15). Opinion: Sexist dress codes erode school pledges of equity, excellence. *Atlanta Journal-Constitution*. https://www.ajc.com/education/get-schooled-blog/opinion-sexist-dress-codes-erode-school-pledges-of-equity-excellence/LST6LA7NXFH3LHDR5BWEXORTI4/

Doyle, A.C. (1890, February). *The sign of the four; or The problem of the Sholtos. Lippincott's Monthly Magazine*.

Draper, H. (1987). *The 'dictatorship of the proletariat' in Marx and Engels*. Monthly Review Press. https://www.marxists.org/subject/marxmyths/hal-draper/article2.htm

Dunckley, V. L. (2015). *Reset your child's brain: A four-week plan to end meltdowns, raise grades, and boost social skills by reversing the effects of electronic screen-time*. New World Library.

Dunne, L. (2009). Discourses of inclusion: A critique. *Power and Education, 1*(1), 42–56.

Durkin, K., & Barber, B. (2002). Not so doomed: Computer game play and positive adolescent development. *Applied Developmental Psychology, 23*, 373–392.

Durlak, J. A., Weissberg, R. P., Dymnicki, A. B., Taylor, R. D., & Schellinger, K. B. (2011). The impact of enhancing students' social and emotional learning: A meta-analysis of school-based universal interventions. *Child Development, 82*(1), 405–432.

Dutton, Y. C., & Heath, C. (2010). Cultural evolution: Why are some cultural variants more successful than others? In M. Schaller, A. Norenzayan, S. J. Heine, T. Yamagishi, & T. Kameda (Eds.), *Evolution, culture, and the human mind* (pp. 49–70). Psychology Press.

Dyson, A. H. (1990). Weaving possibilities: Rethinking metaphors for early literacy development. *Language Arts, 81*(2), 100–109.

Easterbrook, S. (2020). *75th anniversary of ENIAC*. https://twunroll.com/article/1361498261010399235

Eckert, P. (1989). *Jocks & burnouts: Social categories and identity in high school*. Teachers College Press.

Edenborg, E. (2022). Putin's anti-gay war on Ukraine. *Boston Review*. https://bostonreview.net/articles/putins-anti-gay-war-on-ukraine/

Edmondson, H. T. (2006). *John Dewey & the decline of American education: How the patron saint of schools has corrupted teaching & learning*. Intercollegiate Studies Institute.

Elbow, P. (1973). *Writing without teachers*. Oxford University Press.

Elliott, J. E. (1986). On the possibility of Marx's moral critique of capitalism. *Review of Social Economy, 44*(2), 130–144.

Ellis, G., & Solms, M. (2018). *Beyond evolutionary psychology: How and why neuropsychological modules arise.* Cambridge University Press.

Emig, J. (1971). *The composing processes of twelfth graders.* NCTE Research Report No. 13. National Council of Teachers of English.

Emig, J. (1977). Writing as a mode of learning. *College Composition and Communication, 28*(2), 122–128.

Engels, F. (1925/1978). *Dialektik der natur* [*Dialectics of nature*]. Dietz Verlag.

Erbil, D. G. (2020). A review of flipped classroom and cooperative learning method within the context of Vygotsky theory. *Frontiers in Psychology,* https://www.frontiersin.org/articles/10.3389/fpsyg.2020.01157/full, https://doi.org/10.3389/fpsyg.2020.01157

Escobar, A. (1995). *Encountering development: The making and unmaking of the Third World.* Princeton University Press.

Everett, S. (2018). "Untold stories": Cultivating consequential writing with a Black male student through a critical approach to metaphor. *Research in the Teaching of English, 53*(1), 34–57.

Ewing, E. T. (2001). Restoring teachers to their rights: Soviet education and the 1936 denunciation of pedology. *History of Education Quarterly, 41,* 471–493.

Ewing, E. T. (2002). *The teachers of Stalinism: Policy, practice, and power in Soviet schools of the 1930s.* Peter Lang.

Farr, M. (1993). Essayist literacy and other verbal performances. *Written Communication, 10*(1), 4–38.

Faulkner, W. (1951). *Requiem for a nun.* Random House.

Felepchuk, E. (2021). Autism-as-machine metaphors in film and television sound. *Ought: The Journal of Autistic Culture, 2*(2), Article 9. https://scholarworks.gvsu.edu/ought/vol2/iss2/9

Figes, O. (1997). *A people's tragedy: The Russian Revolution: 1891–1924.* Viking Penguin.

Fish, S. (1980). *Is there a text in this class?: The authority of interpretive communities.* Harvard University Press.

Fitt, R. A. (2020, October 19). Conservative activists in Texas have shaped the history all American children learn. *The Washington Post.* https://www.washingtonpost.com/outlook/2020/10/19/conservative-activists-texas-have-shaped-history-all-american-children-learn/

Fitzpatrick, S. (1979). *Education and social mobility in the Soviet Union 1921–1934.* Cambridge University Press.

Flaherty, C. (2018, July 18). The evolving English major. *Inside Higher Ed.* https://www.insidehighered.com/news/2018/07/18/new-analysis-english-departments-says-numbers-majors-are-way-down-2012-its-not-death

Flavell, B. (2022, January 15). The logic of atheism. *Atheist Alliance International.* https://www.atheistalliance.org/blog/the-logic-of-atheism/

Fleer, M., González Rey, F., Veresov, N. (2017). Continuing the dialogue: Advancing conceptions of emotions, perezhivanie and subjectivity for the study of human development. In M. Fleer, F. González Rey, & N. Veresov (Eds), *Perezhivanie, emotions and subjectivity: Advancing Vygotsky legacy* (pp 247–261). Springer.

Flores, M. (2022, May 30). The New World Order: The historical origins of a dangerous modern conspiracy theory. *Middlebury Institute of International Studies Center on Terrorism, Extremism, and Counterterrorism.* https://www.middlebury.edu/institute/academics/centers-initiatives/ctec/ctec-publications/new-world-order-historical-origins-dangerous

Four Arrows. (2020). *The red road: Linking diversity and inclusion initiatives to indigenous worldview.* Information Age Publishing.

Four Arrows (Ed.). (2006). *Unlearning the language of conquest: Scholars expose anti-Indianism in America.* University of Texas Press.

Francois, C. (2022, May 9). Opinion: George Washington University needs a new name. *The Washington Post.* https://www.washingtonpost.com/opinions/2022/05/09/george-washington-university-needs-new-name/

Freeman, E. (2005). No child left behind and the denigration of race. *Equity & Excellence in Education, 38*(3), 190–199.

Freire, P. (1970). *Pedagogy of the oppressed.* (M. B. Ramos, Trans.). Herder & Herder.

Gallagher, C. (1997). The history of literary criticism. *Daedalus, 126*(1), 133–153.
Galvin, S., & Greenhow, C. (2020). Writing on social media: A review of research in the high school classroom. *TechTrends, 64,* 57–69. https://doi.org/10.1007/s11528-019-00428-9
Gardner, H. (1983). *Frames of mind: The theory of multiple intelligences.* Basic Books.
Gates, H. L. Jr. (1988). *The signifying monkey: A theory of African American literary criticism.* Oxford University Press.
Gaupp, R. (1908). *Psychologie des kindes* [*Psychology of children*]. https://babel.hathitrust.org/cgi/pt?id=ucl.$b123699&view=1up&seq=5
Gayol, Y., Rosas, P., & Smagorinsky, P. (Eds.) (2020). *Developing culturally and historical sensitive teacher education: Global lessons from a literacy education program.* Bloomsbury.
Gilbert, M. (1994). *The First World War: A complete history.* Henry Holt and Company.
Gilligan, C. (1982). *In a different voice: Psychological theory and women's development.* Harvard University Press.
Gilligan, C. (2020). Classics@9: Carol Gilligan, looking back to look forward: Revisiting *in a different voice. The Center for Hellenic Studies, Harvard University.* https://chs.harvard.edu/classics9-carol-gilligan-looking-back-to-look-forward-revisiting-in-a-different-voice/
Glaude, E. S. (2016). *Democracy in Black: How race still enslaves the American soul.* Crown.
Glick, J. (1997). Prologue. In *The collected works of L. S. Vygotsky. Volume 4: The history of the development of higher mental functions* (R. Rieber, Ed.; M. J. Hall, Trans.). Plenum.
Goffman, E. (1959). *The presentation of self in everyday life.* The Overlook Press.
Golec de Zavala, A., Lantos, D., & Keenan, O. (2021). Collective narcissism and the motivational underpinnings of the populist backlash. In J.P. Forgas, W.D. Crano, & K. Fiedler (Eds.), The psychology of populism: The tribal challenge to liberal democracy (pp. 105–122). Routledge.
Gómez, S. A. (2018, May 19). Ten Marxist ideas that define the 21st century. *Monthly Review Online.* https://mronline.org/2018/05/19/ten-marxist-ideas-that-define-the-21st-century/
González Rey, F. (2011). A re-examination of defining moments in Vygotsky's work and their implications for his continuing legacy. *Mind, Culture, and Activity, 18,* 257–275.
González Rey, F. (2017). Advances in subjectivity from a cultural-historical perspective: Unfoldings and consequences for cultural studies today. In M. Fleer, F. González Rey, & N. Veresov (Eds.), *Perezhivanie, emotions and subjectivity: Advancing Vygotsky's legacy* (pp. 173–195). Springer.
Goodlad, J. (1984). *A place called school: Prospects for the future.* McGraw-Hill.
Gould, S. J. (1977). *Ontogeny and phylogeny.* The Belknap Press of Harvard University Press.
Gould, S. J. (1981). *The mismeasure of man.* Penguin.
Graham, L. R. (1987). *Science, philosophy, and human behavior in the Soviet Union.* Columbia University Press.
Graham, S., & Perrin, D. (2007). A meta-analysis of writing instruction for adolescent students. *Journal of Educational Psychology, 99*(3), 445–476.
Graves, D. (1983). *Writing: Teachers and children at work.* Heineman.
Green, M. S. (2021). *Lincoln and Native Americans.* Southern Illinois University Press.
Griffith, M. D., Kuss, D. J., & King, D. L. (2012). Video game addiction: Past, present and future. *Current Psychiatry Reviews, 8*(4), 308–318.
Groenke, S. L., Haddix, M., Glenn, W. J., Kirkland, D., Price-Denis, D., & Coleman-King, C. (2015). Disrupting and dismantling the dominant vision of youth of color. *English Journal, 104*(3), 35–40.
Grossman, P. L., Smagorinsky, P., & Valencia, S. (1999). Appropriating tools for teaching English: A theoretical framework for research on learning to teach. *American Journal of Education, 108*(1), 1–29.
Grzymala-Busse, A. (2019, April 17). Once, the 'Judeo-Christian tradition' united Americans. Now it divides them. *The Washington Post.* https://www.washingtonpost.com/politics/2019/04/17/once-judeo-christian-tradition-united-americans-now-it-divides-them/
Gvozdetsky, V., & Budreyko, E. (2021). "Whoever is not with us is against us": (In commemoration of the 90th anniversary of the Case of the Industrial Party)," *2021 International Conference Engineering Technologies and Computer Science (EnT),* Moscow (pp. 65–71). https://doi.org/10.1109/EnT52731.2021.00018

Haidt, J. (2012). *The righteous mind: Why good people are divided by politics and religion.* Pantheon Books.

Hallinan, M. T. (1996). Race effects on students' track mobility in high school. *Social Psychology of Education1*, 1–24. https://doi.org/10.1007/BF02333403

Hall, K. S., Sales, J. M., Komro, K. A., & Santelli, J. (2016). The state of sex education in the United States. *Journal of Adolescent Health, 58*(6), 595–597.

Hanebrink, P. (2018). *A specter haunting Europe: The myth of Judeo-Bolshevism.* Harvard University Press.

Harré, R., Moghaddam, F. M., Cairnie, T. P., Rothbart, D., & Sabat, S. R. (2009). Recent advances in positioning theory. *Theory & Psychology, 19*(1), 5–31.

Hata, M. (Dir.) (1986). *The adventures of Milo and Otis.* Columbia Pictures.

Hedegaard, M. (2007). The development of children's conceptual relation to the world, with focus on concept formation in preschool children's activity. In H. Daniels, M. Cole, & J. V. Wertsch (Eds.), *The Cambridge companion to Vygotsky* (pp. 246–275). Cambridge University Press.

Heekes, S.-L., Kruger, C. B., Lester, S. N., & Ward, C. L. (2020). A systematic review of corporal punishment in schools: Global prevalence and correlates. *Trauma, Violence, & Abuse, 23*(1), 52–72.

Herrnstein, R. J., & Murray, C. (1994). *The bell curve: Intelligence and class structure in American life.* The Free Press.

Heuer, C. J. (2007). *BUG: Deaf identity and internal revolution.* Gallaudet University Press.

Higgins, C., & Mazhulin, A. (2022, October 16). Russian troops kill Ukrainian musician for refusing role in Kherson concert. *The Guardian.* https://www.theguardian.com/world/2022/oct/16/russian-troops-kill-ukrainian-musician-yuriy-kerpatenko-for-refusing-role-in-kherson-concert

Hillig, G. (2000). Opfer des Stalinistischen Terrors: Ein internationales Forschungsprojekt des Makarenko-Referats über die Verfolgung ukrainischer Pädagogen. *Marburger UniJournal, 5*, 10–13.

Hillocks, G. (1986). *Research on written composition: New directions for teaching.* National Conference on Research in English and ERIC Clearinghouse on Reading and Communication Skills.

Hillocks, G. (1987). Synthesis of research on teaching writing. *Educational Leadership, 44*(8), 71–82.

Hillocks, G. (1995). *Teaching writing as reflective practice.* Teachers College Press.

Hillocks, G. (2011). *Teaching argument writing, grades 6–12.* Heineman.

Hines, D. E., & Wilmot, J. M. (2018). From spirit-murdering to spirit healing: Addressing anti-Black aggressions and the inhumane discipline of Black children. *Multicultural Perspectives, 20*(2), 62–69. https://doi.org/10.1080/15210960.2018.1447064

Hirsch, E. D. (1987). *Cultural literacy: What every American needs to know.* Houghton Mifflin.

Hitler, A. (1925/1999). *Mein kampf.* (R. Manheim, Trans.). Houghton Mifflin. https://www.sjsu.edu/people/mary.pickering/courses/His146/s1/MeinKampfpartone0001.pdf

Holmes, L. E. (2005). School and schooling under Stalin, 1931–1953. In B. Eklof, L. E. Holmes, & V. Kaplan (Eds.), *Educational reform in post-Soviet Russia: Legacies and prospects* (pp. 56–101). Frank Cass.

Holowinsky, I. Z. (1988). Vygotsky and the history of pedology. *School Psychology International, 9*, 123–128.

Holowinsky, I. Z. (2008). *Psychology in Ukraine: A historical perspective.* University Press of America.

Holzman, L. (2008). *Vygotsky at work and play.* Routledge.

Homma, I., & Masaoka, Y. (2008). Breathing rhythms and emotions. *Experimental Physiology, 93*(9), 1011–1021.

Horowitz, I. L., & Suchliki, J. (Eds.) (2009). *Cuban communism: 1959–2003* (11th ed.). Transaction Publishers.

Howard, R. W., Berkowitz, M. W., & Schaeffer, E. F. (2004). Politics of character education. *Educational Policy, 18*(1), 188–215.

Howard-Hill, T. H. (2006). Early modern printers and the standardization of English spelling. *The Modern Language Review, 101*(1), 16–29.

Hull, G., & Rose, M. (1990). "This wooden shack place": The logic of an unconventional reading. *College Composition and Communication, 41*(3), 287–298.

Husserl, E., (1913/1963). *Ideas: A general introduction to pure phenomenology.* (W. R. Boyce Gibson, Trans.). Collier Books. From the German original of 1913 *Ideas pertaining to a pure phenomenology and to a phenomenological philosophy*, First Book. http://dhspriory.org/kenny/PhilTexts/Husserl/Ideas1.pdf

Ilf, I., & Petrov, E. (1980 [1928]). Dvenadtsat' stul'yev [Twelve chairs]. *Khudozhestvennaya Literatura.* [In Russian]

Ives, S. (2023, February 20). *Ruthless: Monopoly's secret history.* PBS: American Experience. https://www.pbs.org/wgbh/americanexperience/films/ruthless-monopolys-secret-history/

Izaguirre, A., & Gomez Licon, A. (2022, August 15). *So-called 'Don't Say Gay' law confuses some Florida schools. Associated Press.* https://apnews.com/article/health-education-ron-desantis-gender-identity-49dfb9a4f63b2497846df8e96fd652cc

Izzard, E. (1999). Do you have a flag? In E. Izzard, *Dress to kill* (L. Jordan, Dir.). PolyGram. https://www.youtube.com/watch?v=UTduy7Qkvk8

Jacobs, D. T. (1998). *Primal awareness: A true story of survival, transformation, and awakening with the Rarámuri shamans of Mexico.* Inner Traditions.

Jacobs, D. T., & Jacobs-Spencer, J. (2001). *Teaching virtues: Building character across the curriculum.* Scarecrow Press.

Jaensch, E. R. (1930). *Eidetic imagery and typological methods of investigation: Their importance for the psychology of childhood, the theory of education, general psychology, and the psychophysiology of human personality.* Harcourt.

Jennings, H. S. (1906). *Behavior of the lower organisms.* Columbia University Press & Macmillan.

Johnson, A. (2019, March). Leon Trotsky's long war against antisemitism. *Fathom.* https://fathomjournal.org/the-fathom-long-read-leon-trotskys-long-war-against-antisemitism/

Johnson, T. S. (2008). *From teacher to lover: Sex scandals in the classroom.* Peter Lang.

Johnson, L. L., Chisam, J., Smagorinsky, P., & Wargo, K. (2018). Beyond publication: Social action as the ultimate stage of a writing process. *L1-Educational Studies in Language and Literature, 18*, 1–21.

Johnson, L. L., & Kim, G. M. (2021). Experimenting with game-based learning in preservice teacher education. *English Teaching: Practice & Critique, 20*(1), 78–93.

Johnson, T. S., Smagorinsky, P., Thompson, L., & Fry, P. G. (2003). Learning to teach the five-paragraph theme. *Research in the Teaching of English, 38*, 136–176.

John-Steiner, V. (1987). *Notebooks of the mind: Explorations in thinking.* Harper & Row.

Juluka. (1984). Kilimanjaro. On *Stand your ground.* Warner Bros. Records.

Kaiser, R. A. (1967). *Student physiological response to metaphor in reading.* Unpublished doctoral dissertation, University of Pittsburgh.

Kanu, Y. (2011). *Integrating Aboriginal perspectives into the school curriculum: Purposes, possibilities, and challenges.* University of Toronto Press.

Kaplan, D. E. (2018). Piagetian theory in online teacher education. *Creative Education, 9*, 831–837.

Keller, B. (1989, February 4). Major Soviet paper says 20 million died as victims of Stalin. *New York Times.* https://www.nytimes.com/1989/02/04/world/major-soviet-paper-says-20-million-died-as-victims-of-stalin.html?auth=login-google1tap&login=google1tap

Kellogg, D., & Veresov, N. (2019). Setting the stage. In L. S. Vygotsky, *L. S. Vygotsky's pedagogical works: Volume 1: Foundations of pedology* (pp. v–xx). (D. Kellogg & N. Veresov, Trans.). Springer.

Kennett, J. (2002). Autism, empathy and moral agency. *The Philosophical Quarterly, 52*(208), 340–357.

Kennicott, P., & Cappucci, M. (2021, July 16). Examining the elements of breathtaking art: Weather patterns can help us understand what's going on in these classic images. *The Washington Post.* https://www.washingtonpost.com/arts-entertainment/interactive/2021/weather-patterns-in-art/?itid=hp_special-topic-chain2

Kilpatrick, W. H. (1918, September). The project method. *Teachers College Record, 19*, 319–335.

Kim, M. S. (2012). Cultural–historical activity theory perspectives on constructing ICT-mediated metaphors of teaching and learning. *European Journal of Teacher Education, 35*(4), 435–448. https://doi.org/10.1080/02619768.2011.643393

Kim, G. M., & Johnson, L. L. (2021). Playful practices: Reimagining literacy teacher education through game-based curriculum design. *Research in the Teaching of English, 55,* 241–264.

Kimmerer, R. W. (2015). *Braiding sweetgrass: Indigenous wisdom, scientific knowledge and the teachings of plants.* Milkweed Editions.

Kingsley, T. L., & Grabner-Hagen, M. M. (2015). Gamification: Questing to integrate content knowledge, literacy, and 21st-century learning. *Journal of Adolescent and Adult Literacy, 59*(1), 51–61.

Kinloch, V. F. (2005). Revisiting the promise of students' right to their own language: Pedagogical strategies. *College Composition and Communication, 57*(1), 83–113.

Kirkland, D. E. (2014, November). *The lies "big data" tell: Rethinking the literate performances of black males through a modified meta-analysis of qualitative "little" data.* Paper presented at the annual convention of the National Council of Teachers of English, National Harbor, MD.

Klein, A. (2020, June 2). Why principals worry about how mobile devices affect students' social skills, attention spans. *Education Week.* https://www.edweek.org/technology/why-principals-worry-about-how-mobile-devices-affect-students-social-skills-attention-spans/2020/06

Kleinspehn-Ammerlahn, A., Riediger, M., Schmiedek, F., von Oertzen, T., Li, S.-C., & Lindenberger, U. (2011). Dyadic drumming across the lifespan reveals a zone of proximal development in children. *Developmental Psychology, 47*(3), 632–644.

Klosterman, C. (2016). *But what if we're wrong?: Thinking about the present as if it were the past.* Penguin.

Knox, J. E. (1993). Translator's introduction. In L. S. Vygotsky & A. R. Luria, *Studies on the history of behavior: Ape, primitive, and child* (V. I. Golod & J. E. Knox, Eds. & Trans.) (pp. 1–35). Erlbaum.

Kochman, T. (1981). *Black and white styles in conflict.* University of Chicago Press.

Koffka, K. (1934). *Foundations of mental development,* Russian translation (unattributed). Moscow-Leningrad.

Kohlberg, L. (1958). *The development of modes of thinking and choices in years 10 to 16.* Unpublished doctoral dissertation, University of Chicago.

Köhler, W. (1917). *Intelligenzprüfungen an anthropoiden* [*The mentality of apes*]. Royal Prussian Society of Sciences.

Kolbanovsky, V. N. (1968). A valuable work on the history of psychology. *Voprosky Psikhologii, 6,* 143–145.

Kompridis, N. (2006). *Critique and disclosure: Critical theory between past and future.* MIT Press.

Korey, W. (1972). The origins and development of Soviet anti-Semitism: An analysis. *Slavic Review, 31*(1), 111–135.

Kotik-Friedgut, B., & Friedgut, T. H. (2008). A man of his country and his time: Jewish influences on Lev Semionovich Vygotsky's world view. *History of Psychology, 11*(1), 15–39.

Kozulin, A. (1986). The concept of activity in Soviet psychology: Vygotsky, his disciples and critics. *American Psychologist, 3,* 264–267.

Kozulin, A., & Gindis, B. (2007). Sociocultural theory and education of children with special needs: From defectology to remedial pedagogy. In H. Daniels, M. Cole, & J. V. Wertsch (Eds.), *The Cambridge companion to Vygotsky* (pp. 332–362). Cambridge University Press.

Kozyrev, V., & Turko, P. A. (1936). "Pedologicheskaia shkola' Prof. L.S. Vygotskogo. *Vysshaia Shkola, 2,* 44–57. Republished in *Journal of Russian & East European Psychology* as "Professor L.S. Vygotsky's 'Pedological School,'" 2002, 3838.

Kracke, W. H. (2006). To dream, perchance to cure: Dreaming and shamanism in a Brazilian indigenous society. *Social Analysis, 50*(2), 106–120.

Kraus, M. W., Côté, S., & Keltner, D. (2010). Social class, contextualism, and empathic accuracy. *Psychological Science, 21*(11), 1716–1723.

Krementsov, N. (1997). *Stalinist science.* Princeton University Press.

Kristeva, J. (1969). *Séméiôtiké: Recherches pour une sémanalyse*. Seuil. [*Desire in language: A semiotic approach to literature and art*, Columbia University Press, Blackwell, 1980.]
Kroeber, A., & Kluckhohn, C. (1952/63). *Culture: A critical review of concepts and definitions*. Vintage Books.
Krylenko, N. V. (1930). Indictment of Industrial Party members. *Soviet Union Review*, *8*(1), 199–201. https://books.google.com/books?id=8kLjAAAAMAAJ&pg=PA200&lpg=PA200&dq=Victor+A.+Larichev+The+Industrial+Party+Trial&source=bl&ots=SSPbv0_Wfq&sig=ACfU3U2fi3FM69S5KGiGf07aUODaej_d-g&hl=en&sa=X&ved=2ahUKEwjh4PO2wI37AhWjRzABHRR3Bt8Q6AF6BAguEAM#v=onepage&q=Victor%20A.%20Larichev%20The%20Industrial%20Party%20Trial&f=false
Kushen, R. A. (1993). The death penalty and the crisis of criminal justice in Russia, *Brooklyn Journal of International Law*, *19*(2), 523–581. https://brooklynworks.brooklaw.edu/bjil/vol19/iss2/4
Laal, M., & Laal, M. (2012). Collaborative learning: What is it? *Procedia - Social and Behavioral Sciences*, *31*, 491–495.
LaBerge, M. (2018, June 27). Chimps, humans, and monkeys: What's the difference? *Jane Goodall Institute*. https://news.janegoodall.org/2018/06/27/chimps-humans-monkeys-whats-difference/
Lamarck, J. B. (1914). *Zoological philosophy: An exposition with regard to the natural history of animals*. (H. Elliot, Trans.). Macmillan and Co. https://archive.org/details/b22651433/mode/2up
Langer, J. A., & Applebee, A. N. (1983). Instructional scaffolding: Reading and writing as natural language activities. *Language Arts*, *60*(2), 168–175.
Langer, J. A., & Applebee, A. N. (1987). *How writing shapes thinking: A study of teaching and learning*. National Council of Teachers of English.
Lave, J. (1988). *Cognition in practice*. Cambridge University Press.
Law, I. (2012). *Red racisms: Racism in communist and post-communist contexts*. Palgrave Macmillan.
Leachman, M., Masterson, K., & Figueroa, E. (2017). *A punishing decade for school funding*. Center on Budget and Policy Priorities. https://www.cbpp.org/sites/default/files/atoms/files/11-29-17sfp.pdf
Lee, C. D. (1993). *Signifying as a scaffold for literary interpretation: The pedagogical implications of an African American discourse genre*. National Council of Teachers of English.
Lee, C. D. (2008). The centrality of culture to the scientific study of learning and development: How an ecological framework in education research facilitates civic responsibility. *Educational Researcher*, *37*(5), 267–279.
Lee, C. D. (2010). Soaring above the clouds, delving the ocean's depths: Understanding the ecologies of human learning and the challenge for education science. *Educational Researcher*, *39*(9), 643–655.
Lee, H. (1960). *To kill a mockingbird*. J. B. Lippincott & Co.
Lehrer, T. (1965). Introduction to "Clementine." On *That was the year that was*. Reprise Records.
Lenin, V. I. (1906). *The crisis of Menshevism*. https://www.marxists.org/archive/lenin/works/1906/crimensh/index.htm
Leont'ev, A. N. (1932/2005a). Letter from A.N. Leontiev to L.S. Vygotsky (N. Favorov, Trans.). *Journal of Russian and East European Psychology*, *43*(3), 70–77.
Leont'ev, A. N. (1971). Introduction. In L. S. Vygotsky, *The psychology of art* (Scripta Technica, Inc., Trans.) (pp. v–xi). M.I.T. Press.
Leont'ev, A. N. (1981). *Problems of the development of mind*. Progress Publishers.
Leont'ev, A. N. (1986). Problem of activity in the history of Soviet psychology. *Voprosy Psikhologii*, *4*, 109–120.
Leont'ev, A. N. (1997). On Vygotsky's creative development. In R. W. Rieber & J. Wollock (Eds.), *The collected works of L. S. Vygotsky, Volume 3: Problems of the theory and history of psychology* (R. van der Veer, Trans.) (pp. 9–32). Plenum.
Leont'ev, A. N. (2005b). Study of the environment in the pedological works of L. S. Vygotsky. *Journal of Russian and East European Psychology*, *43*(4), 8–28. https://www.marxists.org/archive/leontiev/works/leontiev-lsv-env.pdf

Leont'ev, A. N. (2005a). The genesis of activity. *Journal of Russian & East European Psychology, 43*(4), 58–71.

Leont'ev, A. N., & Luria, A. R. (1956). Psychological views of L. S. Vygotsky. In A. N. Leont'ev & A. R. Luria (Eds.), *Vygotsky: Selected psychological works* (pp. 4–36). Academy of Pedagogical Sciences of the Russian Soviet Federated Socialist Republic.

Leontiev, A. A., & Leontiev, D. A. (2003). A myth about a falling out: A.N. Leontiev and L.S. Vygotsky in 1932 [In honor of the 100th anniversary of the birth of A.N. Leontiev]. *Psikhologicheskii Zhurnal [Psychological Journal], 24*(1), 14–28.

Levesque, B. (2022, October 1). Putin slams LGBTQ+ people in Ukrainian annexation speech. *Los Angeles Blade*. https://www.losangelesblade.com/2022/10/01/putin-slams-lgbtq-people-in-ukrainian-annexation-speech/

Lévy-Bruhl, L. (1922). *La mentalité primitive*. Félix Alcan.

Lickona, T. (1991). *Educating for character: How our schools can teach respect and responsibility*. Bantam.

Lieberman, P. (2007). The evolution of human speech: Its anatomical and neural bases. *Current Anthropology, 48*(1), 39–66.

Lim, N. (2016). Cultural differences in emotion: Differences in emotional arousal level between the East and the West. *Integrative Medicine Research, 5*(2), 105–109.

Linnane, R. (2021, March 3). Wisconsin students wanted to make a schoolwide virtual presentation on Black History Month. Their principal shut them down. *Milwaukee Journal Sentinel*. https://www.jsonline.com/story/news/2021/03/03/wisconsin-principal-stops-high-school-black-history-month-presentation/6863956002/

Lipsitz, G. (2009). *The possessive investment in whiteness: How white people profit from identity politics, revised and expanded edition*. Temple University Press.

Lipsitz, G. (2011). *How racism takes place*. Temple University Press.

Loewen, J. (1999). *Lies across America: What our historic sites get wrong*. The New Press.

Loftus, E. F., Miller, D. G., & Burns, H. J. (1978). Semantic integration of verbal information into a visual memory. *Journal of Experimental Psychology: Human Learning and Memory, 4*, 19–31.

Loftus, E. F., & Pickrell, J. E. (1995). The formation of false memories. *Psychiatric Annals, 25*, 720–725.

Lopez-Zafra, E., Garcia-Retamero, R., & Berrios Martos, M. P. (2012). The relationship between transformational leadership and emotional intelligence from a gendered approach. *The Psychological Record, 62*, 97–114.

Lovaas, O. I. (1987). Behavioral treatment and normal educational and intellectual functioning in young autistic children. *Journal of Consulting and Clinical Psychology, 55*(1), 3–9.

Love, B. (2019). *We want to do more than survive: Abolitionist teaching and the pursuit of educational freedom*. Beacon Press.

Lovell, S. (2015). *Russia in the microphone age: A history of Soviet radio, 1919–1970*. Oxford University Press.

Luria, A. R. (1976). *Cognitive development: Its cultural and social foundations* (M. Cole, Ed.; M. Lopez-Morillas & L. Solotaroff, Trans.). Harvard University Press.

Luria, A. R. (1928). Psychology in Russia. *The Pedagogical Seminary and Journal of Genetic Psychology, 33*(3), 347–355.

Luttenberger, S., Wimmer, S., & Paechter, M. (2018). Spotlight on math anxiety. *Psychological Research in Behavioral Management, 11*, 311–322.

Lutz, C. A. (1988). *Unnatural emotions: Everyday sentiments on a Micronesian atoll & their challenge to Western theory*. University of Chicago Press.

Lynd, A. (1953). Who wants progressive education? The influence of John Dewey on the public schools. *The Atlantic*. https://www.theatlantic.com/facebook-instant/article/640458/

Lyons, E. (1967). *Workers' paradise lost: Fifty years of Soviet communism: A balance sheet*. Funk and Wagnalls.

Macleod, I. (1965, December 3). 70 m.p.h. *The Spectator*. http://archive.spectator.co.uk/article/3rd-december-1965/11/70-mph

Majors, Y. J. (2015). *Shoptalk: Lessons in teaching from an African American hair salon*. Teacher's College Press.

Makalela, L. (2019). Uncovering the universals of ubuntu translanguaging in classroom discourses. *Classroom Discourse*, *10*(3–4), 237–251. https://doi.org/10.1080/19463014.2019.1631198

Mamonova, T. (1988). *Russian women's studies: Essays on sexism in the Soviet culture*. Teachers College Press.

Mampaey, J., & Zanoni, P. (2016). Reproducing monocultural education: Ethnic majority staff's discursive constructions of monocultural school practices. *British Journal of Sociology of Education*, *7*, 928–946.

Marquart, M., Diaz Meyer, M., Schneider, M., & Hilgemann, R. (2016). Learning handwriting at school: A teachers' survey on actual problems and future options. *Trends in Neuroscience and Education*, *5*, 82–89.

Marshall, J. D., Smagorinsky, P., & Smith, M. W. (1995). *The language of interpretation: Patterns of discourse in discussions of literature*. NCTE Research Report No. 27. National Council of Teachers of English.

Martinez, X. (2017). *We rise: The Earth guardians guide to building a movement that restores the planet*. Rodale.

Martinez, J. G. R., & Martinez, N. C. (1987, April). *Are basic writers cognitively deficient?* Paper presented at the Annual Meeting of the Western College Reading and Learning Association, Albuquerque, NM. https://files.eric.ed.gov/fulltext/ED285179.pdf

Martins, J. B. (2013). Da relação Vigotski e Leontiev – Alguns apontamentos a respeito da história da psicologia soviética. *Revista Interamericana de Psicología/Interamerican Journal of Psychology*, *47*(1), 43–52.

Marx, K. (1843). A contribution to the critique of Hegel's philosophy of right. Marxists.org. https://www.marxists.org/archive/marx/works/1843/critique-hpr/intro.htm

Marx, K., & Engels, F. (1848). *Manifesto of the Communist Party*. Communist League. https://www.marxists.org/archive/marx/works/download/pdf/Manifesto.pdf

Marx, K. (1867/1887). *Das Kapital* [*Capital: A critique of political economy*]. Dietz Verlag.

Marx, K., & Engels, F. (1985). *Marx & Engels collected works vol 20: Marx and Engels:1864–1868*. Lawrence & Wishart.

Maxouris, C., & Christina Zdanowicz, C. (2022, February 5). Teachers are leaving and few people want to join the field. Experts are sounding the alarm. *CNN*. https://www.cnn.com/2022/02/05/us/teacher-prep-student-shortages-covid-crisis/index.html

McCagg, W. O. (1989). The origins of defectology. In W. O. McCagg & L. Siegelbaum (Eds.), *The disabled in the Soviet Union: Past and present, theory and practice* (pp. 39–62). University of Pittsburgh Press.

McCarney, J. (2003). Hegel's racism? A response to Bernasconi. *Radical Philosophy*, *119*, 32–35.

McCutchen, D., Teske, P., & Bankston, C. (2008). Writing and cognition: Implications of the cognitive architecture for learning to write and writing to learn. In C. Bazerman (Ed.), *Handbook of research on writing: History, society, school, individual, text* (pp. 451–470). Erlbaum.

McGuigan, F. J. (1969). *Covert oral behavior during silent reading*. Final Report. Hollins College. https://files.eric.ed.gov/fulltext/ED038267.pdf

McLean, C. (2022, April 28). How parents' views of their kids' screen time, social media use changed during COVID-19. *Pew Research Center*. https://www.pewresearch.org/fact-tank/2022/04/28/how-parents-views-of-their-kids-screen-time-social-media-use-changed-during-covid-19/

Mecacci L., & Yasnitsky A. (2011). Editorial changes in the three Russian editions of Vygotsky's "Thinking and Speech" (1934, 1956, 1982): Towards authoritative and ultimate English translation of the book//*Психологический журнал Международного университета природы, общества и человека «Дубна»*. ISSN 2076-7099.

Meckler, L. (2018, November 5). Montessori, long a favorite for wealthy families, struggles to expand its reach. *The Washington Post*. https://www.washingtonpost.com/local/education/montessori-long-a-favorite-of-wealthy-families-struggles-to-expand-its-reach/2018/11/05/51a5ae02-ccc9-11e8-920f-dd52e1ae4570_story.html

Medinsky, Y. N. (1954). *Public education in the USSR*. Foreign Language Publishing House.

Mercer, N., & Fisher, E. (1992). How do teachers help children to learn? An analysis of teachers' interventions in computer-based activities. *Learning and Instruction, 2*, 339–355.

Mickelson, R. A., & Everett, B. J. (2008). Neotracking in North Carolina: How high school courses of study reproduce race and class-based stratification. *Teachers College Record, 110*(3), 35–570.

Mikhailov, F. T. (2006). Problems of the method of cultural-historical psychology. *Journal of Russian and East European Psychology, 44*(1), 21–54. (S. D. Shenfield, Trans.).

Milner, H. R. (2006). The promise of Black teachers' success with Black students. Educational Foundations, Summer-Fall, 89–104. https://files.eric.ed.gov/fulltext/EJ794734.pdf

Milner, H. R. (2010). *Start where you are, but don't stay there: Understanding diversity, opportunity gaps, and teaching in today's classrooms*. Harvard Education Press.

Modell, A. (2005). Emotional memory, metaphor, and meaning psychoanalytic inquiry. *Psychoanalytic Inquiry, 25*(4), 555–568.

Moffa, E. D. (2022). Hard history in hard contexts: Teaching slavery and its legacy in a Neo-Confederate space. *The Journal of Social Studies Research*. https://doi.org/10.1016/j.jssr.2022.01.002

Moffett, J. (1968). *Teaching the universe of discourse*. Houghton Mifflin.

Moll, I. (1995). Cultural people and cultural contexts: Comments on Cole (1995) and Wertsch (1995). *Culture & Psychology, 1*, 361–371.

Moll, L. C. (1990). Introduction. In L. C. Moll (Ed.), *Vygotsky and education: Instructional implications and applications of sociohistorical psychology* (pp. 1–27). Cambridge University Press.

Moll, L. C., & Whitmore, K. F. (1993). Vygotsky in educational settings: Moving from individual transmission to social transaction. In E. Forman, N. Minick, & A. Stone (Eds.), *Contexts for learning: Sociocultural dynamics in children's development* (pp. 19–42). Oxford University Press.

Moll, L. C. (2000). Inspired by Vygotsky: Ethnographic experiments in education. In C. Lee & P. Smagorinsky (Eds.), *Vygotskian perspectives on literacy research* (pp. 256–268). Cambridge University Press.

Molloy, M. (2021, May 3). Creative punishments for students in school. *My Town Tutors*. https://www.mytowntutors.com/creative-punishments-for-students-in-school/

Momaday, M. S. (1969). *The way to Rainy Mountain*. University of New Mexico Press.

Montessori, M. (1912). *The Montessori method*. Dover Publications.

Moore, K. (2011). Frameworks for understanding the inter-generational transmission of poverty and well-being in developing countries. *Chronic Poverty Research Centre Working Paper No. 8*. https://papers.ssrn.com/sol3/papers.cfm?abstract_id=1754527

Münsterberg, H. (1909). *Psychology and the teacher*. D. Appleton and Co.

Murray, D. M. (1980). Writing as process: How writing finds its own meaning. In T. R. Donovan & B. W. McClelland (Eds.), *Eight approaches to teaching composition* (pp. 3–20). National Council of Teachers of English.

Nardoto, G. B., Sena-Souza, J. P., Kisaka, T. B., Viana Costa, F. J., Duarte-Neto, P. J., Ehleringer, J., & Martinelli, L. A. (2020). Increased in carbon isotope ratios of Brazilian fingernails are correlated with increased in socioeconomic status. *NPJ Science of Food, 4*(9), 1–3. https://doi.org/10.1038/s41538-020-0069-1

National Center for Educational Statistics. (2005). *Rates of computer and internet use by children in nursery school and students in kindergarten through twelfth grade: 2003*. Author. https://nces.ed.gov/pubs2005/2005111.pdf

National Institutes of Health. (2022, October 17). Hair straightening chemicals associated with higher uterine cancer risk. *Author*. https://www.nih.gov/news-events/news-releases/hair-straightening-chemicals-associated-higher-uterine-cancer-risk

National Symposium on Neurodiversity at Syracuse University. (2011). *What is neurodiversity?* https://neurodiversitysymposium.wordpress.com/what-is-neurodiversity/

Nell, V. (1999). Luria in Uzbekistan: The vicissitudes of cross-cultural neuropsychology. *Neuropsychology Review, 9*, 45–52.

Nettleton, A. (2010). Life in a Zulu village: Craft and the art of modernity in South Africa. *The Journal of Modern Craft, 3*(1), 55–78.

New London Group (1996). A pedagogy of multiliteracies: Designing social futures. *Harvard Educational Review, 66,* 60–92.

Newell, G. E., Bloome, D., Kim, M.-Y., & Goff, B. (2019). Shifting epistemologies during instructional conversations about "good" argumentative writing in a high school English language arts classroom. *Reading and Writing, 32,* 1359–1382.

Newman, D., Griffin, P., & Cole, M. (1989). *The construction zone: Working for cognitive change in school.* Cambridge University Press.

Nikiforova, O. I. (1960). Role of inner speech in the reconstruction of literary images. *Psychological Abstracts, 34,* 395–396.

Nishimura, T., Tokuda, I. T., Miyachi, S., Dunn, J. C., Herbst, C. T., Ishimura, K., ... Fitch, W. T. (2022). Evolutionary loss of complexity in human vocal anatomy as an adaptation for speech. *Science, 377*(6607), 760–763. https://doi.org/10.1126/science.abm1574

Nolan, J. D. (1973). Conceptual and rote learning in children. *Teachers College Record, 75*(2), 251–258.

Nurfaidah, S. (2018). Vygotsky's legacy on teaching and learning writing as social process. *Langkawi, 4*(2), 149–156.

Nystrand, M. (1997). *Opening dialogue: Understanding the dynamics of language and learning in the English classroom.* Teachers College Press.

Nystrand, M. 1986). *The structure of written composition: Studies in reciprocity between writers and readers.* Academic Press.

Nystrand, M. (2022). History as a dialogic process: The case of Frank Lloyd Wright. *Bakhtin Gazette, 7,* 1–31.

Oakes, J. (2005). *Keeping track: How schools structure inequality.* Yale University Press.

Ojose, B. (2008). Applying Piaget's theory of cognitive development to mathematics instruction. *The Mathematics Educator, 18*(1), 26–30.

Okamura, M. (2013, July 25). Video games: Good entertainment or distraction from the real world? *Athgo.* http://athgo.org/video-games-good-entertainment-or-distraction-from-the-real-world/

Orwell, G. (1938). *Homage to Catalonia.* Secker and Warburg.

Orwell, G. (1945). *Animal farm.* Secker and Warburg.

Osher, D., Bear, G. G., Sprague, J. R., & Doyle, W. (2010). How can we improve school discipline? *Educational Researcher, 39*(1), 48–58.

Overton, W. F. (2015). Processes, relations, and relational-developmental-systems. In W. F. Overton & P. C. M. Molenaar (Eds.), *Handbook of child psychology and developmental science, Vol. 1: Theory and method* (pp. 9–62). John Wiley and Sons.

Ozer, M., & Perc, M. (2020). Dreams and realities of school tracking and vocational education. *Palgrave Communications, 6,* Article 34. https://doi.org/10.1057/s41599-020-0409-4

Pannekoek, A. (1934). *The theory of the collapse of capitalism.* https://www.marxists.org/archive/pannekoe/1934/collapse.htm#:~:text=The%20collapse%20of%20capitalism%20in%20Marx%20does%20depend,determine%20the%20will%20to%20revolution%20of%20the%20proletariat

Parkhurst, H. (1922). *Education on the Dalton Plan.* E. P. Dutton & Company.

Pearce, J. (2017, July 30). Why do progressives hate the West so much? *The Imaginative Conservative.* https://theimaginativeconservative.org/2017/07/west-progressives-joseph-pearce.html

Peddie, R. L. (1952). The relation of haptic perception to literary creative work. *British Psychological Society Bulletin, 3,* 19–21.

Peirce, C. S. (1931–1935; 1958). *The collected papers of Charles Sanders Peirce.* Vols. I–VI (C. Hartshorne & P. Weiss, Eds., 1931–1935); Vols. VII–VIII (A. W. Burks, Ed., 1958). Harvard University Press.

Perles, K. (2013, July 30). *Character education: Good hearts lead to good grades.* Education.com. https://www.education.com/magazine/article/character-education-classroom-improve-academic/

Perrillo, J. (2019). At home on the range: Cowboy culture, Indians, and the assimilation of enemy children in the Cold War borderlands. *American Quarterly, 71*(4), 945–967.

Perrine, L., & Arp, T. R. (1956). *Sound and sense: An introduction to poetry*. Harcourt, Brace, & World.

Peters, V. (1956). Education in the Soviet Union. *The Phi Delta Kappan, 37*(9), 421–425.

Pew Research Center. (2020). *Parenting children in the age of screens: 1. Children's engagement with digital devices, screen time*. Author. https://www.pewresearch.org/internet/2020/07/28/childrens-engagement-with-digital-devices-screen-time/

Piaget, J. (1973). *The psychology of intelligence* (H. Weaver, Trans.). Littlefield and Adams.

Pollack, T. M., & Zirkel, S. (2013). Negotiating the contested terrain of equity-focused change efforts in schools: Critical Race Theory as a leadership framework for creating more equitable schools. *The Urban Review, 45*(3), 290–310. https://doi.org/10.1007/S11256-012-0231-4

Portes, P., & Salas, S. (Eds.) (2011). *Vygotsky in 21st century society: Advances in cultural historical theory and praxis with non-dominant communities*. Peter Lang.

Portes, P., & Smagorinsky, P. (2010). Static structures, changing demographics: Educating for shifting populations in stable schools. *English Education, 42*, 236–248.

Potebnya, A. A. (1862). Мысль и язык *[Language and thought]*.

Potter, D. (1977). *The impending crisis: America before the Civil War*, 1848–1861. HarperCollins.

Pound, P., Langford, B., & Campbell, R. (2016). What do young people think about their school-based sex and relationship education? A qualitative synthesis of young people's views and experiences. *BMJ Open, 6*(9), 1–14. https://bmjopen.bmj.com/content/bmjopen/6/9/e011329.full.pdf

Probst, R. E. (2004). *Response and analysis: Teaching literature in secondary school*, second edition. Heinemann.

Purdie, N., & Hattie, J. (2002). Assessing students' conceptions of learning. *Australian Journal of Educational & Developmental Psychology, 2*, 17–32.

Purves, A., & Beach, C., R. (1972). *Literature and the reader: Research in response to literature, reading interests, and the teaching of literature*. National Council of Teachers of English.

Rabinowitz, P. J. (1987). *Before reading: Narrative conventions and the politics of interpretation*. Ohio State University Press.

Rabinowitz, P. J., & Smith, M. W. (1997). *Authorizing readers: Resistance and respect in the teaching of literature*. Teachers College Press.

Raby, R. (2010). "Tank tops are ok but i don't want to see her thong": Girls' engagements with secondary school dress codes. *Youth Society, 41*, 333–356.

Radzikhovsky, L. A. (1979). About early stages of L. S. Vygotsky's scientific creativity. *Voprosy Psikhologii, 1*, 99–106.

Ransom, J. C. (1937, Autumn). Criticism, Inc. *The Virginia Quarterly Review*. https://www.vqronline.org/essay/criticism-inc-0

Ransom, J. C. (1941). *The new criticism*. New Directions.

Ratner, C., & Silva, D. N. H. (Eds.) (2017). *Vygotsky and Marx: Toward a Marxist psychology*. Routledge.

Razmyslov, P. (1934). O "kul'turnoistoricheskoi teorii psikhologii" Vygotskogo i Luria. *Kniga I Proletarskaia Revoliutsiia, 4*, 78–86. Republished in *Journal of Russian and East European Psychology* as "On Vygotsky and Luria's 'cultural-historical theory of psychology'" 2002, 3838.

Reconstruction: America After the Civil War. (2019). H. L. Gates, Jr. & D. McGee (executive producers), J. Marchesi (Dir.), R. Rapley, S. Holman, & C. Readdean (Producers/Directors). Inkwell Films and McGee Media.

Reed, J. (1919a/2011). "Ten days that shook the world." In *Writings of John Reed: "Ten days that shook the world," and other essays* (pp. 93–290). Red and Black Publishers.

Reed, J. (1919b/2011). Aspects of the Russian Revolution. In *Writings of John Reed: "Ten days that shook the world," and other essays* (pp. 67–76). Red and Black Publishers.

Reed, J. (1919c/2011). A new appeal. In *Writings of John Reed: "Ten days that shook the world," and other essays* (pp. 57–63). Red and Black Publishers.

Reed, J. (1919d/2011). Soviet Russia now. In *Writings of John Reed: "Ten days that shook the world," and other essays* (pp. 87–92). Red and Black Publishers.

Repovš, G., & Baddeley, A. (2006). The multi-component model of working memory: Explorations in experimental cognitive psychology. *Neuroscience, 139*(1), 5–21. https://doi.org/10.1016/j.neuroscience.2005.12.061

Repucci, S., & Slipowitz, A. (2022). *The global expansion of authoritarian rule*. Freedom House. https://freedomhouse.org/sites/default/files/2022-02/FIW_2022_PDF_Booklet_Digital_Final_Web.pdf

Rettig, P., & Montoya Talavera, M. (2023, June 8). Opinion: U.S. classrooms' value on individual effort isn't norm everywhere. *Atlanta Journal-Constitution*. https://www.ajc.com/education/get-schooled-blog/opinion-us-classrooms-value-on-individual-effort-isnt-norm-everywhere/O34ZKWZ6CJD3BDKY74K3XMQSNQ/

Ricoeur, P. (1983). *Time and narrative* (Vol. 1; K. McLaughlin & D. Pellauer, Trans.). University of Chicago Press.

Rieber, R. W., & Wollock, J. (1997). Prologue: Vygotsky's "crisis," and its meaning today. In R. W. Rieber & J. Wollock (Eds.), *The collected works of L. S. Vygotsky, Volume 3: Problems of the theory and history of psychology* (R. van der Veer, Trans.) (pp. vii–xii). Plenum.

Riess, R. (2022, August 19). Public schools receive 'In God We Trust' poster donations as new Texas law requires their display. *CNN*. https://www.cnn.com/2022/08/19/us/texas-schools-in-god-we-trust/index.html

Robb, M. (2019, October 29). Tweens, teens, and phones: What our 2019 research reveals. *Common Sense Media*. https://www.commonsensemedia.org/kids-action/articles/tweens-teens-and-phones-what-our-2019-research-reveals

Robinson, G. C., & Norton, P. C. (2019). A decade of disproportionality: A state-level analysis of African American students enrolled in the primary disability category of speech or language impairment. *Language, Speech, and Hearing Services in School, 50*(2), 267–282.

Rodina, K. A. (2006, June). *Vygotsky's social constructionist view on disability: A methodology for inclusive education*. Paper presented at the European Learning Styles Information Network (ELSIN) 11th Annual Conference, Oslo. http://lchc.ucsd.edu/mca/Paper/VygotskyDisabilityEJSNE2007.pdf

Rogoff, B. (2011). *Developing destinies: A Mayan midwife and town*. Oxford University Press.

Rose, M. (2004). *The mind at work: Valuing the intelligence of the American worker*. Penguin.

Rosenblatt, L. (1938). *Literature as exploration*. D. Appleton-Century Co.

Roth, W.-M. (2007). Emotion at work: A contribution to third-generation cultural-historical activity theory. *Mind, Culture, and Activity, 14*(1–2), 40–63.

Roth, W.-M., & Jornet, A. (2017). *Understanding educational psychology: A late Vygotskian, Spinozist approach*. Springer.

Rousseau, J.-J. (1762). *Émile,ou, De l'education* [*Émile, or On Education*]. https://brittlebooks.library.illinois.edu/brittlebooks_open/Books2009-08/rousje0001emile/rousje0001emile.pdf

Rubin, J. Z., Provezano, F. J., & Luria, Z. (1974). The eye of the beholder: Parents' views on sex of newborns. *American Journal of Orthopsychiatry, 44*, 512–519.

Rudneva, E. I. (1937). Pedologicheskie izvrashcheniia Vygotskogo. *Gosudarstvennoe uchebno-pedagogicheskoe izdatel'stvo*, 3–32. Republished in *Journal of Russian and East European Psychology, 38*(6), 75—94. (M. E. Sharpe, Inc., Trans.)

Ruotsila, M. (2000). Lord Sydenham of Combe's World Jewish conspiracy. *Patterns of Prejudice, 34*(3), 47–64.

Russell, L. (2013, August 26). Police: 8-year-old shoots, kills elderly caregiver after playing video game. *CNN*. https://www.cnn.com/2013/08/25/us/louisiana-boy-kills-grandmother/index.html

Saavedra, A. R., & Opfer, V. D. (2012). Teaching and learning 21st century skills: Lessons from the learning sciences. *Asia Society*. https://www.opsba.org/wp-content/uploads/2021/02/RAND-Paper.pdf

Sala, G., Aksayli, N. D., Tatlidil, K. S., Tatsumi, T., Gondo, Y., & Gobet, F. (2019). Near and far transfer in cognitive training: A second-order meta-analysis. *Collabra: Psychology, 5*(1), 1–22.

Salomon, G. (Ed.) (1993). *Distributed cognitions: Psychological and educational considerations*. Cambridge University Press.

Salyer, J. (2022, August 12). John Dewey's dehumanizing project and public education. *The Catholic World Report*. https://www.catholicworldreport.com/2015/09/15/john-deweys-dehumanizing-project-and-public-education/

Sankararaman, S., Mallick, S., Dannemann, M., Prüfer, K., Kelso, J., Pääbo, S.,... Reich, D. (2014). The genomic landscape of Neanderthal ancestry in present-day humans. *Nature, 507*, 354–357. https://doi.org/10.1038/nature12961

Sannino, A. (2015). The principle of double stimulation: A path to volitional action. *Learning, Culture and Social Interaction, 6*, 1–15.

Santayana, G. (1905). *The life of reason*. https://www.gutenberg.org/files/15000/15000-h/15000-h.htm

Sanz, C. M., Call, J., & Boesch, C. (Eds.) (2013). *Tool use in animals: Cognition and ecology*. Cambridge University Press.

Saqlain, N. (2015). A comprehensive look at multi-age education. *Journal of Educational and Social Research, 5*(2), 285–290.

Saunders, W. (2003). Sexual sins. *Catholic Education Resource Center*. https://www.catholiceducation.org/en/culture/catholic-contributions/sexual-sins.html

Schuessler, J. (2021, November 9). Bans on Critical Race Theory threaten free speech, advocacy group says. *New York Times*. https://www.nytimes.com/2021/11/08/arts/critical-race-theory-bans.html

Scribner, S. (1985). Knowledge at work. *Anthropology and Education Quarterly, 16*(3), 199–206.

Scribner, S., & Cole, M. (1981). *The psychology of literacy*. Harvard University Press.

Searle, D. (1984). Scaffolding: Who's building whose building? *Language Arts, 61*, 480–483.

Seed, A., & Byrne, R. (2010). Animal tool-use. *Current Biology, 20*. https://reader.elsevier.com/reader/sd/pii/S0960982210011607?token=DD425AF8DAD3919E1C578695533A7B9CB818F757E3624E58F7926811E584ADF0499AE38676426DF554C728E71BB7A731&originRegion=us-east-1&originCreation=20220429153057

Segal, S. L. (1986). Mathematics and German politics: The national socialist experience. *Historia Mathematica, 13*, 118–135.

Serin, H. (2018). A comparison of teacher-centered and student-centered approaches in educational settings. *International Journal of Social Sciences & Educational Studies, 5*(1), 164–167.

Sewell, R. (2005, July 8). What is dialectical materialism? *Marxist University*. https://www.marxist.com/what-is-dialectical-materialism.htm

Shanahan, T. (2013). Letting the text take center stage: How the Common Core State Standards will transform English language arts instruction. *American Educator, 4–11*, 43.

Shanon, B. (2009). The knot in the handkerchief. *Metaphor and Symbolic Activity, 5*(2), 109–114. https://doi.org/10.1207/s15327868ms0502_4

Shemesh, A., Talmon, R., Karp, O., Amir, I., Bar, M., & Grobman, J. Y. (2016). Affective response to architecture – Investigating human reaction to spaces with different geometry. *Architectural Science Review, 60*(2). https://doi.org/10.1080/00038628.2016.1266597

Shevchenko, N. (2021, December 31). 10 Soviet TABLETOP GAMES that you need to play NOW. *Russia Beyond*. https://www.rbth.com/lifestyle/334597-soviet-tabletop-games

Shevchenko, N. (2022, January 2). Look at these MILITARISTIC & PATRIOTIC board games of the early SOVIET era. *Russia Beyond*. https://www.rbth.com/history/334599-militaristic-patriotic-board-games-ussr

Shields, D. L., Bredemeier, B. L., Lavoi, N. M., & Power, F. C. (2005). The sport behavior of youth, parents, and coaches: The good, the bad, and the ugly. *Journal of Research in Character Education, 3*(1), 43–59.

Shif, Zb. I. (1935). *Razvitie nauchnykh ponjatij u shkol'nika. [The development of scientific concepts in the schoolchild]*. Gosudarstvennoe Uchebno-Pedagogicheskoe Izdatel'stvo.

Sigel, I. E., & Cocking, R. R. (1977). *Cognitive development from childhood to adolescence: A constructive perspective*. Holt, Rinehart & Winston.

Silberman, S. (2015). *NeuroTribes: The legacy of autism and the future of neurodiversity*. Avery.

Singal, A., & Arora, R. (2015). Nail as a window of systemic diseases. *Indian Dermatology Online Journal, 6*(2), 67–74. https://doi.org/10.4103/2229-5178.153002

Singer, E. (2013). Play and playfulness, basic features of early childhood education. *European Early Childhood Education Research Journal, 21*, 172–184.

Skerrett, A., & Smagorinsky, P. (2023). *Teaching literacy in troubled times: Identity, inquiry, and social action at the heart of instruction.* Corwin.

Skyer, M. (2022, July 19). *Multimodal transduction in deaf education.* Paper presented at the Annual Meeting of the Society for Text and Discourse [online]. https://www.researchgate.net/profile/Michael-Skyer-2/publication/361938313_MULTIMODAL_TRANSDUCTION_in_Deaf_Pedagogy_Symposium_1_Deaf_and_Hard_of_Hearing_Readers_Session_4_Multimodal_Multilingualism_Language_and_Literacy_Development_of_Deaf_Learners_S4_-Members_Scott_Dostal_H/links/62cd953f6151ad090b95fc44/MULTIMODAL-TRANSDUCTION-in-Deaf-Pedagogy-Symposium-1-Deaf-and-Hard-of-Hearing-Readers-Session-4-Multimodal-Multilingualism-Language-and-Literacy-Development-of-Deaf-Learners-S4-Members-Scott-Dostal.pdf

Smagorinsky, P. (1992). Towards a civic education in a multicultural society: Ethical problems in teaching literature. *English Education, 24*, 212–228.

Smagorinsky, P. (1995a). Constructing meaning in the disciplines: Reconceptualizing writing across the curriculum as composing across the curriculum. *American Journal of Education, 103*, 160–184.

Smagorinsky, P. (1995b). The social construction of data: Methodological problems of investigating learning in the zone of proximal development. *Review of Educational Research, 65*, 191–212.

Smagorinsky, P. (1998). Thinking and speech and protocol analysis. *Mind, Culture, and Activity, 5*, 157–177.

Smagorinsky, P. (2001). If meaning is constructed, what is it made from? Toward a cultural theory of reading. *Review of Educational Research, 71*, 133–169.

Smagorinsky, P., Cook, L. S., & Johnson, T. S. (2003). The twisting path of concept development in learning to teach. *Teachers College Record, 105*, 1399–1436.

Smagorinsky, P. (2009a). The culture of Vygotsky. *Reading Research Quarterly, 44*, 85–95.

Smagorinsky, P. (2009b). Is it time to abandon the idea of "best practices" in the teaching of English? *English Journal, 98*(6), 15–22.

Smagorinsky, P. (2010a). The culture of learning to teach: The self-perpetuating cycle of conservative schooling. *Teacher Education Quarterly, 37*(2), 19–32.

Smagorinsky, P. (2010b). A Vygotskian analysis of the construction of setting in learning to teach. In V. Ellis, A. Edwards, & P. Smagorinsky (Eds.), *Cultural-historical perspectives on teacher education and development: Learning teaching* (pp. 13–29). Routledge.

Smagorinsky, P. (2011a). *Vygotsky and literacy research: A methodological framework.* Sense.

Smagorinsky, P. (2011b). Vygotsky's stage theory: The psychology of art and the actor under the direction of perezhivanie. *Mind, Culture, and Activity, 18*, 319–341.

Smagorinsky, P. (2011c). Confessions of a mad professor: An autoethnographic consideration of neuroatypicality, extranormativity, and education. *Teachers College Record, 113*, 1701–1732.

Smagorinsky, P. (2012). Vygotsky, "defectology," and the inclusion of people of difference in the broader cultural stream. *Journal of Language and Literacy Education* [Online], 8(1), 1–25. http://jolle.coe.uga.edu/wp-content/uploads/2012/05/Vygotsky-and-Defectology.pdf

Smagorinsky, P. (2013a). The development of social and practical concepts in learning to teach: A synthesis and extension of Vygotsky's conception. *Learning, Culture, and Social Interaction, 2*(4), 238–248.

Smagorinsky, P. (2013b). What does Vygotsky provide for the 21st century language arts teacher? *Language Arts, 90*, 190–202.

Smagorinsky, P. (2014a). Who's normal here? An atypical's perspective on mental health and educational inclusion. *English Journal, 103*(5), 15–23.

Smagorinsky, P. (2014b, November 26). Taking the diss out of disability. *Teachers College Record.* http://www.petersmagorinsky.net/About/PDF/TCR/TCR2014.html

Smagorinsky, P. (Ed.). (2016a). *Creativity and community among autism-spectrum youth: Creating positive social updrafts through play and performance.* Palgrave Macmillan.

Smagorinsky, P. (2016b). Huck and Kim: Would teachers feel the same if the language were misogynist? *English Journal, 106*(2), 75–80.

Smagorinsky, P. (2017). Misfits in school literacy: Whom are U.S. schools designed to serve? In D. Appleman & K. Hinchman (Eds.), *Adolescent literacy: A handbook of practice-based research* (pp. 199–214). Guilford.

Smagorinsky, P. (2018a). Deconflating the ZPD and instructional scaffolding: Retranslating and reconceiving the zone of proximal development as the zone of next development. *Learning, Culture and Social Interaction, 16,* 70–75.

Smagorinsky, P. (2018b). Is instructional scaffolding actually Vygotskian? And why should it matter to teachers? *Journal of Adolescent & Adult Literacy, 62*(3), 253–257.

Smagorinsky, P. (2018c). Literacy teacher education: "It's the context, stupid". *Journal of Literacy Research, 50*(3), 281–303.

Smagorinsky, P. (2018d). Emotion, reason, and argument: Teaching persuasive writing in tense times. *English Journal, 107*(5), 98–101.

Smagorinsky, P. (2018e). *Teaching English by design: How to create and carry out instructional units* (2nd ed.). Heinemann.

Smagorinsky, P. (2018f). Inclusion, "defectology," and second language learners. In J. Lantolf & M. Poehner (Eds.), *Handbook of sociocultural theory and second language development* (pp. 551–564). Routledge.

Smagorinsky, P. (2019). Vygotsky, "defectology," and the Soviet approach to human difference. In P. Smagorinsky, J. Tobin, & K. Lee (Eds.), *Dismantling the disabling environments of education: Creating new cultures and contexts for accommodating difference* (pp. 47–64). Peter Lang.

Smagorinsky, P. (2020a). *Learning to teach English and language arts: A Vygotskian perspective on beginning teachers' pedagogical concept development.* Bloomsbury.

Smagorinsky, P. (2020b). Neurodiversity and the deep structure of schools. *Ought: The Journal of Autistic Culture, 2*(1), Article 4. https://scholarworks.gvsu.edu/ought/vol2/iss1/4

Smagorinsky, P. (2021a). The great equalizer of the conditions of [humanity]: How transformative can schools be when society itself remains inequitable and quarrelsome? In D. C. Berliner & C. Hermanns (Eds.), *Public education: The cornerstone of American democracy* (pp. 69–83). Teachers College Press.

Smagorinsky, P. (2021b). The relation between emotion and intellect: Which governs which? *Integrative Psychological & Behavioral Science, 55,* 769–778.

Smagorinsky, P. (2021c, February 3). OPINION: Strengthening teacher pipeline won't matter if destination is a sewer. *Atlanta Journal-Constitution.* https://www.ajc.com/education/get-schooled-blog/opinion-strengthening-teacher-pipeline-wont-matter-if-destination-is-a-sewer/HKTUADQ5OZBSTIBOABHWJZGJLU/

Smagorinsky, P. (2022). The creation of national cultures through education, the inequities they produce, and the challenges for multicultural education. *International Journal of Multicultural Education. 24*(2), 80–96.

Smagorinsky, P. (2023a). My life as a gardener. In J. Avila (Ed.), *Leaders in English language arts education: Intellectual self portraits.* Brill.

Smagorinsky, P. (2023b). Talking and listening for civic engagement. *English Journal, 112*(3), 57–63.

Smagorinsky, P., Cole, M., & Braga, L. W. (2017). On the complementarity of cultural historical psychology and contemporary disability studies. In I. Esmonde & A. Booker (Eds.), *Power and privilege in the learning sciences: Critical and sociocultural theories* (pp. 70–92). Routledge.

Smagorinsky, P., Johannessen, L., Kahn, E., & McCann, T. (2010). *The dynamics of writing instruction: A structured process approach for the composition teacher in the middle and high school.* Heinemann.

Smagorinsky, P., & Johnson, L. L. (2021). Empathic framing during concept development in book club discussions in a service-learning teacher education class. *Language and Sociocultural Theory*, *8*(2), 206–238.

Smagorinsky, P., & Lang, M. (2023). Learning to create environments for deafness among hearing preservice teachers: A defectological approach. Learning, Culture, and Social Interaction.

Smagorinsky, P., McCann, T., & Kern, S. (1987). *Explorations: Introductory activities for literature and composition, grades 7–12*. National Council of Teachers of English.

Smagorinsky, P., & O'Donnell-Allen, C. (1998a). The depth and dynamics of context: Tracing the sources and channels of engagement and disengagement in students' response to literature. *Journal of Literacy Research*, *30*, 515–559.

Smagorinsky, P., & O'Donnell-Allen, C. (2000). Idiocultural diversity in small groups: The role of the relational framework in collaborative learning. In C. D. Lee & P. Smagorinsky (Eds.), *Vygotskian perspectives on literacy research: Constructing meaning through collaborative inquiry* (pp. 165–190). Cambridge University Press.

Smagorinsky, P., & Taxel, J. (2004). The discourse of character education: Ideology and politics in the proposal and award of federal grants. *Journal of Research in Character Education*, *2*(2), 113–140.

Smagorinsky, P., & Taxel, J. (2005). *The discourse of character education: Culture wars in the classroom*. Erlbaum.

Smagorinsky, P., Tobin, J., & Lee, K. (Eds.) (2019). *Dismantling the disabling environments of education: Creating new cultures and contexts for accommodating difference*. Peter Lang.

Smagorinsky, P., Wilson, A. A., & Moore, C. (2011). Teaching grammar and writing: A beginning teacher's dilemma. *English Education*, *43*, 263–293.

Smith, A. (1776/1977). *An inquiry into the nature and causes of the wealth of nations*. University of Chicago Press.

Smith, L.T. (2005). Building a research agenda for indigenous epistemologies and education. *Anthropology and Education Quarterly*, *36*(1), 93–95.

Smith, M. W. (1989). Teaching the interpretation of irony in poetry. *Research in the Teaching of English*, *23*(3), 254–272.

Smitherman, G. (1977). *Talkin and testifyin: The language of Black America*. Houghton-Mifflin.

Smith, P. K., Singer, M., Hoel, H., & Cooper, C. L. (2003). Victimization in the school and the workplace: Are there any links? *British Journal of Psychology*, *94*(2), 175–188. https://doi.org/10.1348/000712603321661868

Snyder, T. (2010). *Bloodlands: Europe between Hitler and Stalin*. Basic Books.

Snyder, T. (2015). *Black earth: The Holocaust as history and warning*. Crown.

Snyder, T. (2018). *The road to unfreedom*. Crown.

Snyder, T. (2021, June 29). The war on history is a war on democracy. *The New York Times Magazine*. https://www.nytimes.com/2021/06/29/magazine/memory-laws.html?utm_source=substack&utm_medium=email

Snyder, T. (2022a, April 22). The war in Ukraine has unleashed a new word. *New York Times*. https://www.nytimes.com/2022/04/22/magazine/ruscism-ukraine-russia-war.html

Snyder, T. (2022b, October 10). *Russia's Crimea disconnect*. https://snyder.substack.com/p/russias-crimea-disconnect

Soboleva, M. (2017). Concept of the "New Soviet Man" and its short history. *Canadian-American Slavic Studies*, *51*, 64–85.

Social and Character Development Research Consortium. (2010). Efficacy of schoolwide programs to promote social and character development and reduce problem behavior in elementary school children. *U.S. National Center for Education Research & Institute of Education Sciences*. https://ies.ed.gov/ncer/pubs/20112001/pdf/20112001.pdf

Solnick, S. L. (1991). Revolution, reform and the Soviet telephone system, 1917–1927. *Soviet Studies*, *43*(1), 157–175.

Solzhenitsyn, A. I. (1973). *The Gulag archipelago Volume 1: An experiment in literary investigation* (T. P. Whitney, Trans.). Harper & Rowe.

Sonnenborn, T. M. (1975). *Herbert Spencer Jennings 1868–1947: A biographical memoir.* National Academy of Sciences. http://www.nasonline.org/publications/biographical-memoirs/memoir-pdfs/jennings-herbert.pdf

Souto-Manning, M., & Smagorinsky, P. (2010). Freire, Vygotsky, and social justice theories in English education. In S. J. Miller & D. Kirkland (Eds.), *Change matters: Critical essays on moving social justice research from theory to policy* (pp. 41–51). Peter Lang.

Special Collections at the University of Washington Libraries. (n. d.). *Fairytales and the five-year plan: Russian children's literature exhibit.* https://content.lib.washington.edu/exhibits/russian-childrens-lit/index.html

Spencer, H. (1864). *Principles of biology.* https://www.gutenberg.org/files/54612/54612-h/54612-h.htm

Spinoza, B. de (1677/1955). *On the improvement of the understanding. The ethics. Correspondence.* Dover.

Spranger, E. (1914). *Lebensformen [Types of men].* (P. J. W. Pigors, Trans.). G. E. Stechert Company.

Springston, R. (2018, April 14). Happy slaves? The peculiar story of three Virginia school textbooks. *Richmond.com.* https://richmond.com/discover-richmond/happy-slaves-the-peculiar-story-of-three-virginia-school-textbooks/article_47e79d49-eac8-575d-ac9d-1c6fce52328f.html

St. John-Bond, M. (2018, October 1). Stalin and Putin's attitudes towards national minorities: A comparative essay. *The Historical Opinion.* https://historicalopinion.wordpress.com/2018/10/01/stalin-and-putins-attitudes-towards-national-minorities-a-comparative-essay/

Stern, W. (1927). *Psychologie der frühen Kindheit bis zum sechsten Lebensjahre* (4th ed.). Verlag von Quelle und Meyer.

Stitzlein, S. M. (2022). Divisive concepts in classrooms: A call to inquiry. *Studies in Philosophy and Education, 41,* 595–612. https://doi.org/10.1007/s11217-022-09842-8

Strauss, V. (2014). For first time, minority students expected to be majority in U.S. public schools this fall. *Answer Sheet of the Washington Post.* https://www.washingtonpost.com/news/answer-sheet/wp/2014/08/21/for-first-time-minority-students-expected-to-be-majority-in-u-s-public-schools-this-fall/?utm_term=.806a5f82624e

Street, B. V. (1984). *Literacy in theory and practice.* Cambridge University Press.

Street, B. V. (2003). What's "New" in New Literacy Studies? Critical approaches to Literacy in theory and practice. *Current Issues in Comparative Education, 5*(2), 77–91.

Strother, G. B. (1949). The role of muscle action in interpretative reading. *Journal of General Psychology, 41,* 3–20.

Stubbs, R. (2019, April 17). A wrestler was forced to cut his dreadlocks before a match. His town is still looking for answers. *The Washington Post.* https://www.washingtonpost.com/sports/2019/04/17/wrestler-was-forced-cut-his-dreadlocks-before-match-his-town-is-still-looking-answers/

Swindle, J.M. (2003). A rhetorical use of women in Tacitus' Annales. *Studia Antiqua,* 3(1), 105–115. https://scholarsarchive.byu.edu/studiaantiqua/vol3/iss1/10

Tagami, T. (2021, June 3). Georgia education board passes resolution to limit classroom discussions of race. *Atlanta Journal-Constitution.* https://www.ajc.com/education/state-board-passes-resolution-to-limit-classroom-discussions-of-race/L4HYBED74BBFLEYTK5JSNDTK44/

Tagami, T. (2023, February 16). School librarians could face criminal charges under Georgia bill. *Atlanta Journal-Constitution.* https://www.ajc.com/education/school-librarians-could-face-criminal-charges-under-georgia-bill/6KPSAZSZGBAF5OZE2DBQ724AIE/

Taine, H. A. (1873). *A tour through the Pyrenees* (J. Safford Triske, Trans.). Henry Holt.

Talankin, A. A. (1931). Diskussiia o polozhenii na psikhologicheskom fronte [Discussion of the turnaround on the psychological front]. *Sovetskaia Psikhonevrologiia, 2–3,* 15. Republished in *Journal of Russian & East European Psychology* as "On the Vygotsky and Luria Group," 2002, 3838

Tartakower, A. (1971). The Jewish problem in the Soviet Union. *Jewish Social Studies, 33*(4), 285–306.

Tate, W. F. (1995). Returning to the root: A culturally relevant approach to mathematics pedagogy. *Theory Into Practice, 34*(3), 166–173.

Taylor, C. (1985a). *Human agency and language: Philosophical papers 1.* Cambridge University Press.

Taylor, C. (1985b). *Philosophy and the human sciences: Philosophical papers 2.* Cambridge University Press.

Taylor, K. (2015, October 29). At a Success Academy Charter School, singling out pupils who have 'got to go.' *New York Times.* https://www.nytimes.com/2015/10/30/nyregion/at-a-success-academy-charter-school-singling-out-pupils-who-have-got-to-go.html?ref=nyregion

Taylor, K. (2018). American political development and black lives matter in the age of incarceration. *Politics, Groups, and Identities, 6*(1), 153–161.

Taylor, J. M., Gilligan, C., & Sullivan, A. M. (1997). *Between voice and silence: Women and girls, race and relationship.* Harvard University Press.

Teo, P. (2016). Exploring the dialogic space in teaching: A study of teacher talk in the pre-university classroom in Singapore. *Teaching and Teacher Education, 56,* 47–60.

The Council for Global Equality (n. d.). The facts on LGBT rights in Russia. *Author.* http://www.globalequality.org/component/content/article/1-in-the-news/186-the-facts-on-lgbt-rights-in-russia

The Great Soviet Encyclopedia Wiki. (n. d.). *Population (USSR).* https://greatsovietencyclopedia.fandom.com/wiki/Population_(USSR)

The Phyllis Schlafly Report. (1993, May). What's wrong with outcome-based education? *Author, 26*(10). https://eagleforum.org/psr/1993/may93/psrmay93.html

Thomas, A. (2017). *The hate U give.* Balzer + Bray.

Thomas, G. E. (1983). The deficit, difference, and bicultural theories of Black dialect and nonstandard English. *Urban Review, 15*(2), 107–118.

Thorndike, E. L. (1906). *The principles of teaching based on psychology.* A. G. Seiler.

Tingting, Y. (2021, December 29). Why long fingernails were all the rage in ancient China. Sixth Tone: Fresh Voices from Today's China. https://www.sixthtone.com/news/1009319/why-long-fingernails-were-all-the-rage-in-ancient-china-

Tolstoy, L. (1862). *Who should teach whom to write: We the peasant children or the peasant children us?* [*Komu u kogo uchit'sia pisat'—krest'ianskikh rebiatam u nas ili nam u krest'ianskikh rebiat*]

Toulmin, S. E. (1958). *The uses of argument.* Cambridge University Press.

Toulmin, S. E. (1978, September 28). The Mozart of psychology. *New York Times Review of Books.* https://www.nybooks.com/articles/1978/09/28/the-mozart-of-psychology/

Treleaven, K. (2022, August 1). Rise of the 'jackhammer parent.' *Answer Sheet of The Washington Post.* https://www.washingtonpost.com/education/2022/08/01/meet-the-jackhammer-parent/

Tripathy, M. (2018). Building quality teamwork to achieve excellence in business organizations. *International Research Journal of Management, IT & Social Sciences, 5*(3), 1–7.

Trudgill, P., & Hannah, J. (2017). *A guide to varieties of English around the world,* Sixth edition. Routledge.

Tsai, J. (n. d.). Culture and emotion. *Nobaproject.* https://nobaproject.com/modules/culture-and-emotion

Tucker, R. C. (1990). *Stalin in power: The revolution from above, 1928–1941.* W. W. Norton.

Tuller, D. (1996). *Cracks in the iron closet: Travels in gay and lesbian Russia.* University of Chicago Press.

Tulviste, P. (1991). *The cultural-historical development of verbal thinking.* Nova Science Publishers.

Tunç, B., & Ülker, S. (2020). Ignored discrimination in schools: Tracking. *Political Economy and Management of Education, 1*(2), 16–36.

Tyler, R. W. (1949). *Basic principles of curriculum and instruction.* University of Chicago Press.

The Wiener Holocaust Library. (n.d.). *Juden Raus! board game.* https://wienerholocaustlibrary.org/object/obj046/

U. S. Bureau of Labor Statistics. (2021, April 27). College enrollment and work activity of recent high school and college graduates summary. *Author*. https://www.bls.gov/news.release/hsgec.nr0.htm#:~:text=The%20participation%20rates%20for%20male%20and%20female%20graduates,2020%2C%20about%209%20in%2010%20were%20full-time%20students.

Umrikhin, V. V. (1991) 'Nachalo kontsa" povedencheskoi psikhologii v SSSR. In M. G. Iaroshevskii (Ed.), *Represirovannaia nauka* (pp. 136–145). Nauka.

United Nations. (1948). *Universal declaration of human rights*. https://www.ohchr.org/en/human-rights/universal-declaration/translations/english

United Nations. (2022). *Progress on the sustainable development goals: The gender snapshot 2022*. Author. https://unstats.un.org/sdgs/gender-snapshot/2022/GenderSnapshot.pdf

Vad Vashem. (2021). Gomel. *Vad Vashem: The World Holocaust Remembrance Center*. https://collections.yadvashem.org/en/untold-stories/community/14621614-Gomel

Van der Lely, H. K. J., Rosen, S., & McClelland, A. (1998). Evidence for a grammar-specific deficit in children. *Current Biology, 8*(23), 1253–1258.

Van der Spek, E. D., & Van Oostendorp, H. (2011). Measuring learning in serious games: A case study with structural assessment. *Educational Technology Research and Development, 59*(6), 741–763.

Van der Veer, R. (1997a). Translator's foreword and acknowledgements. In L. S. Vygotsky, *Collected works* (Vol. 3: Problems of the theory and history of psychology) (pp. v–vi) (R. W. Rieber & J. Wollock, Eds.; R. van der Veer, Trans.). Plenum.

Van der Veer, R. (1997b). Some major themes in Vygotsky's theoretical work. An introduction. In R. W. Rieber & J. Wollock (Eds.), *The collected works of L. S. Vygotsky, Volume 3: Problems of the theory and history of psychology* (R. van der Veer, Trans.) (pp. 1–7). Plenum.

Van der Veer, R. (2002). Editor's introduction: Criticizing Vygotsky. *Journal of Russian & East European Psychology, 38*(6), 3–9.

Van der Veer, R. (2007). Vygotsky in context: 1900–1935. In H. Daniels, M. Cole, & J. V. Wertsch (Eds.), *The Cambridge companion to Vygotsky* (pp. 21–49). Cambridge University Press.

Van der Veer, R. (2014). *Lev Vygotsky*. Bloomsbury.

Van der Veer, R. (2015). Vygotsky, the theater critic: 1922–3. *History of the Human Sciences, 28*(2), 103–110.

Van der Veer, R. (Ed.) (2020). *Vygotsky's pedology of the school age* (R. van der Veer, Trans.). Information Age Publishing.

Van der Veer, R. (2021). Vygotsky, Luria, and cross-cultural research in the Soviet Union. In D. McCallum (Ed.), *The Palgrave handbook of the history of human sciences* (pp. 1–21). Palgrave Macmillan. https://doi.org/10.1007/978-981-15-4106-3_82-1

Van der Veer, R., & Valsiner, J. (1991). *Understanding Vygotsky: A quest for synthesis*. Blackwell.

Van der Veer, R., & Yasnitsky, A. (2011). Vygotsky in English: What still needs to be done. *Integrative Psychological and Behavioral Science, 45*(4), 475–493.

Van der Veer, R., & Yasnitsky, A. (2016). Translating Vygotsky: Some problems of transnational Vygotskian science. In A. Yasnitsky & R. van der Veer (Eds.), *Revisionist revolution in Vygotsky studies* (pp. 143–174). Routledge.

Van der Veer, R., & Zavershneva, E. (2018). The final chapter of Vygotsky's *Thinking and Speech*: A reader's guide. *The History of the Behavioral Sciences, 54*(2), 101–116.

Van Oers, B. (2001). Contextualisation for abstraction. *Cognitive Science Quarterly, 1*, 279–305.

Vasiliev, N. L. (2018). M. M. Bakhtin as a university professor. *Dialogic Pedagogy: An International Online Journal, 6*, 1–7. https://doi.org/10.5195/dpj.2018.234

Veresov, N. N. (2017). ZBR and ZPD: Is there a difference? *Cultural-Historical Psychology, 13*(1), 23–36. https://doi.org/10.17759/chp.2017130102

Veresov, N. N., & Kellogg, D. (2019). Leaving the stage. In L. S. Vygotsky, *L. S. Vygotsky's pedagogical works: Volume 1: Foundations of pedology* (pp. 143–155). (D. Kellogg & N. Veresov, Trans.). Springer.

Vernon, W. (2023, January 23). Russia: Putin's Kremlin targets LGBT in new crackdown. *BBC*. https://www.bbc.com/news/world-europe-64345693

Vine, N. (2009). Psychology under the Third Reich. *Psychology*. https://web.wpi.edu/Pubs/E-project/Available/E-project-102609-144251/unrestricted/PsychologyUndertheThirdReich.pdf

Vogel, S. M. (1997). Baule: African Art Western eyes. *African Arts*, *30*(4), Special Issue: The Benin Centenary, Part 2, 64–77, 95.

Von Vugt, M., & Van Lange, P. M. A. (2006). The altruism puzzle: Psychological adaptations for prosocial behavior. In M. Schaller, J. A. Simpson, & D. T. Kenrick (Eds.), *Evolution and social psychology* (pp. 237–262). Psychology Press.

Vorländer, K. (1904). *Marx und Kant [Marx and Kant]*. Verlag der 'Deutschen Worte'.

Vygodskaya, G. (n. d.). *His life*. https://lchc.ucsd.edu/mca/Mail/xmcamail.1998_08.dir/0033.html

Vygotsky, L. S. (1925/1986). *Psikhologija iskusstva*. Iskusstvo.

Vygotsky, L. S. (1926). O vlijanii rechevogo ritma na dykhanie. In K. N. Kornilov (Ed.), *Problemy sovremennoj psikhologii* (pp. 169–73). Gosudarstvennoe Izdatel'stvo.

Vygotsky, L. S. (1930). *The instrumental method in psychology*. Presentation at the Krupskaya Academy of Communist Education. https://www.marxists.org/archive/vygotsky/works/1930/instrumental.htm

Vygotsky, L. S. (1934a). *Myshlenie i rech': Psikhologicheskie issledovaniya [Thinking and Speech: Psychological investigations]*. Gosudarstvennoe Sotsial'no-Ekonomicheskio Izdatel'stvo.

Vygotsky, L. S. (1934b/1987). Preface to Koffka: The problem of development in structural psychology. A critical investigation. In L. S. Vygotsky, *Collected works* (Vol. 1, pp. 195–232) (R. Rieber & A. Carton, Eds.; N. Minick, Trans.). Plenum.

Vygotsky, L. S. (1962). *Thought and language* (E. Hanfmann & G. Vakar, Eds. & Trans.). MIT Press.

Vygotsky, L. S. (1966). Play and its role in the mental development of the child. *Voprosy psikhologii*, *12*(6), 62–76. From a stenographic record of a lecture given in 1933 at the Hertzen Pedagogical Insti- tute, Leningrad.

Vygotsky, L. S. (1971). *The psychology of art* (Scripta Technica, Inc., Trans.). M.I.T. Press.

Vygotsky, L. S. (1978). *Mind in society: The development of higher psychological processes* (M. Cole, V. John-Steiner, S. Scribner, & E. Souberman, Eds.). Harvard University Press.

Vygotsky, L. S. (1986). *Thought and language* (A. Kozulin, Ed. & Trans.). MIT Press.

Vygotsky, L. S. (1987). Thinking and speech. In L. S. Vygotsky, *Collected works* (Vol. 1, pp. 39–285) (R. Rieber & A. Carton, Eds.; N. Minick, Trans.). Plenum.

Vygotsky, L. S. (1993). *The collected works of L. S. Vygotsky. Volume 2: The fundamentals of defectology (abnormal psychology and learning disabilities)* (R. W. Rieber & A. S. Carton, Eds.; J. E. Knox & C. B. Stevens, Trans.). Plenum.

Vygotsky, L. S. (1997a). *Educational psychology* (L. S. Vygotsky & V. V. Davydov, Eds.; R. Silverman, Trans.). St. Lucie Press.

Vygotsky, L. S. (1997b). *The collected works of L.S. Vygotsky. Volume 3: Problems of the theory and history of psychology* (R. van der Veer, Trans; R. W. Rieber & J. Wollock, (Eds.). Plenum.

Vygotsky, L. S. (1997c). *The collected works of L. S. Vygotsky. Volume 4: The history of the development of higher mental functions* (R. Rieber, Ed.; M. J. Hall, Trans.). Plenum.

Vygotsky, L. S. (1998). *The collected works of L. S. Vygotsky. Volume 5: Child psychology* (R. Rieber, Ed.; M. J. Hall, Trans.). Plenum.

Vygotsky, L. S. (1999). *The collected works of L. S. Vygotsky. Volume 6: Scientific legacy* (R. W. Rieber, Ed.; M. J. Hall, Trans.). Plenum.

Vygotsky, L. S. (2004). *The essential Vygotsky* (R. W. Rieber & D. K. Robinson, Eds.). Kluwer & Plenum.

Vygotsky, L. S. (2019). *L. S. Vygotsky's pedagogical works: Volume 1: Foundations of pedology*. (D. Kellogg & N. Veresov, Trans.). Springer.

Vygotsky, L. S., & Luria, A. R. (1993). *Studies on the history of behavior: Ape, primitive, and child* (V. I. Golod & J. E. Knox, Eds. & Trans.). Erlbaum.

Waks, L. J. (2013). John Dewey and the challenge of progressive education. *International Journal of Progressive Education, 9*(1), 73–83.

Wallace-Wells, D. (2022, August 3). It's been a 'summer of disasters,' and it's only half over. *New York Times.* https://www.nytimes.com/2022/08/03/opinion/floods-climate-summer-kentucky.html

Ward, G. M. (2013). *A study of teachers' perspectives on Montessori students' transition to a traditional high school.* Unpublished doctoral dissertation, University of South Carolina.

Washington Post Editorial Board. (2022, August 15). Opinion: Youngkin's toxic school 'tip line' is shrouded in secrecy. *The Washington Post.* https://www.washingtonpost.com/opinions/2022/08/15/youngkin-school-tip-line-secret/

Watson, J. B. (1930). *Behaviorism* (revised edition). University of Chicago Press.

Weaver, C. (1996). *Teaching grammar in context.* Heinemann.

Wells, H. G. (1895). *The time machine.* William Heinemann.

Welsh, R. O., & Little, S. (2018). The school discipline dilemma: A comprehensive review of disparities and alternative approaches. *Review of Educational Research, 88*(5), 752–794.

Wertsch, J. V. (1984). The zone of proximal development: Some conceptual issues. In B. Rogoff & J. V. Wertsch (Eds.), *New directions for child development: No. 23. Children's learning in the "zone of proximal development"* (pp. 7–18). Jossey-Bass.

Wertsch, J. V. (1985). *Vygotsky and the social formation of mind.* Harvard University Press.

Wertsch, J. V. (1991). *Voices of the mind: A sociocultural approach to mediated action.* Harvard University Press.

Wertsch, J. V. (1994). The primacy of mediated action in sociocultural studies. *Mind, Culture, and Activity, 1*(4), 202–208.

Wertsch, J. V. (1995). Vygotsky: The ambivalent enlightenment rationalist. *Volume XXI, Heinz Werner Lecture Series* (pp. 39–62). Clark University Press.

Wertsch, J. V. (1996). The role of abstract rationality in Vygotsky's image of mind. In A. Tryphon & J. Voneche (Eds.), *Piaget-Vygotsky: The social genesis of thought* (pp. 25–43). Psychology Press.

Wertsch, J. V. (1997). Foreword. In L. S. Vygotsky & A. R. Luria, *Studies on the history of behavior ape, primitive, and child* (V. I. Golod & J. E. Knox, Eds. & Trans.) (pp. ix–xiii). Erlbaum.

Wertsch, J. V. (1998). *Mind as action.* Oxford University Press.

Wertsch, J. V. (1999). Revising Russian history. *Written Communication, 16*(3), 267–295.

Wertsch, J. V. (2000). Vygotsky's two minds on the nature of meaning. In C. D. Lee & P. Smagorinsky (Eds.), *Vygotskian perspectives on literacy research: Constructing meaning through collaborative inquiry* (pp. 19–30). Cambridge University Press.

Wertsch, J. V. (2007). Mediation. In H. Daniels, M. Cole, & J. V. Wertsch (Eds.), *The Cambridge companion to Vygotsky* (pp. 178–192). Cambridge University Press.

Wertsch, J. V. (2021). *How nations remember: A narrative approach.* Oxford University Press.

Wertsch, J. V. (2022). The narrative tools of national memory. In H. L. Roediger & J. V. Wertsch (Eds.), *National memories* (pp. 454–471). Oxford University Press.

Wertsch, J. V., & Sohmer, R. (1995). Vygotsky on learning and development. *Human Development, 38,* 332–337.

Whalen, J. (2022, April 10). Russian students are turning in teachers who don't back the war: The cases are part of a Soviet-style hunt for 'traitors' who oppose the Kremlin's invasion of Ukraine. *The Washington Post.* https://www.washingtonpost.com/world/2022/04/10/russia-war-dissent-opposition-crackdown/

Whorton, D. (2015, November 9). Years of cheating by Russian track and field athletes detailed in report. *Los Angeles Times.* https://www.latimes.com/sports/la-sp-wada-report-russia-doping-20151110-story.html

Wiens, E. (2012, July 20). I won't hire people who use poor grammar. Here's why. *Harvard Business Review.* https://hbr.org/2012/07/i-wont-hire-people-who-use-poo

Wilhelm, J. D., Baker, T., & Dube, J. (2001). *Strategic reading: Guiding students to lifelong literacy*. Heinemann.

Wilkinson, C. (2020). LGBT rights in the former Soviet Union. In M. J. Bosia, S. M. McEvoy, & M. Rahman (Eds.), *The Oxford handbook of global LGBT and sexual diversity politics* (pp. 233–248). Oxford University Press.

Winn, M. T. (2018). *Justice on both sides: Transforming education through restorative justice*. Harvard Education Press.

Winston, A. W. (2020). Why mainstream research will not end scientific racism in psychology. *Theory & Psychology, 30*(3), 425–430.

Wissler, C., & Duvall, D. C. (1908). *Mythology of the Blackfoot Indians*. Anthropological Papers of the American Museum of Natural History, v. 2, part 1.

Witte, S. P. (1992). Context, text, intertext: Toward a constructivist semiotic of writing. *Written Communication, 9*(2), 237–308.

Wixted, J. T., Mickes, L., & Fisher, R. P. (2018). Rethinking the reliability of eyewitness memory. *Perspectives on Psychological Science, 13*(3), 324–335.

Wood, D., Bruner, J. D., & Ross, G. (1976). The role of tutoring in problem solving. *Journal of Child Psychology and Psychiatry, 17*, 89–100.

Woods, C. (Editor) (2010a). *Visible language: Inventions of writing in the ancient Middle East and beyond*. The Oriental Institute of the University of Chicago. http://oi.uchicago.edu/pdf/oimp32.pdf

Woods, C. (2010b). Introduction: Visible language: The earliest writing systems. In C. Wood (Ed.), *Visible language: Inventions of writing in the ancient Middle East and beyond* (pp. 15–27). The Oriental Institute of the University of Chicago. http://oi.uchicago.edu/pdf/oimp32.pdf

Worrell, B., W. Collins, W., & Clinton, G. (1975). *Ride on. On Parliament, Chocolate City, Side 1, Track 2*. Casablanca Records.

Worsley, P. (1982). *Marx and Marxism*. Routledge.

Worthy, J., Lammert, C., Long, S. L., Salmerón, C., & Godfrey, V. (2018). "What if we were committed to giving *every* individual the services and opportunities they need?" Teacher educators' understandings, perspectives, and practices surrounding dyslexia. *Research in the Teaching of English, 53*(2), 125–148.

Yacovone, D. (2022). *Teaching white supremacy: America's democratic ordeal and the forging of our national identity*. Pantheon Books.

Yaden, D. B., Reinking, D. P., & Smagorinsky, P. (2021). The trouble with binaries: A perspective on a science of reading. *Reading Research Quarterly, 56*, 119–129.

Yagelski, R. P. (2007). A thousand writers writing: Seeking change through the radical practice of writing as a way of being. *English Education, 42*(1), 6–28.

Yan, H. (2022, May 31). There's talk of razing Robb Elementary School and rebuilding it. Here's what happened after other school massacres. *CNN*. https://www.cnn.com/2022/05/31/us/schools-after-mass-shootings-uvalde-texas/index.html

Yaroshevsky, M. G. (1989). *Lev Vygotsky* (S. Syrovatin, Trans.). Progress Publishers.

Yaroshevsky, M. G., & Gurgenidze, G. S. (1997). Epilogue. In R. W. Rieber & J. Wollock (Eds.). *The collected works of L.S. Vygotsky. Volume 3: Problems of the theory and history of psychology* (R. van der Veer, Trans.) (pp. 371–392). Plenum.

Yasnitsky, A. (2009). *Vygotsky Circle during the decade of 1931–1941: Toward an integrative science of mind, brain, and education*. Thesis. Department of Curriculum, Teaching and Learning, Ontario Institute for Studies in Education. University of Toronto.

Yasnitsky, A. (2012). The complete works of L.S. Vygotsky: PsyAnima complete Vygotsky Project. *Dubna Psychological Journal, 3*, 144–148.

Yerkes, R. M., & Learned, B. W. (1925). *Chimpanzee intelligence and its vocal expressions*. Williams & Wilkins Co. https://doi.org/10.5962/bhl.title.6965

Young, Y. A. (2003). *The minds of marginalized Black men: Making sense of mobility, opportunity, and future life chances*. Princeton University Press.

Youngkin, G. (2022, January 25). Opinion: Glenn Youngkin: Virginia's parents can decide what's best for their children. *The Washington Post.* https://www.washingtonpost.com/opinions/2022/01/25/glenn-youngkin-virginias-parents-can-decide-whats-best-their-children/

Zamoyski, A. (2009). *Poland: A history.* Hippocrene Books.

Zavershneva, E. (2010). The Vygotsky family archive: New findings. Notebooks, notes, and scientific journals of L.S. Vygotsky (1912–1934). *Journal of Russian and East European Psychology, 48*(1), 34–60. https://doi.org/10.2753/RPO1061-0405480102

Zavershneva, E., & Van der Veer, R. (Eds.) (2018a). *Vygotsky's notebooks: A selection.* Springer.

Zavershneva, E., & Van der Veer, R. (2018b). Not by bread alone: Lev Vygotsky's Jewish writings. *History of the Human Sciences, 31*(1), 36–55.

Zinchenko, V. (2007). Thought and word: The approaches of L. S. Vygotsky and G. G. Shpet. In H. Daniels, M. Cole, & J. V. Wertsch (Eds.), *The Cambridge companion to Vygotsky* (pp. 212–245). Cambridge University Press.

Zisels, J., Suslensky, A., Adamovsky, A., Chervonenko, E., Dukhovny, A., Stamov, R., … Kerez, I. (2014, March 5). *Open letter of Ukrainian Jews to Russian Federation President Vladimir Putin.* https://maidantranslations.com/2014/03/05/open-letter-of-ukrainian-jews-to-russian-federation-president-vladimir-putin/

Živkoviü, S. (2016). A model of critical thinking as an important attribute for success in the 21st century. *Procedia: Social and Behavioral Sciences, 232,* 102–108. Published from a paper presented at the International Conference on Teaching and Learning English as an Additional Language, GlobELT Antalya, Turkey.

Zyphur, M. J., & Pierides, D. C. (2020). Statistics and probability have always been value-laden: An historical ontology of quantitative research methods. *Journal of Business Ethics, 167,* 1–18.

Index

Note: Page references with "n" denote endnotes.

ableist/ableism 44, 78, 241, 243–244, 254
abstraction/abstract 55, 60, 71, 130, 139–140, 190–191, 229, 301; concepts 280; formal schooling 104; knowledge 116; signs as form of 85; thinking 88, 129, 134
acculturation 159
activity-based practical learning: in historical contexts 161–162; in social contexts 161–162
activity in classrooms 164–165
activity theory 6, 23, 277
addressivity 226
adolescence 185–186; biological maturity 128; cognitive stages 100; concept development in 100–102; imaginative play 129–130; and sexuality 175; as transitional age 100; Vygotsky on 42, 82; youth words use in 87
The Adventures of Milo and Otis 64
affordance 59, 65, 93, 140, 159, 168, 216, 219, 224–225, 227, 266, 311–312
African Americans 32, 66, 204
age 169–170; and higher mental functions 169; passport 144, 168–169, 265, 268–269; transitional 43, 82, 100, 102, 129, 174, 185
agency 20, 74, 84, 93, 147, 179, 182, 297
Age of Reason 14, 37, 107, 120, 271
Alfred The Great, king of the Anglo-Saxons 26
alphabetic texts 225–228, 234; production of 225–228
Amelina, Victoria 5
American Society for the Prevention of Cruelty to Animals (ASPCA) 63
anatomy 77, 261
Animal Farm (Orwell) 40, 263
animals 63–65
anti-Leninism 275
anti-Marxism 275–277
anti-Semitism 9, 45, 56, 216; of Tsarist Russia 12

anti-Stalinism 275
apes 84, 94
apperception 187
applied psychology 160
appropriation 14, 59, 130
arena 140, 252, 297
argumentation 214, 216, 230
art: Asian/African 205; essence of 201–205; folk 14; Native American 205; verbal 87
artefacts 23, 24, 27, 64, 73, 86, 314; ideal 24; material 24
articulation 85–86, 210
artificial: devices 158; mental functions 81; school as 158; signaling stimuli 189
Asperger's Advantage 246
atheism or atheistic 11, 234, 302
Atherton, J. S. 23
attention 186–188
authorial reading 215
authoritarianism/authoritarian xxii, 14, 136, 145, 157, 163–164, 177, 188, 278, 314
autodidactic/autodidacticism 163, 170
autodidacts, children as 168–169
autonomous meaning 98
autonomous model of literacy 221
autonomous text 98

Bacon, Francis 22n9
Bakhurst, D. 15
Baldwin Effect 58, 67n2
banking model 162
barbarism/barbarian 31, 200, 220, 236
Barber, B. 134
behaviorism 39, 41, 160, 184, 307
Berkenkotter, C. 23
Bernstein, B. 45
best practice 27
binary sexual orientation 39, 80, 132, 174
biological stage theories 78, 83, 100, 243, 307
biology 32–33
Black History Month 253

Black linguistic justice 230
blindness/blind 33, 44, 89, 144, 206, 239–244, 246, 254, 264, 285, 313
Blonsky, Pavel xxivn2
Boas, Franz Uri 67n4
Bolshevik Revolution 17, 35, 56, 242, 299
Bolshevism/Bolsheviks 4, 7, 12, 16–17, 25, 35, 129, 238, 259, 261, 281, 296
bourgeoisie/bourgeois 19, 21, 48, 55; anti-Marxist 273–289; elimination of 18; social class 5
bourgeois nationalism 280
bourgeois psychology 17, 41, 287, 304
breathing: easy 208–209; patterns 209; rates 208
British "growth model" 232
Burke, K. 64
The Butterflies of Zagorsk 144, 149–150

cancel culture 265
canonical literature/canonical texts 214
capitalism 4, 25, 37; and Vygotsky 48–49
catharsis 199, 210–211, 217–218, 313
Catherine the Great 9, 13
Cazden, C. B. 143
Central Asian research 266–267
Central Committee 261, 273, 275–276, 278, 284–285, 305
character/character education 46–48, 95, 104, 109, 111, 121, 135, 170–172
Chicago School of Criticism 204
children as autodidacts 168–169
children's literature 201
chimpanzees 82
Christian Romanovs 9
Christians/ Christianity 40, 50, 55–56
chronological age 169, 265
Churchill, Winston 95
civilization 14, 31, 38, 65, 77, 190, 200, 220
class analysis 42–47
class size 185, 272
clay modeling 223, 234
coaffect 211
code-meshing 229
code-switching 229
co-education 175
cognition 62, 76, 217, 226; cold 107, 119; cultural 100; disembodied 39; emotions corrupt 107; inner-speech-mediated 303; and social environment 43
cognitive map 192
cognitive psychology xvi, 71, 168, 184, 188–189, 191
cold cognition 107, 119
Cole, Michael xxii, 6, 23–25, 30, 80
collective evolution, and culture 28–29
collective labor and play 126–127

collectivism/collectivist 12, 20, 23, 95, 262, 264, 279; farms 41, 55, 59; Marxist 181; mentality 78
collectivist farms 41, 55, 59
Collins, Bootsy 66
colonialism/colonial 54, 230; empire 248; heritages 25, 95; impositions 29; peoples 293
colonization/colonizing 87, 248; European 36, 58
Common Core State Standards 216
Communism 20–21
compensation, defined 37
complex: concept development 96–97; education, in world 31–32; emotional 202; phenomenon, mind 97
concept(s): as cultural schemata 99–100; development 95–105, 301–304; scientific (academic) 95–96; spontaneous (everyday) 95–96
concept development 95–105, 301–304; in adolescence 100–102; and ideology 102–105; lower and higher mental functions 97; scientific (academic) concept 95–96; spontaneous (everyday) concept 95–96; twisting path 96–97; words in developing higher mental functions 97–99
conditional response xxiii, 113
confirmation bias xv, 119
consciousness 7–8, 208, 288; collective 290n8; and cultural mediation 27; development of 109; and phylogenesis 94; social 125, 213; social construction of 213
constraint 65, 129, 140, 159, 188
construction zone 266
constructivism/constructivist 23, 75, 164, 171–172, 182, 215
context 20; cultural xxii; for ontogeny 93; social 28, 52, 77, 85, 105, 131, 148–149, 152, 179, 259, 271; Soviet, Vygotsky in 16–21, 35–50
contradiction/contradictory: dialectical 209; and education 31–32; emotionally based 109, 208
controversial topics 120
Cooper, R. 131
Cossacks 10
Covid pandemic 170, 179, 230
creative/creativity 129, 206; imaginations 191; reconstruction 191
crises: and capitalism 48; defined 48
crisis in psychology 76
critical pedagogy/critical theory 296, 302
critical race theory (CRT) 31, 205, 249
cross-disciplinary learning 176–178
Culotta, E. 31

cultural assimilation 74–75
cultural capital 249, 313
cultural development 79
cultural evolution 53–55
cultural factors in Vygotsky's conception 219–221
cultural-historical activity theory (CHAT) 23
cultural-historical psychology 71–91; higher mental functioning 74–81; human development 72–74
cultural mediation 27, 53, 56, 59, 120, 199, 211, 311
cultural phylogeny 30–31, 59
cultural relativism 34
cultural schema/schemata 96, 99–100, 104; concepts as 99–100
cultural tool kit/cultural tools 14, 29, 64–65, 86–87, 148–149, 158, 212, 234–235
cultural unity 60–63
culture 23–31; cancel 265; and collective evolution 28–29; cultural phylogeny 30–31; defined 23–24; dominant 25, 32, 42, 120, 167, 205, 220–221, 236, 248, 251–252, 254; and education 26–27; European 13–14; pedology 284–286; and power differentials 29–30; *prolepsis* 25–26; ranking of 284–286; social hierarchies 24–25; *telos* 25–26
Culture Wars 175

daily lesson planning 145
Daniels, H. 20
Darwin, Charles 20, 28, 82, 93–95
Davydov, V. V. 13
deafness or deaf 89, 241–243, 313
deep structure of school 26
defectology 10; German 240–242; inclusive 242–245; Soviet 240–242
demise of the school 275, 296, 303, 305–308
denunciation 19, 263, 279
Descartes/Cartesian 164, 208
designative tradition 15, 236
development, end of 300–301
diagnostic tests 46, 265–270, 277–282, 313
dialectical materialism 36, 39–40, 77, 80, 286
dialectical psychology 39, 72
dialectic synthesis 36–42
dialogism/dialogic 161–162, 289
diapers 80
Díaz, Porfirio 26
'dictatorship of the proletariat' 16–20, 296
difficult children 66, 261
digital media 224
digital tools 224
disabilities, people with 10
Disability Studies 78, 240, 243, 245, 246–247; secondary disability beyond 246–247

disposition theory 243
diversity 253–254; of cultures 103; individual human 231; and mission statements 247; and schools 248–249; society's 133
diversity, equity, and inclusion (DEI) initiatives 249, 252
doctrine: Marxist 20, 261; Marxist-Leninist-Stalinist 304; Soviet 17, 48, 55, 57, 76, 102, 116, 157, 221, 279, 287, 305
dominant culture 25, 32, 42, 120, 167, 205, 220–221, 236, 248, 251–252, 254
Don't Say Gay legislation 176
double stimulation 292, 296
doubling of experience 84
Doyle, Arthur Conan 107
drama: formal 212–213; in life 108–109; in theater 108–109
Draper, H. 16
drawing/draw 222–225, 234
dreams 61–62
dress codes 26, 175, 254
Dubois, W. E. B. 66
Durkin, K. 134
dysphoria 244, 313

East/Eastern: culture 113; Europe 3, 6, 10, 14, 254; Mediterranean 200
eclecticism/eclectic xiii, 50, 260, 287, 289
education: in complex and contradictory world 31–32; and culture 26–27; definition of 158–160; ethics in 170–172;
in European and colonized English world's schools 27; of the feelings 116–119; mass 26; morality in 170–172; multicultural 26–27; occupational 131, 138–139, 141; outcomes-based 160; Vygotsky on 158–160
educational environment: foregrounding 162–164
Educational Psychology (Vygotsky) 109, 110
egocentric emotions 113, 212, 281
eidetic images 88–89
embodied reading 208–212
embodiment/embodied: literacy research 210; reading 208–212; scaffolding 142
emotion(s) 110–111, 211; and cognition 107; egocentric 113, 212, 281; of formal drama 212–213; human development 109; and intellect 110–111; intelligent 199, 211, 218, 313; and learning 118–119; and maturity 111–112; and reason 107–108, 114–116; and socialization 112–114
emplotment 192
enculturation 137, 151, 182, 219
environment 32–33, 294–300
equilibrium 11, 110, 191–192

ernstspiel 122
essayist tradition 226
essence of art 201–205
ethics: in education 170–172; social 170
ethnicity 42, 56, 62
ethnocentric 15, 54, 62, 221
eugenics 243, 282, 305
Eurocentrism 57
European Enlightenment 14, 31, 108, 214, 241
European/Europe: culture 13–14; Nazi movement in 56; rationalism 14–15
evolution: collective 28–29; cultural 53–55; human phylogenetic 53
exploratory speech 313
expressive tradition 232

factory workers 17, 40, 59
fantasy 88, 129–130
fascism/fascist 36, 304
Faulkner, William 52
feelings 116–119; *see also* emotion(s)
feminist psychology 65
fingernails 298–299
first Russian Revolution 7
five-paragraph theme 231
flow: cultural, of school 181; defined 218; emotional 115; Vygotsky's educational psychology 161
foregrounding the educational environment 162–164
formal drama, emotion of 212–213
formalism/formalist 120, 196, 198, 203–204, 206–207, 213, 215, 227–228, 232
Foundations of Mental Development (Koffka) 39
freewriting 227, 231
Freud, S. 30, 107, 191, 211
fun: classrooms as 122; and play 122–123; Vygotsky on 131
future orientation 84, 190; and imaginative play 139; and play 125; Vygotsky's developmental focus 181

games 131–137; and emotions 136–137; and moral development 135–136
gamification 131
garden/gardening 104, 180
Gates, Henry Louis, Jr. 66
genetic: developmental 72, 75, 90, 92, 126; differences 21; domains 63; inheritance 82
genocide 58, 95, 170, 233
genre 205–208
genre theory 205
German defectology 240–242
German/Germanic 3–4, 216; defectology 240–242, 244; notion of *kultur* 13
gestalt 39
Gilligan, C. 30, 65

Glick, J. xix
global warming 105
goal congruence 186
Gomel, Belarus xi, 4–7, 9–10
Goodlad, J. 120
grades 32, 138, 148, 172, 176, 181–182, 234
grammar 228–230, 234, 306
Great Purge 14, 18
Great Terror 170, 200, 259, 274–275, 287
Great War 3–4
guide on the side 164–165
Gulag 24, 41, 57, 262–263, 275
Gurgenidze, G. S. 77, 86

habits 182–183, 193–194, 228, 261
Haeckel, Ernst Heinrich Philipp August 106n1
Haidt, J. 119, 121
Hamlet (Shakespeare) xi, 38, 198, 201, 207
hammer and sickle 17
handwriting 223–224, 227, 234
Hebrew Bible's *(Old Testament)* 37, 57, 240
Hegel, Georg Wilhelm Friedrich 36, 39, 81, 172, 289
Hegelian xv, 36–37, 40, 292
heterogeneity 59
hidden addressivity 226
hidden figures 66
hierarchies 17; cultural 59, 62, 152; psychological 26; racial 282; social 24–25, 62
higher mental functions 29, 32–34, 74, 101, 137, 150, 153; and age 169; concept of 80–81; culture's 177; and pedology 270–271; "primitive" people's 54, 59; proletarian children 44; role of literacy 225; and social order 72; words in developing 97–99
Hirsch, E. D. 26
historical exclusion 247–249
historical revisionism 52
Hitler, A. 3, 11, 238, 243, 273–274, 278, 304–305
homophobia 251
Huckin, T. 23
Hughes, Bryan 34
human action: people 82–85; primates 82–85; signs 82–85; speech 85–90; tools 82–85
human development 28, 72–74, 93–95; biology 78–79; labor in 137–140; nature in 75–77; nurture in 75–77; play in 122–137; social norms 78–79
Husserl, Edmund Gustav Albrecht 51n4
hybridity/hybrid 7, 50, 59, 236

ideal artefacts 24
idealism 39–40
ideal sign 189, 235

identity politics 280
ideology/ideological 102–105, 169, 176, 213–214; Bolshevik 25; communist 41; and concept development 102–105; of cultural cognition 100; Marxist 11, 55, 180; Soviet 20–21, 44–45, 182; state 5–6, 181, 289
imagination 129–131
imitation 130, 132, 231; in socialization 74–75
inclusion/inclusive 241–242, 251–252, 254–255; defectology 242–245; errors of 96; ethos of 245; mission statements 247; modern movement 250; social norms 99
inclusive defectology 242–245
Indian Schools 248
Indigenous scholarship 61
inductive 174; approach to learning 172; inquiries 177; virtuous children 172
information processing 99, 104, 142, 148, 168
in loco parentis 160
inner speech 85–86, 133, 220, 225, 228, 303
instructional scaffolding xii, 142, 143, 145–146, 150–152, 234, 311
instrumental method 158
integrated functioning 160
integrative theory 76
intellect: and emotion(s) 110–111
intellectual traditions 15
intelligent emotions 199, 211, 218, 313
intelligentsia 5, 10, 14, 17–19, 259, 263–264, 278, 282, 286
intercontext 73, 233
interests 183–186
intersubjectivity 150, 153, 233, 254
intertextuality/intertextual 206, 214
IQ tests/intelligence tests 286, 295
irony/ironic 207, 214
Islam/Muslims 55–56

Jacobs, D. T. 61
Jaensch, Erich Rudolf 88, 91n4, 291, 304–305
James-Lange theory of emotions 107, 121n1
James Webb space telescope 115
Jennings principle 294
Jewish: heritage, Vygotsky's 9–12; and Nazis 243, 304–305; Ostracism 10–11; sacred text 56
Jewish problem 11
Jewish question 56
John-Steiner, V. 87
Journal of Russian and Eastern European Psychology xxi
Judaism 11–12
Judeo-Bolshevism 56
Judeo-Christian heritage 57, 220

"The Kaffir" 62
Kant, Immanuel 107
Keats, John xiv
Kellogg, D. 9, 144, 149, 152–153
Kerpatenko, Yuriy 5
Khmelnitsky Uprising 10
kleptocracy 38
Kluckhohn, C. 23
knotted handkerchief 188
Knox, J. E. 58–59, 93, 94
Koffka, Kurt 39
Kohlberg, L. 30
Köhler, Wolfgang 91n2
Kornilov, Konstantin Nikolaevich 22n4
Kozulin, A. 8–9
Kroeber, A. 23
Krylenko, Nikolai Vasilyevich 18–19
kulaks 102, 106n3, 265
Kulish, Mykola 5
kultur 13, 19, 216

labor 137–140; collective 126–127; human 140; in human development 137–140; Marxist notion of 40, 49; material 45; physical 40, 46; tool-mediated 84, 161
Laboratory for Study of the Psychology of Abnormal Childhood 242
labor camps 5, 8, 187, 289
Lamarckian evolution 286
larynx 82
Latiné: population 249; students 204
law of sociogenesis of higher forms of behavior 79
learning: cross-disciplinary 176–178; and morality 172–174; rote 188, 197
learning by doing 161
learning loss 32, 170
learning to write 222–225
Lehrer, Tom 14
Lenin, Vladimir 4, 7, 10, 53, 106n3, 279, 283, 288, 296, 302–304; anti-intellectualism of Soviet Union 18; Bolshevik agitations 261; on materialism 36; *monumentálnaya propaganda* 190; oppressing intellectuals 18; 'Philosophical Notebooks' 77; on proletarian revolution 17; Red Terror 18; "Red Terror" 18; Soviet New Economic Policy 290n13; statues of 190
Leninism 35
Leont'ev, A. N. 5–6, 23, 33, 35, 37, 81, 103
Letters to the Next President 2.0 campaign 253
Lévy-Bruhl, Lucien 67n3
LGBTQ+: books 80, 247; population 247–248; rights 103, 133
lightness standard 78
linguistic determinism 45

linguistic psychology 103, 198
literary criticism 6, 199, 205–206, 213, 216, 313
literary interpretation or analysis 147, 168
logic/logical thinking 58, 77, 102, 107–108, 111, 119, 214, 229–230, 252, 271, 304
logocentric 198
Lovaas Applied Behavioral Analysis 78
love 174–176
Lovell, S. 14
lower mental functions 9, 97
Luria, A. R. xx, 5–6, 55, 60, 86, 94

Magie, Lizzie 123
Makalela, L. 28, 29
male bias 65–66
Manager 123–124, 134
Mann, Horace 26, 42, 248, 299
Marx, Karl xiii, 16, 20, 35, 93; on economic and social classes' struggle 37
Marxism xiii, 1, 4, 8, 17, 20, 35, 37, 39–40, 116, 170, 279, 304–305, 312; orthodox 56; as post-capitalism 40–42; Soviet 287; in Soviet context 35–50; and Vygotsky 8, 40–42
mass education 26, 57, 74, 180, 236, 241
mass schooling 104, 159, 181, 306
material artefacts 24
materialism 35, 39–40; dialectical 36, 39, 40, 77, 80; historical 261
material productivity 140
meaning 16, 84–86, 95–99, 102–103, 127–129, 202–211, 225–226
mediation xvi, xxiii; cultural 27, 53, 56, 59, 120, 199, 211, 311; explicit 15; implicit 15; psychological 14; semiotic 85; social 93, 97, 189, 206
medical model 78, 240, 243
meme xv–xvi, 218
memorization (memorize) 163, 188; of information 190; piecemeal and temporary 196; through mental repetition 192
memory 188–193
memory laws 53
Mensheviks 7, 296
mental functions 270–271
mental health 78, 174, 212, 246–247, 254
metacognition/metacognitive 104, 134
meta-experience xxii
metaphors 149–151
meta-theory 76
methodological reporting 291–293
Mikhailov, F. T. 23
mind 38, 40, 59, 61–64, 71–72, 97; as machine 168; people's frames of 77; post-capitalist frame of 98–99; presentism 241; social formation of 74; Soviet 3, 20, 120, 129

Mind in Society (Vygotsky) xii, xv, xvi, xx, 3, 122, 142–143, 149, 151
mismeasurement/mismeasure 269
Moll, L. C. 23, 150
monarchial Romanovs 294
monoculturalism 56–57
monoculture 31, 54, 78, 221, 236, 248; assertion of 220; educational 121; Soviet approach to 219–220
monologism/monologic 161, 289
Monopoly 123–124, 133–134
Montessori/Montessori School 177–178, 181, 313
monumentálnaya propaganda (propaganda through monuments) 190
monuments/statues 64, 190–191
moral development: and games 135–136
morality: education in 170–172; learning and 172–174
Morrison, Scott 95
Moscow xi, 4–5, 7, 9, 11, 13, 16–17, 25, 42, 48, 179, 219, 234, 238–239, 263, 287
Moscow Film School 301
motivation 164, 196, 226–227, 312
motive of the setting 298
mountains 190, 200, 211
Mr. Spock 107
multi-age classrooms 170
multicultural education 26–27
multiculturalism 56–57
multiliteracies 87, 237
multimodality 87, 90, 237
mythbusting 4–6
myth/mythology 5, 55, 103, 190–191, 252

narrative 4–5; historical 52, 190; Southern heritage 192; structure of 192–193
national identities 40, 104, 131, 281
nationalism 35, 49, 116, 280
National Writing Project 253
Native American culture 221
nature 77–78, 108, 243; and age-based stages 186; in human development 75–77
Nazi 3, 132; anti-Semitic 305; "Jews will not replace us!" slogan 34; rise of 278, 290n7
needs 29, 183; community 31; ontogenetic 32; organic 113; societal 54
neoliberalism 38
neopositivists 283
neuro-atypical 246
neurodiversity 246–247
neurotypical 246
New Criticism/New Critical 201, 204, 206, 216
New Soviet Man 12, 21, 25, 31, 39, 105, 117, 120, 126–127, 181, 187, 262, 280, 295–296, 305

Next Zone of Development (NZD) 144–145
nurture 79–80; in human development 75–77

obstacles 7, 37–38, 134, 137, 166–168; to inclusive education 249; and student activity 164–165
occupational education 131, 138–139, 141
October Revolution 11, 21n1, 35, 201, 296
ontogeny 293–294
orientation 180–183
Orwell, George 40
outcomes-based education 160
Overton, Joseph 67n8
Overton Window 64, 80, 103

Pale of Settlement 9, 10
paper shortage 293
paradox 4, 30, 119, 135, 203, 206–207
paradoxical 140, 203, 207, 209; account 31; conclusion 112, 217
"Paradox of the Actor" 212
Paris Commune 16
Parliament 107
parrot or psittaceous 83, 96
passport age 144, 168–169, 265, 268–269
Pavlovian reflexology 5, 7, 22n4, 110, 158, 182, 287
pedagogical distortions xiii, 275
pedagogy: critical 296, 302; Vygotsky on 160–161
pedological writing 265–270
pedology: diagnostic tests 265–270; and higher mental functions 270–271; movement, Soviet political context of 262–265; ranking of cultures 284–286; and social class 282–284
Pedology Decree 273–275; concept development 301–304; demise of the school 305–308; end of development 300–301; methodological reporting 291–293; ontogeny and phylogeny 293–294; person and environment 294–300; Vygotsky and Jaensch 304–305
Peirce, Charles Sanders 86
people 82–85
People for the Ethical Treatment of Animals (PETA) 63
perezhivanie xxii
person and environment 294–300
Peters, V. 25
phylogeny 93–95, 293–294
Piaget, Jean 29, 39, 100; biology 32–33; environment 32–33
Piagetian developmental conception 243
pipelines 254; leaky 247; school-to-prison 298; for teachers of color 247

play: and collective labor 126–127; defined 122–125; and future orientation 125; games 131–137; in human development 122–137; imagination 129–131; symbolic 127–129
Plekhanov, Georgi Valentinovich 57
pluralistic societies 101, 167, 306
pogroms 9, 11; anti-Semitic 199; genocidal xi
Polish-Bolshevik War 7
Portes, P. 23
positioning theory/positional theory 243
positive social updraft 173, 254
post-capitalism/post-capitalist 4, 39, 40–42, 59, 98, 170
post-colonialism/post-colonial 51n2
post-Pavlov/post-Pavlovian 98, 111, 301
Potebnya, Alexander 91n5
Pound, Ezra 36
power differentials and culture 29–30
practical labor 81
presentism 64, 67, 241
presentist 65–66, 90, 121n3
primary disability 244
primates 82–85
primitive people: higher mental functions 54, 59; Vygotsky's on 58–60
primitivism 58
problem isomorph 27
products/processes in writing 230–233
progressive education/educators 56–57, 164, 178, 179, 183, 195–196, 220–221, 236, 271
prolepsis 25–26
proletariat 4, 7, 12, 44, 48, 55, 284; in collectivist farms 55; 'dictatorship of the proletariat' 16–20, 296; practical labor of 81; rural agrarian 25; Stalin's valorization of 278; status 139
propaganda 41, 53, 190, 311
Protocols of the Learned Elders of Zion 11
proto-composition 222
pseudoconcept 96, 153, 290n10
psychiatry 211
psychological mediation 14
psychological tool 84
The Psychology of Art (Vygotsky) xi, 14, 87, 108–109, 199–201
psychotechnics 267
psychotechnology 120
punishment 26, 136, 173–174, 184; banishment 173; behaviorist 78; harsh and deadly 263
Putin, Vladimir xxi–xxii, 4, 9, 12–13, 174, 190, 293

race 44, 48, 56, 101, 173, 243, 253, 267, 297, 313
racism 31, 36, 120, 191, 215, 251, 298, 312; scientific 106n1, 290n15
ractice (praxis) 12, 96–97, 136–137, 139
Rarámuri shamans 61
rationalism 14–15
rationalist delusion 119–120, 216
reactions: aesthetic 209; conditional 98, 159; emotional 63, 109–113, 118; knee-jerk 94, 116; socially mediated 98; stimulus-response 84
reader response 201–202
reader's critique 198
reading: authorial 215; embodied 208–212; selective 149, 291, 311
reason: 21st century view of 119–120; and emotion(s) 107–108, 114–116
reciprocity principle 233
Reconstruction: America After the Civil War 66
Red Terror 18
Reed, John "Jack" 4, 16, 17, 21n1
reflexology 5, 7, 22n4, 110, 158, 182, 287
relativism/relativist 34, 53, 60, 62, 266, 312
relevance 193–195
religion 55–56, 108, 235, 313
revisionism 52
revolution from above 50, 276
rewards 78, 131, 184
Rieber, R. W. 40
Rodina, K. A. 23
Romanovs/Romanov dynasty 13–14, 16, 18, 238, 311; Christian 9; monarchial 294; and Polish-Bolshevik War 7, 35
romanticism/romantic 15, 200, 233, 267
romantic science 267
rote learning 188, 197
roundabout mediation 89
Rowling, J. K. 36
Rus 13
Russian Civil War 10
Russian naming traditions xxi–xxii
Russian Revolution ix, 106
Russian Revolution of 1905 7
Russo-Japanese War 7
Ruthless: Monopoly's Secret History 123

sage on the stage 164
Salas, S. 23
Sapir, Edward 67n5
satire/satirical 49, 206
Saussure, Ferdinand de 86
scaffolding 145–149
schema 53, 99, 193
school board meeting 236, 251
school budget 185
Science of Reading 76

scientific concepts 95–96, 301–303
scientific method(s) 261
Scientific Revolution 14
scope-and-sequence charts 170
secondary disability 244, 246–247
Second International 17, 22n11
Second Russian Revolution 7
selective reading 149, 291, 311
self-regulation 127–129
semiotic mediation 85
semiotics 86–87
setting xxiii, 27, 30, 32, 98, 100, 103, 297–298; activity-based 164; coeducational 176; cultural 245; educational 170, 301; egalitarian 261; group 131; high-stakes 188; historical 47, 73; ideological 47; industrial 141; Montessori-style 313; rule-bound 123, 133; school 116, 181, 244; social 74, 109, 299
Sewell, R. 37
sex education 174–176
sexual drives 73, 89, 94, 130, 262
sexuality 174–176
sexual maturation 33, 77, 88, 101, 130, 174, 186
Sherlock Holmes 107
Sherlock Holmes (Doyle) 107
Sherrington, Sir Charles Scott 67n7
sign language 89
signs 82–85; and hearing 89–90
single-case comparative method 269
slave trade/slavery 36, 102–103
smartphone/cell phone 179, 182, 197, 224
Snyder, T. 12, 53
Soboleva, M. 12
social: cultural nature of being 73–74; historical nature of being 73–74
social class 42–47; barriers 21, 180; biases 30; bourgeoisie 5; differences 18, 39, 221, 267, 280, 282, 299, 311; distinctions 20, 24, 48, 297, 300; divisions 276; elimination 234; hierarchical 170; immobility 281; inequities 18, 279; issues 17, 42, 264; movement 34; often-privileged 48; and pedology 282–284; relations 302
Social-Emotional Learning (SEL) 216, 249
social hierarchies 24–25
social interest 245, 255n2
socialism 4, 11, 37–38, 171, 260, 263, 276, 281, 297
socialization: and emotion(s) 112–114; imitation in 74–75
social languages 26, 98
social media 196, 219, 224, 226, 235–236
social mediation 93, 97, 189, 206

social norms 78–79
social status 44, 99, 244, 278, 298
societal norms 268
society's shit 278
sociocultural history 59, 63, 92
Sohmer, R. 25
Solnick, S. L. 14
Solzhenitsyn, A. I. 18, 19, 136
Soviet defectology 240–242
Soviet dissident 8, 26, 41, 50, 136, 140, 190
Soviet doctrine 17, 48, 55, 57, 76, 102, 116, 221, 279, 287, 305
Soviet political context of the pedology movement 262–265
Soviet Union 3–4, 8–10; decriminalized same-sex relationships xxi; Vygotsky's works modified in xv
special education xiv, 6, 270, 277; and biological stage development 78; educators 240; medical model of 78; modern-day 243; Russian 10; teachers 243
speech 85–90; inner 85–86, 133, 220, 225, 228, 303; operation levels 86
speech genres 26, 98, 254
Spencer, H. 28
Spencerian evolution 250
Spinoza, Baruch 22n10, 114
spiral curriculum 195
spontaneous concepts 95–96, 301
Spranger, Eduard 51n5
stage theory of development 39, 100, 169
Stalin, J. 18; Great Purge 14, 18
Stalinism 35
standardization 228, 254, 306
standardized: measures 267; schooling 306
standardized tests 216, 249, 254, 282
standards: APA 291; creative/aesthetic 201; cultural 136; literary 214; moral 170; textbook 229
Stasevska, Dalia 5
status errors 232
Stern, William Lewis 91n1
structural analysis 208
struggle 37, 51n1; class 56, 280, 288; dialectical 39, 77; internal/external dramatic 109; social 40
student activity in midst of obstacles 164–165
Studies on the History of Behavior: Ape, Primitive, and Child (Vygotsky and Luria) 82, 94
subjective: construction 35, 191; experience 7, 186, 297; preferences 210
subjectivity 198, 201–202, 211, 297–298
Sumerian classroom 161
survival of the fittest 28, 250
Sverdlov, Yakov 18

tacit socialization 80
talented tenth 66
Taylor, C. 15
teaching: about love and sexuality 174–176; literature 198–218; writing 219–237
technology 57–58, 60–61, 87, 93, 120, 142, 197, 224, 245, 299; modern 77
teeth 28, 33, 64, 77, 167, 223
telos 25–26
terministic screens 64–65
texts: alphabetic 225–228; and genre 205–208
theater 17, 122, 198, 212–213, 301
theatrical: audience 213; codes 212; drama 109; interpretations 124; performances 122, 124, 213; production 213; texts and fables xi
think-aloud method 168
Thinking and Speech (Wood, Bruner and Ross) xii, 127
Thorndike, Edward 106n2
The Time Machine (Wells) 60
tongue 89, 93, 142, 210
tools 82–85; psychological 84
"trained revolutionary thinkers" 4
transitional age 43, 82, 100, 102, 129, 174, 185; *see also* adolescence
translation xv, xvi, xviii–xxiv
troika 5
Trotsky, Leon 4, 56
Trump, Donald 53
Tsarist Russia 9, 12, 14, 88
Tsarist schools 179, 182, 188
tuberculosis xiv, 6, 9, 121n2, 199, 216, 289, xviin4
Tulviste, P. 45, 93
twenty-first century literacies 41–42
twisting path: concept development 96–97; defined 96
typewriter 224, 241

ubuntu 28–29, 250, 269
Understanding Vygotsky: A Quest for Synthesis (Van der Veer and Valsiner) xxiii, 38
unit of analysis xxii, 97, 292
Universal Declaration of Human Rights 103
utterance 84, 98, 162, 225–226, 275, 279

Valsiner, J. xxiii, 57, 89–90, 93, 98, 102, 119
Van der Veer, R. xv, xix, xxi, xxiii, 4–5, 6, 7, 8, 20–21, 38–39, 41, 57, 89–90, 93, 98, 102, 119
variation 60–63
Veresov, N. N. xviii, xx, 9, 144, 149, 152–153
vocational education 138
Vygodskaya, Gita xvii

Vygotsky, L.S.: activity-based practical learning 161–162; background xi; balance of materialism and idealism 39–40; biology 32–33; and capitalism 48–49; career of 4–9; children as autodidacts 168–169; complications in reading in English xiv–xvi; concept development (*see* concept development); cross-disciplinary learning 176–178; cultural-historical psychology 71–91; definition of education 158–160; education in ethics and morality 170–172; on emotions (*see* emotion(s)); environment 32–33; foregrounding the educational environment 162–164; German and Soviet defectology prior to 240–242; hierarchical views 52–67; human development 93–95; and inclusive defectology 242–245; inclusive vision on people with disabilities 10–11; issue of age 169–170; and Jaensch 304–305; Jewish heritage 9–12; and Marxism 8; obstacles 166–168; path to Moscow 7–8; pedagogy 160–161; pedological writing 265–270; play (*see* play); publications accuracy/reliability xviii–xxi; relation between learning and morality 172–174; role of student activity in the midst of obstacles 164–165; secular Judaism 11–12; in Soviet context 16–21, 35–50; Soviet idealism 12–13; teaching about love and sexuality 174–176

Vygotsky the bourgeois 286–289

Wagner, Richard 36
Washington, George 65
Watson, John Broadus 51n3
Wells, H. G. 60
Wertsch, J. V. 8, 15, 23, 25, 29, 52, 59, 62–63, 87, 98

Western decadence 15
West/Western 3, 13; cultural values 241; culture 20, 56; notions of community 29; pedagogue 312; science 48; society 170, 266
Whorf, Benjamin Lee 67n6
Wollock, J. 40
Woods, C. 148, 150, 152
words xiv–xv, xxii, 85–86, 87–89, 103–104, 127–129, 234; in developing higher mental functions 97–99; multiple roles of 102; as paramount, in contrast with multimodal understandings 87–89; and play 127–129; as psychological mediators 7; as signs 24, 86–87, 190
working class 4, 14, 17, 21–22n1, 44–49, 269–270, 282, 301; adolescents 42–43; dictatorship of 17; society 201; women 30
workplace literacy/workplace learning 305
World War I/Great War xi, 3–4, 7, 10, 21n1, 178n2, 200, 242
World War II 4, 11
wrecking 14, 272n5, 278
writing: defining 221–222; pedological 265–270; products and processes in 230–233
writing to learn 232, 235

Yaroshevsky, M. G. 77, 86, 109
Yasnitsky, A. xix
Yiddish performances 198
Young Communists 12, 19, 290n9
Young Pioneers 12, 290n9

Zamoyski, A. 35
Zimmerman, M. 131
zone of intellectual imitation 75
Zone of Next Development (ZND) 144
zone of proximal development (ZPD) xii, xvi, xx, xxiii, 69, 75, 142–153, 162, 234

For Product Safety Concerns and Information please contact our EU representative GPSR@taylorandfrancis.com
Taylor & Francis Verlag GmbH, Kaufingerstraße 24, 80331 München, Germany

www.ingramcontent.com/pod-product-compliance
Lightning Source LLC
Chambersburg PA
CBHW080922300426
44115CB00018B/2919